READINGS IN CULTURAL GEOGRAPHY

READINGS IN

CULTURAL GEOGRAPHY

*Edited with Introductions
and Translations by*

Philip L. Wagner

and

Marvin W. Mikesell

 *The University of Chicago Press
Chicago and London*

International Standard Book Number: 0-226-86931-8
Library of Congress Catalog Card Number: 62-9740

THE UNIVERSITY OF CHICAGO PRESS, CHICAGO 60637

The University of Chicago Press, Ltd., London

Dedicated to
ERHARD ROSTLUND, 1900–1961
Perceptive Student
and Inspiring Teacher of
Cultural Geography

Cultural geography is not a new subject. This generalization holds true whether we define "subject" to mean a recognized scholarly discipline or simply a point of view. In the latter sense of the word, cultural geography was well established in antiquity; in the former sense, its roots are as deep as those of academic geography as a whole. To verify these points it is sufficient to recall the concern for cultural differences—indeed culture areas—in the writings of Herodotus and Strabo, or the more explicit statements of Ratzel and Vidal de la Blache. The reader will also notice that many of the contributors to this volume are senior scholars who have been active in geography or related fields for many years. It is something of a paradox, therefore, that cultural geography has not yet been blessed with a definitive treatise or an effective guide to the literature. The subject is not treated specifically in *American Geography: Inventory and Prospect,* nor has it been elaborated in any of the presidential addresses given before the Association of American Geographers.

To explain the paradox of a subject that is recognized and yet unrecognized, old and yet new, we must attempt to answer two questions: first, what do we mean by "cultural geography," and second, how has this interest been pursued? Substantial answers to both questions are given in our General Introduction under the heading "Themes of Cultural Geography." In this preliminary note it is sufficient to indicate that we do not use cultural geography as a synonym for general human geography. Cultural geography, like economic and political geography, is but a subdivision of that broad field. According to this restricted view, cultural geography is defined by the fact that it demands explicit recognition of culture, in contrast to the implicit recognition given by scholars in the other sub-fields. In other words, cultural geographers are identified not by the phenomena they study, but by the integrating concepts and processes that they stress. The object of their interest, shared by most geographers, is the varied and changing environment of man.

These considerations help to explain why cultural geography should be regarded as a distinctive subdivision of human geography, but they do not explain why so few attempts have been made to define or clarify its particular role. To explain this aspect of the problem, we must refer not to the data and theory of cultural geography, but to the preferences of those geographers who have tried to answer questions in cultural terms. One point is clear: cultural geographers, perhaps more than other geographers, have preferred to deal with substantive rather than methodologic or pedagogic themes. During our consideration of possible selections for this book, we easily compiled a list of more than two hundred substantive works, but we could find few general statements on strategy or rationale. Fortunately, the absence of textbooks and the poverty of programmatic statements does not mean that cultural geographers have avoided generalization or theory, as most of the selections in this volume reveal. Nevertheless, a great need exists for specific treatment of the subject, and we felt that a collection of substantive works, grouped around concepts of its character and capacities, would be the logical way to begin such a task.

One more consideration is necessary before we attempt to explain the content and design of this book. The practice of cultural geography has not been limited to geographers per se. On the contrary, progress has resulted from frequent movement across disciplinary frontiers. To use an appropriate simile, we may say that this volume has profited from in-migration, and that desirable outward movements have also taken place. The common frontiers of geography, anthropology, archeology, ecology, and history have never been and doubtless never will be sharply defined. Let us hope that cultural geographers and all who share their interests will continue to move across these frontiers.

With respect to the anthology itself, we should indicate first of all that it was conceived as a contribution to the training of advanced students in American universities. We sought articles that could serve as a foundation for specialized study and also provide orientation for students primarily interested in other fields. The selection reveals personal limitations—linguistic, academic, and intellectual—but it was made without conscious regard for discipline or nationality, and we believe that the balance between work by geographers and non-geographers, Americans and non-Americans is both desirable and reasonable.

In general, we selected works of wide interest rather than "case studies," but we made no effort to achieve complete topical, regional, or temporal coverage. Our first concern was that the book should include articles that define research problems and indicate procedures for their solution. In addition, we felt that each article should be reproduced in full. Since there is no rule without exception, we granted ourselves special dispensation with respect to two selections that are autonomous parts of longer essays. However, we did not feel that we should extract sections of books or monographs. The reason for reproduction of full and in some cases expanded documentation is obvious: we hope that the selections will be used as well as read. Indeed, the footnotes to the articles, taken together, give a good indication of training requirements in cultural geography. Finally, we should confess that our selection was influenced negatively by such practical considerations as the length of articles and the quality and quantity of illustrations.

It is a pleasure to express thanks to many persons who encouraged and facilitated our work. We are indebted to Norton S. Ginsburg for suggesting that this effort should be made and to other colleagues at the University of Chicago for subsequent encouragement. Special thanks are due to Reine Mikesell for assistance in translation and the checking of footnotes, and to Karl Gudenberg for cartographic work. We are, of course, deeply indebted to the contributors to this volume, as well as their editors and publishers, for agreeing to let us use their work. Additional thanks are due to those scholars who consented to check our translations. Finally, we are keenly aware that this effort was inspired by our training in cultural geography at the University of California.

P. L. WAGNER

M. W. MIKESELL

Davis, California
Chicago, Illinois

CONTENTS

THE THEMES OF CULTURAL GEOGRAPHY

For those who practice and profess it, cultural geography is not susceptible of easy definition.[1] It is a shared curiosity and set of preferences more than an explicit program or doctrine. One important and distinctive feature, however, is common to the writings assembled in his volume, and to the particular tradition of cultural geography which they follow. In this tradition, *cultural geography is the application of the idea of culture to geographic problems.*

Cultural geography, like all subdivisions of geography, must be "earthbound." The features of the earth, in particular those produced or modified by human action, are of great significance. The study of these man-made geographic features takes account of differences among the human communities that create or have created them and formulates the special ways of life of each as "cultures." Cultural geography compares the changing distribution of "culture areas" with the distribution of other features of the earth's surface, in order to identify environmental features characteristic of a given culture and if possible to discover what role human action plays or has played in creating and maintaining given geographic features. It distinguishes, describes, and classifies the typical complexes of environmental features, including the man-made ones, that coincide with each cultural community, as "cultural landscapes," and looks behind them into "culture history" for origins. Finally, it may study the specific processes in which human manipulations of environment are involved, together with their implications for the welfare of the community and humanity, as "cultural ecology."

These five implicit themes—culture, culture area, cultural landscape, culture history, and cultural ecology—together constitute the core of cultural geography.[2]

[1] Although there is a considerable diversity of opinion on the proper content of the subject, we believe that the present essay—without insisting on a single rigid definition at the outset, but taking its departure from one particular point of view—will demonstrate the mutual compatibility and complementary quality of the various conceptions of cultural geography that are employed in practice.

[2] The headings of this essay correspond in general to the sections into which this volume is divided, but the latter are necessarily broader and more arbitrary than the former. For example, space limitations have prevented us from making a clear distinction between landscape studies and cultural ecology. The latter theme is more fully developed in Philip L. Wagner, *The Human Use of the Earth* (Glencoe, Ill.: Free Press, 1960), and William L. Thomas, Jr. (ed.), *Man's Role in Changing the Face of the Earth* (Chicago: University of Chicago Press, 1956).

1

CULTURE

Whether it is considered an inherent property or possession of human beings, or merely an intellectual device for convenient generalization about human attitudes and behavior, "culture" is a key to systematic understanding of differences and similarities among men.[3] The notion of culture focuses attention not on isolated individuals and whatever personal characteristics they happen to possess, but instead on communities of persons occupying a certain extended and usually continuous space and on the numerous features of belief and behavior that are held in common by member of such communities. In other words, the concept of cultures offers a means of classifying human beings into well-defined groups according to verifiable common characteristics and also a means of classifying areas according to the character of the human groups that occupy them.

Culture is an outcome of the ability of human beings to communicate among themselves through symbols.[4] When people seem to think and act alike, they do so because they live and work and talk together, learn from the same companions and teachers, gossip about the same events, issues, and personalities, see around them the same meaningful kind of man-made objects, participate in the same rituals, and remember the same past. Conversely, major differences in outlook and activity usually reflect the absence of common symbols and language. Therefore, culture also rests upon a geographic basis, for habitual and shared communication is likely to occur only among people who occupy a common area.

A community of persons sharing a common culture may exist encapsulated as a single isolated village, in which all the inhabitants are in direct daily contact, or it may extend over a vast territory within which people, objects, and ideas circulate more or less freely and continually. A culture spreads as those who share it move about, or as its corresponding sphere of communication, and the symbols embodied therein, come to prevail over those of other cultures in new territories.

Language, as an essential medium of human communication, is obviously a critical component of any culture. The exact influence of language upon culture

[3] The best introduction to thought on "culture" is Alfred L. Kroeber and Clyde Kluckhohn, *Culture: A Critical Review of Concepts and Definitions* ("Papers of the Peabody Museum of American Archaeology and Ethnology," Vol. XLVII, No. 1 [1952]). For some individual interpretations, see Leslie A. White, *The Science of Culture* (New York: Farrar, Straus, 1949), and David Bidney, *Theoretical Anthropology* (New York: Columbia University Press, 1953). See also A. L. Kroeber's *The Nature of Culture* (Chicago: University of Chicago Press, 1952), esp. pp. 118–35. Perhaps the most lucid non-technical discussion is Edward T. Hall's *The Silent Language* (New York: Doubleday, 1959). Among other "popular" treatments, special mention should be made of Clyde Kluckhohn, *Mirror for Man* (New York: McGraw-Hill, 1949; "Primier" paperback, 1957), and Walter Goldschmidt, *Man's Way* (Cleveland and New York: World Publishing Co., 1959).

[4] This notion is championed especially by Leslie White (*op. cit.*). It is ably developed from the viewpoint of the communications specialist in Karl W. Deutsch, *Nationalism and Social Communication: An Inquiry into the Foundations of Nationality* (New York: Wiley, 1953).

has been guessed at but never clearly established;[5] in any case, language in its turn is strongly affected by other aspects of a culture. Whatever these interrelations may be, the speech of a community is one of its distinguishing traits. A culture, to be sure, may embrace or overlap several different linguistic groups, as long as some sort of equivalence among the coexisting symbolic systems is maintained; likewise, one linguistic group may be divided among several dissimilar cultures.[6]

It is impossible to partition off word-language from the other mechanisms of communication always associated with it.[7] Exclamations, gestures, facial expressions, and the like are also language; in another direction, so are pictures, emblems, and everything that is regularly recognized as "meaning something." Ultimately, objects and behavior of all kinds enter into communication. Culture ascribes meaning to everything, from deliberately articulated vocal sounds to beings, objects, and places.[8]

The ascription of meanings, inherent in culture, guides action (whether seen as symbolic or utilitarian) and results thereby in such concrete expressions as systems of belief, social institutions, and material possessions. The character of these elements of culture, therefore, must largely be inferred upon the basis of the significant features of communication and symbolization—from verbal formulas to costumes and gestures—associated with them.

The degree of "conventionality" implicit in these ideological and institutional elements of culture is still very much less than that in language itself. There are, in other words, more possible ways of satisfactory and significant performance of a ritual, and many more ways of holding and stating a belief, than there are ways of enunciating a given word or rendering a particular grammatical construction; in the former two instances, the range of permitted variation is much wider than in language. Cultural constancy may thus be thought of as tapering off from a highly arbitrary and conventional linguistic usage, through institutional behavior and traditional belief—where the weight of personal experience and the pressure of immediate material circumstances exert more influence on performance—toward the ordinary daily behavior of individuals, in which the circumstantial factors greatly modify and even mask the ideal cul-

---

[5] The chief advocate of linguistic influence on thought and action was B. L. Whorf; see *Language, Thought and Reality: Selected Writings of Benjamin Lee Whorf,* ed. J. B. Carroll (New York: Wiley, 1956). See also the articles in Harry Hoijer (ed.), *Language and Culture* (American Anthropological Association Memoir No. 79 [Chicago: University of Chicago Press, 1954]).

[6] Such cases of cultural overlapping as those of Switzerland and Belgium immediately come to mind, but much distinctiveness remains, in linkage with the several linguistic groups concerned. The English and Spanish languages, on the other hand, are each shared by several well-defined communities; but here again the members of the various cultural groups are distinguishable according to their speech habits.

[7] See especially Hall (*op. cit.*) on this point.

[8] As David Lowenthal puts it, "The surface of the earth is shaped for each person by refraction through cultural and personal lenses of custom and fancy." See his "Geography, Experience, and Imagination: Towards a Geographical Epistemology," *Annals of the Association of American Geographers,* LI (1961), 241–260, ref. to p. 260.

tural patterns. The notion of culture in general does not allow prediction and rational explanation of individual behavior in most spheres to the same degree that linguistic rules allow abstract statements of the possibilities and requirements for particular utterances.

For the purposes of geography, habitual individual behavior and that controlled by institutions are of greater significance than linguistic systems, ideologies, or social institutions in themselves. Geography usually has to deal with just those elements of culture that appear to be most diluted by chance and circumstance. Seldom, therefore, is it possible to predict in a positive sense, or even adequately explain in retrospect, the kind of human behavior that is geographically consequential. The "patterns" of such behavior are much too vague and variable to serve as certain guides.

Geographers and culture historians often mention "levels" or "stages" of culture.[9] The value and advantage of such formulations are that they are retrospective and comparative. It has proved feasible and convenient to analyze the geographic manifestations of past cultures from the standpoint of their maximum technical and organizational potential, rather than their specific patterns of action. Any culture is limited in its capacity to transform habitats by technical knowledge, institutional management and organization, preferences and prohibitions, and so on. The negative determinants of human action under a particular culture can often be ascertained, and they tend to be constant and compelling.[10] Thus, although it is seldom possible to say what an individual or a group may do, it is relatively easy to predict confidently what they will not do, or even be able to do, given adequate knowledge of their culture. In the geographic study of culture, therefore, such matters as taboos, avoidance of certain foods, restrictions on the use of lands, absence of certain techniques, prohibitions on particular occupations, lack of certain kinds of tools, organizational impediments to development, and the like are important.[11] The comparison and ranking of cultures in regard to their potential for affecting habitats is an essential operation in cultural geography, whether motivated by a desire to understand the past effects of man or by an interest in present differentials in productivity and welfare.[12]

[9] See Hans Bobek's article ("The Main Stages in Socioeconomic Evolution from a Geographic Point of View") in Part III of this volume.

[10] The use of negative reasoning in science has been advocated especially by the philosopher Karl R. Popper. See his *The Logic of Scientific Discovery* (New York: Basic Books, 1959).

[11] H. Epstein's article ("Domestication Features in Animals as Functions of Human Society") in Part III of this volume shows the importance of negative reasoning. In this connection see also the articles by Richard Weiss ("Cultural Boundaries and the Ethnographic Map") and Morton Fried ("Geography, Land Tenure, and Ecology in the Contact of Cultures") in Parts II and III. The delineation of areas where milking is not practiced because of aversion or taboos is a classic theme. It was accomplished for Asia by Eduard Hahn, *Die Haustiere und ihre Beziehungen zur Wirtschaft des Menschen* (Leipzig: Duncker & Humblot, 1896), and more recently for Africa by Frederick J. Simoons, "The Non-Milking Area of Africa," *Anthropos*, XLIX (1954), 58–66.

[12] In the final selection of this volume ("The Agency of Man on the Earth"), Carl O. Sauer assesses historical differences in culture as a factor of habitat change. See also Alexander Spoehr's essay on "Cultural Differences in the Interpretation of Natural Resources" in *Man's Role in Changing the Face of the Earth*.

Cultural geographers have also devoted much effort to the study of the origin and dispersal of particular culture traits. Another strategic use of negative reasoning is apparent here. By establishing the real or probable history of migrations and diffusions, it is possible to map the distribution of such traits at given periods and so, by elimination, to infer what means of transformation and development existed at a determined time and place.[13] A thorough knowledge of the historical geography of cultures and cultural features defines and limits further the potential human behavior that may account for geographic transformations and reduces still more the need for reconstructing obscure patterns of behavior.

Obviously, both these essentially negative strategies can be employed in an opposite fashion to suggest influences otherwise not evident. Positive inferences concerning migration and diffusion, or cultural preferences and capacities, may arise from distributional studies or comparisons of cultures and thus point the way toward further search for evidence.

The cultural geographer is not concerned with explaining the inner workings of culture or with describing fully patterns of human behavior, even when they affect the land, but rather with assessing the technical potential of human communities for using and modifying their habitats. In order to achieve such an assessment, cultural geography studies the distribution in time and space of cultures and elements of cultures.

CULTURE AREA

Although the simple facts of location do not, as sometimes is supposed, comprise the sum of geographic knowledge, accurate determination of site and area underlies all geographic study. Accordingly, the first essential step in cultural geography is an investigation of the past and present distribution of culture traits, which constitutes the basis for recognition and delimitation of culture areas. The latter may be defined as territories inhabited at any given period by human communities characterized by particular cultures.

Given the dependence of cultural homogeneity on immediate communication, and the dependence of communication in turn on geographic contiguity or technical substitutes therefor, "culture area" implies a relative uniformity rather than an absolute one. Relative cultural similarity appears in different degrees, from virtual identity of attitudes and aptitudes within a small territory to general resemblances or wide dissemination of individual traits or elements of culture over larger areas.

The locational problem basic to cultural geography, therefore, concerns the

[13] A classic in this field is Carl O. Sauer's *Agricultural Origins and Dispersals* (New York: American Geographical Society, 1952). See also the articles by V. Gordon Childe ("A Prehistorian's Interpretation of Diffusion"), Hans Bobek ("The Main Stages in Socioeconomic Evolution . . ."), I. H. Burkill ("Habits of Man and the Origins of the Cultivated Plants of the Old World"), Hugh Cutler ("Food Sources in the New World"), and Dan Stanislawski ("The Origin and Spread of the Grid-Pattern Town") in Part III of this volume. See also J. E. Spencer and G. A. Hale, "The Origin, Nature, and Distribution of Agricultural Terracing," *Pacific Viewpoint*, II (1961), 1–40.

distribution at any period of human populations sharing similar or related cultures, or single related culture traits or complexes. The three types of spatial categories common to all geography come into play in this connection: *points* serving as cultural hearths and centers, *lines* or *avenues* of cultural dissemination and penetration, and continuous or interrupted *areas* of distribution of given culture types or elements. All three are seen as varying through history. Furthermore, the centers, avenues, and areas of individual traits and cultures often fall together into larger realms in which certain common features prevail widely, so that a kind of areal hierarchy of culture types emerges.[14]

Because of the flexibility and relativity of the culture concept itself, and of the various uses to which it may be put—including the emphasis of cultural influences on material features—the world and its culture-bearing populations will never lend themselves to a single, exact, complete, and thoroughly consistent scheme of classification or regionalization. A fixed and finite list of culture areas for any period of history cannot exist, and the same can be said for a universal and explicit list of all natural or "geographic" regions.

At the two extremes of generality in classifying culture areas lie, respectively, the plotting of the distribution of single traits of human societies or objects of human manufacture, and the division of the world or major parts of it into realms for each of which a limited range and basic similarity of culture type have been adduced. Trait-distribution study begins atomistically with consideration of well-defined individual items. A number of individual distributions of this kind may coincide or nearly coincide and may lead to a postulation of relatedness among the cultures concerned, common sources of the traits, or even over-all cultural similarity. Plotting of trait distributions at different periods may expose the process of diffusion.[15]

A step beyond the study of the distribution of single traits is the investigation of cultural complexes. Social usages or technical procedures and products, consisting of a number of different characteristic elements which form a complex so elaborate and idiosyncratic that it would be very unlikely to recur ac-

---

[14] In addition to the study of hierarchies defined by cultural criteria, attention may be directed to the cultural aspects of hierarchies defined by other criteria: for example, urban hierarchies defined by relative complexity of functions and the range of goods. The static models that have been designed to interpret interrelations among cities or between cities and their hinterlands have obvious, if implicit, relevance to the themes of cultural geography. See Bert F. Hoselitz: "Generative and Parasitic Cities," *Economic Development and Cultural Change*, III (1955), 278–94; and the articles by Rhoads Murphey ("The City as a Center of Change") and Torsten Hägerstrand ("The Propagation of Innovation Waves") in Part III of this volume.

[15] See the articles by Richard Weiss and Carl O. Sauer ("Middle America as a Culture Historical Location") in Part II of this volume. The various "Culture Element Distribution" studies of A. L. Kroeber and others, published in the "University of California Anthropological Records," illustrate this procedure. A recent example is Harold E. Driver and William C. Massey, "Comparative Studies of North American Indians," *Transactions of the American Philosophical Society*, Vol. XLVII, Part 2 (1957). Kroeber's classic study, *Cultural and Natural Areas of Native North America* ("University of California Publications in American Archaeology and Ethnology," Vol. XXXVIII [1939]), can still be read with great profit.

cidentally in widely separated places, provide a stronger demonstration of cultural affinity or common evolution than do individual culture items.[16]

Comprehensive classifications of cultures into a few major, and sometimes further minor, groups most often rest on the combined distributions of a variety of individual diagnostic traits. Such classification may be taken to imply only an analogous evolution (necessary or accidental) of the cultures grouped together, or it may serve as an argument for genetic relationships among the cultures concerned. Thus the several well-known classifications of stages of cultural, and especially technical, development do not usually assert that the cultures of all nomadic herders or all horticultural planters have descended in a single common line; they tend instead to imply that cultural evolution necessarily proceeds through a series of determined stages.[17] On the other hand, such a doctrine as that of the *Kulturkreislehre* proposes that all the cultures of the world fall into a small number of different "circles," in which all the member cultures are of common descent, and genetically rather distant from non-member cultures.[18] In the former case, the argument is evolutionary; in the latter it is genetic. Both tendencies in the classification of cultures and culture areas require acceptance of certain limiting premises. Other, less restrictive, methods of culture area classification are thus desirable for geography.

Geography employs the notion of the "cultural landscape," as will be seen, as one device for distinguishing and classifying cultural regions, but it also requires other ways of establishing culture areas, even for study of the cultural landscape itself. The fact that participation in a given culture demands participation in a community built on communication suggests the availability of

[16] The question of a "breaking point" between innovations that are sufficiently complex and arbitrary to overrule separate development and those that may have occurred independently has been the subject of prolonged but inconclusive debate. See the articles by V. Gordon Childe, Hans Bobek, and Dan Stanislawski in Part III of this volume.

[17] The classic statements of evolutionary doctrine are contained in Lewis Henry Morgan's *Ancient Society* (New York: Holt, 1877), and Edward B. Tylor's *Primitive Culture* (London: Murray, 1871). For recent statements see V. Gordon Childe, *Man Makes Himself* (New York: Mentor Books, 1951), and Leslie A. White, *The Evolution of Culture* (New York: McGraw-Hill, 1959). Julian H. Steward has suggested that classical or neo-classical evolutionism should be replaced by a concept of "multilinear evolution." He assumes that "certain basic types of culture may develop in similar ways under similar conditions but that few concrete aspects of culture will appear among all groups of mankind in a regular sequence." See his *Theory of Culture Change* (Urbana: University of Illinois Press, 1955), *passim*, ref. to p. 4. See also the articles of A. L. Kroeber ("Evolution, History and Culture"), Gordon R. Willey ("Historical Patterns and Evolution in Native New World Cultures"), Robert J. Braidwood ("Levels in Prehistory: A Model for the Consideration of the Evidence"), Robert M. Adams ("The Evolutionary Process in Early Civilizations"), and Julian H. Steward ("Evolutionary Principles and Social Types") in Sol Tax (ed.), *The Evolution of Man*, Vol. II of *Evolution after Darwin* (Chicago: University of Chicago Press, 1960).

[18] The leaders of this school were Father Wilhelm Schmidt and Franz Graebner. See Schmidt's *The Cultural Historical Method of Ethnology* (New York: Fortuny's, 1939; first published as *Handbuch der Methode der kulturhistorischen Ethnologie* [Münster: Aschendorf, 1937]), and Graebner's *Methode der Ethnologie* (Heidelberg: Winter, 1911). See also Clyde Kluckhohn: "Some Reflections on the Method and Theory of *Kulturkreislehre*," *American Anthropologist*, XXXVIII (1936), 157–96, and Wilhelm Koppers, "Diffusion: Transmission and Acceptance," in William L. Thomas, Jr. (ed.), *Current Anthropology* (Chicago: University of Chicago Press, 1956), pp. 169–81.

a rough index to cultural distribution in the distribution of linguistic communities. To be sure, knowledge of a language or dialect does not represent the only vital factor in communication, nor is communication itself the only factor in influencing cultural participation. Nevertheless, a negative consideration applies again: except in cases where an elaborate translation mechanism has developed, an inability to communicate in a given language virtually precludes cultural participation in the community where it is spoken.[19] Thus the map of language distribution displays a less fine division into culture areas, and less particularity in regard to them, than would a map of culture areas themselves, but it is likely to be consistent with larger cultural divisions.[20] However, linguistic barriers, in many cases, mask fundamental similarities of culture that cross them freely.[21] For example, the propagation of the world's major religions often raced far ahead of the languages intimately connected with them. A striking lag of this sort is found in the explosive expansion of Islam, and the less rapid or extensive diffusion of Arabic speech. Often only historical study of former linguistic distribution, and especially of processes of cultural translation, migration, and diffusion, can explain these departures from expected patterns.

The distribution of linguistic communities at a given period, and such linguistic evidences of antecedent patterns as are found, for example, in place names and non-standard rustic vocabularies, thus serve as indices of culture areas.[22] Sometimes, at a rather more general level, other elements of culture, like religion, technology, and economy, have an extended distribution and serve to bind together in some degree subordinate culture areas.[23] The material remains left by past cultures also play a large role in delineating former culture areas. Archeological indicators are widely used in reconstructing culture distributions.[24] Accordingly, the archeologists have contributed most, perhaps,

[19] See the article by C. M. Delgado de Carvalho ("Geography of Languages") in Part II of this volume, and Philip L. Wagner: "Remarks on the Geography of Language," *Geographical Review,* XLVIII (1958), 86–97.

[20] In this connection it may be noted that anthropologists have used language more often than any other culture element to delimit culture areas, even when some of the traits under consideration have no clear connection with language. See, for example, A. L. Kroeber's *Handbook of the Indians of California* (Washington, D.C.: Bureau of American Ethnology, 1925).

[21] Note, for example, the polyglot character of some historic nomadic confederations in Central Asia (e.g., the Hsiung Nu), and the overlapping of linguistic, religious, social, and political patterns in parts of Southeast Asia. For clarification of the Central Asian pattern, see Wolfram Eberhard, *Conquerors and Rulers: Social Forces in Medieval China* (Leiden: Brill, 1952); for Southeast Asia see the article by Jan O. M. Broek ("Diversity and Unity in Southeast Asia") in Part II of this volume; E. R. Leach, *Political Systems of Highland Burma* (London: G. Bell & Sons, 1954); and Herold Wiens, *China's March toward the Tropics* (Hamden, Conn.: Shoestring Press, 1954).

[22] The problems and prospects of place-name study are treated by Ivan Lind and Wilbur Zelinsky in Part II of this volume.

[23] Cf. the articles on religion by Paul Fickeler and on the world's major agricultural regions by Derwent Whittlesey in Parts II and IV of this volume.

[24] See, for example, Gordon R. Willey and Philip Phillips, *Method and Theory in American Archaeology* (Chicago: University of Chicago Press, 1958).

not only to the substantive knowledge of past cultures and their spatial and temporal positions but also to the development of areal concepts applicable to cultures.[25] The correlation of genetic and functional relationships among cultures, inferred from such artifacts as pottery and stonework, with their spatial and temporal relations, is one of the main goals of archeology.

In addition, archeologists are paying increasing attention to the nature of the geographic milieu in which the cultures that they investigate occurred. The question of the milieu is also paramount for the geographer. For one thing, the distribution of a particular culture inferred from the indications mentioned often takes insufficiently into account the variability of natural environments within the boundaries found and so does not necessarily represent a single uniform way of life. Small differences of environment—seashore versus inland, hill country versus flood plain, steppe versus woodland—have come to be recognized as extremely significant archeologically, and also ethnologically.[26] Geographers are attentive to such differences. In addition, they maintain an interest in past environments for their own sake, and in the effect that human action has had on them.[27] The culture area, for a geographer, is always also a "cultural landscape."

THE CULTURAL LANDSCAPE

A culture area, in geographic terms, may constitute a "region." It forms a definable unit in space, characterized by relative internal homogeneity in regard to certain criteria, by some system of internal movement coextensive with it, or by interaction among elements within its limits. The typical association of concrete geographic features within a region, or in any other spatial subdivi-

---

[25] In addition to Willey and Phillips (*op. cit.*), see Willey (ed.), *Prehistoric Settlement Patterns in the New World*, ("Viking Fund Publications in Anthropology," No. 23 [New York, 1956]), and the articles of V. Gordon Childe, and Beardsley *et al.* ("Functional and Evolutionary Implications of Community Patterning") in Parts III and IV of this volume.

[26] A concern with past environments is very evident in the archeological investigations of Robert J. Braidwood and his associates; see, for example, their *Prehistoric Investigations in Iraqi Kurdistan* (Chicago: University of Chicago Press, 1960). The significance of environmental differences in ethnography is clearly demonstrated by Leach (*op. cit.*).

[27] Many studies by geographers could be cited here. For example, Hans Bobek, "Klima und Landschaft Irans in vor- und frühgeschichtlicher Zeit," *Geographischer Jahresbericht aus Oesterreich*, XXV (1954), 1–42; Hermann von Wissmann; "The Role of Nature and Man in Changing the Face of the Dry Belt of Asia," in *Man's Role in Changing the Face of the Earth*, pp. 278–349; H. C. Darby, "The Clearing of the Woodland in Europe," *ibid.*, pp. 183–216; Herbert Wilhelmy, "Das Alter der Schwarzerde und der Steppen Mittel- und Osteuropas," *Erdkunde*, IV (1950), 5–34; Carl O. Sauer: "The Theme of Plant and Animal Destruction in Economic History," *Journal of Farm Economics*, XX (1938), 765–75; *idem*, "Early Relations of Man to Plants," *Geographical Review*, XXXVII (1947), 1–25; *idem*, "Environment and Culture during the Last Deglaciation," *Proceedings of the American Philosophical Society*, XCII (1948), 65–77; *idem*, "The End of the Ice Age and Its Witnesses," *Geographical Review*, XLVII (1957), 29–43. We should also mention a classic early study of Robert Gradmann, "Beziehungen zwischen Pflanzengeographie und Siedlungsgeschichte," *Geographische Zeitschrift*, XII (1906), 305–25.

sion of the earth, may be described as a "landscape."[28] This term comprehends both the distinctive features that serve to set a region apart and those not confined to a particular region but occurring there. The cultural landscape, then, connotes the geographic content of a determined area, or a geographic complex of a certain type, in which the choices made and changes worked by men as members of some cultural community are manifested.[29]

The study of the cultural landscape serves several different ends simultaneously and inseparably. Apart from its function of systematic description, it provides for regional classification, affords an insight into the role of man in geographic transformations, and throws light upon certain aspects of culture and cultural communities in themselves. It looks for differences in landscape that can be attributed to differences of human conduct under different cultures, and it looks for departures, caused by man, from expected "natural" conditions.

Since cultural geography selects for study those differences among landscapes, and those component features of landscapes, that cannot be attributed to "natural" influences, and likewise considers the interferences of man with the free play of those influences, the character of the subject implies a categorical rejection of environmental determinism.[30] If "environmental influences" evoked an "adaptation" by the human community to its surroundings, the emphasis would have to fall upon the study of those influences themselves as a key to all else. The stress, however, is placed by cultural geographers on the human group and its activities. Physical geography is essential to cultural geography, but not as a primary source of explanation for the condition of man. At the same time, the alternative of "cultural determinism" fails to provide satisfactory explanations, for, as previously remarked, the idea of culture is not adequate to explain human behavior, but only to formulate some limiting

[28] We accept Hartshorne's recommendation that "landscape" should be equated with the German *Landschaftsbild* rather than *Landschaft,* since the latter term is used synonymously with "area" or "region." "Landscape" and *Landschaftsbild* refer to the appearance of an area, not to the area itself as a delimited entity. Hence our distinction between "culture area" and "cultural landscape" as research themes. See Richard Hartshorne, *Perspective on the Nature of Geography* (Chicago: Rand McNally for the Association of American Geographers, 1959), *passim.* The conception of "landscape" as the appearance or scenery of an area is exemplified by the magazine of that name, published by J. B. Jackson of Santa Fe, New Mexico, since 1952.

[29] The notion of the "cultural landscape" was introduced to American geography by Carl O. Sauer. See his *Morphology of Landscape* ("University of California Publications in Geography," Vol. II, No. 2 [1925]), and "Recent Developments in Cultural Geography," in E. C. Hayes (ed.), *Recent Developments in the Social Sciences* (New York: Lippincott, 1927), pp. 154–212. Note also the discussion by Robert S. Platt in Part I of this volume. The antecedents of Sauer's interpretations appear mainly in works of Siegfried Passarge, e.g., *Grundlagen der Landschaftskunde* (3 vols.; Hamburg: Friederichsen, 1919–21); *Vergleichende Landschaftskunde* (5 vols.; Berlin: Reimer, 1921–30); and *Die Landschaftsgürtel der Erde* (Breslau: Hirt, 1923). See also the substantive application of the concept in Jan O. M. Broek, *The Santa Clara Valley, California: A Study in Landscape Changes* (Utrecht: A. Oosthoeck, 1932).

[30] The inherent weakness of environmentalist reasoning is exposed by Carl O. Sauer ("Cultural Geography"), Robert S. Platt ("The Rise of Cultural Geography in America"), and Erhard Rostlund ("Twentieth Century Magic") in Part I of this volume.

factors that affect it.[31] The cultural landscape, then, is a concrete and characteristic product of the complicated interplay between a given human community, embodying certain cultural preferences and potentials, and a particular set of natural circumstances. It is a heritage of many eras of natural evolution and of many generations of human effort.

A landscape, under the influence of man and culture, may show a gross configuration closely similar to what might develop under natural influences alone: the over-all pattern of hills and valleys, streams and lakes; the climate; the ocean coasts. The skyline displays the same ridges and crests, or the same immensely broad horizon that has existed for eons. The rains and winds, the heat and cold, come and go at their own seasons. Already in these major physical configurations, however, some human influence may show: a scarred hillside, a mine-dump, a river dammed, a smoky atmosphere. But evidence of human influence is most strikingly revealed in the character of vegetation. Great expanses have been cleared of prairie, forest, or shrub cover and planted to crops. Much of the "wild" cover that remains is damaged or impoverished, or still recovering from human interference. Reflecting the manner of its disturbance and replacement, the vegetative cover thus tends to exhibit patterns distinctive to particular human communities.[32]

The cultivated lands that appear so prominently in many landscapes testify not only to a radical change in plant cover but also to the presence of clearly artificial elements: orchards, gardens, furrowed fields, walls and fences, paths and roads, granaries, stables, dwellings, and entire settlements, all in orderly array. In any cultural landscape, the arrangement, style, and materials of these features tend to reflect the presence of a distinctive way of life, or *genre de vie,* interacting with a given natural setting.[33] Engineering works, architecture, cultivated plants, domestic animals, implements, vehicles, costumes, and much else help to diagnose particular cultures.

Many questions can be asked about the features of a landscape: What is ancient and what is recent? What is typical and what is exceptional? What is accidental and what is intentional? What is transient and what is permanent? What has been imposed by man and what has been given by nature?

These questions mark the path toward understanding a way of life and

[31] As Kroeber remarks, the cultural approach "is a selective approach, fruitful because of its selectiveness, but for the same reason not unlimited in its scope" (*The Nature of Culture,* p. 135). It would be absurd to imagine that economic theory, for example, should be given up for any more generalized theory of culture.

[32] Such patterns are described by several authors in *Man's Role in Changing the Face of the Earth.* Another illustration appears in Marvin W. Mikesell, *Northern Morocco: A Cultural Geography* ("University of California Publications in Geography," Vol. XIV [1961]).

[33] See Max. Sorre's article on *genre de vie* in Part IV of this volume. Settlement forms and features, in particular, have long been used as indicators of cultural differences. See the article by Fred B. Kniffen ("Louisiana House Types") in Part II, and those by H. J. Fleure ("Social Organization and Environment"), Albert Demangeon ("The Origins and Causes of Settlement Types"), and Glenn Trewartha ("Types of Rural Settlements in Colonial America") in Part IV of this volume.

toward comprehension of some processes of geographic change. The answers (or partial answers) to such questions are deciphered from fragmentary evidence imbedded in the landscape, or from historical reconstruction, cultural comparison, physical or biological reasoning, and other means. Like any study dealing with the world as it is, cultural geography must piece together its account from available evidence and accept the aid of any valid and useful reasoning.

The methods most commonly employed in cultural geography generally are those constantly used by most geographers: the plotting of single and joint distributions and densities of given features; the delimitation and comparison of regions by various criteria; the mapping of the spatial arrangement and organization of complexes of related or connected features; the charting of movements; the identification of physical and biotic zonation. These operations reveal the orderly patterns, the regular coincidences of features, the departures from the expected "natural" situation, and the geographic similarities among different places and regions that constitute effects of culture. When culture areas themselves are matched against the spatial units thus defined, the culture concept furnishes a means of grasping processes at work in forming cultural landscapes. For example, if one plots the distribution of different kinds of vegetation in an area, a definite zonation, usually concentric on the local settlements, is likely to emerge. The sequence may be: completely artificial urban plantings, interspersed with streets and buildings; fringe wastelands; various kinds of crop land in succeeding bands; woodland, forest, or other vegetation, at first much disturbed, then increasingly abundant and intact; at last, perhaps, a "virgin" forest. The explanation for the nature of the cover in the several zones lies in different uses of the land and spatial dispositions under the corresponding culture.[34]

The various geographic techniques all fit together automatically, as in this example. Plotting of a distribution leads to establishment of a zonation, created with a definite organizational pattern that has been brought about by regularities of movement by human beings. The whole scheme may be summarized as defining a minor "nodal" region of human activity and landscape type, and a larger area in which such patterns are recurrent may qualify as a relatively homogeneous region. If several such regions, separated by some distance, show a landscape development similar in these respects, they may attest to cultural similarity between their respective inhabitants. The same apparent effects, however, may spring occasionally from different circumstances, and so the cultural controls involved, as well as natural factors, have to be investigated.

The chief advantage in the reasoning that combines ordinary geographic

[34] See Edgar Anderson's article ("Man as a Maker of New Plants and New Plant Communities") in Part IV of this volume, and George F. Carter, "Ecology—Geography—Ethnobotany," *Scientific Monthly,* LXXII (1950), 73–80. A specific illustration of zonation is given in Philip L. Wagner, "Natural and Artificial Zonation of Vegetation: Chiapas, Mexico," *Geographical Review,* LII (1962), in press. In his "Early Relations of Man to Plants" (*op. cit.*), Carl O. Sauer describes a hypothetical sequence and zonation of biotic and edaphic disturbance centered on campsites.

methods with cultural ones is that it permits extrapolation of results. When a given type of cultural landscape has been studied and its formative processes have become clear, a similar development elsewhere may be considered likely wherever the same or very similar conjunctions of natural and cultural circumstances occur. Within a limited area or region this amounts almost to a canon of sampling procedure; over larger distances the probabilities decrease.

A correlation established between a given culture and its landscape thus serves on the one hand for inferences of culture from known landscape types, and on the other for predicting the character of landscape where cultural and natural determinants are known. Even more important practically, the same kinds of problems, connected with the same particular processes of landscape change, usually arise where similar culture types and similar natural circumstances coincide. Thus, for instance, shifting cultivation in the tropics or the reclamation of middle latitude desert lands both pose rather similar problems wherever found, because in each case the most influential factors are basically similar. Even the vast issues of economic development concern cultural landscapes and can be studied as a problem of the influence of certain aspects of culture on the character and scope of artificial processes that transform landscapes. A study of economic development that disregards the relation of culture to landscape is losing something vital.[35]

Few present cultural landscapes are entirely products of the work of contemporary communities. The evolution of a landscape is a gradual and cumulative process—it has a history. The stages in that history have meaning for the present landscape as well as for those of the past. Moreover, the present cultural landscapes of the world reflect not only local evolutions but also a multitude of influences carried by migration, diffusion, commerce, and exchange. Behind most culture areas of today lies a long succession of different cultures and cultural developments. Culture history, accordingly, must enter strongly into cultural geography.

CULTURE HISTORY

The reconstruction of the local and regional succession of cultures and of the history of cultural origins and dispersals employs many of the same indices as does the definition of contemporary culture areas. Thus, through documents, place names, or other linguistic evidence investigators may discover sequences in the occupation of an area by different groups and may link these groups

---

[35] This is not to say that such relationships are easy to comprehend or that all, or even most, of the variables involved in them may be quantified. It goes without saying, therefore, that economic development must be defined very largely in economic, demographic, and technological terms; cf. Norton S. Ginsburg, *Atlas of Economic Development* (Chicago: University of Chicago Press, 1961). In this case, once again, culture may function as a restrictive or inhibiting force. See Bert F. Hoselitz, "Problems of Adapting and Communicating Modern Techniques to Less Developed Areas," *Economic Development and Cultural Change,* II (1954), 249–69; Ernest Beaglehole, "Cultural Factors in Economic and Social Change," *International Labour Review,* LXIX (1954), 416–30; and Charles J. Erasmus, *Man Takes Control: Cultural Development and American Aid* (Minneapolis: University of Minnesota Press, 1961).

14

with peoples in other areas showing similar characteristics. More cautiously, the linguist may interpret connections in the past as evidence for cultural relationships and contacts, without implying necessarily migration and replacement of older populations. The linguistic history of the former Roman Empire, for example, provides a sensitive index to the early cultural penetration and the later waning of the central dominance of Rome, without affording any grounds for thinking that the pre-Roman populations disappeared and were replaced by people from central Italy *en masse*. The histories of the Spanish language in the New World and of the Arabic language in North Africa are patently the same in this regard.

Archeology affords another kind of index to the cultural distribution and movements of the past, but provides a much less certain indication than that of language for the actual unity and individuality of particular communities of people. Peoples speaking very different languages, and thinking and acting very differently, may leave behind a similar kit of tools. However, since the materials recovered by archeology are usually precisely those instruments connected with the modification and improvement of environment, the archeological record is also important from a geographic standpoint. The cultural geographer tries to amplify and extend that record to include all possible facts relating to environments of former cultures.

The inference of cultural identity from artifacts is never certain, and an everlasting dispute rages between proponents of repeated independent invention and the champions of unique invention combined with diffusion. It is in fact logically impossible to show whether a given artifact has been invented in a place or introduced, without external evidence. On the negative side, of course, it is often possible to demonstrate by evidence from elsewhere that a given trait was *not* first invented at a given time and place. However, by establishing chronology and areal distribution conjointly, archeology is able to trace the evolution of techniques and organization, if not precisely of societies themselves.

The problems of diffusion versus independent invention can be investigated by another means that takes advantage of modern genetics. Plants or animals evolve through chromosome mutations and related processes. No two species-populations of organisms that have evolved apart for long are likely to coincide even in their gross morphology, much less in finer details. A cultivated plant or domestic animal population that can be established as genetically distinct testifies, therefore, to an independent evolution of some age, and on occasion may support the inference of a long independent development in the cultural community with which it is associated.[36] Conversely, and even more conclu-

[36] See the articles on the origin and dispersal of cultivated plants by I. H. Burkill and Hugh Cutler in Part III of this volume. For more general statements on theory and method see Sauer, *Agricultural Origins and Dispersals;* Anderson, *Plants, Man, and Life;* D. C. Darlington and A. P. Wylie, *Chromosome Atlas of Flowering Plants* (London: Allen & Unwin, 1955), and D. C. Darlington, *Chromosome Botany* (London: Allen & Unwin, 1956).

sively, the possession by two spatially separated cultural communities of plants or animals that are genetically very similar or identical validates hypotheses of former interchange and contact. The most convincing evidence of intercourse between the New World and the Old before Columbus, for example, is undoubtedly the presence of certain domesticated plants (e.g., the sweet potato) on both sides of the Pacific at the time of first European contact.

The same genetic considerations should find application in the case of human races, but racial differentiation in man appears to be such a gradual process, and so much mixture must have intervened to blur the picture without entailing major cultural change, that human racial indicators on the whole have not illuminated much of culture history. Culture and race are often poorly matched in man.

Another form of evidence for cultural affinities, and therefore also for historical connections, are resemblances in culture traits and culture complexes between different areas. As previously noted, such resemblances may suggest diffusions or a common genesis of several cultures. But only when such evidence is overwhelming does it justify assumption of a single origin and common early history for the cultures concerned.

Culture history, by piecing together such evidence as has been described, from trait and complex distribution, the biology of domesticates, archeology, linguistics, place names, documents, oral traditions, and other sources, seeks to discover four kinds of facts: the origin in time and place of given cultural features; the routes, times, and manner of their dissemination; the distribution of former culture areas; and the character of former cultural landscapes. The problems of culture history concern all of human time. Relatively little is yet known about some of the topics mentioned, even for recent periods. The culture historian may require collaboration not only from the archeologist and paleolinguist, but from economic historians, agronomists, and ethnologists, who deal with more recent phenomena. The question of the culture history of cultivated plants provides an illustration. For the majority of common crop plants of the modern Occident, the original centers of domestication and the early history of diffusion are somewhat better chronicled, perhaps, than the routes and means of later introductions of these plants into parts of the world distant from their homelands. The approximate dating of such late introductions rests, of course, on much more reliable evidence, since, with few exceptions, the well-authenticated base line is the Age of Discovery. The determination of original centers is based on combined genetic and distributional analysis, aided on occasion by archeology and linguistics; reconstruction of the history of later diffusions has to depend on scarce documents, occasional linguistic evidence, and infrequent archeological testimony.[37]

[37] The details of post-Columbian diffusion have, however, been worked out for some crops. For examples, see Redcliffe N. Salaman, *The History and Social Influence of the Potato* (London: Cambridge University Press, 1949), and William O. Jones, *Manioc in Africa* (Stanford: Stanford University Press, 1958).

The important problem of the migration of peoples has a strong bearing on other historical problems, for the simplest demonstration of the spread of culture is the proof of movements by the people who possess it. But migration, often, is an easy assumption rather than a demonstrated fact, and so its invocation can mislead research. Individual cultural elements and complexes can become widely distributed through contact of peoples and by acculturation without any major population movements taking place—consider the spread of North American and European techniques around the world in recent decades, or the drift of Roman goods far beyond the imperial frontiers.[38] In contrast, migrations of great scope have occurred without noticeably deranging the pattern of culture areas; the European immigration to the United States in the last hundred years is a case in point.

On the other hand, it cannot be denied that large-scale redistribution of human populations has often had a great effect on culture areas, as in the initial European settlement of North and South America, Siberia, South Africa, and Australia, or the Arab and Chinese expansions. It is useful to describe the final phases of these movements as "frontiers," and distinguish between frontiers of *inclusion* or *assimilation,* illustrated by Arab and Spanish colonization, and frontiers of *exclusion,* illustrated by the colonization of Europeans in areas occupied by less numerous and technically inferior peoples. The fact that the last open frontiers of European expansion occurred primarily in mid-latitude grasslands suggests interesting problems for comparative study.[39] Within the same context of European expansion, it is useful to distinguish between "colonies of settlement," like the United States and Canada, and "colonies of exploitation," like India or tropical Africa. In the latter, Europeans could not displace native peoples. They became administrators, plantation owners, merchants, teachers, or missionaries—in short, a ruling class in "dual" or "plural" societies.[40]

The importance of transplanted cultural communities depends upon the maintenance of cultural integrity. Thus, the study of recent foreign immigrant groups in American cities, though it possesses great romantic appeal, will not uncover many important additions to North American culture and will not reveal a great deal about the former cultures of the immigrants, diluted and recast as they become in new surroundings. Any immigrant group in the United States represents a transient and probably unique subcultural unit, allied both

[38] Sir Mortimer Wheeler, *Rome beyond the Imperial Frontiers* (Harmondsworth and Baltimore: Penguin Books, 1955).

[39] For further discussion and bibliography, see Marvin W. Mikesell, "Comparative Studies in Frontier History," *Annals of the Association of American Geographers,* L (1960), 62–74.

[40] The most influencial statement on the economic aspects of "dualism" is J. H. Boeke's *Economics and Economic Policy of Dual Societies* (New York: Institute of Pacific Relations, 1953). A collection of essays on various aspects of "pluralism" appears in *Ethnic and Cultural Pluralism in Intertropical Countries* (Brussels: International Institute of Differing Civilizations, 1957). A specific illustration of pluralism is given by David Lowenthal ("The Range and Variation of Caribbean Societies") in Part II of this volume.

to America and the former home community. It loses touch rapidly with the latter and tends to fossilize "old country" ways no longer practiced in the homeland. Such lesser cultural units exist wherever a living community preserves its ways. In some societies they survive longer than in the United States. The history of segregated Jewish communities in the urban centers of the Old World illustrates a very different situation.[41]

In the United States, immigrant neighborhoods are probably less significant from the standpoint of cultural geography than many other kinds of subcultural units that are based on local or regional communities and social stratification, and are bound closely into more or less separate communication systems.[42] This situation may have been true more or less throughout history; innovation and differentiation in place have certainly played an important role in the evolution of culture areas.

However the mechanisms of cultural differentiation and cultural exchange and standardization may have operated in particular instances, two major facts stand out in culture history: ideas and techniques tend to diffuse, and the cultural heritage of peoples tends to increase cumulatively. Both by internal evolution and by diffusion, culture grows and spreads. When one speaks of "stages," therefore, the implication is usually not that one complex replaces and obliterates another, but rather that new cultural complexes and traits are added to the old and coexist with them. Eventually new patterns may emerge, but in them older elements remain. Except in what are probably rare cases of total and abrupt replacement of one population by another (we are no doubt partly blinded by the example of the United States), cultural fusion and gradual development seem to be the rule. "Cultural succession" usually betokens only a convenient subdivision of a historical continuum.[43]

The history of cultural landscapes, intimately related to the foregoing themes, remains in many cases most obscure. As in the study of present cultural landscapes, the reconstruction of the landscapes of the past demands a close co-operation with physical geography. Often the study of purely physical problems provides the first and most rewarding clues for culture history. The question of the peopling of America, for instance, must await the clarification

[41] The importance of this situation in urban geography, and especially urban morphology, is demonstrated by Rosemarie Künzler-Behncke, *Entstehung und Entwicklung fremdvölkischer Eigenviertel im Stadtorganismus* ("Frankfurter Geographische Hefte," Vols. XXXIII–XXXIV [1961]).

[42] For example, see Walter M. Kollmorgen, "A Reconnaissance of Some Cultural-Agricultural Islands in the South," *Economic Geography*, XVII (1941), 409–30, XIX (1943), 109–17.

[43] On this point see especially Bronislaw Malinowski, *The Dynamics of Culture Change* (New Haven: Yale University Press, 1945). Andrew H. Clark's remarks on the distinction between "cross-section" and "process" orientation in historical geography are also relevant; see his chapter on "Historical Geography" in Preston E. James and Clarence F. Jones (eds.), *American Geography: Inventory and Prospect* (Syracuse: Syracuse University Press for the Association of American Geographers, 1954), pp. 71–105, ref. to p. 85. In addition, note Hans Bobek's preference for "evolution" rather than "revolution" in his discussion of the transition from food collection to food production in Part III of this volume.

of the glacial history of North America.[44] Likewise, only when the character of the corresponding physical environments is known can the place and time of origin of any kind of agriculture be identified reliably.[45]

Past cultural landscapes, if they can be reconstructed, furnish a valuable index to culture areas. In addition to the archeological remains of buildings, irrigation systems, walls, and so on, past disturbance of the soil and vegetation may leave its traces. Unfortunately, except for the reports of archeologists, there exist few studies in detail of landscapes of the distant past. An adequate knowledge of an ancient landscape could provide an insight into many aspects of human history at present poorly understood. For instance, the rise, achievements, and decline of Maya civilization or the relation of irrigation works to early empires could be more satisfactorily interpreted if the corresponding cultural landscapes were better known.

In cases where documentary evidence supplements material relicts, former cultural landscapes and landscape changes sometimes are successfully deciphered. The work of H. C. Darby and his associates on the landscapes of England during the early Middle Ages is perhaps the most effective illustration of such reconstruction.[46] A distinguished early illustration is provided by Victor Hehn's reconstruction of the development of the exotic vegetation of the Mediterranean region.[47] On the whole, however, the cultural landscapes of any past time are poorly known.

Awareness of the effects of human action can be of practical value; it profits humanity to know what it has done to the world. In order to identify and describe any of the processes that have helped to create a landscape, and especially those processes in which human interference is involved, the sequence of antecedent conditions must be known. Attempts to check accelerated soil erosion, for example, require consideration of former uses of the soil as well as present cultivation practices and their apparent effects. Contemporary farmers cannot always be blamed for soil destruction or deterioration, nor will changes

[44] See, for example, Carl O. Sauer's "A Geographic Sketch of Early Man in America," *Geographical Review*, XXXIV (1944), 529–73, and the revision of this study, based on more recent geologic evidence, in "The End of the Ice Age and Its Witnesses," *ibid*, XLVII (1957), 29–43.

[45] In this connection, it may be noted that Braidwood's archeological investigations have been enriched by contributions from geologists, botanists, and zoologists. See the reports of Herbert E. Wright, Jr. ("Climate and Prehistoric Man in the Eastern Mediterranean"), Hans Helbaek ("The Paleoethnobotany of the Near East and Europe"), and Charles A. Reed ("A Review of the Archaeological Evidence on Animal Domestication in the Prehistoric Near East") in Braidwood, *op. cit.* Note also his plea for co-operation between natural scientists and archeologists in "Near Eastern Prehistory," *Science*, CXXVII, No. 3312 (June, 1958), 1419–30.

[46] *The Domesday Geography of England* (Cambridge: Cambridge University Press, 1952———). At the time of this writing, four volumes covering eastern, midland, southeastern, and northern England have appeared. A volume on southwestern England and another summarizing the entire work are planned.

[47] Victor Hehn, *Kulturpflanzen und Hausthiere in ihrem Übergang aus Asien nach Griechenland und Italien sowie in das übrige Europa*, (7th ed.; Berlin: Gebrüder Bornträger, 1902). Published in English as *The Wanderings of Plants and Animals from Their First Home* (London: Swan Sonnenschein, 1888).

in their practices alone always restore or preserve the soil.[48] Conversely, knowledge of past landscapes, for example those of Roman Africa and of the Negev of Nabataean times, has suggested practical solutions to some modern problems of land management.[49]

The joint application of physical-biological and cultural knowledge to the study of processes at work in landscapes and their implications for human communities constitutes another major theme of cultural geography.

CULTURAL ECOLOGY

Culture history, by revealing the character of past culture areas and cultural landscapes and tracing them through space and time provides one kind of answer to a question that confronts every geographer: What happened here? A historical answer re-creates the procession of recognized major events that have had something to do with a place, an area, a community of people, or a geographic feature. It names the actors in the geographic drama in the order of their appearance, identifies their status and relationships, and sometimes summarizes their characters. Another kind of answer describes the action of the drama.

The study of cultural landscapes is concerned not only with the actors but also with the actions that have made and continue to make landscapes. Cultural ecology, therefore, hears in our question different implications: How do we name, how do we describe, what happened here? While culture history (if not all history) deals with a *sequence* of events, cultural ecology (as an application of the scientific mode of thinking) concerns the *process* implied in a sequence of events.[50]

Any geographer who studies and describes landscapes affected by man cannot help reporting observations in terms of actual processes, although the statements may be very simple: "These fields are plowed twice a year." "The government is building a dam." "Every year ten thousand tons of coal are extracted from the mine." "The extent of forests in the region has been greatly reduced by commercial lumber operations in the past 75 years." Such statements tell what has happened or is happening to a landscape. Likewise, we are familiar with geographic statements implying or naming a process or a given

[48] See Carl O. Sauer's article in Part IV of this volume. Mention should also be made of Walter C. Lowdermilk, "Lessons from the Old World to the Americas in Land Use," *Annual Report of the Smithsonian Institution for 1943* (Washington, D.C., 1944), pp. 413–29; and Sherburne F. Cook, *Soil Erosion and Depopulation in Central Mexico* ("Ibero-Americana," No. XXXIV [1949]). See also the articles by Paul Sears ("The Processes of Environmental Change by Man") and Arthur N. Strahler ("The Nature of Induced Erosion and Aggradation") in *Man's Role in Changing the Face of the Earth*.

[49] Cf. Jean Baradez, *Fossatum Africae: Vue-aérienne de l'organisation romaine dans le sud-algérien* (Paris: Arts et Métiers Graphiques, 1949), and M. Evenari *et al.*, "Ancient Agriculture in the Negev," *Science*, CXXXIII, No. 3457 (March, 1961), 979–96.

[50] For a slightly different, but compatible, interpretation of this theme, see Julian H. Steward's essay, "The Concept and Method of Cultural Ecology," in *Theory of Culture Change*, pp. 30–42.

landscape condition that affects the inhabitants of a region: "The annual yields of foodstuffs barely support the population at a subsistence level." "Mosquitoes breeding in the swamps and stagnant ponds are vectors of malaria, which afflicts a high percentage of the population." "Industrial development has resulted in a considerable increase of per capita income."

Cultural ecology, like other subfields of cultural geography, begins its work with careful comparison of observational data. It sifts through numerous cases to find what landscape conditions are invariably associated with certain known practices; what kinds of human action appear in all available instances to be linked, or at least coincident, with given landscape developments; what concrete techniques of land and resource use and artificial development are associated with different cultural and social systems; what conditions of livelihood are consistently associated with a particular kind of cultural landscape; what, if any, special natural circumstances are regularly coincident with any aspect of human activity or welfare under one, some, or all societies and cultures. Correlation, or, rather uniform coincidence of this kind, proves nothing, but it leads toward other avenues of insight.

In one direction, cross-checking of cultural landscape features serves to identify the requisite or necessary conditions of a given process. By comparison of closely similar cases in which a few critical differences stand out, the investigator may be able to show, for example, that the lack of certain kinds of tools (e.g., metal blades) or the presence of a prohibition (e.g., religious taboos) has acted to protect forests in a region, or that only where a certain commercial function is carried on do people exploit a particular mineral. Again, the present world distribution of most commercial crops can be correlated with distributions of climates, soils, techniques, and economies.[51] The incidence of some important diseases has also been shown to reflect various natural and cultural circumstances.[52]

The ultimate goal of reasoning in this direction is the identification of conditions necessary to produce a given phenomenon. The product of such reasoning is a division of the world or any part of it into companion-zones of possibility and impossibility: zones where the process or feature considered can occur, and those in which, barring stipulated changes, it could not occur. Negative reasoning operates once more.

The second strategy in cultural ecology is direct: it discovers, describes, and analyzes actual processes.[53] Thus a careful study of farming techniques often reveals just how a soil is degraded or gradually enriched and stabilized; investigation of the skilful pursuit and systematic utilization of fish or game demon-

[51] See Derwent Whittlesey's discussion of major agricultural regions in Part IV of this volume.

[52] Jacques May, *The Ecology of Human Diseases* (New York: M.D. Publications, 1959).

[53] See, for example, Carl O. Sauer's "Man in the Ecology of Tropical America," *Proceedings of the Ninth Pacific Science Congress, Bangkok, 1957*, XX (1958), 104–10; and Harold Conklin's article on shifting cultivation in Part IV of this volume.

strates how a given people multiply and prosper in a stern habitat; observation in detail of the use made of a woodland by a human community and its livestock brings into clear relief the impact of their cutting, culling, burning, foraging, seed-dispersal, and other interferences with the constitution of the flora and the physiognomy of the vegetation.

By following step by step the process that creates a given feature, the investigator can grasp at least one set of sufficient conditions. In order to establish a secure correlation, however, he must go a step further, and show that no other conjunction of circumstances could produce the feature he considers. It is relatively easy to show that cutting, followed by persistent annual burning and by pasturing of cattle above a certain density at appropriate seasons can turn a thriving tropical forest into a uniform grassland.[54] Does this imply that all tropical grasslands have arisen thus or by related mechanisms of human intervention?

The possibility of confident explanation runs down a gradient from geographic features clearly and explicitly of human handiwork (like engineering works which we easily recognize as products of well-known techniques under a specific culture and thoroughly apparent social mechanisms), to features and circumstances in which the mark of man is only dimly visible (as in the now almost uninhabited rain forests of Yucatan, with their suspicious-looking clusters of trees perhaps once favored by the Maya). The study of transformation processes anywhere along this gradient brings rewards.

A similar gradient may exist for the interpretation of the influence of the environment on man, although the rejection of any *automatic* assumptions in this regard must stand. Careful and persistent investigation of some technologically simple cultures (in Australia and the North American deserts) has impelled some scholars to assert regular relationships between the character of environment (largely unmodified by man) and the security, welfare, and organization of the human groups concerned.[55] Others, more conditionally, have supported the idea of definite environmental limitations on the development of farming cultures (e.g., in the Maya area and the Amazon basin).[56] Obvious connections also exist between the productivity and protectiveness of

[54] Cf. André Aubréville: *Climats, forêts et désertification de l'Afrique tropicale* (Paris: Éditions Maritimes et Coloniales, 1949), and Carl O. Sauer, "Grassland Climax, Fire, and Man," *Journal of Range Management,* III (1950), 16–21.

[55] See Joseph B. Birdsell, "Some Environmental and Cultural Factors Influencing the Structuring of Australian Aboriginal Populations," *American Naturalist,* LXXXVII (1953), 171–207, and Steward, *op. cit.*

[56] See Milton Altschuler, "On the Environmental Limitation of Mayan Cultural Development," *Southwestern Journal of Anthropology,* XIV (1958), 189–98; Angel Palerm and Eric R. Wolf, "Ecological Potential and Cultural Development in Mesoamerica," in *Studies in Human Ecology* (Washington, D.C.: Pan American Union, 1957), pp. 1–38; and Betty J. Meagers, "Environment and Culture in the Amazon Basin: An Appraisal of the Theory of Environmental Determinism," *ibid,* pp. 71–90. A different interpretation of some of the data presented in these essays is given by James M. Blaut, "The Ecology of Tropical Farming Systems," in *Plantation Systems of the New World* (Washington, D.C.: Pan American Union, 1959), pp. 83–97.

environments extensively modified by artificial means, and the prosperity and material security of their inhabitants.[57] Although it may not be necessary, or perhaps even desirable, to formulate these various relationships into any general theory, their implications deserve attention at least because of their practical and humane value.

The amelioration of human living conditions and the relief of human misery and material want cannot fail to count among the important, if implicit, goals of cultural geography.[58] Value judgments of a practical kind necessarily arise from the observations and reflections of cultural geographers, and in particular from the analysis and assessment of processes that distinguish cultural ecology. Cultural geography provides to some extent already, and can aspire to provide on a far greater scale, a critique of the utilization of environments by humanity, a "geographic feedback" that can illuminate and guide man's development and enjoyment of space. To be sure, in our society various branches of technology and planning already treat these matters amply. But ordinary geographic methods of observation and investigation, emphasizing spatial order and zonation, both bring to light and help to solve problems that otherwise go unperceived. The wide perspective of cultural ecology qualifies it as an instrument for study of the problems of our own technological order, because cultural ecology provides a correction for the narrowness and overspecialization of outlook that would arise from concentration on Western society and its geographic manifestations.

No really detached comparative understanding of our Western commercial cultures has yet been achieved, although we know countless details about them. Cultural ecology can only give a meaningful interpretation to our technology and its effects when more about the cultures concerned becomes known. It therefore tends to concentrate upon other societies for which the cultural data are more complete and in this way comes to share the interests of anthropology. There is a close kinship between anthropology and cultural geography because the two studies relate to different and complementary aspects of the same concrete problems.

Cultural ecology, as a meeting point of these two disciplines, devotes itself to problems of the habitat of cultural communities of every stage and condition. If it seemingly withholds its emphasis from modern highly technical societies, the causes lie at once in their peculiarity and complexity, and in the fact that other means of self-analysis have become incorporated into them. Because of the difficulty of applying the cultural concept to the study of such complex communities—so far, at any rate—geographers have had to deal with them

[57] See Max. Sorre's article on *genre de vie* in Part IV of this volume and the articles by E. Estyn Evans ("The Ecology of Peasant Life in Western Europe"), Gottfried Pfeifer ("The Quality of Peasant Living in Central Europe"), and Pierre Gourou ("The Quality of Land Use of Tropical Cultivators") in *Man's Role in Changing the Face of the Earth.*

[58] See, for example, Max. Sorre's article on the "Geography of Diet" in Part IV of this volume.

in a different manner and have had to develop economic and technological, rather than cultural, concepts as research tools.[59] This difficulty in the application of cultural thinking may account for the widely differing interpretations given to the terms "cultural" and "human" geography in the United States.

THE CULTURAL GEOGRAPHER

There is one very important difference between cultural geography as presented in this discussion and other subdivisions of human geography. For explanatory purposes, a logical division of the former subject into five allied and complementary, but separate, themes has been proposed. Work on any of these themes may properly constitute "cultural geography." But what sets apart the cultural geographer of the tradition represented in this volume is the fact that when he encounters any one of these five themes, *he thinks automatically of all the others.*[60] For these cultural geographers, any sign of human action in a landscape implies a culture, recalls a history, and demands an ecological interpretation; the history of any people evokes its setting in a landscape, its ecological problems, and its cultural concomitants; and the recognition of a culture calls for the discovery of traces it has left on the earth.

Cultural geography is first and always geographic. It deals essentially with the earth, employing methods used by all geographers. Indeed, the geographer who studies only culture area, cultural landscape, or cultural ecology may justly call himself a cultural geographer, even though he disregards connecting themes, for his subject is the earth under the influence of culture. The majority of geographers who deal with cultural landscapes do so without any explicit attention to culture, culture areas, or culture history. Their work achieves its purpose well, however, as long as the area they study remains approximately constant in culture throughout, and their conclusions respect this limitation on their generality. Within a given culture area—especially a well-homogenized modern Western one—human geography can function successfully without any mention of culture. Indeed, most geographers in the United States practice it in this way. Cultural geographers, on the other hand, prefer to reach toward more general and comprehensive methods and conclusions.

The human geography that limits itself to a single culture area, without comment on culture or culture history, is not nearly so indifferent to cultural considerations as might appear at first. The geographer himself is a product of a given culture, and the less he thinks about other cultures or the abstract idea of "culture," the more likely his thinking is to be saturated with and expressive of the assumptions, preferences, and prohibitions of his own culture. A great many North American and European geographers demonstrate clearly

[59] For clarification of this point see Philip L. Wagner, *The Human Use of the Earth, passim.*

[60] Hence the impossibility of segregating the substantive studies in the balance of this volume into categories corresponding to each theme. As already indicated, most of the articles illustrate more than one theme.

in their published opinions that they are strongly indoctrinated and impregnated with beliefs in "progress," "efficiency," and "economic growth";[61] some
noticeably abhor the "untidiness," "langor," and "frivolity" that they see in
other countries.[62] There is no "cultural geography" in our sense in the U.S.S.R.,
but Soviet geographers are careful to express a cultural orientation emphasizing
utilitarian and egalitarian virtues. In the United States, the very choice of
economic aspects as the core of most human geography tells a great deal about
North American culture. The cultural tradition in geography, of course, itself
exemplifies a long-established trend in Western thought toward comparative
study, explicit assumptions, and detached examination of experience as applied
to the study of man.

Geographers who do not consciously employ the notion of culture in their
studies often allege that the cultural tradition belongs in anthropology rather
than geography. They overlook the fact that cultural geography, of any school,
concerns the earth and does not claim to put forth new generalizations about
the intrinsic character and development of cultures or cultural communities as
such. They disregard as well the predominant role that standard geographic
methods play in any cultural geography. Nevertheless, there is an affinity of
great importance between cultural geography and anthropology, just as there
are bonds between economic geography and economics, political geography
and political science, and between other subdivisions of geography and neighboring fields.

Using the culture concept wherever possible, and welcoming all the help he
can get, the cultural geographer surveys a world-wide panorama of man's works
and asks Who? Where? What? When? and How? The themes of culture,
culture area, cultural landscape, culture history, and cultural ecology respond
to these queries. The geographic study of culture exposes challenging problems,
suggests procedures for their solution, and opens the way to an understanding
of the processes that have created and are creating new environments for man.

[61] The essays of Clarence J. Glacken ("Changing Ideas of the Habitable World") and Alexander
Spoehr ("Cultural Differences in the Interpretation of Natural Resources") in *Man's Role in
Changing the Face of the Earth* help to clarify this problem. Note also Aldo Sestini's reaction to
prevalent ideas of "progress" and "growth" in his essay, "Regressive Phases in the Development of
the Cultural Landscape," in Part IV of this volume. It is surprising that so little attention has been
directed to the explicit assumptions of "our way of life." For a modest but important effort along
these lines, see Shephard B. Clough, *Basic Values of Western Civilization* (New York: Columbia
University Press, 1960).

[62] For a clear exposure of this line of thinking and its implications, see Joseph E. Spencer, "The
Cultural Factor in 'Underdevelopment': The Case of Malaya," in Norton Ginsburg (ed.), *Essays
on Geography and Economic Development* (University of Chicago, Department of Geography Research Paper No. 62 [1960]), pp. 35–48.

PART 1

ORIENTATION

In this part of the anthology we have brought together four essays that provide orientation to some of the basic problems of cultural geography. The first, by Carl O. Sauer, presents a criticism of the idea that geography should be defined as a study of relationships and recommends a research program based on comparative and genetic studies. In the second essay, Robert S. Platt reviews the development of cultural geography in the United States and argues for an eclectic program combining functional and historical studies. In the third essay, Max. Sorre rephrases the question of the relevance of historical analysis and answers it in ecological terms. Finally, Erhard Rostlund takes a fresh look at the works of the environmentalists and their critics and indicates some reasons why serious discussion of this issue should be resumed.

Perhaps the most important point to emphasize about Sauer's essay is that it recommends repudiation of a trend that developed in American geography during the first quarter of the twentieth century. During this period, American geographers moved away from their initial interest in physiography and many redefined their concern as an attempt to understand the relationship of man to his physical environment. To Sauer, this development represents a denial of the proper task of the discipline, which is to study "those elements of culture that give character to an area," or, more generally, to understand "the areal differentiation of the earth." He argues that geography cannot claim an independent status if it is preoccupied with a particular causal relationship and fails to provide an explanatory description of the data of areal occupation. In his view, the movement from physiography to human geography followed two diverging paths. The first entailed a shift of interest from objective analysis of the phenomena of the variable surface of the earth to an attempt to proclaim a causal relationship between nature and the works or activities of man. The second trend, exemplified by the writings of European geographers,[1] entailed no radical reorientation of method or rationale but merely a shift of attention from geomorphology to culture-morphology. According to this interpretation, the genetic and comparative procedures of physiography could also

[1] The different methodology of American and European (especially German) geography before, during, and immediately after this period constitutes the main theme of Richard Hartshorne's monograph, "The Nature of Geography," *Annals of the Association of American Geographers,* Vol. XXIX (1939, and subsequent reprintings).

25

be applied to culture, or at least to material culture, and there is no need to accept the deterministic doctrine. In other words, the goal of cultural geography should be an understanding of the cultural processes that produce "cultural landscapes," just as physiography had sought to understand the natural processes that produce "natural landscapes." The "working program" suggested by this analogy had already been elaborated as a study of the "morphology of landscape." [2]

Not all of the suggestions made in this essay are in harmony with current views, or indeed with Sauer's later views. [3] For example, few geographers have accepted the idea that economic geography is "merely cultural geography carried down to date," and the suggested definition of "human geography" has not been generally applied. [4] The meaning of "landscape" has been the subject of prolonged debate, and today few geographers deny that it has subjective overtones. [5] Perhaps the most challenging feature of Sauer's argument is his assertion that cultural geography, if not all geography, should be historically oriented and proceed from a reconstruction of origins.

Platt's essay differs from Sauer's in several respects. In the first place, his view is retrospective, whereas Sauer outlines a new program, appropriate to the tastes of a new generation but consistent with geography's methodological heritage. Writing in 1952, Platt could survey the accomplishments of that generation and review the reasons for the collapse of environmentalism. The immediate result of that collapse was a strong reaction against broad generalizations of any sort, and a marked predilection for field studies that combined intensive survey and inventory. This reaction, exemplified by V. C. Finch's "Montfort Study," entailed detailed mapping of small areas. [6] From surveys of

[2] Carl O. Sauer, *The Morphology of Landscape* ("University of California Publications in Geography," Vol. II, No. 2 [1925]).

[3] Cf. his "Foreword to Historical Geography," *Annals of the Association of American Geographers*, XXXI (1941), 1–24, and "The Education of a Geographer," *ibid*, XLVI (1956), 287–99.

[4] Actually, "human geography" has little meaning apart from the fact that it implies interest in human works or activities rather than natural phenomena or processes per se. At present, few geographers use this vague designation, but refer instead to "cultural," "economic," "political," "commercial," "industrial," "urban," and "agricultural" geography as topical fields. It goes without saying that none of these fields has been or should be "enclosed." Moreover, as Hartshorne remarks, while some features of the earth "are largely independent of man and others are products of man's work, few are either purely 'natural' or purely 'human.'" See his *Perspective on the Nature of Geography* (Chicago: Rand McNally for the Association of American Geographers, 1959), pp. 48–80, ref. to p. 80.

[5] For clarification of this point see J. O. M. Broek, "The Concept Landscape in Human Geography," *Comptes rendus du Congrès International de Géographie, Amsterdam, 1938* (Leiden: Brill, 1938), II, Sec. 3a, 103–9; and the extensive discussion in Hartshorne's methodological works.

[6] In his "Forward" to this study, Charles C. Colby speaks of a trend in Middle Western geography, "which led away from broad generalizations based on cursory examination of large areas" and "emphasized the findings derived from a quantitative examination of small unit areas" (*Geographic Surveys*, Bulletin No. 9, Geographic Society of Chicago [Chicago: University of Chicago Press, 1933], p. vi). It is interesting that Platt's study, "Magdalena Atlipac," in the same volume emphasizes dynamic functional relationships and is based upon extensive reconnaissance as well as intensive field work. In a recent study, Platt identifies and illustrates the following primary types of field work in American geography: (1) "Exploratory Traverse," (2) "Area Survey," (3) "Explanatory Physical," (4) "Explanatory Human," (5) "Analytical Economic," (6) "Areal Uni-

27

this sort, designed to demonstrate static uniformity or diversity, concepts of areal organization and generic regions, both products of functional analysis, gradually emerged. But the generalizations thus formulated lacked a vital dimension, for they failed to account for process or genesis. Correspondingly, the culture-historical school perhaps tended to neglect functional and generic studies, although it redefined "culture" to include ideas and institutions as well as visible manifestations of human enterprise. Platt's essay exposes and recommends a procedure for overcoming the dichotomy represented by these two trends. It may be added that the synthesis he advocates is exemplified by several articles in this volume.

Platt's appeal for eclectism is rephrased in Max. Sorre's discourse on the role of historical explanation. The argument he presents is based on a comparison of the procedures of geography and ecology.[7] Perhaps "comparison" is a poor word, for he believes that the procedures are essentially the same. His basic premise is that understanding in either case should be comprehensive. In the study of vegetation this implies a satisfactory explanation of specific composition, associations or groupings, and environmental aptitudes, on the one hand, and evolution, migration, and succession, on the other. Having demonstrated the interplay of ecological and historical explanation in this case, he turns to human geography and presents the same argument with different examples.

It must be stressed that Sorre's analogy refers to procedures of analysis, not to animate and inanimate matter as such. Plant associations are obviously aggregates only of plants, and although hybridization may occur, the plant world offers no counterparts of learning and communication (i.e., culture). Cultural evolution differs from biological evolution "in respect of selection and mechanisms of change, of transmission of the old and incorporation of the new, of the presence of diffusion and a consequent tendency to convergence as against divergence, of the immensely increased importance of mind and mentifacts, notably the accumulation and better organization of knowledge, and in many other ways."[8] Nevertheless, ecologists have developed tools and methods that are relevant for geographers, and understanding in either case demands consideration of development through time. As Kniffen remarks, "The absence of a time-range concept compresses expanding novelties together with fading relics into a common flatness."[9]

formity," (7) "Areal Organization," and (8) "Cultural Origin." See his *Field Study in American Geography: The Development of Theory and Method Exemplified by Selections* (University of Chicago, Department of Geography Research Paper No. 61 [1959]).

[7] The sketchiness of this essay is justified by the fact that its subject is given full treatment in *Les fondements biologiques: Essai d'une ecologie de l'homme,* Vol. I of *Les fondements de la géographie humaine* (Paris: Colin, 1947). The balance of this monumental work includes a second volume in two parts on *Les fondements techniques* (1948–50), and a third volume on *L'Habitat* (1952), which includes a general résumé.

[8] Julian S. Huxley: "Evolution, Cultural and Biological," in William L. Thomas, Jr. (ed.), *Current Anthropology* (Chicago: University of Chicago Press, 1956), pp. 3–25.

[9] Fred B. Kniffen, "Geography and the Past," *Journal of Geography,* L (1951), 126–29, ref. to

28

Sauer's essay shows an unfavorable reaction to the rise of the environmentalists, while Platt's chronicles their decline and fall.[10] The tone of Rostlund's article, like that of Sorre's, indicates a detachment from the controversy. Sorre's detachment is perhaps explained by the fact that French geographic scholarship benefited from prompt rejection of the environmentalist doctrine, and a substitution of possibilism for determinism.[11] The clarity of Rostlund's view is enhanced by the fact that it was taken in 1956, long after environmentalism had ceased to be a subject of heated controversy.

Rostlund's re-examination does not refute the basic criticisms of the 1930's, but it corrects the record on one important point: "Environmentalism was not disproved, only disapproved." The problem remains, for it cannot be said that it has been solved. The paradox of this situation, as Rostlund indicates, is that scholars in other fields, as well as the general public, tend to associate geographers with a problem that they no longer recognize as an important aspect of their interest. The methodological argument against defining geography as a study of environmental influences, or any other causal relationship, must stand, but this does not mean that such influences or relationships do not exist. In this connection it is rewarding to recall that the major works of the environmentalists were based in large part upon data collected during the nineteenth century. Because comprehension of the world has increased substantially since that time and geographers have developed more efficient and powerful tools, it follows that the theories and generalizations of the environmentalists may be worthy of re-examination in accordance with the objective procedures of modern science. As Rostlund indicates, "We need a fresh start, but we need not start all over again." His prophecy is limited to a warning that geographers may be drafted to undertake this inquiry or surrender it to scholars in other fields. The most likely prospect is an interdisciplinary effort, like that already underway in cultural ecology, medical geography, and physiological climatology. In any case, geographers will not be able to confine their attention

p. 126. See also the substantial statements of H. C. Darby, "On the Relations of Geography and History," *Transactions and Papers of the Institute of British Geographers,* XIX (1953), 1–11 (reprinted in Griffith Taylor [ed.], *Geography in the Twentieth Century* [2d ed.; New York: Philosophical Library, 1957], pp. 640–52); Andrew H. Clark, "Historical Geography," in Preston E. James and Clarence F. Jones (eds.), *American Geography: Inventory and Prospect* (Syracuse: Syracuse University Press for the Association of American Geographers, 1954), pp. 70–105; Richard Hartshorne, *Perspective on the Nature of Geography,* pp. 81–107; and Carl O. Sauer, "Foreword to Historical Geography."

[10] In this connection see also Platt's "Environmentalism versus Geography," *American Journal of Sociology,* LIII (1948), 351–58, and "Determinism in Geography," *Annals of the Association of American Geographers,* XXXVIII (1948), 126–32. Without attempting to extend what could be a very long list, we should also mention Emrys Jones, "Cause and Effect in Human Geography," *Annals of the Association of American Geographers,* XLVI (1956), 367–77; H. C. Montefiore and W. W. Williams, "Determinism and Possibilism," *Geographical Studies,* II (1955), 1–11; and the relevant discussion in the methodological works of Hartshorne.

[11] In addition to the works cited by Rostlund, see the brief account of the history of French thought in George Tatham, "Environmentalism and Possibilism," in Griffith Taylor (ed.), *Geography in the Twentieth Century* (New York: Philosophical Library, 1951), pp. 128–62.

to critical reviews. Whether real or imagined, environmental influences have never ceased to impress and fascinate man. Geography has a vested interest in this problem, for no other discipline can claim a richer heritage of trials and errors.

CARL O. SAUER

CULTURAL GEOGRAPHY

In the past century the geographers have been dislodged from their earlier carefree encyclopedic state, in which they discriminated only in terms of personal interest and made camp wherever the prospect pleased. The scientific tendencies of the time have brought external criticisms and internal compulsions and a large methodologic literature which marks the process of intrenchment within a recognizable realm. The earlier volumes of the *Geographische Jahrbücher* (Gotha, 1866———), especially the articles by Hermann Wagner, are much concerned with questions of objective and method. The most comprehensive epistemology is that of Alfred Hettner.[1] In these discussions essential unity has not been attained, and to this day there are irreconcilable camps. Therefore the question as to what geography is must continue to be asked, because the answer determines the premises under which the data have been assembled.

Geography is approached in various ways and to various ends. On the one hand, there is an attempt to find the limitation of study in a particular causal relationship between man and nature; on the other, the effort is to define the material of observation. This cleavage has attained increasing dimen-

sions year by year and threatens perhaps to form a gulf across which no community of interests may be maintained. The situation dates from the beginning of modern geography but has grown acute only in the present century. The one group asserts directly its major interest in man: that is, in the relationship of man to his environment, usually in the sense of adaptation of man to physical environment. The other group, if geographers may be divided into simple classifications, directs its attention to those elements of material culture that give character to area. For purposes of convenience the first position may be called that of human geography, the second that of cultural geography. The terms are in use in this manner, although not exclusively so.

Carl Ritter, holder of the first academic chair in geography, especially emphasized human activity as physically conditioned. The thesis of the environment that molds civilization is of course very old but received special attention from the rationalism of the eighteenth century and found able spokesmen in Herder, Montesquieu and later in Buckle. Ritter's position was vigorously attacked by Froebel and Peschel as impressionistic and unscientific. Even around the middle of the last century there existed a polemic literature concerning the physical environment as the field of geographic study.

Friedrich Ratzel in his *Anthropogeographie* outlined the framework in which human geography in the narrower sense has moved since that time, a set of categories of the environment—ranging from abstract

Reprinted, with permission of the author and publisher, from *Encyclopaedia of the Social Sciences*, VI (1931), 621–23 (copyright, 1931, by the Macmillan Company, New York). The author is professor emeritus of geography at the University of California, Berkeley.

[1] Alfred Hettner, *Die Geographie: ihre Geschichte, ihr Wesen und ihre Methoden* (Breslau: F. Hirt, 1927).

concepts of position and space to climate and seacoasts—and their influence on man.[2] By this one work he became the great apostle of environmentalism, and his followers have largely overlooked his later cultural studies, in which he concerned himself with movements of population, conditions of human settlement and the diffusion of culture by major routes of communication. The effect of Ratzel's environmental categories was not great in his own country; in France it was tempered by Vidal de la Blache's acute substitution of *possibilisme* for the original determinism;[3] but in England and the United States the study of the physical environment as the goal of geography became well nigh the mark of recognition of the geographer. Apparently Ratzel did not regard his *Anthropogeographie* as anything more than a stimulus and an introduction to a human geography that was to be based on a study of culture. Whereas anthropologists have made large use of his analysis of the diffusion of culture, western geographers think of him only as an environmentalist. In the United States the *Annals of the Association of American Geographers* (published since 1911) show the rapid spread of human geography. So far the high point of this invasion has been marked by H. H. Barrows' presidential address before that body in 1923, a frank plea to constitute the subject solely on the basis of environmental adjustment.[4] So prevalent has this view become in English-speaking lands, and so different is the objective of the continental body of geographers that the work done by the one group is largely ignored by the other.

The rejection of the environmentalist position in geography is based not on any denial of the importance of studies in environment but simply on the following methodological grounds: (1) no field of science is expressed by a particular causal relation; (2) the environmentalist inquiry lacks a class of data as field of study, there being no selection of phenomena but only one of relations, and a science that has no category of objects for study can lead, in Hettner's words, only a "parasitic existence"; (3) nor is it saved by a method that it can claim as its own; (4) special pleading is most difficult to avoid by reason of the fact that success lies most apparently, or at least most easily, in the demonstration of an environmental adjustment. Theoretically the last objection is least serious; practically it has been most so, as is illustrated by a flood of easy rationalizations that certain institutions are the result of certain environmental conditions. In this regard those students who have least troubled themselves with knowledge have reaped the greatest apparent success. The polemic against the position of geography as the study of environmental relations has received its sharpest definition by Schlüter,[5] Michotte,[6] and Febvre.[7]

The other school continues the major tradition of the subject. It therefore does not claim that it represents a new science but rather that it attempts the cultivation of an old field in terms acceptable to its age. It is not anthropocentric; rather it has shown at times excessive tendencies in the other direction. Cultural geography is only a chapter in the larger geography and always the last chapter. The line of suc-

[2] Friedrich Ratzel, *Anthropogeographie* (2 vols.; Stuttgart: J. Engelhorn, 1882–91; 2d ed., 1899–1912).

[3] Paul Vidal de la Blache, *Principes de géographie humaine, publiés d'après les manuscrits de l'Auteur par Emmanuel de Martonne* (Paris: Armand Colin, 1922). Translated by Millicent T. Bingham as *Principles of Human Geography* (New York: Henry Holt, 1926).

[4] Harlan H. Barrows, "Geography as Human Ecology," *Annals of the Association of American Geographers*, XIII (1923), 1–14.

[5] Otto Schlüter, *Die Ziele der Geographie des Menschen* (Munich: R. Oldenbourg, 1906).

[6] P. L. Michotte: "L'Orientation nouvelle en géographie," *Bulletin de la Société Royale Belge de Géographie*, XLV (1921), 5–43.

[7] Lucien Febvre and Lionel Bataillon, *La terre et l'évolution humaine: introduction géographique à l'histoire* (Paris: La Renaissance du Livre, 1922). Translated by E. G. Montford and S. H. Paxton as *A Geographical Introduction to History* (New York: Alfred A. Knopf, 1925).

cession passes from Alexander von Humboldt through Oskar Peschel and Ferdinand von Richthofen to the present continental geographers. It proceeds from a description of the features of the earth's surface by an analysis of their genesis to a comparative classification of regions. Since the day of Richthofen it has been customary also to use the term "chorology," the science of regions. During the latter half of the past century the work carried on was overwhelmingly physical, or geomorphologic, not because most geographers thought that the study of genesis of physical land forms exhausted the field but because it was necessary to develop first a discipline to which the physical differentiation of the earth's surface would yield. Geographers are now in possession of a method by which the origin and grouping of physical areas can be determined and in which successive steps in their development are identified. Processes have been identified, measures of the intensity and duration of their activity have been determined, and the grouping of land forms into assemblages which constitute unit areas that can be genetically compared is well advanced.

The latest agent to modify the earth's surface is man. Man must be regarded directly as a geomorphologic agent, for he has increasingly altered the conditions of denudation and aggradation of the earth's surface; and many an error has crept into physical geography because it was not sufficiently recognized that the major processes of physical sculpturing of the earth cannot be safely inferred from the processes that one sees at work today under human occupation. Indeed, a class of facts which Brunhes labeled "facts of destructive occupation," such as soil erosion, are most literally expressions of human geomorphosis.[8] The entire question of narrowing subsistence limits which confronts man in many parts of the world, apart from the

question of the greater number of human beings among whom the subsistence may need to be divided, is directly one of man as an agent of surficial modification. Even the most physically minded geographer is driven therefore to this extent into the examination of human activity.

There has, however, never been a serious attempt to eliminate the works of man from geographic study. The Germans have long had a phrase, "the transformation of the natural landscape into the cultural landscape"; this provides a satisfactory working program, by which the assemblage of cultural forms in the area comes in for the same attention as that of the physical forms. In the proper sense all geography is physical geography under this view, not because of an environmental conditioning of the works of man, but because man, himself not directly the object of geographic investigation, has given physical expression to the area by habitations, workshops, markets, fields, lines of communication. Cultural geography is therefore concerned with those works of man that are inscribed into the earth's surface and give to it characteristic expression. The culture area is then an assemblage of such forms as have interdependence and is functionally differentiated from other areas. Camille Vallaux finds the object of inquiry to be the transformation of natural regions and substitution therefor of entirely new or profoundly modified regions.[9] He considers the new landscapes which human labor creates as deforming more or less the natural landscapes and regards the degree of their deformation as the veritable measure of the power of human societies. In this sense then he finds the physical area expressed through two sorts of modalities, those that limit and those that aid the efforts of the group. A persistent curiosity as to the significance of the environment is unaffected here by any compulsion to dress up the importance of the environment. The facts of the culture area are to be explained by

[8] Jean Brunhes, *La géographie humaine* (Paris: Felix Alcan, 1910; 3d ed., 1925). Translated by T. C. LeCompt as *Human Geography* (Chicago and New York: Rand McNally, 1920).

[9] Camille Vallaux, *Les sciences géographiques* (Paris: Felix Alcan, 1925).

whatever causes have contributed thereto, and no form of causation has preference over any other.

Such a method of approach is entirely congenial to the geographer. He has been accustomed to regard the genesis of the physical area and he extends similar observations to the cultural area, which has a somewhat simpler and more exact form than the culture area of the anthropologist. The geographic culture area is taken to consist only of the expressions of man's tenure of the land, the culture assemblage which records the full measure of man's utilization of the surface—or, one may agree with Schlüter, the visible, areally extensive and expressive features of man's presence. These the geographer maps as to distribution, groups as to genetic association, traces as to origin and synthesizes into a comparative system of culture areas. The experience in geomorphologic study provides the necessary technique of observation and a basis for evaluating the modalities stated by Vallaux. A geography such as this is still an observational science utilizing skill in field observation and cartographic representation, and geographic therefore in methods as well as objective.

The development of cultural geography has of necessity proceeded from the reconstruction of successive cultures in an area, beginning with the earliest and proceeding to the present. The most serious work to date has concerned itself not with present culture areas but with earlier cultures, since these are the foundation of the present and provide in combination the only basis for a dynamic view of the culture area. If cultural geography, sired by geomorphology, has one fixed attribute it is the developmental orientation of the subject. Such a slogan as "Geography is the history of the present" has no meaning. An additional method is therefore of necessity introduced, the specifically historical method, by which available historical data are used, often directly in the field, in the reconstruction of former conditions of settlement, land utilization, and communication, whether these records be written, archeologic or philologic. The name *Siedlungskunde* has been given by the Germans to such historical studies and they have been furthered especially by Robert Gradmann, editor of *Forschungen zur deutschen Landes- und Volkskunde,* and Otto Schlüter. A compact view of attainments and problems is given by the former in "Arbeitsweise der Siedlungsgeographie." [10] August Meitzen gave great impetus to field studies by asserting the extraordinary persistence of field forms (*Flurformen*) and village plans as culture relics.[11] Although many of his conclusions have fallen, the inertia of property lines has proved a most valuable aid in determining inherited conditions. Whereas much has been attained in the reconstruction of rural culture areas, the anatomy and phylogeny of the town as a geographic structure are less well advanced to date. They are at present being pioneered by numerous studies, most particularly in France and Sweden. Important generalizations have not yet appeared, but a technique of analysis is emerging.

A logically integrated development is also under way in economic geography as participating in the culture geography program.[12] Localization of production and industry is no longer the major aim as in the familiar economic geography, which taught distributions of commercial products and analyzed them. This now becomes a device in synthesis, not an objective in itself. The economic geography that is in the making is nothing else than culture geography carried down to date, for the culture area is essentially economic and its

[10] Robert Gradmann, "Die Arbeitsweise der Siedlungsgeographie in ihrer Anwendung auf das Frankenland," *Zeitschrift für Bayerische Landesgeschichte,* I (1928), 316–57.

[11] August Meitzen, *Siedlung und Agrarwesen der Westgermanen und Ostgermanen, der Kelten, Römer, Finnen und Slawen* (3 vols. and atlas; Berlin: W. Hertz, 1895).

[12] Gottfried Pfeifer, "Über raumwirtschaftliche Begriffe und Vorstellungen und ihre bisherige Anwendung in der Geographie und Wirtschaftswissenschaft," *Geographische Zeitschrift,* XXXIV (1928), 321–40, 411–25.

structure is determined by historic growth as well as by the resources of the physical area. The title of pioneer belongs to Eduard Hahn, who broke the purely speculative culture stages of gathering, nomadism, agriculture, and industry and formulated a set of economic form associations, of which the system of hoe culture has become best known. Also he disproved a general succession in culture stages and demonstrated the lateness of nomadism as a culture form.[13]

Cultural geography then implies a program which is unified with the general objective of geography: that is, an understanding of the areal differentiation of the earth. It rests largely on direct field observations based on the technique of morphologic analysis first developed in physical geography. Its method is developmental, specifically historical in so far as the material permits, and it therefore seeks to determine the successions of culture that have taken place in an area. Hence it welds historical geography and economic geography into one subject, the latter concerned with the present-day culture area that proceeds out of earlier ones. It asserts no social philosophy such as environmentalist geography does but finds its principal methodic problems in the structure of area. Its immediate objectives are given in the explanatory description of the data of areal occupation which it accumulates. The major problems of cultural geography will lie in discovering the composition and meaning of the geographic aggregate that we as yet recognize somewhat vaguely as the culture area, in finding out more about what are normal stages of succession in its development, in concerning itself with climactic and decadent phases, and thereby in gaining more precise knowledge of the relation of culture and of the resources that are at the disposal of culture.

[13] Eduard Hahn, "Die Wirtschaftsformen der Erde," *Petermanns Mitteilungen,* XXXVIII (1892), 8–12 and map; *Die Entstehung der Pflugkultur* (Heidelberg: Carl Winter, 1909); *Von der Hacke zum Pflug* (Leipzig: Quelle & Meyer, 1914; 2d ed., 1919.)

ROBERT S. PLATT

THE RISE OF CULTURAL
GEOGRAPHY IN AMERICA

The meaning of the term "cultural geography" has changed greatly in the past thirty-five years. Before World War I the word "culture" had a very specific meaning to American geographers, but quite unimportant and quite different from the meaning as generally understood now. Since that time the subject of cultural geography has grown up and assumed importance in America.

Before 1915 American geographers were familiar with the word "culture" as designating the "works of man" on topographic maps of the United States Geological Survey, in contrast with the land and water forms of nature. On these maps "culture" is printed in black—as compared with nature, represented in brown for relief, shown by contour lines, and blue for water features (Fig. 1).

In this clear-cut, objective classification into cultural and natural features there was no necessary implication for or against cause and effect relations, environmental determinism, or historical genesis. However, it was easier to find or imagine environmental relations between culture and nature, relations apparently simple and di-

rect between the black lines of roads and the brown contours of valleys, than to discover any signs of historical antecedents. Accordingly, in the days of environmental interpretation, culture was looked upon as things built by man in relation to nature but not necessarily arising from a past sequence of history.

In World War I, geographers who worked on military maps continued to distinguish cultural from natural features and to draw them in *de facto* space relations to each other.[1]

Meanwhile, even before the war, a revolt against environmental determinism had begun, accompanied by a demand for empirical data collected without bias of causal theory. Ringleaders in the movement were Wellington D. Jones and Carl O. Sauer, first associated as graduate students.

Soon after the war, environmentalism was generally discredited in favor of a more objective study of the content of areas. Regional inventory and analysis arose and flourished. The Michigan Land Economic Survey was organized as a pioneer project in land planning, with the co-operation of geographers. The classification of items to be inventoried or mapped was only slightly different from that used before: instead of the distinction between culture and nature

Reprinted, with permission of the author, from *Proceedings of the Seventeenth International Geographical Congress, Washington D.C., 1952* (Washington, D.C., n.d.). A variant of this paper translated by Wilhelm Müller-Wille under the title "Die Entwicklung der Kulturgeographie in Amerika" was published in *Erdkunde*, VI (1952), 260–62. The author is professor emeritus of geography at the University of Chicago.

[1] Example: The map of Fort Leavenworth, Kansas, used for topographic instruction in World War I. See Clarence O. Sherrill, *Military Topography for the Mobile Forces* (4th ed.; Menasha, Wis.: George Banta, 1921).

there were separate maps of land cover and the land itself.[2]

In such regional inventory there was explicit repudiation of cause and effect theory, environmental or otherwise. But the obvious spatial relations remained, culture in relation to nature, and there was still no introduction of a time factor, culture traced in a sequence of history.

The ultimate expression of the theory of land inventory and analysis was Carl Sauer's monograph distinguishing the natural landscape and the cultural landscape as successive phenomena but analyzing and relating them in space as currently observable and not calling particular attention to the historical integrity of culture in the sequence of time.[3] Diagrammatic illustration was furnished in a pair of formulas, as follows:

and the arrangement indicates a sequence. But the form of expression is that of a formula in physical science in which causal factors produce a certain effect, subject to repetition.

In the study of landscape and land use another step taken in the 1920's made a small but significant modification in the system of mapping: substituting one map of culture and nature together for the two or more separate maps of land cover and the lay-of-the-land. In this consolidated map each circumscribed area represented a uniform association of land use and land character, designated as to type by a key number. For instance, number 1 for cultivated lowland, number 2 for cultivated upland, number 5 for pasture on steep land, etc.[4] In later maps, made in the same way, the single numbers were replaced by sym-

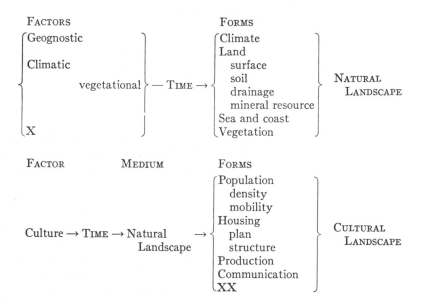

In this scheme the word "time" appears

bols in the form of a fraction, in which the numerator stood for the land cover and the denominator for the land itself (Fig. 2).

Like the previous method of mapping

[2] Example: Michigan Land Economic Survey, Antrim County, 1923. A cover map of what is on the land, mainly cultural features, and another map of the land itself, the soil and lay-of-the-land, natural aspects.

[3] Carl O. Sauer, *The Morphology of Landscape* ("University of California Publications in Geography," Vol. II, No. 2 [1925]).

[4] Wellington D. Jones and V. C. Finch, "Detailed Field Mapping in the Study of the Economic Geography of an Agricultural Area," *Annals of the Association of American Geographers,* XV (1925), 148–57.

land use, this also was intended to be an objective, empirical record, without environmental bias. But the emphasis on field mapping of small units of area, supposedly uniform in both cultural and natural aspects, seemed to suggest environmental re-

Economic Survey, has been used widely.[5] In urban geography there has been even more use of equivalent mapping method.[6]

The fractional code method, combining land use and land character on one map, has also continued in use and been im-

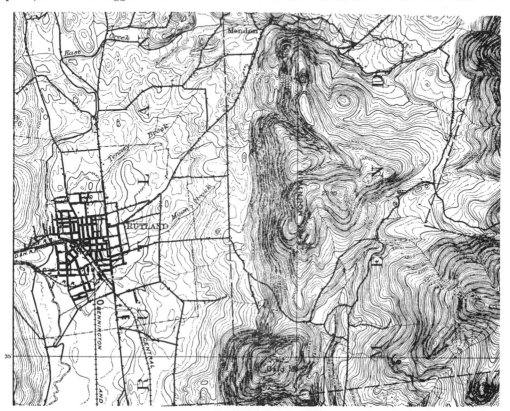

Fig. 1. Part of the Rutland, Vt., Sheet, U.S. Geological Survey, 1893. In this example the hill contours and streams of nature are distinguishable from the roads and houses of "culture," even though the brown and blue colors of the original are not reproduced.

lations even more direct, simple, and locally detached than the previous mode of study. So the idea of a mosaic pattern of small uniform areas did not advance the understanding of cultural geography, however useful this idea may have been in the development of better field technique.

This and the other kinds of maps which appeared before 1925 have continued to flourish and are still important in all kinds of geographic study, particularly in regional planning and applied geography. Regional inventory, like that of the Michigan Land

proved for greater usefulness. In more generalized form it was applied in surveys for the Tennessee Valley Authority, particularly in connection with aerial photography.[7] More recently the Land Use Survey of Puerto Rico has used the same system combining land use and land character in

[5] Example: Wisconsin Land Economic Inventory, Vilas County, 1931.

[6] Example: Philadelphia City Planning Commission, Land Use in Philadelphia Metropolitan District, 1944 (Philadelphia, 1949).

[7] Example: Tennessee Valley Authority, Rural Land Classification, Harriman Quadrangle, 1936.

EXPLANATION OF FRACTIONAL SYMBOLS
NUMERATOR

Left-hand Digit MAJOR USE TYPE	Second Digit SPECIFIC CROP OR USE TYPE		Third Digit CONDITION OF CROP
1. TILLED LAND	1. CORN (MAIZE) 2. OATS 3. HAY, (IN ROTATION) 4. PASTURE (" ") 5. BARLEY 6. WHEAT	7. PEAS (Mainly for canning). 8. SOY BEANS 9. POTATOES T. TOBACCO X. SUDAN GRASS 4/5. OATS AND BARLEY MIXED	1. GOOD 2. MEDIUM 3. POOR
2. PERMANENT GRASS LAND	1. OPEN GRASS PASTURE 2. PASTURE WITH SCATTERED TREES OR BRUSH 3. WOODED PASTURE 4. PERMANENT GRASS CUT FOR HAY		1. GOOD 2. MEDIUM 3. POOR
3. TIMBER LAND	1. PASTURED 2. NOT PASTURED		1. GOOD 2. MEDIUM 3. POOR
4. IDLE LAND	1. IS CAPABLE OF USE		

DENOMINATOR

Left-hand Digit SLOPE OF LAND	Second Digit SOIL TYPE (Wis. Soil Survey terminology).	Letter X (If indicated). CONDITION OF DRAINAGE
1. LEVEL, 0° TO 3° 2. ROLLING, 3° - 9° 3. ROUGH, 0° - 15° 4. STEEP, Over 15°	1. MARSHALL SILT LOAM 2. KNOX " " 3. " " (STEEP PHASE). 4. LINTONIA " " 5. WABASH " " 6. ROUGH, STONY LAND	X POOR XX VERY POOR

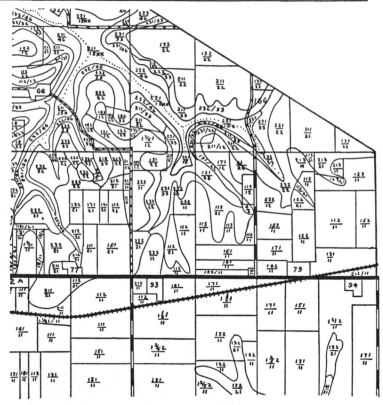

FIG. 2. Part of "A Map Showing the Utilization of Land in the Service Area of Montfort, Wisconsin, in Its Relation to Conditions of Slope, Soil, Drainage, and Roads." Each circumscribed area is judged to be characterized by its complex symbol, in which the numerator describes land use and the denominator land character. Plate 1 in V. C. Finch, "Montfort: A Study in Landscape Types in Southwestern Wisconsin," Geographical Society of Chicago, Bulletin No. 9 (University of Chicago Press, 1933).

one complex symbol.[8] Of course through all these decades from before World War I, there have been broadly generalized studies and maps of geographic regions, combining ideas of land use and land character.[9]

So much for modes of study which originated before 1925. These are all valuable for classifying, surveying, and generalizing on areas, and they still form an indispensable part of the equipment available for geographic study. But that equipment was not yet complete in 1925 for geography as now studied. There was need of additional ideas and devices to be supplied by development along different lines.

Soon after 1925, advance was made along two lines at least to meet this need. One line led from the study of quasi-homogeneous units of area, sharply defined in a static mosaic of spaces, to the study of areas of organization, nodal units, expressing human occupance in its setting, a functional pattern of points of focus and lines and limits of movement, showing phenomena even more localized than in the mosaic of small unit areas but not detached from more extensive space relations.

The roots of this development before 1925 lay in commercial geography, in such studies as those of seaports. After 1925 equivalent ideas were applied to land occupance studies (Fig. 3). These have dealt in most cases with a town and its district or with a focal establishment and its service area, such as a sugar mill and its plantations or an airport and its connections.[10] Work from this viewpoint was initiated under the leadership of C. C. Colby. Recent development is well illustrated in the work of E. L. Ullman.[11]

The second line of geographic thought after 1925 led directly from work in anthropology done long before by Alfred L. Kroeber. A preface written in 1923 for a book begun about 1906 contained the following statement:

It is not a history in the usual sense of a record of events. . . . The book is a history in that it tries to reconstruct . . . the scheme . . . in which these people . . . lived. . . . There being no written documents, the element of time enters . . . less than in works which it is customary to designate historical. In the stead of time, the geographical factor looms large. It is not that this dimension is necessarily more important in savage life than that of chronology; but it is a hundred times more readily operated in. . . .[12]

By the term "geographical factor" the author referred evidently to the space dimension and not to environmental influence. The work presented the concept of culture as a phenomenon originating, spreading, and evolving in time and space, understandable in time but traceable in space, and understandably localized in space.

This concept came into geography from anthropology, particularly through the contact of Carl Sauer with Professor Kroeber. In a study by Sauer and Brand, "Pueblo Sites in Southeastern Arizona," published in 1930 from field work done in 1928 and 1929, findings were based on the collection and identification of potsherds "with benefit of counsel from Professor Kroeber."[13] This included maps more like previous ex-

[8] C. F. Jones, *The Rural Land Classification Program of Puerto Rico* ("Northwestern University Studies in Geography," Vol. 1 [1952]), 1–77.

[9] Examples: C. R. Dryer, *High School Geography: Physical, Economic, and Regional* (New York: American Book Co., 1911), Fig. 307; C. Langdon White and Edwin J. Foscue, *Regional Geography of Anglo-America* (New York: Prentice-Hall, 1943), Fig. 12.

[10] Examples: Robert S. Platt, "Geography of a Sugar District: Mariel, Cuba," *Geographical Review*, XIX (1929), 603–12; idem, "Problems of Our Time" *Annals of the Association of American Geographers*, XXXVI (1946), 1–43.

[11] E. L. Ullman, "Mobile: Industrial Seaport and Trade Center" (Ph.D. diss., University of Chicago, 1943).

[12] A. L. Kroeber, *Handbook of the Indians of California* (Smithsonian Institution, Bureau of American Ethnology, Bulletin No. 78 [Washington, D.C., 1925]), p. v.

[13] Carl O. Sauer and Donald D. Brand, *Pueblo Sites in Southeastern Arizona* ("University of California Publications in Geography," Vol. III [1930]), 415–58.

amples by Kroeber[14] than like previous maps by Sauer (Fig. 4).

Thus soon after the publication of Sauer's "Morphology of Landscape," and while the analytical study of landscape was still proceeding among geographers else-

publications of scholarly excellence and great value in geography.[15]

So in the years following 1925 there arose at least two schools of thought in geography: first, in California attention was directed to the works of man as phenomena

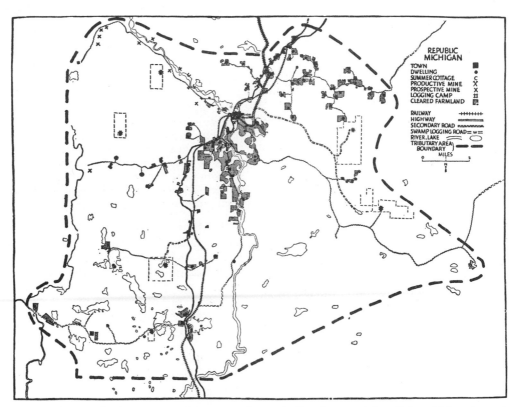

Fɪɢ. 3. Map of land occupancy, the pattern of organization in a nodal unit in which a town is the focus of interests, represented by lines and limits of movement as well as uniform areal types. From Robert S. Platt, "Field Study of Republic, Michigan: A Community in the Marquette Iron Range," *Scottish Geographical Magazine,* XLIV (1928), pp. 193–204.

where, work was launched from a different viewpoint, one concerned with the origin and spread of culture and more closely allied to culture history. This line of study likewise has continued, giving rise to many

of cultural development—buildings and crops were distinguished according to their origin and their spread was traced historically; second, in the Middle West attention was directed to the works of man as

[14] Example: Kroeber's map of "cremation and earth burial in California" showing spread of the custom of burial into the area from a culture hearth farther northwest and a spread of cremation into the area from the south (*Handbook of the Indians of California,* Fig. 70).

[15] Example: Fred B. Kniffen, "The Diffusion of the Covered Bridge in America," *Geographical Review,* XLI (1951), 114–23. The map on p. 119 indicates a culture hearth on the Atlantic coast and diffusion of covered bridges inland during succeeding decades.

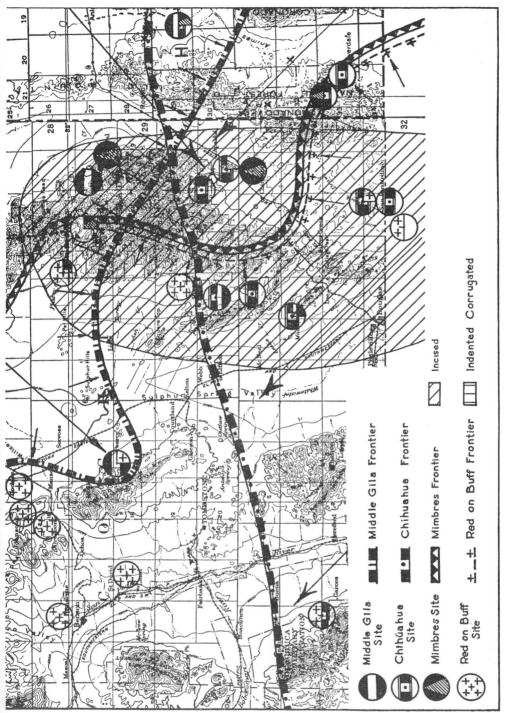

FIG. 4. Part of a map of culture affiliations, of the ruins, and attempted reconstruction of the limits of the several culture areas, showing sites of Gila culture in the northeast spreading from a culture hearth outside the area to a frontier toward the southwest and sites of Red on Buff culture in the west spreading to a frontier toward the east, exemplifying a concept of the historical integrity of culture in origin and spread, without regard for any correlation with local environmental diversity. From Sauer and Brand, "Pueblo Sites in Southeastern Arizona," Fig. 3.

phenomena of human activity applied directly to functional problems in the local environment—to types of buildings and crops distinguished according to their utility and ecological setting.

Both lines of approach seem to offer serviceable keys to aspects of knowledge, though reaching results less comprehensive when used separately than in combination with each other. How can the student of functional pattern understand his data without reference to their cultural origin; and how can the student of cultural origin understand his data fully without appreciation of the functional pattern of human enterprise to which they belong?

Gradually those geographers interpreting occupance in terms of function have come to realize that human activity meeting the needs of life in a local environment is not a direct response to that local environment but a conditioned response depending on available equipment and ideas already in mind, inherited from predecessors in that place or elsewhere.

Those geographers in particular who dealt with human occupance in regions of exotic culture were confronted promptly with conspicuous evidence of the historic ties of culture rather than the natural ties of direct response to local needs. Later it became evident that even geographers dealing with familiar regions of their homelands also are confronted with phenomena of specific cultural heritage rather than direct response to local needs. Even the urban scenes and farmsteads which have been taken for granted from childhood as normal objects of ordinary human life are found to have historic ties of culture and to be understandable in terms of cultural origin and spread—a fact to be reckoned with in the American Middle West no less than in such obvious cases as the bizarre folklands of strange tribes or the European countryside marked by remnants of medieval occupance.

Meanwhile geographers in the other line of approach, studying works of man from the viewpoint of culture history, find that they are dealing not merely with discrete inherited forms but with an active enterprise of people living and making themselves at home in an earthly habitat, drawing on their cultural inheritance to create and carry on a going concern expressed in a coherent functional pattern.

Synthesis of the two lines of approach is not complete. But the need is recognized and the trend is clear. All culture has developed and continues to grow in the functional pattern of active human enterprise. And all human enterprise functions through the medium of culture. Full understanding involves both aspects. Geographers undertaking study in an area now commonly seek answers to both kinds of questions: (1) What is the functional pattern of human enterprise going on in this environment, and (2) What is the cultural origin of this way of life?

These questions imply radical changes of thought since World War I, not only departures from environmentalism, but also movement from the concept of static uniformity to that of functional organization, and from the concept of culture as the works of man on topographic maps to that of culture in its more specific sense as the social heritage of objects, and ideas produced, modified, and selectively passed along by human enterprise.

These questions do not imply a permanent dichotomy between the two lines of approach, between functional organization and cultural origin. On the contrary they are directed toward the understanding of a single phenomenon: human occupance in its earthly setting, carried on by people who have drawn upon their heritage of equipment from the past to make themselves at home in the present in the place where they live, a functional-cultural pattern in space and time, a coherent dynamic entity in the multidimensional spatial-temporal frame.

Studies taking account of both of these aspects of human enterprise are made with increasing facility. For example, a tropical plantation is viewed as a functioning establishment of modern mechanized economy and as a cultural embodiment of forms and practices inherited from the past, all occupying a definite place in the world. Similarly a new frontier settlement is viewed as an active enterprise by a group of people making themselves at home here by recourse to ways of living inherited from past experiences elsewhere and adapted somehow to this place.[16] The objective is to make progress in understanding the world pattern of occupance, produced by people differing in experience working together with inherited equipment.

So cultural geography takes its place in America, as in Europe, not as a vague or separate subject but as a well-conceived, integral part of all human geography, adding not merely a time element in a sequence of occupance but a dimension of cultural process in a dynamic pattern of human enterprise on the earth.

---

[16] Examples: Robert S. Platt, "Reconnaissance in British Guiana, with Comments on Microgeography," *Annals of the Association of American Geographers,* XXIX (1939), 105–26; *idem,* "Reconnaissance in Dynamic Regional Geography: Tierra del Fuego," *Revista Geográfica* (Instituto Pan-Americano de Geografía e História), V (1949), 3–22.

MAX. SORRE

THE ROLE OF HISTORICAL
EXPLANATION IN HUMAN
GEOGRAPHY

While collecting my ideas on the mobility of the *oikoumene* for a study of human migration, I was led to reflect again on the role of historical explanation in human geography. It seemed to me that the terms of the old controversy between historians and geographers were much too restrictive and that it would be rewarding to consider the problem in all its generality. In order to achieve this goal, we must deliberately disregard pedagogic considerations, which have dominated and distorted the debate. We are concerned with questions of method and scientific philosophy; particular academic disciplines are not the issue here. As will be seen, the discussion to follow could be transposed and applied to the problem of the relations of geomorphology and geology. It will also bring to mind the old and nearly forgotten quarrel on "actualism." The history of science shows that, in spite of differences of terminology, we always come back to the same fundamental problems.

Within the group of natural and social sciences—to which human geography belongs—we use two types of explanation which are not opposed but complementary. Whatever the observed phenomenon may

be, it is recorded in a temporal series, it is the result of a long evolution, and it is explained by a series of anterior states. When we describe a phenomenon in these terms, we give it a genetic explanation; let us say historical explanation for it is basically the same thing, history in a large sense being only the restoration of a succession. But the same phenomenon appears at the same time in a spatial context. It maintains multiple connections with its environment, ranging from simple juxtaposition to causality. It is not possible to conceive of it apart from the equilibrium established in this complex: its ties to the environment are indissoluble. Consequently, there is a place for an explanation drawn from the relations of a being to its environment—reciprocal relations because we are presented with a mass of complex actions, reactions, and interactions. This explanation, actualist by definition, is basically ecological. The word must be understood in the full sense that was given to it by its creator Haeckel.[1] Historical and ecological explanation are the two types of explanation invoked by all the sciences of living things.

One could group the latter in two great categories according to whether they appeal

Translated, with permission of the author and publisher, from "Le rôle de l'explication historique en géographie humaine," in *Mélanges géographiques offerts à Philippe Arbos* (2 vols.; Clermont-Ferrand: Imprimerie G. de Bussac, 1953), II, 19–22. The author is professor emeritus of geography at the Sorbonne.

[1] [See Ernst Haeckel, *The History of Creation*, translated by E. R. Lankester (2 vols.; New York: Appleton, 1876), II, 354, in which ecology is defined as the science of "the correlations between all organisms living together in one and the same locality and their adaptation to their surroundings."]

more or less to one or the other type. Geology, human paleontology, paleo-ethnology, prehistoric anthropology, and history are placed on one side. And I note in passing that there is really no reason to separate history *stricto sensu* from the rest of the group. The fact that it works only with written documents does not change its character. Ethnology, sociology (with all its branches, including economics, somatic and physiological anthropology), and above all human geography belong to the other group. Human geography strives to describe the physiognomic complex centered on man or the human group. It unravels the entangled relations established within this complex. It remains very close to the concrete, for it is primarily descriptive: as soon as it takes on an explanatory character, i.e., scientific, it becomes an ecology. The specific type of explanation in human geography is an ecologic explanation.

However, these oppositions are matters of degree. These two types of explanantion are complementary. It is clear that one cannot put aside the weight of the past in analyzing the present without danger of serious distortion of reality. Less commonly, we can see that the converse is also true. At each moment of the past a phenomenon can be explained only if one replaces it in the midst of its contemporary phenomena. The present complex is the fruit of history, but history itself is the succession of past complexes.

Such are the general formulas. They become intelligible if we take the example of a discipline with a rather clear and well-established methodology: botanical geography, or, as it is also called, plant sociology. Its objective is the study of vegetative communities. It begins by recognizing them through determination of their specific composition, i.e., by defining plant associations. This done, it explains them. It investigates how these communities, when characterized not from a systematic point of view as associations, but physiognomically as formations, correspond with characteristics of

site, climate, and soil. Plant communities exhibit these influences in their appearance and behavior during the course of the year. They are in more or less precarious equilibrium with them. In our latitude, the evergreen oak forest is linked rather closely with Mediterranean climate. The pattern of its morphological and functional adaptations is dependent on the pluvio-thermic properties of this climate. Thus we determine the ecology of the community, one of the essential tasks, if not the principal one, of plant geography. But this knowledge is not sufficient for a total understanding of the community and its localization. Under the same Mediterranean climate and under generally analogous conditions there exist side by side groups of different specific composition—forests, *garrigue* or *maquis*, suffrutescent formations, or even very degraded grasslands. Observation shows that there is a genetic connection among them, and that, in the absence of intervention by man and his helpers, they proceed toward a forest climax. A certain number of these communities are therefore stages in a succession. Moreover, floristic analysis shows that the terminal community includes species from diverse sources. They have arrived in it after wanderings in the course of geologic time. We arrange them according to age and affinity. We divide the community into elements, each with a past that retraces plant paleontology and particular ecologic relations. Thus we have introduced the principle of historical explanation in two forms: (1) remote historical explanation, accounting for the initial provenience of the species; (2) a more proximate historical explanation, tracing the evolution of ecological groups. During these two operations we have come to a total explanation of the vegetation. This example seems to me particularly appropriate to show the interplay between historical and ecological explanation in the study of a natural community.

The same applies in human geography. A human group, rooted in its regional milieu, contracts unbreakable bonds with its environment. It acts vis-à-vis its environment as a powerful transforming agent, even at lower technological levels, but at the same time is subject to environmental pressures. The geographic complex, which is organized around the human group, likewise carries the weight of all its past so that many traits of the complex cannot be explained without reference to evolution. In our agricultural countries of temperate Europe we frequently come across a disharmony between the traits of the agrarian structure and elements of the present system of cultivation. The apparent disharmony is cleared up when we find in this agrarian structure a survival of now vanished economic and social systems and techniques of production. It has acted as an element of crystallization and immobilization. In other words, the geographic complex appears as an assemblage of elements of various ages, each with its own history —and it is not by accident that here again we use the word "element," which carries the same meaning in the vocabulary of plant sociology. The natural tendency of the geographer—an ecologist by definition —is to seek among the traits of the geographic complex the one that seems to be dominant (e.g., climate, soil, working techniques) and then to unravel the tangle, that is, to deduce from it all the other traits. In this work he always finishes by coming up against resistance, which reveals the role of the past, of history. In the picture of our agricultural activity the Middle Ages still survive, and even in our industrial life we still find many archaic distributional traits. English authors sometimes speak of what they call "inertia" in their country. This is a mechanistic way of saying the same thing. Let us say that historical explanation completes ecological explanation and prevents its excesses.

Hence the necessity for giving a large place in the education of the geographer to the formation of the historical sense. I should like this word to be understood in the widest way. Geography is the description of the earth, not of this or that canton of our temperate countries. Let us not restrict our field. And how could we understand, or rather how could we try to understand anything about African or Indonesian societies without some knowledge of the methods of paleo–ethnology and its provisional results? Perhaps we have to go all the way to the Neolithic to grasp the origins of even the local complex that surrounds us. In all the countries of northwestern Europe there is a certain family resemblance: much has been attributed lately to the Northern-Mediterranean contrast. For my part, I am strongly impressed by the originality of the Atlantic world. But this world is very old. Everything we learn about the culture of the dolmens or of the spread of campanuliform vases into another area invites us to go back to very ancient times.

Thus history is important, and not only what is written in the archives, although this should of course come first. But the condition must be imposed that history, true to its vocation, should be total. We shall not banish political history. For the geographer who is describing the swarms of workers on the Franco-Belgian frontier, it is indispensable to know how the frontier was fixed. And we know, too well to neglect them, what terrible breaks in the evolution of human societies are brought about by wars. But what matters to us more than the events is social history, economic history, or culture history. This is the real historical baggage of the geographer. We must hope that historians, anxious not to break the bonds between the two disciplines so long united, will be inspired by these necessities. There are pedagogic formulas to discover.

We can also believe that they will not fail. The example of a very fine recent historical book on the Mediterranean at the time of Philip II shows how application of the methods of the geographer, in unraveling the traits of the present complex, can

prove fruitful for the study of past societies.[2] Is not this manner of conceiving history as a succession of geographies a triumph of the ecological spirit? So, let us
have no false dichotomies, but, with clear
awareness of the autonomy of each discipline, a true collaboration for common
profit.

[2] [Fernand Braudel, *La Méditerranée et le monde
méditerranéen à l'époque de Philippe II* (Paris:
Colin, 1949).]

ERHARD ROSTLUND

TWENTIETH-CENTURY MAGIC

On the first page of this magazine is the statement, "Human geography is the study of the earth's surface as modified by man the inhabitant." Most of the geographers in this country would agree with this excellent definition, but the question that needs to be asked is what other Americans think geography is, and what might be the reason for their opinion. It seems best to approach the question by way of a detour among the scholars in the field.

Fifty years ago the leading American geographers were professed environmentalists who had chosen as their field of study the problem of geographic influence on human culture. In 1903 Miss Ellen Churchill Semple published *American History and Its Geographic Conditions*, and in 1911 she published *Influences of Geographic Environment*.[1] Albert Perry Brigham's *Geographic Influences in American History* also appeared in 1903, and in 1907 Ellsworth Huntington published *The Pulse of Asia*.[2] Both men became presidents of the Association of American Geographers, and in their presidential addresses, given in 1914 and 1923, respectively, both of them dealt with problems of environmentalism.[3] But by this time the task of geography was being redefined. In 1924, Carl O. Sauer criticized the premature generalizations resulting from the bias of environmentalism, or geographic determinism, as the theory was also called.[4] He pointed out that to define geography as the study of environmental influences is to assume in advance that such influences do operate, and that a science cannot be based upon or committed to a preconception. Sauer's presidential address of 1940 emphasized human geography as a culture-historical study concerned with "the works of man, or the cultural landscape."[5] In 1954, the half-century mark of the Association, the American geographers took stock of their work in *American Geography: Inventory and Prospect*.[6] In this book, which "represents the combined

Reprinted, with permission of the author and publisher, from *Landscape*, V (1956), 23–26 (copyright, 1956, by J. B. Jackson). The author (1900–1961) was a member of the Department of Geography at the University of California, Berkeley.

[1] Ellen Churchill Semple, *American History and Its Geographic Conditions* (Boston and New York: Houghton Mifflin, 1903); *Influences of Geographic Environment* (New York: Henry Holt, 1911).

[2] Albert Perry Brigham, *Geographic Influences in American History* (New York: Chautauqua Press, 1903). Ellsworth Huntington, *The Pulse of Asia* (Boston and New York: Houghton Mifflin, 1907).

[3] Albert Perry Brigham, "Problems of Geographic Influence," *Annals of the Association of American Geographers*, V (1915), 3–25; Ellsworth Huntington, "Geography and Natural Selection," *Annals of the Association of American Geographers*, XIV (1924), 1–16.

[4] Carl O. Sauer, "The Survey Method in Geography and Its Objectives," *Annals of the Association of American Geographers*, XIV (1924), 17–33, esp. 18–19.

[5] Carl O. Sauer, "Foreword to Historical Geography," *Annals of the Association of American Geographers*, XXXI (1941), 1–24.

[6] Preston E. James and Clarence F. Jones (eds.), *American Geography: Inventory and Prospect* (Syracuse: Syracuse University Press, 1954).

thoughts of hundreds of professional geographers," the term "environmentalism" is scarcely to be found except in a few references to earlier writers.

Two points must be remembered. To say that a study of environmental influences is not the proper task of geography is not the same as saying that there are no such influences. The European critics of determinism—Lucien Febvre,[7] P. Vidal de la Blache,[8] Jean Brunhes[9]—did not say that, and neither did Carl Sauer. In 1927 he wrote: "There is, of course, no intention to belittle environmental influences. . . . The notion of environmental significance is really a commonplace to which everyone subscribes. Those who deny it are as readily refuted as those who exaggerate it . . . [But] we object to the assumption that geography is commissioned to general environmental studies alone."[10] What seems to have happened in recent years is that the disciples have become more doctrinaire than the teachers in their attitude toward environmentalism, and in their wish to "refute," "discredit," and "exterminate" the idea. (All the terms have been used.) To keep the record clear: environmentalism was not disproved, only disapproved.

The other point is that not all geographers have discarded the theory. Another mid-century survey was made in 1951, *Geography in the Twentieth Century,* in which twenty geographers participated,

seven of whom are Americans.[11] In this book we find a whole chapter devoted to environmentalism, and several other chapters showing that determinism, in one form or another, is by no means a dead issue among professional geographers. Other signs indicate that the idea is also very much alive outside the profession.

It is highly probable that many Americans would be puzzled by the definition of human geography given above, for it does not express their idea of what geography is. Contact with many students and conversations with people in general have led me to believe that the current ideas of what geography is concerned with can be grouped into several categories. Some people confuse geography with geology and assume that geography is a study of rocks. Others, who obviously retain memories from their elementary-school days, think that geography is useful because it teaches us that coffee comes from Brazil, Lima is the capital of Peru, and the like. Still others are likely to raise questions of how geography influences literature, affects international relations, and shapes the destiny of peoples. In this group, I believe, are those who continued to read books on geography after they left elementary school. The question is, which books do they read?

In his review of Ellsworth Huntington's *Mainsprings of Civilization,* Fred Kniffen says: "For many working in other fields Ellsworth Huntington is the voice of American geography. Furthermore, there is a wide circle of laymen who read his works with pleasure and conviction."[12] Kniffen is undoubtedly right. I do not know exactly how large the circle of readers is or how commonly the idea of environmentalism is accepted, and can only report some signs that have caught my attention.

There are, in the first place, statements by some of the geographers. Griffith Taylor,

[7] Lucien Febvre and Lionel Bataillon, *A Geographical Introduction to History* (New York: Alfred A. Knopf, 1925). First published as *La terre et l'évolution humaine: introduction géographique à l'histoire* (Paris: La Renaissance du Livre, 1922).

[8] P. Vidal de la Blache, *Principles of Human Geography* (New York: Henry Holt, 1926). First published as *Principes de géographie humaine* (Paris: Armand Colin, 1922).

[9] Jean Brunhes, *Human Geography* (Chicago and New York: Rand McNally, 1920). First published as *La géographie humaine* (Paris: Félix Alcan, 1910).

[10] Carl O. Sauer, "Recent Developments in Cultural Geography," in E. C. Hayes (ed.), *Recent Developments in the Social Sciences* (Philadelphia: Lippincott, 1927), pp. 154–221, ref. to p. 172.

[11] Griffith Taylor (ed.), *Geography in the Twentieth Century* (New York: Philosophical Library, 1951).

[12] Fred B. Kniffen, review of Ellsworth Huntington's *Mainsprings of Civilization,* in *American Antiquity,* XI (1946), 269–70.

whose books are also widely read, describes himself as a "geographer who has always been primarily interested in environmental control." [13] Other examples are: "In Northwest Europe the natural environment is less decisive than in the Mediterranean lands. . . . Instead of shaping its inhabitants of whatever origin to a uniform pattern, it has permitted variety of economic use of the land and in contingent social structures." [14] "The primary assumption of geography is that social structures and events which are tied to specific locations must thereby be adjusted to, and inter-related with, the 'attributes of place' possessed by such locations." [15] No doubt many professional men in other fields have the same impression of geography as Marston Bates, who says, "The geographer perhaps tends to stress the ways in which physiography and resources have shaped cultural patterns." [16]

There are signs of environmentalism in other types of literature. "The land, the mountains, with all their climates—all at work, molding men, shaping their bodies, brains, habits, characters, occupations, attitudes, scales of values, social organizations." [17] "History is a social expression of geography, and Western geography is violent. . . . You could love such a country but you were bound to hate it, too—and the splits in the Western soul begin right

here." [18] "The California writers do not somehow seem to carry a weight proportionate to the bulk of their work. Why is this? All visitors from the East know the strange spell of unreality which seems to make human experience on the Coast as hollow as a trollnest. . . . This is partly no doubt a matter of climate: the empty sun and the incessant rains; and of landscape: the dry mountains and the void of the vast Pacific." [19] "In a word, it was inevitable that his environment should have bred in the American settler a fixed idea and a trait. . . . The trait was the prodigal disregard for not merely game but wildlife of all sorts." [20] "Thus environment [in New England] stepped in to alter an historical architectural procedure. Farther south, in Maryland and Virginia, the climate induced a different social and economic system." [21] "With the knowledge before us we know that the populous nation which can keep its citizens in ideal climatic conditions, whether indoor or outdoor, will have a great opportunty to lead the world in health, energy, trade and culture." [22] An advertisement in the *New York Times* describes *A Geography of Europe* by Jean Gottman with these words: "An eminent geographer analyzes the influence of the continent's physical features on the people." Mr. Gottman does no such thing, but the advertisement reveals what the blurb writer thinks the geographer is doing.

Signs of geographical determinism can

[13] Griffith Taylor, *Our Evolving Civilization: An Introduction to Geopacifics* (Toronto: University of Toronto Press, 1946), p. 3.

[14] Derwent Whittlesey, *Environmental Foundations of European History* (New York: Appleton-Century-Crofts, 1949), p. 28.

[15] C. Langdon White and George T. Renner, *Human Geography: An Ecological Study of Society* (New York: Appleton-Century-Crofts, 1948), p. vi.

[16] Marston Bates, "Human Ecology," in A. L. Kroeber (ed.), *Anthropology Today* (Chicago: University of Chicago Press, 1953), pp. 700–13, ref. to p. 704.

[17] T. K. Whipple, *Study Out the Land* (Berkeley and Los Angeles: University of California Press, 1943), p. 36.

[18] Bernard De Voto, Introduction to B. A. Botkin (ed.), *A Treasury of Western Folklore* (New York: Crown Publishers, 1951).

[19] Edmund Wilson, *Classics and Commercials* (New York: Farrar, Straus, 1950), pp. 45–46.

[20] Edward H. Graham, *The Land and Wildlife* (New York and London: Oxford University Press, 1947), p. 12.

[21] Rexford Newcomb, "Regionalism in American Architecture," in Merrill Jensen (ed.), *Regionalism in America* (Madison: University of Wisconsin Press, 1952), pp. 276–77.

[22] S. F. Markham, *Climate and the Energy of Nations* (London: Oxford University Press, 1942), p. 133.

also be detected in discussions, reports, and term papers of some university students, but perhaps not so commonly now as in former years. These students seem to have acquired the concept before arriving on the campus, and if this is true it is puzzling, for to my knowledge the idea that geography is a study of environmental influences is not taught, or at least not particularly stressed, in the secondary schools. They must have picked up the idea elsewhere.

We thus find ourselves in a curious situation. A part of the reading public, which may be much larger than we think, believes that geography is one thing, and most of the geographers say it is another. There are several reasons for this situation. One of them is doubtless the type of geographical literature that is most readily available to the American people. In one of the larger public libraries in the West, I recently found twenty-five works of Ellsworth Huntington, six of Griffith Taylor, and the principal writings of Ellen Churchill Semple. There are several copies of some of the works, the books are well worn, and the cards in them indicate that they have been borrowed by many people. It would be embarrassing to list the works of other leading geographers of our time: there are hardly any. To judge from this library, Ellsworth Huntington *is* the voice of American geography, or at least the voice most widely heard.

And there is a reason for this wide circle of readers, as Kniffen put it. People read with pleasure, because these authors write in a clear and vigorous style; people read with conviction, because these works seem to provide answers to questions that interest the readers. Furthermore, these authors do not address an inner circle; they speak to the American people. I am not referring to so-called popular editions; it is the main works of the environmentalists that are on the shelves of the public library. One might look askance at facile generalizations, but not at the fact that the books are read, nor at the authors for addressing themselves to

the public. So eminent a geographer as Alexander von Humboldt did: the opening line in *Kosmos* reads, "In the late evening of an active life I offer to the German public a work, which in vague outline has been in my mind for almost half a century." [23] Humboldt also suggested that "thoroughness does not unconditionally demand pallor in style of writing." [24]

The prestige of ancient lineage is behind the environmentalists: Friedrich Ratzel, Thomas Buckle, Montesquieu, Jean Bodin, Aristotle. But other geographers have an equally old tradition and can also claim part of Ratzel's heritage, perhaps the better part. It is not clear, however, that the prestige of ancient scholars is a reason for the appeal of environmentalism. I would suggest that we are dealing with something older than Montesquieu or Aristotle, something more deeply rooted, which may be a significant reason. Many primitive peoples believed in something in the physical world around them that influenced human affairs, forces that might be in the sun, the moon, the sky, the sea, the forest. Among some peoples the forces were conceptualized and named, such as the *mana* of the Polynesians, the *huaca* of ancient Peru, the *manitou* of the Algonkians, or the *wakan* of the Sioux. These influences had various forms: they might be invested in persons or associated with things, and they were attributes of places. It is not a far cry to the "attributes of place" we find in some of the modern geography books. My suggestion is that the popular belief in the influence of the environment today may not stem from Miss Semple or Ellsworth Huntington at all, but is likely to have more ancient roots. It may well be that one of the reasons for the wide circle of readers is that these writers are saying what people have always believed.

Perhaps the most important reason for

[23] Alexander von Humboldt, *Kosmos* (London: George Bell & Sons, 1880), I, ix. (1st ed.; Stuttgart and Tübingen, 1845.)
[24] *Ibid*, p. xi.

the prevalence of the belief in geographical influences is that the spirit of our time is congenial to such ideas. Other types of environment are commonly thought to exert their effects on people. If Johnny is bad at school, the reason may be that his home environment is bad. If a man commits a crime, the chances are that the cause lies in his childhood environment. If the economic environment is wretched, people turn to communism. If a competitive environment prevails, whether in business, industry, or other walks of life, it develops the best qualities in man. The precise definition of good and bad may vary among the people holding these opinions, but what does not vary is the belief that a significant cause-and-effect relationship exists; in short, that man is largely the product of his several environments. It is not strange that a belief in geographical influences thrives in this society, which believes in the effects of so many other environments.

It would be a mistake to dismiss such ideas as popular notions lacking significance. Environmentalism is a dogma on which action is based. In primitive society it was possible to do something about the environmental forces, provided one knew the correct and prescribed procedure that is called magic, and usually it was known only to certain experts. Correct magic could bestow many benefits: it could cause rain to fall, crops to grow, game to become plentiful, sickness to disappear, children to grow brave and handsome, and many other results that man wished for. Whether or not magic really or "scientifically" worked is immaterial; magic was a force and mainspring in primitive culture because men believed in it. In our society, too, we have experts in environmental control who bestow benefits on mankind in a prescribed way, and it looks as if the way may become more and more prescribed. The action is based on the proposition: man is largely the product of his environment; therefore, if we improve the environment we shall have better men. This is Twenti-

eth-Century Magic, and it is a force in our society because we believe in it.

We must distinguish between the normal and surely commendable human desire to improve the lot of man, and the intention of doing it by action based on a particular and prescribed theory, which may or may not be true. And there can be no doubt that there is such an intention, for the signs are all around us. S. F. Markham, quoted above, was not concerned with the climate for academic reasons; as secretary to one of the prime ministers of Britain he was interested in legislation. A recent editorial in one of the leading New York dailies points out that what is needed in Vietnam is not only land reform and agricultural engineering, but social and anthropological engineering; and almost any day we can hear or read about what is needed in the Near East, Africa, India, Asia, not to mention what is needed in this country. A common term in these discussions is "conditions," and conditions are part of the environment. The problem discussed is never how to save the values of native culture, but how to rescue the native from his miserable old environment, and we propose to do it by changing the environment. The question is never how to preserve the wooden plow and the native attitude toward the land, cattle, family, and tribe, but how to get tractors and commercial fertilizers on the land, break down tribal organization, and get industries started. What is doubtful is not the need but the remedy; the problems have become standardized and the solutions prescribed, and at bottom the prescription rests on environmentalism. The critical question before us is not whether the environment is the mainspring of civilization, but whether environmentalism will become, or perhaps already is, the mainspring of our society.

A return by way of the detour we came takes us back to geography. We know from the publication of *American Geography: Inventory and Prospect* what the men in the profession are doing and plan to do.

Most of them are preoccupied with specialized studies, which can be grouped into two major types. On the one hand we find contributions in economic, political, historical, urban geography, and related fields, all of which are essentially inquiries into certain aspects of human culture. On the other hand are climatology, geomorphology, and studies in soil, water, plant, and animal geography, which are concerned with certain aspects of nature. American geography at mid-century, then, is a study of nature on the one hand and culture on the other, but the question of whether or not there is a significant relation between nature and culture has been left out. The key is presumably to be found in Preston James's remark about geographic determinism: "In a relatively stable environment, no example of positive determinism has been demonstrated by acceptable method and consequently the concept is no longer considered useful as a guide to geographic understandings." [25] The significant words are "by acceptable method," and I believe it is true that we have no geographical technique that is adequate for dealing with the question. It might also be said that there is no reason for leaving this problem on the

[25] *American Geography: Inventory and Prospect*, p. 13.

doorstep of geography, for it belongs as much to anthropology, history, or any other discipline concerned with man. But the problem has not disappeared because an acceptable method of dealing with it has not been found, and perhaps it has not been found because we have not searched. Douglas H. K. Lee makes the suggestion that some of the thought-provoking generalizations of the early determinists "must now be re-examined in the light of newly acquired knowledge." [26] His point is well taken. We need a fresh start, but we need not start all over again. We need no more polemics about what geographers should study, no more declarations affirming environmentalism from one side or exterminations from the other. The task is to search for the truth wherever it lies. Meanwhile the engineers of human destiny are not waiting for the outcome of academic debates; and if they have their way, one of the prospects, which is no longer unimaginable, is that geographers may be told what to study.

[26] Douglas H. K. Lee, "Physiological Climatology," in *American Geography: Inventory and Prospect*, pp. 471–83, ref. to p. 473. [See also his recent study of *Climate and Economic Development in the Tropics* (New York: Harper & Bros., 1957)].

PART **2**

CULTURE AREAS AND DISTRIBUTIONS

Each of the nine articles in this section deals with the problem of identifying and delimiting culture areas. The topics considered range from cattle-collars and house types to entire cultural complexes, and the scale of the studies shifts from Switzerland and Louisiana to major realms of the world. Diversity of this sort is an inevitable consequence of the varied interests of cultural geographers and the innumerable aspects of culture, both material and non-material, that may be studied geographically. In spite of the abrupt transitions, these essays illustrate common purposes and procedures.

The most generally applicable method in cultural geography is to map the distribution of some traits that are thought to characterize a given people. Since all traits are differentiated areally, there is no logical limit to the number that may be considered, and in fact it is often impossible to predict which traits, elements, or complexes will provide tangible evidence of cultural areas or groupings. In practice, attention is most often directed to elements of broad or even universal importance, such as livelihood, settlement patterns, language, and religion. These basic elements of culture can be used for the identification of gross patterns or "culture worlds." [1] For example, religion "forms a common bond among the faithful, manifests itself in social institutions, and gives sanction to custom." [2] Consequently, the realms of such faiths as Islam, Buddhism, and Christianity give at least a crude approximation of major culture areas. More refined distributions are derived from studies that elucidate differences within or across such areas. By means of interviewing and further mapping, tertiary boundaries and areas are established. Regardless of the scale, the delimitation of culture areas proceeds inductively by determination of the limits of individual traits and the establishment of boundaries or transition zones.

This procedure is demonstrated by Richard Weiss in his study of cultural

[1] Large-scale distinctions of this sort have been used primarily in pedagogic works. Cf. Richard J. Russell and Fred B. Kniffen, *Culture Worlds* (New York: Macmillan 1951), and Preston E. James and Nelda Davis, *The Wide World: A Geography* (New York: Macmillan, 1959). The former is designed for use in colleges and the latter in high schools.

[2] Jan O. M. Broek, "Progress in Human Geography," in Preston E. James (ed.), *New Viewpoints in Geography* (Twenty-ninth Yearbook of the National Council for the Social Studies, Washington, D.C., 1959), pp. 34–53, ref. to p. 43.

distributions in Switzerland.[3] The major finding of his study is an unexpected cultural boundary that coincides with an old political demarcation rather than with the more conspicuous religious and linguistic frontiers. He also demonstrates that objective distributions may be unintelligible if one fails to account for the subjective evaluation of traits by the peoples who are exposed to them. In Switzerland, as elsewhere in the world, an innovation may be accepted or rejected, not on the basis of its form and content or its compatibility with established custom, but because of its affiliation with desirable or undesirable groups. The identification of playing cards and cattle-collars as "Protestant" or "Catholic" is merely one manifestation of a universal tendency. Consciously or unconsciously, all peoples select certain traits to serve as symbols of their identity. Wherever several traits of this sort coincide, one is justified to speak of a "cultural boundary," and the territories delimited by such boundaries have explicit meaning as "culture areas."

Linguistic differences are both a cause and a consequence of the cultural discontinuities and uniformities that characterize any sizable area of the world. Language not only enables man to communicate with his neighbors, but it also permits him to learn from the experiences of his ancestors and communicate his own knowledge to successive generations. Language responds to existing symbols and serves as a mechanism for the creation of new ones. Moreover, linguistic distinctions, like biologic distinctions, reflect and provide evidence of cultural origins and dispersals.[4] It is not surprising, therefore, that language has been used more often that any other human attribute as an "index of culture." Nor is it surprising that carefully designed linguistic maps provide the cultural geographer with his most powerful tool.

The article of C. M. Delgado de Carvalho clarifies and elaborates these points. It cannot be said that his statement is exhaustive, but it defines a number of research problems and gives concrete illustrations of what linguistic investigation can reveal. Geographers have special reason to be familiar with the problems associated with attempts to relate language and nationality, for they have pioneered in the study of this particular theme.[5] The author's remarks on linguistic evolution and the relation of language to other elements of culture and to nature are less familar but no less relevant. His case studies

[3] It is unfortunate that we are unable to reproduce the excellent maps on which this essay is based, for the *Atlas der schweizerischen Volkskunde* is a triumph of cartography as well as scientific research.

[4] In this connection it is interesting to note that many of the evolutionary and taxonomic principles of philology were formulated prior to Darwin's time. For example, the common origin and diverging descent of the Indo-European languages were recognized in the latter half of the eighteenth century—an insight, as A. L. Kroeber indicates, "which grouped species of idioms into genera and genera into a family." See his essay on "Evolution, History and Culture," in Sol Tax (ed.), *The Evolution of Man,* Vol. II of *Evolution after Darwin* (Chicago: University of Chicago Press, 1960), pp. 1–16, ref. to pp. 8–9.

[5] See, for example, Leon Dominian, *The Frontiers of Language and Nationality in Europe* (New York: American Geographical Society, 1917), and H. R. Wilkinson, *Maps and Politics: A Review of the Ethnographic Cartography of Macedonia* (Liverpool: Liverpool University Press, 1951).

of the Portuguese, French, and English languages illustrate processes of evolution, diffusion, and differentiation that are of universal importance.[6]

Religion deserves an important place in cultural geography, for no other element of culture more completely permeates human life.[7] Perhaps the main reason for the relative neglect of this topic is a lack of general awareness that religion has material as well as non-material manifestations. The imprints of religion may not be conspicuous to the inhabitants of a particular religious realm, but to a visitor of another faith—say, a Moslem in Europe or an American in India—landscapes seem to be impregnated with religious symbolism.

This reaction is demonstrated in Paul Fickeler's sensitive study of religious manifestations in Asia. In his consideration of such concepts as holiness and sacredness, and tolerance or intolerance, he outlines problems that should be of interest to cultural geographers. In his analysis of the symbolic meanings of light and fire, colors, sounds, directions and positions, numbers and times, motions, plants and animals, and, finally, entire landscapes, he demonstrates that religion plays a prominent role in conditioning the varied habitats of man. He might also have considered the religious aspects of such basic philosophical concepts as "fate" and "progress" for they too influence the way men use their resources and time.[8] Religion, like language, also deserves serious consideration from students of cultural evolution and diffusion. Moreover, the religious aspects of sectionalism and regionalism may be of considerable importance even in a seemingly well-homogenized Western country like the United States. Indeed, in such cases the distribution of religious bodies reveals basic cultural distinctions that other features of national life tend to mask.[9]

Another indicator of cultural differences is provided by the names that particular peoples give to the sites of their settlements and the natural and artificial features of their habitats. From study of such names, retrospective knowledge

[6] For further discussion of linguistic methods and their relevance in studies of cultural distributions see William E. Bittle, "Language and Culture Areas: A Note on Method," *Philosophy of Science,* XX (1953), 247–56. The results of recent quantitative studies are summarized by D. H. Hymes in "Lexicostatistics So Far," *Current Anthropology,* I (1960), 3–44.

[7] Cf. Pierre Deffontaines, *Géographie et religions* (Paris: Gallimard, 1948); H. J. Fleure, "The Geographical Distribution of the Major Religions," *Bulletin de la Société Royale de Géographie d'Egypte,* XXIV (1951), 1–18; Xavier de Planhol, *The World of Islam* (Ithaca, N.Y.: Cornell University Press, 1959; first published as *Le Monde Islamique: Essai de géographie religieuse,* Paris: Presses Universitaires de France, 1957); and Erich Isaac, "Religion, Landscape, and Space," *Landscape,* IX (1959–60), 14–18.

[8] In this connection much can be learned from critical reading of Max Weber's classic work, *The Protestant Ethic and the Spirit of Capitalism,* trans. Talcott Parsons (New York: Scribner's Sons, 1930) [first published in the *Archiv für Sozialwissenschaft und Sozialpolitik,* Vols. XX–XXI (1904–5)]. See also R. H. Tawney, *Religion and the Rise of Capitalism* (New York: Harcourt, Brace, 1926; Mentor Books, 1947), and Shepard B. Clough, *Basic Values of Western Civilization* (New York: Columbia University Press, 1960). Data from the realms of other religions are presented by Deffontaines and De Planhol.

[9] See Wilbur Zelinsky, "An Approach to the Religious Geography of the United States: Patterns of Church Membership in 1952," *Annals of the Association of American Geographers,* LI (1961), 139–93, and Andrew H. Clark, "Old World Origins and Religious Adherence in Nova Scotia," *Geographical Review,* L (1960), 317–44.

is acquired of culture areas and movements. In some cases such evidence is virtually all that we can hope to obtain.[10] In the fourth article in this section Ivan Lind discusses some of the challenges and frustrations of place-name study. His witty and learned essay excites interest in place names and illustrates the substantial scholarship that such study requires. In this type of inquiry much is gained by collaboration between "amateurs" and "professionals," but it is essential that the former realize the limitations of untrained eyes and ears.

A concrete illustration of the value of place-name study is given by Wilbur Zelinsky in his analysis of generic terms in the place names of the northeastern United States. His examination is particularly valuable because it shows that such terms can be sorted into regional and temporal categories even in a region "where cultural areas have had scant opportunity to crystallize." Moreover, Zelinsky's study suggests that comparable results might be obtained in other areas and by study of other classes of names.[11] For example, there is ample evidence from elsewhere that place names can facilitate reconstruction of past environments and landscapes.[12] Skilled analysis of place names is both an adjunct to and a prerequisite of any serious study of cultural distributions and movements in the past.

The number of material traits that may be used as a basis of cultural differentiation is unlimited, for most of man's creations embody custom and tradition, and some objects have added importance as symbols of collective identity. Richard Weiss's study of cattle-collars and playing cards may be recalled in this connection, and it may be added that cultural differences have been elucidated by studies of many features of the rural landscape.[13] Among these features none has received greater consideration than house types. The importance of dwellings is self-evident: they usually represent the most elaborate and valuable possession of man. It is rarely possible to describe houses as mere shelters, for, as Spencer remarks, "into his houses man has built many ideas, hopes, and dreams far beyond the satisfaction of simple protective needs." [14]

The rich geographical literature on house types includes studies of floor plan and external form,[15] studies that emphasize component features of houses as

[10] Cf. John Corominas, "La toponymie hispanique préromane et la surviance du basque jusqu'au bas moyen âge," *Sixth International Congress of Onomastic Sciences, Munich, 1958* (Munich: Beckschen, 1960) I, 105–46.

[11] For further discussion see Meredith F. Burrill, "Toponymic Generics," *Names*, IV (1956), 129–37, 226–40.

[12] See, for example, Leo Waibel, "Place Names as an Aid in the Reconstruction of the Original Vegetation of Cuba," *Geographical Review*, XXXIII (1943), 376–96, and H. C. Darby, "The Clearing of the Woodland in Europe," in William L. Thomas, Jr. (ed.), *Man's Role in Changing the Face of the Earth* (Chicago: University of Chicago Press, 1956), pp. 183–216.

[13] See, for example, Fred Kniffen, "The American Covered Bridge," *Geographical Review*, XLI (1951), 114–23; and Eugene Cotton Mather and John Fraser Hart, "Fences and Farms," *Geographical Review*, XLIV (1954), 201–23.

[14] J. E. Spencer, "House Types of Southern Utah," *Geographical Review*, XXXV (1945), 444–57, ref. to 445.

[15] Cf. Jorge Dias, "Contribution to the Study of Primitive Habitation," *Comptes Rendus du Congrès International de Géographie, Lisbonne, 1949*, I (Lisbon, 1951), 107–11.

well as complete units,[16] studies that consider form and materials only incidentally and focus on the functions that houses are designed to perform,[17] and studies that deal with evolution and transformation as well as distribution of types.[18] In any case, it is clear that houses have usually been studied not for their own sake, but rather as a means to facilitate understanding of cultural groupings and areas. For this reason, we have reproduced Fred Kniffen's classic study of house types and culture areas in Louisiana. It hardly needs to be stated that the procedures demonstrated in his study are applicable to houses elsewhere and to many other features of the landscape.[19]

Geographers, like all scholars, must deal with generalities as well as specifics, and on occasion they must attempt to clarify and solve complex problems of vast scale. In such efforts the inductive procedures outlined by Weiss, Delgado de Carvalho, Fickeler, Lind, Zelinsky, and Kniffen are invaluable, but it becomes necessary to consider entire complexes as well as individual elements or traits. This difficult task is undertaken by Jan Broek in his study of diversity and unity in Southeast Asia.

The rationale of his effort, understandable today as well as at the time of writing, is to demonstrate that the student of international affairs must consider social and economic issues as well as immediate political problems, for "peoples are first of all a part of their local cultural pattern, each with its own traditions, institutions, and ways of making a living." In his attempt to unravel these patterns in Southeast Asia, Broek considers environment and population distribution, and the relation of race, language, and religion to patterns of migration and external pressures. These elements of diversity form the background for his consideration of the prospects for economic and political unity. His conclusions are timeless, for they demonstrate the relevance of geographic analysis to research problems that are not amenable to any definitive solution.[20] He also demonstrates—for the first time in this anthology—that cultural analysis may be incorporated into broader inquiries that include consideration of environmental, economic, and political variables.

Diversity and unity also form the main theme of David Lowenthal's ac-

[16] Cf. J. E. Spencer, "The Houses of the Chinese," *Geographical Review*, XXXVII (1947), 254–73.

[17] Cf. Albert Demangeon, "L'Habitation rural en France," *Annales de Géographie*, XXIX (1920), 352–75.

[18] Cf. Edna Scofield, "The Evolution and Development of Tennessee Houses," *Journal of the Tennessee Academy of Science*, XI (1936), 229–40.

[19] In the study of rural house types Italian Geographers have been outstanding pioneers. Since 1938 twenty monographs have been published in the series *Ricerche sulle dimore rurali in Italia* (present publisher, Leo S. Olschki, Florence). See Edward T. Price, "Rural Dwellings in Italy," *Geographical Review*, LI (1961), 435–37.

[20] For additional discussion of the problems of cultural diversity in Southeast Asia see Elizabeth Bacon, "A Preliminary Attempt To Determine the Culture Areas of Asia," *Southwestern Journal of Anthropology*, II (1946), 117–32; A. L. Kroeber, "Culture Groupings in Southeast Asia," *Southwestern Journal of Anthropology*, III (1947), 175–95; J. E. Spencer, *Asia East by South: A Cultural Geography* (New York: Wiley, 1954); and Norton Ginsburg et al., *The Pattern of Asia* (Englewood Cliffs, N.J.: Prentice-Hall, 1958).

count of Caribbean societies, but he extends the dimension of the problem to include vertical as well as horizontal planes. In any society "one or more determinants of social stratification, such as color, descent, wealth, occupation, age, or sex, may inhibit freedom of choice or expression more or less completely in various realms of activity." These inhibiting factors may serve to distinguish one or more groups and be based on one or more diagnostic traits. Accordingly, one may speak of duality, pluralism, or simply of diversity. In any case, cultural identity is maintained by barriers to free movement of peoples, objects, and ideas.

That such barriers should be artificial as well as natural should occasion no surprise. Every West Indian is born into an island world, but his insularity cannot be equated with that of all other islanders; for example, with that of the Polynesians or the inhabitants of the Aegean Islands. Consequently, even the physical aspects of Caribbean diversity are conditioned by culture. The social and economic aspects are not only conditioned by culture: they are manifestations of culture. In the Caribbean region, as elsewhere, the objective attributes of groups or communities acquire meaning as a result of cumulative, subjective evaluations. It is from such unions of fact and fancy that most, if not all, cultural distinctions are born.[21]

The discussions of Broek and Lowenthal take account of evolution and diffusion, but both authors place greater emphasis on differentiation among contemporary societies. Sauer's study of cultural patterns in Middle America is more clearly historical, and within this temporal framework he minimizes development *in situ* and maximizes the significance of migration and diffusion. Broek analyzes territorial patterns, while Lowenthal looks for layers or shadings within such patterns. Sauer interprets his distributions as a consequence of cultural ebb and flow, and describes Middle America as a zone of interpenetration of peoples and institutions, mainly originating elsewhere. He finds abundant evidence of displacement and blending but relatively little of endemism. In short, he is impressed with the importance of movement, and poses questions concerning whence, whither, and along what routes movement has taken place.

To answer these questions, Sauer, like Broek, examines many features of the natural environment: relief and drainage, winds and currents, climate and soils, flora and fauna. These considerations support a postulate that the Central American isthmus has served as one of the world's great corridors for human migrations. Not surprisingly, Sauer's account of physical conditions and cultural movements also leads to some critical observations on the concepts of culture area and stage. As an alternative mode of thinking, he recom-

---

[21] The theme of diversity or pluralism is developed by several authors in the monograph from which this article is drawn. See also the related discussion and bibliography in David Lowenthal (ed.), *The West Indies Federation: Perspectives on a New Nation* (New York: Columbia University Press, 1961).

mends that emphasis be placed on accretion and synthesis, for in Middle America the available evidence does not support the hypothesis of autochthonous culture areas passing through parallel stages of development.[22] Perhaps the most important generalization in this essay is an emphatic statement on the relative importance of isolation and exposure.

[22] A stimulating discussion of similar problems in an adjacent area is offered by Paul Kirchhoff (with comments by Ralph L. Beals, Carl O. Sauer, and A. L. Kroeber) in "Gatherers and Farmers in the Greater Southwest," *American Anthropologist*, LVI (1954), 529–60. See also Homer Aschmann, "The Subsistence Problem in Mesoamerican History," in *Middle American Anthropology*, II (Washington, D.C.: Pan American Union, 1960), pp. 1–9.

RICHARD WEISS

CULTURAL BOUNDARIES AND THE ETHNOGRAPHIC MAP

If we ask a man—say a farmer planting potatoes, a bureaucrat drafting a letter, or a cooper putting on a hoop—why he is working the way he is, instead of an answer we will probably receive an astonished look, or at best the reply: "That's the way it's done." But if we explain to the same man, concretely and practically, that his work is performed somewhere else in an altogether different way, then he will either dismiss the way of working that we have described as "impossible," for more or less sound reasons, or he will begin to think it over. In any case, a conversation about his work is under way.

By a confrontation with a different way of doing things, a "border clash" between what is his and what is alien, we have brought our informant out of his traditional unconsciousness and into an awareness of the peculiarity of his way of working. Awareness of distinctiveness is always aroused as a result of border-contact with what is different. This is true both for the distinctiveness of the individual and that transcending the individual, and linked with society or expressed in the landscape, and this is what interests us about our informant.

When our informant recognizes that *he* is different, he also recognizes the distinc-

tiveness of his way of working, by virtue of which he belongs to certain areal tradition [*Traditionskreis*].[1] In the process it may strike him intuitively that he belongs to a cultural community and to a culture area or landscape. At any rate, he knows this much: that he and his like are not alone in this world, that right in the next town "other people" dwell, who can be recognized as different by this or that speech habit, by the accent of their "good day," by the way they cook their soup, the sound of their church bells, and other symptoms of this sort.

This is just the way the man from Zurich feels about the man from Basel, and the Basler about the Zürcher. The Basler would not enjoy his famous Shrovetide Carnival [*Fastnacht*] if he did not have Zurich's attempt at a carnival and Zurich people in general as a subject for his jokes. On the other side, the Zürcher can enjoy pride in his intercontinental airport when he thinks of the Baslers, who have the first Swiss sample-fair but no such airport. Everyone, with his own property and peculiarities, takes himself as a "Middle Kingdom" as against the less worthy stranger, the *fremder Fötzel*, as people in the old Swiss cantons still sometimes call any citizen of another canton or a foreigner.

This is the spirit of oldtime village rail-

Translated with permission of the author, from "Kulturgrenzen und ihre Bestimmung durch volkskundliche Karten," *Studium Generale*, V (1952), 363–73. The author is professor of ethnology at the University of Zurich, Switzerland.

[1] I have expressed my concept of the "areal tradition" in *Volkskunde der Schweiz* (Erlenbach-Zurich: Eugen Rentsch, 1946), pp. 23 ff.

lery,[2] surviving also in cities as well as in larger regional or national areas, where a pronounced *Lokalgeist*, kindled in friction with a neighboring *genius loci*, prevails. Inter-village scuffles, overshadowing all internal enmities, are the purest expression of local community feeling set off sharply against that of a neighboring local community. In these matters we see what will occupy us further: that the fixing of boundaries is based not only on objective differences in natural conditions, culture traits, or inherited way of life, but on a subjective motive, the very awareness of being distinctive, which in certain spheres makes it possible to perceive and experience people and things as proper and trustworthy, i.e., as "homely."

The awareness of one's distinctiveness is, so to speak, a flash of lightning that illuminates the realm of objective difference. It makes one's own space, and even more all other space, appear in an individual, and often very arbitrary, light. This applies both to the narrow local and the wider national feeling of distinctiveness. What villagers in their local joking allege to characterize their neighbors are almost always massive vices, or traits considered as vices, such as drunkenness, gluttony, stupidity, thievishness, filthiness, poverty, sour wine —in short, "vices" that make one's own "virtues" appear all the brighter. Nationality definitions move on exactly the same level of summary partiality and primitive presumption in the characterization of neighbors: for instance, the various images of "the Swiss," [3] "the Frenchman," "Ivan,"

and the "Ami" [American]. National pride does not differ in the least from village pride in its causes and its territorial functions, and every village bounds off what is its own from what is "foreign" with the same egocentric overrating of itself as in the former "Middle Kingdom" that felt exalted above the surrounding barbarian world.

Local pride, which tries to glorify a local community and fill it with exclusiveness, is the expression of a drive for self-preservation. It can likewise derive special stimulus from an inferiority complex. Thus the sense of difference in the small and old Swiss half-canton of Nidwalden, which has about 19,000 inhabitants, is conditioned by an inferiority complex of the "nid" (i.e., lower) part of the forest core [*Kernwald*] toward its twin canton in Obwalden. One of Nidwalden's sons, the psychiatrist Jakob Wyrsch, has demonstrated that this inferiority is rooted in an unawareness of medieval history.[4]

In fact, Nidwalden and Obwalden are alike as twin brothers in natural setting, speech, and religion. A whole series of peculiarities of these ancient peasant communes is involved in the structure of their quarrel, over which the headmen of both half-cantons came into collision as they were crossing together to Schwyz during the 650th anniversary celebration of the Swiss Confederation in 1947. The issues range from the cult of a local "saint" of the Nidwalden folk (blessed brother Konrad Scheuber) as against the successful and generally venerated Klaus von Flüe of the Obwalden people, to Nidwalden's finally successful campaign to secure an electric plant, the Bannalp Power Station, as against the initially much more profitable Lungern plant of Obwalden. Other bases of rivalry include: the contrast between the histrionic tendencies of Nidwalden with its Stanser Clowns' Society and the "realism" of its twin; and the fact that Nidwalden

---

[2] The spirit of local joking patterns is ably presented, with much supporting material, in Hugo Moser, *Schwäbischer Volkshumor: die Necknamen der Städte und Dörfer* . . . (Stuttgart: Kohlhammer, 1950). The *Atlas der schweizerischen Volkskunde* will include a map of "yokel" or "hick" [*Schildbürger*] places and tales. Especially deserving of mention is an article, with a map, by Paul Geiger and Richard Weiss in the *Schweizerisches Archiv für Volkskunde* XLIII (1946), 221–70.

[3] "Nachbarliche Charakterisierungen der Schweizer," in Richard Weiss, *Volkskunde der Schweiz*, pp. 353 ff.

4. J. Wyrsch, "Das Volk von Unterwalden," *Schweizerisches Archiv für Volkskunde*, XLIII (1946), 1 ff.

waged a desperate struggle against a French
army in 1798—a battle fought with unex-
ampled heroism and terrible sacrifices on
the part of the whole population, although
there was no hope of success—, while at
the same time the "realists" of Obwalden
remained calm, even under Napoleonic me-
diation, and annexed the Engelberg monastery lands that belonged naturally and
entirely to Nidwalden. Another source of
grievance was the secession of the Nidwalden people, by decision of their local commune, from the Swiss Confederation in
1815.

So we discover from small examples—
and who can help thinking about the fate
of greater lands and peoples?—how a culture area, with its visible culture content,
can be conditioned, formed, and limited
from within, from its spiritual center. This
often happens because of a historical experience, engraved as it were upon the collective consciousness of the communal being, which takes effect (even if the history
books are silent about it) in each individual
who lives under the influence of a place
and is conditioned by its destiny, without
his even being aware of it.

It is understandable that much less sense
of distinctiveness is found in the interior
of such areas—i.e., the core areas in which
the stamp of distinctiveness has originated
—than on their edges and borders. For
example, the French Alsatian more consciously or demonstratively represents
French civilization than the Frenchman of
Île-de-France, the German abroad makes
himself out to be more German than someone in the German core area, and the Catholic of the Diaspora or of mixed or border
areas of religious affiliation is a "better"
Catholic than one within the great realms
of Catholicism.

In addition, the borders and frontier
zones of culture areas often pose for the
first time the question of culture area for
an outsider. From the train we notice distinctive house types and settlement forms,
and first become attentive to differences between one area and another. The person

who stands outside—and this is where we
are as soon as we take the scientific view
—tries to take account objectively of the
visible characteristics on one side or the
other and their local preconditions.

Thus we wish to ask ourselves in the following discussion whether and how culture
areas and cultural boundaries can be identified objectively, and how they can be
"explained"; meanwhile we shall not forget the foregoing considerations on the
internal distinctiveness of culture areas.

As joint editor of the *Atlas of Swiss
Ethnography*,[5] I take my departure from
the standpoint of the ethnographic cartographer, whose tedious work rests on the
postulate that one can "see" culture areas
and cultural boundaries on ethnographic
maps. In what follows I draw support from
familiar ethnographic maps, knowing that
I cannot comprehend all realms of culture
thereby; but I believe that these examples
enable me to say something basically important about the formation of culture
areas and cultural boundaries.

BOUNDARIES AND AREAS ON ETHNOGRAPHIC MAPS

The same thing happens to a person who
draws ethnographic maps as to anyone who
occupies himself with the tedious and tire-
some task of translating statistical material
into a topographic picture of space: he
feels rewarded and delighted if "areas"
and "boundaries" appear on his sheet, if
things that are alike arrange themselves
from the warp-material of the incomprehensible local notes in such a way that he
can put them together into patches on
paper representing geographic space and
surround these patches with lines, or
boundaries. The joy of the draftsman has
its basis in the often startling recognition
of spatial order in material that cannot be
seen as a whole. Such a recognition could
not be had, really, without the help of the
map, or could only be obtained with the

[5] Paul Geiger and Richard Weiss (eds.), *Atlas
der schweizerischen Volkskunde* (Basel: Schweize-
rische Gesellschaft für Volkskunde, 1950–   ).

aid of an uncommon capacity for spatial imagination.

The scientific cultural and ethnographic cartographer will not be content with his pleasure in relatively neat "areas" and "boundaries." He will concede that his areas of distribution and boundaries are simplifications of reality, like all pictures. The falsification is reduced if the information is not laid out in areal units—which make a more striking graphic composition —but rather appears truly as points on the map. The "point style," true to place, as used in the *Atlas of Swiss Ethnography*,[6] is less attractive than the "area style," but more realistic and hence should be the obvious choice for research maps. Even so, it already contains enough generalization.

As an example of areas of distribution let us take the map of "Ways of Hitching Cattle for Draft" [*Zugvorrichtungen für Rindvieh*], published in the prospectus for the *Atlas*, although we are unable to reproduce it here. This map shows the distribution of the three ways of hitching cattle that occur in Switzerland: horn-yoke, neck-yoke, and collar [*Kummet*]. The "area" in which the collar is in general use for the hitching of cattle and where it has replaced the older horn- or neck-yoke is first of all not a closed and unitary one. Districts without cattle or without draft-cattle remain empty; here and there only a few small farmers have draft animals, but elsewhere cattle (oxen) are frequently used for draft. Therefore, the area of distribution of the collar misrepresents unlike conditions as being alike. Above all, there are usually no sharp boundaries, but rather transitional zones, in which, for example, the collar is already used in part, and the neck- or even the horn-yoke is still employed. Such transitional zones can nevertheless be regarded as "areas" in them-

selves, namely, as "areas of mixture."[7] Areas of mixture would then border a "pure area" on each side.

The same farmer often has both ways of hitching in current use, according to terrain (upland or valley), kind of animals (young or old, oxen or cows), purpose (plowing, manure-spreading, breaking-in of young draft animals), while in the same place another farmer with level land and progressive ideas uses no cattle at all for draft, and performs all his draft work with a tractor. Finally in our critique of areas of distribution and their boundaries, we must include individual differences in local custom. The ethnographic map, which aims at giving the "average" of custom, cannot, and is not intended to, represent these individual variants. To be sure, they may be important, since new areas, e.g., new districts showing some predominant custom, may be created by such individual divergences—as in the case of a newly arrived harness maker who has introduced a new collar among his customers.

If the ethnographic map gives only a very coarse image of spatial distribution or topographic location of material collected statistically, then it can surely not take in all other referents of the object within a cultural structure, or at least it can only give an indication of them. To be sure, one may draw "sociological," "psychological," or "historical" maps along with pure distributional ones, in so far as such has been the purpose while collecting the material.[8] Thus we may have a map that shows where the animal-collar is diffused only among small farmers, and where it occurs also among large farmers (social coordination), or maps that represent the evaluation of the animal collar in comparison to the yoke as "more aristocratic," "less cruel to the animal," or "more modern"

---

[6] On the advantages and disadvantages of areal and point style on ethnographic maps, see H. Schlenger, "Methodische und technische Grundlagen des Atlas der deutschen Volkskunde," *Deutsche Forschung: aus der Arbeit der Notgemeinschaft der Deutschen Wissenschaft*, XXVII (1943), 122 ff.

[7] For types of areas, see Schlenger, *op. cit.*, pp. 142 ff., and earlier writings of W. Pessler, the pioneer of ethnographic cartography in Germany.

[8] On this differentiation of maps according to their function, see the introductory volume to the *Atlas der schweizerischen Volkskunde*, p. 98.

(psychological co-ordination). Finally, the chronology of the disappearance of a way of hitching animals can also be represented historically in a cartographic spatial picture.[9] But such efforts, even if they could all be united synoptically on a map, still do not show totality of culture, which ethnography seeks to comprehend through the study of folk culture. Critics of the illustration of areal connections will continue to say that "it leaves out the unity of the culture."

We are always thoroughly conscious that the spatial view of things is dearly bought. The depiction of spatial relationship and the informative inspection of the distributional picture must be purchased at the price of dismembering the object or dissecting it and its relationships out of the rich complexity of the organic cultural whole. The map will never be able to show why in this or that district in the Freiamt (southeastern part of Aargau) peasants still hold fast to their *Jöchli* (yokes), in spite of tractors and animal-collars, and why, in contrast to the neighboring Protestants of Aargau who have accepted the modern collar, the yoke appears to the Catholic peasants as something of their own, belonging to their homeland, even as something "Catholic."

Only the intensive local monograph can approach the ideal of a comprehensive presentation of the unity of culture in the fullness of its relationships, but it thereby loses the spatial overview. It is impossible to achieve at one time both the comprehensive viewpoint of the whole culture and the spatial outlook. Nevertheless, we shall always keep in mind the great relevance of the spatially restricted, intensive mode

[9] Such a map of the disappearance of the horn-yoke is provided for the commentary on the map of hitching-methods. In French ethnography, such cartographic representation of stages in the disappearance of folk culture traits, on a local-temporal basis—*cartes de régression*—has become the main type of ethnographic maps, which I think is unjustified. See André Varagnac, *Civilisation traditionelle et genres de vie* (Paris: A. Michel, 1948).

of study for the living grasp of a culture area, even though we first take advantage of the possibilities of the analytical and extensive distribution map, in order finally to put it again at the service of a total view of culture.

We have an established procedure for looking at the ethnographic map and its distributional picture. We first try to form the distributional picture as comprehensively as possible. To stay with our example, we would establish the distribution of the animal-collar beyond our limited Swiss sector and throughout the world, which in practice is an exceedingnly difficult task. Then, from this *momentaneous distributional picture* (1) we pose the question of the origin of the pattern of distribution and its momentary boundaries. Adding the time dimension, we enquire into the *spatio-temporal process of diffusion* (2). If we are able to track down the course of the diffusion, we may discover its place and perhaps also time of origin, the *center of diffusion* (3). Thus in the retrospective historical interpretation of the map we grasp a segment of the progression of a culture, and receive a partial but accurate insight into its development in time and movement in space. In schematic form this procedure appears as follows:

Genetic Explanation ↑ | (1) Distributional area ↑
| (2) Process of diffusion | Historical Development
↓ | (3) Center of origin |

As we turn the present-day still snapshot of the distribution map into the moving picture of the passage of time—with the help of information from earlier periods and historical sources—and interpretatively let the film run backwards, then the distributional picture of today shrinks, theoretically, back to the place of origin, to the location of the inventor. In practice the origin, in this sense, cannot be established precisely for most items of folk culture, but it can probably be bracketed more or less accurately in space and time.

Our cattle-collar developed from the horse-collar. We do not know where this secondary modification was first carried out. According to material and linguistic indices, the horse-collar, along with other objects and words connected with transport (e.g., whip, carriage), comes from the Slavic area. With the help of a study by Haudricourt,[10] we can follow the course of its provenience farther, to the nomadic peoples of Inner Asia, from whom so many peculiar traits of pastoral culture are derived. Among the Mongol and Altaic peoples, the word for a bast camel saddle, *qom,* was later applied to the horse collar, known as *gamyt* in Kirgiz, *khomut* in Russian, and finally *Kummet* in German, while the short form of the word, with rather variable meaning, can be found in the English *hame,* the Dutch *haam,* and the Croatian, Hungarian, and Rumanian *ham.* On the basis of linguistic arguments, we can reconstruct, at least in rough outline, how the horse-collar and after it the cattle-collar spread over most of Europe. In southern Italy horses are still harnessed in the manner of antiquity, with the withers-yoke— the way of hitching that was transferred to cattle and supplanted the horn-yoke.

Thus all the problems of cultural movement [*Kulturwanderung*] are posed together. How does a legless thing "move"? Can it move only with its bearers, or be spread only with movements of peoples, as was formerly believed? Or does diffusion take place through contact-transfer, with one person learning by watching another? These questions cannot be answered here.[11]

In regards to the relationship between area of distribution and culture area, I should only like to remark that items do not wander in empty space. Between object and object, object and man, or man and man, there arise and pass away hundreds of relationships caused by direct or indirect contact in the culture area. Countless people have devoted their efforts to the simple matter of cattle hitching, and have used and valued it. Countless people absorb it into their world in daily habit, and experience it as a homely thing that seems indispensable, something that "belongs." In short, a thing does not wander in or enter a vacuum, but a culture area that already has its culture content, its distinctive cultural stamp, and probably also its boundaries.

Why do different areas react so differently to the cattle-collar, which is everywhere the same? We find first that in the western area of Switzerland the predominantly large, or rather medium, peasant enterprises favor the cattle-collar modeled on the horse harness, while the predominance of small peasants in central and eastern Switzerland explains the retention of the yoke.

However, it is disconcerting for us that the collar comes to a standstill in its progress from west to east along a line or border zone that acts as a barrier for entirely different objects, not related to agriculture. This border belt runs from the lower course of the Reuss through the present canton of Aargau, then continues over the extensive mountain mass of the Napf and across the watershed of the Brünig Pass, along the boundary between Bern and the inner Swiss cantons of Lucerne and Unterwalden.

This "Reuss-Napf-Brünig Line," or "Reuss border" for short,[12] is a barrier for the penetration of diffusion impulses from east and west. So far we have demonstrated this bordering of distributional areas on eighteen maps. But new bits of evidence are always coming in from the most diverse realms of popular culture, so

[10] André G. Haudricourt, "Contribution à la géographie et à l'ethnologie de la voiture," *Revue de géographie humaine et d'ethnologie,* I (1948), 54–64.

[11] Important reasons for the various possibilities of cultural diffusion are given by E. Spranger, "Probleme der Kulturmorphologie," *Sitzungsbericht der Preussischen Akademie, Philosophisch-Historische Klasse,* 1936, pp. 2 ff.

[12] Richard Weiss, "Die Brünig-Napf-Reuss-Linie als Kulturgrenze zwischen Ost- und Westschweiz auf volkskundlichen Karten," *Geographica Helvetica,* II (1947), 153–75.

that we have begun to speak of a "cultural boundary." How and with what justification was it defined?

From Distributional Boundary to Cultural Boundary, or from Area of Distribution to Cultural Area

We speak of a cultural boundary, in our case of the "Reuss border," because many limits of distribution coincide or come close together here, so that a "bundle of lines" appears on the map. Our usage corresponds to an established practice, especially among linguistic geographers, of describing such accumulations as cultural boundaries. In this manner we have a simple objective procedure for localizing cultural boundaries: we superimpose as many maps as possible of different traits and establish boundaries where "bundles" cluster.[13] Within these "bundles" of lines, taken as cultural boundaries, it should be possible to find culture areas. A great many distributions must coincide, so that the objective substance of culture agrees in certain respects.

Much can be said against this outwardly and schematically attractive procedure. Nevertheless, I shall keep returning to it and try to reinforce cultural boundaries through reference to an increasing number of cartographically established boundaries of distribution. However, we should not try to make this procedure into an unduly massive or self-sufficient technique. For this reason I have taken care that the following reflections on the example of the "Reuss border" should not become too farfetched.

Our cultural boundary, the "Reuss border," as determined on ethnographic maps, results from the fact that diffusion impulses from west and east come to a stop, permanently or temporarily, on one side or the other of this critical line, at least as seen during the interval of our survey

(1937–42). Behind the distributional boundaries that cluster in this zone there are also distributional areas, and each must have its center.

Can we deduce culture areas from the accumulation of distributional areas, and cultural centers from distributional centers, as we deduced cultural boundaries from distributional boundaries? To answer these questions, I will carry over the interpretative scheme applied to single areas of distribution (distributional boundaries and areas ⇄ diffusion process ⇄ center of distribution) to the whole complex, as follows:

(1) Cultural boundary or area
(2) Cultural movement
(3) Cultural center

Cultural centers are places from which issue many impulses of diffusion; in this case let us take our western Swiss region: Bern, Geneva, and their connection with Paris—which is not to say that these cities, or cities in general, are the only culture centers of the area. Such culture centers, thanks to the quantity of diffusion processes that issue from them like waves, create culture areas. Where these waves—in this case the diffusion boundaries—run into or cut across those coming from other centers, we can demonstrate the existence of a cultural boundary produced by the accumulation of distributional boundaries. Seen in this light, the cultural boundary seems to be in motion, as a critical zone or state of cultural diffusion.

To illustrate and reinforce this idea, we must now investigate our "Reuss border," using the single distributional pictures that share in this cultural boundary. It would be a subject for a monograph to trace all the items of the pertinent eighteen or more maps back from their current distributions toward their centers of distribution, as was done for the cattle-collar. Here only a few examples will be given to illustrate practical difficulties and also problems or revelations that result from this interpretative procedure.

[13] For this purpose we have had the maps of our *Atlas* made in a transparent version that allows us to overlay any map on any other.

Gift-giving at New Year's[14] is predominantly a West-Swiss[15] trait, not because it extends across the linguistic boundary as far as the Reuss border, but because it has drawn back that far from eastern Switzerland. A process of withdrawal in the opposite direction, from west to east as far as the Reuss line, is evident in the maps of Christmas customs, many of which have been pushed back as far as the Reuss border, probably in large part as a result of Calvinist influence from Geneva. A positive attitude in western Switzerland toward New Year's customs—not only gift-giving mentioned previously, but also the wearing of masks on New Year's Day—goes along with the west Swiss aversion to Christmas. Where Christmas masks have been driven out, New Year's masks are much more certain to remain, as if according to a rule that the sum of "vices" must be constant.

This example of competing customs shows clearly the importance of comparative interpretation of maps and their picture of distributions, or in other words, the importance of keeping in mind the whole of culture.

This generalization seems especially apt when an attempt is made to answer the question of why a cultural boundary should stand out at one particular place rather than elsewhere—in our example, along the Reuss-Napf-Brünig boundary rather than along the German-French linguistic boundary. The question concerns how cultural boundaries are established. To answer it, we should again begin with distributional boundaries and their determinants, and piece together synthetically and comparatively the establishment of the cultural boundary. Factors favoring or restricting diffusion are not likely to be the same for cattle-collars, playing-cards, New Year's customs, and cuisine; yet the different factors entering into the establishment of a cultural boundary must somehow harmonize.

To show what reasons may be critical for the localization of a cultural boundary, and first of all for a distributional boundary, let us take the unpretentious example of the playing-cards used in *Jass*, a game found almost everywhere in Switzerland. When we first published the simple distribution map of the so-called "German" and "French" *Jass*-cards in the first proofs of the ethnographic atlas in 1937–38, we were astonished to notice that the two types are separated by the Reuss border. This line between western and eastern Switzerland had not yet been noticed scientifically —except in dialect geography[16]—because it was naïvely assumed that the German-French linguistic line, running about 100 kilometers to the west, must be the most important cultural boundary.

In the case of the *Jass*-cards, the establishment of the striking Reuss border resulted from the historical circumstance that until 1798 (the year of the collapse of the "Old Confederation") the eastern boundary of the Bern territory reached eastward to Reuss, exactly as far as the present distribution of French *Jass*-cards. The cards were probably introduced from Bern, at a time unknown to us, as an item subject to the monopoly-tax. We have thus been able to connect this distributional boundary with a territorial boundary that disappeared 150 years ago. It is also notable that this onetime territorial boundary, running through the present canton of Aargau, con-

---

[14] The examples following are more thoroughly interpreted and mapped in Weiss, "Die Brünig-Napf-Reuss-Linie. . . ."

[15] By "West Swiss" I mean the whole west of Switzerland beyond the Reuss, both the German-Swiss part with the canton of Bern and the French-Swiss part, that is, the French and German linguistic areas of Switzerland.

[16] This refers to the so-called dialect boundary of the Schild, which is a boundary between single and double plural forms of the verb, running in the neighborhood of the Reuss. Other dialect peculiarities of German-speaking east and west Switzerland join in making a division here. But most of these dialect boundaries reach somewhat farther east than the ethnographic distributional boundaries in the Reuss area. Certain basic differences between dialect and ethnographic boundaries seem to come out here. See R. Hotzenköcherle in *Vox Romanica,* IV (1939), 123–29; and Weiss, "Die Brünig-Napf-Reuss-Linie . . . , p. 156 n.

tinues to operate as a religious boundary; the formerly Bernese western part of the canton, with its French playing-cards, is Protestant, whereas the eastern, non-Bernese part, with German cards, is Catholic. The consequence is that along this boundary playing-cards are distinguished as "Catholic" or "Protestant," and receive a new evaluation and character in connection with folk culture of the Catholic or Protestant stamp. So playing-cards, like cattle-collars, cannot be looked at in isolation, but only in their cultural connections.

The same holds true for the establishment of their distributions and distributional boundaries. Bern is not only a secondary center of diffusion for the "French" type of playing-card, but also a cultural center, and, because it serves as the administrative center of the territory and thus becomes a focus for traffic,[17] other impulses make their way through this territory as far as its boundaries.

The old Bernese state, and also the smaller present canton of Bern, thus constitute a "cultural province," in the sense of this expression used in the pioneer cultural geographic study of the area of the Rhineland archbishoprics by Aubin, Frings, and Müller.[18] It might also be described as a "historical landscape," as this expression is used in a recent study by H. Schlenger.[19] We shall say nothing about Bern's role as the capital of the Swiss Confederation after 1848.

Mention of the Bernese cultural province

does not give a complete explanation of the Reuss line as a cultural boundary. One may ask why the old boundary of Bern should reach as far as the Reuss, the Napf, and the Brünig, and first of all one may ask about the natural basis for this territorial structure.

The Napf massif, reaching into the center of the country, appears even in prehistoric times as a barrier that hinders traffic between eastern and western cultures. In the Middle Ages it coincided with the boundary between zones of Alamannic and Bergundian influence. But no extreme importance in boundary formation needs to be attributed to the barrier function of the Napf area, if we take into consideration the fact that even higher and more difficult mountain massifs did not become boundaries, and that to the south of the Napf neither the Brünig Pass nor the level passage from the Emmental into the Entlebuch represents a decisive obstacle. The Reuss River is no real obstacle, any more than the Rhine has to be a political or cultural boundary for the German Rhineland.[20] On the contrary, the old Bernese border town of Brugg, lying on the Aare, a continuation of the Reuss, does not have its name (meaning "bridge") for nothing; since Roman times it has handled the traffic and trade between east and west, which have moved along the waterways of the Limmat and the Aare. This is a pronounced "passage boundary." [21]

No political boundary would have arisen here without a free desire to organize, or without political choices that have taken advantage of natural border zones back through the Middle Ages into prehistory. The religious division followed the already

[17] The importance of traffic, especially of modern railroad traffic and in particular its "density" (railroad index figures), has recently been expressed in a striking way on ethnographic maps by H. Plath, "Verbreitungsgesetze in Brauch- und Wortgeographie Niedersachsens und angrenzender Gebiete," *Neues Archiv für Niedersachsen,* XV (1950) (Festschrift für P. Pessler), 51 ff.

[18] Hermann Aubin, Theodor Frings, and Josef Müller, *Kulturströmungen und Kulturprovinzen in den Rheinlanden* (Bonn: L. Röhrscheid, 1926).

[19] H. Schlenger, "Die geschichtliche Landeskunde im System der Wissenschaften," in *Geschichtliche Landeskunde und Universalgeschichte: Festgabe für Hermann Aubin zum 23, Dezember 1950* (Hamburg: "Wihag"-Buchdruckerei, 1950).

[20] This is shown in Aubin, Frings, and Müller, *op. cit.*

[21] This expression comes from H. Maurer, "Zur Wertung der oberösterreichischen Grenzen," *Oberösterreichisches Heimatblatt,* II (1950), 125 ff., as it concerns proposed terminology for territorial boundaries. Important and concrete contributions to Swiss boundary problems in various respects are made by different authors in *Geographica Helvetica,* I (1946), 350–59.

present territorial boundary according to the principle *cuius regio eius religio*. In the so-called Common Domains along the Reuss a Catholic barrier developed in the interior of Switzerland, between the federated Protestant cities of Bern in the west and Zurich in the east. This religious boundary still operates as a cultural boundary, as a division between a Catholic and a Protestant folk culture, even in the area between Mellingen and the cantonal boundary of Lucerne and Bern where it has neither a natural nor a political basis.

Expressed more generally, this means that natural features like mountain barriers and waterways favor natural traffic units and traffic boundaries, which in their interplay with political-territorial development can be overlapped or strengthened into culture areas or cultural boundaries.

The development and determination of the Reuss border are nevertheless much more complex, as we have shown. We have spoken only of the area of Bern and its influence, not of the influence of Calvinist (or modern) Geneva or that of Paris (in our *Atlas* most apparent in articles of fashion), which surge out as "cultural currents" through and beyond Bern to the Reuss border. On the other side, the corresponding countercurrents from eastern Switzerland and from beyond Switzerland should be considered. This whole complicated matter of opposing currents will probably undergo much clarification through further monographic and comparative study of our maps. In any case, we are convinced that cartographic efforts toward objective comprehension of culture dynamics and cultural boundaries are not in vain.

With all the modesty proper to any scientific effort, we may still say that although we do not "see" cultural boundaries on our maps, we nevertheless discover important indices for them, just as one cannot "see" a disease in its psycho-physical totality on an X-ray, but only "shadows" of it.

The shadows, in this case the distributional areas and boundaries of otherwise insignificant objects, are not an end in themselves but become important for us as keys to recognition of a causal complex and its limits. Ethnographic distributional boundaries, to keep the medical simile, are merely symptoms. They are symptoms in the literal sense of the term, since they "coincide" in a cartographically demonstrable congruence with other boundaries, such as natural, traffic, economic, territorial, religious, and linguistic boundaries. This external, objectively demonstrable congruence is a symptom of an inner unity of culture. Man creates the spiritual bond between natural conditions and objective cultural items, so that the cultural landscape with his stamp upon it can be seen, to use the terminology of the philosophy of culture, as "objectified intelligence." [22]

Thus we come back to the subjective motive with which we began, for neither culture nor cultural boundaries can be understood without it. Alongside the objective cartographic determination of culture areas and cultural boundaries we must set, as a necessary supplement, the subjective experience of the culture area and its boundaries. This is seeing from within, from the standpoint of the "home." The subjective home area and its boundaries also can become an object of investigation.[23]

OBJECTIVE CULTURE AREA AND SUBJECTIVE HOME AREA; CULTURAL BOUNDARIES FROM WITHIN AND WITHOUT

To stay with our examples, the simple cattle yoke on the stable wall or the greasy playing-cards on the farmstead table can be experienced as something of one's own, distinctive, trusted, and homely, especially in contrast to things that are different. The

[22] Martin Schwind, "Kulturlandschaft als objektivierter Geist," *Deutsche Geographische Blätter*, XLVI (1951), 5–28; *idem*, "Sinn und Ausdruck der Landschaft," *Studium Generale*, III (1950), 196–201; Carl Troll, "Die geographische Landschaft und ihre Erforschung," *Studium Generale*, III (1950), 163–81.

[23] Kurt Stavenhagen, *Heimat als Lebenssinn* (2d ed.; Göttingen: Vandenhook & Ruprecht, 1948).

object thus becomes larger than itself. It is included within the wealth of references locked together into the subjective oneness of the home area through awareness of the distinctiveness and the feel of "home."

We have already shown that the old fashioned *Jöchli* and the German playing-cards along the religious boundary are thought by the neighboring Protestants to be "Catholic," and hence included in the complex of a Catholic folk culture, just as "tippling" and numerous snacks between meals[24] are viewed in the same area as peculiarities of one's Catholic neighbors. These symptoms—which we can also show objectively on maps to be more nearly predominant in Catholic areas—therefore have their subjective side. The Protestant will regard his abstemiousness and industriousness as something special of his own, and will even boast about them, as against the frequent meals and uninhibited use of alcohol among his Catholic neighbors, poor on the whole but rich in children. One can say that such things become emblems of the individuality of the homeland, acknowledged and vaunted, or censured by others. Thus these emblems are subjectively experienced symptoms, which are raised up consciously as signs proclaiming the distinctiveness of oneself and of the familiar homeland as "typically Protestant," "especially like Zurich," *"bien génévois,"* etc. So, for instance, the greeting "adieu" is emphasized as good Genevan, although in objective cartographic fact it is not confined to the area of Geneva. In Basel the greeting *grüezi* is mocked as "Zurich boorishness," an emblem of the differentness of Zurich, as in all the local raillery previously mentioned. The inhabitants of an area use its food specialties, e.g., cheese, as an emblem, although this does not mean that the particular cheese is unique. Similarly, Protestant "sobriety" is boasted of, in contrast to Catholic "untidiness," or German

"sincerity" in contrast to Latin "maliciousness."

Regardless of their nature or whether they conform to reality or are obviously unreal, these emblems still remain as signs and tokens of a local, and hence spatially circumscribed, awareness of distinctiveness, which we have now established as a fact, and must pursue further.

The opposite face of the culture area seen from without is the home area seen from within. But what is "home"? We find a satisfying answer in the work of Kurt Stavenhagen,[25] to whom ethnology is deeply indebted, although it has not yet fully recognized or acknowledged the fact.

To use our example again: The peasant who hitches his cattle in the yoke thinks of the *Jöchli,* in contrast to the cattle-collar, as something of his own, but not only proper and familiar to him alone, but rather common to other peasants who also retain the yoke, and so he regards it as homely.

The whole cultural makeup of the world of home, from the *Jöchli* to dogmas, is branded with familiarity, and is therefore homely. It is not the speck of earth as such that is familiar and beloved as "home." Things become familiar only as part of surroundings that are stamped with the spiritual experience of familiarity and security. The reason for "home" is not in things (stream, forest, house, language, custom), but in the home community; it is not primarily a relationship of man to thing, but rather of man to man. This relationship is built outward from the most intimate relation between mother and child[26] to larger and larger communal circles: family, neighborhood, village commune, linguistic, religious, and national communities. All the things in the surroundings that have to do with the feeling of

---

[24] The cartographic presentation of these dietary specialties is given by maps I, 12 ("Snack at Noon") and I, 14 ("Drinks at the Inn") of the *Atlas der schweizerischen Volkskunde.*

[25] Stavenhagen, *op. cit.*

[26] The health-education work of Julia Schwarzmann, "Die seelische Auswirkung der Heimatlosigkeit im Kindesalter und ihre Auswirkungen" (diss., University of Zurich, 1948), should be cited on this point.

community (family house, street, village, city, and country, with their natural and cultural content) receive a stamp of familiarity and become homely. The *Jöchli* or the family home are familiar not because of their usefulness or beauty or other objective qualities, but because they are experienced in homely familiarity. Wherever one is secure, no matter how simple the place, it is also beautiful.

Thus a home area is created, like a snail's shell, organically growing outward from its innermost coils; for many the "home" is limited to their own village or valley, but for others it reaches as far as the oases of the Sahara.

In this connection, a question arises concerning the relationship between subjective home area and objective culture area. Are they spatially related? One can connect objective culture areas with certain cultural boundaries, as we have tried to show, although the various distributional boundaries never coincide but make bundles of lines or, in dynamic terms, overlapping waves.

A similar picture characterizes the home area as it is experienced. No one inhabitant of a given district will have exactly the same domain of familiarity, and so the same home area, as any other. But the home areas of the various inhabitants of a given place, seen from that place and according to individual horizons, would spread out like waves, concentrically, or would overlap. Are there not "bundles" of lines in this case too, i.e., a zone within which the familiarity-relation of most of the inhabitants of a place is particularly intensive? We believe that we can speak of a home area in this sense, just because the familiarity-relation rests on a feeling for a local community. Thus Zurich people who are not only settled in the place but have roots there will think of the city itself, then the canton, then Switzerland as a country, and within it the Protestant and German-Swiss areas as especially familiar. On the other hand, the Swiss even regards districts speaking languages other than his own, but within his country, as more familiar than foreign districts using his language.

It all depends upon where and to what extent people with a locally fixed cultural type can feel familiar and at home without great difficulties of adaptation. We can disregard experiences of familiarity under the very special circumstances that are possible even in altogether alien cultural milieus. Thus there are certain nearby or distant, subjectively felt home areas that are not only of individual kinds but depend on the cultural peculiarities of the local community. The relation with the objective culture area results from the fateful circumstantial conditions of such local distinctiveness—one's home is one's fate. The place that is home is likewise a cultural center, i.e., a center of distribution of certain objective traits that are the subject of the feeling of familiarity and the mark of the familiar. Culture areas are not only spatially determined by their center, core, and areas of radiation, but they are also, as seen cartographically, qualitatively stamped by certain cultural dominants like religion, speech,[27] and political, economic, or natural unity that carry a mass of cultural symptoms. There is a "Catholic culture," a "German culture," a "farming culture," an "Alpine culture," and so on. Such dominants can be experienced or endured unconsciously, or used consciously to delineate the homely. In other words, they function as emblems.

To be sure, we commonly find an incongruence of subjective with objective space: what is subjectively felt to be a "specialty" of a district need not be distributed, objectively, throughout or only within the district. A plane or linear congruence between (subjective) home areas or borders and (objective) culture areas or boundaries cannot be imagined, because we cannot,

[27] I have dealt with the relation between ethnographic and linguistic boundaries especially in "Sprachgrenzen und Konfessionsgrenzen als Kulturgrenzen," in *Laos, Études comparées de folklore ou d'ethnologie régionale*, I (Stockholm: Almqvist & Wiksell, 1951), 96 ff.

at least not yet, apply the topographic and statistical measures of the map to subjective areas.

But emotionally potent home areas—i.e., religious areas ("religious landscapes"),[28] national areas, "historical landscapes," or cultural provinces—doubtless also have a tendency to set themselves apart objectively in their cultural character. On the other hand, the familiarity of the home will enter above all where the objective cultural harmony of community feeling as well as natural conditions favor it. Objectively speaking, there is no Swiss yodel, no Swiss song, no Swiss house, any more than there are Swiss Alps of a type peculiar to Switzerland and only Switzerland. We do not want for Switzerland a leveling of Swiss diversity into a unified national culture, but on the contrary, the spectre of a *Culture fédérale* or *Bundeskultur* that is caricatured on walls only serves to reinforce in cultural matters the federalism that has been handed down from the past, and has become a basis for the state. Nevertheless, objective unification makes undeniable progress in areas with strongly or even offensively conscious cultural dominants of a national, religious, landscape, or other character. On the other hand, objective unity makes it possible for one to find familiar things in nature or culture and so to feel subjectively at home. Reciprocal effects thus do occur between objective, cartographically grasped, culture areas and subjective home areas. It is a task for cultural morphology in social science, and for geography concerned with cultural landscapes, to illuminate this fabric from various sides.

Even though the highly complicated interweaving of men and objects in the cultural unit may never be comprehended as a single whole, we shall go on trying, as cultural cartographers, to understand objective culture traits in their spatial circumstances and limits, and to proclaim them on maps. The investigation of cultural forms, in the sense of the theory of culture (cultural morphology), can have no foundation without the delineation of these forms in circumstantial culture areas represented by the map. Distributional boundaries of particular culture traits are symptoms of critical zones of cultural distribution. The joy of the cartographer in dealing with such boundaries is therefore not an idle one.

[28] Paul Fickler, "Grundfragen der Religionsgeographie," *Erdkunde,* I (1947), 121–44 [translated in this volume; see pp. 94–117 below].

C. M. DELGADO DE CARVALHO

THE GEOGRAPHY OF LANGUAGES

"Geography of languages" and "linguistic geography" do not seem to me to be equivalent expressions. Both belong to the domain of human geography, which takes in all cultural manifestations differentiated geographically. But the geography of languages assumes the history of the formation of the geographic area of certain languages, independent of linguistic phenomena proper, while linguistic geography is applied rather to the geographic influences that modify words, terms, or expressions and alter, in space or rather in use, their meaning and pronunciation. "Linguistic geography," said Albert Dauzat, "has as its essential purpose to reconstruct the history of words, flexions, and syntactical groupings, according to the distribution of present forms and types. This distribution is not the result of chance; it is a function of the past, and also of the geographic conditions and the milieu to which men belong." [1] As an example he cites the word for "bee," called, according to the region of France considered, *mouche à miel, avette, abelho,* or *essette.* The field of the geography of languages is rather the study of present geographical distributions, determined by the expansion of languages and resulting from environmental conditions,

which, we may add, do not remain strangers to linguistic geography.

An interesting and suggestive investigation of *Geografia linguística* was made in Brazil by Comandante Eugênio de Castro.[2] In the first part of his study he looked into the technical vocabulary of the Brazilian navy for words and terms coming from the three principal sources that he was studying: the Vikings, Scandinavian navigators of the eighth and ninth centuries; the Normans, in the tenth century; and the Mediterranean sailors of the thirteenth to the eighteenth centuries. In the second part of the work, De Castro examines the seacoast, a factor in the "mestization" of the Portuguese language, where each center presents its own characteristics according to the nature of the predominant social influences. Then he examines the Sertão, where he distinguishes certain linguistic foci: the "geography of cattle" as a radiation from the valley of the São Francisco, the "geography of the banners" principally as a radiation of the Paulistas, and the "geography of the canoe or horseman" penetrating by the Maranhão and Amazonia. In studying the linguistics of the Sertão, De Castro determines which influences belong to the life of the *engenho,* the mines, the coffee plantations, the coastal people, the soldiers, and the ox drivers.

Two languages belong to the same family when they are differentiations of a sin-

Translated, with permission of the author, from "Geografia das linguas," *Boletim Geográfico,* I (1943), 45–62. The author is professor of contemporary history at the University of Brazil, Rio de Janeiro. All the footnotes to this article are supplied by the editors.
[1] Albert Dauzat, *La géographie linguistique* (Paris: Flammarion, 1922), p. 27.

[2] Eugênio de Castro, *Ensaios de geografia linguística* (São Paulo: Campanhia Editora Nacional, 1941).

gle langauge that was formerly spoken, Latin, for example, was the language spoken and used by the cultivated classes in the most important centers of the western Roman Empire. In each of the provinces—Gaul, Spain, Africa—it found itself in a different situation, and gradually evolved.

When the restoration of classical studies was attempted in the ninth century, the Franks noticed that the language they spoke was no longer correct Latin, but "Romance." The transition from Latin into Italian, French, Spanish, Portuguese, and Rumanian was imperceptible, because the provincials continued to think that they were speaking the same language.

But it is not always possible to trace the origin and formation of a language. The Slavic family illustrates the difficulty encountered in attempting to demonstrate historically the existence of a common tongue. The resemblance of Russian, Polish, Czech, Serbo-Croatian, and Bulgarian leads to the supposition that a common Slavic language existed before the ninth century of our era. In spite of the differences of pronunciation, grammar, and vocabulary, there are so many concordances that we cannot fail to admit one original language, unknown to us because it escaped for so long the influences of Mediterranean civilization.

In the same way there must have existed down to the fourth or fifth century B.C. a common Germanic language, from which German, English, Flemish-Dutch, Danish-Norwegian, and Swedish have evolved (e.g., *Durst—thirst—torst*). It is in general in the oldest forms of these now differentiated languages that points of contact are found. The case of Anglo-Saxon, with its declensions, is typical. When these links are missing, the demonstration of contact by historical means is more difficult.

Since, however, certain languages of the Indo-European group began to be written seven centuries before the time of Christ (e.g., vedic texts, the Iranian of Darius, the texts of Zoroastrianism, the language of Homer), the archaic forms fixed in writing have allowed us to trace the prehistory of the group. Thence comes the fact that this is the best-known and most studied group; thence, too, a tendency for philologists to want to trace Aryan origins for many languages where they do not fit, like Etruscan and Basque. The Semitic and Finno-Ugrian groups also disagree with the primitive common Indo-European. In the present state of our knowledge, it cannot be said that all spoken languages are continuations of one ancestral tongue.

Geographical conditions act on the evolution of languages and their differentiation in the following way: when they remain the same for a long time with few changes, it is because the populations that use them have undergone little mixing, as in the case of the Polynesians. On the other hand, when populations are not homogeneous, idioms are juxtaposed and many people have to adopt a new tongue. The same happens in a period of great social changes, as was the case, for example, with Latin from the first to the ninth century. Thus there are periods when changes of language are greater and more rapid, and others of slower alteration. The case of Caxton, who in his old age no longer understood the language of his infancy, is typical.

LANGUAGE AND RACE

There is no necessary connection between language and race. For example, English is the product of British, Anglo-Saxon, Scandinavian, and Franco-Norman elements. Nevertheless, the language is Germanic. The juxtaposition of French is interesting, and leads to curious reimportations (e.g., *bougette*, "a small leather bag," gave *budget* in English, and was reimported into France with the parliamentary vocabulary).

Often certain languages remain as isolated islands (e.g., French in Canada). It would be of little use to group the languages spoken according to the physical type of their speakers, but nevertheless some relationship exists. These relationships result from the divergent evolution of a small number of more ancient languages which were influenced by historical and geographic factors that also determined differences in the human groups. But the limits of a language never coincide perfectly with the limits of a somatic type.

There is much talk of a "Jewish race," yet there is no real Jewish language. The Jews speak the languages of the groups among which they live. The Hebrew that some of them speak, or cultivate, was learned for the sake of nationalism or the desire to maintain a tradition; like the Latin of the Middle Ages, Hebrew is also a dead language.[3] As for Yiddish, the commonest language among Jews, its origin is German and medieval. It was the language spoken by the Jews from the Rhineland who emigrated to Poland. During the first Crusades, mostly at the end of the twelfth century, German Jewish communities formed a current of migration to Kraków, Poznań, Kalisz, and Siberia. Because of their numbers and intellectual superiority, the Jews soon occupied an intermediate social position between nobles and serfs. The jargon of Jewish traders was thus a transplanted branch of Low German, with Germanic vocabulary and construction as well as Hebrew expressions and Slavic additions. These elements, geographically segregated, built up a literature of legends and prayers, rich in its sources but without grammar or fixed rules. It was in the beginning of the nineteenth century that a renewal movement, the Haskalah, began in Berlin to make the language a literary one by means of good translations (e.g., those of Moses Mendelssohn). After 1880, there was also a renaissance of Yiddish, involving stories (*Spector*), poetry (*Frug*) and novels, in Russia. In the United States it became a journalistic and theatrical language. The case of Yiddish thus offers a typical example of the dispersal of the Jewish people,

[3] The reader should bear in mind that this article was published in 1943, prior to the formation of the state of Israel and the adoption of Hebrew as its official language.

and marks one of the episodes of its migration about the world.

Social differences do not constitute an obstacle to the perfect unity of language. Gaul and Spain, with little Latin blood, accepted the Latin language as the vehicle of Latin culture. Nor is it correct to speak of an Aryan race simply because a common language existed—Aryan, the Indo-European language from which came the present languages, and Sanskrit as an older form.

In the course of history there is no people that has not changed its language more than once. Variations go on from one generation to another, although in recent centuries the press has had an influence in the standardizing, fixing, and preservation of literary languages.

LANGUAGE AND NATION

A relation does exist, however, between a language and a people, or a national group. The Austro-Hungarian Empire contained within itself elements of decomposition symbolized by its different languages: German, Czech, Slovene, Italian, Hungarian, Rumanian, Polish. When nationalist or separatist spirit reaches a certain strength in a region it tries to embody itself in a national language; this is what Ireland is attempting to do; but it is hard to revive a dying language.

On the other hand, the fact that the Bretons and Provençals in France keep their own languages does not weaken their patriotism. The same is true in Switzerland and Belgium. This is because there is besides the concept of the people that of the Nation, which is loftier and more precise. Peoples mix, nations do not. Language is not indispensable for living together, although it is a great help; the will is what makes the nation; at most, language, like religion, customs, and traditions, makes a people. Where linguistic differences decrease, other differences also decrease, and the national spirit becomes consolidated. Language characterizes a people and not necessarily a nation, because the spoken and written language is what determines the unity of culture. The Roman Empire, was Latin in language only in its western and Italic parts; the east remained Greek, despite the loss of its political independence.

A culture can hardly survive the conditions that created it; hence the difficulty of maintaining artificially the language that represented it; this is the case of Yiddish in the United States. Still, a language is worth as much as the culture it represents. In France, for example, in the thirteenth century Provençal was the language of a brilliant culture, and the learned language then was Latin; but when the French of the north also became a learned language, the special culture of the south declined; today only vestiges and poetic works remain. For the same reasons Egyptian and Armenian declined, whereas Arabic continues to live.

The wider its geographic area, the more useful a language is. On the other hand, populations that live in regional geographic isolation, if they wish to participate in the civilization of their times and to keep their language, must be bilingual. This is the situation of many groups in countries of old cultures like France and Germany. In these countries the school, the army, the government, and business in general (where only the national language is used) are unifying agents for language. The common language is the only one that the inhabitants of different regions can use to communicate among themselves. The linguistic unity of the Roman Empire was the result of relatively rapid communications, and especially good roads.

The cities, because of their business, the afflux of population from different regions, and their multiple contacts, are centers for the formation of common languages. Rural regions, in contrast, escape more easily the action of the state and business and are able to keep their speech-ways longer. Great commercial routes connecting cities also encourage linguistic unification. Regions that remain remote keep their local dialects for longer periods of time but differences gradually disappear. Some dialects, when their vocabulary is further removed from that of the common language, can put up more resistance because they do not suffer so readily from the influence of a related tongue. For a common language to be able to win out over local languages and become universal (i.e., be understood abroad), it is indispensable that it become rigid and fixed, and that any deviation be considered an error.

In the Roman Empire, the widespread use of Latin resulted from the necessity on the part of the inhabitants of distant regions without a common language to understand one another and communicate. Where there existed a common language (e.g., Greek) Latin was not borrowed, but it continued to be more prominent than local dialects in the western part of the empire. The Roman colonies were points of diffusion; the Gaulish nobility adopted Latin to keep its privileges and culture. In Great Britain and the Pyrenees, where the Roman occupation was less complete, Celtic and Basque subsisted. Northern French was more directly influenced by Latin because of the military occupation of the defensive line of the Rhine. The same happened in Illyria and Dacia, where the Danubian legions implanted Latin—today's Rumanian.

On this subject, Porfessor Ernesto Faria says in a recent book:

With the Roman expansion, and the transmission of Latin by the legionnaires to a large part of Western Europe, as far as Betica and Lusitania, and also to a good part of Eastern Europe, the idiom of *Latium* had to become the official language of all the Roman Empire, which would thus form a great linguistic unit equal to the political unit.

This did not happen, however. If Latin was easily implanted in the west, it did not succeed in being adopted by the local populations in the east, because of the presence there of Greek, the language of a civilization superior to that of Rome. Everything in the Roman Empire that was of Greek civilization remained faithful to Hellenism, except the Greek cities of the southern coast of Italy and of the coasts of Sicily. The separation of the empire into the Eastern Empire, of Greek speech, and the Western Empire, of Latin speech, corresponded to reality.[4]

Once Latin, the language of a great civilization, was accepted by the peoples of the west, it rapidly became a decisive factor in the process of Romanization. Notable centers of Roman culture developed in the provinces, which is proved by the origin of a number of Latin poets and prose writers. What V. Chapot says of the cities of Spain can be extended to a large part of the west: "The cities amalgamated a cosmopolitan population, of which Latin was necessarily the common language." [5]

With time, as the work of Romanization was completed, the native languages gave way entirely, taking refuge in the mountains, and Latin dominated entirely in its two forms: the *sermo nobilis* language of literature, treaties, and the schools, and the *sermo rusticus, plebius* or *castrensis,* the speech of the legionnaires, colonists, and the local populations. This happened not because the other languages ceased entirely to be employed, but because, as Bourciez observes, "they no longer fitted the needs of a new civilization, nor the relations that became more frequent between the different parts of the Empire, and, above all, with the metropolitan center." [6]

With the fall and dismemberment of the Roman Empire in the fifth century A.D., Latin, no longer having the centralizing and revitalizing power of Rome, nor the influence of the schools, began to develop independently in each province. In addition to the great Romance tongues, it gave rise to a host of dialects. This differentiation is also explained by historical, ethnological, and political or commercial factors. Meyer-Lübke does not accord much im-

portance to the first two factors, affirming in regard to the historical that "the different age of Latin in the various countries can explain differences within the Romance languages, but not the actual differences of these languages among themselves." Of the second factor he adds that "until the present it has been possible to prove ethnological influence only in the most limited cases." On the other hand, he makes much of the third factor, because he finds that "an important aspect, perhaps the most important, is furnished to us by 'commercial relations.' " [7] Brugmann expresses the same opinion in his comparative grammar of the Indo-European languages.[8] Bourciez, on the contrary, insists on the ethnological aspect: "The various countries being occupied by different kinds of invaders, and subjected to their own political regimes, the people no longer communicated with one another as they had done in the times of the Empire; thus it happened that the differentiation that already existed in embryo in the various parts of the Roman world was rapidly accelerated."

This was the general situation. Nevertheless, Latin continued to be studied, read, and written. Being the language of the law, it was that of the notaries—not the classical or popular Latin, but rather the barbarous Romance. Despite a lowering of the cultural level, the notaries still tried their best to approximate the good norms of the language of the Roman jurists. Furthermore, it is known that in the time of Charlemagne, Alcuin, who was encharged with the restoration of learning, provoked a small renaissance of Latin studies. Elsewhere, a more or less classical Latin continued to be written in the monasteries. Finally with the creation of universities Latin was destined to gain numerous adherents once again; since that time it has

[4] Ernesto Faria, *A renovação atual dos estudos latinos* (Rio de Janeiro: Ministério de Educação e Saúde, Serviço de Documentação, 1945).

[5] V. Chapot, *Le monde romain* (Paris: Renaissance du Livre, 1927), p. 481.

[6] Edouard Eugène Joseph Bourciez, *Eléments de linguistique romane* (2d ed.; Paris: C. Klincksiek, 1923), pp. 25–32.

[7] Wilhelm Meyer-Lübke, *Einführung in das Studium der romanischen Sprachwissenschaft* (Heidelberg: C. Winter, 1901), pp. 19–22.

[8] Karl Brugmann and Berthold Delbruck, *Grundriss der vergleichenden Grammatik der indogermanischen Spachen* (6 vols.; Strassburg: K. J. Trübner, 1886–1900).

been the language of science and has lasted as such up to the beginning of the past century. The predominance of Latin for twenty centuries in Western Europe could not help having appreciable consequences. It is a fact, as Ernesto Faria indicates, that "all the modern languages of Western Europe are full of Latin, even those which most appear to be entirely independent of it."

Thus the language of Rome served as a nucleus for the formation of the various languages, which geographical separation and difficulties of communication (caused by the decadence of Roman civilization), impelled to spring up in the different provinces of the empire. The implantation of a common language is rather the result of the interests of individuals and thus of a political imposition, and its duration is linked with this interest, plus the political services, and the cultural and social prestige that it represents. Thus it is that Arabic continues to hold on principally as a language of religion and culture.

History seems to show that commerce does not impose a language so much as it encourages its diffusion. In antiquity, Phoenician, in spite of its expansion, never conquered Greek; in the Middle Ages, the Hansa never fostered Low German, which remained a dialect.

In addition, the social tendency of men to imitate encourages study of the languages of civilization and reserves local languages for private relations. Local languages are not only influenced in their vocabulary by the languages of civilization, but they even tend to disappear when bilingual generations are succeeded by generations that despise the local speech.

One frequently encounters islands of languages on the way to extinction. Linguistic enclaves persist in mountainous regions (e.g., the Alps, Calabria, the Balkans) and certain islands. The same thing happens among small immigrant groups in a new country, which tend, at least for a certain time, to conserve their own language.

There are, then, in the course of history, marked alternations of the unification and differentiation of languages. Languages grow, attain their apogee, decay, and die.

INFLUENCE OF THE MILIEU

Putting to one side the general characters that the forms of topography can give to a language, it may be said that the area or surface of the territory itself has a noticeable influence on the language spoken within it.

The extensiveness of the area permits the formation of numerous dialects, and when a language results from them, it becomes considerably enriched. This is what happened with German, the result of several languages spoken by different Germanic tribes. In the case of England, the languages spoken by the different peoples —Angles, Saxons, Jutes—were also enriched by the superposition of French, the entirely different language of the Norman conquerors. Thence comes the notable richness of the language of Shakespeare, which is in fact a double language.

With the extension of territory, new relations, and the creation of new interests and needs are reflected in new terms. Languages evolve, and only crystallize when there is national stagnation. In contrast, expansion and movement perpetuate languages.

The American contribution to present-day English is considerable. The same happens with "Brazilian" in relation to Portuguese. These influences, it is true, act on more perfect languages through slang and argot, but crudeness is a sign of youth and does not cease to enrich when it fails to be recognized.

A language planted in a distant area, in a "New World," is transformed to some degree in the new milieu and remains sheltered from changes that are taking place in the country of origin. We have examples of this in our language. The French Canadian speech of today is the French of the eighteenth century with Indian terms, English words, and incorrect phonetic and grammatic features. The same retardation of the basic language is seen in the Dutch of the

Boers in South Africa. The *taal* is a deteri-orated language, formed of Old Dutch, Hottentot, and Kaffir. In this case, one of the symptoms of deterioration is the impossibility of expressing abstract ideas.

One of the relations of territory and language is the political use that the rulers of the territory try to make of the language for unification. We will cite only the attempts, sometimes violent, at Russification made in the times of the tsars in Poland and Finland. In fact language is an element of resistance and national vitality; it was the passive obstacle that Poland presented to Russia, Bohemia to Austria, Schleswig to Prussia, and Flanders to Belgium. But the geographic force that territory represents in the distribution of languages is profoundly natural and resists artificial solutions. The unification of the Italian language did away with the languages spoken in the different districts of Italy in antiquity, but today in the unified language itself new dialects stand out, and they are distributed topographically like the languages spoken before unification. The same process has affected the dialects of modern Greece.

The influence of the milieu is as complex as the milieu itself. But that of the spiritual or moral environment, if one exists, is stronger than the influence of the physical environment. This is true of the languages of countries that are invaded. Victory, from the intellectual and linguistic point of view, belongs to the more advanced, whether they be conquerors or conquered. The Germanic tribes that invaded Italy (Ostrogoths and Lombards) became Italians; the Frankish and Celtic tribes in France became French; the Wends became Germans.

The physical environment has a pronounced influence on vocabulary. Abstract ideas always depend for their expression on the state of civilization, but concrete words are related to the necessities and possibilities of the environment. Thus it is that the pastoral Herrero of Africa, and the Dinka pastoralists of the White Nile, possess an extremely rich vocabulary to designate their animals. In northern Siberia, the Samoyed, a population of advanced barbarians, have more than ten terms to describe the brown and grey shades of their reindeer. The Malay vocabulary, thanks to the maritime life of the insular populations of Malaya, is especially rich in nautical terms. The Kirgiz pastoralists of the Tien Shan have no less than four terms for mountain passes and defiles. These terms include in addition an indication of the relative difficulty of the passage: *daban* is a difficult and rocky defile and *art* is a very high and dangerous one, while *bel* is low and easy of passage and *kuktal* is a wide opening between low hills.

Different kinds of land forms have more or less intense influence in languages. Rivers, for example, are very rarely a dividing line between languages. The lower Danube perhaps constitutes an exception, but this fact is explained historically by its having been chosen as a military frontier and artificially colonized by Trajan. Mountains are no more effective as limits, but produce curious effects of isolation upon languages. Mountains give refuge and protection to social groups that are distinctive for one reason or another. When mountains give passage by their passes and defiles to migrations, great ethnic and linguistic complexity reigns in a mountain area. But when a group separates itself in one of the valleys and remains isolated, it becomes as a captive there, and crystallizes, sheltered from outside influences for centuries. Customs and languages are conserved in more or less perfect form, but the speech forms of neighboring groups become at last unintelligible to one another. This occurs in the Caucasus, in Nepal, in the Hindu Kush, in the Alps, and so on. Afghanistan, a region of passage between India and Mesopotamia, has stored in its complicated terrain small social units that even today betray by different idioms their different ethnic origins.

In the Alps, this phenomenon has been more completely studied. For example, three linguistic currents are represented in Switzerland's 41,000 square kilometers, but in its valleys thirty-five different dialects of German, sixteen dialects of French, and five of Romansch or degenerated Latin have been formed. In the eastern Alps the same fact is realized, with Slavonic taking the place of French. In the mountains of Formosa, where the Malays took refuge during the Chinese invasion, the valleys also encouraged the survival of Malay dialects.

Plains exercise a diametrically opposite effect: they tend to unify languages. Thus it is that in the vastness of Russia the Slavic population employs only two principal dialects (Great Russian and Little Russian or Ukrainian). But when a plain happens to be a desert, units tend to disperse, forming islands, and a language becomes diversified into dialects.

Swamps are real frontiers against the expansion of languages. Because of them there were preserved in the Baltic provinces and Lithuania dialects or even languages that are much closer to the original Sanskrit than the other Aryan languages. As a consequence of similar conditions, the dialect of the Dutch islands of Frisia approximates old Anglo-Saxon, which was carried to the British Isles.

The sea is a powerful agent in the propagation of languages as of all other human institutions. But the destiny of a transplanted language depends very much, as we have seen, on the later facilities offered by navigation and the state of regular communication. Thus islands and sometimes peninsulas have become foci of isolation, which has a profound influence on language.

Insular peoples have a noticeable propensity to form distinct dialects. On the isles of the English Channel we still find variants of the *langue d'oïl* of medieval France, i.e., northern French before the unification of the language. In the fourteenth century the Portuguese voyagers noted that the inhabitants of the Canary Islands had various dialects and, because of the lack of easy communication among the islands, could not understand each other. Even today in the Philippines the natives of Visaya do not understand the natives of Cebú. Japanese has affinities with the Altaic languages, as English has affinities with the Germanic; however, insularity in both cases encouraged distinct languages, Japan abandoning the agglutinative forms, and England the inflectional ones.

The survival of archaic forms of speech is one of the notable consequences of insularity. I have already mentioned the case of the Channel Islands. In the case of Sardinia we find two series of vestiges—inflections that the Latin languages have already lost, and Spanish words left by the Spanish domination. On the Balearic Islands the Catalan language has been preserved in more pure form than in eastern Spain. In Iceland one still finds the pure Norwegian of the ninth century.

The extremities of peninsulas, especially when they are mountainous, serve as shelter for populations during invasions. There languages are preserved and dialects are formed. For example, the populations of Celtic speech are all sheltered by the western mountain chains of Europe (Brittany, Cornwall, Wales, Ireland, Scotland). Today ancient Celtic forms two groups of dialects: the "Gaelic" group (Irish, Manx, and Scots) and the "Cymric" group (Welsh, Cornish [now extinct], and Breton).

Insular isolation caused by insufficiency of nautical equipment sometimes produces curious phenomena. For example, in Madagascar a largely African population adopted Malay dialects. It is true that the Hovas on the eastern part of the island are Malays, but the Sakalavas on the western side are Africans. The Malay language is predominant because the Malays are navigators, and because the Africans became definitely separated from the African continent by the Mozambique current which they could not conquer. Hence the predominance, all over the island, of archaic Malay.

By virtue of their geographic position, some islands lend themselves to internationalism in speech. The islands of the Mediterranean furnish good examples of polyglot populations: Cyprus, Crete, Malta, Corfu, and Sicily are typical. They attracted a great many conquerors and merchants. Cyprus, for example, was successively Phoenician, Greek, Assyrian, Persian, Roman, Byzantine, Venetian, Turkish, Egyptian, and finally British (from 1878). In Malta any language of the Mediterranean is spoken, indifferently. Maltese is made up of Phoenician, Arabic, and Italian words. In Corsica, French and Italian are spoken equally. In Formosa, Japanese, Chinese, and Malay are on the same footing.

The linguistic internationalism of islands is also found on coasts. At times commercial cosmopolitanism determines the formation of a special language. Thus was born the "lingua franca" (a mixture of Italian, Greek, Arabic, and Turkish) in the Levant of the Mediterranean, at the time of the commercial supremacy of the Italian cities. It is still spoken today in Smyrna.

For the same motive, the Swahili of Zanzibar became the language of the East African coast. On the western coast of Africa Negro-English prevails, which has a Far Eastern cousin in so-called Pidgin English, a Chinese adaptation of English, Portuguese, and Malay words.

In Brazil the same process affected the Tupi language, which became the *Lingua Geral* ("general language") of communication with the Indian. Border life in colonial Brazil, depending essentially on maritime communications, preserved Portuguese from any great alterations. To this we owe the notable unity of our language, despite its great territorial extension.

CONSTITUTION AND GEOGRAPHIC AREA OF LANGUAGES

A German linguist who studied the distribution of the Indo-Germanic languages in 1872 announced a "wave theory" to explain the propagation of linguistic phenomena (*Wellentheorie*), according to which events take place in waves, without any perceptible limits.[9] There exist also "isogloss" lines, just as there are isotherms and isobars.

Common languages superpose themselves on dialects, and the latter are distinguishable from special languages. A special language is a slang-like form used by a group of individuals in special circumstances. It develops against the common background of a living language. At times there are not slangs but technical languages, or even different tongues, spoken side by side. Thus among the Caribs the men spoke Carib and the women Arawak; among the Masai of East Africa, different words are employed, according to the age of the speaker, for the same objects. In certain religions there are linguistic taboos. These are dualisms that segment a language.

Dialects grow up spontaneously, says J. Vendryes, by the natural play of linguistic action.[10] It is not easy to define a dialect. Various criteria are necessary to fix its geographic limits: they mark out veritable natural regions. Such limits become more precise when they coincide with a political division—which they often outlive.

The common language adopted in a country has been imposed by a certain number of special conditions, and it grows out of a prevailing dialect. For example, the history of common French is closely linked in its geographical expansion with the political and economic history of the country. The movement spread out from the capital, and the dialect of the Île-de-France was adopted as neighboring provinces were added to the kingdom. And it was the French of a certain social class—the bourgeoisie—that won out. Fixed in the eighteenth century in the *Cité*, it was later accepted by the court and the provinces. It was the writers of the *Grand Siècle* who imposed the language; it became free of other dialect influences.

[9] Johannes Schmidt, *Die Verwandschaftsverhältnisse der indogermanischen Sprachen* (Weimar: H. Böhlau, 1872).

[10] Joseph Vendryes, *Le langage: introduction linguistique à l'histoire* (Paris: Renaissance du Livre, 1921), pp. 288–93.

Spanish was formed before French. The peninsula presented three groups of dialects: Galician on the west, Catalan on the east, and a central group. A northern dialect won out, that of Castilla la Vieja, which became common Spanish, spreading fanwise southward and separating the members of the central group, today found in separate but similar vestiges in León and Aragón. Thanks partly to Alfonso X, Castilian became a literary language in the thirteenth century. It failed to absorb only Portugal, where old Portuguese related to Galician was renewed and fixed in the sixteenth century, with Lisbon as its center.

English is distinguished from French and Spanish in having been influenced by several dialects. This is explained geographically by the fact that London, where the common language was formed, was the meeting place for migrants from all directions. This is also why the pronunciation of English has been so diversified since the eighteenth century, and thus perhaps explains the present difficult nature of the language. The position of London from the standpoint of contact and interchange explains the extension of its language.

German did not have a capital to serve as a center of geographic radiation. It was not political unity that gave it value; what counted most was that German was a written language for religious reasons and because of colonization. The German of Luther, based on the language used in the chancelleries of cities and principalities prevailed. Having rid itself of numerous dialectal peculiarities, German continuously pushed the Slavic languages eastward as the borderlands were colonized, beginning in the fourteenth century under Charles IV. The printing press solidified these conquests.

Russian belongs to the eastern group of Slavic languages, including Ukrainian and Belorussian (White Russian). The primitive language gave way phonetically and was simplified morphologically under the influence of Old Bulgarian, a liturgical language that had the same influence on the formation of Russian that Latin had on French or English. But of all the Slavic languages, Russian was the one that received the most alien elements: its letters came from alterations of the Greek, Latin, and Cyrillic alphabets; the vowel *a* has Finnic characteristics when it replaces the *o* of primitive Slavic; Tataric left vestiges in sentence structure; and the scientific language is spattered with German words.

The formation of Russian took place as recently as the eighteenth century, when a compromise was established between the Slavonic (of the church) and the popular language. Thereafter the language was written as it was spoken. This development had two consequences: the fixation of an emancipated language, and the adoption of a spoken speech identical with the literary language. One of the characteristics of Russian is that it is a language of colonization, that is, it has spread through migrations and the occupation of the soil, without allowing provincial corruptions. In fact, Russian has barely two dialects, which differ only slightly. This is a remarkable linguistic uniformity for such an extensive area, in which, however, sixty different languages are spoken by ethnic minorities.

Italian is a common language of different origin; it is purely literary—the result of the prestige of writers like Dante, Petrarch, and Boccaccio—and dates from the fourteenth century. The language that became established was Tuscan because of the strategic position of Florence—a link in the chain that connected Rome and Bologna—and because of the city's prosperity, its writers, and also the resemblance of Tuscan speech to Latin, which facilitated the replacement of other dialects by a common tongue.

It was principally the nineteenth century that saw the national languages definitively constituted and fixed. As a nation becomes conscious of itself, its written language, being the language of culture, appears as an essential element. The first language that became thus fixed and formed a people, if not a nation, was Greek, when Attic succeeded Ionian.

The utility of a common language soon becomes apparent in a state when the language of a restricted number of privileged people differs from the vulgar language of the lower classes. As democracy advances, it imposes the utility of a knowledge of the language of the elites, so that the citizens do not find themselves politically in a condition of inequality before the administration. For public use, for assemblies, for examinations, a common language is indispensable.

In Norway, Danish-Norwegian is still the tongue of the old bourgeoisie, and the *landsmal* or pure Norwegian is the popular language. In the Orient, the diffusion of common languages like Pali had religious propaganda as a determining cause, through translated texts. In the Occident, the role of religion was less important in the fixation of languages. It was in the Middle Ages that the national languages of the Occident began to be written. Literature and the chancelleries, that is, secular factors, spread them. In the sixteenth century the press gave them new strength of expansion and independence, principally when Latin was replaced as an erudite language.

The use of a dead language as a language of learning offers great inconveniences because only a living language can evolve and keep up with the sciences, which are in perpetual evolution. If instead of pretending to make itself classic and correct, Latin had adapted itself to the necessities of a world of change, it would perhaps have held out as the international language of learning. The preoccupation with Ciceronianism was its fatal weakness. It was interposed between thought and a new reality, principally in the natural sciences, where it was able to interpret only painfully and imperfectly. By getting out of contact, it created difficulties. Hence the victory of living languages in the field of science.

DISTRIBUTION OF LANGUAGES

The most widely spoken language is probably Chinese. Among the modern languages of commercial importance and practical usefulness in international business, we mention the following:[11] English, spoken by about 225 million persons; Russian, spoken by about 160 million persons; German, spoken by about 80 million persons; Spanish, spoken by about 80 million persons; French, spoken by about 62 million persons; Portuguese, spoken by about 50 million persons; and Italian, spoken by about 40 million persons.

These approximate numbers do not translate exactly the real importance of each of the languages because some are not spoken but merely "understood." French, for example, is not only spoken by 62 million Frenchmen, Belgians, Swiss, Canadians, Haitians, etc., but because it is a diplomatic language, possessing a popular literature, and is also of considerable scientific value, it is understood by a good portion of the elite of large countries (Latin America, Russia, Spain, etc.). German does not have the general popularity that its scientific production merits. English has lately been penetrating South America and is conquering places in university training that formerly belonged to French. Portuguese is little known beyond the foreign circles that are directly interested in it.

THE PORTUGUESE LANGUAGE

Two centuries before Christ, the Iberian Peninsula was Romanized, and the Latin imported by the conquerors, after having evolved into a popular and barbarian language, became the language of the Celtic population of so-called Lusitania. Isolated on the western coast in the second century, it evolved separately from Hispano-Roman and formed the "Portuguese dialect" which

[11] The editors have made no attempt to bring these figures up to date. Current information on this subject may be found in many reference books.

became a language in the twelfth century when a Portuguese nationality was constituted. Consequently, dialect differentiation has been going on for two thousand years—that is, the disintegration of the mother language into its derivatives, of which Portuguese is one. In its slow transformations, the language obeyed the three principles enunciated by Eduardo Carlos Pereira:[12] the principle of least effort (softening, syncope, loss of final consonants, obliteration of declensions with persistence of accusatives, etc.); the principle of the persistence of the tonic syllable; and the principle of analysis, with its regularizing tendency. Two currents can be noted: from the fifth to the thirteenth centuries the "popular stream," the unconscious action of the people in the evolution of the Latin lexicon, obeying rhythm and analogy, and from the fourteenth century onward the "learned stream," the conscious action of the Latinists against popular changes in their translations. Thus we have a double, or sometimes a triple or quadruple vocabulary, making the richness of the language. (Examples: *ministerium, ministério, mister; fratrem, frade, freire, frei; maculam, mácula, mágua, malha, mancha.*)

Since Hispano-Roman has split into various dialects, Portuguese could not remain unaffected by influences from the languages spoken on the banks of the Minho, Galician-Portuguese or Gallego, to which it was very similar. Later, the Arabs also came to influence Portuguese, chiefly in toponymy and in the speech of certain southern provinces. But the unity of Portuguese, which may be said to date from the reign of Alfonso III (1248–79), nevertheless allowed the persistence of "dialects," which are still used today and fall into three groups: (1) the "continental" dialects (*transmontano, interamnense, beirão, meridional*), (2) the "insular" dialects (*açoriano, madeirense*), and (3) the "overseas" dialects (Indo-Portuguese).

Carried to Brazil by discoverers and colonists, Portuguese now constitutes the "Brazilian language," which is in fact a co-dialect of the Portuguese of the sixteenth century. Under the influence of factors of the milieu, it continues to differentiate itself from the language of Portugal in vocabulary, prosody, and syntax. Brazil received its popular language when the period of syncretism of vocabulary was already ended, during which forms derived from the same word multiplied because of uncertainty and oscillating pronunciation; Brazil acquired the "classical language" of the *Quinhentistas* under the influence of the renaissance of letters in a time of grammatical discipline. Hence the regularity and relative uniformity of our language.

Certain tendencies, however, have manifested themselves in the last four centuries. The most characteristic among them, according to Clovis Monteiro,[13] was the simplification of the flectional system, that is the "analytic tendency." "In the speech of the people," says our distinguished linguist, "what is evident at every moment is the force with which the analytic tendency in syntax, present in our language from the beginning, is expanding. Through the schools and the style of good authors, the popular spirit in Brazil becomes familiar with certain prenominal forms that are the last vestiges of the Latin declensions." But the author justifies us in the following way: "One should notice that it is nowhere else but in the solecisms of the Latin of the people, in the vices of the vulgar language, that the literary syntax of the Romance languages rests today."

Concerning the geographical expansion of our language, Jacques Raimundo writes:[14]

[12] Eduardo Carlos Pereira, *Gramática histórica,* (8th ed.; São Paulo: Companhia Nacional Editora, 1933).

[13] See Clovis do Rego Monteiro, *Português da Europa e português da America: aspetos da evolução do nosso idioma,* (2d ed.; Rio de Janeiro: Departamento de Imprensa Nacional, 1952).

[14] Jacques Raimundo, *A língua portuguesa no Brasil: expansão, penetração, unidade e estado atual* (Rio de Janeiro: Departamento de Imprensa Nacional, 1941), pp. 21, 77, 82, 84.

In São Vicente, to the south, as well as in Recife and its neighborhood to the north, and in Baía in the center, the savages who made use of it in their relations with the white man were already quite numerous. . . .

The life that went on at the seashore and along the coast, in the neighboring lands, or inland in the settled neighborhoods and bush clearings, had already constituted the imperious cause of an expansion of the vocabulary among the colonists, even showing up in official documents and reports submitted to the court.

There were names of trees, animals and objects, and of whatever had to do with customs, problems, industry, commerce, and other activities of the native; but whatever the colonist or administrative agent heard or learned, badly or imperfectly, molded itself to the phonetic type and entered into frequent use in accordance with the morphological character of the invading language. The new words were reshaped, sometimes adjusting themselves by analogy to a gender, sometimes being inflected, with the proper affix, for number and even for the appropriate case.

The acquisition of the new elements went on, as in the Orient and Africa, because of the necessity of expressing ideas for which no suitable or satisfactory denominations existed, the word coming in as a term sometimes with two or more forms. Since then numerous Tupí divergencies and variants have made themselves felt, creating difficulties as to their meaning because they are rather differing in aspect. Besides the frequent mutilations, there occurred among other things an irregular transliteration of the guttural *i* of the savage, as the Portuguese *i* or *e*.

In relation to the native and African contributions, the same author says:

The American portion grew immediately, rapidly, and prodigiously. From Brazilian Indian languages, the major contributors, local names of plants, animals, and topographic features were already an appreciable, rich, incomparable, and precious patrimony. As for toponyms, it should be remarked that it was not these languages that were the principal sources, but rather the missionaries and the people who went into the *sertão*, both settlers and those in search of riches. The diligence of the *bandeirante*—whose vocabulary would be worth investigating as another proof of his

lively and tireless activities—is no doubt what was responsible for the preservation of the native names for relief features, confirming them in one place, conferring them in another, inventing them in some other place, and renewing them somewhere else. Incomparably more precious, however, were the terms which, by infiltrating and spreading into daily speech, produced others that followed the models of Portuguese morphology, or those incrusted in ready-made phrases that fixed their lasting meanings, enlivening local shades of meaning and reconfirming the ethnos of a race.

As to Spanish influence, Jacques Raimundo adds:

The intromission of Castilianisms makes itself felt, coming sparsely down the Amazon Valley, insinuating itself along the border region of Mato Grosso, or expanding abundantly over the Pampas of Rio Grande do Sul; but, once considered as *"platinismos"* (peculiarities of speech from the Rio de la Plata), they mostly became regionalized there, conforming in general to the type of Portuguese, which was the victorious language. The influence of the latter was so strongly characteristic that even today, in a frontier city like Santa Ana do Livramento, which is separated from the Uruguayan city of Rivera only by a street, the exact limit of the Brazilian side agrees with the extent of Portuguese speech.

The African languages also made their bequests:

The introduction of the Negro slave, first to São Vicente in 1532, and then transported to all the colony, created a new source of enrichment.

There came Negroes from upper Guinea, and these seem to have been the first; they were from the Guinean and Sudanese ethnic groups. But the more numerous shipments were of Dahomeys, Yorubas, and Hausas. From lower Guinea, Congolese and Angolans were transported; from the eastern coast Mozambiques were later imported. The Bantu furnished the largest number of words, and some of them were used in the capital, and were well received even in the works of the best authors, like *zombar* and *zombaria*, from a root *izomba* (singular: *kizomba*) meaning a prank, a joke, a boyish trick; from this must have come *zomba*, which did not take hold, except perhaps ephemerally in the language of the lower classes of the people. . . .

The Guinea-Sudanese, proud of their traditions and customs, spirited and intractable in their attitudes, profoundly attached to their own national religion and rites, (some to animism and others to Maleism or Mussulmanism, a counterfeit of Islam), exerted little influence despite their moral and social achievements, and this influence persisted in the language of immediate relations. What there was and is from the Hausa is mostly restricted to them, and consists mostly of words of Arabic origin. From the rare Mandingos, in the few places where they appeared, may have come the term *bá,* an affectionate name for a "Black Mammy," which spread rapidly. As for *banana,* a word common to Wolof and Peul, its long use in Portuguese shows that the Portuguese introduced it, allowing several hybrid compounds to develop in Brazil. A copious number of words was borrowed from the Yorubas, but for use among themselves, being things to do with religion and their cult; cookery became indebted to them for several names of delicacies and condiments to excite the appetite, as well as of several drinks.

With this author, we may conclude that:

The dominance of the Portuguese language was accentuated since the beginning of colonization, by the imposition of its words, its phonetic model, its morphological type, and its syntactical form. It did not become transformed, but kept its essential characteristics: for example, the same prosody or exactness of the tonic accent, except for a few minutiae of pronunciation, such as the failure to distinguish between tonic and atonic vowels that are today absorbed or elided overseas, as they were not in the sixteenth century; the survival of the morphology, keeping the flectional type of number, gender, and case unaltered, and the gains made by the process of derivation by affixes or deverbalization, which added or adopted American Indian and African words; the respect for the pattern of sentence construction, with its original turns and shapes, except for the uniformizing effect of analogy and certain inaccuracies in the use of the governing particles. In general, no differentiation took place that would justify thinking of a dialect in Brazil; there are some groups which, because of small variations or peculiarities, are like jargons grading into regional speech

types, like the Amazonian, Northeastern, Central (Caipira, Capiau, or Goiano), Sul-Riograndense, or Gaúcho. Only those deserving major attention, that are mentioned in special books or articles, or in notes and appendixes of fictional works and regional literature, are cited.

Today Portuguese, spoken by eight million people in Portugal itself and understood by about nine million Portuguese colonials, is the language of 43 million Brazilians. Thus we are the depositaries of a unique language, spoken in America in 8.5 million square kilometers, without local dialects and hardly even slight changes of pronunciation and intonation. As a living language it goes on being enriched not only with terms of Indian (principally Tupí) origin, but also with foreign terms which continue to impose themselves during the evolution of the Western civilization to which we belong.

In Brazil itself, the Portuguese language is influencing the speech of the foreign colonists who have established themselves here. The "German" of the Teuto-Brazilians, for example, is undergoing alterations according to the zone in which it is spoken. In certain parts of Santa Catarina, the German of the immigrants is preserved in a relatively purer form than elsewhere. In these eighty years, however, despite the literary or intellectual contact maintained with Germany, the speech of the colonists has continued to adopt in Germanized forms our words of common use (e.g., *tabeljong = tabelião; pushen = puxar; kapinen = capinar; kashir = caixeiro; carnesek = carne sêca; reemen = remar;* not counting geographic terms: *barre, devolutes land, pikade, riberong, pantanne,* etc.) In other places, like Petrópolis, the decadence of the German language is more marked, and the language even tends to disappear. The geographic factor of interaction militates against the perpetuation of the language, for when life with the Luso-Brazilians is intimate, resistance is reduced, and contact with Germany is almost lost, especially since there has been no influx of immigrants to maintain the spiritual connections. In Rio Grande do Sul, assimilation results from a systematic effort by the public authorities of the state.

The case of the German language in Brazil is repeated for Portuguese in India. It is an identical influence of the geographic milieu on the language of a community of Portuguese and of natives converted by the Portuguese who are submerged in the Indian milieu, where other maternal languages exist like the Gujerati of Damão and the Konkani of Goa. There are several dialects, since the Portuguese colonies are far apart: northern Creole in Bombay, Damaense in Damão and Diu, Macaista in Maco, Goanese, etc. In Damão, Portuguese is the maternal and domestic language of the Catholic population; in Goa Portuguese is not a school language and is considered foreign.

The decadence of Portuguese in the Indies, contrasting so strikingly with its vitality in Brazil, is marked by the suppression of phonemes in different positions (*curção = coração, boc = bôca, caz = casa, palau = palavra, imbúl = embrulho*). There are no surd vowels in Indo-Portuguese (*butá = botar; tucá = tocar*). As a rule there is no formal distinction of gender or number (*port jinél = portas e janelas; dois criad = dois criados* or *duas criadas*). In the Macaista dialect the plural is at times made by reduplication of the substantive (*fifio = filhos* and *filhas*), by influence of the native languages. The definite article is seldom used, the verb loses its final consonant, etc. These examples are sufficient to show the growing imprecision of Indo-Portuguese, and its crumbling in the different colonies, a result of being lost in a native world. The language of Camões has not been carried to a greater perfection or to higher destinies, in spite of the deep influence that this language had in the past on the native languages of Asia.

Brazilians speak a single language. There are few languages which are understood over so vast an area without considerable alterations. It is evident that we have dialect forms, local speech forms, and regional expressions; but more rapid communication, education, the radio, the press, and the airplane are bringing the popular language every day closer to the literary. Under these several influences, in environments distant from the metropolis, and in diverse geographic conditions, a language has been formed with a different accent, a mild accent which changes syntax by mixing up the oblique cases of personal pronouns, which changes phraseology, but keeps a remarkable unity.

Antenor Nascentes, taking a total of 100,000 words of the Brazilian language as a base, calculates that 80 per cent is formed by Latin elements, 16 per cent by Greek, 2 per cent by European elements, and 2 per cent by Asiatic, African, American, and others. From Arabic, Nascentes calculates that the language has received 609 elements, from French 657, from Spanish 400, and from Italian 383.

The present phenomenon of regional linguistic diversity permits us to study Brazilian geo-linguistics in which the geographic factor still plays a marked part. "Thus it is territorial continuity, ease of communications, by land, sea, and river, and at last the mixing of ethnic elements from diverse parts of the Federation, that can and must explain for us the phenomenon we are dealing with," says Rodolfo Garcia, concerning Brazilianisms.

In certain zones the influence of one of the ethnic elements predominated. In the extreme north it was the Indian, in others it was the African element, which in the south disappears in the variety of European cultures represented there by immigrants. The dialect map drawn by Antenor Nascentes[15] divides the country into five dialect regions: north, northeast, river, south, and Sertão. "If," says Renato Mendonca, "there is a palpable difference between the singsong of the north and the unhurried speech of the south, no less noticeable is

[15] Antenor Nascentes, *O idioma nacional*, vol. IV, *Gramática histórica* (2d ed.; Rio de Janeiro: Livraria Alves, 1933), p. 244 (map).

the difference between the speech of a Cearense and a Baiano, between the language
of a Paulista and that of a Gaucho." For
this author, besides the principal divisions,
transition zones must be noted in the north,
in Maranhão and east of Piaui, and, in the
south, in Paraná and the north of Santa
Caterina.

According to Renato Mendonca, the linguistic division should be: (1) "Amazonica"; (2) "Maranhense-piauiense," transitional; (3) "Cearense"; (4) "Nordes-
tina," up to Alagôas; (5) "Baïana," with
Sergipe; (6) "Fluminense"; (7) "Caipira"
with São Paulo and the frontier of Minas;
(8) "Mineira" and São Francisco baïano;
(9) "Paranaense" with the north of Santa
Catarina; (10) "Gaúcho"; and (11) "Ser-
taneja," Goiaz, and Mato Grosso.[16] This
author asserts that the transitional zone of
Maranhão "keeps well lighted the flame of
Lusitanian" and "is characterized by the
absence of dialect traces." He thinks that
the most notable linguistic trait in the vocabulary of Paraná is the presence of Gua-
rani terms, many of which are connected
with the maté industry and are common in
Paraguay. He adds that Amazonica is distinguished at first glance by the fact that
50 per cent of its ordinary speech is formed
of Tupí terms and expressions, and that
Rio Grande shows 60 per cent of Rio de la
Plata terms in its everyday vocabulary.

Peculiar zoologic names are significant
in our different linguistic regions because
they reflect everyday life. Thus by means
of them we can follow the waves of linguistic diffusion, noting their points of origin.
In a study by Rodolfo von Ihering[17] we
see that the Amazonian, northeastern, and
southern regions use names that have affinities. Thus the marimbondo is a caba in
Amazonia and a sabiá carachué. In the

northeast, the gambá of the south is a
timbú, and it is micura in Amazonia. The
tainha of the north is paratí, bacurau, and
curiango in the south. In zoological terminology there is a subregion of Reconcavo
baïano where a strong African influence
stands out (caxinguelê, congolo, sarné). In
conclusion, Ihering thinks that the preference for native names is 50 per cent in the
south, 70 per cent in the northeast, and
87.5 per cent in Amazonia.

DIFFUSION OF THE FRENCH LANGUAGE

When a common language is integrated
in a region occupied by a social group, it
takes on a material substance and a geographic extension. In one of his volumes
on the history of the French language,
Ferdinand Brunot[18] studies the propagation of the language and the geographic
conditions that conditioned it. More than
any other linguist he considers language a
geographic phenomenon that adapts to the
features of the soil and the economic evolution of the country.

In the eighteenth century, although
French became the language of diplomacy
and of the culture of the European elites,
it did not propagate in the same way in
France itself. Monarchial centralization,
which was effective as a process of political
and national unification, did not cause
linguistic unity to progress so far as might
appear at first sight. In the eighteenth
century the administration paid little attention to establishing the moral unity of
the French people on the basis of a "king's
language"; the linguistic question did not
exist, the patois continued in all the provinces, and the common language gained
ground only slowly.

It was the creation of a net of highways
in the eighteenth century that had a profound influence on the propagation of the
language. Brunot says that "the civil engineers served the interests of the language

[16] Renato Mendonça, O português do Brasil:
origens, evolução, tendéncias (Rio de Janeiro:
"Civilisação Brasileira," 1936).

[17] Rodolfo and Hermann von Ihering, As aves
do Brasil (São Paulo: Typografia do Diário Official, 1907). The species referred to are native
birds.

[18] Ferdinand Brunot, Histoire de la langue
française des origines à 1900 (12 vols.; Paris:
A. Colin, 1905).

more than many members of the Academy." Overcoming the great difficulties of communications, and establishing by the ordinance of 1775 a regular schedule of passenger transport, the government contributed much to the linguistic unification of the country. The new highways did not all radiate from Paris as a center, as had been the case in the previous century; transverse highways were established between principal cities. These highways permitted the establishment of direct contacts between the capital and provincial cities, passing through extensive rural zones. They provoked, besides, a certain mobility of labor in a country in the process of industrialization.

The postal service constituted an advantage that everyone could appreciate, but nobody remembered to write letters in local dialect. The "public scribe" himself was an agent in the diffusion of the common language. From the sixteenth century on, the ordinances and administrative acts were no longer written in Latin, and highway commerce brought about the use of the spoken national idiom. A document of 1793, cited by Brunot, says that "what is making the Bretons less savage is their more frequent communication with the cities, and the great highways constructed in Brittany in these last thirty years are one of the causes of this communication."

It is essential to remember that the road net of the time constituted one form of the industrial movement. The circulation of workers brought on the disappearance of the dialects. Where workmen from different provinces congregated for great works, the use of French soon prevailed. The mountaineers of Auvergne and the Alps migrated in winter to the urban centers, and returned to their native fields "Frenchified." So a fluctuating population is a powerful vehicle for the geographic spread of a language.

However, certain dialects in particular regions did not cease to hold out merely for this reason. An important distinction made by Demangeon in his studies of human

geography applies here.[19] The habitat can, he thinks, be dispersed or concentrated. Now in the case of the diffusion of French the application of this criterion is significant, and the philologist Brunot did not fail to point up this contrast.

Local speech persists where the geographic situation and the social structure are opposed to outside influences. In agglomerated agricultural villages of farmers or wine growers there is communication and interchange. Such contacts are not enjoyed in a community of cattle raisers with scattered and more or less isolated houses. It was the dispersed settlement pattern that helped the Basque, Breton, Flemish, and other regions to keep their dialects. Isolation also acts in the same way when factors of insularity or peninsularity are effective, as is still the case in Brittany and Corsica.

FORMATION OF THE ENGLISH LANGUAGE

The English language is not of British origin, i.e., it was not the first language spoken by the inhabitants of the British Isles. On the contrary, it was imported there by invaders who emigrated from the European continent. Before English, two languages were spoken in what is now England: Celtic and, to a certain degree, Latin. English was introduced to the island in A.D. 449.

Teutonic, or Germanic, was the language spoken in the fifth century of our era by the populations dwelling near the mouths of the Rhine, the Weser, and the Elbe, and the present Schleswig. They were Saxons, Jutes, and Angles who had a rude and guttural vocabulary of about two thousand words. Like all languages, Teutonic evolved, and in its migrations it became differentiated, forming three great groups of languages: (1) High German (old, medieval, and modern German), (2) Scandinavian

[19] Albert Demangeon, "La géographie de l'habitat rural," *Annales de Géographie*, XXXVI (1927), 1–23, 97–114. [See the translation in Part IV of this volume.]

(Old Norwegian [extinct], Icelandic, Danish, Swedish, etc.), (3) Low German, to which Dutch, Flemish, and English belong.

Thus it can be seen that English could be defined and classified as "a language of the Low German group, belonging to the Teutonic branch of the Aryan family." English is the "lowest" of the Low German dialects. Low German is the German of lower Germany, i.e., the northern plains of Europe. The future English, then a simple dialect, went down the rivers to the sea, turning into Dutch and Frisian in the Low Countries, and, crossing the Channel, became the foundation for English.

On the large island of Britain, the Jutes established themselves in the southeast, in Kent, and on the Isle of Wight. The Saxons occupied the central and southern part, forming three kingdoms: Essex, Wessex, and Middlesex and Sussex (the ending "-sex" marks the Saxon origin). As for the Angles, they formed the two "peoples" of the northeast, the people of the north or North Folk (the present Norfolk) and the people of the south or South Folk (the present Suffolk), which together constituted the monarchy of East Anglia. There were then three Teutonic groups, forming seven monarchies, together with Mercia (the "Seven Kingdoms," which in fact never existed), speaking different Teutonic dialects that little by little with the shift of political pre-eminence from one group to another became fused to form the English language.

We emphasize the Teutonic branch, from which English came, because it is remarkable that the island has always been conquered by races of the same group: first, Anglo-Saxons; second Danes and Norwegians; and at last the Normans, the only ones who spoke a language not of their race—French.

When the decedent Roman Empire was invaded and conquered by the Barbarians, the Germanic tribes occupied Western Europe; the Franks defeated the Romanized Celts of Gaul, and the Angles, Saxons, and Jutes subjected the Romanized Celts of Britain. But although the Franks abandoned their primitive language and adopted the Latin spoken by the conquered, the Jutes, Angles, and Saxons imposed their Germanic language on the subjugated populations. The Gaulish territories thus turned out to have a stronger intellectual culture than the conquerors at the time of the invasion. This situation was repeated in the tenth century when the Norman conquerors, imitating the Franks, abandoned their language to adopt the Latin that was spoken in France.

In the territories of Britain, however, it was always the invader who was able to impose his language and culture, and this fundamental difference in medieval social contacts is revealed in linguistic consequences.

The various invasions pushed the Celtic elements of the primitive population back into the mountains of the west and north, and into Ireland. Thus in modern Ireland, Wales, and Scotland, Celtic languages are still spoken: Irish or Erse, Welsh, Gaelic, and Manx (on the Isle of Man).[20] Monasteries and intellectual centers like York in Northumbria were refuges of Latin, called *laeden* by the Angles, while they knew their own language as *aenglisc*.

Thus the territory lost on the Continent by Low German was reconquered to advantage overseas. Today approximately a hundred and fifty million people speak modern English. On the Continent High German developed later than Low German, and at the expense of other Teutonic languages. It is the language most spoken in Central Europe, thanks to its geographic expansion.[21]

In sum, the geography of languages is one of the parts of human geography which seems destined for a particularly rapid and decisive growth, because it links the present

[20] The Celtic language of Cornwall became extinct about A.D. 1750.

[21] A brief discussion of linguistic atlases in the original version of this article has been omitted.

more logically to the past and because it points up the influences that have been effective and the directions followed. It is more complex than the geography of ethnic groups and more significant than the geography of religions. In a country like Brazil, in which all the processes we study are in full activity, and in which the elements already "sedimented" in other countries are in active movement, it becomes more useful and opportune to study the geography of languages.

PAUL FICKELER

FUNDAMENTAL QUESTIONS
IN THE GEOGRAPHY
OF RELIGIONS

Religion and geography appear at first to have hardly any point of contact, and this is probably also true for the lofty concept that "the Kingdom of God is within" (Luke 17:21). But since all religions in the course of their development have created a more or less manifest cultus that is spatially and temporarily perceptible in the form of magical and symbolic events, objects, and behavior, religious phenomena appear in a real relationship with the earth's surface, and so can be studied geographically. The investigation and exposition of the relations between religion and geography is the scientific task of the geography of religions, which thus forms a branch of cultural geography.

The relations between religion and environment are mutual, so that their investigation can be approached under two main headings: How does the environment, including the people, the landscape, and the country, affect a religious form? And how, reciprocally, does a religious form affect a people, landscape, and country? The investigation of the first topic is a task for the science of religion, to which geography furnishes the necessary particulars about landscapes and regions; the investigation

Translated, with permission of the editor, from "Grundfragen der Religionsgeographie," *Erdkunde: Archiv für wissenschaftliche Geographie*, I (1947), 121–44. The author (1893–1959) was a free-lance scholar and writer who traveled extensively in Asia. He is best known for his monograph "Der Altai: eine Physiogeographie," *Petermanns Geographische Mitteilungen, Ergänzungsheft* 187 (1925).

of the second problem, in contrast, is more a task of the geography of religions, to which the science of religion and other cultural sciences provide the necessary foundation.

Religions and their distributions have long received notice in geographical works, textbooks, and atlases, but most of these hardly go beyond a more or less detailed factual description and seldom give an indication or explanation of geographical effects. At the other extreme, numerous attempts are made—and with the best intentions—to apply geographical causality in order to provide interpretations, which are often too simple, easy, distorted, or downright incorrect in cases where a diversity of non-geographic conditions and causes exists.

In a few recent works on the regional geography of Asia there is evidence of an increased effort to devote proper attention to religious phenomena and to evaluate them geographically. Despite this encouraging concern and the progress made, we are still aware of noticeable defects of content and method. On the other hand, travel descriptions and non-geographic writing about most countries of Asia offer such a wealth of isolated observations, and both used and untouched material, that it is really surprising that the results of such work have not long since been incorporated into regional geographic studies. The amount of material is so vast that it would be worthwhile to work on it separately and present it as a "Religious Geography of

Asia," thus supplementing and deepening regional and cultural geography. However, my preliminary work on this topic very soon disclosed the methodological necessity for summarizing systematically the basic phenomena common to all the Asiatic religions, and preceding the specific aspects of this work with a general comparison.[1] The large number of religions in Asia justifies the application of understandings derived from them to all the religions of the earth and their distributions. Reference should be made to all levels of religion, including nature-religions, because even they produce direct effects in the landscape, and are indirectly essential for deeper understanding of the development of the higher religions as a whole and many of their individual aspects. For the same reasons, the most important ancient religions, from those of prehistory to and beyond those of classical antiquity, have to be considered, and frequent side glances have to be cast toward Europe and ancient Egypt, where religion still marks the modern landscape in impressive fashion. Indeed, ancient Egypt and the Near East provide magnificent examples from the historical geography of religions, which can throw considerable light on many present situations. The abundance of material and problems permits consideration of only a few basic questions in an article of this length.[2]

CEREMONIALISM AND THE SACRED

If every religion has a side dealing with personal conduct (ethical) and a side dealing with worship (ceremonial)—an external and internal aspect, which can be contrasted, following Kant, as the "visible church" and the "invisible church"—, then the geography of religions is concerned above all with ceremonial religion, and must deal with the most important ceremonial ideas that are expressed geographically. For this purpose, several concepts taken over from the science of religion must be more accurately defined, and many phenomena must be more clearly subdivided and outlined through the reformation of underlying assumptions and synthetic concepts, as for instance those connected with consecration, ceremonialism, toleration, and so forth.

The concept of holiness and sacredness, quantitative and qualitative, is among the basic ideas. Following H. Rust, we can distinguish the sanctity of nature-magic, rooted in a particular space or thing, and historical-religious holiness, linked through a historical personality (e.g., the founder of an institution or a saint) with a certain place since a definite time or with an event (a birth, a miracle, or an enlightenment).[3] The first kind of sacredness is characteristic of most natural sanctuaries and shows an indestructible permanence in time and space (the law of persistence); on the contrary, the second can pass away with the disappearance of the religious form that determined it, although it seldom does. Both kinds of sacredness, however, can become superimposed or fused and enhance one another mutually, as for example in the case of most natural sanctuaries, which have been taken over by the higher religions (e.g., hilltop sanctuaries). Sacredness, especially of the nature-magic type, can have two effects: first, in the sense of "dangerous power" which, like an electrical high tension field, deals out fatal shocks and should be avoided; and second, in the sense of "sanctifying power" which, on the contrary, calls for the most intimate possible contact and seeking-out of the holy thing. On the first-named kind of sacredness, with the effect of taboo, rest all avoiding and keeping clear of natural sanctuaries, and their inviolability, immutability, avoidance,

[1] [The author was preparing such a work when this was written, but it has not been published.] See also Werner Leimbach, "Landeskunde von Tuwa," *Petermanns Geographische Mitteilungen, Ergänzungsheft* 222 (1936), 91.

[2] [A detailed discussion of the German literature on the geography of religions follows. The interested reader should consult pp. 122–124 of the original article.]

[3] Hans Rust, *Heilige Stätten* (Leipzig: Quelle & Meyer, 1933).

and protection—for instance of sacred hill-tops, waters, plants, animals, and so forth; on "sanctifying holiness," on the other hand, is based all frequenting of sacred places, from daily ceremonial visits to the god's house to the world-wide traffic of pilgrims toward Mecca, or the making of an extensive cultural landscape by covering holy places with graves, temples, and monasteries.

Another essential feature of holiness lies in its transferability (sanctification), although this may differ greatly in degree. It occurs directly, so to speak, through a kind of irradiation or induction, and indirectly through mediating devices, such as water (e.g., holy water), consciously dedicated to it. On this fact, in the final analysis, rest all contagious sanctification, transferred sanctification, desanctification, and resanctification of places or people by priests of a single religion or of differing ones, in succession or existing parallel through time, and their incorporation into different ceremonial forms or exclusion from them.

We are here within the conceptual realm of the ceremonial [*kultisch*], as part of which can be counted everything connected with religious ceremony in the narrowest or widest sense: religious pictures and symbols, ceremonial things (objects and practices), ceremonial places, ceremonial rules (commandments and prohibitions), and much more. Here, too, among other things, belongs the important underlying notion of ceremonial or ritual purity, which is essential for deeper understanding of many phenomena of religious geography. Such purity is a requirement of many religions and has its basis in the essence of the sacred and the godly, of which it is one of the characteristic features. To the divinity, conceived as absolute, immaculate and pure, and to its cult places, man may approach only in a condition of the greatest possible outward and inward purity, especially for ceremonial acts, if he is to find a response from sympathetic magic. This is altogether the deepest and most original sense and purpose of ritual purification. It is required

for all things that are in any way connected with the sacred, and applies to men, sacrificial animals, priests, ceremonial equipment, ceremonial garments, cult practices, and ceremonial places. It causes, along with fear and respect, numerous prohibitions on contact or even approach, the keeping of one's distance from holy places in nature, prohibitions on climbing holy hilltops, on sailing on holy lakes (e.g., in Central Asia), and on trespassing on certain burial grounds or temples (e.g., in ancient Greece). Where access is nevertheless permitted, it demands in certain religions a previous outward purification, and an inner one by magic and symbolic means. We can cite the numerous ceremonial washing requirements of the adherents of the Japanese Shinto, of Hinduism, or of Islam (e.g., washing of the feet and arms with running water or, where it is lacking, with pure sand, before each of the five daily prayers performed while oriented toward Mecca). We should also mention the arrangements for the necessary washing wells or bathing ponds by religious buildings (e.g., the temple pools in ancient Egypt and India). In a wider sense, the sharp division among Indian castes also rests upon this basis, especially the segregation of the "impure" caste of the Untouchables. Indeed, the ideal of ceremonial purity in a religion can so permeate its communicants that for them, as in the case of Moslems or Hindus, all who believe in another faith may be considered "impure." This attitude, together with other circumstances, can become a source of constant friction in religiously mixed areas, as in northwestern India between Moslems and Hindus, and can lead to bloody disturbances especially at times of religious festivals. This was one reason for the political division that took place in 1947 between Islamic Pakistan—i.e., "Land of the Pure," from the Persian *pak*—and Hindu India. In this case the external purity of an overdrawn ceremonialism stifles and overwhelms the inner purity of the heart.

The state of ceremony in a religion or

confession, that is, the total of ceremonial-religious arrangements and their application by the faithful, can be expressed at any time by the comprehensive and collective concept of ceremonialism, with various effects depending on circumstances. The kind of ceremonialism can concern external, perceptible phenomena serving the cult—i.e., sacred natural and artificial places with the whole wealth of their colors, sounds, fragrances, numbers and directions, flowers, animals, and man (e.g., the cult of saints), mountains, bodies of water, groves, religious buildings and graves, places of pilgrimage and whole ceremonial landscapes, cult activities, and pilgrim traffic. They are all conditioned and perpetuated by more or less numerous and strict precepts (commandments and prohibitions), which regulate many aspects of religious and worldly life, from the cradle to the grave, in the smallest details. Thus, in a general way, we can distinguish a religious ceremonialism that is oriented to sensory life, especially to the eye and ear, and a symbolic ceremonialism (e.g., religions of nature and paganism, Hinduism, Lamaism), from a preceptual ceremonialism more oriented toward commands and prohibitions (e.g., the Mosaic religion of law and Islam), but we must remain aware that both kinds of ceremonialism mutually condition and enter into each other in every possible way. The ceremonialisms dedicated to faith (in the sense of unconditioned acceptance of certain religious ideas) and directed to the inner man, as for example Protestantism and its sects, can have the effect, although indirectly, of favoring a certain economic spirit like capitalism.[4] The degree of ceremonialism of a religion depends upon the loyalty and zeal of its practice by living adherents, which, depending on their co-operation, may be weak, medium, or strong, and as a last stage of growth, mature into an excessive ceremonialism, like the monastic Lamaist

religion of Tibet, which overwhelms the worldly life. Thus historical development, in this case the growth of ceremony, can lead to a strengthening of ceremonialism, but also—mostly after a high point has been attained through moral resolution and renovating transformation by significant personalities (reformers)—to a weakening, going as far as an abandonment of the cult. Not only do religions, their tenets, and the areas upon which they set their mark, differ qualitatively and quantitatively as to ceremonial, but so also do the adherents of one and the same faith within its realm. Notable differences in ceremonialism may coincide with differences of race, national character, landscape, and country, as for example among the nature-religions of northern, middle, and southern Asia; between northern and southern Buddhism; between the iconoclastic, strict Sunnite Islam of the Near East and the less strict and more pictorially inclined Shiite Islam of Persia and Indonesia; or between the Roman Catholic Christians of northern and central Europe and those of southern Europe, e.g., in Sicily. In general, the acceptance of image-cults is relatively strongest in religions of the Asiatic monsoon lands (higher nature religions of East Asia, Hinduism, southern and eastern Buddhism and, to be sure, the over-sacral Lamaism of the frigid high steppes of Tibet as well), while the acceptance of preceptual religions (Israel's religion of law, and Islam) predominates in the dry steppes of western Asia. The moderately ceremonial nature-religions (i.e., shamanism) occupy an intermediate area.

An extremely important basic concept for the geography of religions is that of religious tolerance. It is altogether decisive for the relations of religions and creeds among themselves, and the manner and extent of their spatial distribution, which takes place either peacefully through preaching and missions (as in Buddhism and Christianity), or by force and battle (e.g., religious wars, the "holy wars" of Islam), or both together (Islam, Christi-

[4] Max Weber, *Gesammelte Aufsätze zur Religionssoziologie* (3 vols.; Tübingen: Mohr, 1920–21).

anity). It is also significant for the mutual relations of religions and states, with the limiting case of the religious state (monastic Tibet, the monkish republic of Athos, the church-state of Rome) and that of state religions (Babylon, Egypt, Greece, Rome, and eastern Asia). Toleration of whole religions, or of one or another of their parts (creeds, sects, orders, movements, and communities), can differ according to realm, time in history, and relation to other religions or their parts. In general, nature-religions, paganism, mixed religions, and mystical movements tend to be more tolerant than the monotheistic religions of revelation and scriptures, with their firm conviction of being chosen people, and the dogmatic infallibility of their churches and reformed creeds or sects (although historical fluctuations and exceptions can of course occur). Religions chiefly dedicated to image and saint cults are notably more tolerant than preceptual churches. The reciprocal relation of tolerance is apparent in the characteristic designation of adherents of a religion. The series runs from respected "co-believers" and "comrades (brethren) in the faith" through the tolerated "persons of another faith" in a church that also possesses sanctifying power, to those who are "unbelievers" in the mind of the intolerant "strict and true believer" and of his uniquely sanctifying church. Here is reflected the whole spectrum of religious toleration, from benevolent respect through indifference, disdain, resistance, and persecution to eradication by banishment, forcible ejection, and annihilation, with all their profound effects on people and country, state and culture, especially with respect to external aspect and distribution.

CULT SYMBOLISM: LIGHT AND FIRE

Religious symbols in the widest and most general sense play a large role in cult-religious life, and here we should concern ourselves with those phenomena that are perceptible and fundamental in the landscape: sacred lights, colors, tones, fra-

grances (i.e., qualities) and furthermore the sacred directions, numbers, motions, and times that serve in ceremonial. All of these symbols retain even today their original and ancient meaning as an expression of ideas that are difficult or impossible to convey in words, and they keep their magical-causal purpose alongside their later function, whether consciously or unconsciously, as a selfless, symbolic honoring of the divine. This magical-aesthetic primal meaning and purpose of all cult symbolism must always be taken into account.

Sacred lights are used by all religions, both for purposes of magic and for worship, the former predominating in the nature-religions and the latter predominating more in the higher religions, where they have mostly kept their double meaning (e.g., storm candles). In antiquity, extreme examples of light-religions were the Egyptian (with illuminations at festivals in the open air) and the light-and-darkness religion of Zarathustra, with its giant outdoor fire altars. Today the religion of inner enlightenment, Buddhism, most commonly practices the cult of external illumination with lights on temples and stupas (e.g., festivals of the boats-of-light in Siam, butter-lamp feasts in Lhasa, lantern-lighting in Buddhist temples and Shinto shrines in Japan). Buddha is the "light of the world" of Mahayana doctrine. But Islam, too, for a full month in the fasting time of Ramadan, allows the ritual lights of its mosques to shine out into the night, as does Christianity ("I am the light of the world," John 8:12) by the illumination of such cult buildings as St. Peter's on June 29, by grave-lights at All Souls', by processions of lights, and by illuminated Christmas trees, so that their lights answer the celestial lights beyond the earth, whose mark once inspired and formed these cults.

SACRED COLORS

If the cult lights play a relatively modest role in the landscape of night and appear mostly at certain ceremonial seasons, then the colors of a cult have much greater significance for the landscape of daytime, where they show up outdoors especially in ceremonial costumes and buildings. In this respect, most religions favor a particular color that is especially distinctive and characteristic, and which, bound up with certain sacred places (sanctuaries and places of pilgrimage) and ceremonial periods (cult feasts), stands out 'as being bright and gay. It will be worthwhile here to give at least a short survey of the most important main ceremonial colors, although the uncommonly complex and extremely inviting subject of ceremonial color in the landscape has not yet received the attention in regional studies that it deserves.

Among all peoples and in all times, by far the holiest and most widespread ceremonial color is white, or, with metallic sheen, silver. As the symbolic color of diffused light and reflection, of light and what is bright in general, of the supermundane and celestial, the absolute and the pure, white is the sign of the supreme gods of heaven and the things of nature and of culture that are assigned, dedicated, and consecrated to them (sacred natural sites or holy ways of life; garments; edifices). Since the dead are often considered to be connected with the celestial powers, white is also, by the law of correspondence, the symbolic color of death, and so of mourning, among many simple and higher nature-religions throughout Eurasia, especially in East Asia, South Asia, and ancient Europe (including ancient Germany). White was therefore already the ceremonial color of the "light" gods and priests in ancient Egypt, of the doctrine of light and darkness of Persia and the modern Parsees, and in Germany, where white animals were considered holy—for example the horse (cf. "the man on a white horse") or the swan (the carrier of souls; later the symbol was transformed into a stork, as the bringer of children). In present-day nature-religions of Asia, white marks out the scene of shamanistic ceremonies, which in northern Asia is usually a lonely clearing in the birch forest where white hares' pelts and

bleached white horse skulls hang, and white or lightly colored animals, mostly horses, are sacrificed. In the higher nature-religions of China and Japan, both of which show many common Asiatic traits, white predominates as a color for magical protective charms, as the symbolic color for the west, and as the color of the dead, mourning, graves, and temples. Thus many white buildings, like the Heavenly Altar at Peking, as well as commemorative gates, and extensive fields of graves glisten in the landscape. The same is true of Japan's Shinto, the nature-religion of ritual purity (sacred white animals, and priestly, ceremonial or mourning costumes), Hinduism (priests' clothing, caste marks, temple structures), and especially Buddhism (the white lotus blossom, the white elephant, white stupas, dagobas, pagodas, *chortas*, prayer-walls, monasteries, and entire monastic settlements and landscapes). The landscape upon which Islam is stamped is strongly marked by white: e.g., white turbans as a badge of the faithful, the white garments (*ihram*) of pilgrims to Mecca, white gravestones, and snow-white mosques with minarets that reach up into the heavens like slim church candles.

Next to white in sacredness and effect on the landscape stands yellow and especially gold with its metallic luster. It embodies in a color symbol light itself, the stars, and especially the sun—whatever radiates, sparkles, or shines—and the godly and sacred things connected with these. Yellow or gold becomes the symbol of the religious inner light and enlightenment, of the spiritual sun and godly wisdom, and also of religious fervor and hope, of faith and of redemption. In all the religions which have joyous ceremonies, it serves along with white and red, especially, in the festive worship of the "Most High" of the time, and His radiant majesty. Because of their sensory and behavioral effect and symbolic affinity, gold and white often appear together and can mutually enhance each other's effect and be substituted for each other. Already in prehistoric and antique cults, gold symbolized the sun (cf. the sun-cart of the Bronze Age, or the sun god Ra in Egypt); in China it symbolized the zenith, the heavens, and the Son of Heaven, the emperor. Thus it is that the roofs of the imperial palace in the Forbidden City at Peking, and certain temples like that of Confucius, are covered with glazed yellow tiles. Since Buddhism's goal is the inner enlightenment of the spirit through meditation, it is no accident that yellow has also become its main ceremonial color. The ancient yellow ritual clothing of monks and priests, already in use before the time of Buddhism, prevails, therefore, in the domain of southern Buddhism ("Lanka [Ceylon] shines with yellow garments"), and also in the reformed "yellow church" of Lamaist northern Buddhism and the domain of eastern Buddhism in Japan (Nichiren sects).

This symbolic color attains its greatest effect in landscape in the gilded religious buildings of southern Buddhism, as for example on top of the seventy-meter white stucco Ruwanweli dagoba, the "Golddust Dagoba" of Anuradhapura in Ceylon, or the high pagodas (dagobas) of Burma, including the Shwe Dagon in Rangoon, which rises to 112 meters, the highest tower of light in Buddhism, and spreads the rays of Enlightenment and the Doctrine far into the landscape. The gilded Kuthodaw pagoda at Mandalay is surrounded by 729 smaller white pagodas. This evident superordination of gold over white clearly demonstrates our idea that gold symbolizes more the radiant light, and white, on the other hand, the diffuse light. Instead of being gilded, however, pagodas may also be left white, in accordance with the interchangeability of gold and white. Northern Buddhism, too, develops the magic of glistening golden roofs on the temples of the Lama monasteries of Kumbum and Sera, or on the Potala at Lhasa, where the highest ceremonies of the golden church, in the seat of the Dalai Lama, rise to a festive symphony in gold and yellow. It is understandable, I am convinced, from the nature

of this religion of enlightenment, why so many statues of "the Enlightened one" and "the Light of the World"—from the smallest to the greatest sitting and standing figures, giant "rock-Buddhas" over fifty meters high, and countless bodhisattvas—are either white, or partly or entirely gilded.

The more abstract Islam has also not renounced the festiveness of this symbol of light, and has crowned many mosques and mausoleums, especially Shiite ones, with golden cupolas, as for example in Karbala (Iraq), Qum, or Mashhad, and other places in Persia. It is easily understood that the Christian world religion, whose founder made himself known as the "Light of the World," puts golden cupolas, spires, crosses, or weathervanes on top of its churches; thence, too, comes the golden halo, the aureole in pictures of Christ and the saints. It is also not by accident that high and lofty, vaulted and spired religious structures are, by preference, gilded, and especially their upper parts and tips (pagodas, cupolas, spires), because only they can fully develop the splendor of gold, especially against the background of a blue sky. If such gold cupolas shimmer faintly even in diffuse light, in bright sunlight they sparklingly reflect the rays in all directions, and appear to the faithful like the light of promise.

Red as a symbolic color is much older in culture history than yellow, and follows just after white in its ceremonial religious significance. Red is the ancient color symbol for fire, the glow of the sun, and, as the color of blood and the life fluid, it became the symbolic color for life. Because of its stimulating effect, it also became the symbolic color of love and joy. Red and white are therefore often employed together in ceremonial symbolism, and red, like yellow (gold), may substitute for or even replace white, as the nature-religions, such as shamanism and the higher religions of interior and eastern Asia that it underlies, especially Shinto, clearly demonstrate. Red therefore appears noticeably in the landscape as a color of ceremonial garments, buildings, and ritual decor, and, with a metallic luster, especially in copper implements. The shamans in the Mongolian Altai wear red caps, the Singhalese in Ceylon employ red and white in temple processions, and the Jaray (Moi) forest folk of Southeast Asia have graveposts painted red and white.[5] The great Shiva temple in Madurai (South India) with gate-towers over fifty meters high covered with figures of the gods, which once shone with many colors under the tropical sun, is surrounded by an outer wall painted with red and white perpendicular stripes; and in Banaras on the steep banks of the holy Ganges stands the lovely Durga temple, with three red towers rising into the tropic heavens. In Chinese universism, red is the symbolic color of the overhead noonday sun, and so of the *yang* as the bright, warm, heavenly, manly, and creative principle. Here red is the color symbol of joy and happiness. Hence, in Peking red walls surround the sanctuary of heaven and the Forbidden City of the emperor. The red of the south-facing façades of many Chinese temples shines in the landscape. In Japan's Shinto, many shrines and archgates (*torii*) have either the sacred natural white color of hinoki wood, as at the great shrine of Ise, or the red ceremonial color, like all Inari shrines and the *torii* belonging to them, as well as the sacred bridges that lead to the sanctuaries of Nikko. The same is true of the "red arrow gates" and the red-painted wooded pillars of Buddhist religious structures in Korea.[6] Lamaism, saturated with the demonic and magical lore of the Bon religion, has conserved the ancient ceremonial red color of shamanism until today in the "Red Church." *Chortas* (stupas) in white and red enliven holy places. The white exterior walls of the haughty monkish castles are trimmed above with a wide horizontal frieze of red, with red corner posts and red pennants.[7] In Lhasa, on a base of glistening white buildings, the Red Palace of the Dalai Lama, with golden roofs, rises into the dark blue highland sky.[8] These structures served as models for the monasteries of the Red Church far northward, as far as the source region of the Yenisei in Tuva. In ancient Greece, according to Plutarch, the gods were decorated with red on feast days; the same color was also used for the priestly garb and ritual tent, or ark of the covenant, of the Jewish pastoral nomads. In the Roman Catholic Church, red serves as the symbolic color of love and of blood on the feast of the Holy Ghost and the "sorrowful" feasts of Christ and the Martyrs; it is also used as a ceremonial cult-adornment outside religious buildings during processions, particularly on Corpus Christi.

A much more modest role is played by the cult-color blue in the landscape. It became the symbolic color for heaven, air, and wind, and also for the breath—and so, because of its psychological effects, the color symbol of the spiritual, ineffable, secret, and eternal, of the irrational and metaphysical. But blue has always kept its ancient meaning as a magical defense against the Evil Eye, not only in the ancient Egyptian religious cult, but also in the Babylonian star religion. In the Babylon of Nebuchadnezzar (605–562 B.C.), the high walls of the Ishtar Gate and the side walls of the 300-meter procession street leading to it were covered with dark blue glazed tiles, and on the highest platform of the 90-meter cubic tower, the supreme sanctuary of the city's god, Bel-Marduk, 15 meters high and blue in color, was widely visible over the holy city. Since in Chinese color symbolism blue corresponds to heaven and the east, certain parts of religious

[5] Georg Buschan, *Illustrierte Völkerkunde* (Stuttgart: Strecker & Schröder, 1923), II, 927.

[6] Hermann Lautensach, "Religion und Landschaft in Korea," *Nippon: Zeitschrift für Japanologie*, VII (1942), 204–19.

[7] Sven Hedin, *Transhimalaja* (3 vols.; Leipzig: F. A. Brockhaus, 1909–12), II, 348, with color plate. [English edition, 2 vols.; New York: Macmillan, 1909–13.]

[8] Ernst Schäfer, *Geheimnis Tibet* (Munich: F. Bruckmann, 1943), p. 178, plate 31.

buildings are covered with blue glazed bricks or tiles, as on the floors of the top three terraces of the Heavenly Altar, the triple roof of the temple of the Good Year, and the red encircling wall of the Celestial Sanctuary in Peking. In Lhasa, too, the blue glazed tile roofs of Chinese houses stand out from those of the Tibetans. In Islam, blue monastic cowls symbolize in their color the turning of the soul toward heaven, and in Islamic religious architecture, especially that of the Saljuq period, blue shades predominate, as is shown in the minarets of the great Musallah of Herat, Afghanistan, built in 1212, or the cobalt blue of the Sunnite "Blue Mosque," in Tabriz, Persia.

In all the Mediterranean region, and in western Asia and India, blue has served from ancient times till now as the color for defense against the Evil Eye, as has been noted, so that here not only do many people wear turquoise jewelry—any jewelry is in the final analysis developed from the use of magic amulets—but domestic animals too, like the holy zebus in India, go around through the streets of the cities with necklaces of blue glass beads. In Asia Minor in 1934 I saw even droshki-horses with from one to five blue strings of beads around their necks and on other parts of their harness, and indeed even automobiles with blue beads on the front of the radiator.

Still less are the significance and employment of the cult color green. As the color of the plant world it is symbolic of reawakening life and growth, of creation and also of heavenly rebirth. It is effective especially in seasonally cold or dry countries having a fall of leaves, where it contrasts with the color of the surroundings. In ancient Egypt, where the contrast between the fertile green of the Nile Valley and the ocher-colored steppe or red of the sand desert springs to mind, green things were considered "blessed," in contrast to those of red color, which was despised.[9] Similar landscape differences in the predominantly

⁹ Adolf Erman, *Die Religion der Ägypter* (Berlin and Leipzig: W. de Gruyter, 1934), p. 39.

steppe-like area of Islam's distribution may have contributed to the fact that, along with white, green has become a main characteristic color of that religion. Green is even today the color of the prophet's flag, and the main color of all Islamic peoples. Often the roofs of the mausoleums and towers of shrines, the *Turbes*, are green, like the 30-meter conical tiled roof of the funereal tower of the "Green Turbe" in Konya or Bursa in Asia Minor. In the realm of Christendom, Maytime green must also be taken in account as a religious decoration, and also the Christmas tree. We should also take account of the roofs, cupolas, and spires of churches and mortuary buildings, clothed with a patina of copper or malachite green, like those that so strikingly characterize, or once characterized, the urban scene of Munich, Hanover, or Lubeck.

In contrast to all the ceremonial colors so far discussed, black seldom occurs as a ceremonial color on religious buildings, but on the other hand it appears commonly in ceremonial clothing out of doors. As the color of darkness, of the night, it becomes symbolic of the underworld, the earthly, and dark depths of the waters, and thus of spiritual and moral darkness, of what is evil and false, of the impure and the imperfect, of sin and all the divinities and powers ("black magic") connected with it. This contrast with the white and yellow (or gold) of what is heavenly and bright has since ancient times found its classical expression in the light-and-darkness doctrine of Zarathustra. In all religious cults, therefore, black animals are sacrificed to the gods and powers of the underworld, according to the rule of sympathetic magical affinities. In China, black is the symbol color of the night, of winter and the north, of *Yin*, which as the principle of dark and cold, earthy and damp, female and passive is opposed in a thoroughgoing polarity to the bright, light *Yang* principle of the south (red or white). Magical protection must be sought or produced against the harmful power of the *Yin*, as through the provision of protective groves, trenches, or artificially built defensive hillocks (for instance the so-called "Hill of Ashes" in front of the north gate of the Forbidden City of the "Son of Heaven," the emperor in Peking.)[10] Since black and darkness decrease visibility and cause unclarity, they also generally become the symbolic color of backwardness and obscurity, and thus of suffering, expiation, and grief, already appearing among the Greeks and the Romans and the early Christians, the latter of whom only later suppressed the original white mourning color in the rest of Europe. Thence black became the color of mourning in the world-wide reaches of Christendom, where, in funeral processions and feasts of mourning, and especially in churchly days of mourning and feasts of the dead, it marks the scene of graveyards and the neighborhood of churches and their approaches by the presence of people clad in black. In accordance with the precepts of Islam, and on the basis of the segregation and exclusion from public view of women, women's clothing worn outside the house is dark, mostly a great brown or black mantle with a headdress or even a veil made of black horsehair. For this reason, the daily street scene in Islamic settlements is strikingly distinctive. Besides blue and brown, black also belongs to the preferred colors of the enamel decorations used by the Saljuqs on the outer walls of mosques.

CEREMONIAL SOUNDS

All religions having an orderly form of general or at least simultaneous worship (religious communes) employ in greater or lesser degree certain characteristic ceremonial sounds, not only during religious services themselves, but also in the periodic announcement of the beginning and end of religious services and seasons. These ceremonial sounds are important for the geography of religions only when they ring through the countryside and so characterize the landscape. This audible ceremonial landscape must also be considered in a comprehensively planned regional or cultural geographic account, even if only briefly.

In nature-religions, ceremonial defensive noises from human voices (yells) or from objects (rattling, creaking, clacking, popping, shooting, ringing, tolling, blowing, etc.) are used together as a means of scaring away all the things of earthly or unearthly nature that are regarded as alive, and particularly demons or ghosts that threaten man or his possessions with disease, the landscape with bad weather, or the heavenly bodies with extinction of their light. This ceremonial defensive noise has been preserved until today, mostly unconsciously, even in the higher religions, and plays a role in many ceremonial practices, like the tolling of bells during a storm, ringing bells at the transubstantiation, or all ritual shooting for processions (originally to ward off demons who wanted to disturb holy proceedings). Besides defensive noise, ceremonial music itself is widely used. The sounds of percussion instruments are more used for predominantly rhythmical activities, chiefly magical-religious dances, while those of string and wind instruments are used in predominantly melodical activities, symbolic services of worship, and church music proper. In connection with outdoor ceremonies and worship, processions, pilgrimages, burial rites, and so on the ritual music of the religions of all peoples and times is also brought into the landscape. In its effect on the landscape religious music is surely far behind the sounds used to announce services, which are supposed to be heard by as many adherents of the sect as possible, and therefore to reach as far as possible. The source of the sound, its loudness, and its location, are critical.

The most natural and the weakest sound for announcing services, the human voice of the one who calls to prayer from the rampart of the minaret (muezzin)—more like a song with a high nasal tone than a

[10] Wulf D. Castell, *Chinaflug* (Berlin: Atlantis-Verlag, 1938). pp. 64–65.

call—carries at most a few hunderd meters. According to press reports, in 1937 the
callers to prayer were replaced in some noisy
cities like Singapore by large loudspeakers
able to drown out street noise over almost
two kilometers. The call to prayer sounded
regularly five times every day from all
minarets is characteristic of all Moslem
settlements or sectors within the Islamic
realm. There is also the cannon-shooting
that announces the beginning and ending of
fasting every morning and evening in the
fast-month of Ramadan.

In the realm of Lamaism, besides the
dull tone of the shell trumpet, one hears,
especially from the monastery temple roofs
in Tibet, the tones of brass trumpets (up
to several meters long and reminiscent of
our wooden Alpine horns), which sound
deep and joyously through the surrounding
countryside, like the peals of an organ.[11]
The Mosaic religion also used the sound
of trumpets of burnished silver on the
"Trumpet Festival" or the "Sabbath of the
Blowing," especially at the beginning of
the sacred "Year of Jubilee": "In the day
of atonement shall ye make the trumpet
sound throughout all your land" (Lev.
25:9). But the ceremonial sounds of percussion instruments also have an effect in
the landscape, smaller, to be sure, with the
dull tones of the shaman's drum of nature-
religions than in the sounds from the drum
towers (*koro*) of Japan. The wooden resonator used by the earliest Christians is also
heard, preserved until today in the Christian convents of the East as a wooden or
metal disk, the small or large *semanterium*.
The sounds of such metal resonators as the
tomtom or gong, in East Asia or the Lamaist monasteries of inner Asia, resound far
and wide.

The ceremonial tones of the moving
metal resonator, the bell, are aimed at the
greatest effect over a distance. The bell is
ancient, and is attested from Babylon for
the ninth century B.C. It is also used in
East Asia. The giant 74-ton bell of the
main temple of the Chinzei-Ta sect, which

hangs in a bell-tower of the year 1618 amid
a temple grove in Kyoto and rises above
the noises of the city with is deep tones, is
famous. The combined effect of bells, giant
drums, and gongs around the Buddhist
cloisters in Korea is well described by
Lautensach.[12] The bell has experienced its
strongest development, though, in connection with Christian church life. The oldest
ritual use of bells, in the Christian monasteries of North Africa, is assigned to about
the year 500; from there they came to
southern Italy, whence, despite their early
defects and especially their lack of sonority,
they reached Gaul, Spain, and Britain in
the sixth century, and Germany in the seventh. Until the twelfth century church bells
were beehive-shaped, short, and thick; in
the thirteenth century they received—out
of the centuries-long search for the best
tone—the so-called "Gothic" or "German
rib," and thus the swinging form of bell
that has lasted until now. The sound of
medium-sized bells one meter in diameter
carries within a radius of at least two kilometers under favorable conditions (i.e.,
high tower, open belfry, and level country),
or even to five or six kilometers; indeed the
hardest peals can be audible up to ten kilometers away, so that the range of audibil-
ity of middle to large bells, like the "German Bell on the Rhine"—the bell of St.
Peter in Cologne cathedral—can reach
twenty kilometers. According to the peculiarities of the bells' sounds, the special features of their timbre and tone, their use of
major or minor key, their melodic or har-
monic pealing, the strength with which they
ring and the distance over which they can
be heard, and finally the whole way in
which the bells are rung, and other characteristics like the community of sounds in
the neighborhood, one might work out diagnostic differences by landscape and even
whole countries, for example Germanic and
Latin. The regular sound of bells on Sundays and feast days, and for special cult
and mourning festivals, characterizes the
landscapes of all of Christendom, and the

---

[11] Hedin, *op. cit.*, I, 39, 53, Fig. 5.

[12] Lautensach, *op. cit.*, p. 215.

additional ringing thrice daily for services, as well as the differing tones of special bells (the *Ave* bell, the transubstantiation bell, the bell for the dead) are especially noticeable in landscapes and countries influenced by the Roman Catholic creed. So the region of almost any religion, or the landscape through which its sounds ring becomes more or less unmistakable and recognizable, even for a blind man.

DIRECTIONS AND POSITIONS

Sacred directions or cult directions also belong to the essence of what is ceremonial and influential in the landscape. They dominate ceremonial space, and they not only influence the directions of prayer and movement but acquire great significance for the cultural landscape because of corresponding alignment of the main axes and outlooks of graves and religious buildings, sacred settlements, parts of towns, and finally even cities. Thus far this matter has received too little attention, or none at all, in cultural and regional geography.

Among all possible directions in space, the vertical upward direction of the glance or the head and also the whole body, plays a significant and general role as the direction of prayer. Upon its nature and effects, which Theodor Lipps studied deeply and presented in his book,[13] ultimately rests all cult of the heights, in the widest sense, as well as star and mountaintop cults, and the preference for tall religious buildings, from the simplest nature-religions to the world religions. The other class of sacred cardinal directions lies in the plane of the horizon, where two chief groups can be distinguished: ceremonial directions determined naturally, and those determined culturally. The naturally determined ones are set by extraterrestrial or earthly orientation points, the three major points on the sun's trajectory predominating in the first-named group. Among these, the rising place of the life-dispensing star of day in the

[13] Theodor Lipps, *Raumaesthetik und geometrisch-optische Täuschungen* (Leipzig: J. A. Barth, 1897).

east was so important that it acquired a prominent religious-ceremonial meaning as the most important point of orientation among all peoples. Upon this rests the ceremonial turning to the east, in prayer, sacrifices, or burials, beginning with the nature-religions and extending to the orientation of the main axes of religious buildings in Greece, Rome, Jerusalem, and many Christian churches. Alignment toward the south stands in second place, and plays such a vital role among the higher East Asiatic nature-religions, especially in the universism of the Chinese peasant folk worshipping the sky and earth, that we must speak here of a "southing" cult. The observance of the ceremonial north-south orientation of the main axes of religious buildings and whole settlements (for example in Peking) gives a special stamp to them because of the south-facing façades. Less important is the ceremonial alignment toward the setting sun, or "westing." Where the land of the dead is imagined to lie in the west, the dead are put into the grave facing westward. Thus the cities of the dead of the ancient Egyptians lie westward of the towns, and the cemeteries and funeral pyramids are on the west bank of the Nile. As against the ceremonial directions set by extraterrestrial reference points, those determined by terrestrial reference points have a more regional or local meaning. What determines their orientation is first of all sacred nature-places, which, because they can ultimately be reached, fix the directions also of pilgrimage trips and routes, (cf. the holy mountain of the gods, Kailas, across the sacred lakes in the Himalayas).

Alongside the naturally determined sacred directions, with more natural sanctity, the culturally determined ceremonial directions with more historical religious sanctity play a great, in fact by far the greatest, role. To them belong, in the areas of all religions, both isolated smaller holy places and graves of saints, stupas, religious buildings, and cemeteries, that fix a smaller or larger surrounding region as a point of orientation and pilgrimage, from the smallest local or district sanctuaries through the great national ones (like Karbala for the Shiites) and up to the greatest supreme sanctuaries of the world religions: Peking, Banaras, Lhasa, Jerusalem, Rome, and Mecca. Although all ceremonial directions aiming at extraterrestrial points run parallel to each other (east, south, and west orientation) and their goal points themselves are physically unattainable, all ceremonial directions aimed at a point on the earth, or a natural or cultural holy place, run together centripetally into their pole of orientation. They resemble, so to speak, the lines of a magnetic field. Thus we can aptly compare all direction-setting holy places with a ceremonial "pole," and the whole area of distribution belonging to and affected by it to a ceremonial "field of force," in which the sacred directions, as ceremonial "lines of force," seek their "pole." The areal extension of such a "field of force" then depends upon the strength, that is, the importance (kind and degree of sacredness) of its pole. While smaller or medium-sized sanctuaries can only influence a surrounding district corresponding to their importance, the great world sanctuaries, as centers of religions and major "poles," create gigantic "fields," and their "lines of force" stream through the whole realm if not beyond—e.g., the role of Mecca in the realm of Islam.

All sacred places, taken as a foreseen goal, can also be walked around and looked at from all sides, so that the direction of cult circulation, with or against the apparent direction of rotation of the starry heavens (and the sun), is added as a further orientation, depending upon whether sacred precepts demand that the sanctuary should lie to the right or the left of the one who goes around it, and whether a directional harmony or at least a correspondence of cult and cosmic motion (the way of the stars and the living way) need be sought or not. Circulation takes place in circles, spirals, or, in connection with climbing, in helical lines. The displacement of a histori-

cal and religious pole (e.g., that from Jerusalem to Mecca for the Moslems), or its obliteration (which seldom happens because of the power of persistence of an established holy place), or finally, and more commonly, the rise of a new place of pilgrimage through reports of miracles (e.g., Lourdes) causes a more or less strong change in the ceremonial "field of force," and thus in its sacred directions.

NUMBER, TIME, AND MOTION

The idea exists among all peoples that numbers, in addition to their value as a key to order, have a deeper symbolic meaning; they have a great influence in the life of culture as symbolic numbers. Especially significant for the geography of religions are the sacred numbers or cult numbers, which as the basis for the subdivision of ceremonial space (religious buildings and settlements) and especially of ceremonial time, and also activities (prayer and sacred dance movements, religious travel, etc.) deeply condition the general ceremonial life, and also have an effect, directly and indirectly, in the landscape. Without going further into the intriguing field of the significance of sacred numbers for the geography of religion, to say nothing of the history of symbolism and of religions, let it be noted here that certain numbers, mostly uneven ones, among the digits, especially three, five, and seven, have played a significant role both in nature-religions and higher religions since ancient times. This is true not only for Chinese universism, in which these numbers are attributed to the heavenly powers as being perfect, good, and manly (and in which the number of parts in religious edifices and groups of them is thoroughly determined, as for example the Heavenly Altar in Peking, with three circular terraces of which the proportions of diameters are the sacred $7:5:3$, with three-part ritual gates, three-story temple roofs, and so on), but also for the world religions. Just think about the significance of the numbers three and seven (the seven-day week!) in Mosaic, Islamic, and Christian religion, or of the number four and its multiples, especially eight, in Buddhism.

Sacred bodily movements, or cult movements, belong within the framework of a consideration of the geography of religions, as motion of the human body in time and space in so far as they take place in the open air. Ceremonial movements, along with ceremonial sounds, are the most important carriers of cult activity. They are strongly conditioned by sacred directions, numbers, and times, be they sacred bodily movements in the smallest space (e.g., the conduct of prayer), in somewhat larger areas (ceremonial dances), or in the largest spaces (i.e., religious travel or pilgrimages). In this case, too, only a few suggestions can touch on the major problems. In the whole area of the distribution of Buddhism, especially of northern Buddhism or Lamaism, the most prayer-centered religion ("Om mani padme hum"), the individual worshipper with his prayer devices (i.e., rosary or hand prayer wheel) and the prayer machines driven by wind or water (prayer drums) are an everyday phenomenon in both the monastic settlements and the open landscape. In the realm of Islam, every Moslem must, in conformity with the scriptures, perform his prayer ritual— not an easy one—five times a day, indoors or out, wherever he is, after first ceremonially purifying himself with "living" (i.e., running) water or, if necessary, clean sand. Spreading a prayer rug especially brought for the purpose, the Muslim faces toward Mecca, and must touch the ground with his forehead as he prays. Large masses of the white-clad faithful carrying out their prayer ritual together, with the precision of well-drilled soldiers, in the streets or open spots in front of mosques and other holy places, present a truly impressive picture. But praying movements are also brought into the landscape in the realm of Catholic Christianity, through kneeling, genuflection, or removal of the hat before country crosses, chapels, stations of the cross, and so on, along with the use of prayer devices (prayerbooks, rosaries), and prayers spoken and sung, especially at places of pilgrimage and in their neighborhood, by individuals, groups, or masses of people (processions, dancing processions, pilgrimage, funerals). Even more impressive are the movements in performance of ceremonial dances, mostly much livelier, and often accompanied by ritual music. They contribute, even though usually in but modest degree, to the enlivenment of the nearby surroundings at religious activities and festivals, from the magical religious charm-dances of the shamans in the areas of nature-religion to the symbolic and reverent temple dances in the regions of the world religions. Ceremonies in holy places and pilgrimage centers are especially enhanced by ritual dance costume and perhaps dance masks. The religious practices of all peoples have given rise to ceremonial dances; indeed, the colorful and artistic fantasy of India has given birth in the Brahma cult to a manifestation of the highest god, Shiva, in the form of the dancer-god, Nataraja ("lord of the cosmic dance"), who destroys and always re-creates the world. He is so represented in Indian ritual art.

Ceremonial movement as progressive movement, i.e., cult traffic proper from that in small spaces up to long-range pilgrim travel, requires a detailed discussion in itself, which can best follow only after a discussion of the goals of the traffic (natural and cultural holy places).

The same holds for sacred times, or ceremonial times, dedicated to the moments in life that are significant to man (birth, puberty, marriage, death), to the cycle of the year (e.g., solstices), to agriculture (e.g., planting, growth, harvest), or to the commemoration of particular historical religious personalities or events. They are founded on the need of man for magical intervention in natural processes (defense or furtherance), or for symbolic veneration of the divinity through the interruption of active work and the establishment of religious and secular holidays for the purpose of inner recollection, edification, and momentary respite. They all produce a temporary growth and intensification of ceremonial religious life, and have a noticeable effect in ceremonial settlement, traffic, and economy. According to the length of the ceremonial seasons, the beginning, middle, and end of which are usually denoted by typical ceremonial sounds, we can distinguish: sacred times of day (like the five praying times of Muslims, with their calls to prayer, and the three praying times of Catholics, announced by tolling bells); sacred days, including certainly the regularly recurring weekly day of rest (the Jewish sabbath, Christian Sunday, Islamic Friday, etc.), and the sometimes variable feast days of the year of many religions (for example, the Christmas, Easter, and Pentecost festivals of Christians); sacred weeks (Christian Holy Week and the Chinese New Year's feast); sacred months (the October "Month of the Gods" in the Shinto province of Idzumo, or the Islamic fast-month of Ramadan); and sacred years (e.g., the "Horse Year" every twelve years for the Hindus and Tibetans, the Jewish "Year of Jubilee" every fifty years, and the Catholic *Anno Santo* every twenty-five years). Not only the content but also the name of the sacred times have to do mostly with their holy character; the names of the days refer to heavenly bodies and divinities (the sun, the moon, Mars, Zeus, Donar, Freya, etc.), and the beginning of calendrical reckoning is often, as among the Jews, Christians, or Moslems, fixed by occurrences in the history of religions. The profane work year stands in contrast to the cult, or church, year.

Sacred times, depending on the way and width of ceremonial, have uncommonly abundant effects, both in settlement (for instance, often through a complete alteration of the normal settlement structure, not only at the sacred places themselves but also in the other settlements of the whole area as well) and in ceremonial traffic, through a powerful increase in local

and long-distance cult travel. But even economic life is more or less strongly influenced by sacred times. The ceremonial economy that works directly for the needs of the cult (for instance industries built around Christmas or pilgrimages) is fostered; the rest of the economy is, indirectly, both fostered and hindered, according to the sort of ecclesiastical significance of sacred times and the strictness of their observance (e.g., reduction of work, or bans on work), their duration, number, and distribution through the year. If, for instance, in the area of higher East Asiatic nature-religions, the regular weekly day of rest is lacking, and there is only the twelve-day Chinese New Year's festival in its place, as against the fifty-two Sundays and the average fifteen other holidays—a total of about sixty-five non-working days—in the Christian Year, then such differences make themselves highly prominent in economic life. The same is true for the realm of Islam, where in addition there is a great disturbance of the whole productive system during the fast-month of Ramadan. In the realm of Catholic Christianity, the ninety prescribed fast-days of the year (fifty-two Fridays and about forty days of fast before Easter) influence certain branches of the economy through increased demand for fasting-foods, especially fish and snails. We can make only an allusion here to the ecclesiastical origin of markets and fairs and note that church fairs and trade fairs arose in the twelfth and thirteenth centuries.

Landscape and Ceremonial

We have already seen by many examples in how many different ways the religious ceremonial theme can be connected with the phenomena of existence. The most important of these connections, for our problem, are the linkages between religion and landscape. From the first, the sacred has been implicit in the natural landscape, both in single landscape features (e.g., mountains, waters, groves) and in whole landscapes. The veneration of single landscape features or sacred places in nature is based on their individual peculiarity and distinctiveness, which strikingly set them off from their surroundings in their whole being, and in their symbolic manifestation, according to form, color, size, potency, etc. This property can be enhanced by position in the landscape, chiefly through individualization; so that each such presence, self-contained, rounded off, reposing island-like unto itself and visible if possible in a single glance, is favored by holiness in the widest and narrowest sense: the arresting lonely cliff or mountain peak in surroundings of a different sort, a lake in a lonesome forest, steppe, or mountain landscape, a solitary isle amid broad waters, an island of woods in the steppe, or a clearing in the forest, and so on. In addition, peculiarity, remoteness, loneliness, and especially inaccessibility, favor the sanctity of places in nature. Space forbids me to go further into the deeper aspects of nature-sacredness and the very stimulating matter of the religious ideas involved. Let me only recall what was said about the nature of sanctity and sanctification, and about the "fields of force" and ceremonial "pole." Many transitions and types exist between the demonic and the festive, holy, transfigured landscapes and parts of landscapes.

The heavenly bodies beyond the earth, the constellations, as visible parts of the unclouded heavens by night and by day, and venerated as sacred, also play a large role. Not only have they, as remarked above, indirectly promoted the veneration of sacred lights, fires, colors, directions, numbers, and movements, and especially the subdivision of ceremonial times—or even inspired these things—but they have also evoked a widely distributed star cult (e.g., the Babylonian star religion and Chinese universism), for the service of which there are special cult buildings (temple-observatories, sun and moon temples, altars of heaven, and so on). We can go no further into this matter, or the veneration of smaller sacred nature-places of the earthly landscape—sacred cliffs, stones, caves, and such; only the cults of sacred mountains,

waters, plants, and animals, with some of their effects for the geography of religions, can be briefly described.

The veneration of sacred mountains (the mountain cult) is the main form of all veneration of high places. In all religions mountains play a greater role than all the rest of natural sanctuaries together, and their cult has such an effect in the landscape that it is surprising that it has not long since received a special comprehensive geographic treatment, like what was done on the ethnological side in the work of Ferdinand von Adrian.[14] The origin of the veneration of mountains lies in the nature of mountains in general, in their numerous individualities in particular, and, to be sure, in their significance for the bodily and especially the spiritual life of men, as Ferdinand von Richthofen noted.[15] Striking mountain shapes, particularly the profiles of peaks, which may recall geometric or other significant cult-symbolic figures, have much to do with their degree of sanctity: round or bell-shaped summits (e.g., Mount Tabor in Palestine), pyramids (*kailas*), sharp points (e.g., Adam's Peak), or cones (e.g., Mount Fuji). Other features of significance are similarity to animate bodies or their parts (e.g., human heads or birds' wings) or pertinence to other cult features such as sacred numbers (for example, three or five, in China—*Wu Tai Shan* is "the five-finger mountain"); these characters may be accentuated by impressive coloring, accumulations of snow, or frequent envelopment in cloud (the holiest sacred color being white), along with great relative height over the visible landscape, which is of more importance in this case than absolute height above sea level; and they may even be set off by fire, as are volcanoes. Since the most ancient times mountains have been considered a seat of the gods, wrapped

[14] Ferdinand von Andrian, *Der Höhencultus asiatischer und europäischer Völker* (Vienna: C. Koneger, 1891).

[15] Ferdinand von Richthofen, *Vorlesungen über allgemeine Siedlungs- und Verkehrsgeographie* (Berlin: D. Reimer, 1908), p. 107.

in mystery—especially of the bright and heavenly gods and powers toward whom men looked upward from below, and who gazed down upon men, blessing them. The Babylonians conceived of the earth as a "mountain of many lands" sticking up into the heavens, upon the peak of which the highest god of Heaven, Enlil, sat enthroned. This world-mountain motif became the basis for the stepped-temple tower in ancient Babylon, as well as for the stepped roofs and pyramids of southeast Asia, where the holy mountain, Meru, as the "world mountain," forms the basis for the entire higher religious architecture. In Israelite religion holy mountains (Sinai, Nebo, Hermon, Lebanon, Zion, Olives, Carmel, and Tabor) also play a large role; their veneration is echoed in many places in the Bible, and receives its finest expression in the beginning of the 121st Psalm: "I will lift up mine eyes unto the hills, from whence cometh my help."

The veneration of mountains is expressed either in avoiding the sacred mountain or in frequenting it, befitting the degree and manner of its sanctity. The avoidance of the holy (i.e., dangerous) upper portion, especially the summit—where the peace and purity of the divinity may not be disturbed without punishment—is then a religious cult prohibition, representing an inviolability and unapproachability either imposed by the nature of the peak (i.e., snowy pinnacles that are hard to climb) or freely elected. The prohibition also applies to airplane flights over the peak; a report of a planned flight over Mount Everest, the sacred Chomolungma (Valley of the Gods) by two English airplanes raised a great stir in India and Tibet in 1934. In such cases, European mountaineering expeditions can recruit no native guides, or can get them only with difficulty or under certain reservations, and are not permitted to lay out shelter huts or religious structures. On the other hand, sanctifying holiness causes frequenting of the mountain and a regular pilgrim traffic to, around, and up the mountain, especially to the summit. The ceremo-

nial circle tour around a mountain (circle pilgrimage) at its foot or on the lower slopes (e.g., on Kailas),[16] or ceremonial mountain climbing—the peak pilgrimage—then becomes a cult command, and for certain congregations a religious duty. An example is the pilgrimage to the summit of the most sacred mountain of Japan, Fuji San (3,778 meters) which is carried out every year by many thousands of white-clad pilgrims, and is the main ceremonial activity of the Fuji-Ko brotherhood. A plan for a funicular railway to the summit was angrily rejected throughout Japan in 1936 as a desecration of the holy mountain. The Ontake brotherhood, also, is said to have three million members, seventy thousand of whom yearly make a pilgrimage to the peak of Ontake (3,063 meters) during the period from mid-July to mid-September.

The mountain cult attains its greatest effectiveness in the landscape where it leads to the construction of religious structures, either on mountains themselves as mountain sanctuaries on their feet, slopes, or peaks, or else in the immediate neighborhood. These sanctuaries may be archgates (*torii*), chapels, summit crosses, graves, temples, or monasteries, mostly with adjoining dwelling houses and work buildings. The mountain sanctuaries of the four Buddhist and the five ancient Chinese holy mountains in China, covered with temple and monastery sites and visited the year round by flocks of pilgrims from all parts of the country, offer magnificent examples,[17] as do the cloister-dotted Diamond Mountains in central-northeast Korea,[18] and especially the numerous Tibetan monasteries at the feet, on the slopes, and upon the peaks of mountains, such as those on Kailas, Chomolungma (Everest), or Minya Gongkar.

The veneration, or cult, of sacred waters

[16] Hedin, *op. cit.*, II, 164–67.
[17] Ernst Boerschmann, *Baukunst und Landschaft in China: eine Reise durch zwölf Provinzen* (Berlin: E. Wasmuth, 1926), pp. x–xiii.
[18] Lautensach, *op. cit.*, p. 213.

is less important than the mountain cult, but it also plays a notable role in all religions and has abundant direct and indirect pertinence in the geography of religions. There is no geographic writing on this, and the cultural sciences offer only skimpy summaries. The origin of water-veneration has many roots, and all can be explained by the critical meaning of water for all life, as a beneficial and destructive element of nature, and for spiritual life in particular; it has something unfathomable and mysterious about it, so that all peoples attribute a high magical and symbolic significance to it (cf. Goethe's "Der Fischer" and "Gesang der Geister über den Wassern"). So water has an important meaning in religious life simply as a substance: in the water cult as a magical-religious material ("magical water") and as a means of transmitting sacredness; as baptismal water and religious miracle water (e.g., water from the Ganges or the Jordan, from Mecca, Lourdes) and a means of purification in ritual washing; and in the landscape as holy springs (cf. the cult of springs) as well as sacred bodies of water (with their cult). There is no space here to go deeper into the matter of the fascinating symbolic significance of flowing and standing waters (e.g., the cults of rivers and lakes). Standing waters are generally considered a symbol of peace and womanliness, and flowing ones, on the contrary, symbols of movement and of manhood. In contrast with the veneration of heights and summits in the landscape, which stand for masculinity and the Apollonian principle of light, the veneration of waters can be characterized as a cult of what is deep and wide, embodying in symbol what is moist and female, the chthonian principle of earth and night.

Like the cult of high places, the water cult, according to the manner and degree of its sacredness, brings about either avoidance or frequenting of sacred waters. Avoidance, in many nature-religions, effects a cultural prohibition on any kind of alteration of the natural waters through such activity as adding embankments, divert-ing or rerouting of streams, or fishing and travel (e.g., on almost all the lakes of inner Asia); thus there is a ceremonial-religious "protection" of the waters. For example, on a winter crossing of the frozen Kosso Gol, the largest lake in Mongolia, the Tuvan native always used to carry some container for performing his biological necessities, in order not to desecrate the sacred lake. Women, who in nature-religions are often considered "impure," have to stay away from the banks of the sacred waters.[19] Indeed the Toba Lake in northwestern Sumatra was considered so sacred by the natives that it could not be looked upon by any stranger.[20] On the other hand, the frequenting of sacred waters calls for the closest possible contact with them, and brings into being the many sacred and healing "miracle waters," ritual baths in holy rivers (e.g., Ganges and Jordan), lakes, and artificial bathing pools (as in the temple baths of ancient Egypt and India), and ritual washing in "living" water —that is, running water and the flowing springs connected with them, as in Islam and Shinto. The sacredness of the Ganges attracts countless pilgrims to Banaras, who take their ceremonial baths of purification there, on the ghats along the banks, making the pilgrimage in the evening of life or being brought as corpses to be burned and have their ashes scattered in the holy streams (cf. also the water burials in eastern Tibet). This is also the basis for all sorts of construction on the banks of sacred waters (e.g., cult buildings, temples, monasteries and graves, of which there are numerous examples in most religions), miniature replicas of sacred lakes in artificial holy pools, grave-pools in ancient Egypt and India (at Taj Mahal), temple, church, or chapel pools (in Egypt, India, Christendom, and the Moslem world) and finally the monastery pool (in Buddhist and Christian countries, in the latter case

[19] Leimbach, *op. cit.*, pp. 55, 68, 78, 88, 91.
[20] K. Helbig, "Sichtbare Religion im Batakland auf Sumatra," *Zeitschrift für Ethnologie*, LXV (1934), 231.

serving also an economic-ceremonial end:
fish for fast-days). Water and bodies of
water not only can confer blessings, but in
most religions may also be blessed. We can
cite the water-blessing of the Mongols, or
that of Greek Catholics on January 6
(Epiphany), which includes even the
"Blessing of the Sea" at the harbor of
Piraeus—the inspiration, perhaps, of the
"Marriage of the Doge with the Sea" in
medieval Venice. There is no space here to
deal even briefly with these subjects or with
the meaning of sacred islands.

SACRED PLANTS AND ANIMALS

A short discussion of the religious-geographic significance of sacred plants (plant
cult), cannot be passed over. In all religions, plants enter into ceremonial life for
magical ends, for symbolic worship, or for
festive decoration. Both single plants, intact or as parts (e.g., root, stem, twig, leaf,
flower), and groups of plants may be venerated as sacred, and protected. Among
them are plants that exhibit ceremonially
important symbolic colors (red, yellow,
white, etc.), symbolic shapes—for instance
the ray form of many Compositae as a
symbol of the sun—or pleasant odors, and
some even combine several such symbolic
properties. This applies especially to the
lotus blossom. The lotus sends its stem up
from the muddy dark bottom into the
bright surface of the water and here brings
to blossom in a single night its large white
flower, with golden stamens, a symbol of
the rising sun and purity. For this reason
it was sacred already in ancient Egypt and
was used architecturally in lotus column-
capitals, as well as in the Babylonian-As-
syrian louts frieze and in India, where it
became the seat and attribute of several
divinities (Brahma, Vishnu, and Ganesha,
among others). Buddha, too, the "Pure
One" born into the impure world, is so
commonly represented as sitting in the
lotus blossom in religious contemplation,
with various gestures (*mudras*), that
"Buddha in the Lotus" has become by far
the most important and widespread symbol

and cult image in Buddhism and is spread
over the gigantic area of Buddhist influence
in the earth's most frequently spoken and
spun-out prayer, "Om mani padme hum."
Thus the next-to-the-last incarnation of
Buddha, the sacred young white elephant,
is commonly pictured standing in the lotus
blossom, as are the numberless disciples,
the boddhisattvas, and the Kwannon statues in Japanese Buddhism.

Still more important than sacred flowers
are sacred trees and the cult of trees. In
north Asiatic nature-religions the birch, because of its white bark, is especially venerated and is used in shamanistic rites of
exorcism. This is also true of the sacred
conifer, hinoki (*Chamaecyparis obtusa*
S. & Z.), with the white wood of which the
most important sanctuaries of Shinto—the
shrines of Ise and many others, with accompanying arch-gates (*torii*)—are constructed. In one of the imperial forests in
the same Kiso Mountains where the sacred
pilgrimage-mountain Ontake is located, in
an area of mixed woods about eighty-five
square kilometers in extent that has long
been strictly guarded and is destined purely
for the Ise sanctuary, the *Chamaecyparis*
logs best-suited for the rebuilding of the
shrine that takes place every twenty years
are raised. With much ceremony, they are
selected according to strict ritually prescribed measurements (sacred numbers!)
and flawless proportions of growth (appropriate to the flawlessly pure sun goddess
Amaterasu) and are shipped to Ise.[21] The
sakaki-bush (*Cleyera japonica*) is also sacred to Shinto, and its smaller branches are
used in many ceremonies. Handsome old
specimens of the sugi, a needle-leaf tree,
and of *Cryptomeria,* five to six meters in
circumference and with trunks forty-five
meters tall, surround the temples and line
the avenues approaching them, for instance
in the world-renowned *Cryptomeria lane,*
35 kilometers in length, between Kanuma
and the temple landscape of Nikko, 120

[21] *Goryorin Taikan* (Survey of the Imperial
Forests) (Tokyo, 1934), pp. 192–98, Figs. 1–7,
and map. In Japanese.

kilometers north of Tokyo. Another illustration is provided by the giant camphor trees of Nagasaki's temple groves. The Indian fig (*Ficus indica* and *F. bengalensis*) is sacred to the Brahmin Hindus, and Buddhists revere the mango (*Mangifera indica*), with its panicles of white flowers, and particularly the sacred fig tree (*F. religiosa*)—the Bodhi or Bo-tree (*bo-gaha*)—under which Buddhi attained *sambodhi,* the highest stage of enlightenment. The latter tree grows wild in the Himalayan forests, but its plantings have been carried with Buddhism to many cult centers as far south as Ceylon and as far north as Japan. The Singhalese of Ceylon plant the so-called temple tree (*Plumeria acutifolia* Pori) and the ironwood tree (*Mesua ferrea* L.) for their pleasantly scented white flowers, which are sacrificed by predilection in the temples.[22] How much religion can sometimes influence the nature and composition of a plant community is shown by the occurrence of the decoratively white-flower-crowned teak tree (*Tectona grandis*) in Siam; although it ordinarily grows there only in the tropical mixed monsoon forest, it enters into the composition of formations in the holy groves that are connected with former or still standing Buddhist temple centers, and that therefore certainly arose through artificial planting.[23] The evergreen spruce was dedicated in Greece to Poseidon, and it was also sacred to the Germans. As a solstice-feast and Christmas festival tree, connected with the cult of the light that is victorious over the evil forces of darkness and midwinter, it lives on, though in an altered form, as our Christmas tree[24]—seven million of which used to sparkle each

winter in Germany alone, making the city streets and squares green for weeks. After what has just been said, we might distinguish between the more independent individual trees that were holy and venerated in themselves, like most impressive isolated trees in the regions of nature-religion, for instance the Donar-oaks in Germany, and the less autonomous sacred "companion" trees that are linked especially with religious buildings (temples and monasteries) or graves; but here there are many intermediate stages.

Still more than the single sacred tree, groups of three or more holy trees, and even more holy natural forests (especially virgin forests) or lighter, natural or artificially planted sacred groves, have moved men to veneration. The twilight mood and stirrings that prevail in the forest make it so fit as a resort of demons, gods, and spirits that it fills the imagination of primitive man with respect and dread, and even the adherent of the higher religions experiences a "pious shudder." For this reason certain independent groups of sacred trees and woods, or even whole forests in areas of nature-religions (e.g., shamanism) and pagan religions, like those of ancient Greece and Germany, tend to enjoy veneration and the protection of the cult. I am convinced that out of these ancient forests sanctuaries, in the course of time there probably arose all those subsidiary sacred groves that are laid out to accompany graves, temples, and monasteries, the ultimate meaning of which is enclosure within a magic circle for protection against the demons and other harmful powers. Therefore all of these sacred attached groves were originally magic protective groves, which only subsequently took over other functions as well, such as that of shutting out the noises of the world. Among them should be counted, for example, all the "town groves" in China which, following the geomantic Wind and Water Doctrine (*Fung Shui*), stand in and around settlements amid otherwise almost treeless surroundings. The second type in this category is the widespread cemetery

[22] Paul and Fritz Sarasin, *Ergebnisse naturwissenschaftlicher Forschungen auf Ceylon* (3 vols.; Wiesbaden: C. W. Kreidel, 1887–93), III, 25.

[23] R. Reinhard, "Die Tiekwälder und ihre Nutzung," *Wissenschaftliche Veröffentlichungen des Museums für Länderkunde zu Leipzig,* N.F., IV (1936), 27.

[24] Otto Laufer, *Der Weihnachtsbaum in Glauben und Brauch* (Berlin and Leipzig: W. de Gruyter, 1934), p. 24.

grove. The basic idea and the effect on the landscape are the same from the cemetery groves of antiquity (ancient Egypt), through the shamanistic funereal groves on high hills in the unforested portions of Siberia or Indonesia and the innumerable cemetery groves, grave-mound groves, and groves on emperors' graves in China—the only islands of forest enlivening the dreary expanse of the economic landscape—to the cemeteries and forested graveyards of Islam (cf. the cypress grove cemeteries in Eyup near Istanbul, or at Uskudar, and the mausoleum grove of the Taj Mahal), and of Christendom (e.g., the forest-cemeteries at Ohlsdorf near Hamburg, or at Munich). As a third type, the temple grove is widely distributed. In the Mediterranean area it already surrounded many cult centers in Greece, Rome, and Egypt in antiquity—for example, at Thebes in Egypt[25]—and it still surrounds with green most temples of the higher nature-religions of East and South Asia. To this category also belong the church and chapel groves in the realm of Christendom, like those of the morainic hill crests of the Alpine foreland in Upper Bavaria. As a fourth class associated with these we have the monastery grove, which affords not only magical protection against demons but exclusion of the noises of the world (*claustrum*) and the necessary peace for meditation, and so also becomes a "meditation grove." Since the days of Gautama Buddha, who experienced the highest enlightenment during inner meditation under the sacred Bodhi tree, and since the time of the first Buddhist forest communities and cloisters,[26] the monastery grove has become a widely visible landscape marker of the most pronounced monastic religion of the globe in the gigantic area of Buddhism. In contrast to these groves, the Christian monastery forests, such as those in Bavaria

(e.g., Ettal, Benedikbeuren, Tegernsee, or the great forest of the cloister of Niederaltaich), are very much economic forests, which no longer have anything to do directly with religious matters.[27] Out of sacred attached groves, probably, in the course of time there developed the gardens and parks that produced today's landscape gardens. We can go no further here into such questions as: the further effects of the plant cult for forest protection or reforestation, of which Hermann Lautensach brings a characteristic example from Korea;[28] the possibility of a botanic and plant geographic investigation of the present composition of the plant communities of forests protected by religion, and thus the possible reconstruction of the formerly much more widespread original forest cover of their near and even more distant surroundings and, indirectly, of their animal life; the significance of representations of plants in religious architecture and graphic arts for the former distributions of plants and the culture history of economic plants (pictures of bananas, for instance, on reliefs in Borobudur, or date palms in the religious art of ancient Sumeria and Egypt *ca.* 3000 B.C.).

The same holds true for the significance and effect, in the geography of religions, of the veneration of sacred animals (the cults of animals), about which one might write a whole book. Out of the overabundance of material and questions on this subject, let it be noted here only that the veneration of bears (bear cult) in northern Asia, culminating in the ceremonial "bear feast," and of the tiger in East and South Asia (tiger cult), can frequently lead to actual worship, invocation ("Tiger, help me . . . !"), and protection of the animal. The local overabundance of cattle-stealing tigers in northwestern Sumatra, resulting from this attitude, meant constant decimation of the draft animals necessary for

[25] Ermann, *op. cit.*, p. 197.

[26] Hermann Oldenberg, *Buddha: sein Leben, seine Lehre, seine Gemeinde* (6th ed.; Stuttgart and Berlin: J. G. Cotta, 1914), pp. 161–63, 408–16, 435. [English version; London: Williams & Norgate, 1882.]

[27] J. Kostler, "Geschichte des Waldes in Altbayern," *Münchener historische Abhandlungen,* VII (1934), 128.

[28] Lautensach, *op. cit.*, p. 210.

plowing, so that the Batak, for instance, had to go over from plow cultivation and *Sawah* ("wet rice") economy to hoe culture and *ladang* ("burning and dry rice") economy in many areas, a change that resulted in an extensive destruction of forests.[29] The veneration of animals has profound effects on the economy. Cattle, sheep, pigs, and horses must first have become domesticates because of the veneration of wild animals. Most prohibitions on the killing and eating of certain animals, like the cow in India (where there is a cow cult) or the pig among Jews and Moslems, are determined by ceremonial, for rejection originally occurs in such a case not because of the bodily impurity of the pig, but on account of its sacredness and its association with the divinities of vegetation in the pre-Mosaic cult and in the cults of the peoples geographically contiguous to the people of Israel, who had a preference for the pig as a sacrificial animal. "Impure" thus means the same here as "formerly sacred." Under the influence of Judaism, Islam also rejected the pig (cf. *Koran*, II, 168), and indeed even more rigorously, so that for a Moslem even touching a pig with one's body or clothing requires ritual purification, and the training and customs to which they have been used for centuries have created in many of the faithful a real natural antipathy, even a feeling of disgust.

In the avoidance of swine's flesh and pork fat by Jews and Moslems, the physical uncleanness of this omnivore,[30] the unwholesomeness and rapid spoilage of the fat encouraged by the subtropical climate, or such diseases of swine as trichinosis and redleg play a lesser role. This is shown by the way pork is prized among adherents of other religions who were and are distributed in the subtropics and even the tropics, and who have even stricter rules of ritual purity (e.g., the purity-religions

of the ancient Near East or Japanese Shinto). The fact that the full loss of the pig as an important domestic animal among about 260 million people was ultimately for cult reasons and not those of health is proved, furthermore, by the circumstance that among these very same pastoral nomads sacred sheep, and indeed the fat-tailed sheep bred specially for this purpose, have taken over as the source of animal fats.

The ancient bull cult that played a large role in Egypt (Apis), Babylon (cf. the ceremonial picture tiles of the Ishtar Gate), ancient Israel (cf. the Golden Calf), Greece (e.g., Dionysos), Rome (in the suovetaurilia and taurobolium), and ancient India, is still alive today in India. Here the bull is sacred to the wild and frightful god Shiva. There is no temple of Shiva in front of or within which Nandi, the holy bull, is not chiseled in stone, usually larger than life-size. The holy bulls of Shiva, with chains of glass beeds of the protective color of turquoise around their necks, wander about today unmolested through the streets of Banaras. If one or more of these sacred bulls or cows happen to lie down in the middle of a busy street, all traffic must carefully go around such "ceremonial barriers" or be routed over other streets. In 1935 the English authorities required the establishment of "cow-free streets," which aroused the opposition of the population. Not only are temples erected to sacred wild animals or their divinities, like the many tiger temples in eastern Asia but certain animals themselves are kept, alive, in temples (like the serpent and monkey temples of India), or at sanctuaries in temple groves or gardens, e.g., the Sika deer (*Pseudaxis sika* Temn. Schl.) in Japan. Our present-day zoos and animal parks have probably evolved from this religious cult.

More important is the role of animals in religious art, like the long double rows of more than life-size stone figures of animals that border the sacred approaches to graves (e.g., Chinese emperors' graves) or

[29] Helbig, *op. cit.*, pp. 234–35.
[30] B. W. Gebel, "Der Islam: die Religion der Wüste," *Beiheft zu dem Jahresbericht der Schlesischen Gesellschaft für vaterländische Kultur*, I (1922), 104–33.

temples (cf. the lane of rams in front of the Amon temple at Karnak, *ca.* 1250 B.C.), as magic protection, landmarkers, and signs of honor. The cult art of all religions, from the classical animal worship of ancient Egypt and India up to the representations of animals on Gothic cathedrals (gargoyles), offers countless examples. Among the birds, in most religious cults white water birds play the role of bearers of souls and omens or emissaries of the gods. But the cock has attained by far the greatest ceremonial meaning. Because of its early morning crowing, it is considered by most peoples of Eurasia to be the one who frightens away all night-prowling evil spirits and demons of the darkness and is the animal symbolic of the rising sun, the east, and manliness. For this reason cocks are not lacking in any Bonbo cult, and in east Tibet, because of the Buddhist prohibition of the use of meat (a consequence of the belief in reincarnation), and the ban on living things, cocks are kept only for their crowing.[31] The Chinese nature and ancestor cult has also taken them in. Indeed, in China no coffin is without a living white cock as watcher of the dead and frightener of demons.[32] Thus it plays the same role as the gilded metal cock looking far out into the landscape from the tips of many Christian church steeples.

PROTECTED LANDSCAPES

The sacred portions of the landscapes, so far considered separately for methodological reasons, often or even mostly occur bound up together, that is, a sacred countryside may be linked with holy waters, fire, or plants, in every possible way (like a "sacred island" and "sacred fishes" with a "sacred lake," or a "holy grove" or "sacred fire" with "holy mountains" and so forth). In this case, sacredness is not restricted to separate small places in nature, but may extend (through the impor-

tant religious principle of contagious sanctification) to neighboring portions of the landscape and perhaps beyond. Such sacred natural landscapes then become religiously determined nature-protection areas, which represent regular islands of undisturbed nature in the midst of the economic landscapes more or less transformed by man. They are known especially from the areas of the nature-religions, for which I introduce a typical example from Todja at the confluence of the Bei-kem in the upper basin of the Yenisei:

In Todja two areas are holy, with boundaries marked by trees and stones draped with different colored ribbons (offerings to the souls that live in this district). These protected areas, where hunting and woodcutting are strictly forbidden, insure that the deer will not be exterminated. It is likewise forbidden to relieve oneself and so commit a desecration. Therefore the Tuvans avoid these areas. Generally every peak sticking out of the woods is also sacred, and the divinity living on especially holy mountains watches over the game preserve and punishes whoever trespasses on it. It is a sin even to give any information about sacred mountains.[33]

The examples could be multiplied from other areas of nature-religion in the interior, eastern, and southern parts of Asia. For example, the American scholar H. M. Smith explored a mountain range in Siam that was avoided by the natives, who considered it to be inhabited by nature spirits; in this peculiar nature preserve he found a rich fauna, with many rare and even some unknown birds. Pre-Islamic Arabia also had holy places and natural areas (*haram, hima*), where a permanent truce of God prevailed, and no animals could be hunted or no wood cut. Whoever entered a *haram* area had to subject himself besides to certain restrictive rules regarding clothing, care of the body, and sexual intercourse.[34]

[31] Albert Tafel, *Meine Tibetreise* (2 vols.; Stuttgart: Union Deutsche Verlagsgesellschaft, 1914), II, 153, 231 n.

[32] *Ibid,* I, 84.

[33] Leimbach, *op. cit.,* pp. 65–66.

[34] Pierre Daniel Chantepie de la Saussaye, *Lehrbuch der Religionsgeschichte* (4th ed. edited by A. Bertholet and E. Lehmann, 2 vols.; Tübingen: Mohr, 1925), I, 653; English version; London: Longmans, Green, 1891. French version, Paris: A. Colin, 1904.

The nature-worship of Germany also knew sacred landscapes to which respect and avoidance were due, and where no animal might be killed; it was said of the sacred places in Iceland that "no one might look therein without having washed himself." [35] The same was true in Greek paganism, where holy landscapes and portions of landscapes were abundant, especially around sacred places; Xenophon described one of them, the holy district of Olympia.[36]

Sacred natural landscapes are supplemented in the most varied possible combinations by sacred cultural landscapes, transformed by man—graveyards, temples, and monasteries. There are cultural landscapes in which the religious motif appears as a single point, in the form of a lone sanctuary like a tomb, temple, chapel, or church, or as an elevated sanctuary like the Würmlinger mountaintop chapel near Tübingen, or a tower-like religious building such as a Buddhist high pagoda or Christian church spire, stressed as by an exclamation point. The varied possible arrangements of several graves or cult buildings into unified, ceremonial groups of the same type and kind, or of different types and kinds in larger cult districts, can substantially fill relatively large portions of a landscape, up to a quarter or a half, or even three quarters, of the ground surface; they can even fill it altogether in an extreme grave-landscape like those made by the religions of the ancestor cult and the cult of the dead in eastern Asia—where one must often speak of the "settlement geography of the dead"—or it can become a temple landscape, also at home in eastern and southern Asia, and finally a monastery landscape in the gigantic area of the extreme monastic religion of Buddhism. To the picture of these "ceremonial landscapes," then, belong the figures, gates, pillars, walls, *obos, chortas,* temples, altars, prayer drums, crosses, and many more things that often appear outside of a cult landscape or holy place. They include, furthermore, the sacred avenues, the grave and temple streets, the procession routes and ways of the stations of the cross, with holy trees, pools, and animals, and the colorful throng of ceremonial costumes, ritual activities, and cult sounds. The character and amount of ceremonial expression of a people, a landscape, or an entire country or realm depends not only on the kind and degree of religious ceremonialism and its consequences, but also on the character of the landscape. The capacity to impose the stamp of a religious cult is a measure of religious-geographic significance. The original spirituality and intensity of a religion thus by no means always provide an index of its later progress as a cult, or of its ultimate acceptance and the strength of its impact on the landscape. Thus, for instance, Buddhism, a religion of the greatest intensity and self-forgetfulness, which originally was nearly free of ceremonial, later became ever more ceremonialized, and at last through extreme alienation has reached the strongest degree of impact on its territory, quantitatively and qualitatively, of all religions. But the tremendous area of the sacred cultural landscape and the cult landscape forces us to conclude that the discovery and presentation of the relations between religion and settlement, economy, and traffic is a fascinating task in itself. I have tried merely to discuss some important basic questions in the geography of religions and to indicate a few of its problems.

[35] *Ibid,* II, 568.
[36] Xenophon *Anabasis,* V, 3, 11–13.

IVAN LIND

GEOGRAPHY AND
PLACE NAMES

The mischievous German who twisted a well-known definition of the geographical sciences into "die oberflächliche Wissenschaft von der Erde" would surely nod knowingly at our title. It is true, indeed, that place names do not belong to the essentials of what seems to be the geographer's concern; and he takes certain risks when, usually without linguistic training, he meddles with the interpretation of names in order to give support to an argument, or to make the picture he has painted richer or more lush.

A place name can of course be extremely misleading if its modern, apparent meaning is different from its original and genuine one. Thus the author of the latest great description of Spain's physical geography enters a linguistic blind alley when he suggests that *Sierra Morena*, through its very nature, constitutes the reason for its own name (literally "dark mountain").[1] The name really arose from *Mons Marianus*, of which the latter part is derived from a personal name, as place names ending in *-anus* commonly are; by an unusual circumstance we know who this Marius was, a Roman mine-owner. One other example in Spain concerns the name of the highest part of the Pyrenees, which

on maps[2] may be called *Montes Malditos* ("cursed mountains")—a term, like *Sierra Morena*, constructed through a folk-etymology, in this case upon *Maladeta*, in which **mal/mala*[3] is considered a "Mediterranean" (i.e., pre-Latin) word for "mountain"; the rest of it is even more obscure.

The translation of *Buenos Aires* as "fresh air" is not altogether fitting. The city's name, in its full form *Santa Trinidad y Puerto de la Santísima Virgen de los Buenos Aires*, alludes to an image of "the most holy Virgin" in a church, where sailors before a long, dangerous voyage light candles to obtain "good weather." A little misleading, too, are the Spanish *Santander*, which does not refer to St. Andrew but to St. Emeterus, and some well-known names of Alpine peaks. For example, *Monte Rosa* has nothing to do with the rosy-glowing *Alpenglühn*, but probably with Old High German *(h)rosa*, "ice crust," and *Die Jungfrau* is not altogether so poetic as one might think; it refers to the nuns (virgins, *Jungfrauen*) in the Interlaken convent, and so it was logical to call a neighboring summit *Der Mönch* ("the monk"). I mention in this regard the Russian *Orel* and the Finnish *Kotka*, both corresponding in the respective languages to a word that means "eagle." But the old form of *Orel* shows a

Translated, with permission of the author and editor, from "Geografi och Ortnamn," *Svensk Geografisk Årsbok*, 1953, 23–35. The author, now retired, taught geography in the Swedish high schools.
[1] L. Sole Sabaris, *España: Geografía física*, Vol. I of Manuel de Teran (ed.), *Geografía de España y Portugal* (Barcelona: Montanes y Simon, 1952), p. 257.

[2] For example see the map in A. Amorim Girão, *Geografia de Portugal* (2d ed.; Porto: Portucalense Editora, 1949–50).

[3] An asterisk (*) signifies that a name form has been scientifically reconstructed, but not demonstrated. The sign < means "derived from" or "developed from."

different origin, and *Kotka* is presumably a translation of the Swedish *örn,* meaning "eagle," but also "sandy beach," of which there are many in the archipelago nearby.

It often happens that linguists cannot suggest any rendering, or offer only most uncertain ones. This is too frequently the case for the names of the most important countries and towns, which are sometimes so transformed, because of their age, that they are impossible to recognize. Paris, Marseilles, Lisbon, Ankara, Damascus, Aden, and Delhi are examples of perplexing names, though guesses by linguists are not lacking, and it is believed possible in some cases to place the name in linguistic context. Thus the old *Parisii* had a name with Illyrian connections; *Massalia* points toward Italian and Greek names of similar sound (for example the *Mons Massicus* known from Horatio); and *Lisbon* <*Olisipo* had many relatives in the Iberian Peninsula, such as *Sisipo,* which now has the Arabic name *Almaden,* from *al-maden,* "the mine."

It is natural that the Mediterranean world in particular offers some riddles that are hard to solve. We know that *Portugal* comes from the name of the river-crossing that the Romans called *Portus Cale,* but what *Cale* means no one knows for sure. *Hispania* has been suspected since ancient times of being Phoenician, and of reflecting the country's abundance of rabbits; but this is very uncertain, like the derivation of *Madrid* (oldest known form *Magerit,* tenth century A.D.) from a Celtic **magetoritum,* which may have meant "the big ford." *Italia* was originally the name of a part of the present Calabria. The identification of it with the Latin *vitulus* ("calf"), and the interpretation of the name as "oxland" or "country of bull-worshippers" is no more than possible. The name *Graecia* has a history reminiscent of that of *Italia.* In ancient Epirus lived a Hellenic tribe, the *Graoi* or *Graioi* (perhaps "the shepherds" if derived from the Greek root *graein,* "graze"), who were known to the ancient inhabitants of Italy as the Balkan

people *par préférence.* The Greeks call their country *Hellas* and themselves *Hellenes,* a name that was first applied to a small tribe in Thessaly and is of unknown meaning. *Athens,* the ancient and modern Greek *Athenai,* has probably most often been interpreted as (Pallas) Athena's city, but it has also been traced through an ancient *attanon* ("pottery vessel"), which reminds one of the city's ceramic industry. Yet another Mediterranean land which goes under a foreign name is Egypt, the old Greek *Aigyptos,* which first referred to the Nile and perhaps had an old Egyptian word as its basis. The modern Arabic name is *Al-misr,* which originally meant "place," "country," or "border."

Even in northern latitudes obscure cases are found. To explain *Londinium* (London), a Celtic personal name **Londinos* is constructed, which is perhaps more plausible than to connect such a northern name with a supposed "Mediterranean" root **lon/lun* ("marsh"?). *Berlin* has somewhat surprisingly been linked, in the second edition of the *Svensk Uppslagsbok,*[4] with the Slavic *bereg* ("shore"). In any case, there is probably no reason to distinguish it from the numerous Slavic names ending in *-in* that are generally derivatives of personal names. One West Slavic language has a word *berlo* (with the root *berl-*), a "pole" or "stick," which may have been used as a personal name (like the Swedish word "stake" and the root *kij* in Kiev, which also means a pole). *Moskva* is properly a river name, and it is probably simplest to connect it with a Slavic root *mosk-* ("moist"), but it could also be Finnish like a good many other river names ending in *-va.* Among the most variously interpreted names I should also cite the name of a country, *Belgium.* After the state was founded in 1830, the inhabitants went back to the important Celtic tribe of the *Belgae* to create a suitable name. It was supposed to be related to the Swedish *bälg* ("bel-

[4] G. Carlquist and J. Carlson (eds.), *Svensk Uppslagsbok* (2d ed., Malmö: Forlagsguset Norden, 1947), III, 791–810.

lows") and to suggest something large and extensive, but whether it represents the people as "numerous," "powerful," "widely roaming and unruly," or simply as being "dressed in voluminous clothes," we do not know.

It is natural that in their explanations of names linguists, like other professors, are of several opinions, and there is nothing to object to in it; but less justified is the disagreement that originates in nationality differences. It is not always easy for Swedish and Finnish researchers to agree on the origins and historical implications of certain obscure town names in Finland. In large parts of Central Europe, controversies exist over German versus Slavic origin. For example, *Schlesien* (Polish *Śląsk = Silesia*) can be referred to the Germanic *Silingers* (cf. *Silinge* in Södermanland, Sweden), which is also supposed to be the origin of the mountain and river name *Śleza*. Or is it originally Slavic, and the source of the landscape name? And in Moravia, which one is the original form, the German *Brünn* ("a well") or the Czech *Brno* ("a muddy place")? The fieriest nationalism of this kind is perhaps encountered in and around Hungary, where the dispute between Hungarians and Rumanians is especially intense, but where also the Slavs (and Germans) have strong interests to protect. Among the names hard to interpret is *Tatra;* a Rumanian scholar points to *turtur* ("dove"), but it is surely more nearly correct to link the name (earlier *Tritri*) with *toltry,* a West Ukrainian word for certain hills of Tertiary limestone, and some similar south Slavic hill names (also the Greek *terthron*).

Confusion of place names on another level is caused where speech territories come together, or where places go under unlike names, or under names with different forms in several languages. Such a case occurs above all in Europe's great north-south shatter zone, where German, Slavic, Finno-Ugric and Romance languages break in upon one another. Estonia gives a good example in *Tallinn* and *Tartu.* The first

name recalls the short-lived Danish dominion (*taani linn,* "Danish castle"); the Germans obviously took up Old Estonian *Räpelä* (from *rebane,* "fox"?) in the form *Reval,* while the old name of the Russians (of Estonian origin) is *Kolyvan. Dorpat* and *Tartu* have come down from a personal name, **Tarbatu* or something like it, while the Russian name was *Yuriev* (from *Juri,* "George"). Swedish school children are not alone in thinking that it is difficult to learn *Szczecin* (supposedly connected with *szczyt,* "a summit") and *Wrocław,* formerly Stettin and Breslau. The latter is nearly the same name as *Bratislava,* a linguistically new construction based on the old Slavic-German *Brezalauspurc* and recalling a Moravian duke of the tenth century; it becomes *Pressburg* in the mouths of the Germans. From my own experience I know that the high school student is interested in Lemberg's dissimilar forms: the Ukrainian *Lwiw,* the Polish *Lwów* (pronounced Lvoov), and the Russian *L'vov,* all alluding to a duke Lev or Leo of the thirteenth century. Farther away we find *esh-Sham* ("to the left," i.e., north) as the Arabic name for Damascus, *Allahabad* as the Persian name for the Indian *Préag* (the "union" between the Ganges and the Djamna), *Batavia* as a Dutch name for which the Persian-Indian *Djakarta,* "fruit of victory," has now been substituted.

The case of *Wien* gives an example of the way in which dissimilar languages can be helpful in interpretation. R. Much performed a fine piece of detective work when, with the help of the Czech form of the name, *Videň,* and the Polish *Wiedeń,* he was able to figure out that the Danube's tributary, the Wien, had the Celtic name **Vedunia* ("forest" or "wild river"), from which the name of the city came at second hand.[5]

It often happens that distortions and

[5] R. Much, "Die Namen im Weichbilde Wiens und ihre Entstehung," in Othenia Abel (ed.), *Wien: sein Boden und seine Geschichte* (Vienna: Wolfrum-Verlag, 1924), p. 253.

false etymologies are consequences of national or linguistic mixing. The Finnish
Käkisalmi ("cuckoo's sound") became the
Swedish *Kexholm*. The Turks simplified
Constantinople to *Istambul* (which also
can be explained by the Greek *eis tan polis,*
"to the city," an expression that the Turks
often heard), or sometimes *Islambul*. The
probably pre-Semitic *Urushalim* ("Shalem's
settlement") was turned by the Hebrews
into *Jerusalem* ("home of peace"), and the
Chinese *Hsiang-Kang* ("fragrant harbor")
was deformed by the Europeans into *Hong
Kong*. Sometimes new creations can become
amusing. The Pomeranian *Liebesseele* (literally, "soul of love," in German) is a combination of the Slavic *lipa* ("linden") and
selo ("village"). In Mecklenburg the German *Kuhschwanz* ("cow's tail") has as
its base the personal name *Chotibanz*. In
North America French names have been
distorted by English speakers: for example,
Bay Despair (Labrador) was originally
called *Baie des espoirs,* and *Picketwire*
(Colorado) was *Purgatoire!*

A change of name can not infrequently
be a cause of trouble. Just consider now
formations that are Russian or Russian-
influenced. The Caucasian *Vladikavkaz*
("Rule the Caucasus") got called *Ord-
zhonikidze* after one of Stalin's early
Georgian co-revolutionists, but was re-
christened after his death as *Dzaudzhikau,*
when the relationship between the two companions had cooled. As Ossetia's capital it
has acquired this Ossetian (and thus
Iranian) name, meaning "Dzawag's place."
Such renaming strikes us as banal or dis-
respectful, but it has numerous precedents
in other quarters: Constantinople, Maria-
Theresiopol (the Serbian *Subotica,* after a
sixteenth-century warrior, *Subota*), Karls-
bad, Oskarshamn. More appropriate are
personal names in newly founded places:
Karlsruhe, Washington, and many others.
A troublesome problem sometimes arises
from the vagaries of African Negro place
names. A river, for example, may perpetu-
ally change its name—it is said that one
river in the Belgian trusteeship territory of

Ruanda has at least a dozen names within
less than two miles along its course; and
towns as a rule have two names, that of the
place itself and that of the chief. Many a
traveler has encountered a frustrating problem when he wanted to follow the good rule
of using native names in so far as possible
on his maps.

As the reader discovers, so far we have
been concerned with mere vexations in the
relationship between geography and topo-
nymics. But there is another side to the
coin—otherwise this article would not have
been written.

It is a rather common occurrence for
place names to arouse interest among
geographers. I shall pick out a few names
from the pile. The great teacher of my
young days, Friedrich Ratzel, devoted a
still useful chapter in his *Anthropogeographie* to "die Versteinerung der Sprache,"
"die Leitfossile." [6] His great contemporary,
Ferdinand von Richthofen, investigated the
significance of names when he traveled
through China and got so well into knowledge of the language that he was able, on
linguistic grounds, to venture certain theories about the origins of the Chinese people,
which theories, however, are given a failing
mark by the linguist B. Karlgren. Richthofen's disciple Sven Hedin taught himself East Turki, scattered notes about place
names richly through his writings, and
secured for himself in *Eine Routenaufnahme durch Ost-Persien*[7] the collaboration of the orientalist K. V. Zetterteen on
linguistic identification and interpretation
of names. Hedin's great "competitor," Sir
Aurel Stein, who was not, to be sure, a
geographer, liked to put information about
place names in his books. A third desert
specialist, the Dane O. Olufsen, published
a word list of Bukhara Turkic words of

[6] Friedrich Ratzel, *Anthropogeographie* (4th
ed.; 2 vols.; Stuttgart: J. Engelhorn, 1921–22),
II, 348–72.
[7] Sven Hedin, *Eine Routenaufnahme durch
Ostpersien* (2 vols.; Stockholm: Generalstabens
Litografiska Anstalt, 1918–27).

geographic interest. In his elegant *Géographie humaine de la France*, Jean Brunhes gives frequent illuminating asides on names, especially those of classical origin.[8] To the more recent period belongs Hermann Lautensach,[9] who in his great monograph on Portugal sets forth the testimony of place names concerning settlement history. In Sweden, the journal *Ymer* has for decades contained much about Swedish place names, and J. Raquett's article in this yearbook's fifth number was concerned with more exotic names.

On the other hand, there are, of course, many geographic studies that disappoint a reader who has an interest in name interpretation. To the extent that an author's reticence stems from a consciousness of the risks involved in handling place names, this is quite respectable.

My task here is to try to suggest the reasons for the geographer's onomatological interest. In the first place, it may be a certain general human inclination to puzzle over the meaning of names that one always has in his mouth or meets accidentally. A primitive liking for etymology results in explanations of names that for the most part are reasonably simple and banal, but sometimes can show ingenuity or imagination. Everyone in Sweden knows the old Latinizing explanation of the curious name *Hjo* (possibly etymologically related to *hjon*, and so meaning "home" or "household"), as in the initials of *hic jacet otium*, "here lies repose": in Hjo one rested, indeed, before the crossing to Hästholmen. Sometimes the explanations expand into a legend, like the one about conspicuous erratic blocks thrown by a giant at some odious newly built church. The usual explanation of the name *Dahomey* illustrates how the kingdom got its name from a place

where a chief named *Da* was buried with a gashed abdomen (*omi*). Such an etymology may be well grounded, but it leaves considerable doubt.

The geographer often does not stop with the explanation itself, even though it is both imaginative and poetic; he desires to make use of it for his own purposes, to incorporate it into his geographic synthesis in broad or profound allusions, and he may be aided in this endeavor by the actual linguistic forms.

However, names are of widely differing value. Some of them turn out to be *leerer Schall*, empty of content, without literally being able to give any illumination about either a locality or the people who gave it a name. We do not get much pleasure from *Fridhem* ("peaceful house") or *Annero* ("Anne's rest"), neither from the more genuine Finnish *Vesijärvi* (near Lahti) or its literal Norwegian equivalent *Vandsjö* ("water lake," near Moss). Many examples of banal, affected, and sometimes misleading name creations are given by Mencken in *The American Language*,[10] and Erich Mjöberg tells of a cartographer in Australia who gained the favor of young women by promising to put their names on the map of the barren hill country that he had to chart. When ancient, difficult names are at last interpreted, the etymologies can occasion disappointment, since the expected meanings are altogether simple—"hill," "dale," "water," "river." This is because most names at first had a restricted local range and were valid in only one village, where it was sufficient to talk about "the river" or "the hill." The eminent Celtic scholar, J. Vendryes, must not have had this clearly in mind when, in a criticism of E. Ekwall's *English River Names*,[11] he found the author's explanations inadequate, because they turned out to have such gen-

[8] Jean Brunhes, *Géographie humaine de la France* (2 vols.; Paris: Société d'Histoire Nationale, 1920–26).

[9] Hermann Lautensach, "Portugal: auf Grund eigenen Reisen und der Literatur," *Petermanns Mitteilungen, Ergänzungsheft* 213 & 230 (1932, 1937).

[10] H. L. Mencken, *The American Language: An Inquiry into the Development of English in the United States* (4th ed., New York: Alfred Knopf, 1936).

[11] Eilert Ekwall, *English River Names* (Oxford: Clarendon Press, 1928).

eral content and therefore to be "trivial." He might have thought about all the *don*-rivers—Donau, Dn-estr, Dn-epr, Don (and the much smaller Ossetian Don)—where the root is probably the early Iranian *danu*, "water," "river." Primitive naming sticks to geographic details. For example, the Indians around Puget Sound have no name for "the Sound" as a whole, but have names for nearly all of its promontories and bays.[12]

A great many names become instructive through their form, which allows the linguist, using ever more refined methods, to draw conclusions about their origin and age. Names like *Korinthos, Parnassós, Larissa* are taken back to the putative pre-Greek "Pelasgic" language. A characteristic group are the French words ending in *-euil* (*Verneuil, Auteuil,* etc.) which can be placed as compounds of a Celtic suffix *-ialon* ("clearing," "field") with a prefix in most cases known through the scarce relics of Gaulic speech, or a Latin word.

To the extent that one succeeds in interpreting them—and this is being done with increasing success—names also give, through their content or form, some information concerning one or the other, or both, of the geographer's two chief interests, nature and mankind, and in large view more often about the latter. A rough division according to content can treat names as being naturally or culturally determined, along with names that have both natural and cultural elements. To the first group belong, for example, *Ahus* <*a-os, Arhus* <*ar-os* ("river mouth"), *Bremen* (from *bräm*, "edge," "border"), *Szeged* (from *sziget*, "island"); to the second group belong *Birmingham* (*Bermingeham*, "the settlement of Berm's band"), *Bordeaux* (probably late Latin *burdigalum*, "fish-pond"), *Beograd* ("white castle"), *Budapest* (Slavic; rendered as a personal name, "Buda," and an "oven," which refers to the limekiln at Gellerthegy). To the third

group of names belong *Amsterdam* (*Amstelredam,* "the dike on the banks of the Amstel"), *Brussels* (*Brokzele,* cf. the German *bruch,* "breech" or "clearing," and the old Swedish *sal,* "big farmstead"). In most European languages "cultural names" are preponderant as designations for settlements, and the same is no doubt true in most speech areas of any significance outside our part of the world. As tolerably sure exceptions I think I can give—without statistics to support it—Japanese, Malayan, and American Indian names.

All sorts of natural features are glimpsed in names, representing such as had practical meaning for the people who gave the names, or things that were impressed on their imagination. Places on water belong to the most important sources of names, for example *Shanghai* ("foremost on the sea"), *Hamburg* ("castle at the river bend", if the word is to be associated with the German *Hamm* or the abundant English *ham,* where the meaning has developed into "streamside meadow"), *Tiflis* (Georgian, *Tbilisi,* "hot springs"), *Quebec* (Algonkian, *Kebek,* "the sound"), *Pará* (in full, *Belém do Grão Pará,* "Bethlehem-by-the-Big-River"). Scarcely less often appear landforms, e.g., *Poland* (Polish, "a plain"), *Kazań* (Turco-Tartar, "a kettle"), *Zagreb* ("beyond the ditch or depression"), *Montevideo* (*Mont Ovidio,* after an old bishop).

Rather more seldom is geologic information given, but *Limfjorden, Limhamn,* and *Lima* in Dalarna, Sweden (where there is limestone), show an important natural influence. That the plant world is an amply stocked source of names is self-evident, just as it is no surprise that trees turn up especially often in Malay names (e.g., *Malacca,* originally a city called after the tree *Phyllanthus emblica*). Leipzig (Slavic, *Lipsk*) means "the place of lindens," and *Dresden* (*Draždjany*) a "forest dweller." That animals, as primitive man's friends or enemies, often become commemorated in names is equally natural. Certain newly discovered data are considered to give support to the old derivation of *Bern* from the

[12] T. T. Waterman, "The Geographical Names Used by the Indians of the Pacific Coast," *Geographical Review,* XII (1922), 175–94.

German *Bär* ("bear"), which was long regarded as a folk etymology.

People may sometimes doubt the interpretations of names, because natural circumstances have been altered since the names were given: e.g., no woods are to be found, or in any case no oaks grow in a place; beavers or bears, not to mention bison and aurochs, have not occurred there in the memory of man; or bogs and probably here and there lakes are gone. Many names ending in *-woude* (cf. the German *Wald*) in Holland speak of the former occurrence of forests, and in Germany and northern Europe forests now appear in many places that were formerly covered with heath, as is shown by names with *Heide*, "heath," "heather."

Thanks to the information it offers, a place name can be an aid in one's first orientation on the map. Anyone in Sweden who is interested in glacio-fluvial deposits, but has no geologic map, can direct his steps to places with *sand, ör, mal, malm, mo* (all meaning sand of various grain size), *hed* ("sandy plain"), and sometimes *gryt* (an old word; cf. the English "grit") in their names. Nevertheless, it must be admitted that names generally do not give much information about nature that one does not get more reliably and better by other means. Wilhelm Troll observed with interest, however, the way in which the *-loh* in South German names (e.g., *Hohenlohe*) indicated light oak forest, sometimes holy groves, while places with names ending in *-buch* and *-heide* had a different natural setting.[13] The geographer J. V. Eriksson, well known to an older generation of Uppsala students, collected the Swedish names that pinpoint the former distribution of the yew tree.[14]

However, as has been said, it is mostly

human matters that are touched on. Often a founder's name appears in a place name. I have already mentioned a couple of the many Slavic names that consist of personal names, sometimes slightly changed, and I can adduce *Potsdam < Podstupim, Posen (Poznań)*, and (presumably) *Warszawa*. A couple of Romance counterparts are *Dijon < Divio* and possibly *Avignon < Avennio*, Derivations from personal names or nicknames are common in different languages. Here belong in general the common Germanic ones ending in *-ing, -inge, -ingen*, and the like, e.g., *Göttingen < Guddinga* (like the Swedish *Göinge*), *Reading*. Many places in France, northern Spain, and northern Italy also have names ending in *-ing*. A similar derivation in formerly Celtic countries is the (Latinized) one ending in *-iacum*, which is encountered in the mass of southern French and northern Spanish names ending in *-ac*, e.g., *Armagnac < Erminiacum*, "of Erminius" (*fundus*, "farm," is understood), and northern French ones ending in *-y*, e.g., *Vitry < Victoriacum*. Derivations ending *-anus, -anicus, -inus*, and so on in different genders and numbers are Latin, for example *Perpignan < Perpinianum*, "Perpinius' (farm)," and *Medellin*, "Metellus' (farm)." In Rumania an important suffix of personal names is *-eşti*, e.g., *Bucureşti*, derived from the personal name *Bucur*, "cheerful."

Still more common, no doubt, are similar derivations in the Slavic countries. The Polish *Katowice* (German, *Kattowitz*) is a double derivative from the personal name *kat* (+ *ov* + *ice*). This *-ov, -ev* element is found alone in a great many names, e.g., *Kraków*, "the Krak village." (The derivation *-in* in Berlin has already been noted.) In Finnish, village or farm names are overwhelmingly personal names or their derivatives, for example the numerous ones in *-la, -lä* (Anjala, Värälä); and in Arabic a significant group of place names is formed of derivatives of personal names.

Another sort of personal names, with a wider scope, is folk and tribal names, which are a very motley group. Above all one has

---

[13] Wilhelm Troll, "Die Bedeutung der Ortsnamen für die pflanzengeographische Forschung," *Zeitschrift für Ortsnamenforschung* (later: *Namenforschung*), II (1926–27), 12 ff.

[14] J. V. Eriksson, "Ortnamnsforskning och Vaxtgeografi," *Svensk Botanisk Tidskrift*, VII (1913), 321–36.

to distinguish between the name a group gives to itself, and those used by others. The usual development is that a group calls itself "the humans," "the real humans," "those who know how to speak," etc. The name of the Swedes belongs here, for according to a plausible explanation by Tacitus, *Suiones* is equated with the Latin *suus*, "his," and is also supposed to mean "one's own" or "we" (similarly, cf. the Germanic tribe of the *Suebi*, the later *Swabians*). The word *tysk*, meaning "German" in Swedish, has been developed out of *diotisc*, "belonging to the people (*thiod*)." Often the name is characterized by a more or less explicit self-esteem, not to say boasting, as is probably the case with *Franks* ("brave," "fierce"), and *Turks* and *Mongols* (both "strong"). In many cases the name given by a neighboring people has become the established one, although it does not always amount to a compliment. The Lapps keep their own name, *Same*, although they do not know the theory of the Finn, Karsten, that *Lapps* is a derogatory Germanic appellation. *Iowa* is the name of a branch of the Dakota tribe, *Ahioba*, which is supposed to have been called "the sleepy people" by malicious neighbors. As we know, names like *Preussen, Sachsen, Böhmen, Ungarn* are plurals of Germanic origin, and Gaulic tribal names have in many cases become names of cities, displacing older Celtic names, e.g., *Paris*, from *Parisii*, instead of *Lutetia*. In many countries places bear names of foreign peoples and reflect peaceful or warlike contacts. Not far from Reims are *Villers-Franquex, Aumenancourt, Gueux,* and *Sermiers,* names that are evidence of Franks, Alamanni, Goths, and Sarmatians of the *Völkerwanderungen*.

Behind a name may sometimes be traced the most far-reaching historical connection, as a couple of examples will show. Evidence of pre-Celtic names is found in a V-shaped territory, from Portugal and Ireland to the areas around the lower Danube and ancient Galatia (here, however, none survived as far as is known). Arabic names occur from *Dakar* (which, if my opinion is correct,

comes from a word for "plowshare," and is a name for Cape Verde) and the *Jellala* Falls in the Congo (*jillal*, "waterfall"), to southeast Asia, where *Kra* (Isthmus and Cape) is possibly a southern Arabian word for "village." Thanks to either the Arabs or the Indians, Persian names reach as far as Java; the second syllable in *Djakarta* is the Persian *kert*, originally "made," and later "founded" (of a town). Indian names occur from *Zanzibar* (from the Persian *zenj*, "black" and the Indian *bar*, "land"), across Farther India to the Philippines. *Ayuthia* in Siam is almost surely the ancient Indian *ayodhya*, "invincible."

Names, often very modestly, can give historical information in other ways. The meanings of *Cairo* (Arabic, *al-Kahira*, "the victorious") and *Rangoon* (*Yan-gun*, which is believed to be Indian and is thought to mean "end of the battle," in memory of a war of liberation) are related. With great hopes, the Roman colonies of *Florentia* and *Valentia* were founded, as well as the later castle, *Belfort* ("beautiful-strong"), Kashmir's capital *Srinagar* (supposedly "sun-city"), and *Addis Ababa* ("new flower"; it was the Negus Menelik's consort who called it by this name). But on the other hand we find names with a gloomy sound, like the French *Malaise* ("discomfort") and *Maurepas* ("bad eating").

The total picture of a people's naming practice furnishes a not uninstructive index to their psychology. Frenchmen appear clever even in their name-giving, which is considerably more lively and subtle than that of the Germanic peoples. The names of Negro villages have often arisen from actual events, and may be dramatic phrases, more vivid than the Turkish ones of the same kind, but shorter. The Kikongo-French dictionary of the missionary K. E. Laman gives many good examples.[15] In comparison with these, American Indian names as a whole show a tendency to be matter-of-fact, although they may be very long. Contrasts between names given by

[15] Karl E. Lamen, *Dictionnaire kikongo-français* (Brussels: Librairie Falk Fils, 1936).

the Negroes and the Indians are like those a traveler encounters when he comes from Havana, with its Negro-influenced cheerful humor, to the Indian tranquillity of Vera-cruz. The world of names which spans the widest registry is that of the Chinese (plus Annamite), embracing on the one hand high-sounding names like *Tientsin* ("heavenly ford"), *Wuchang* ("warlike splendor"), and on the other hand drastically realistic ones, like the common *Su Ho,* "snot (mucus) river."

Not the least important name-making force in intellectual life has been religion, from its lower stages where trolls and ghosts, nymphs and elves exist, to the highest stage of religious feeling. *Pontianak* (Borneo) is the name for a dangerous spirit, originally the soul of a woman who died in childbirth. *Lhasa* means "spirit world." The Nordic *Helge å* ("holy river") and *Helgenas* ("holy isthmus") correspond to Finland's *Pyhäkoski, Pyhäjärvi* ("holy river," "lake"). India is deeply steeped in religion, and this influence is clearly evident in its place names. *Bombay* is thought to be named after a goddess (Mombai), *Cawnpore* after Vishnu (under the name Kanha), and *Amritsar* means "the immortal pond" (*amrita saras*). Most of the divine names of antiquity have been displaced as a result of the advent of Christianity, but *Porto Venere* (Italy) and *Port-Vendres* (France) recall the easily understood role that Venus-worship played in connection with seamen's voyages. Many Celtic places were called *Lugdunum,* evidently a compound of the name of the god of light, *Lug,* with *dunum* ("a hill"), and the most important of them became *Lyons.*

With the coming of Christianity, a wave of saints' names overran the nations (Islam has counterparts of this). The Catholic countries fairly swarm with such names, among other things because discoverers and colonists liked to resort to day-names from the calendar in their name-giving—hence names like *Santiago* and *Buenaventura* (after the scholastic philosopher and saint)—but they also used other concepts

of religious significance, for example *Ascension* (from Christ's Ascension) and *Asunción* (from the Assumption of the Virgin Mary). In Protestant countries this kind of name has been to a considerable degree replaced, but certain others have sometimes come in their place, like *Providence* and *Salem* in Puritan New England; there are also many names with "church" or "priest," while "convent," "monk," etc., are comparatively rare. Without having any statistics to lay on the line, I suspect that the Celtic countries, above all such modern ones as Ireland and Brittany, and some ancient ones as well, are most thickly studded with church names.

The worldly order of course often shows up in names. In a great many cases the subjects are emperors (*Zaragoza* < *Cesarea Augusta,* Turkey's *Kaysarije,* now *Kayseri*), kings (many *Kingstons, Montreal, Monterrey*), dukes (*Hercegovina*), princes (*Port au Prince*), counts and other nobles, and on down the social scale to the common man. The English *Carlton* was at first "the farm of a *churl*," i.e., a "free man," while *Knighton* was a "knight's," i.e., a servant's, residence. The precise significance of different words for settlement forms that enter into place names in Sweden and most other Germanic countries—e.g., *-sta, -by, -torp, -bo, -boda, -rum, -måla*—are of course not easy to treat, and in some cases it is certain that many steps have preceded the fixation of one meaning. The German *dorf,* like the Swedish *torp,* originally meant a "pioneer farm," which became a village and in many instances a city, e.g., Düsseldorf on the Düssel, the "roaring" river. In the same way the Latin *villa* ("farm" or more properly "manor") in various Romance languages became a widespread and fashionable word for "village" (in Germany in the form *Weiler*), and thus often "city," alongside the Latin *vicus* ("village," which enters for instance into *Vichy, Norwich,* and also *Braunschweig* < *Bruneswic* ("Bruno's village"). The work of the Norwegian Magnus Olsen is a distinguished example of what place-name research can do to reconstruct the settlement history of a country.[16] Works by Hans Krahe, Carlo Battisti, and many others give an idea of the possibilities of place-name study to assist history (and prehistory) in throwing light upon the dark early ages of the Mediterranean world.

A host of names points to a military origin. The Latin *castia, castellum* lives on in many forms within the old boundaries of the Roman Empire, from *Castilla* to *Manchester* and *Newcastle,* with the Germanic *borg* (Burgos), the Slavic *grad* (Graz, Novgorod), and the Greek *pyrgos* (Bulgarian *Burgas*) as rivals.

It would require a whole book to show the testimony of place names about economic life. They illuminate many steps in the spread of agriculture where other sources are silent, and speak very often of "clearings" or "burnings" (for example, *Bayreuth, Praha* or *Prag*) and other preparations of the ground (*Novara,* "new fields"). What was grown at the time of naming is often reported: *Bergen* < *Biorgin* ("mountain meadow" likewise many other Nordic names ending in *-vin*); *Zermatt* ("by the grass pasture," and thence *Matterhorn*); *Afyon-Karahisar* ("opium-black castle"); *Carmel* ("orchard"). Animals can be recognized in *Goa* (where "cow" is probably the source of the name), *Ispahan* (in which *asp,* "horse," supposedly enters), the *Faeroes* ("sheep islands"), and many others. The most important mineral was for a long time salt, and the *-hall* in *Halle, Reichenhall,* and many other names possibly means a store of salt, while *Szolnok* in Hungary and *Salford* in Warwickshire must have lain along the routes of the salt trade. Very often a primitive industry is represented in a name, e.g., in *Calcutta,* which, according to the latest explanation known to me, is connected with Bengali *kali* ("seashells for lime-burning") and *kata* ("lime ready for slaking"). *Nor-*

way—*Norvegr*—is far from being the only country or territory that takes its name from "way"; in Japan's *Hondo* the last syllable originally meant "way," and later "territory." Fords usually play a less important role in southern European names than in more northern lands, where well-known examples are *Oxford* and *Schweinfurt* (cf. the Swedish *Svennevad* < *Svinavad,* "swine ford"), and *Vejle* (corresponding to the German *-wedel* in many names). The same root as in *-furt* is found again in Latin *portus,* which not only occurs in countless port names but is also applied to mountain passes, particularly in the Pyrenees, and the German *Pforzheim.*

This sample collection of name categories cannot be lengthened, but before I conclude, I shall allow myself to point out another value—perhaps considered unscientific—that can be derived from the study of place names: the psychological-aesthetic value. Many kinds of rhythms and intonations are played upon, all the way from the polysynthetic names of the Eskimos and many Indians (e.g., Quohquinaspassakesaannannaquog, a river in Massachusetts) to the Chinese two- or three-part word compounds which become hard knots after a thousand years of handling. The prize for beauty I should give to Italian names: Milano, Vallombrosa, Montecatini, Sannazaro. The slight measure of competence in place names that the geographer acquires contributes above all to giving the study of maps a deep dimension, but it also provides one more superficial pleasure of the eye and ear.

Finally, it must be said that the geographer is not simply the receiving party; he can also give. A linguistic rendering of a name must be confirmed by *die Realprobe,* a demonstration that the interpretation agrees with geographic reality, and here the geographer with his trained glance, and in the appropriate case his ability to interpret the meaning of maps, has something to offer, particularly when it can be concluded that the natural conditions of a locality have changed over the centuries or millen-

[16] Magnus B. Olsen, *Aettegård og helligdom* (Oslo: Aschehoug, 1926).

niums that have passed since the giving of a name. In more than one work of an onomatological nature I have found that geographic insights and the geographic point of view would have been useful for the exposition. The geographer can also help in the compilation of suitable maps showing the derivation and routes of dispersal of name types, and since, as his profession requires, he has many names in his head, he can at one time or another supply facts for enlighening comparisons.

WILBUR ZELINSKY

GENERIC TERMS IN THE PLACE NAMES OF THE NORTHEASTERN UNITED STATES

For many years American toponymy has been the domain of students of language who have been concerned almost exclusively with specific names.[1] There is much in the best of such research to interest geographers, but the even more promising topic of generic terms—the common nouns— used to denote geographic features in the United States has been strangely neglected by geographers and linguistic specialists alike.[2] As major items in any cultural landscape, these terms deserve close scrutiny for

Reprinted, with permission of the author and editor, from "Some Problems in the Distribution of Generic Terms in the Place-Names of the Northeastern United States," *Annals of the Association of American Geographers*, XLV (1955), 319–49. The author is professor of geography at Southern Illinois University, Carbondale.

[1] All except the most recent materials on the subject are listed in Richard B. Sealock and Pauline A. Seely, *Bibliography of Place Name Literature, United States, Canada, Alaska, and Newfoundland* (Chicago: American Library Association, 1948). Much of the more important work is summarized in George R. Stewart, *Names on the Land* (New York: Random House, 1945) and in H. L. Mencken, *The American Language* (4th ed.; New York: Knopf, 1947), and *The American Language, Supplement II* (New York: Knopf, 1948).

[2] Some pioneering essays were written by geographers early in this century, but they failed to stimulate further investigation. The most important of these are Herbert M. Wilson, "A Dictionary of Topographic Forms," *Journal of the American Geographical Society*, XXXII (1900), 32–41, and R. H. Whitbeck, "Regional Peculiarities in Place Names," *Bulletin of the American Geographical Society*, XLIII (1911), 273–81.

their own sake; but of even greater importance are the complex, uncharted interrelationships among place names and other phases of culture and the possibility that their study may illuminate significant aspects of American cultural history and geography.[3]

It is the purpose of this exploratory essay to survey the distribution of a selected group of generic terms over an important section of the United States, to speculate about their significance, and to note some of the problems to be encountered in their further study. The fact that several hundreds of thousands of place names exist in the United States has made it necessary to limit this reconnaissance to a single major region immediately productive of challenging facts and problems—specifically the northeastern United States—and to a single readily accessible source of data—the large-scale topographic sheets of the Geological Survey and the Corps of Engineers. It is recognized that such an approach represents a crude compromise between two earlier types of studies, both conducted in

[3] Interesting work along these lines, based chiefly on specific elements in place names, is reported in Alfred H. Meyer, "Toponymy in Sequent Occupance Geography, Calumet Region, Indiana-Illinois," *Proceedings of the Indiana Academy of Science*, LIV (1945), 142–59, and H. F. Raup and William B. Pounds, Jr., "Northernmost Spanish Frontier in California as Shown by the Distribution of Place Names," *California Historical Society Quarterly*, XXXII (1953), 43–48.

considerable depth: the analysis of a single term over its entire range in time and space[4] and the intensive inventory of all specific and generic terms within a restricted territory.[5] Obviously, the ultimate synthesis of American place-name study will require a great many more monographs

of the final edifice, or at least afford the builders an overview of their task.

LIMITATIONS OF THE STUDY IN TERMS OF AREA, TOPIC, AND SOURCE MATERIALS

The area encompassed by this study (shown in Fig. 1) is that contiguous and

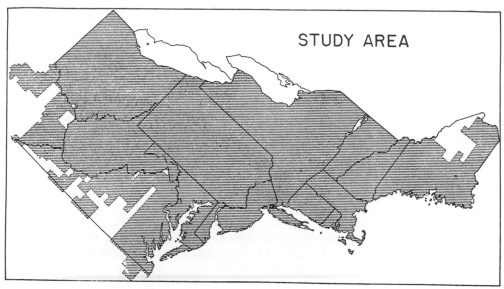

FIG. 1.

of both types. The utility of the present paper lies in its providing a rough scaffolding that may somehow indicate the shape

[4] Robert C. West, "The Term 'Bayou' in the United States: A Study in the Geography of Place Names," *Annals of Association of American Geographers*, XLIV (1954), 63–74.

[5] The most outstanding example is Frederic G. Cassidy, *The Place-Names of Dane County, Wisconsin* (Greensboro, N.C.: American Dialect Society, Publication No. 7, 1947), a study based not only on written and cartographic sources but also on painstaking field work. Among the more important studies based largely, if not entirely, on documentary materials are George Davis McJimsey, *Topographic Terms in Virginia* (New York: Columbia University Press, 1940); Hamill Kenny, *West Virginia Place Names* (Piedmont, W. Va.: Place Name Press, 1945); and E. Wallace McMullen, Jr., *English Topographic Terms in Florida, 1563–1874* (Gainesville: University of Florida Press, 1953).

more or less compact territory in the northeastern United States for which topographic sheets of a scale of 1:62,500 or larger were available in 1953. Fortunately, this region happens to include the sites of the earliest permanent European colonization in the United States (except that in Florida) and also constitutes an area that furnished settlers to most of the rest of the nation. In addition to being a culture hearth, the northeastern United States is also characterized by a degree of cultural diversity well above the average for the country and is rivaled in this respect perhaps only by Louisiana.

Specific terms were eliminated as a topic of study and also such generic terms as are applied casually in vernacular speech to features of the landscape without being incorporated into particular names, e.g., such usages as *rise, dip,* or *neighborhood.*[6] In other words, only those generic terms appearing on topographic maps as a portion of a geographic name have been studied. Their number has been further reduced by the omission of terms describing the internal features of towns, for lack of adequate coverage, and of that large group applied to coastal features. Because of the enormous number of places named on highly detailed coastal charts and the peculiar cartographic problems involved in depicting their essentially linear distributions, it was deemed best to bypass these terms at present, but not without voicing the hope that they will soon receive the attention they merit. Two final limitations have been the elimination of most terms that occur with great rarity or as minority elements in restricted tracts and, on the other hand, those that are universal in the sense that they occur abundantly wherever their use is appropriate. No doubt many intrinsically important terms are left out by such a policy; but this decision was dictated by a concentration of interest in the major regional variations in the place-name cover.

It is readily demonstrated that the topographic sheets used for this study are in many respects gravely deficient as sources of place names. The relative completeness and accuracy of the names on a given sheet will vary with its scale, date, and the particular area involved. Furthermore, since

the collection of place names was of incidental interest to government agencies concerned primarily with such matters as relief, hydrology, and material culture, the quality of the toponymic content may differ greatly from one surveyor or map editor to another. In more exacting studies these topographic sheets must be supplemented by a wide variety of other maps, local literature and archival materials, and intensive field work, not only to fill in the details of the contemporary place-name pattern but also to trace the all-important changes that have occurred in the past. Notwithstanding these reservations, the maps accompanying this text afford a meaningful, if crude, approximation of the more or less contemporary distribution of some of the more regionally significant generic terms within the study area.

STREAM TERMS

Any observant map-reader who compares large-scale maps of the United States with those of Western Europe will be struck by the relative paucity of place names on the former—even making generous allowance for omissions by map-makers.[7] This difference, which is difficult to define quantitatively, may be attributed to the recency of settlement and the simpler history of America, the lower average population densities (and, hence, the coarser grain of the cultural landscape), and, in many areas, the less complex character of physical features.

Among the various classes of physical features in the northeastern United States, streams appear to be the most often named.[8] Since a generic term is invariably appended when these names are formally

---

[6] The interesting but vexing problem of the relationships between vernacular "topographic" language (using the word in its extended sense) and the generic terms employed in place names has apparently been left wholly unexplored. A large body of valuable material on vernacular usage is now available in the work of the group headed by Hans Kurath, viz., *Linguistic Atlas of New England* (6 vols.; Providence, R.I.: Brown University Press, 1939–43), subsequently referred to as *LANE,* and *A Word Geography of the Eastern United States* (Ann Arbor: University of Michigan Press, 1949). The correlation of such material with the generic usages in place names will provide a major research problem in the years to come.

[7] John K. Wright, "The study of Place Names: Recent Work and Some Possibilities," *Geographical Review,* XIX (1929), 141.

[8] A valuable discussion of the psychology of naming or not naming particular features is found in George R. Stewart, "What is Named?—Towns, Islands, Mountains, Rivers, Capes," *University of California Publications in English,* XIV (1943), 223–32.

FIG. 2.

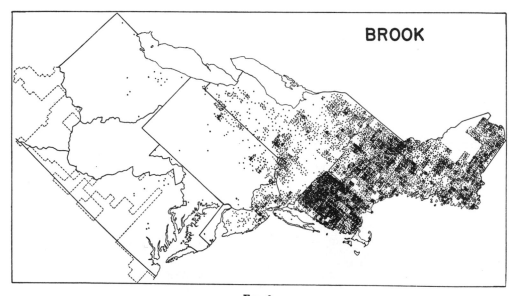

FIG. 3.

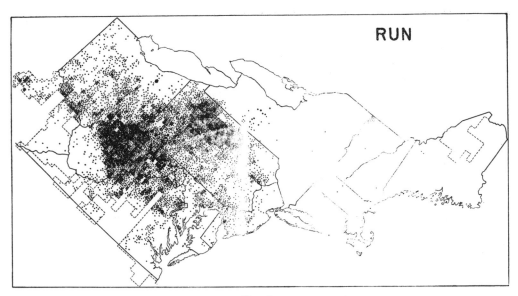

Fig. 4.

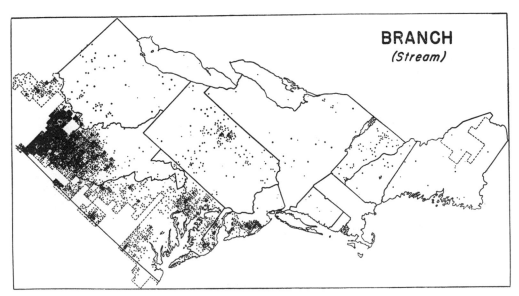

Fig. 5.

133

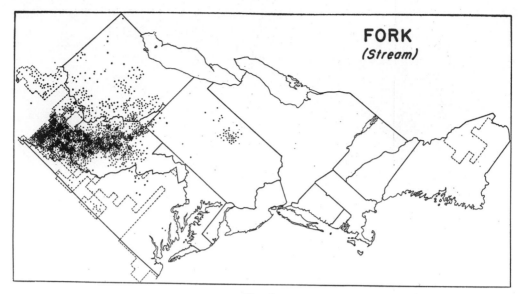

Fɪɢ. 6.

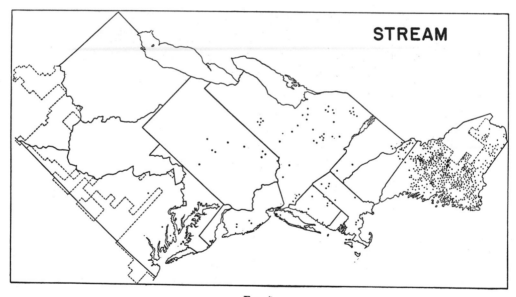

Fɪɢ. 7.

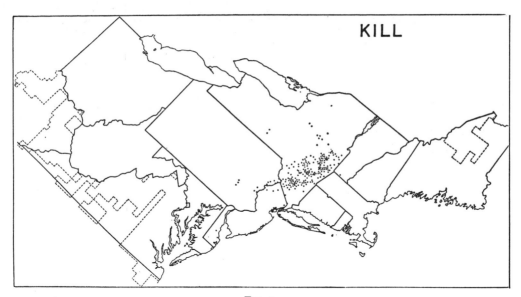

FIG. 8.

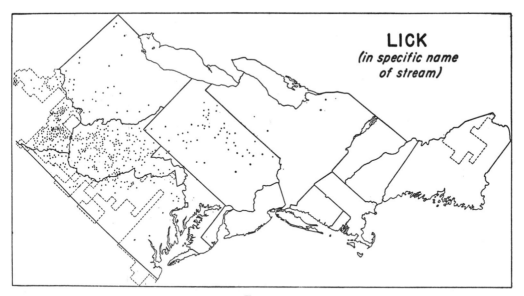

FIG. 9.

recorded on maps,[9] a large mass of stream terms await the attention of place-name geographers. Although a total of perhaps no more than a score of terms are in use for the many thousands of streams in the study area, some of them rather rare and special, it is important to note the existence of some significant sub classes within this restricted group of words.

First, different terms may denote distinctions in the size of streams. Thus in the Deep South the terms *river, creek,* and *branch* (or *fork*) form a hierarchy expressing decreasing magnitude.[10] In Maryland the series is augmented by *run* as an intermediate category between *creek* and *branch*.[11] Farther northward, such series as *river-creek-run* or *river-brook* are prevalent, with the term *river* always unrivaled as a label for the largest streams.[12]

A major distinction must also be made between terms applied exclusively to tributaries and those that may be used for either tributaries or master streams. There are many cases where a tributary acquires a name wholly independently of the main stream (in which event the size hierarchy of terms comes into play); but such terms as *branch, fork,* or *prong* are frequently used to denote tributaries, often in conjunction with some directional adjective, such as "right" or "left," "north" or "south," or "upper" or "lower." [13] The matter is

complicated, however, by the fact that in some regions *branch* and *fork*, through a process whose history is most obscure, have acquired the status of full generic terms, as in "Grassy Fork" rather than "West Fork" of So-and-So Creek. As will be seen, these variant usages depart sufficiently in areal distribution from the parent forms so that they may be accepted as distinct terms.

The choice of a generic term for a stream may also be affected by its velocity or some other physical characteristic. Thus, in his study of Maryland stream names, Kuethe discovered that *run* was applied to streams of high velocity (in the mountains and Piedmont), while *branch* was most frequently adopted for those of moderate current, and *creek* was used for the most sluggish (in the Coastal Plain).[14] In southeastern Virginia and in other parts of the South not covered by this survey, streams which flow slowly through swampy areas may receive the appellation *swamp*. In the glaciated country of New England and northern New York the terms *deadwater* and *flowage* are sometimes employed for streams that have been partially obstructed so that they have swollen nearly to the dimension of lakes. Elsewhere within this same region the terms *inlet* and *outlet* are used aptly enough for streams entering or leaving glacial lakes. Where streams pass by "a spot to which animals resort to lick the salt or salt earth found there," [15] the word *lick* is often used as part of a compound specific name, e.g., "Elk Lick Branch," and sometimes, but less frequently, as a pure generic term, e.g., "Elk Lick." In those parts of Tidewater Virginia and the Eastern Shore where ditches have been dug intermittently to drain low ground, it is sometimes impossible to distinguish artificial from natural channels,

[9] Although sometimes omitted or suppressed in local vernacular usage, James B. McMillan, "Observations on American Place-Name Grammar," *American Speech,* XXIV (1949), 241–48.

[10] Much overlap in usage may exist, but in the aggregate the size distinctions implicit in these terms are unmistakable.

[11] J. Louis Kuethe, "Runs, Creeks, and Branches in Maryland," *American Speech,* X (1935), 256–59.

[12] Because of this universal usage, the term *river* has not been mapped in this study. A problem of some interest is the regional variation in the size of streams to which a given term (*river* among them) may be assigned.

[13] But seldom, if ever, are ordinal numbers employed, as in the Far West. George R. Stewart, "Nomenclature of Stream-forks on the West Slope of the Sierra Nevada," *American Speech,* XIV (1939), 191–97.

[14] Kuethe, *op. cit.,* pp. 258–59.

[15] James A. H. Murray (ed.), *A New English Dictionary on Historical Principles* (10 vols.; Oxford: Clarendon Press, 1888–1928). Hereinafter referred to as *NED.*

and the term *ditch* may occasionally be used for the latter.[16]

Since large streams are almost invariably designated as *rivers* in the northeastern United States, our attention here is limited to the distribution of terms for medium- and small-sized streams. Of these, probably the most important is *creek* (Fig. 2),[17] for it occurs in considerable numbers almost everywhere west and south of the Adirondacks and Hudson River in association with medium-sized streams.[18] Like many other important generic place terms, *creek* is an Americanism in the sense that the British word has acquired an entirely novel connotation on this side of the Atlantic. There are hundreds of instances along the American coast of *creek* being used in its original sense of salt-water estuary or embayment, but its application to fresh-water inland streams is a North American innovation. Students of the American language have not yet fully accounted for this shift in meaning, but the *NED*'s surmise is the most probable and widely accepted explanation:

Probably the name was originally given by the explorers of a river to the various inlets and arms observed to run out of it, and of which only the mouths were seen in passing; when at a later period these 'creeks' were explored, they were often found to be tributaries of great length, and 'creek' thus received an application entirely unknown in Great Britain.

Such a hypothesis is strengthened by the near absence of the term in interior New England (as noted in *LANE*). The gradual merging of brackish estuaries with inland streams that occurs within the broader coastal plains to the south is a rarity along the rugged New England coast, and so too the opportunity for extending the term inland. Not much significance need be read into the variations in the frequency of

creek outside New England, for most of these are caused by shortcomings in map sources or by variable numbers of nameable streams. The decreased importance of the term in the central portion of the study area is largely the effect of strong competition from *run,* which is used for medium-sized as well as small streams.

The distribution of the important stream term *brook* (Fig. 3)[19] is in most respects the converse of that of *creek,* for it is well represented in New England, New York, New Jersey, and northern Pennsylvania but is relatively uncommon elsewhere.[20] Within the area of its principal concentration, *brook* is used in the common English sense of a small stream or rivulet—in southern New England almost to the exclusion of other terms.[21] The distributional pattern is closely coincident with that of the New England culture area and with its westward expansion during the late eighteenth and early nineteenth centuries. Since the original sense of *brook* is "a torrent, a strong flowing stream" (*NED*), the term was much less applicable in the coastal territories south of New York Harbor and, although in occasional use there, had a slimmer chance of being adopted and spread inland than in hilly New England.

Southwestward of the region dominated by *brook,* the great majority of small streams are termed *runs* (Fig. 4).[22] The substitution of this usage for the equally appropriate *brook* throughout most of the central portion of the study area is difficult to explain. In Great Britain, the term is confined to northern England and portions of Scotland, specifically Yorkshire, north Lincolnshire, Norfolk, and Lanark, where

[16] McJimsey, *op. cit.*

[17] In this map, as in subsequent ones, each dot corresponds to a single occurrence of the usage.

[18] Not only within the study area but throughout most of Anglo-America.

[19] Kurath, *Word Geography of the Eastern United States,* Fig. 93.

[20] Although occurrences as far south as Florida can be found. McMullen, *op. cit.*

[21] The unusually heavy concentration of *brooks* in southern New England in Figure 3 is probably as much the result of superior map coverage for that area as of any pronounced areal differential.

[22] Kurath, *Word Geography of the Eastern United States,* Figs. 18 and 93.

it is regarded as dialectal.[23] Further research into the British history of *run* is necessary before its American distributional pattern can be accounted for; but two hypotheses suggest themselves: (1) *run* may have been a waning but still widespread term in Great Britain at the time of its introduction into America where, for unknown reasons, it failed to gain much of a foothold except within its present range,[24] or (2) the term was taken to Pennsylvania and Maryland by the Scotch-Irish immigrants who were familiar with it in their homeland and thence carried westward by the advancing frontiersmen.[25] At any rate, it is tempting to correlate the area dominated by *run* with the Midland speech demarcated by Kurath in his *Word Geography of the Eastern United States* and to seek a common origin for both. It is especially interesting to note the unusually sharp boundary dividing *run* from its equivalent term *branch* in Virginia and West Virginia.

The use of *branch* in the English sense of a tributary and in conjunction with a directional specific is so widespread within the study area that its occurrence was not plotted. The second major usage of *branch*, as a full-fledged generic term, is an Americanism with a curiously spotty distribution (Fig. 5).[26] Although there is a decided preponderance of *branches* in the nomenclature of small streams in most of the

southern part of the study area[27]—and particularly in the Appalachians—there are sizable clusters of occurrences in southern New Jersey, parts of Vermont and New Hampshire, and that north-central Pennsylvania region which will presently be seen to be anomalous in other respects. Within its more southerly range, the important concentration in Maryland and the Eastern Shore is striking.

It is noteworthy that even in the zone of greatest frequency, *branch* (in its full generic sense) does not dominate nearly so much as *brook* or *run* do in their respective areas, for it faces severe competition from both *fork* and *creek*. A fragmented distributional pattern and the complex series of physical connotations may well indicate a complicated history. It is obvious that *branch* in its full generic sense stems directly from the original tributary term, but the locus and method of the transition are uncertain, as is the question of whether a single or multiple origin can be ascribed to it. Neither are there sufficient data on hand to settle the major problem of the dominance of *branch* in the southeastern United States.

In spite of lower frequency and greater restriction of range, the term *fork* presents an interesting parallel to *branch* (Fig. 6). Again a word with a purely tributary sense in Great Britain has retained its original usage rather generally but has been transformed locally into a full generic term. In this case, however, the Americanism is apparently wholly absent from the northeastern half of the study area—except for the aberrant north-central Pennsylvania tract —and is almost completely an inland, montane phenomenon. The absence of *fork* in the oldest colonial regions suggests the pos-

[23] *NED;* and Joseph Wright (ed.), *The English Dialect Dictionary* (New York: Putnam's Sons, 1898–1905).

[24] In this connection the few New England occurrences and those in the Mohawk Valley may be of considerable significance. Cf. Edward E. Hale, Jr., "Dialectical Evidence in the Place-Names of Eastern New York," *American Speech,* V (1929), 154–67.

[25] The fact that Kurath (in *Word Geography of the Eastern United States*) notes isolated occurrences of *run* in those portions of eastern North Carolina settled by Scottish immigrants would seem to support such a hypothesis.

[26] Also see Kurath, *Word Geography of the Eastern United States,* Fig. 93.

[27] And throughout the remainder of the southeastern United States. *Webster's New International Dictionary of the English Language* (2d ed., unabridged), hereinafter referred to as *Webster;* and Maximilian Schele de Vere, *Americanisms: the English of the New World* (New York: C. Scribner, 1872).

sibility of a relatively late origin along an inland frontier.[28]

The closely similar term *prong* is much less current than either *branch* or *fork*. In its basic sense of a tributary, only twenty-six occurrences are noted on maps of the study area—all within its southern half.[29] Thirteen cases of the use of *prong* in the full generic sense of stream have been recorded—eight in Delaware and five in Virginia. The lateness of the earliest *DAE* and McJimsey citations (1725 and 1770 respectively) would make this appear to be another relatively recent term.

In Maine and northern New Hampshire the term *stream* is applied to many and sometimes a majority of medium-sized watercourses; but its use is greatly restricted in other parts of New England and in New York, New Jersey, Pennsylvania, and Virginia, and it is unknown elsewhere in the study area (Fig. 7). This distributional pattern is not only unexplained but scarcely noticed in American place-name literature.[30] There is nothing unusual in the physical context of *stream* to help solve the question;[31] but recency of the first recorded occurrence in Virginia (McJimsey, 1820) may be an important clue, for the northern New England tract in which *stream* achieves its greatest prominence is one of recent settlement.

In contrast to *stream*, the limitation of the term *kill* to the Hudson Valley, Catskills, and upper Delaware Valley (Fig. 8) can be accounted for quite readily. This Dutch equivalent of *brook* or *run* is almost exactly coterminous with the region of sig-

nificant, or even transient, Dutch settlement. It is interesting to note occurrences as far afield as the Mohawk Valley, Delaware, and Berks County, Pennsylvania. The relative scarcity of *kills* along the lower Hudson Valley and on Long Island is not so easily explained, although detailed historical investigation might show that Dutch toponymy was more thoroughly supplanted by English terms here than in less accessible areas.

The term *lick* has already been cited as one used not only in its strict original sense but also quite often within the specific name of a stream (Fig. 9) so as to take on some generic attributes. Until a study has been made of the geography of salt licks and their place in the frontier economy, it will be difficult to determine how closely *lick* as an element in stream nomenclature coincides with the physical and economic entity. What does appear certain from the map is that *lick* is a Southernism, probably of late origin along the frontier.[32] The use of *lick* as a full generic term for stream occurs in scattered localities in West Virginia and in the adjoining portions of Virginia, Kentucky, Ohio, and western Maryland—as well as in north-central Pennsylvania.

Among the remaining minor terms used for drainage features, one of the more interesting is *ditch*. The ambiguity of its connotations on the Eastern Shore has been mentioned previously, but the same phenomenon occurs in poorly drained sections of northern and northwestern Ohio (and other middle western areas). A parallel term—*drain*—is found infrequently within the study area but abounds in the formerly swampy tracts of southeastern Michigan.

LAKE TERMS

The percentage of lakes endowed with names within the northeastern United

---

[28] An hypothesis bolstered by the rather late date for the earliest occurrences yet recorded, viz., 1697, in Sir William A. Craigie and James R. Hulbert, *A Dictionary of American English on Historical Principles* (4 vols.; Chicago: University of Chicago Press, 1936–44), hereinafter referred to as *DAE,* and 1721 (McJimsey).

[29] Thus supporting the *NED*'s contention that *prong* is a southernism.

[30] Hale, *op. cit.*, p. 165, mentions the occurrence of *stream* in the Adirondacks without comment.

[31] *Webster* equates the term with *brook*.

[32] A recent origin is suggested by the dates of the earliest citations: 1747 in McJimsey, 1747 in Mitford M. Matthews (ed.), *A Dictionary of Americanisms on Historical Principles* (Chicago: University of Chicago Press, 1951), and 1750 in *DAE*.

States is almost as high as that of streams, even though only two generic terms—*lake* and *pond*—are in common use.[33] *Lake*, a widely current English term, is applied in the British Isles to larger bodies of water, but in America to specimens of almost any size. The term may precede or follow the specific in a name but is most often found in a terminal position.[34] *Pond* is, in a sense, an Americanism, for its common meaning in England is "a small body of still water of artificial formation" (*NED*) and only locally is it equivalent to a small lake. In studying the highly divergent patterns of *pond* and *lake* in Figures 10A and 10B, it must be remembered that lakes are an important phenomenon only in the glaciated northern section of the study area. Within this region, *pond* predominates greatly throughout all New England, except northeastern Maine, and in eastern New York. Although *lake* is generally reserved in New England for larger bodies of water, there is an extremely wide overlap in usage, many a *pond* being larger than a *lake*. The manner in which this special, local English term came to dominate in New England (and the more lacustrine portions of the Chesapeake Bay region) at an early date[35] remains a mystery. *Lake* is used most frequently in northeastern Maine, the western Adirondacks, northeastern Pennsylvania, and northern New Jersey—the outer rim of the lake zone of the northeastern United States.[36]

The extent to which hills, mountains, and

other eminences have been named in various regions of Anglo-America presents interesting irregularities. The majority of eligible places in New England possess names, as do most of those throughout the Folded Appalachians; but in that hilliest of areas, the Appalachian (i.e., Allegheny and Cumberland) Plateau, only a small minority of highland tracts are dignified with names.[37] Among the array of generic terms used for upland features, several are so widespread as to lack regional significance. The most notable example is the ubiquitous *mountain;* but *top* (along with its derivative *roundtop*), *peak*, *mound*, and *rock* are also important. The widely prevalent *ridge* offers the interesting problem of a single term covering a multiplicity of features from an insignificant line of sand dunes or a river levee to a huge mountain rampart.

The term *hill* is favored throughout the United States for protuberances of less than mountain size; but in New England—and particularly the southern half of the region —*hill* is employed for a wide variety of landforms of great range in magnitude, far outstripping all competitive terms (Fig. 11A). In the Southern Appalachians *hill* yields precedence to *knob* (Fig. 11B), an Americanism that appears to be of late origin.[38] The term *mount*, used in Great Britain for "a more or less conical hill of moderate height rising from a plain" (*NED*), occurs widely throughout the United States, with an especially large concentration in New England and eastern New York. *Mount* is perhaps unique in that the word is obsolete in the vernacular except for its survival in place names (*DAE*).

[33] *Tarn, pool, mere, loch,* and *zee* occur, but with great rarity.

[34] McMillan, *op. cit.,* p. 247.

[35] The *DAE* records the use of pond in 1622; Clarice E. Tyler, "Topographic Terms in the Seventeenth Century Records of Connecticut and Rhode Island," *New England Quarterly,* II (1929), 382–401, in 1644.

[36] Figure 10B records only those cases where *lake* is used in a terminal position; but the areal pattern for antecedent cases is much the same. The term *mill pond,* used apparently in the original English sense, is scattered throughout the older portion of the study area, with the largest number of occurrences in the Chesapeake Bay region.

[37] Possibly because of the generally uniform size and appearance of hills.

[38] The *NED* cites *knob* thus; the earliest recorded by McJimsey and *DAE* are 1777 and 1796, respectively. J. D. Whitney, *Names and Places: Studies in Geographical and Topographical Nomenclature* (Cambridge, England, 1888) states (pp. 106–7): "There is an occasional 'knob' in the eastern United States, both in the White Mountains and in the Catskills; but the topographical use of this word is decidedly a southwestern [i.e., south-central United States] peculiarity."

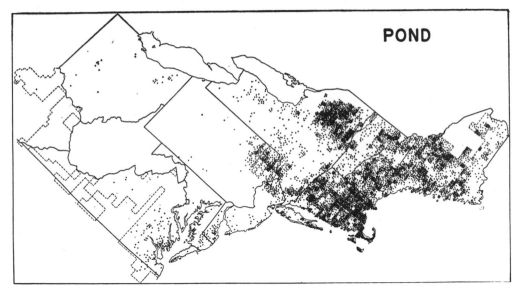

FIG. 10A.

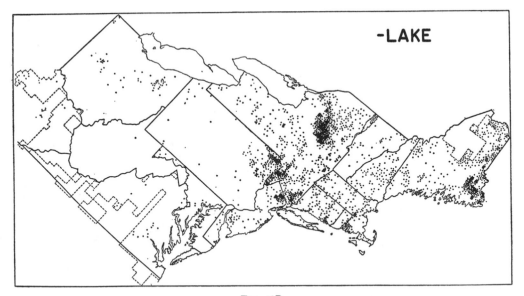

FIG. 10B.

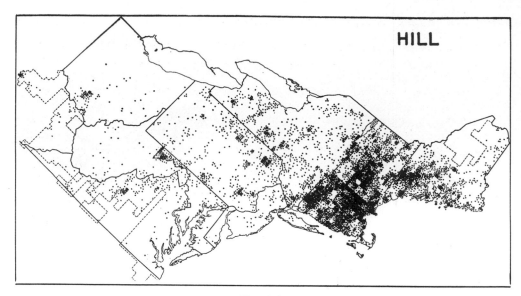

FIG. 11A.

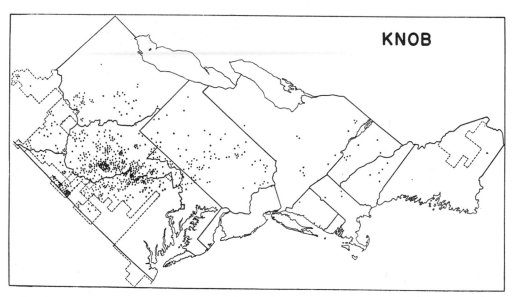

FIG. 11B.

The influence of biblical nomenclature on the popularity of the term in New England would bear investigation.

Perhaps the most curious term used as a synonym for *hill* within the study area is *cobble,* which is defined by the *DAE* as "a round hill . . . name applied to a hill or other moderate elevation whose sides have a covering of loose or cobble stones." The generic term is evidently unknown in

"shelf-like projection on the side of a rock or mountain" (*NED*), or sometimes the whole eminence, may be termed a *ledge* (Fig. 12), a thoroughly English usage, while in the Southern Appalachians the Americanism *spur* is applied to the rib-like flanks of some mountains.[41] Passes across ridges and mountains are only occasionally bestowed with names, and then in those areas where they are of particular impor-

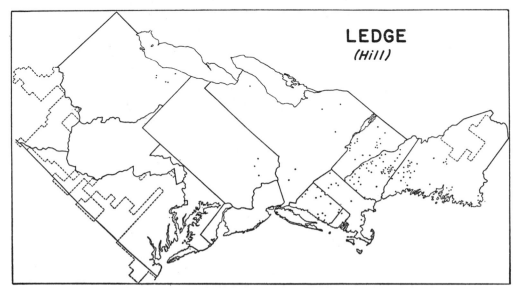

LEDGE
(Hill)

Fɪɢ. 12.

the British Isles, and a German or Austrian derivation is suggested by the *DAE* and Whitney.[39] The fact that the thirty or forty occurrences discovered in this survey are limited to eastern New York and western New England might suggest diffusion from a Dutch source in the Hudson Valley.[40]

Unlike some mountainous regions of Europe, there is a distinct scarcity of names for the component sections of individual hills and mountains in the United States. In the northern half of the study area a

tance in the local routing of communications. The term *pass* occurs in all appropriate sections of the study area, but less often than might be expected.[42] Within New England the Americanism *notch* is greatly favored,[43] especially in the White Mountains, but the term also appears in New York and Pennsylvania (Fig. 13). A rather late origin is indicated for *notch*[44] in contrast to the antiquity of almost all other New England

[41] A late origin is likely since the earliest examples in McJimsey and the *DAE* both date from 1737.

[42] The only locality in which it appears to outnumber the alternative terms in the Adirondacks, according to Hale, *op. cit.,* p. 164.

[43] Whitney, *op. cit.,* p. 135.

[44] The earliest citation in the *DAE* is 1718, in McJimsey, 1832.

[39] Whitney, *op. cit.,* pp. 109–11.

[40] Within the same general area there are numerous cases where *cobble* is used as a quasigeneric term in the specific portion of a place name.

terms. Within the Appalachians southward from central Pennsylvania—and to a lesser extent in the Poconos, Catskills, and northern Vermont—passes are denoted as *gaps* (Fig. 14). This term does occur infrequently in Great Britain but did not achieve widespread popularity in the United States before the mid-eighteenth century.[45]

Lowland tracts, basins, valleys, and the like have gone nameless in a great majority of the places where they lack strong physical individuality. Since it is difficult to decide which lowland areas merit proper names—outside such obvious candidates as the Appalachian valleys—it is likewise difficult to determine which generic terms are regionalized and which relatively universalized in distribution. An additional complication is created by the widespread habit of regarding stream names as adequate labels for lowland areas, which often are not otherwise designated.[46] Thus it is uncertain whether the three most popular terms—*valley, hollow,* and *bottom*—display any genuine regional concentration. All are abundant in the rougher areas south and west of New England and poorly represented in the latter region. Clearly, a more refined definition of these terms and their relationship to river and pass terms is called for.

Other lesser terms do, however, cluster within more limited ranges. Thus *gorge, gulf,*[47] *glen,*[48] and *gully*[49] are restricted to the northern section of the study area, especially western New York;[50] and *clove,* from the Dutch *klove* or *kloof,* is used for "a

rocky cleft or fissure; a gap, ravine" (*NED*) in and near the Catskills. Within the Southern Appalachians the term *cove* is current for a rather uncommon landform, "a recess with precipitous sides in the steep flank of a mountain."[51] A curious distributional puzzle is posed by the term *draft* which has been adopted for mountain ravines (and also watercourses) in two widely separated tracts: north-central Pennsylvania and an area in the Folded Appalachians along the Virginia-West Virginia boundary between parallels 37° 30′ and 38° 30′—and almost never elsewhere.[52]

VEGETATIONAL FEATURES

One of the more striking peculiarities of American toponymy is the near-absence of generic terms for vegetational features.[53] Such terms in the northeastern United States as do have any floristic connotations refer primarily to drainage characteristics. Thus, the term *swamp* indicates, in general, "a tract of rich soil having a growth of trees or other vegetation, but too moist for cultivation" (*NED*). Although the term has gained almost universal acceptance throughout North America, its greatest concentration appears along and near the Atlantic Seaboard. The etymology and areal source of the word are both obscure. Although it may possibly have been in local use in England around 1600 (*NED*), no documentary proof for this claim has been forthcoming, and the oldest citations yet

---

[45] McJimsey's earliest citation is dated 1741; that of the *DAE,* 1750.

[46] Indeed, it is sometimes impossible to judge whether a given term refers to the valley or the stream, e.g., *draft,* for which the *DAE* cites both meanings.

[47] "Deep and wide, between mountains," *LANE.*

[48] "Small and thickly wooded," *LANE;* originally a Gaelic term, *NED.*

[49] Usually used for valleys containing intermittent streams, *LANE;* possibly an Americanism.

[50] Whitney, *op. cit.,* pp. 157–58.

[51] *NED.* The same source also attributes the sense of "gap" or "pass" to *cove* in the United States but is probably incorrect in doing so. The term appears to have originated in the English Lake District, *DAE* and Whitney, *op. cit.,* p. 163.

[52] Although the term, alternatively spelled *draught,* is not so noted by the *NED,* the fact that the earliest citation dates from 1801 suggests the likelihood that it is an Americanism.

[53] J. K. Wright, *op. cit.,* pp. 143–44. The only important exception is provided by national and state forests. There are, however, innumerable allusions to plant life in the specific elements of American place names.

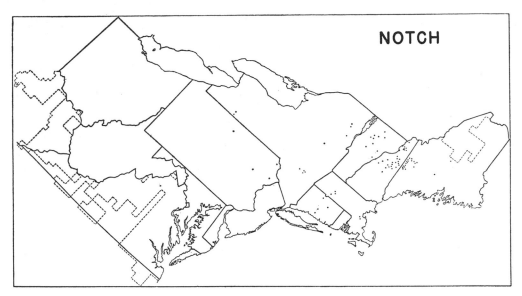

FIG. 13.

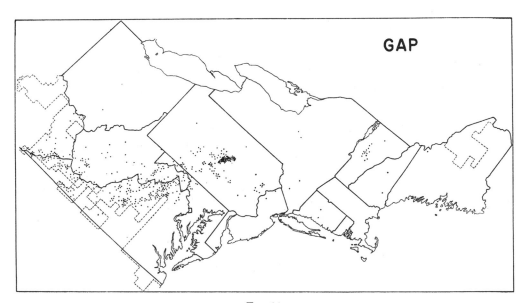

FIG. 14.

discovered are in the early colonial records of Virginia.[54]

The widely used English term *meadow* was transferred to the American colonies at an early date but with some change in emphasis, for its American sense is defined as "a low level tract of uncultivated grass land, especially along a river or in marshy regions near the sea" (*NED*), and the *LANE* states that the "exact meaning varies considerably with the character of the country." At any rate, *meadow*—usually denoting a grassy, often poorly drained tract devoid of trees—failed to penetrate far into the interior of the study area, and today it is found mainly along the Atlantic Seaboard northward of Cape May, New Jersey.

The term *marsh,* like *swamp,* is widely prevalent in the United States, but almost always as a designation for an unforested, water-logged tract, either fresh or salt. Within the study area its primary concentration is in the Chesapeake Bay region. Once again within the Hudson Valley a Dutch term *vly* (or *vlie*) is applied to swamps and marshes. Notable by its absence in the study area is *slough,* a term of wide currency in the Middle West. In southeastern Virginia and thence southwestward along the coastal plain, the Algonquin term *pocosin*[55] is applied to poorly drained interfluves. Within New England and portions of New Jersey and New York fresh or brackish tracts "grown with tufts of grass (hummocks), cranberries, or blueberries, or without any growth" (*LANE*) and too small to be called *swamps* or *marshes* are designated as *bogs,* a usage not too far from the English.

It is interesting to note a few instances of the use of the venerable English term

fen in Maine and Rhode Island. A rather more perplexing problem is posed by the use of the term *heath* within northeastern Maine (but evidently not in neighboring New Brunswick). The *NED* attributes no particular floral significance to the term, which in Great Britain apparently denotes a flat, rather bleak upland tract with or without heather or some other shrubby growth. In New England *heath* seems to be applied solely to level interfluves covered by cranberries, blueberries, or heather (*LANE*), but field work is needed to establish the precise physical connotations of the word. There is no explanation at hand for its presence in Maine and absence in other American regions.

Agglomerated Settlements

If considerable uncertainty surrounds the historical geography of many generic terms describing the relatively immutable physical features of the northeastern United States, then there is even greater scope for confusion in the study of most terms applied to the cultural landscape. The difficulties are particularly impressive in the study of the class of objects with the most diversified nomenclature—agglomerated settlements: There are great variations in the areal density of towns (Fig. 15); the names of individual places often have undergone one or more changes; and, in many cases, the generic element in the name is implicit rather than stated, as in, say, "Brewster," instead of "Brewster Village" or "Brewster City." Thus, a fairly exacting study of the distributional significance of various settlement terms would require the drafting of a time series of maps showing the number and location of all instances of a given usage as against the total number of settlements containing explicit generic terms in their names; and some account would have to be taken of settlement size and morphology—altogether a task of heroic dimensions. Because of this fact, the following statements are merely reasonable guesses.

[54] *NED*. According to Robert Krapp (as quoted by Martha J. Gibson in " 'Swamp' in Early American Usage," *American Speech,* X [1935], 303–5), the term was not used in Great Britain because all "swampy" tracts had long since been reclaimed and put under cultivation.

[55] Among the several spellings, the chief variants are *poquosin* and *pocoson.*

Certain terms for agglomerated settlements can be safely characterized as universal, viz., *junction, crossing, landing,* and *forge* or *furnace,* as they occur in a large percentage of suitable situations. The suffix *-ton* probably falls into the same category, since there is scarcely a corner of the study area lacking this usage.[56] Another suffix, *-boro* or *-borough,* is much less common but seems to be as widely distributed. The status of *-ville,* perhaps the most popular

in widely scattered portions of the study area.[57]

A clearly regionalized pattern appears in the distribution of *corner* or *corners* in the names of villages (Fig. 17), for numerous clusters occur throughout New England, New York, Ohio, northern Pennsylvania, New Jersey, and the Chesapeake Bay region, while almost no examples are found in Kentucky, West Virginia, or southern Pennsylvania. Particularly not-

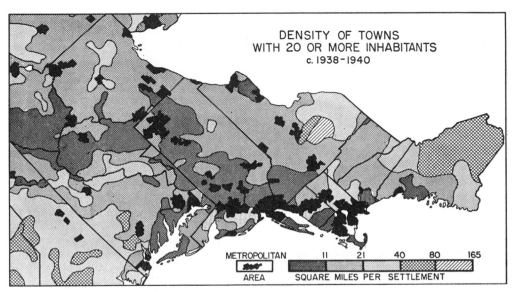

FIG. 15.

term for a settlement in the northeastern United States, is more doubtful (Fig. 16). There is a high degree of correlation between the pattern for *-ville* and that for the totality of agglomerated settlements (Fig. 15), but the unusually heavy concentration in southeastern Pennsylvania invites further investigation. Another ostensibly universal term is *green,* for some twenty-five occurrences have been recorded

able is the strong concentration in south-central Maine. Nothing is known of the history or cultural significance of *corner* except that it is an Americanism entirely unknown in England.[58]

A less complex pattern prevails for another Americanism, *center,* which is distributed widely, though not in vast num-

[56] In plotting *-ton* on manuscript maps, a careful distinction was made between towns whose names were formed by the addition of the suffix and those where *-ton* was part of a borrowed name. By this definition "Ironton," for example, would qualify, but "Hamilton" would not.

[57] The origin and morphological connotations of the term are obscure inasmuch as none of the dictionaries define *green* in the sense of a settlement; but it is possibly derived from "village green."

[58] The earliest citation in the *DAE* dates from 1841, but the term was certainly in use long before then.

bers, throughout the entire northern half of the study area (Fig. 18).[59] Although the fact may not help explain the distribution, it is interesting to note that *center* frequently occurs as the designation for one of a cluster of toponymically related villages. Thus, to quote a fictional example, a "Colchester Center" may lie within a mile or two of "Colchester" which, in turn, is flanked by "North Colchester" and "South Colchester."

Other town terms with essentially New England concentrations are *village* (Fig. 19) and *common,* the latter of which is found only in Vermont, Massachusetts, and Rhode Island. In portions of western New York and northern Vermont and Maine the term *settlement* is used for some relatively diffuse groupings of houses, a usage apparently related to frontier conditions.

Two of the most important terms for settlements, *-burg*[60] (Fig. 20) and *-town* (Fig. 21), occur in nearly all sections of the study area, but for reasons that are not at all clear their major concentrations lie within the central portion. Possibly the essentially urban significance of these terms is more apposite in this region of well-developed urban culture than elsewhere. The term *city* shows an even stronger clustering within the central area (Fig. 22). This Americanism[61] is used not only for genuine cities but also as "a grandiose or anticipatory designation for a mere hamlet or village" (*DAE*). In southeastern Pennsylvania, the adjacent part of New Jersey, and southeastern New England, there appear a number of villages with the designation *square* in obvious reference to the town square around which the settlement is arranged.

Few generic terms for towns are centered

in the southern portion of the study area since settlement is generally sparse and a larger than average proportion of places lack generic elements in their names. The term *crossroads* is one of the few, for even though scattered as far north as Maine and New York, most occurrences are in Tidewater Virginia and Delaware. Within the same Tidewater Virginia region, the term *forks* is attached to many small villages and hamlets situated at road intersections. Because of the wide intervals between genuine towns, the numerous rural stores of the South often take on certain urban functions; and if a small settlement should arise near one, it frequently receives the appellation *store* or *shop* (Fig. 23).

HIGHWAYS

Since such phenomena as bridges, wharves, farms, mills, dams, and other areally conspicuous works of man have received universal terms when they have been named by mapmakers, the only important class of artifacts remaining to be discussed is rural highways.[62] Although most of these are designated at the present time only by means of letters and numbers, a variety of generic terms for roads have survived from earlier days or have been recently revived. The most areally restricted is *tote road,* a term for "a rough temporary road for conveying goods to or from a settlement, camp, etc." (*NED*) that occurs only in northern Maine[63] and is documented only as far back as 1862 (*DAE*). The terms *turnpike*[64] and its derivative *pike*[65] obviously refer to the improved toll

---

[59] Once again the *DAE*'s earliest citation—1791 —seems unreasonably recent.

[60] The term is unusual etymologically in that it may derive from German, Dutch, and French sources as well as English. It is also interesting to note that it is closely akin to *-boro.*

[61] The earliest citation dates from 1747 in New Jersey (*DAE*).

[62] Under the rubric of non-material culture, some atypical terms for political units, e.g., *town* (for *township*), *borough,* and *hundred,* and for tracts of real estate, e.g., *grant, patent,* or *gore,* might logically be discussed; but their distributional traits and the factors controlling them are so special that they merit independent treatment.

[63] Except for a single example in the anomalous north-central Pennsylvania region.

[64] First recorded in England in 1748 (*NED*) and in the United States in 1785 (*DAE*).

[65] Described by the *NED* as dialectal, colloquial, and an Americanism; first known adoption in the United States in 1836 (*DAE*).

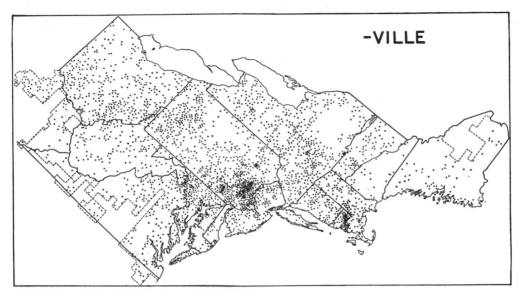

FIG. 16.

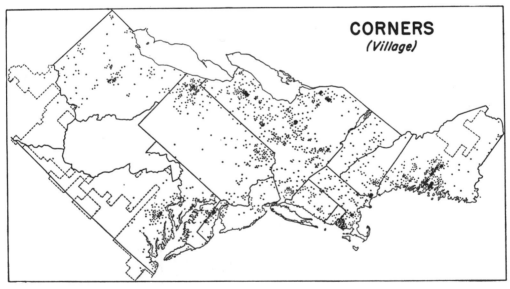

FIG. 17.

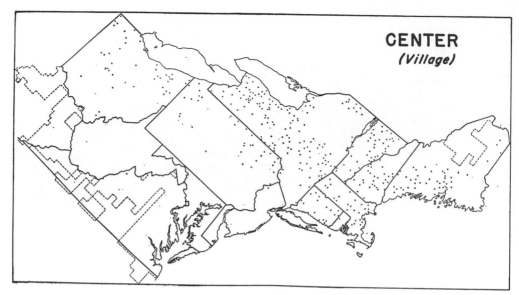

Fig. 18.

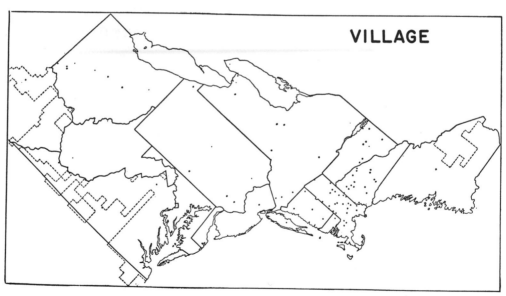

Fig. 19.

150

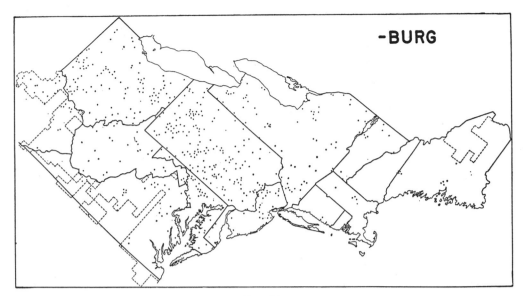

FIG. 20.

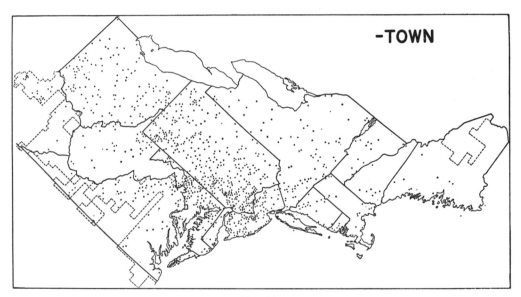

FIG. 21.

151

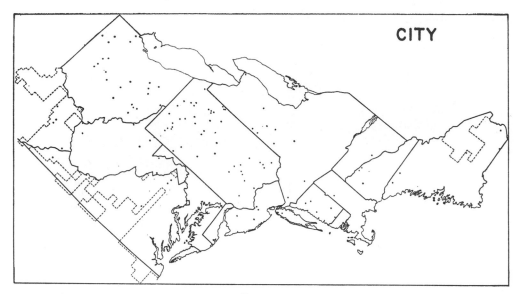

FIG. 22.

FIG. 23.

152

roads constructed since the latter part of the eighteenth century. The contemporary distribution of the terms is markedly uneven: *turnpike* occurs in every state within the study area, but notable concentrations are found only in southeastern New England, the immediate hinterland of Baltimore, and in west-central Ohio; *pike* remains important only in the territory adjoining the Massachusetts-Rhode Island boundary, the Blue Grass region of Kentucky, and western Ohio.

Avenue, which has much the same distribution pattern, except for an extension into New Jersey and Maryland, has never been recorded in the sense of a rural road by lexicographers in either Great Britain or the United States. The use of *lane* for rather short public roads extends along the Atlantic Seaboard from New Hampshire to the Potomac and recurs, after a wide gap, in the Blue Grass country of Kentucky (Fig. 24). The only definition recorded for England is "a narrow way

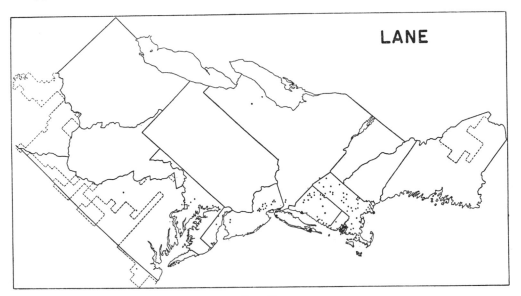

FIG. 24.

Another group of road terms is current only within the older portions of the northeastern United States, particularly New England. *Street,* the most important of these, is found in considerable profusion in the rural tracts of Massachusetts and Connecticut and in western New York, an altogether remarkable phenomenon in view of the fact that this relic of the Roman occupation of Britain has long been obsolete in the vernacular of that country.[66]

[66] *NED.* This dictionary's definition of *street* as "a paved road, a highway" would seem to apply. Hale's contention (*op. cit.*) that the term is used as an equivalent for hamlet in certain parts of New York and Connecticut cannot be confirmed by a study of the maps of those states.

between hedges or banks" (*NED*); but in this country the *LANE* describes it as a private road and the *DAE* as a Southernism meaning "a road which has a fence on each side." The list of such terms is rounded out by *way* which occurs infrequently in southeastern New England.

CONCLUSIONS

It is evident from the foregoing series of maps and descriptions that no two of the terms studied have identical or even nearly identical patterns of distribution. This is true not only because of the areal non-equivalence of the various phenomena named, but also because of rapid and often complex linguistic shifts in many terms in a region where migration has been vigorous and settlement so recent that cultural areas have had scant opportunity to crystallize. Nevertheless, it is equally evident that the majority of terms discussed can be sorted into a few rough regional and temporal categories. First, it appears that the Atlantic Seaboard, and especially its New England sector, contains many Anglicisms and archaic terms and that it more closely

which occupy a small but distinctive region, these regionalized groupings may be tabulated as follows:[67]

It is tempting to press further and endeavor to establish definite boundaries for culture areas on the basis of place-term distributions; but such an experiment must be deferred because of the inadequacies of the map data and the means for tracing the chronological shifts in the importance and areal extent of the terms.

Old Colonial (Entire Seaboard)

| Corner | Marsh (?) | Mill pond |
| Lane | Meadow | Pond |

New England

Avenue	Common	Hill	Street
Bog	Corner	Ledge	Village
Brook	Creek (near	Mount	Way
Center	absence of)	Pond	
	Heath		

Midland

-burg	Square
City	-town
Run	

South

Branch (in non-	Forks (for hamlet)
tributary sense)	Pocoson
Crossroads	Swamp (for stream)

Northern Frontier

Center	Flowage	Gully	Notch	Settlement
Cobble	Glen	Inlet	Outlet	Stream
Corner	Gorge	Mount	Pond	Tote road

Southern Frontier[68]

Branch (in non-tributary	Fork (in both tributary and	Knob
sense)	non-tributary senses)	Lick
Cove	Gap	Spur
Draft		

resembles the home country toponymically than do the interior regions. In areas settled some time after about 1760 (Fig. 25) there is an important group of Americanisms and terms with a strong frontier flavor. If one excludes the Dutch terms,

[67] Some terms are recorded as being characteristic of two regions. The term "Midland," used for the central portion of the study area, is borrowed from Kurath, *Word Geography of the Eastern United States.*

[68] North-central Pennsylvania may be regarded as an outlier of this region.

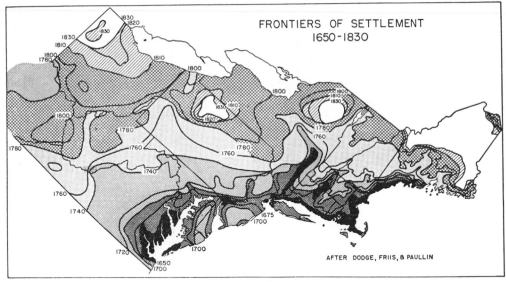

FRONTIERS OF SETTLEMENT
1650-1830

AFTER DODGE, FRIIS, & PAULLIN

FIG. 25.

A variety of research problems are suggested by the provisional data presented here. Most urgent is the need for a series of careful studies of the toponymy of a selected group of communities that will include generic terms, specific names, and vernacular topographic language and will treat these subjects in their full geographic and historical context. In addition, much is to be gained by investigating the historical geography of important individual generic terms over their full North American range. Although abundant documentary materials exist for the study of generic terms in Great Britain, their analysis has been neglected in favor of an exhaustive survey of all individual specific names of the country.[69] If this deficiency were to be remedied, the study of American toponymy could be greatly advanced. Corollary to such studies, there should be research on the source, routing, and destination of the settlers of the United States, with particular attention to the culture and the social psychology of those who were the most active namers.

Among other unanswered problems is the interaction of differing European cultures in the United States. Why have no minority cultures except the Dutch survived in the generic terms of the study area, and specifically why the failure of German, Swedish, and aboriginal terms? [70] Furthermore, why have these non-English cultures survived in specific names? And what is the relationship between specific and generic nomenclature not only as regards cultural survival but also in a more general sense? A host of interesting linguistic problems with geographic overtones are offered by generic terms—particularly

[69] The English Place-Name Society's *Survey of English Place-Names.* The closest approach to a discussion of generic terms is found in *Introduction to the Survey of English Place-Names: Part II, the Chief Elements Used in English Place-Names* (Cambridge, 1924).

[70] There are, of course, isolated exceptions, such as *pocoson,* a single case of *-berg* (for mountain in the Pennsylvania German country), and a few *lacs* and *rivières* near the Canadian border. In other parts of the nation Spanish and French terms may locally assume great importance. See Raup, *op. cit.;* West, *op. cit.;* Mary Austin, "Geographical Terms from the Spanish," *American Speech,* VIII (1933), 7–10; and Edward E. Hale, "Geographical Terms in the Far West," *Dialect Notes,* VI (1932), 217–34.

the process of change in the meaning of old terms and the invention of new ones in the transfer of settlers overseas to a relatively similar physical environment and the further changes with the penetration of the interior. The paramount problem, however, and one that may never be fully answered, is the nature of the interrelationships among toponymy, other cultural phenomena, and the physical environment. It is to be hoped that some way can be found to approach this problem so as to delimit accurately the past and present culture areas of the nation and to document the whole marvelously intricate process of cultural evolution.

FRED B. KNIFFEN

LOUISIANA HOUSE TYPES

Perhaps nowhere else in the United States does the landscape so clearly reflect the imprint of varied cultural strains as it does in Louisiana. French expansion followed the waterways, and to this day the cultural pattern of the lowlands stands in marked contrast to that of the pine hills, settled originally by overland migrants from the deep and border South. The theretofore sparsely populated prairies of southwestern Louisiana received an influx of settlers from northern states during the last quarter of the nineteenth century; the cultural imprint is highly reminiscent of the Midwest.

The diversity of cultural pattern is obvious even to the casual observer; to the trained geographer it presents a challenge in the matter of a critical evaluation and classification of the elements responsible for the differences. The logical approach to culturogeographic[1] regions would appear to be through the quantitative and qualitative consideration of the cultural forms of the landscape, by a method analogous to that employed by anthropologists in arriving at

culture regions, or in establishing culture relationships.[2]

For Louisiana, house types are an element of culture possessing great diagnostic value in regional differentiation. Hence, they were employed as the opening wedge in the attack, and it is with the identity and distribution of house types in Louisiana that this paper is concerned.

METHODOLOGY

The first attempt at classification involved the detailed analysis of several hundred houses. A card file was devised, embracing headings for each of the constituent elements of the individual house: plan, roof, chimney, porches, appendages, paint, windows, height, etc. As each of these elements was encountered in new form it was given a card and number under its proper heading. On the field sheets each dwelling was analyzed by means of the index. The location of each house was recorded to the nearest tenth of a mile, to permit of relocation and to facilitate mapping.

Almost the sole virtue of this system is its completeness. It is slow; it involves an unwieldy mass of data; and its very detail obscures the ready perception of the es-

Reprinted, with permission of the author and editor, from *Annals of the Association of American Geographers*, XXVI (1936), 179–93. The author is professor of geography and chairman of the Department of Geography and Anthropology at Louisiana State University, Baton Rouge.

[1] The term "culturogeographic" is advanced to fill the need for a word importing the cultural forms of the geographic landscape. A culturogeographic region differs from a geographic region in that only cultural forms are considered.

[2] Notably exemplified in the works of Erland Nordenskiöld and members of his school. For a stimulating study along these lines, see S. Klimek and W. Milke, "An Analysis of the Material Culture of the Tupi Peoples," *American Anthropologist*, XXXVIII (1935), 71–91.

sential form of the structure. In place of the index system there was gradually developed a largely graphic method of representing the form of the dwelling. A few strokes are sufficient to indicate all essential details concerning plan, roof, porches, appendages, height, etc. Separate columns on the new field sheets provide for the classifi-

route, map, Fig. 1), with a grand total recording of about 15,000 houses. To effect a thorough sampling every dwelling visible from the road was included, and old roads were alternated with modern highways.

Urban centers were disregarded in the enumeration, not because they are not significant, but because they introduce com-

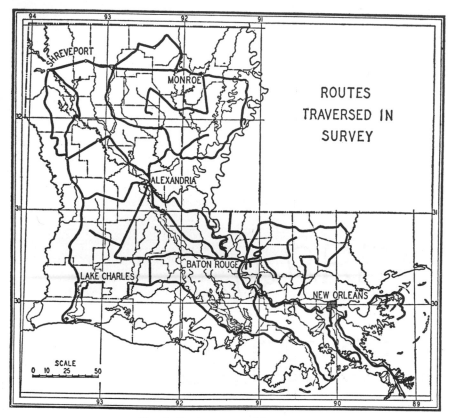

Fig. 1. Routes traversed in survey.

cation of each structure according to broad categories of age and class. Qualities other than the aforementioned were largely neglected, being noted only where regionally conspicuous. The defection is not so serious as might first appear, since it was early learned that certain elements show little variation, and may be disregarded.

Employing the new system it was possible to proceed much faster, some 1,700 houses being registered on the banner day. The state was thoroughly traversed (see

plexities out of all proportion to the areas they occupy. Also cities, and even large towns, frequently maintain a large measure of independence of local cultural environment, exhibiting the varied ideas of a heterogeneous population, and aping the practices of groups far removed. Louisiana is a highly rural state; the inclusion of urban centers could in nowise seriously alter the results. At most, cities would appear on the maps as inconspicuous islands.

The analysis of the field data brought

forth many difficult problems. Neither houses nor other cultural forms can be classified in a manner exactly analogous to that used by biologists. The biologist never finds the tail of a lion grafted to the body of a cow; the classifier of cultural forms has no such assurance. He must judiciously generalize, and he can never be completely objective. Without the necessary historical and comparative data he cannot safely accept apparent genetic relationships. In his morphologic data he must look for central themes, and must temporarily obscure minor variations in the individual forms. The correctness of his selection of central themes or *motifs* may find support in the facts of distribution: That is, should he find that what he suspects to be the minor variants of a theme have a common areal distribution, he may with some assurance group them together.

A preliminary examination of the field data revealed that virtually every structure would fall into one of four general classes: (1) those with sideward-facing gables; (2) those whose gables face the front; (3) those having pyramidal roofs; and (4) those with shed roofs. The latter two classes are numerically insignificant, while the first two show considerable regional overlap. It was immediately evident that further division was necessary.

Of those structures with sideward-facing gables one element showing great diagnostic possibilities was the method of construction of the front porch. The statistical proof of the assertion lies in the marked areal concentration of the variants of porch construction. Another element showing similar diagnostic qualities was the open passage of the familiar "two pens and a passage" (Fig. 6), while still another was two-storey construction. Other elements, such as appendages, failed as distinguishing markers of types largely because they did not show sufficient variation or segregation.

The houses with frontward-facing gables were divisible on the basis of width: the "shotgun" house, a single room wide; and the bungalow type, two rooms in width.

Though each of these types shows individual differences, such as a variety of methods for construction of front porches, the data failed to reveal significant areal concentration.

Houses with pyramidal roofs are sparingly represented over most of the state, but nowhere do they reach dominance. Houses with shed roofs belong almost exclusively to one simple unvarying type, highly restricted in distribution.

Summary forms were prepared, embracing the above-mentioned types and a number of subtypes, based on differences in width, length, etc., some fifty in all. Also, provision was made for cognizance of age and class. Each field sheet was independently summarized, totaled, and the percentage of each type and subtype computed.

Still, fifty types defied handling. It seemed advisable to reduce the number by both combination and elimination. It was deemed permissible to disregard variation in length, width, and type of appendage, where the diagnostic element or elements remained obviously the same. Since form was the essential thing, age and class were justifiably omitted from consideration. Types differing too widely in form to permit of combination stood alone, or were eliminated, if their percentage distribution fell consistently below twenty.

After combination and elimination there remained nine types or, better, groups of morphologically similar types:

1. *Built-in Porch.*—For a very considerable group of houses with sideward-facing gables this feature appeared statistically as the critical element. In this type the front porch is an integral part of the structure (Figs. 2, 3, 5).[3] The use of this feature as a criterion of type is justified by its numerical dominance over extensive areas (Fig. 13). Also, the built-in porch is independent of class, appearing alike on small and large houses.

2. *Attached Porch.*—This differs from

[3] Grateful acknowledgment is made to Mr. J. A. Ford for his skillful execution of the series of house-type drawings.

FIG. 2. Built-in porch type.

FIG. 3. Built-in porch type.

Fig. 4. Attached porch type.

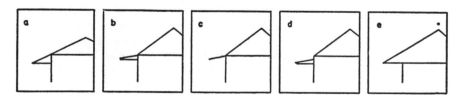

FIG. 5. Four common methods of attaching porches. Figures *a, b, c,* and *d* illustrate the four common methods of attaching porches, while *e* illustrates the built-in porch.

FIG. 6. Open passage type; double log pen.

FIG. 7. Single log pen.

FIG. 8. Midwestern or "i" type.

FIG. 9. Shotgun type.

FIG. 10. Bungalow type.

FIG. 11. Trapper type.

162

FIG. 12. Oysterman type.

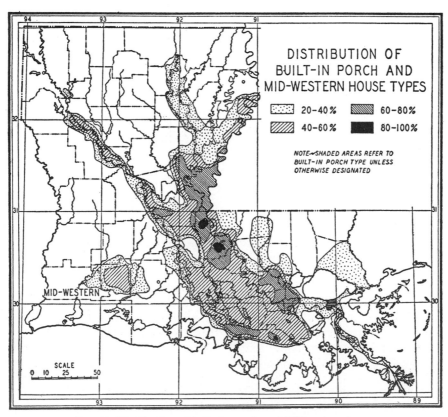

FIG. 13. Distribution of built-in porch and Midwestern types.

163

164   *Fred B. Kniffen*

the above only with respect to the manner of constructing the front porch (Fig. 4). Morphologically the two types are similar or vary within the same limits, as regards other elements. Included within this second type are four closely related methods of attachment of the front porch (Fig. 5),

distinctive trait is the presence of an open passage running from front to rear (Fig. 6). It is to be found in the primitive double log pen and in the more modern frame house. In addition to the distinctive open passage this type is characteristically marked by a high gable, with the steep

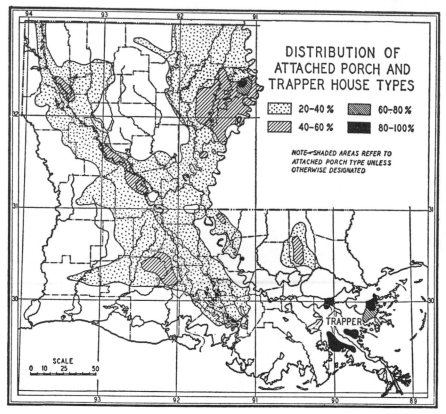

FIG. 14. Distribution of attached porch and trapper types.

their combination into a single type justified by their coincident areal distribution.

3. *Porchless.*—This type differs from the preceding two only in the absence of a front porch. Its inclusion as a type was dictated by its attaining a twenty to sixty per cent frequency over an extensive area (Fig. 15).

4. *Open Passage.*—Referable to the same general class of houses having sideward-facing gables, and at least occasionally exhibiting all the varying characteristics of the three preceding types is the fourth. Its

roof projecting on either end and extending downward to form porches on either side. Included with this type is the single log pen (Fig. 7) and its frame equivalent, the inclusion justified by morphologic similarity (high gable and steep projecting roof) and coincident distribution.

5. *Midwestern.*—The genetic implication of this name is justified in fact. Its morphologic distinction rests in its two storeys, a feature strikingly foreign to the simpler folk house types native to Louisiana. United by this common feature are two

different structures showing similar areal extent. The first, and numerically much more important, is the "i" (Indiana-Illinois-Iowa)[4] house (Fig. 8). It possesses the features of sideward-facing gables and one-room depth, in addition to its two storeys. The second and numerically less significant

type belongs to the general group of houses possessing frontward-facing gables. It differs in having a width of two rooms. It is two or more rooms deep (Fig. 10). The type appears to be recent in Louisiana, and if it has roots in older folk types of the state they are not obvious.

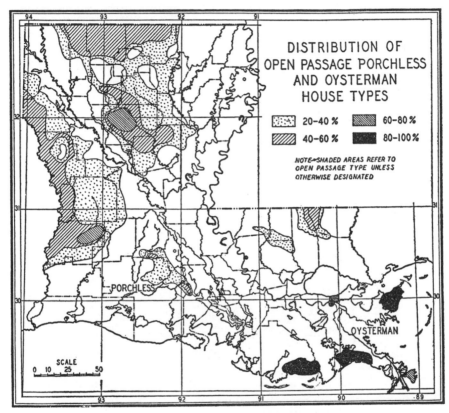

Fɪɢ. 15. Distribution of open passage, porchless, and oysterman types.

two-storey house is square with a pyramidal roof.

6. *Shotgun.*—The folk-term here employed is commonly used in Louisiana to designate a long, narrow house. It is but one room in width and from one to three or more rooms deep, with frontward-facing gable (Fig. 9). Additional data will very likely suggest several subtypes.

7. *Bungalow.*—Like the preceding this

8. *Trapper.*—This type is so-called because it is constructed and used by the trappers of Louisiana's coastal marshes and bayous. Its distinguishing feature is its shed roof (Fig. 11). It is commonly square with but a single room. Though most frequently constructed of tar-paper over siding, it is occasionally reproduced in palmetto thatch.

9. *Oysterman.*—The distinctive feature of this coastal type is the pile-supported platform on which the house proper rests (Fig. 12). The latter is most frequently a

[4] It is not intended to imply that this house type is restricted to, or originated in, the three states named.

single-room shotgun type, though occasionally it takes another form.

After combination into these nine types the unassigned residue was so small as to be disregarded without seriously affecting the final picture.

As the next step in the analysis of the

The final step was a synthesis of the distributions of the individual types, a map (Fig. 17) showing areas and extent of domination of one or two forms, and areas of mixture. For the sake of legibility it was found necessary to omit from the final map the lower percentage bracket, all below

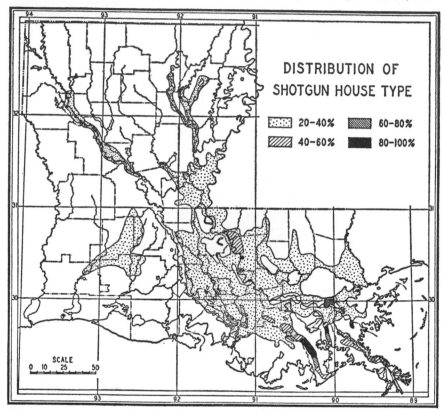

FIG. 16. Distribution of shotgun type.

data the percentage distribution of each house type was entered on a map. The base was a route map of the survey traverses, while the unit area, or rather distance, was the space covered by each field sheet, with an average of about thirty houses to each. On the basis of the plotted data isopleths were drawn, interpolation between the traverses resting on the judgment of the observer. Isoplethic intervals of 20 per cent were found to fit the data best. The unexpected ease with which the isopleths were entered is indicative of the correctness of the classification (Figs. 13, 14, 15, 16).

forty. The distribution of the bungalow type was not considered, for the reason that it may be regarded as a constant, and hence of no value in regional definition. It occurs everywhere in the state, but only in the vicinity of urban centers does it attain the higher percentage groups.

DISTRIBUTION OF TYPES

It may be worthwhile to point out certain facts with regard to the distribution of the individual types (see index to regions, Fig. 18):

The type distinguished by the built-in

porch is rather closely confined to the flood plain of the Mississippi, fingering northward along the valleys of the Ouachita and Red (see Fig. 13). It would appear to be distinctly a Lower Mississippi Valley form, since it fades into insignificance before reaching the northern boundary of Louisi-

in a broad band occupying the Mississippi flood plain. Observation indicates its presence at least as far north as Missouri.

The Midwestern type is strikingly and sharply confined to the heart of the prairie region of southwestern Louisiana (Fig. 13), whither it was imported from the

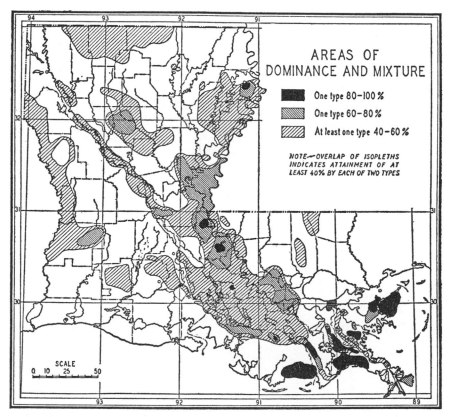

Fɪɢ. 17. Areas of dominance and mixture.

ana. Its absence in the pine hills and prairies is noteworthy. In the coastal marshes it is confined to the agricultural "islands" associated with small areas of high ground.

The type with the attached porch (Fig. 14) also attains its greatest prominence in the flood plains, but it is by no means so confined, since it spreads generously into the pine hills and prairies. Like the preceding this type is sharply restricted in the coastal marshes, but unlike the former it reaches the northern boundary of the state

Corn Belt about forty years ago. Outside this immediate area it was encountered no more than a dozen times throughout the remainder of the state.

The open-passage type (Fig. 15) is restricted to the three pine hill areas of Louisiana: the Florida Parishes; the region between the Mississippi and the Red; and the belt along the western margin of the state (Fig. 18). There is no extension of this type into the valleys, the prairies, or the coastal marshes. As might be inferred from the map, the double pen extends into the neighboring states of Mississippi, Arkansas, and Texas. It is well known in the states of the deep and border South.

The porchless type is very localized, reaching mapable significance in only one section (Fig. 15). It should be pointed out that it is largely coincident with, and partially peripheral to, the type having the attached porch.

may represent a case of mistaken identity, but more likely it marks a migrant group of people. The general distribution of the type would indicate that it belongs to the Lower Mississippi Valley.

CONCLUDING REMARKS

The final map may seem to leave rather large areas unmarked, but it is intentionally

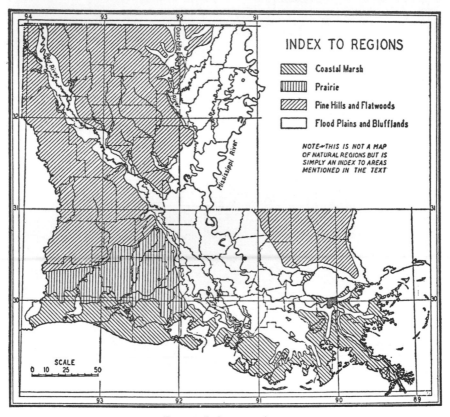

FIG. 18. Index to regions.

The trapper (Fig. 14) and the oysterman (Fig. 15) types are very specialized, and are entirely restricted to the navigable waterways of the immediate coastal region.

The shotgun house (Fig. 16) is strikingly associated with the state's waterways, attaining marked dominance along the coastal bayous, but also significantly extending in narrow bands far up the Ouachita and Red. The island in the western part of the state

so. The cores or centers of frequency distribution are clearly indicated; the intervening areas are properly undefined zones of mixture.

Possible objections may be forestalled by pointing out that this study is not intended to be *descriptive* of specific areas, but rather it is one step in the attempt to *define* the culturogeographic regions of Louisiana. Nor is it entirely a materialistic listing and classification of the house types of Louisiana. It is also an attempt to get at an areal expression of *ideas* regarding houses—a groping toward a tangible hold on the geographic expression of culture.

The study is avowedly confined to present-day Louisiana, with but slightest concern for time and extraregional relations. The house types are set up on the basis of morphologic comparison and distribution. The difficult consideration of historical genesis, it seems likely, can but combine into families and genera, or divide into species and varieties—to use the biologic analogy.

The best indication of the soundness of the methodology would seem to be that it works. The maps exhibit no inexplicable anomalies, while the final results agree with the observations of those familiar with the state.

That the general method is applicable outside Louisiana is confirmed by the experiences of several extended trips, where the same tendency for house types to cluster was observed.

JAN O. M. BROEK

DIVERSITY AND UNITY
IN SOUTHEAST ASIA

The first half of the 1940's may prove to be the most momentous period in the history of Southeast Asia. At the beginning of this decade the lands between China, India, and Australia were, with the exception of the buffer state Thailand, under the direct control of Western nations. Then, in a few months, the 150 million inhabitants of this region were brought under the rule of Japan. Will the expulsion of the Japanese mean a full turn of the wheel of fortune, a return to the situation of 1940? Obviously not; the war has brought such changes in economic, cultural, and political relations and mental attitudes, in the East as well as in the West, that a return to the *status quo* of prewar years is not only undesirable but impossible.

The colonial question is therefore of greater importance than ever. It is perhaps to be expected that the discussions should center on the subject of political independence, but it is unfortunate that this topic proves so absorbing that little attention is being devoted to equally important economic and social issues. The anticolonial tradition in American history naturally expresses itself in a strong emotional protest against the existence of dependent areas. This attitude can be a powerful lever for progress if it is understood that we are dealing here not with a fortuitous and

Reprinted, with permission of the author and editor, from the *Geographical Review*, XXXIV (1944), 175–95 (copyright, 1944, by the American Geographical Society of New York). The author is professor of geography at the University of Minnesota, Minneapolis.

immoral political relationship but with a deep-rooted cultural and economic complex. The colonial relation is essentially one form of the acculturation process, and as such it is a transitory phase. It was as a dependency of Rome that Western Europe was "exploited," but also enriched, by the more advanced Mediterranean civilization. In time it threw off the Roman yoke, and eventually it surpassed the old Empire.

Southeast Asia is now in the stage of "imperial devolution." The preoccupation with the political aspect of this process obscures, however, the problem in its totality. If one looks at Thailand or at some of the republics of tropical America, it is plain that for the masses a higher standard of living and more democratic procedures do not automatically result from political sovereignty. The Philippine commonwealth, while moving rapidly to political independence, has remained economically dependent on the United States. In the other parts of Southeast Asia prosperity was not based so overwhelmingly on the right of free access to one market, but collectively these lands were in the same position to the Western countries as the Philippines were to the United States. Japan now grants "independence" generously all over Southeast Asia, but at the same time it insists on a "co-prosperity sphere" in which, obviously, it will rule while the native peoples will remain the hewers of wood and drawers of water. In turn the Western nations attempt to counteract Japanese propaganda strategy by also making political promises. Thus we may anticipate the strange phenomenon that after the defeat of Japan the ambition of the native people for political freedom will be stronger than ever but their economic dependence on the Western nations will be the same, if not greater, than before. This divergence of political ideals and economic realities will be the most baffling problem of postwar tropical Asia.

A one-sided approach, focusing on political doctrines, must inevitably lead to disillusionment. The people of the liberated countries will discover that independence has not diminished the need for markets, capital, and trained personnel and that it has not solved the problem of security. And the American people, once again, will be dismayed by the persistence of evils that were supposed to disappear when this war for freedom had been won.

It is often assumed that independent sovereignty for all peoples must be the ultimate aim of a just world order. Yet the Soviet Union, with its great variety of peoples, shows a markedly different, and apparently satisfactory, solution on the basis of equal partnership. We cannot a priori rule out the possibility that some peoples of Southeast Asia may prefer a similar interdependent relationship. However, whether the future is to be one of equal partnership or of independence, there must be a period of preparation before such adult status can be attained. The roads to this goal as well as the time required to reach it will differ for different peoples, depending as much on their social-economic structure as on their political cohesion.

These considerations are all too often forgotten in the oratorical demands for freedom now and everywhere. Modern means of communication have made the earth a unity, but they have not created uniformity. The recent discovery that the earth is "global" does not change the fact that peoples are first of all a part of their local culture pattern, each with its own interdependent relationships of man to man and man to nature, its own traditions, institutions, and ways of making a living. Terms such as "democracy," "self-deter-

mination," and "independence" receive their meaning from local experience, not from global charters. Instead of offering universal, ready-made schemes that are likely to prove misfits, we must analyze the specific regional problems and lay plans accordingly.

REGIONAL DIVERSITY IN SOUTHEAST ASIA

In the last year or so various plans have been advanced to fuse the former dependencies into one or two political units administered or supervised by an international authority or mandatory power until the countries are ready for complete self-rule.[1] Quite aside from other difficulties, such schemes do not take sufficient account of the diversity of Southeast Asia.

The natural environment shows a great variety of conditions. The dominant fact is the fragmentation of the lowlands by either seas or mountains. Great plains at one time existed where we now find the drowned Sunda and Sahul shelves, but the present plains beyond the amphibious coastal swamps are relatively small. Within the lowlands there are strong contrasts in soil fertility.[2] The best soils are those derived from volcanic deposits. These are found along the inner curve of the great southern island arc, from Sumatra east to the "fishhook" around the Banda Sea, and in the northern arc (part of the East Asiatic island festoons) running from Formosa through the Philippine Islands south to northern Celebes and Halmahera (Fig. 1).

[1] See, for instance, "The United States in a New World, II: Pacific Relations," *Fortune*, Supplement, August, 1942; Ely Culbertson, *Total Peace* (Garden City, N.Y.: Doubleday, Doran, 1943), pp. 323–34.

[2] E. C. J. Mohr, "Climate and Soil in the Netherlands Indies," *Bulletin of the Colonial Institute of Amsterdam*, I (1937–38), 241–51; *idem, De bodem der tropen in het algemeen, en die van Nederlandsch-Indië in het bijzonder* (2 vols. in 6 parts; Koninklijke Vereeniging Koloniaal Instituut, "Mededeeling," Vol. XXXI [Amsterdam, 1933–38]), translated by Robert L. Pendelton as *The Soils of Equatorial Regions, with Particular Reference to the Netherlands East Indies* (Ann Arbor: Edwards Brothers, 1944).

In contrast, British Malaya, Borneo, and western New Guinea are non-volcanic; moreover, the heavy equatorial rains have thoroughly leached the soils, limiting the range of suitable crops and resulting in lower yields than in the volcanic lands.

Burma, Thailand, and French Indochina have no active volcanoes, and their alluvial deposits are on the whole less rich than those of, say, Java; on the other hand, their soils are less leached than those of the equatorial zone.

Settlement, largely determined by the search for wet rice fields, reflects these differences. The population is highly concentrated on the alluvial plains, except those of New Guinea, Borneo, Sumatra, and Malaya, where swamps or leached soils prevail (Fig. 3). External forces have accentuated rather than smoothed out the contrasts. The Chinese arts of dike building and intensive farming have enlarged the carrying capacity of the Red River delta and the Annam coast; Java and Luzon, the most favored islands of Malaysia, have become centers of colonial development and have seen their populations increase tenfold since the beginning of the nineteenth century. In these three areas population pressure has reached the danger point. In lower Tongking and Java the average density to a square mile is about 1,000 people. In central Luzon it is 600, but unsatisfactory conditions of land tenure add to a pressure that otherwise would seem comparatively moderate.

There are signs, however, that the peak of concentration has been reached. The census figures of recent decades indicate— even if ample allowance is made for errors in enumeration—that the average annual rate of population growth has been much higher in certain sparsely populated areas than in the traditional cores (Fig. 4). This is not to say that the trend is toward an even distribution throughout the region; even a small absolute increase in numbers in an almost empty district will result in a substantial percentage of growth. It does mean, however, that the spread of modern

civilization, in such forms as roads, hygiene, or development of resources, raises some potentially favorable areas to a higher level of opportunity, either for the local population or for immigrants. The high rate of increase in southern Sumatra and, especially, in Mindanao reflects the immigration of Javanese and Filipinos, respectively. In western Malaya and eastern Sumatra around Medan the rate is also strongly influenced by immigration, but here most of the immigrants have been "birds of passage," who arrived in large numbers during the boom years of rubber estates and tin mines and left in times of depression such as the early 1930's. Elsewhere the high rates of growth, if not the result of erroneous census estimates, seem to be largely caused by increase of the local population.

It should be repeated that the sparse settlement of, for instance, the plains of Borneo and New Guinea is no accident; their carrying capacity is inherently lower than that of the present areas of concentration. Proper regard for the rights of the local populations demands extensive reservation of arable lands for their future needs. This means that the area available for resettling the surplus population of the present crowded districts is much more restricted than would appear at first glance. It underscores the invalidity of Japanese claims for living space in these southern regions and serves as a warning against schemes for colonization by European refugees after the war.

The racial distribution also reflects the natural environment. The rugged and heavily forested uplands act as barriers between the lowlands. This is particularly true of the mainland, where north-south ranges have imposed a linear pattern on the migrations. In the archipelago the sea has acted as a link rather than as a barrier, so that here we find a more nearly concentric pattern of coastal and interior peoples. The consecutive eastward migrations of different racial groups have all left their mark on the region, from the oldest recognizable

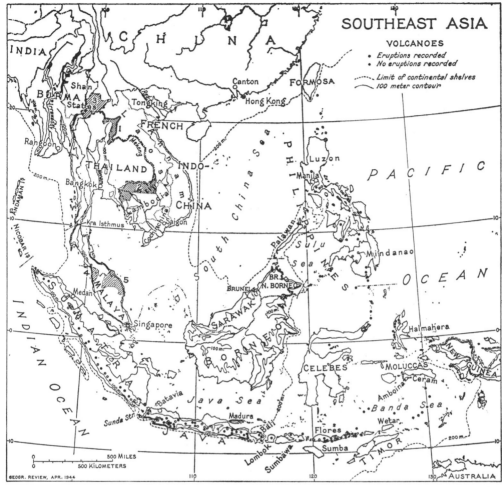

FIG. 1. Orientation map. The 100-meter contour line (omitted for the smaller islands) brings out the small extent of lowland areas in Southeast Asia. The 200-meter bathymetric line indicates the extent of the continental shelves. Tectonic movements in these shelves have subsided; the uplands are dominated by erosional activity, and relatively extensive coastal plains have resulted from deposition. In the zone between the Sunda shelf on the west and the Sahul shelf on the east, and continued to the north in the Philippines, recent and continuing vertical movements are reflected in the mountainous island chains, separated by deep sea basins.*

* The distribution of volcanoes is based on W. D. Smith: "The Philippine Islands," *Handbuch der regionalen Geologie,* III (Heidelberg, 1910), 13 ff.; F. von Wolff: *Der Vulkanismus* (Stuttgart, 1923), II, part 1, 159 ff.; *Atlas van Tropisch Nederland,* 1938, Sheet 5; L. M. R. Rutten: *Voordrachten over de geologie van Nederlandsch Oost-Indië* (Groningen, 1927). The large number of volcanoes in northern Celebes necessitated the use of smaller symbols in that area.

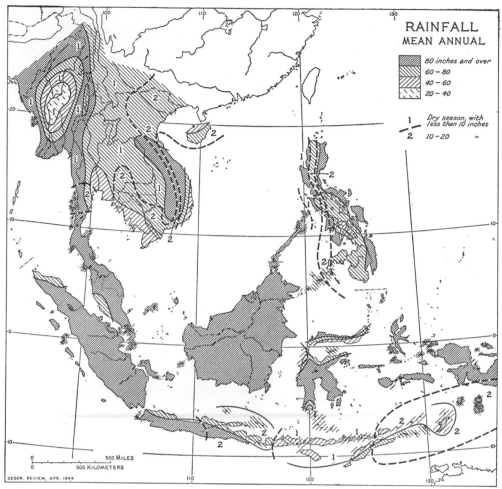

FIG. 2. Rainfall. The rainfall for the dry season is based on the six months May to October in the Northern Hemisphere and November to April in the Southern Hemisphere. The areas marked *1*, including Burma, most of Thailand and interior French Indochina, the northwestern Philippines, and the middle part of the Lesser Sunda Islands, have a pronounced "dry monsoon." Where these areas are well exposed to the rain-bearing winds (Burma coast, western Philippines), the rainfall during the wet monsoon is so large that the annual total is more than 80 inches and often is greater than the precipitation in equatorial areas (e.g., Akyab, on the Arakan coast, 207 inches).

Areas marked 2 have a less pronounced dry season and are transitional to the areas with "year-round" rainfall. Java, for example, is under the influence of the Asiatic (N.W.) monsoon from October to May; from April to November the southeast monsoon prevails, which brings rain to the south coast but in general is drier than the northwest monsoon. As a result, western Java and the entire south coast has a high annual rainfall (more than 80 inches) and no dry season, but the northeast has a rainfall between 60 inches and 80 inches and some months that are practically dry.*

* This highly generalized map is an adaptation from *Philips' Comparative Wall Atlas of Asia* (Climate), edited by J. F. Unstead and E. G. R. Taylor; *Oxford Wall Maps: Asia, Mean Annual Rainfall,* compiled by A. J. Herbertson and E. G. R. Taylor, 1909; C. Braak: "Klimakunde von Hinterindien und Insulinde," *Handbuch der Klimatologie,* IV, part R (Berlin, 1931).

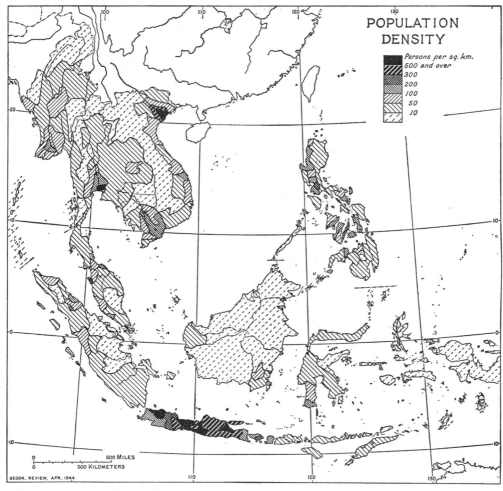

POPULATION
DENSITY

Persons per sq. km.
500 and over
300
200
100
50
10

500 MILES
500 KILOMETERS

GEOGR. REVIEW, APR. 1944

FIG. 3. Population Density In order to present a comparable picture for the whole of Southeast Asia, the year 1940 or 1941 was chosen, and densities were calculated for administrative districts. The use of administrative districts for the sake of uniformity explains, for instance, the rather low density of the Annam coastal region, where the districts include large areas of sparsely settled uplands adjacent to the crowded coastal strip. The scale of the map required, of course, some generalizations where there were many small districts with differing densities (Tongking, Cochinchina, Java). Cities, where they formed separate census units, were included in the adjacent districts.*

* *Yearbook of Philippine Statistics, 1940,* p. 7; *Malayan Year Book, 1939,* pp. 36–37; *Statesman's Year-Book, 1943,* pp. 90–92, 182–194; *Verslag van de volkstelling* [Netherlands Indies], 1930 (figures of this census were multiplied by 1.12 for the Indonesian population, 1.13 for "Europeans," and 1.14 for "Chinese and Other Foreign Asiatics" to obtain the 1940 estimate); *Annuaire Statistique de l'Indochine, 1930–1931, 1937–1938,* pp. 51–52, 15–16 (the percentage of increase between 1931 and 1936 was used to compute the population figures for 1941); *Statistical Year Book—Siam, 1933–1935, 1936–1937,* pp. 71–72, 50–51 (estimate based on rate of increase between census years 1929 and 1937); *Census of India, 1931,* XI, Burma, Part 2, pp. 2–3 (estimate computed on basis of increase between census years 1921 and 1931. Certain remote areas were, however, excluded from the census. See explanatory note, Part 2, p. 1, and Part 1, Report, p. 223).

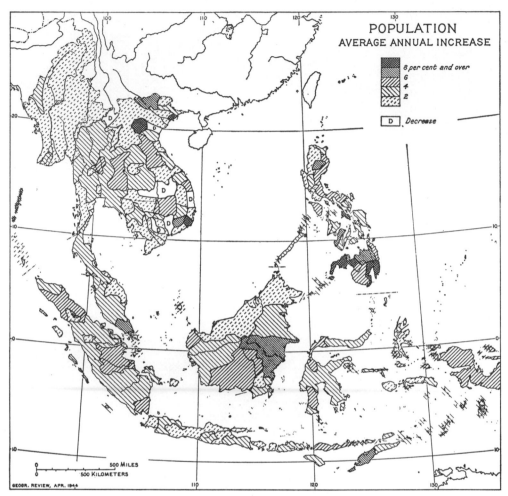

FIG. 4. Population change. This is, so far as known, the first attempt to give a comprehensive view of the crude rate of population growth in Southeast Asia, but the map cannot rise above the level of available information. The cartographic presentation points up clearly the doubtful quality of census data over large parts of this region (see, for instance, French Indochina or the contrast between Burma and Thailand). However, the enumeration methods employed in the Philippines, Java, Bali, most of Sumatra, northern and southern Celebes, British Malaya, and Burma proper indicate reasonable accuracy. In Burma and the Netherlands Indies the rates of growth refer to the periods 1921–31 and 1920–30 respectively. The increase shown in southern Sumatra (Lampongs) is doubtless below the rate that prevailed in the 1930's, when Javanese immigration was accelerated. Altogether, the rates are high, as the correspondign percentages for some other countries show: Japan proper, 1.12; India, 1.5; Italy, 0.98; U.S.A., 0.72; Great Britain, 0.4. The map is based on the crude gain (or loss) between the two most recent official censuses.*

* For source see page 175.

element, the Negrito, in remote jungle re-treats, to the latest, and dominant, group of Mongoloid peoples. Of more significance for the postwar world, however, are the language groups, because these are an important factor in the pattern of nations, existing or emerging, in Southeast Asia (Fig. 5).

The isolated valleys of the Irrawaddy, the Menam, the Mekong, and the Red River and the narrow coastal plain of Annam have served as migration routes, as cultural cores, and as political key areas for, respectively, the Burmese, Thai, Cambodians, and Annamese. The numerous migrations and cultural impacts have created a highly complex situation. The early settlers have either been absorbed by the later groups or been pushed into the uplands. The Mon-Khmer peoples now appear as fragments all over Farther India, their once solid hold on the region ripped apart by invasions of Burmese, Thai, and Annamese. The continental offshoot of the Malayo-Polynesian language group in French Indochina (the Cham and related peoples) now lives on as a much reduced group in the mountain refuge of the central Annamese range. The most recent immigrants seem to be the Miao-Yao tribes, who have been moving into the northern part of our area during the last centuries, probably under pressure of the Chinese proper.

In contrast with the extreme complexity of the mainland, the island world is rather simple in its basic language features, demonstrating again the unifying function of the sea. Over the entire area, from the Malay Peninsula northward to include part of Formosa and eastward to include the Moluccas (with the exception of northern Halmahera, of "Papuan" speech), the languages belong to one common stock, the so-called Malayan division of the Malayo-Polynesian group.

Within this division there exist, of course, a multitude of languages: in the Philippine Islands there are at least 60 different languages and dialects, and in the Netherlands Indies some 25 languages and about 250 dialects are reported.[8]

The social crazy quilt we see today in Southeast Asia is, however, only partly a result of the wanderings of what are now considered the indigenous peoples. One can go even further and say that the differences between them would be rather small had it not been for the impact of outside forces, first of more advanced Oriental civilizations, later of the Western world.

Before the Westerners found the way to tropical Asia, it had been for centuries a "colonial area" for both Hindus and Chinese. That meant—just as it does today—on the one hand exploitation by profiteering merchants and tribute-seeking conquerors but on the other hand cultural enrichment, whether directly through active proselytizing or indirectly through imitation and adaptation. It was particularly the Hindu expansion in the early centuries of our era that introduced to the primitive, pagan, tribal societies of Southeast Asia the higher forms of religion, philosophy, literature, architecture, and political and social organization. The temples and palaces of present-day Burma, Thailand, and Bali and such classic monuments as Angkor in Cambodia and Borobudur in Java are symbols of the mighty impulses that came from India. These cultural advances were fairly strong in the lowlands but weak and retarded in the uplands. The cultural influence of China was, on the whole, limited but predominates among the Annamese in the coastal area of French Indochina; here Confucianism, Buddhism, and ancestor worship mingle in true Chinese fashion and the Annam court and the mandarin bureaucracy bear clearly the stamp of Chinese tradition.

Later, about the fourteenth century, another outside force, Islam, made its impact on the region. Although its source was in

[8] *Census of the Philippines, 1939*, II, 333; *Atlas van Tropisch Nederland* (Koninklijk Nederlandsch Aardrijkskundig Genootschap in collaboration with the Topografische Dienst in Nederlandsch-Indië, 1938), Sheet 9*b*.

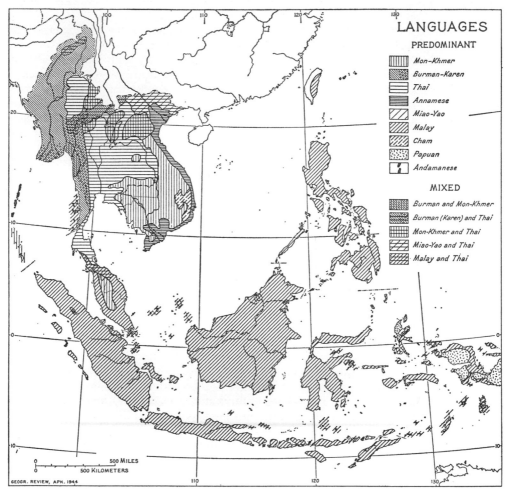

FIG. 5. Languages. This is a simplified version of a more detailed map compiled by Dr. Paul K. Benedict and the author. Small "islands" of foreign language stocks, such as cities and plantations or mining areas, had to be omitted (for instance, one-half of Rangoon's population was Indian, more than three-fourths of Singapore's Chinese). The Andamanese languages had to be given a separate symbol because they have no known affinity to any other language. The 400 native Negritos are now only a remnant, a small minority compared with the 20,000 Indians and Burmese in the penal and free colonies around Port Blair on South Andaman Island. Cham is generally recognized as a branch of the Malayan language family; its location indicates sea-borne migration, perhaps from South China (see P. K. Benedict, "Thai, Kadai, and Indonesian: A New Alignment in Southeastern Asia," *American Anthropologist*, XLIV [1942], 576–601).*

* Sources include: *Atlas van Tropisch Nederland*, 1938, sheet 96; A. L. Kroeber: "Peoples of the Philippines," *American Museum of Natural History, Handbook Series* No. 8 (1919); L. de la Jonquière: *Ethnographie du Tonkin septentrional* (Paris: 1906); Henri Maspéro's chapter on languages in *Un empire colonial français: L'Indochine*, edited by Georges Maspéro, I (Paris and Brussels, 1929), 63–80; Wilhelm Credner: *Siam: das Land der Tai* (Stuttgart, 1935); Paul Schebesta and K. Streit: "Völker- und Stammkarte der Orang-Utan von Malaya," *Petermanns Geographische Mitteilungen*, LXXII (1926), pl. 21; E. H. Man: *On the Aboriginal Inhabitants of the Andaman Islands* (London, 1932); *idem: The Nicobar Islands and their People* (Guildford, 1932?): *Census of India, 1931*, II, The Andaman and Nicobar Islands, and XI, Burma, Part 1, Linguistic Map.

RELIGIONS

	Buddhist
	Hindu
	"Chinese"
	Mohammedan
	Christian
	Primitive

FIG. 6. Religions. For large parts of the region data on religion are either lacking or vague; one reason is, of course, that the subject defies exact definition. What is described in the legend as "Chinese" religion is a mixture of Buddhism, Confucianism, and ancestor worship, and it is hard to say where the boundary lies between this and animistic beliefs. The Annamese language boundary has largely been followed. Such transition zones also exist on the frontiers of other religions. The purpose was, as in Figure 5, to show the broad divisions. There are, for instance, Christian missions all over Southeast Asia, but where they form relatively small minorities, as among the Karen in Burma, the hill tribes of Indochina, or on Java, they have been omitted. On the other hand, Christianity has a strong foothold or even predominance among the Bataks of north-central Sumatra and the primitive tribes of the eastern islands. In this latter area Islam is also still making progress, but mostly in and around local ports. Note the relic area of Hinduism on Bali.*

* The Netherlands Indies census has no complete data on religion but gives detailed information on certain areas with large Christian populations (*Volkstelling, 1930,* Part 4, pp. 83 ff. and Part 5, pp. 91 ff.). Supplementary statistical information can be found in *Indisch Verslag,* II, in the chapter on "Eerediensten." For other countries the data either have been taken from official sources already mentioned or are based on missionary publications, regional descriptions, and information from former residents.

179

the Near East, the new religion and its concomitant social-economic tenets were carried to the Indies by Mohammedan merchants from northwestern India. It spread
steadily from the trade centers along the
Strait of Malacca eastward and northward,
and by the time the Portuguese arrived,
Islam was dominant in the coastal regions
of the Indies and had pushed north as far
as Mindanao.

The political upheaval caused by the advent of Islam no doubt facilitated the penetration by Europeans, who could play the
contending factions against one another.
And, more important, the geographical limits of Islam at the time of the European
invasion go far toward explaining the present peculiar position of the Filipinos in
Southeast Asia. It is well known that Moslems are virtually immune to Christian missionary activity. Spanish colonial policy,
which placed much stress on the spreading
of the Christian faith, was very successful
among the animist population of the Philippine Islands (except for the remote mountain tribes) but was never able to convert
the Mohammedans of Mindanao, Palawan,
and Sulu. The so-called Moros are to this
day a group apart from the Filipinos, and
it appears that this Moslem minority has
grave misgivings regarding its future position in an independent Philippine commonwealth. As to the remainder of the country,
it must be said in justice to the Spaniards
that it was they who, by their conversion
policy, Westernized the Filipinos and
thereby created the spiritual conditions that
led to the revolt against Spain and subsequently made possible the rapid progress
in self-government under the American regime. This is too often forgotten by those
who criticize what they consider the political or educational backwardness in the Indies or Malaya. It is interesting to note
that in the Moro provinces of Cotabato
(Mindanao) and Sulu the rate of literacy
is the lowest in the Philippine Islands: although on the average 50 per cent of the
Philippine population over ten years of age

can read and write, the percentage is 20 or
less for these two provinces.[4]

There are other aspects of Western colonial policy that have tended to increase
the contrasts between the parts of Southeast Asia. The trade of each of the countries shows that there has been very little
exchange within the region. What intraregional commerce did exist was either for
transshipment at Singapore or shipments of
rice from the surplus lowlands of Cochin
China, Thailand, and Burma to such deficit
areas of plantation economy as British Malaya and Sumatra. French Indochina and
the Philippines, because of protectionist
policies, had between one-half and three-
fourths of their trade with France and the
United States, respectively, British Malaya
and the Netherlands Indies were less dependent on their home countries, partly
because of the world-wide demand for their
products and partly because of a long tradition of free trade. Thailand, being outside any empire structure, also had more
diversified trade, but this too was largely
with the industrialized countries of the
middle latitudes. Only Burma had its major market and supply area close by,
namely, in India, which took more than
half its trade. Thus the commercial structure of the countries of Southeast Asia
shows great similarity to that of the raw-
materials-producing countries of Latin
America: they face the world, turning their
backs to one another.

Each colonial power has ruled, developed, or exploited its empire according to
the ideologies and social and economic practices of the home country. The Americans
have stressed political development, the
French cultural assimilation, the British
and Dutch economic progress, the former
more in a laissez-faire manner, the latter
in a more paternal form. No doubt the

[4] *Census of the Philippines, 1939,* II, 298 ff. and
385 ff. Literacy for females is particularly low:
13.1 per cent in Cotabato and 16.1 per cent in
Sulu. It may be added that literacy in the pagan
Mountain Province is 29.1 per cent.

foreign domination has created greater unity *within* each dependency. If the manifold peoples of the Netherlands Indies now begin to feel the bonds of an Indonesian nation, if the native leaders on the Peninsula look forward toward a unified national Malay state, it is due to the unification under Western rule and the penetration of Western ideas of nationalism. At the same time, however, this rising national consciousness within each dependency sharpens the division between the political units of Southeast Asia. For instance, the Malayan peoples of the Peninsula, the Indies, and the Philippines have many basic cultural traits in common, but the different forms of colonial rule have created divergent interests that cannot be ignored. It seems out of the question that the Filipinos, eagerly awaiting their independence, would agree to be part of a Malayan superstate, especially if this were placed under international supervision. And even if they were willing, the Indonesians would most likely reject the scheme because they would fear the power of the politically more advanced Filipinos and the possible friction between Moslem and Christian interests. A union of British Malaya and the Netherlands Indies would not present these particular problems, but —quite apart, of course, from Dutch or British objections—it is doubtful whether the Indonesians would welcome the addition of a substantial and concentrated Chinese minority such as exists in British Malaya.

On the mainland one finds similar hurdles in the path toward a fusion. National consciousness among the Burmese, Thai, and Annamese is relatively strong, rooted in old traditions and fortified by resistance to Western dominance. Japan rewarded Thailand by giving it parts of French Indochina (in Laos and Cambodia), of British Malaya (the four northern states), and of Burma (part of the Southern Shan States). The annexations in Laos and part of the Shan territory may have some ground in that the inhabitants show more affinity to the Thai than to the peoples of Thailand's neighbor states. The other additions, however, are based on tenuous claims of former suzerainty. There is little doubt that this generosity of Japan is resented by Thailand's neighbors. Whatever boundaries result from the future peace conference, they will cause ill feeling and form a hindrance to close collaboration within a federation.

Regional Problems

In view of these contrasts and divergent interests one may well ask whether there is any sense in dealing with Southeast Asia as a regional unit. The answer is that, in spite of all the differences noted, there are certain considerations of a broader nature and of far-reaching significance that give validity to the concept.

There is, in the first place, the "colonial" character of the region. In recent years there has been increasing acceptance of the thesis that "the colonial powers are not only in a position of trustees towards the colonial areas under their rule, but that they also owe a moral obligation toward the rest of the world to account for their stewardship." [5] Although an international administration over the whole region is neither a practical nor a desirable solution, there is much to be said for a regional supervisory organ embodying this "third-party interest," at least if this principle finds application to all colonial areas of the world. In this line of thought the colonial powers, after the expulsion of Japan, would resume charge of their respective dependencies but would be accountable to an international authority.

The function of this international body should not, however, be limited merely to supervising the progress made toward self-

[5] *War and Peace in the Pacific: A Preliminary Report of the Eighth Conference of the Institute of Pacific Relations . . . , Mont Tremblant, December 4–14, 1942* (New York: International Secretariat, Institute of Pacific Relations, 1943), p. 56.

government. Political rights are meaningless unless they rest on a sound social and economic foundation. If the outside powers, in the spirit of the Atlantic Charter, wish to have a part in the political development of the dependencies, they will also have to accept a share in the responsibility for the material welfare of these lands. It would be strange indeed if public opinion, say in the United States, could demand that full democracy be established in Malaya and at the same time disclaim any concern for the economic conditions in that country. This raises the question of the economic future of Southeast Asia to cardinal importance.

ROLE OF RAW-MATERIALS EXPORT

In the past the export of commodities gained from field, forest, and mine has provided the revenues with which to pay for improvements. A peasant society is naturally poor in capital. The investments made by Westerners and to a smaller extent, by Chinese and Indians (the latter mainly in Burma) have, no doubt, been profitable to them. But the native peoples have also gained on the whole, not only by better opportunities for employment, but especially by obtaining roads, ports, waterworks, hospitals, experiment stations, and other durable improvements. There are, of course, differences of opinion as to whether the native peoples have received their fair share of the profits and, if not, how this should be corrected after the war. Nevertheless, improvement of living conditions will still depend largely on the import of capital, equipment, and services. Will Southeast Asia be able to pay for these necessities in the traditional manner?

We are now painfully aware that Southeast Asia had been developed into a veritable treasure house of raw materials. It produced almost all the natural rubber, cinchona bark, abacá (Manila hemp), kapok, teakwood, and pepper of the world, three-fourths of the copra and tapioca flour, more than half the palm oil and tin, and one-third of the agave fibers (sisal and

henequen). The region was also of great importance for natural resins and gums and for essential oils; for instance, most of the jelutong (an ingredient of chewing gum) and three-fourths of the citronella oil came from here. Another product, seemingly minor but actually highly important, was the versatile insecticide rotenone. Its production has expanded rapidly in the last ten years, and British Malaya and the Netherlands Indies had almost a monopoly on the world market.

In addition, Southeast Asia produced considerable quantities of cane sugar (14 per cent of the world production) tea (18 per cent), tobacco, spices, and rare metals such as tungsten (22 per cent).[6]

Southeast Asia has experienced an extraordinary economic development since about the middle of the nineteenth century. While the economy of Latin America stagnated because of the abolition of slavery and the instability of governments, colonial Southeast Asia, brought closer to Europe by the Suez Canal, became the great tropical supply center for Western industry. This paramount position is now seriously threatened from two directions: preparation for war and the war itself have led to the development of synthetic substitutes in the industrial countries and the introduction or expansion of natural production in the tropical parts of India, Africa, and especially, South America. Not all these ventures will succeed, but even if only a part survive the war, it will mean a considerable competition for Southeast Asia. This competition will not be merely on the basis of price and quality—on which tropical Asia might, on the whole, have the stronger position—but will also involve political and national considerations. The lesson of the danger of relying on distant countries for strategic raw materials may result, in Europe as well as in America, in the main-

[6] The percentages refer to 1938 or 1939 and are taken from the *Statistical Year Book of the League of Nations* and the *Agricultural Export Crops of the Netherlands Indies* (annual) for 1940.

tenance of home production of synthetics at whatever cost; concern for the large capital invested in the new industries (for synthetic rubber in the United States some 625 million dollars) would certainly support such a policy. Or, for instance, the "good-neighbor policy" toward Latin America might induce the United States to give preference to the new or revived products of that region. Expansion of trade outlets in other countries may partly make up for the loss elsewhere. For instance, if China is helped to its feet and its transportation system and industry are developed, resulting in greater consuming power, it may become a substantial customer for rubber, fibers, industrial fats and oils, and foodstuffs. Even so, it is hard to see how Southeast Asia can regain its former export volume. The repercussions on the social-economic structure will be severe, unless, as suggested above, the more advanced nations recognize their responsibility for doing more than expressing sympathy with political ideals.

New Opportunities

The future will demand a new approach. It is too early to draw up any specific long-range plans, and the problems differ, of course, for the different countries of Southeast Asia, but some brief suggestions may illustrate the possibilities.

The decline of exporting may, to some extent, prove a blessing in disguise if countered by a constructive readjustment policy. A shift in emphasis from a few export commodities to a more diversified agriculture would increase economic resistance in depression years. The disastrous period of the early 1930's taught a hard lesson, and some beneficial changes occurred, but they were minor compared with those that the postwar period will require. British Malaya, especially, needs more home production of food; normally it imported about two-thirds of its rice consumption.

Another item for a long-range reconstruction program is resettlement, either to relieve the population pressure in overcrowded areas or to furnish a new livelihood for workers in depressed export industries. In the preceding decade energetic efforts were made to promote emigration from Java to Sumatra and from Luzon to Mindanao. The initial results were promising, but too small to afford any material relief as yet.[7] This work will have to be resumed on a much larger scale.

The development of manufacturing industries is another approach to betterment, and more stimulating than the spread of subsistence agriculture under the resettlement schemes. Moreover, it will be a necessity if the shrunken export markets do not provide enough money to buy manufactured goods abroad. The favorable results obtained in Java in the 1930's under a social policy of encouraging small-scale factories for the production of daily necessities are guideposts for the future.[8] In addition to Java, central Luzon, lower Tongking, and possibly the districts around Rangoon, Bangkok, and Singapore may well become centers of consumers' goods industries, selling on the Oriental price level. This activity, in turn, induces the establishment of more basic industries, as the experience of Java has shown. Such industrial centers will also supply the outlying agrarian regions, and closer trade relations

[7] The number of colonists leaving Java rose from 20,000 in 1937 to 53,000 in 1940. For a description of the new resettlement program see "Agricultural Colonization and the Population of Java," *The Netherlands Indies,* Dept. van Economische Zaken, Netherlands Indies, VI (1938), 11 ff.; "Javanese Colonization in the Outer Provinces," *ibid;* G. H. C. Hart, *Towards Economic Democracy in the Netherlands Indies* (Netherlands Indies Paper No. 5, Netherlands Indies Council, Institute of Pacific Relations, 1942); Wilbo Peekema, "Colonization of Javanese in the Outer Provinces of the Netherlands East Indies," *Geographical Journal,* CI (1943), 145–53. In the Philippine Commonwealth, under the auspices of the National Land Settlement Administration, it has been reported that 11,500 persons were settled in Mindanao in 1939 and 1940.
[8] P. H. W. Sitsen, *Industrial Development of the Netherlands Indies* (Bulletin No. 2, Netherlands Indies Council, Institute of Pacific relations, n.d.).

will result. This was already noticeable in
the Netherlands Indies; under the stimulus
of expanding factory production, the value
of Java's exports of manufactured goods
to the other islands rose from 34 million
guilders in 1934 to 70 million in 1940.

The question whether Southeast Asia will
develop a heavy industry is still academic.
The possibilities cannot be discounted
merely because the region has little or no
metallurgical coal and relatively small iron
deposits. These twin elements of the early
Industrial Revolution are becoming less
important as technology advances. Because
of its heavy rainfall and strong relief,
Southeast Asia has considerable potential
water power. In addition, metal alloys and
plastics are bound to play a much greater
role than in the past. The region has many
metals, such as tin, aluminum, chromium,
manganese, and tungsten, and enormous
forest reserves, which some day will yield
the raw material for various kinds of wood
plastics.

Industrialization and the concomitant
changes in social-economic organization
will tend to lower the birth rate, as has
happened in other countries. It is only by
this process that we can hope to break the
vicious circle in which a rise in living standards is nullified by increased survival.

The development of manufacturing will,
again, depend largely on the assistance of
the Western nations in supplying capital,
equipment, and technical assistance. This
may seem an invitation to the present industrial nations to cut their own throats,
but experience has shown that the flow of
trade among industrial countries is greater
than that between industrial and raw-mate-
rials–producing countries.

Toward a Regional Bloc

Although Southeast Asia will thus be
still dependent on Western countries, the
peoples of the region can strengthen and
speed up their progress toward economic
self-determination by regional collaboration.[9] A political, territorial fusion directly
after the war would, as discussed above,
cause more harm than good; but a regional
bloc, working along functional lines, appears as a distinct possibility. Even if an
international colonial authority should not
materialize, a purely regional organization
for consultation and co-ordination could
be set up. The recently created Anglo-
American Caribbean Commission is an example of such regional collaboration. A
number of committees, acting under a
secretariat as the regional clearinghouse,
should examine the problems of the region
as a whole as well as the intraregional
sources of friction.

For instance, although the problem of
raw materials can, obviously, be solved
only by world-wide agreements, a united
stand by the countries of tropical Asia
would considerably strengthen their position at the conference table. Other regional
topics needing discussion and, where feasible, a common policy, are regulation of
immigration, labor conditions, intraregional
shipping, and aviation. Furthermore, there
should be a regular interchange of information on such matters as education, public hygiene, nutrition, resettlement, rural
credit, agricultural methods, and industrial
development in order to promote the rapid
spread of effective welfare policies.

Local Unity

This idea of community of interests—
whether from an internal or an external
viewpoint—also appears in the character of
Southeast Asia as a transit area. This has
long been recognized for the Malay Archipelago and the adjacent Peninsula: these
lands astride the equator act as a barrier
guarding the gateway between the Pacific
and Indian oceans and at the same time

[9] Bruno Lasker, *Welfare and Freedom in Postwar Southeast Asia* (American Council Paper No.
2, American Council Institute of Pacific Relations,
n.d.) ; *idem, International Action and the Colonies*
("Fabian Society Research Series"), Vol. LXV
(1943).

form steppingstones between Asia and Australia. Together with the other two bottlenecks of world shipping—the Caribbean with the Panama Canal and the Mediterranean with the Suez Canal—Malaysia forms the trinity of strategic thoroughfares on which world sea power rests. French Indochina and the Philippines, flanking the South China Sea, guard the portals to the Malacca and Sunda Straits; Thailand borders on the Pacific as well as on the Indian Ocean and controls the Isthmus of Kra, the potential site for a canal linking the two oceans. This strategic position of Southeast Asia has been emphasized in recent years by the emergence of Burma as a transit zone between China and the Indian Ocean. Air transportation will certainly play a large role after the war, but it will not replace land and sea transportation. It would seem that the future system of skyways will even accentuate the position of Southeast Asia as a crossroads center. Here the great-circle route from the Pacific coast of America via Japan to East China, the Philippines, and Singapore meets the transpacific "island hopping" line via Hawaii and also the route from Australia to India and beyond to West Asia and Europe.

These functions give Southeast Asia a vital place in the world's circulatory system and make its security a matter of international concern. In this respect no part of the region can be separated from the whole; when Japan penetrated into French Indochina, the entire structure of Western domination in Southeast Asia was doomed. In the same way, if and when Japan is expelled from either Burma, Sumatra, or the Philippine Islands, its entire newly won empire will start to crumble.

This strategic interdependence has even more direct bearing on the fate of the peoples of Southeast Asia as they approach the stage of self-rule. The historical development points clearly at the eventual emergence of at least six national states in this region. They will be flanked by Australia, India, and China, and to the north will be Japan, which in spite of defeat may remain a potentially formidable nation. If for the moment we leave open the question of Japan's future power and omit Australia as actually only a small nation in terms of population and remote from most of the Southeast Asiatic countries, the contrast between Southeast Asia and its immediate neighbors becomes even stronger.

The thought occurs that the fragmentation of Southeast Asia into six separate states or more may create an "Asiatic Balkans," destined to become a pawn in an eventual struggle for political or economic supremacy between its great neighbors. Speculation on such contingencies can hardly form a compelling argument for the establishment of a regional bloc. We have seen, however, that there are other—and urgent—problems that require regional solution. Co-operation on concrete questions of colonial emancipation, security, and welfare may gradually establish a sense of unity that will transcend local divergences. It is through this organic evolution toward interdependence that Southeast Asia will become strong enough to ward off outside pressure and gain genuine freedom.

The concept of the national sovereign state is essentially a product of European culture. No one will deny the stimulative qualities of a vigorous national life, but neither can anyone fail to see what chaos has been caused by nationalistic anarchy. While the Western world is searching for an escape from this impasse, tropical Asia is struggling toward national self-determination.

Must these peoples travel the same road as Europe did, or will they be able to subordinate patriotism to collective regional interests? It seems not yet too late—if the Western nations recognize their true responsibility—to guide Southeast Asia toward a future in which "interdependence" will be as challenging a word as "independence" is today.

DAVID LOWENTHAL

THE RANGE AND VARIATION
OF CARIBBEAN SOCIETIES

Pluralistic circumstances affect Caribbean societies in a variety of ways. No society is altogether plural or even heterogeneous; if it were, it would not be a society at all, but only an assemblage of functionally unrelated communities. No society entirely lacks institutional diversity; if it did, it would be so homogeneous that it could not survive in any environment. Between these theoretical extremes, however, there is a continuum of possible sociocultural configurations. Some societies exhibit more, or different, evidences of pluralism than others. Aspects and combinations of pluralism vary from place to place in intensity, in structure and interrelatedness, in degree of formal institutionalization, in the extent to which they are locally apprehended, in historical stability, and in functional import. In any particular society, for example, one or more determinants of social stratification, such as color, descent, wealth, occupation, age, or sex, may inhibit freedom of choice or expression more or less completely in various realms of activity.

Elsewhere in this monograph Smith[1] has

Reprinted, with permission of the author and publisher, from "Social and Cultural Pluralism in the Caribbean" (Proceedings of a conference arranged by the Research Institute for the Study of Man, New York, May 27–28, 1959), *Annals of the New York Academy of Sciences*, LXXXIII, Article 5 (1960), 786–95 (copyright, 1960, by the New York Academy of Sciences). The author is a member of the research staff of the American Geographical Socity of New York.

[1] M. G. Smith, "Social and Cultural Pluralism," in "Social and Cultural Pluralism in the Caribbean," *Annals of the New York Academy of Sciences*, LXXXIII, Article 5 (1960), 763–77.

set a theoretical framework; I shall consider how to assess the varieties of sociocultural diversity that actually do occur within West Indian societies. I limit myself to the islands because I know them best, and because their insularity suggests a manageable scheme for analysis. I use the word "diversity" rather than "pluralism" advisedly. The distinction Smith makes between heterogeneous and plural is a valid one, but it is difficult to use. At just what point do differences in ways of life become so incompatible as to make a minority a separate cultural section? How does one decide whether stylistic similarities conceal fundamental diversities? Are the basic institutions the same in one society as in another, and have they always the same relative importance? How much social mobility, actual or perceived, makes a plural society merely heterogeneous? How large must an institutionally distinctive minority be to qualify the whole society as plural rather than merely pluralistic, and does the size of the group effectively measure its significance? [2] It appears to me that non-plural societies grade imperceptibly into plural ones. In any case, diversity is a necessary element of pluralism. This paper concerns both concepts.

To compare societies, one must first decide what one means by a society. No functional hierarchy of social groups properly fits circumstances throughout the West Indies. The role of the family, the estate, the

[2] A. I. Hallowell, "The Impact of the American Indian on American Culture," *American Anthropologist*, LIX (1957), 201–17.

parish, the society, the empire, or indeed of any social or territorial unit, is here crucial, there trivial; its scope or size here extensive, there narrow. Smith's definition of societies as "territorially distinct units having their own governmental institutions" establishes sufficient and perhaps necessary criteria, but does not actually identify them; how potent or inclusive need governmental institutions be to qualify a social unit as a society? I shall instead experiment with an arbitrary geographical measure.

To my mind, the most apposite realm for societies in the West Indies is the island. There are obvious exceptions: Hispaniola and St. Martin, for example, both divided by sovereignty. However, the island does less violence to social reality, involves less Procrustean chopping and stretching than any other topographic category, because insularity is a basic fact of life. An island is a world, to use Selvon's title.[3] The network of social relations seldom survives the sea. Polynesians and Melanesians, more at home with the ocean, make it a highway instead of a barrier; but for West Indians (save, perhaps, in French Martinique and Guadeloupe) the island is in most contexts the most compelling areal symbol. A man who says, "I am a Jamaican," or "I am a Barbadian," is very likely expressing the broadest allegiance he knows.[4]

Each of the smaller islands also has special characteristics, a unique self-image, and a particular view of all the others. What is more, large and small islands are equally conscious of their individuality. Jamaican and Montserratian parochialisms are much alike, although one country has 1,700,000 people and the other only 14,000. Physical insularity intensifies a sense of belonging within each island, whatever its size. To be sure, Jamaicans who live in the

Blue Mountains are unlike inhabitants of the Cockpit Country, and those who dwell in Kingston have little in common with people on Frome sugar estate at the western end of the island. However, these differences do not divide Jamaica into one hundred separate Montserrats; indeed, not even into two or three.

Communities do exist, of course, along with neighborhood self-consciousness, but these microcosms are hard to identify; self-sufficient in no respect, they are socially and culturally integrated with island society as a whole.[5] West Indian communities cannot be understood as worlds in themselves. To be sure, community organization and subregional ties are more important in some islands than in others, though not necessarily in the largest or most populous of them. Barbados, with 230,000 people, is practically one geographical community, despite fairly rigid class barriers, owing to its excellent road network and its historic cultural homogeneity. Dominica, on the other hand, with only 65,000 people, has considerable village and local self-consciousness because population centers are isolated by difficult topography and poor communications and, in part, because of the collapse of the plantation economy that once supported island-wide social institutions. In Jamaica and in Trinidad, physical and social distance notwithstanding, island feeling prevails over local and sectional interests, partly because island radio and newspapers, island government and politics, are omnipresent. However, these unifying forces are weaker in an island such as St. Vincent and practically nonexistent on Bequia, in the Grenadines. One can

[3] S. Selvon, *An Island Is a World* (London: MacGibbon & Kee, 1955).

[4] David Lowenthal, "The West Indies Chooses a Capital," *Geographical Review*, XLVIII (1958), 336–64.

[5] See M. G. Smith, "Community Organization in Rural Jamaica," *Social and Economic Studies* (Institute of Social Research, University College of the West Indies), V (1956), 295–312; R. T. Smith, *The Negro Family in British Guiana* (London: Routledge & Kegan Paul, 1956); and C. Wagley, "Recent Studies of Caribbean Local Societies," in A. C. Wilgus (ed.), *The Caribbean: Natural Resources* (Gainsville: University of Florida Press, 1960).

walk around Bequia in a day, but its 4,000 inhabitants include three mutually exclusive communities. On the other hand, the web of kinship brings the 8,000 people in nearby Carriacou into a close network of associations.

The administrative status of these and other tiny islands is no gauge to the local state of mind. Many constituent parts of the West Indies Federation are themselves island groups: Trinidad includes Tobago, St. Kitts includes Nevis and Anguilla, Antigua has Barbuda, St. Vincent and Grenada share the Grenadines, and both Jamaica and the federation are involved with the Cayman Islands and the Turks and Caicos Islands. Long association or political expediency might promote unit solidarity, but most of these unions are fortuitous or recent; a man from Tobago is apt to think of himself as a Tobagonian, not as a Trinidadian. The primary geographical identification is that with the island, no matter how small or dependent it may be. St. Kitts and Nevis are only two miles apart and are economically interdependent (Nevis grows food for Kittican sugar plantations), but the inhabitants of each island seldom have a good word to say for the other, and both snub Anguillans, who are sixty miles away and a different kind of folk entirely, in their own view and in reality. Grenada and its dependency, Carriacou, likewise have little in common; the difference between the hierarchical social structure of the former and the egalitarianism of the latter is just one of many vital contrasts.[6] At the same time, Carriacou and its own tiny dependency, Petit Martinique, are quite dissimilar; the Petit Martiniquais would seldom call himself a Carriacouan any more than he would a Grenadian. Only the smallest islands and those used as resorts by the "mainlanders" lack this overriding sense of individuality. One scholar termed Lesser

Antillean feeling "a case of insular psychology gone mad."[7]

A sense of individuality does not, of itself, suffice to make an island a society. West Indian islands are not discrete social organisms; they are both more and less than this. There are inter-island family and economic ties throughout the eastern Caribbean. Many small-island elite live elsewhere: Martiniquais own Guadeloupe *sucreries,* important Tobagonians reside in Trinidad, and Petit Martinique is governed by a Grenadian District Officer who visits once a week from Carriacou. However, the social institutions of Jamaica (not just its government) are similarly truncated with respect to Port of Spain and London. Similar qualifications limit most societies. Only the largest nations are entirely self-governing, and even these have myriad links with other peoples: property owned abroad, social, economic, and religious enclaves and exclaves.

The choice of islands as social units is statistically as well as methodologically convenient. There are fifty-one Caribbean islands of whose essential social integrity I am reasonably certain: each of them is an "enduring, co-operating social group so functioning as to maintain itself and perpetuate the species.[8] The units range in population from Cuba, with 6,500,000 people, to Mayreau, one of the St. Vincent Grenadines, with 250. Almost nine-tenths of the 18,700,000 West Indians live in societies larger than 1,000,000 people. Eight per cent inhabit societies ranging from 100,000 to 1,000,000, 4 per cent in societies smaller than 100,000. The picture is quite different when one takes social units as the measure. Only five societies (one tenth of the total) have more than 1,000,000 people; five others have between 100,-

[6] M. G. Smith, *Kinship and Community in Carriacou* (to be published by Yale University Press).

[7] R. H. Whitbeck, "The Lesser Antilles—Past and Present," *Annals of the Association of American Geographers,* XXIII (1933), 21–26, ref. to p. 25.

[8] "Society" (definition 7), *Webster's New Collegiate Dictionary* (1956 edition).

000 and 1,000,000 each, while forty-one societies are smaller than 100,000. Most of these (53 per cent of all the social units in the West Indies) have fewer than 10,000 people each, even though together these small-islands comprise less than 0.5 per cent of the Caribbean population. Of the islands having populations of less than 10,-000, two-thirds have less than 2,500 inhabitants apiece. In other words, more than one-half of all West Indians live in a society larger than 3,000,000 (Cuba or Haiti); but the mean population per society is 366,000 (one-half again as many as Barbados), while the mode is a society of only 7,000 persons (about the size of Anguilla).

The small size of most West Indian societies has a significant bearing on individual heterogeneity and pluralism. Unless they are completely cut off from the modern world, social groups with fewer than 100,000 people face many special problems: a "colonial" relationship with some larger territory or, in the case of the West Indies Federation, with a federal government; a dearth of trained men and of leaders for external as well as for local governmental positions; a lack of cultural focus; and a narrow, conservative outlook and sometimes pathological sensitivity to criticism, exacerbated by small-island feuds and a claustrophobic absence of privacy. Common metropolitan bonds, like economic interests, and analogous social cleavages result in superficial but trivial similarities. Jealousies, rivalries, fears, and, above all, mutual ignorance, tend to make each small island a museum in which archaic distinctions are carefully preserved. It is precisely because so many of the West Indian islands are isolated and miniscule that they exhibit pluralistic features. Geographical and sociocultural heterogeneity reinforce each other.

Colonial status, a frequent feature of pluralism, is likewise linked both with insularity and with small size. It is no accident that of the fifty-one West Indian societies, only the three most populous are politically independent: that is, ruled by their own elites, not by outsiders. The next largest one, Puerto Rico, is semiautonomous. The remainder are in effect colonial, whatever their formal status. A high proportion of the smallest territories (those with populations under 40,000) endure double colonialism as dependencies of dependencies. Indeed, some of the Grenadines are dependencies of dependencies of dependencies. However, neither government nor size is an infallible indicator of sociocultural heterogeneity, much less of pluralism.

There are, however, several more direct approaches to an appraisal of the range of West Indian societies. One method, inherent in Smith's paper, is holistic and functional: to assess the general condition of each society and rank it according to intensity of pluralism, that is, the degree of incompatibility or antagonism between the different cultural sections. This approach demands analysis not of institutional differentiation but rather of the strains to which it leads: the extent to which government is maintained by force rather than by consent; the degree to which the activities and aims of each cultural section offset or negate those of other sections. What is crucial is the relationship between the cultural sections.

Not every disagreement or difference is evidence of pluralism, however, nor is discord an infallible yardstick. Horizontal plural societies, in which cultural sections are not hierarchically arranged, display little strain if there is little contact between the sections. On the other hand, apparent agreement on goals and values in stratified societies is not necessarily an indication that pluralism, much less tension, is absent. The fact that each cultural section in British West Indian societies parades loyalty to the Crown, avoids manual labor when possible, admires white skin, and fancies Christian marriage as an ideal does not indicate that they share a basic way of life or common institutional systems, but rather that each strives to advance by emulating the perceived behavior of the ruling section and by discrediting its own circumstances and ways of life. Cultural unity may mask institutional diversity. What is more, horizontal and vertical pluralism have disparate origins, careers, and terminations. When differences between non-stratified sections become intolerable, partition, as in Israel and to some extent in Canada, is a likely result, while stratified societies, such as that of Haiti, are more apt to suffer revolution.

When one considers that some West Indian societies (notably Trinidad, British Guiana, Surinam, and St. Croix) contain important horizontal as well as vertical sections, and that the character and role of each is constantly shifting, the difficulty of judging the intensity of pluralism becomes evident.[9] A pragmatic, comparative assessment of the incompatibility of sociocultural sections demands prophecy as well as omniscience.

A second approach involves a holistic but synthetic type of analysis. This is to ascertain the extent of sociocultural heterogeneity in each society and then compare the societies with each other, starting, perhaps, with pairs of approximately equal size: Barbados and Guadeloupe, Aruba and Antigua, St. Croix and Montserrat, Bonaire and Bequia, St. Barthélemy and Providencia, Union and Saba. This method raises several questions. For one, heterogeneity is not pluralism; cultural diversity often coexists with institutional unity. Nevertheless, without heterogeneity there can hardly be pluralism; they are correlated. To rank societies according to their degree of internal diversity is certainly relevant to a study of pluralism.

A more serious difficulty is that no one has devised a formula for adding up different sorts of diversity. How many points does one allot to this or that amount of

ethnic heterogeneity, how many points to various differences in rural and urban living patterns, how many to property and kinship systems? Social and cultural elements can hardly be combined quantitatively for any society, let alone for more than one. Any general comparison must be essentially impressionistic, as much a work of art as a product of science. This is probably why it is seldom undertaken in the Caribbean, or elsewhere, except by travelers, novelists, and poets. Social scientists usually find the task temperamentally disagreeable. Nevertheless, we need more such studies by competent observers, especially studies comparing British, French, and Dutch dependencies.

The third approach is particularistic and synthetic. This method is to examine specific aspects of society and culture and to study the range and variation of each throughout the West Indies. This approach yields no generalizations about any particular society as a whole, but it has its uses, nonetheless, and it has the advantage of being possible. It has been tried, for various traits, at various levels of sophistication, and with various degrees of success by Proudfoot[10] for the British and American dependencies; by Kruijer[11] for St. Eustatius, St. Maarten, and St. Thomas; by the Keurs[12] for the Netherlands Windward Islands; by M. G. Smith[13] for Grenada and Carriacou; and by Cumper[14] for the Brit-

[9] H. C. Brookfield, "Pluralism and Geography in Mauritius," *Geographical Studies,* V (1958), 3–19.

[10] M. Proudfoot, *Britain and the United States in the Caribbean: A Comparative Study in Methods of Development* (London: Faber & Faber, 1954).

[11] G. J. Kruijer, "Saint Martin and Saint Eustatius Negroes as Compared with Those of Saint Thomas: A Study of Personality and Culture," *West-Indische Gids,* XXXV (1953), 225–37.

[12] John Y. Keur and Dorothy L. Keur, *Windward Children: A Study of the Human Ecology of the Three Dutch Windward Islands in the Caribbean* (Assen, Netherlands: Royal Vangorcum, 1960).

[13] *Kinship and Community in Carriacou.*

[14] G. Cumper, *Social Structure of the British Caribbean* (Mona, Jamaica: Extra-Mural Department, University College of the West Indies, 1949), Parts 1, 2, 3.

ish Caribbean generally. Two kinds of study are needed: detailed comparisons of all facets of life in a few societies, and broad surveys of particular traits and institutional subsystems for the whole area. Class and color configurations; the roles of minor ethnic groups; metropolitan policies, influences, and images; ecological and economic patterns; religious, legal, and educational systems; mating and kinship; and other aspects of culture and society should be separately scrutinized for each and compared for all West Indian societies.

Let us consider color-class stratification. The classic white-colored-black system of status ranking,[15] significant in many West Indian societies, is unimportant in others. In Cuba, the Dominican Republic, and Puerto Rico, where Negroes are a fairly small minority, the elite is hardly distinguishable, in terms of color, from most of the lower class. Many of the smallest West Indian societies are virtually homogeneous with respect to race and color: Carriacou, San Andrés, St. Eustatius, Barbuda, and Mayreau being almost entirely Negro communities, and St. Barthélemy being almost entirely white.

Elsewhere the pattern and the significance of color heterogeneity vary profoundly. Warner views status systems based on color as the most inclusive and rigid form of social stratification, one in which the position of the individual is fixed and determined by birth.[16] In few Caribbean societies, however, do color-class differ-

ences retain these castelike attributes; all have some measure of mobility and assimilation. The white *békés* of Guadeloupe and Martinique, an endogamous and genealogically self-conscious group, form a closed elite (closed to metropolitan and other Antillean whites as well as to *gens de couleur*) at the summit of an otherwise open class structure. Until recently the mulatto elite in Haiti occupied a similar position. In many of the smaller islands, such as Saba, Bequia, and La Désirade, black, colored and, when present, white groups tend to form separate communities rather than ranked sections within the same community; despite some status difference, each group is essentially classless.[17] In still other societies (St. Croix, St. Thomas, Aruba) special economic circumstances such as tourism or oil refining, together with continual in- and out-migration and skewed age and sex distributions, obscure the color-class pattern and diminish its functional significance.

Even where color-class hierarchies clearly operate, it is difficult to estimate how important they are. Barbados is most self-conscious about color-class distinctions, but other British Caribbean social hierarchies may well be more rigid. Too little is known of the different character and varying roles of the elite in, for example, Barbados, where many whites are not members of it; in Trinidad, where it is deeply divided by nationality; and in Grenada and Dominica, where it is becoming predominantly light-colored. We need comparative studies of the elites of each society in terms of their ethnic and social origins, numbers, proportions to the total population, residential patterns, occupational and economic roles, uniformity or diversity of circumstances, internal solidarity, extent of identification with the whole society (higher in Barbados, for example, than in Trinidad and St. Vincent), affluence relative to others, control of political, educational, and religious insti-

---

[15] See M. G. Smith, *A Framework for Caribbean Studies* (Mona, Jamaica: Extra-Mural Department, University College of the West Indies, 1955), pp. 47–50; *idem,* "Ethnic and Cultural Pluralism in the British Caribbean," in *Ethnic and Cultural Pluralism in Intertropical Countries* (Brussels: International Institute of Differing Civilizations, 1957), pp. 439–47; and L. Braithwaite, "Social Stratification in Trinidad," *Social and Economic Studies* (Institute of Social and Economic Research, University College of the West Indies), II (1953), 5–175.

[16] W. L. Warner, "The Study of Social Stratification," in J. B. Gittler (ed.), *Review of Sociology: Analysis of a Decade* (New York: Wiley, 1957), pp. 234–35.

[17] G. Lasserre, "La Désirade, petite île guadeloupéenne," *Cahiers d'Outre-Mer,* X (1957), 325–66.

tutions, and stereotypes and self-images of the rest of the population.

We also need comparative studies of peoples partly or wholly outside the stratified social order. The extent to which East Indians in Trinidad, British Guiana, and Surinam have been Creolized is debated in this monograph, as it probably will be perennially, but few will deny that these East Indians constitute a separate cultural section. This is not true of East Indians in other West Indian societies, who are generally assimilated to, sometimes integrated with, the Creole lower class.[18] Is it because these East Indians are much smaller minorities (7 per cent in Guadeloupe, less everywhere else)? East Indian minorities (predominantly urban, to be sure) in other parts of the world maintain separate social organizations.

The same is substantially true of other ethnic minorities in the West Indies. The Chinese, Portuguese, and Syrian communities, together do not account for 3 per cent of the population of any West Indian territory, but in many of them they play significant roles.[19] Their virtual monopoly of retail trade in some societies represents, for the Creole majority, a social truncation as serious, perhaps, as the truncation of political functions involved in colonial relationships. On the other hand, the presence of certain minorities may serve to ease other status relationships. If Syrian merchants, for example, are accepted to any extent by the elite, the middle class is also apt to find areas of acceptance; on the other hand, rejection of these "foreign" elements may promote an awareness of common outlook among European and Creoles.[20]

It is interesting that all these West In-

dian minorities have achieved a measure of economic success; however much or little they fit into the general social order, they are not at the bottom of it. There are no West Indian counterparts to the Negroes and Puerto Ricans in northern cities of the United States, the *eta* in Japan, or the Albanians in Belgrade, who perform certain menial tasks that are virtually badges of caste. Until recently the few Javanese in Paramaribo, Surinam, were the only garbage collectors and sewer cleaners, but today they abjure such occupations. Convicts used to perform similar services in French Guiana until the termination of the penal establishment there.

Data are needed from each West Indian society about all of these minorities and about their relative and absolute numbers, their economic roles, and the extent to which they remain aloof from, or merge into, the general social order.

The extent of linguistic differentiation within West Indian societies similarly illustrates their diversity. Language is both a symbol of and an adjunct to status. What proportion in each society speaks the "standard" tongue, and on what occasions? How different is the Creolese variant in pronunciation, vocabulary, and grammar? How do various sections of the population feel and act about the use of patois? There are several fundamentally different situations.[21] In most societies the patois is a dialect of the language of the educated, but in Dominica, St. Lucia, Curaçao, and Surinam the local patois has no relation whatever to the official prestige tongue; the two are mutually unintelligible. Linguistic differentiation is thus formalized, and the gulf between social classes is greater than in societies where the patois is a variant of the metropolitan language. The opposite is true where the lingua franca derives from a European language that is more widely spoken in the region than the local official

[18] G. Lasserre, "Les 'Indiens' de Guadeloupe," *ibid*, VI (1953), 128–58.

[19] M. H. Fried, "The Chinese in the British Caribbean," in M. H. Fried (ed.), *Colloquium on Overseas Chinese* (New York: Institute of Pacific Relations, 1958), pp. 49–58.

[20] I am indebted to Rhoda Metraux, Institute of International Studies, New York, for this suggestion.

[21] See R. B. Le Page, "The Language Problem of the British Caribbean," *Caribbean Quarterly*, IV (1955), 40–49, and E. Efron, "French and Creole Patois in Haiti," *ibid*, III (1954), 199–213.

language. In the English-speaking Netherlands Windward Islands and, to some extent, in San Andrés and Providencia, linguistic differentiation tends to break down rather than to reinforce social stratification, because the values associated with the language of the majority outweigh the prestige associated with metropolitan Dutch or Spanish.

To describe the range and diversity of social institutions and cultural forms is not enough, however; one must also account for them. How is it that pluralism affects one society more than another? How can one explain heterogeneity in one place and homogeneity in another? Why are certain traits diverse in this place and uniform in that one? Answers to such questions require comparative analysis, to avoid oversimplified or excessively functional explanations.

Let me illustrate with data on the European Guianas.[22] Here, I think, comparisons have special validity because these territories are contiguous, because their inhabited areas are remarkably alike physically, and because their settlement for a long time followed similar models, particularly in Surinam and British Guiana, which were drained and diked for plantation agriculture along the same lines until the late eighteenth century.

Ethnic heterogeneity characterizes both British Guiana and Surinam, principally because many indentured laborers were brought in after the emancipation of the slaves. One-half the population of each territory today is of Asian origin, virtually all Indian in British Guiana, while three-tenths is Indian and two-tenths Javanese in Surinam. However, Surinamese society is generally less integrated. In British Guiana, East Indian ways of life have become more and more similar to those of other rural or urban folk, while in Surinam the Creoles, Hindustanis, and Javanese for the most part have their own villages, languages, and even customary garb. British Guianese East Indians refer to their compatriots in Surinam as "good" Indians, that is, closer adherents of old-country fashion and ritual.[23] Unlike British Guianese, Surinamers do not hesitate to assert their separate ethnic interests; political parties are avowedly divided along racial and religious lines; there is scarcely any sense of a general Surinam Society. Occupational and rural-urban ethnic differentiation are also more pronounced in Surinam. Three-fourths of the Creole population is urban, compared with less than one-half in British Guiana, and most of Surinam's rural Creoles are concentrated within a few districts.

Several factors help to account for these differences. For one, slavery lasted twenty-five years longer in Surinam than in British Guiana. In the interim many slaves fled the country and, when emancipation finally came, in 1863, the Negroes still left on Surinam estates were not willing to wait out an additional decade of indenture. In British Guiana, many former slaves pooled their savings to buy up estates and turned to subsistence agriculture; in Surinam, most of them moved off the land.

The delay of emancipation also retarded the introduction of indentured workers. East Indians began to enter British Guiana as early as 1841, but did not reach Surinam until after 1873, and the Javanese came there still later, between 1891 and 1939. Neither group in Surinam has had as long to become assimilated as have the East Indians of British Guiana. Moreover, the East Indians of Surinam (known there as Hindustanis) have found acculturation more difficult for lack of a continuing tie with certain British institutions and aspects of culture. Besides, there is little in common between the Hindustanis and the Javanese. Many of the latter are still first-generation immigrants, for the most part content with their alien status as Indonesian citizens, and are regarded as clannish

[22] David Lowenthal, "Population Contrasts in the Guianas," *Geographical Review*, L (1960), 41–59.

[23] Personal communication from C. Jayawardena.

and unenterprising by Europeans, Creoles, and Hindustanis alike.

Dutch colonial policy is partly responsible for the fact that Surinam's rural villages are, by and large, more homogeneous racially than those of British Guiana. Until after the Second World War the Surinam government promoted residential segregation by leasing abandoned estates to ethnic groups. This practice is now disavowed, but efforts to promote integration have had little success, perhaps because many people still believe, at heart, that the different races simply will not work or live well together.

The linguistic situation displays similar segmentation. In British Guiana English is both the vernacular and the prestige language of the educated, but in Surinam the common Creole tongue (*Taki-Taki,* an amalgam of African, English, and other elements) is utterly unlike the official, upper-class Dutch. Dutch is unimportant elsewhere in America, and *Taki-Taki* is incomprehensible outside Surinam, so it is little wonder that Javanese and Hindustanis prefer to retain their own, more widely spoken, languages. Even the Creoles are divided, some preferring Dutch, others promoting *Taki-Taki* as their "own" tongue, that is, as an appurtenance of nationalism. Lacking a viable common language, Surinam is unlikely to reach a level of social or cultural integration comparable to that in British Guiana, even should Surinamers desire it.

These features represent, of course, only one aspect of social organization in the Guianas. Analogous contrasts can be drawn with respect to the varieties of stratification within the Creole groups and the roles of the European and other minorities. Whatever point of departure one selects, society and culture can be understood best, as Furnivall remarked of colonial practice, when studied both comparatively and historically.[24]

[24] J. S. Furnivall, *Colonial Policy and Practice: A Comparative Study of Burma and Netherlands India* (Cambridge: Cambridge University Press, 1948), pp. 9–10.

CARL O. SAUER

MIDDLE AMERICA AS A CULTURE HISTORICAL LOCATION

To place Middle America as a scene of distinctive human occupations and experience we begin with its geographic position and configuration in the over-all pattern of the inhabited earth. The significance of location needs to be appraised rather than the limits that may be assigned. I shall be concerned only most casually with delineation of area, saying, for the sake of convenience rather than by conviction, that Middle America is bounded by the Bahamas, the Windward Islands, the Gulf of Darien, and the Isthmus of Tehuantepec. This is intended to be only a rough physical identification; it is sufficient for the immediate geographic focus and it defers argument about culture areas and their boundaries. If I thereby dislocate the expected frame of reference, it is to avoid the horns of a contrived dilemma, i.e., Mesoamerican vs. Andean culture area, on which concern with autonomy of cultures would impale us.

POSITION AND CONFIGURATION OF LAND AND SEA

Physically, our area is the space between the two massive Western continents, including the island garland of the West Indies, the Caribbean Sea, and the mainland of Central America, the latter the only

Reprinted, with permission of the author, from *Actas del XXXIII Congreso Internacional de Americanistas, San José, Costa Rica, 1958*, I (San José: Lehmann, 1959), 115–22. The author is professor emeritus of geography at the University of California, Berkeley. The footnotes to this article are supplied by the editors.

isthmus between the world oceans (except for that of Suez). Thus the uniqueness of its position is both intercontinental and interoceanic. Situated on the northern flank of the Tropics, Middle America has similar climatic regimes, whatever the local altitude, as to length of day, march of temperature, and pattern and season of rainfall. In these latitudes also the probability of major change in climate within human times may be discounted. To one coming from the North its plant world, especially in the temperate highlands, appears quite familiar as far south as Nicaragua and to a lesser degree through the Greater Antilles. South American elements of flora and fauna have penetrated northward in mass and diversity, farthest so through the lowlands. Biotically both mainland and islands have been a zone of meeting and mingling of stocks from North and South and centers of endemism only in minor degree.

CORRIDOR AND CROSSROADS

What then of the physical situation and condition as to human attraction, access, and passage? The mainland *Istmo* is an unobstructed passageway, the only way between North and South available to men until they learned to use boats. Mexico is the cone of the funnel, Central America the narrowing tube through which poured all but the later migrants that peopled South America. Perhaps nowhere in the world has there been as narrow, long, and significant a land passageway.

Radiocarbon dates are now assigning

some tens of thousand years to human presence from Texas to California. They are also reducing greatly the time of the last phases of the Ice Age, so that a first peopling of the New World before the beginning of the last (Fourth or Wisconsin) glaciation is no longer a fantastic notion. It should not have taken a great time for men to drift south from Texas and California to and through the inviting Isthmian lands. Through most of human time in the New World people, ideas, and goods have been flowing into and across this mainland bridge. At first, and for quite a time, it was a one-way bridge leading men south.

The corridor of Central America is extraordinarily inviting in the diversity of its terrain, soils, climate, and life. Nature offered no deterrent to man to enter, nor barriers of relief or climate to halt him. Unless and until established peoples blocked the passage of newcomers, such migrants could live and move widely with ease and at their leisure.

The general level of the ocean has risen about 30 meters in the last ten thousand years and probably at least 100 meters in all since the last maximum of glaciation. The coastal swamps, estuaries and widely flooding river valleys of today in the main are the result of recently risen sea levels. The Gulfs of Panama and Darien and the Atrato Valley indicate such progressive late submergence by eustatic rise of sea level, because of the deglaciation in high latitudes. The lowered sea levels during the migrations of Early Men resulted in stream erosion and good drainage of lowlands; the later rise of sea level brought flooding by both sea and lowland streams.

The rain forest between Panama and the Atrato was no serious obstacle. It is more formidable now than it was before the coming of the Europeans. When Columbus discovered the Portobello coast he was impressed by the well-populated and cultivated country, like a *huerta pintada*. The Spanish colony of Darien lived chiefly off the numerous, large, and advanced native villages to the west. Balboa's discovery of

the Pacific was by an easy and well-supplied march. Three centuries later a surveying party of the United States Navy, of which the youthful M. F. Maury was a member, tried much the same route and nearly perished in a trackless and foodless wilderness. By then the Indian populations had disappeared; the present rain forest has repossessed lands of former abundant Indian habitation.

For passage by sea, currents and winds must be considered and also the range of visibility of land across water; the voyaging is thought to have been by drift and paddle. Access to the West Indies island bridge was easiest from the southern bridgehead of Trinidad and Tobago. Because of the strong westward set of current the island of Tobago was most eligible as a starting point for the Windward Islands, the high parts of Tobago and Grenada also being within sight of each other. Thence north to Cuba the passage from island to island presented no difficulty, except for Barbados, somewhat distantly apart, rather low, and lying strongly upwind and upcurrent from the islands to the west. Discovery and possession of the Bahamas, also on the windward side of the large islands, was most feasible from Haiti. These low islands could only be sighted from canoes at close range; that they were nearly all occupied bespeaks seafaring competence and venturesomeness. Jamaica was most easily reached from Haiti; at both ends of this sea passage mountains tower to two thousand meters, and ·brisk and steady winds and currents run straight west. (Note the ease of Columbus' discovery of Jamaica and the difficulties he had in getting back from there to Santo Domingo.) Haiti is thus suggested as the common source of colonization of Jamaica, Cuba, and the Bahamas.

Various passages from the Bahamas to Florida offer no great difficulty, but to come from the northern mainland to the islands against the powerful Gulf Stream was quite another matter. Along the Florida east coast the northward current may exceed a hundred kilometers a day; entry to the Bahamas by canoe from Florida seems quite unlikely, to Cuba from Key West only somewhat less so. The passage to the West Indies from North America, however, seems feasible for primitive man coming by way of Yucatán. Thus speculations would run as follows: Folk moving down the Mexican Gulf coast had become accustomed to knowing and using tropical plants and animals. In Yucatán the access they had to seals and sea turtles along the shores offered an invitation to prowl the shallow seas. Along the east coast of Yucatán a steady drift sets northward, the great outflow of the Caribbean into the Gulf of Mexico. Western Cuba lies northeast of Yucatán, that is, in a favorable position for men at sea to drift across at an easy angle. Also, once such seafarers got well out into the Yucatán Channel the Cuban highlands would be in sight, an advantage lacking for any passage from Florida.

From the east the two equatorial currents, driven by the trade winds, sweep across the Atlantic to and through the West Indies. The equatorial sea drift, deflected by the shoulder of Brazil, running westerly, and picking up the waters of the Amazon and Orinoco, moves at a rate of 50 to 80 kilometers a day as far as Trinidad. West of Trinidad the drift along the north coast of South America continues steadily but with a decreasing rate toward Panama. Within the Caribbean the trade winds become almost easterly, as does the drift; both wind and drift reach the mainland coast of Central America with some vigor. (Note that Columbus, sailing eastward on the north shore of Honduras, named Cape Gracias á Dios in relief at getting out of the windward belt.) We may not exclude from possible attention the narrow passage of the Atlantic and its extraordinarily favoring winds and currents out of Africa.

On the Pacific side a weak sea drift sets from Panama to Tehuantepec during most of the year, with winds prevailing out of the south. Navigation along shore here also may take account of regular daily alterna-

tion of land and sea breezes. Below Nicaragua the highland coast is broken by numerous sheltered bays accentuated by submergence. From the Gulf of Fonseca west-northwestward there are long beaches and attractive lagoons behind great sand bars for coastal voyagers.

EARLY MIGRATIONS

This geographical position and configuration, as I have tried to set them forth briefly, are at the center of the New World stage, whoever the actors and whatever the act and shift of scene. As yet we know almost nothing of the long early times, except the footprints of men that trailed bisons in the fossil volcanic ash of Nicaragua, and some early midden sites that are scarcely reconnoitered. The Isthmus lacks offside pockets of isolation as refuges for what Father Cooper has called "internal margins."[1] Survivals of primitives who passed through are not to be sought here but out in the back woods and far corners of South America; the ancestors of these early peoples must once have inhabited Central America. Nearly the whole of our knowledge of aboriginal Middle America is of later peoples who were agriculturists, in contrast to Mexico and most South American countries.

The exception is presented by the so-called Ciboney, to which name Cuban scholars properly object, as applied to all or any non-agricultural predecessors of the Arawak. Neither the scant historical knowledge nor the scattered archeologic remains of the islands warrant the attribution of everything that preceded Arawak colonization to one culture or one people. By what route, what sort of craft, and at what times may they have come? Whenever they came, the sea passages, winds, and currents were about as they are now. Notable ability to survive at and move by sea seems an inescapable premise. I have suggested above the superior eligibility of Yucatán as point

[1] John M. Cooper, "Areal and Temporal Aspects of Aboriginal South American Culture," *Primitive Man*, XV (1942), 1–38.

of departure. A South American entry has been discounted by the restriction of the known primitive and early sites to the northern, great islands. By whatever bridge-head they came, it is worthy of note that all three mainland approaches have long been occupied by agricultural peoples. It is unlikely that such primitive folk could have forced their way through wide areas occupied by advanced and numerous peoples. Hence the hypothesis may be put forth that these primitive islanders came in before the higher cultures existed. From this it may follow that the early island colonists were already venturesome sea-farers, who stagnated in the isolation of their final homes. At the beginning of European contacts they occupied the western part of Cuba and the southwestern part of Haiti, both areas of highest suitability for Indian agriculture, an adverse comment on the case of independent invention and, subsequent to their contact with the Arawaks, on the readiness to accept new and advantageous learning.

In earlier times, when migrations of peoples were continuing or recurrent by southward displacement and mingling, the sources of population and ways were out of the north. Language is carried by migrants coming as groups, and the historic languages of the Central American corridor should disclose old linkages to Mexico and the north, vestiges of ancient population drift. This is one of the most attractive problems of comparative linguistics and glottochronology, the clarifying of surmises about old linguistic filiations, such as Swadesh is investigating.[2] Of immediate interest is the question of older common roots of the Chibchan group with linguistic stocks to the north; might its member groups in Nicaragua and Honduras be in part not merely a western fringe of Chib-

chan expansion out of South America, but also rear guard remnants from the north? In the cultural substrata of Central America there may also survive techniques and tools of fishing and hunting brought down from the north. On social organization and ceremonial ways I have no competence to make any suggestion other than to urge that such elements, sufficiently identified, be studied as to their overall distribution without regard to the limits of Middle America.

PROVENIENCE OUT OF THE SOUTH

For the later cultural introductions and modifications a preponderance of South American influences is found, aside from southward drives of late aggressive folk (Pipil). South American crop plants mainly vegetatively reproduced, dominate lower Central America, giving way in the north to annual seed plants. A large complex of kinds, techniques, and uses of narcotics, intoxicants, body paints, and unguents centers on South America. Metallurgy, I should think, was derived out of South America. Has it been noted that the prizing of gold had a continuous distribution in the New World, greatest in South America, including all of Middle America, and limited in the north by the Mexican highland high cultures, and that it was not merely related to cultural level or source of metal? What are the distributions and their significances of inclosed towns (by palisades or live hedges), ritual cannibalism, idols of stone or wood, hereditary caciques, and many other traits in and beyond our area?

Let us take one of the available lines of passage of men and ideas, the West Coast, as illustrating questions of distant migration and communication, probably from the south. I should like to begin in the north, with the Hohokam of the Arizona Desert. Their appearance by mass immigration, dated by Gladwin as of the early eighth century A.D., was without any preliminary local antecedents and they remained without notable connection with

---

[2] See M. Swadesh, "Lexico-statistic Dating of Prehistoric Ethnic Contacts," *Proceedings of the American Philosophical Society*, XCVI (1952), 452–63, and Swadesh *et al.*, "Symposium: Time Depths of American Linguistic Groupings," *American Anthropologist*, LVI (1954), 361–77.

neighboring cultures.[3] They came with an elaborate and distinctive culture, at its best in the earliest period, when they colonized rapidly and fully the Middle Gila Basin. It was a nation of implicit social classes and political organization. No comparable ability and enterprise in irrigation engineering is known to the north of Peru and none at all in neighboring areas, except the historic irrigation of Opata and Pima, almost surely derivative from the vanished Hohokam. The lively animation of free hand pottery designs, copper bells, palettes, mosaic, plaques, and other traits also bespeak a distant origin. Could such migrants have come by land northward without leaving trace of their passage or could they have forced their way through already long and well-occupied lands? Or did they come by sea, continuing until they came, at the end of the sea, to a desert sparsely and primitively peopled, which they were able to transform by their irrigation arts and organization of labor?

Farther down the coast, Sinaloa has its southern (?) mysteries: The seemingly aristocratic tumulus of Guasave excavated by Ekholm has elaborate grave furnishings (including lacquer on gourd) strangely out of place in the known simple archeology of northern Sinaloa.[4] In the prehistoric towns of the Culiacán Valley are clusters of great urn burials and on the coast are mounds of slag where sea shells were used in smelting complex sulphide ores difficult to reduce to metal.[5] The nearest source of such ores is well to the east in the mountains; the metallurgy was of an advanced technology. In the State of Colima vault burials

have long been sought and plundered for their anthro- and zoomorphic pottery. These are chambers excavated laterally in rock from vertical shafts, the latter subsequently refilled. They are strongly reminiscent of Colombian huacas, as on the Quimbaya ridge crests.[6] Such are a few of the many items in archeology and ethnology that need to be properly identified and examined as to the whole range of their occurrence. Is it our own agoraphopia and thalassophobia as students of New World culture that have so greatly restricted knowledge and consideration of far connections of culture, of mobility of peoples, of communications of ideas beyond the sheltering limits of so-called culture areas?

LIMITATION OF THE CONCEPT OF CULTURE AREAS AND STAGES

The peoples living about the Caribbean were more separated than connected by the Carib Sea. What is known of movements by sea is that they were peripheral and occasional. Whatever elements of culture the Antilles and Central America held in common came almost wholly from the northern mainland of South America. The islands were quite simply colonial South American. The islanders preserved with little change the culture they brought with them, living largely in isolation from other cultures. Such at least is the picture as it has come down to us. It might be less simple if we knew more. On the Island of Haiti north of Samaná Bay, the Spaniards found the Ciguayos, warlike and differing in customs and speech from the others. The southwestern Haitian province of Xaragua was more aristocratic than the rest and was said to have had intensive irrigation. The Jamaicans were praised for their agricultural skill; here also, elaborately sculptured stone seats are known in some number and

[3] Harold Gladwin, *History of the Ancient Southwest* (Portland, Me.: Bond Wheelright, 1957).

[4] Gordon F. Ekholm, "Excavations at Guasave, Sinaloa, Mexico," *Anthropological Papers of the American Museum of Natural History*, XXXVIII (1942), 23–139.

[5] B. H. McLeod, "Examination of Copper Objects from Culiacán," in Isabel Kelly, *Excavations at Culiacán, Sinaloa*, ("Ibero-Americana," No. XXV [1945]), Appendix II, 180–86.

[6] Robert C. West, "Ridge or 'Era' Agriculture in the Colombian Andes," *Actas del XXXIII Congreso Internacional de Americanistas, San José, Costa Rica, 1958*, I (San José: Lehmann, 1959), 179–82.

seem to be like those from Colombia and Costa Rica. It may be, therefore, that the island Arawak included a number of distinct colonizations, not all wholly Arawakan.

For Central America a southeast-northwest division between Circum-Caribbean and Mesoamerican culture is commonly recognized. (I do wish that a term other than "Mesoamerican" might have come into use for the Mexican-Guatemalan complex.) As a synoptic picture at the time of European contact it has value in introductory orientation. It is, however, only a rough delineation of status at one moment of history, synchronic, not diachronic, as our colleagues like to say in the fashion of the day.

Geography, which basically is concerned with position and areal extension, holds suspect all simplified and inclusive areal generalizations. Schemes of climatic, vegetation, and geomorphic regions, and even more so those of natural and cultural regions, may be useful elementary conveniences in helping to see major patterns of differentiation over the earth and thus as approaches to the processes of such differentiation or conjugation. As with landforms and vegetation, the cultural content of an area is an accretion and synthesis by different and non-recurrent historical events and processes of people, skills, and institutions that are changing assemblages in accommodation and interdependence. Few human groups have lived in isolation, excluding persons and ideas from outside; the more they have done so the less have they progressed. Isolation after a while stifles innovation; this is perhaps the major lesson of the history of mankind and also of natural history. An advancing culture accepts new culture elements without being overwhelmed by them; it adapts as it adopts and thus change leads to invention. The history and prehistory of the Old World are read throughout in terms of the communication of people and culture traits, of their blending and modifications into

new forms as they are farther removed in time and place from their origins. Why should the New World be different; why should there be construed here a congeries of autochthonous culture areas, each passing through independent parallel stages of development?

No part of the New World has been less isolated or self-contained than has Central America. I return to the initial theme that it has always been corridor and crossroads. It needs study as such with the most accurate identifications of its elements of culture and of the total range of distribution of each, however far this may extend into other areas and times and thus of whatever may be learned of their appearance and movements in actual time, and not by reference to inferred or imagined stages.

Since I am strongly impressed by the role of the Isthmus as a cultural passageway, I should assign it the role of culture hearth only in one instance—as the place of origin, at its northern borders, of New World seed agriculture. Much inquiry remains to be carried out on this problem and it may never be resolved, although I am hopeful that it will be. I like placing the origin of the maize-beans-squash complex in southern Mexico and Guatemala. I share the view that vegetative reproduction, that is, planting pieces of the desired plant in the ground, is earlier than seed agriculture. I am struck by the fact that seed agriculture all over the New World is still by planting, and not by sowing processes as in the Old World. It seems probable to me that agriculture by vegetative reproduction was brought into Central America with domesticated plants out of tropical South America. (Central America has added nothing new to the list of such domesticates.) As planting was carried northward into areas environmentally different as to the rainy season, highlands, and native flora, attractive herbaceous weeds appeared in the planted clearings which became the basis of the new seed crops.[7] This is my tentative surmise of the basis of "Mesoamerica."

[7] For elaboration of these remarks see Carl O. Sauer, "Cultivated Plants of South and Central America," in Julian H. Steward (ed.), *Handbook of South American Indians* (Smithsonian Institution, Bureau of American Ethnology Bulletin 143 [6 vols.; Washington, D.C., 1946–50]), VI, 487–543; and *idem, Agricultural Origins and Dispersals* (New York: American Geographical Society, 1952), pp. 40–73.

As these questions of the geographic range of traits and assemblages and of the derivative modifications or variations into new forms and complexes are diffusionist in import, they ask for an examination of the evidence that geographic distributions may bear, wherever identifiable traits are known. Culture history, and this means culture dynamics, may not build Chinese walls.

PART **3**

CULTURAL ORIGIN AND DISPERSAL

In cultural geography studies of areas and distributions merge imperceptibly with studies of origins and dispersals, and in practice the latter may precede the former. In either case determination of the content and extent of culture areas entails consideration of what is alien and intrusive or native and spontaneous. At times migration and diffusion may be of overwhelming importance, but at other times diversification may take place without benefit of external influences. Regardless of their origins, cultural patterns never cease to be in flux. Objects, ideas, institutions, and entire civilizations arise, spread, and fuse. Accordingly, cultural geographers, in common with all students of culture, must attempt to solve problems of genesis and process.

It is appropriate that discussion of these issues should be introduced by an archeologist, for the members of that profession have custody of the longest and most impressive record of cultural growth and change. During the past century archeology has evolved from a treasure hunt to a science, and in recent years archeologists have undertaken distributional and ecological studies that are essentially geographic.[1] To be sure, the data of archeology are meager, fragmentary, and almost entirely material, but the methods that the archeologists have devised are applicable to other materials and other times. As Childe suggests, scholars in many fields can profit from understanding of trends and processes within the vast span of prehistoric time.

These observations apply especially to the study of diffusion. It is seldom possible for an archeologist to understand the precise motives or preconditions of an innovation, but he may be able to locate the place or area of its origin, and reconstruct the direction, rate, and extent of its dissemination. For example, raw materials can be traced to and from places of origin, and the diffusion of manufactured articles can be reconstructed through cartographic and statistical analyses of form, technique, material, and style. Data of this sort may suggest migration, trade, or uncontrolled drift. In any case, they provide proof

[1] For a comprehensive review of the growth of archeology see Glyn E. Daniel, *A Hundred Years of Archaeology* (London: Duckworth, 1950). It is not possible here to give even an abbreviated list of archeological works that employ geographic methods or deal with geographic problems, but mention should be made of Sir Cyril Fox's classic study of *The Personality of Britain* (Cardiff: National Museum of Wales, 1932), and Gordon R. Willey (ed.), *Prehistoric Settlement Patterns in the New World* ("Viking Fund Publications in Anthropology," No. 23 [1956]). See also the article by Beardsley *et al.* ("Functional and Evolutionary Implications of Community Patterning") in Part IV of this volume.

of intercourse between or among human groups. The effect of such investigation is to establish a web of communication that explains, or at least helps to explain, the content of culture areas.[2]

From Gordon Childe's essay on diffusion in prehistory we turn to Hans Bobek's world-wide survey of social and economic evolution. This comprehensive statement plays an important role in the discussion. In the first place, it reviews a large literature and summarizes current thinking on major issues in cultural history. In the second place, it offers some important original ideas on the characteristics of evolutionary stages and the processes that initiate them. The sequence described—from bands of unspecialized hunters and gatherers to modern urban societies—is based on solid historical and comparative evidence. Bobek's emphasis on "rent-capitalism" as a critical feature of peasant and early urban societies is a major innovation. It should also be noted that he stresses evolution rather than revolution, and that he refutes the thesis of a single immanent trend. Within each of his socioeconomic stages, Bobek describes forms of livelihood, social organization, population density and dynamics, and cultural manifestations in landscapes. Each of these considerations presuppose the others, and each raises questions that exceed the scope of the essay. It goes without saying that some of the evidence presented is amenable to different interpretations,[3] and that some of the conclusions may be challenged. Nevertheless, Bobek's statement is "heuristic" in the best sense of that overworked word, and it demonstrates that much of the data of cultural geography can be sorted, classified, and arranged in an evolutionary sequence.[4]

The key consideration in Bobek's discussion is livelihood, and understanding of the evolution and diffusion of livelihood demands consideration of the origin and dispersal of cultivated plants. Today, most scholars agree that most of man's cultivated plants are derived from experiments that were undertaken several thousand years ago. There is also general agreement that domestication has rarely been sporadic or repetitious. From a few well-defined areas of origin, crops and crop combinations were gradually carried to the limits of the habitable world.

The essays of I. H. Burkill and Hugh Cutler review the history of ideas

[2] See, for example, the discussion of "culture contact situations," "cultural stability," and "cultural isolation" in "Seminars in Archaeology: 1955," *Memoirs of the Society for American Archaeology,* XI (1956). The relevant works of Childe are listed in a comprehensive bibliography published just prior to his death in *Proceedings of the Prehistoric Society,* N.S., XXI (1956), 295–304. See also A. L. Kroeber's essays, "Stimulus Diffusion," *American Anthropologist,* XLII (1940), 1–20, and "The Ancient Oikoumene as a Historic Culture Aggregate," *Journal of the Royal Anthropological Institute,* LXV (1949), 9–20; both articles are reprinted in Kroeber's *The Nature of Culture* (Chicago: University of Chicago Press, 1952).

[3] Cf. Julian H. Steward: *Theory of Culture Change* (Urbana: University of Illinois Press, 1955); Leslie A. White: *The Evolution of Culture* (New York: McGraw-Hill, 1959); and Rushton Coulborn, *The Origin of Civilized Societies* (Princeton: Princeton University Press, 1959).

[4] Much of the pioneer work on this theme was accomplished by Eduard Hahn. See, for example, his *Die Entstehung der Pflugkultur* (Heidelberg: Winter, 1909) and *Von der Hacke zum Pflug* (Leipzig: Quelle & Meyer, 1914).

about agricultural origins and evaluate current thinking. In addition, each
author presents some viable interpretations of his own. The foundation of
Burkill's statement is N. I. Vavilov's delimitation of major world centers of
crop diversification and breeding. He re-examines that pioneer work in the
light of more recent investigations and attempts to relate botanic and genetic
evidence to what is known of human migrations. Some of his conclusions are
debatable—for example, the assertions that hunters rather than farmers domesticated the herd animals and that cereals were grown before root crops[5]—
but the basic structure of his essay is consistent with current views. In both
the Old and the New World questions of primacy or ultimate origins tend to
arouse heated controversy, and this is especially true of the problems of transoceanic carriage and the relative importance of the major centers of domestication. The value of the essays of Burkill and Cutler lies not only in what they
describe as "known," but also in their indications of what needs to be known.
In the same spirit, Carl Sauer describes the maps in his study of agricultural
origins and dispersals as "work sheets to be revised as better knowledge comes
to hand of man's plants and animals, of their remains recovered in archeology,
of their implications in different cultures, of the climates, shore lines, and land
surfaces of the prehistoric human past." [6]

In the articles reviewed thus far little attention has been paid to the motives
that inspire or condition cultural innovations, although we have learned from
Weiss, Fickeler, and Lowenthal that cultural distinctions may not be products
of rational or utilitarian thought. In the fifth article in this section H. Epstein
examines the consequences of the selection and breeding of domestic animals
and concludes that many of these accomplishments reflect social or aesthetic
considerations. The evidence is especially striking in this case, for one tends
automatically to describe domestic animals in economic terms. To be sure,
animals are usually raised for draft and transportation purposes or for such
products as meat, milk, and wool, but the motives that have influenced breeding practices also reveal preoccupation with such non-economic considerations
as the color of hide or hair and the shape of horns.[7] Epstein's article demonstrates that knowledge of the origin, variation, and selection of domestic animals provides valuable evidence of culture growth and change. Particular

[5] For discussion of the origins of animal domestication, cf. the articles of the Hans Bobek and H. Epstein in this volume. Arguments for and against the primacy of cereal cultivation in the Near East as against root cultivation in Southeast Asia are presented by Robert J. Braidwood ("Levels in Prehistory") and Edgar Anderson ("The Evolution of Domestication") in Sol Tax (ed.), *The Evolution of Man* Vol. II of *Evolution after Darwin* (Chicago: University of Chicago Press, 1960).

[6] Carl O. Sauer, *Agricultural Origins and Dispersals* (New York: American Geographical Society, 1952), pp. 106–7. See also his more recent statement in "Age and Area of American Cultivated Plants," *Actas del XXXIII Congreso Internacional de Americanistas, San José, Costa Rica, 1958,* I (San José: Lehmann, 1959), 215–29.

[7] The importance of color symbolism has already been considered in Paul Fickeler's study of religion. See also David E. Sopher, "Turmeric: A Geographical Investigation of Cultural Relations in Southeast Asia," *Yearbook of the Association of Pacific Coast Geographers,* XII (1950), 11–15.

breeds of animals, like particular races of cultivated plants, may be living artifacts that have survived the peoples and cultures once associated with them. As products of man's sustained interest, domestic animals always reflect some aspects of culture.[8]

In Morton Fried's study of land tenure, geography,[9] and ecology in the contact of cultures we are reminded once more that diffusion does not take place in a vacuum. Ideas and institutions cannot move far without encountering other ideas and institutions, and unless outright rejection takes place, the contacts thus established result in varying degrees of modification and assimilation. A particularly sensitive factor in any situation of culture contact is the attitude that impinging groups hold toward land. In the cases examined by Fried, land tenure stands out as an index of social organization and a critical factor in the contest between different social systems for control of an area. His analysis is especially revealing because it deals with contacts between cultures of sharply differing degrees of agressiveness and exploitive demand. Contrasts are not always so sharp or change so abrupt, but in lesser degree the processes are universal. The American West during the period of pioneer settlement and China's expanding frontiers are ideal laboratories for the study of acculturation. In addition, this essay deals explicitly with the interaction of social organization, livelihood, and environment—a problem treated previously in this volume and a problem we will encounter again.[10]

It is easy to understand why cultural geographers have devoted most of their attention to rural landscapes, for urban geography is a rich subject in its own right, and many of the methods employed in the study of culture are difficult to apply to the heterogeneous elements of urban life. Nevertheless, cultural geographers have made some notable contributions to urban studies and they may aspire to make more. Most of the work undertaken has been directed to two main problems: differences in urban morphology, and the role of cities in cultural evolution and dispersal.

These considerations are combined in Dan Stanislawski's study of the origin and spread of the grid-pattern town. He asks whether this feature of urban morphology is sufficiently simple to have evolved independently in several

[8] For further discussion and bibliography see Richard Lewinsohn, *Animals, Men and Myths* (New York: Harper & Bros., 1954); Charles A. Reed, "Animal Domestication in the Prehistoric Near East," *Science*, CXXX, No. 3389 (December, 1959), 1629–39; G. H. Bousquet, "Des animaux et leur traitement selon le Judaïsme, le Christianisme et l'Islam," *Studia Islamica*, IX (1958), 31–48; and Frederick J. Simoons, *Eat Not This Flesh* (Madison: University of Wisconsin Press, 1961).

[9] The reader will note that Fried uses "geography" in its atrophied sense to refer only to "natural environmental features." This usage is seldom encountered in current geographic literature. Cf. our introductory statement, "The Themes of Cultural Geography," and the articles by Carl O. Sauer and Robert S. Platt in Part I of this volume.

[10] For further discussion of land tenure in different cultures see Kenneth H. Parsons, Raymond J. Penn, and Philip M. Raup (eds.), *Land Tenure: Proceedings of the International Conference on Land Tenure and Related Problems, Madison, Wisconsin, 1951* (Madison: University of Wisconsin Press, 1951), and the useful *Bibliography on Land Tenure* (Rome: Food and Agricultural Organization of the United Nations, 1955).

areas, or whether it is sufficiently complex to suggest a more restricted origin. In his attempt to answer this question he considers the advantages and disadvantages of the grid, and traces it to the prehistoric urban civilizations of the Middle East. The fact that he can find no proven examples in the New World prior to the European conquest suggests a single era and area of origin. As new archeological evidence is exposed, some features of this reconstruction may have to be changed, but revision or refinement will also have to be based on analysis of form and function through time.[11]

Rhoads Murphey's comparative study of the historical role of cities in Western Europe and China suggests that urban institutions have encouraged innovation in the former case and discouraged it in the latter. Toward the end of the Middle Ages, European cities began to serve as bases for independent groups of entrepreneurs who were able to challenge the authority of the feudal and seignorial order. As towns grew and prospered, a new quasi-democratic order began to spread through the European countryside, and the movement was accelerated by the Industrial Revolution. In China cities with the same general functions tended to play a different role. Murphey's examination of urban functions and influences suggests that the historical role of the Chinese city as a center of political and military power tended to check revolutionary impulses and conserve imperial authority. There could be no counterpart of the European alliance of higher nobles and merchants against minor lords, for in China the latter were also based in towns. Moreover, Chinese merchants and craftsmen were unable to translate their economic influence into political power. This historical pattern differs from that of Europe and, in lesser degree, the Moslem world.[12] Murphey's essay demonstrates that we should not define urbanism or urbanization in universal terms. In spite of their heterogeneous character, cities always function in a broader cultural milieu.[13]

The last two articles in this section treat major historical developments only incidentally and focus instead on modern problems of migration and diffusion. Edgar Kant is concerned with the former problem and his treatment of it is largely taxonomic. His basic interest is in the patterns of rural-urban migration

[11] Cf. the recent study of this problem by George M. Foster in which he argues that the grid pattern in Spanish America represents "not the diffusion of a material trait, but the utilization of an idea in a new context, with specific goals in mind." Foster believes that the grid pattern evolved in the Americas as a result of the process of founding new towns in a colonial setting. See his *Culture and Conquest: America's Spanish Heritage* ("Viking Fund Publications in Anthropology," No. 27 [1960]), pp. 34–49.

[12] See G. E. von Grunebaum, *Islam: Essays in the Nature and Growth of a Cultural Tradition,* (American Anthropological Association Memoir No. 81 [1955]), pp. 141–58; and Xavier de Planhol, *The World of Islam* (Ithaca: Cornell University Press, 1959, pp. 1–41; first published as *Le monde islamique: essai de géographie religieuse,* Paris: Presses Universitaires de France, 1957).

[13] For further discussion of the general problems raised by Murphey's esssay see Robert Redfield and Milton Singer, "The Cultural Role of Cities," *Economic Development and Cultural Change,* II (1954–55), 56–59; Eric E. Lampard, "The Role of Cities in Economically Advanced Areas," *ibid,* pp. 81–136; Bert F. Hoselitz, "Generative and Parasitic Cities," *ibid,* pp. 278–94; and Gideon Sjoberg, *The Preindustrial City* (Glencoe, Ill.: Free Press, 1960).

in modern Europe, but he approaches it by way of a long and revealing detour. From the great migrations of prehistory and the *Völkerwanderungen* of early historic times, he turns to the diverse patterns of pastoral migrations,[14] the flight from highland areas, European colonization overseas,[15] and the profound displacements of population caused by the two world wars. Then he considers the persistent drift toward industrial and urban centers, and the more spectacular movements caused by pronounced cases of depression or "boom." His final comprehensive classification is extended to include the duration or rhythm of migrations as well as their motivation and extent. For the cultural geographer, this study has both implicit and explicit meaning. Implicitly, it identifies and describes some important mechanisms of diffusion. Explicitly, it demonstrates that patterns of migration vary significantly within different culture areas.

Cultural geographers have only rarely sought to define their problems statistically, but this does not mean that such problems are inherently "qualitative." For some important problems adequate quantitative data can be found, and Torsten Hägerstrand's study of the propagation of innovation waves gives a clear indication of how they may be used. He does not claim that his findings are of universal importance, or even that his methods are applicable to other areas or times. Nevertheless, there is good reason to believe that his analysis of the diffusion of automobiles and radios illustrates a more general process that has operated far beyond the borders of Scania. The quantitative study of innovations in process of diffusion is a valid and necessary approach to understanding of the evolution of culture areas and groupings.[16]

[14] The problems and prospects of pastoral nomadism are evaluated by ten authors in "Nomads and Nomadism in the Arid Zone," *UNESCO International Social Science Journal,* XI (1959), 481–585. See also Mohammed Awad, "Settlement of Nomadic and Semi-Nomadic Tribal Groups in the Middle East," *International Labour Review,* LXXIX (1959), 25–56, and Burkhard Hofmeister, "Report on Transhumance: A Selected International Bibliography," *Professional Geographer,* XIII (1961), 37–39.

[15] One of the few studies of intercontinental migration that includes consideration of the homeland as well as the immigrant community is Maurice Edmond Perret's *Les colonies tessinoises en Californie* (Lausanne: F. Rouge, 1950).

[16] Cf. Torsten Hägerstrand, "On Monte Carlo-Simulation of Diffusion," in William L. Garrison (ed.), *Quantitative Geography,* "Northwestern University Studies in Geography" (in press). A more elaborate work in Swedish (*Innovationsförloppet ur korologisk synpunkt* [Lund, 1951]) is summarized by John Leighly in "Innovation and Area," *Geographical Review,* XLIV (1954), 439–41.

V. GORDON CHILDE

A PREHISTORIAN'S
INTERPRETATION
OF DIFFUSION

Discussions of diffusion are apt to degenerate into combats wherein only dust is diffused or else to ascend into an ether so diffuse that the disputants are left balancing probabilities inherently unsusceptible of statistical treatment. Perhaps that is one reason why the privilege of speaking first on this day, devoted to the diffusion of loftier themes, should have been accorded to a prehistoric archeologist. For the mean and unsightly bits of stone or pottery that the spade uncovers from the dust of ages are at least solid and tangible, though always the product of human hands, designed by human brains, and concretely embodying men's ideas.

But there are perhaps more fundamental reasons why the high honor of contributing to this symposium should have been accorded to a prehistorian—and may I say how highly I appreciate this honor not only to myself but to the very youthful science I represent. Prehistoric archeology has effected a revolution in man's knowledge of his own past, comparable in scale to the revolutions achieved by modern physics and astronomy. Instead of the beggarly five

thousand years patchily and fitfully illumined by written records, archeology now offers the historian a vista of two hundred and fifty thousand years; like a new optical instrument it has already extended our range of backward vision fiftyfold and is every year expanding the field surveyed with the new perspective. With the field of historical vision thus deepened and enlarged the sociologist should be able better to gauge both the antiquity of diffusion and its significance as a factor in promoting progress.

Of course, the archeologist's attention is focused primarily on man's material culture —the equipment, the extracorporeal organs that enable human groups to survive and multiply. But within the human species improvement in that equipment takes the place of the hereditary bodily modifications that demarcate genera in the biologist's evolutionary hierarchy. And so such improvement may be taken as a proof of progress in the sense that organic evolution attests a survival of the fittest.[1] But the speed of progress, thus defined, so extraordinarily rapid as compared with organic evolution, seems to be due to the distinctively human capacity of learning from one's neighbor; inventions and devices, created by one society as adjustments to its special environment, can be adopted by another and adapted to its rather different requirements. But that is exactly what I

Reprinted, with permission of the publisher, from *Independence, Convergence, and Borrowing in Institutions, Thought, and Art* (Harvard Tercentenary Publications [Cambridge, Mass.: Harvard University Press, 1937]), pp. 3–21 (copyright, 1937, by the President and Fellows of Harvard College). During his long and productive career, Vere Gordon Childe (1892–1957) held appointments as professor of prehistoric archeology at the universities of Edinburgh and London.

[1] *Man Makes Himself* (London: Watts, 1936 [rev. ed.; New York: Mentor Books, 1952]).

mean by diffusion. To me diffusion means essentially the pooling of ideas, building up from many sides the cultural capital of humanity, or, to use the late Professor Dixon's happy metaphor, diffusion is the process "whereby the achievements of all peoples are distilled into the vessel of Culture." [2]

Now the rigorous proof of diffusion as just defined is essentially a task for archeology. Until quite recent times, the tradition of historiography, derived from the slave-owning societies of Greece and Rome, has tended to ignore as mechanic and banausic the very technical processes the improvement of which has constituted the most objective aspect of progress. Even for a process that affected historiography as directly as did printing we have to appeal mainly to archeological data. Gutenberg's invention had a long line of precursors (sealing, block-printing, and so on) and complex presuppositions (such as ink and paper), ignored by literary historians. In tracing the pedigree of these essential moments in the invention, Carter[3] has had to appeal to documents provided by the archeologists—to actual European block-prints, to analyses of papers dug up in the Fayum, and to texts preserved by Asian deserts. Yet the invention and diffusion of printing is a recent step in human progress. For earlier periods the archeologist is called upon to play an exclusive role in the demonstration of diffusion.

Comparative ethnography has indeed made brilliant contributions toward vindicating the diffusionist thesis. But it is handicapped by its limitation to two dimensions. Only with archeological help can the time factor be reintroduced. The ethnographic protagonist of diffusion cannot hope to convince a hardened evolutionist unless he can bring forward archeological

evidence to show that trait-complexes, today widely dispersed, once occupied a more continuous domain, or at least to prove former intercourse between points of occurrence now isolated. And folk-memory for its part treats as material for myth the processes that classical historiography despises. Our English diffusionists themselves have sometimes been misled by that mythopoeic tendency into advancing as proofs of their case abstractions that have no evidential value. They seem in fact at times to assume that human progress can be resolved into a series of dramatic steps— inventions—any one of which can be exactly located in time and space: discovery of agriculture or the invention of pottery is presented as an event that happened at a given moment and in one precise place. But surely that "heroic theory of invention" is an abstraction.

Official records indeed do enable us to show that all reciprocating steam engines comprise vital parts that are legitimate or illegitimate offspring of an invention patented by James Watt in 1769 in England, and therefore that his invention has been diffused. Without written documents that would hardly be demonstrable. But a large number of Englishmen still believe that "the steam engine" sprang fully formed from Watt's brain as he watched the rattling kettle-lid. Surprisingly few have ever heard of De Caus or Newcomen; still fewer have any clear notion of the social background against which the eighteenth-century inventors worked, of the complex economic circumstances instigating a deliberate search for new sources of power, or of the technical presuppositions for the realization of a working steam engine. Isolated from its context "the invention of the steam engine" is rarefied into an abstraction which the archeologist could never grasp and which the sober historian should dismiss as a myth. Popular tradition today still assigns to Watt and a few other names just the role attributed to Prometheus and kindred heroes in Greek mythology.

Archeology must renounce all hope of

[2] Roland B. Dixon, *The Building of Cultures* (New York and London: Scribner's Sons, 1928).

[3] Thomas F. Carter, *The Invention of Printing in China* (rev. ed.; New York: Columbia University Press, 1931 [2d rev. ed. by L. Carrington Goodrich; New York: Ronald, 1955]).

proving myths or of digging up abstractions. But it can establish the reality of intercourse between distinct communities at very remote periods. And the intercourse thus demonstrated proves at least the possibility of that commerce in ideas which constitutes diffusion on the above definition. Admittedly the archeologist's picture of the prehistoric world from almost the earliest times is a mosaic or rather a kaleidoscope of distinct groups—what are termed in Europe "cultures"; each owes its archeological individuality to its peculiar adjustment to its special historical environment, an adjustment imperfectly reflected in the surviving relics of its material culture—its tools and architecture, its dress and art. Admittedly too the groups thus symbolized are at any given time spatially localized and separated from one another by formidable barriers—the seas, mountains, and deserts that still exist, the no less formidable tracts of swamp and virgin forest that man himself has gradually reduced.

Yet these groups appear neither static nor isolated. Archeology traces with more or less confidence migrations whereby human groups, or at least the "cultures" symbolizing such, were brought into different environments or into immediate contact with other human groups. The demonstration of folk-migrations is so familiar from European archeology that it suffices here to recall that such mass movements almost invariably involve intercourse between differently adjusted communities. Whatever the ultimate fate of either party, invaders inevitably learn something from those whose former territory they traverse or occupy; the older inhabitants, for their part, cannot fail to borrow some items from the newcomers' equipment.

But archeology can also demonstrate intercourse between groups that severally remain fixed in their proper territories. It may be well to indicate briefly the methods of the demonstration. This consists of course in tracing interchange of products between the communities concerned. The most unequivocal of such indications of intercourse is afforded by the transportation of substances far from places where they occur in nature. Even in the Old Stone Age during the last European ice age, marine shells and fish bones have been found far from the sea in the caves of the Dordogne;[4] indeed, Breuil has suggested a regular commerce between the familiar reindeer hunters of the interior and coastal tribes not as yet directly known to archeology. And, of course, by the New Stone Age the transportation of materials over long distances is established by many cases: to the familiar examples like the flint from Grande Pressigny (in west-central France) used in Switzerland, Belgium, and the Channel Islands, or the Mediterranean shells from Danubian graves in Bohemia, central Germany, and the Rhineland new instances are constantly being added. For example, axes made of Preselite (blue stone) from Pembrokeshire in southwestern Wales have recently been identified in North Ireland and in Wiltshire,[5] while axes from stone occurring only at Graig Lwydd on the slopes of Penmaen Mawr, North Wales, were carried as far afield as Wiltshire.[6]

And sometimes this transportation of substances not only reveals the possibility of a commerce in ideas, too, but also explicitly attests actual diffusion. The emmer wheat grown by the earliest neolithic inhabitants of Denmark and the sheep they bred are not descendants of any wild species native to northern or western Europe. The wild ancestors of emmer must be sought in the east Mediterranean region, and the Stone Age sheep of Europe are believed to be of Asiatic stock. Thus in Denmark, and indeed throughout northwestern Europe, the very traits, which on the economic interpretation of prehistory define

[4] Henri Breuil and René de Saint-Perier, *Les poissons, les batraciens et les reptiles dans l'art quaternaire* ("Memoires, Institut de Paléontologie Humaine," Vol. II [1927]).

[5] *Antiquity,* X (1936), 220.

[6] *Archaeologia Cambrensis,* XC (1935), 189.

the New Stone Age, are themselves incontrovertible evidences of diffusion. Here the food-producing economy based on the cultivation of exotic cereals and the breeding of foreign animals cannot have been evolved locally but must have been introduced from without.

But it is the archeological exploration of the Near East and the co-operation therein of geology that are providing the most striking and also the earliest proofs of frequent communication over really substantial distances. In the neolithic settlements around the Fayum Lake, perhaps the oldest yet known and dating from 5000 B.C., Caton-Thompson collected shells brought from the Mediterranean and others from the Red Sea, as well as various exotic stones of still uncertain provenance.[7] A little later obsidian was being used for the manufacture of tools by the earliest inhabitants of the Tigris-Euphrates delta and of Assyria as well as by the predynastic Egyptians. Yet supplies of the volcanic glass are geographically very restricted; the Armenian massif or the island of Melos are the most likely sources. The only recorded sources of lapis lazuli are on the Iranian plateau. Yet this stone was being imported into Egypt and Sumer by 4000 B.C. and during the first half of the third millennium was reaching the Indus Valley, Baluchistan, Russian Turkestan, and Troy, on the Asiatic shore of the Hellespont. It would be tedious to continue this catalogue, to which each well-conducted expedition adds new items.[8] The transportation of exotic materials over long distances thus attested in prehistoric times only foreshadows that intensive importation of raw materials into Egypt and Sumer to which written records also bear witness as soon as they begin.

Scarcely less conclusive proofs of intercourse are afforded by the distributions of manufactured articles. Of course *ex hypothesi* its "country of origin" is not stamped upon a prehistoric commodity, but it can generally be determined with a high degree of probability. Sometimes the actual factories can be located. At Graig Lwydd, for instance, was found not only the sole deposit of the rock used but also the workshop where the axes exported to Wiltshire were fashioned.

But generally the place of origin is determined mainly by statistical and cartographic methods. For instance, we scrutinize closely and compare a large sample of seals from various regions in the Near East. Among several hundred from Mesopotamian sites we notice six or seven differing from the rest in form, technique, material, and style. Only from the Indus Valley can we find many seals exhibiting the same peculiarities, but there they constitute the bulk of the collection. It is therefore a fairly safe inference that the seals in question were manufactured in the Indus cities. The stray specimens from Sumer can only be exports thence or just possibly products of an Indian seal-cutter plying his native craft in Sumer. Or again thousands of sherds of fine knob-ornamented wheelmade pottery from Harappa and Mohenjo-Daro define both the distinctive character and the Indian origin of the fabric; the stray fragments picked up at Eshnuna in Babylonia[9] are as clearly imports as is an English beer-bottle, stamped with the maker's name, picked up in an East African kraal, and their origin is no more doubtful. In practice of course archeologists abbreviate the demonstration. They are sufficiently familiar with their material to recognize whether a type is "distinctive" without setting out mathematically its frequency in a random sample; and they prefer to establish the origin of the type by plotting its

[7] G. Caton-Thompson and E. W. Gardner, *The Desert Fayum* (London: Royal Anthropological Institute, 1934).

[8] Cf. V. Gordon Childe, *New Light on the Most Ancient East* (London: Routledge and Kegan Paul, 1935 [rev. ed.; 1952]); and Alfred Lucas, *Ancient Egyptian Materials* (2d ed.; London: Arnold, 1934).

[9] Henri Frankfort, *Iraq Excavations* ("University of Chicago Oriental Institute Communications," Vol. XVII [1934]).

distribution on a map rather than by tabulating figures. Such abbreviation in no wise detracts from the statistical accuracy of the argument. But of course in prehistory statistics may be just as misleading as in any other science. Certain metal types happen to turn up most frequently in northern Europe although neither the raw materials nor the technical presuppositions for their production were available there.[10] Still, using his statistics judiciously and armed with sufficient knowledge to discount freaks of distribution, the prehistorian can with reasonable confidence recognize a South Russian pin in a neolithic tomb in Denmark,[11] British spearheads in graves or hoards of the Bronze Age in Holstein, the Rhineland, and the Paris basin,[12] Syrian vases in First Dynasty tombs in Egypt, and Egyptian slate palettes in Byblos before 3000 B.C.

Data of the kind just described are submitted as affording rigorous proofs of intercourse between scattered human groups. Considering the limitations of the archeologist's material—furs, feathers, textiles, basketry, and wooden objects that bulk so large in the commerce of contemporary "primitives" have been irrevocably lost— the paucity of likely articles submitted to petrographic or chemical analysis, and the still restricted range of scientific exploration, they establish a remarkable amount of intercourse at surprisingly early periods. And the traffic thus established afforded channels for the diffusion of ideas and inventions as much as of materials and manufactured goods—for modern anthropology shows that the role of "the silent trade" was greatly overestimated by early economists.

And closely related in kind to the argument from the distribution of finished commodities is one that does directly indicate a diffusion of ideas. I refer to the reproduction by distinct groups of arbitrary or specialized types. Archeologists are apt to define a "specialized type" as one whose peculiarities are not obviously conditioned either by the object's function or by its material and the method of its manufacture. Of course, it could be objected that a subjective element has entered into the above definition. But in practice the selection of types for study is controlled by precisely the same statistical and cartographic methods as are employed in determining the provenance of manufactures: the rarity of the selected type within its class would constitute a rough test of the degree of its specialization. Continuity in its geographical distribution would materially enhance the likelihood that all examples are results of copying. In fact, recent excavations have most satisfactorily filled in gaps in the distributions of types assumed on purely formal grounds to be related, so that the two criteria support each other.

Ornaments, such as pins, are particularly well adapted for such treatment. After a survey of a vast number of Bronze Age pins from Europe and western Asia it was soon recognized that those with double-spiral heads were comparatively exceptional. Before the war a few specimens were known from Troy and the Aegean Islands and one was collected by Pumpelly at Anau in Russian Turkestan.[13] Despite the remoteness of the last-named example, its connection with the rest was boldly assumed by Hubert Schmidt in his publication of the Anau finds. His assumption has been justified during the last ten years by the discovery of intermediate specimens at Hissar[14] in

[10] Cf. for instance the remarks of Nils Åberg, *Bronzezeitliche und früheisenzeitliche Chronologie* (Stockholm, 1935), part 5, on the misleading distribution of the early *Griffzungschwerter*.

[11] *Aarbødger for nordisk oldkyndighed og historie* (Copenhagen, 1929), p. 204.

[12] E. Sprockoff, "Zur Schäflung bronzezeitlicher Lanzenspitzen," *Mainzer Zeitschrift*, XXIX (1924), 56.

[13] Raphael Pumpelly, *Explorations in Turkestan* (Carnegie Institution of Washington Publication No. 73 [Washington, D.C., 1908]).

[14] Erich F. Schmidt, "Tepe Hissar: Excavations of 1931," *University of Pennsylvania, Museum Journal*, XXIII (1933).

northern Iran and at Ahlatlibel [15] in central Anatolia. Plotted on a map, the type now appears distributed along a more or less continuous chain of sites. Other specialized types are found to be common to several of these, and all lie on or near the famous caravan route from Central Asia westward through Tabriz. It cannot reasonably be doubted that our double-spiral pins denote intercourse along this historic highway already in the third millennium B.C.

In this case it is not asserted that the pins dug up have themselves been transported from some unidentified factory: the model has been diffused and copied locally at several points. The presuppositions for its adoption—the metallurgical technique and the fashion of using pins— may have been established at the several sites long before the particular type was copied there. Accordingly specialized types are not strictly comparable to the culture traits which play such a prominent role in ethnographic arguments. A peculiar sort of pin need not be an integral constituent of a culture or trait-complex. For example, the cultures of Troy II and Anau III, as defined by the total assemblage of archeological traits, are admittedly quite distinct.

Nevertheless such specialized types may sometimes be invoked as evidence for the diffusion of techniques too. The graves and hoards containing the oldest bronze objects in Bohemia comprise, besides tools and weapons that are either very generalized or else exclusively Central European, also specialized types of pins, lock-rings, earrings, and neck-rings that recur also in Asia Minor;[16] and in this case too excavations in Hungary[17] have filled in gaps in the dis-

tribution of the ornaments even since 1926. The Bohemian specimens are almost certainly copies of Oriental models. In other words, the earliest bronzes manufactured in Central Europe include imitations of Asiatic ornaments. It really looks as if Asiatic smiths, settled in Central Europe and producing for a local market with local ores, had introduced both their metallurgical knowledge and their fashions in ornaments. And that is perhaps as near as prehistory can ever come to a rigorous proof of the diffusion of a major invention like bronze.

One more archeological argument deserves to rank as affording valid evidence of intercourse. Exceptionally alien peoples are recognizably portrayed on the figured monuments of ancient civilizations. The Indus cities have yielded many naturalistic figurines of baked clay. Some of these depict persons of distinctly Mongolian type, and anatomical studies of an actual skull from Mohenjo-Daro have verified the accuracy of the modeler's delineation.[18] Hence intercourse between the urban civilizations of the Indus Valley and Mongolian tribes, presumably already located in Central Asia, is proved for the first half of the third millennium B.C.

Archeology can offer concrete and tangible proofs of intercourse beginning already during the Ice Age and growing ever more intensive and extensive. As fast as excavation advances into hitherto unexplored regions or unplumbed depths of the Old World tangible proofs come to light of intercourse with more familiar regions. Already archeology can demonstrate beyond cavil a web of communications extending from the Atlantic to the Oxus and the Indus by the third millennium before our era as surely as can history from the tenth century thereafter. Systematic excavations in Siberia and China, in North Africa and Arabia, will surely reveal further extensions of the web. And deeper diggings may well demonstrate an enhanced antiquity

---

[15] Hamit Zübeyr, "Ahlatlibel Hafriyati," *Türk Tarih Arkeologya ve Etnografya Dergisi,* II (Istanbul, 1934), 78, 93, Ab. 355. Cf. the map published in *Annals of Archaeology and Anthropology,* XIII (Liverpool, 1936), plate 52.

[16] V. Gordon Childe; *The Danube in Prehistory* (Oxford: Clarendon Press, 1929).

[17] J. Banner, "A Marosvidék bronzkori zsugorított temetkezéseinek sirmelléklétei," *A. M. kir. F. J. Tudomanyégyetem archaeologiai intezeteböl dolgozatok,* VII (Szeged, 1931).

[18] E. Mackay, "Further Excavations at Mohenjo-Daro," *Journal of the Royal Society of Arts,* LXXXII (1934).

for the nexus in all directions. Evidently archeology's rigorous proofs of such ancient and extensive intercourse between discrete human groups lend very material support to ethnographic theories of diffusion based upon observed similarities between contemporary barbarian cultures. It is needless to labor this point. Instead may I briefly turn to the prehistorian's second title to participate in your deliberations, to the role of diffusion as a vital moment in progress itself.

On the enlarged and deepened field of history that archeology is opening up to the judgment of the sociologist, we already receive the impression that the course of man's progress has followed anything but a straight line or a level plain; both temporal and spatial variations in the rate of man's advance toward mastery of his physical environment are perceptible. But the impression is vague not only because of the limitations on archeology's vision but also because our own standards of valuation are nebulous, and that can be corrected. To this end will you accept as a basis of discussion the restriction on culture to the material plane and the analogy between progress in culture and organic evolution adumbrated earlier? By virtue of that analogy cultural adjustments will be adjudged progressive if they further the multiplication of the species in the long run. There would then be a correlation between population which can ideally be plotted as a graph and progress which by itself is scarcely measurable. The population curve would doubtless be an imperfect reflex of cultural progress; discrepancies between the two curves would cancel out in the vast period surveyed by archeology. On the strength of this assumed parallelism the curvature in the rate of progress might be asserted more confidently.

Archeology surveys, say, 250,000 years. For 96 per cent of this almost inconceivable time-span, the Old Stone Age, the improvements in man's equipment were relatively slight. And apparently the species *Homo sapiens* or even the genus *Homo* constituted a small and restricted group among competing mammalian genera and species. Food production—agriculture and mixed farming—represented the first revolutionary advance and was followed by a very marked expansion of the population wherever and whenever the new economy was applied. When the population curve of humanity comes to be plotted over the millenniums, it will surely exhibit an upward kink at this point which may accordingly be termed the "Neolithic Revolution."[19] But this "revolution" began so far back, spread so slowly, and was in reality so complex and gradual that it can still only be studied abstractly.

It is succeeded by a second that can be more accurately located in time and space and examined as a concrete process: small villages of self-sufficing peasants are transformed into populous cities wherein manufacture and commerce rank as equals with farming and fishing. The new cities exceed the old neolithic hamlets and chalcolithic townships as much as modern industrial cities exceed medieval burghs and market towns. The whole scale of human life has been transformed. This Urban Revolution is first discernible in the valleys of the Nile, the Tigris-Euphrates, and the Indus. There it was consummated round about 3000 B.C. Yet on closer inspection the Urban Revolution turns out to be a long and complex process just like the Industrial Revolution to which it may legitimately be compared. Like the latter, it resulted from the application of a variety of distinct but interlocking discovery-complexes. The harnessing by man of non-human motive powers through the sail, the yoke, and the wheel and the metallurgy of copper and bronze takes the part of the steam engine and the power loom, coal and iron, in the modern counterpart. And the recent excavations at Ur and Erech, at Kish and Eshnuna, have revealed explicitly in Mesopotamia pre-

[19] For the economic interpretation of archeological "ages" see my presidential address, "Changing Methods and Aims in Prehistory," *Proceedings of the Prehistoric Society,* I (1935).

paratory stages of the revolution such as
have long been familiar in predynastic
Egypt and must still be assumed in India
too.

At the same time, as fresh excavations
deepen our knowledge of the Egyptian, Sumerian, and Indus civilizations, the distinctness and individuality of each becomes
increasingly manifest. The agreements are
indeed striking—"the organization of society in cities; the continued but sparing
use of stone, side by side with copper and
bronze, for the manufacture of weapons,
tools and vessels; the use of picture signs
for writing; the fashioning of ornaments
out of fayence, shell and various kinds of
stone" and the other common traits enu-
merated by Sir John Marshall [20] form an
imposing array.

But the agreements are of a very abstract
kind. Sumerian cities are obviously organized around temples, Egyptian cities around
the court of Pharaoh or of a feudal lord;
at Harappa and Mohenjo-Daro no such
nucleus of capital accumulation is conspicuous at all. The tools, weapons, and vessels
have quite different forms in the three regions. The symbols of the scripts differ, and
the conventions observed for their use
among the Egyptians are not the same as
those adopted in Sumer. The most popular
types of beads, pendants, and patterns differ as do the parts of the body to be decked
and the whole style of dress. In a word,
apart from a few interchanged commodities, we are confronted with concrete differences embraced within an abstract identity.

No theory of one-sided diffusion will explain such difference within identity. It
would be more preposterous to postulate
an Egyptianization of Sumer[21] to account
for the agreements between Nilotic and
Mesopotamian cultures than to explain similarities between London and Moscow by

[20] *Mohenjo-Daro and the Indus Civilization* (3
vols.; London: A. Probsthain, 1931).

[21] As maintained by the "English diffusionist"
school. The converse view once advocated by Petrie and De Morgan is equally untenable.

the phrase "westernization of Russia." The
traveler from London to Moscow is indeed
struck by similarities of precisely the same
order as those subsisting between, say,
Abydos and Erech. He can point to "the
organization of society in industrial cities;
the continued use of horse-drawn carts side
by side with trains and automobiles as
means of transport; the use of alphabetic
signs for printing; the drinking of tea and
the paraphernalia for its infusion." But on
the one hand closer inspection reveals the
superficiality of the agreements: the nucleus of economic power is in the one case
a class of private capitalists concretely represented in a luxurious West End, in the
other a totalitarian state externally symbolized by a few banners. The printed symbols are different and are not even combined according to the same conventions,
since in Russian each character denotes a
single sound, whereas in English the same
letter may stand for as many as four distinct sounds.

On the other hand, research will certainly
show that the agreements are in truth results of diffusion—borrowed ideas divergently applied—but that the diffusion has
been a most complicated process and the
borrowings by no means unilateral. Tea-
drinking reached England and Russia independently at different times and by different routes. An alphabet was brought to
Britain from Rome, to Russia from Byzantium, and the common origin of the
scripts can be found only a thousand years
or more before the mission of St. Cyril or
even the annexation under Claudius Caesar.
Even the penetration of Russia by Western ideas began long before Peter the Great,
and in the Industrial Revolution itself Russia's role was not entirely passive. Only one
formula really covers the facts. English and
Russian civilizations as we know them
"have resulted from the combined efforts
of many countries, each contributing a
certain quota to the common stock of
knowledge." And that is precisely the formula suggested by Sir John Marshall to
account for the similarities between the

urban civilizations of the Near East five millenniums ago. In fact, just as the historian by ransacking obscure treaties, parish records, and private correspondence can establish intercourse under most varied guises between Russia and Western Europe throughout the last ten centuries, so the archeologist is establishing intercourse between the various centers of Oriental culture in prehistoric times, that is, before the accomplishment of the Urban Revolution, as at the dawn of history.

The revelation of prehistoric intercourse, direct or indirect, between Egypt, Mesopotamia, and even India is indeed by no means the least striking result of recent excavations in the Near East. It is only in the last fifteen years that the prehistory of the Orient has been systematically studied with the same minuteness and with the same co-operation from natural scientists as have been instrumental in establishing the fact of intercourse between the various parts of prehistoric Europe. Yet the earlier Oriental instances already outweigh the European. Before the war the Indus civilization was dreamed of only by a few inspired visionaries. Indeed to the historian the discovery of Harappa and Mohenjo-Daro has opened up a world no less new than that uncovered by Columbus to medieval Europe. Archeology has shown that two thousand years before the earliest hints in cuneiform texts of contact with India, that subcontinent was already sending her manufactures to the lands wherein our own civilization was admittedly cradled. In other words, in the third millennium B.C. India was already in a position to contribute to the building up of the cultural tradition that constitutes our spiritual heritage as she notoriously has done since the time of Alexander. And even since I first wrote these words the excavations of the Oriental Institute near Baghdad have brought to light concrete proofs that the potentiality just envisaged was in truth realized. At Tell Agrab a green steatite vase of typical Sumerian workmanship has been found portraying a humped bull in front of a manger,

a characteristic scene of Indus cult.[22] It shows that by 3000 B.C. such a cult was already being practiced in Mesopotamia itself; in other words, that at least a religious idea had been diffused from India to Babylonia.

In general terms then, archeology demonstrates intercourse between the great riverine centers of population in the period preluding that great acceleration of progress that I termed the Urban Revolution.[23] Surely that intercourse was a factor in promoting the revolution itself. It can hardly be an accident that the earliest evidences of intensive and extensive communications between divergently adjusted human societies are being afforded by the countries of the Ancient East where urban civilization was destined first to blossom. The pooling of ideas for which such communications gave opportunity was perhaps the decisive moment in fomenting the growth of precocious cultures, in the transvaluation of human life.

The environmentalist insisting on soil and climate in his account of the early rise of civilization in the riverine valleys has, as usual, forgotten that the most important element in man's environment is his fellow men. In the case before us it may certainly be conceded that environmental conditions in the Near East—the opportunities for divergent specialization, the dependence of riverine societies on imported raw materials, the desiccation coincident with the melting of the last ice sheets over Europe —were unusually favorable to intercourse precisely during the critical centuries. It suffices here to insist on the proofs of intercourse during the period of urban civilization's gestation. The archeologist submits this observation to the historian as a critical instance that may be indicative of the significance of diffusion as a factor in promoting progress.

[22] *Times* (London), August 1, 1936.

[23] [See V. Gordon Childe, "The Urban Revolution," *Town Planning Review*, XXI (1950), 3–17; and chap. 7 of *Man Makes Himself*.]

HANS BOBEK

THE MAIN STAGES IN SOCIO-ECONOMIC EVOLUTION FROM A GEOGRAPHICAL POINT OF VIEW

Historically, and by its own constantly reiterated choice, geography has the task of describing the inhabited surface of the earth in its endlessly diverse spatial differentiation, and of scientifically expounding it—that is, of comprehending forces at work at present or in the past.

One might well doubt the possibility of achieving such a purpose in a satisfactory way, considering the inexhaustible complexity of the subject; for in this matter are involved not only all the realms of nature, with their varied phenomena and forces, the effects and mutual influences of which are still by no means clearly understood, but also man, who represents a problematical world difficult for science to penetrate. Still, the complex reality is there—on every trip we take it appears as a series of landscapes, of homelands of different peoples, and arouses the curiosity of the human mind. If one sought today to dismiss geography as "an unviable science," tomorrow it would arise again anew.

The greatest difficulty lies in the essential diversity of the elements concerned,

Translated, with permission of the author and publisher, from "Die Hauptstufen der Gesellschafts- und Wirtschaftsentfaltung in geographischer Sicht," *Die Erde: Zeitschrift der Gesellschaft für Erdkunde zu Berlin*, XC (1959), 259–98 (copyright, 1959, by Walter de Gruyter & Co., Berlin). Some minor corrections of the original text have been inserted by the author, who is professor of geography and director of the Geographical Institute at the University of Vienna, Austria.

each of which must be evaluated in its own way, while in geographic fact they are most intimately interwoven or even fused together. The analysis must ultimately make use of a comparative procedure, yet without forgetting the altogether dissimilar characters of the components.

Thus, as we know, the search for strict causalities, a manner of posing problems which works well enough for our purposes in the inorganic world, loses its meaning altogether in the human sphere, since the complicated many-layered structure of the human being denies it any convincing result. Who would dare to trace the pure causality of a single human behavior trait through body and soul, and still distinguish the influences of the physical and social environment? Nevertheless, the geographer must be concerned with the sum of numerous individual items of behavior and human ways within a single segment of space. The illegitimate extension of the causal, natural science way of thinking into the human element has given us many false leads and failures, and the same is true of the one-sided application of biological ways of thought.

However, from the fact that in human affairs we have to reckon not with strict laws but with a composite of motivations of different kinds, and with anything but absolute determinants, it certainly does not follow that everything human on earth is gripped in hopeless individuality and is inaccessible to any rational understanding. Regularities are by no means lacking. The physiognomically oriented study of the cultural landscape has been able to bring them out in abundance. But it is not possible to the same extent as in the case, say, of natural communities or ecological complexes, to explain such regularities of human phenomena in terms of actual functions only. There is left over a considerable, and for real understanding often a decisive, remainder, which can be cleared up satisfactorily only in historical-genetic terms.

Individuals—and also the intermediate groups—receive their characteristic formation and direction in being and behavior from different cultures, carried, practiced, and steadily transformed (but at quite different tempos) by certain societies at any particular time; in such fashion that in different societies or cultures, often a quite different "functioning" in relation to the social and physical environment of the time must be reckoned with. Naturally, there is also a common human denominator at hand—which is meaningful enough—but it is not at all sufficient to comprehend in an orderly way the totality of cultural phenomena throughout the world.

These cultural communities can thus never be understood simply on the basis of their contemporary conditions. They are historical entities, grown up in time and space, in an infinitely complicated succession of drives and impulses, conditions and reactions, hard to understand fully. Any attempt at an understanding or explanation of the human element within geographic reality must first proceed to them, and take its departure again from them, if it is not to be bound to collapse right from the start.

To be sure, the study of cultural communities is not primarily, and certainly not in its full extent, the subject of geography— no more than that of the earth's crust, the atmosphere, or the forms of organic life. Geography is concerned with them, as with the other complexes of elements, only in so far as they constitute parts of geographic

reality, or better, enter decisively into these. As in all other cases, geography will freely make use of all the explanation available from other sciences about these fundamental complexes of phenomena.

Such cultures, or societies, about the relative dimensions and limits of which nothing more will be said here (almost the same problems come up here as in the delimitation of geographic regions), can first be evaluated individually as to their environment-forming power, each by itself, in its full distinctiveness and in its own right. But they can also be evaluated comparatively, leaving aside odd individual peculiarities, since many approximately like complexes of culture content or organizational structure occur in them, so that series of related cultures stand out from others and allow grouping into types. One may arrive thus at more or less highly schematized models of cultural structures, in the same way as landscape study elaborates generalized models of landscape formation.[1]

In a comparative consideration of cultures, not only qualitative but also quantitative differences will be found, so that —purely on the basis of the abundance of expressive forms, achievements, and institutions—poor and rich cultures can be distinguished. An objective basis is thus available (apart from all the possibilities of qualitative evaluation that are subjective as they necessarily relate to the scale of values of a given culture, and so must be challenged) for speaking of more or less advanced or developed cultures or societies.

The erection of "stages" of the development or evolution of culture, therefore, appears to be quite justified, in so far as the enrichment of culture content and the structural evolution of societies occurring in the course of history should be brought into an intelligible system on a purely descriptive basis. The opinion—often dis-

[1] Cf. Hans Bobek, "Gedanken über das logische System der Geographie," *Mitteilungen der Geographischen Gesellschaft in Wien*, XCIX (1957), 122–45.

puted, and especially so at the outset of such a point of view—to the effect that it is a question of a single, necessary sequence immanent in all cultures ("Evolutionism"), has no doubt been justly refuted. This led, however, to an unjustified rejection of all such theories of "stages."

It is inherent in any comparative viewpoint that it cannot pay equal attention to the immense fullness of reality. This must always be reserved to the individual description. It would be a vain concern, therefore, to try to bring all existing cultures, with all their distinctive traits, into one such series of stages of increasing enrichment and evolution. The evolution of reality always follows many more or less parallel paths; impulses overlap, and advances on these different paths are neither contemporary nor alike. It must be left to the various sciences concerned with man and the manifold aspects of cultures to focus their interest on particular kinds of culture content or structure, and, accordingly, to propose quite different series of types or stages.

Geography, too, in looking at man and his cultures, can skip some and aim at other aspects on behalf of those that prominently concern and condition the presence, grouping, and activity of man in the landscape.

It is not intended here to enter into a discussion of the different theories of "stages" which geography previously has partly created for its own purposes, and partly—more often, I think—borrowed from other sciences (chiefly ethnology and economics) and more or less happily adapted. They already contain much that is important. It seems to me rewarding and even urgent, however, in a new attack on the problem, to try to show from a modern point of view the steps in the growth of the basic types in social and economic evolution that are geographically significant, and to assess their meaning. Such an attempt would have the aim of setting up a widespread and necessarily generalized framework into which the actual cases (with the

limitations made above) can be fitted. With the assumption that for any time period the distribution of these most important types might be fixed on a map, a kind of spatio-temporal co-ordinate system for human cultural development, as seen from the geographic standpoint, could be erected. Thus the character of that cultural medium which, like a filter, modifies and largely determines the human impact on the landscape, could be properly elucidated.

From the geographic standpoint, the following elements seem to me to deserve special notice in such an attempt:

1. The existing livelihood forms [*Lebensformen*]. In their number and kind are reflected the arrangement and width of the activities of a society or culture, its wealth of possibilities or its narrowness and monotony. Primary, secondary, and tertiary livelihood forms can be distinguished, according to whether they are given over to the use of the physical environment and acquire their goods thereby, or devote themselves chiefly to their reworking and transformation, or again are occupied in exchange, administration, and other kinds of services.

2. The interplay of the different livelihood groups within society, their ranking in the social hierarchy, and their contribution to the social product. The Marxist school speaks of the "relations of production" [*"Productionsverhältnis"*] which, however, should be understood here in the widest sense. The manner of this interplay is of greatest moment for the efficiency and developmental capabilities of the society.

3. The demographic valence of societies, expressed both in population density and in reproductivity, or dynamics.

4. Finally, the settlement pattern and the rest of the manifestations of the society, or rather the culture, in the landscape. This is a major focus of geographic research, and can obtain worthwhile conclusions from the rich material available on this subject (hardly regarded by other sciences) to serve not only the narrower purposes of geography but also the better knowledge of

mankind and its cultures in general. As the actual form of the cultural landscape is a product of the interaction of different societies with their respective physical environments, or better, with already modified inherited forms of environment, only an allusion to certain basic tendencies peculiar to the different types of societies is possible at such a large scale of generalization.

The following stages of social and economic evolution will be considered as especially significant from the geographic standpoint, since they were or are linked with profound changes in the realm of the foregoing groups of elementary facts:

1. Food gathering stage.
2. Stage of specialized collectors, hunters, and fishermen.
3. Stage of clan-peasantry [*Sippenbauerntum*], with pastoral nomadism as a subsidiary branch.
4. Stage of feudally or autocratically organized agrarian societies [*herrschaftlich organisierte Agrargesellschaft*].
5. Stage of early urbanism and rent-capitalism.
6. Stage of productive capitalism, industrial society, and modern urbanism.

Food Gathering Stage

The cultural development of mankind can be represented by an asymptotic curve that falls off very slowly toward the past and climbs more and more steeply above the zero-line as it approaches the present. Approximately 98 or 99 per cent of the total duration of man's existence, estimated today at around a million years, falls into a cultural stage that is designated as "food gathering" [*Wildbeuterstufe*] in accordance with the character of the means of food supply prevalent in it. Only a few 100,000 people in scattered and mostly very unfavorable backward areas of retreat, and now much distorted in their cultures by influence from the outside, belong to its last survivals, so that today it plays only a minimal part geographically. But in pre-Columbian times things were quite different (see the map). We cannot go into the extraordinary problems connected with

the growth of this first cultural stage of mankind and its spread over the greater part of the later *oikoumene* here,[2] but must be content to characterize this stage in a few lines.

There is only one livelihood form, that of the gatherers and small game hunters, that makes use in omnivorous fashion of all the sources of food offered by nature, without any appreciable care (or domestication) of plants and animals, but also without really destructive exploitation. The only variation results from the biologically based division of labor between the sexes. The only societal groups are on the one hand the family household, ultimately based on the necessity of a rather long period of care for the children, and on the other hand the local group, which is also as a rule the unit of settlement. It arises through a more or less loose association of blood-related or unrelated families on the basis of reciprocity and common interest in a livelihood area. The relation between neighboring local groups also rests on mutual recognition of interests that are in this case spatially separated. The relationship of reciprocity permeates and regulates in general all mutual bonds among human beings. It lends to the local group, through the usual gift-exchange of game and artifacts, the character of an economically closely united community.

The densities of population attained at this cultural stage, as they refer to large areas, remain at a very low level of a few individuals per hundred square kilometers, if one may trust recent estimates. The Australians do not reach even three, and the Ituri Pygmies (who have doubtlessly been crowded back) about ten per hundred square kilometers. From Kroeber's computations for North America at the time of contact with the whites,[3] we can take figures that are in part still lower than those

[2] This refers to the cardinal problem of the origin of humanity and the rise of its races.

[3] A. L. Kroeber, *Cultural and Natural Areas of Native North America* ("University of California Publications in Archaeology and Ethnology," Vol. XXXVIII [1939]).

of the Australians. For settlement groups of about twenty individuals, areas of from a couple of hundred to a couple of thousand kilometers were found, according to this source. But no doubt many areas were more densely settled, and others almost unoccupied. As R. J. Braidwood and C. A. Reed have convincingly suggested of the already somewhat more highly developed early Mesolithic settlement of Star Carr in Yorkshire, England,[4] and as E. S. Deevey also asserted,[5] these low population densities are surely not to be explained by the fact that the upper limit of carrying capacity of the environment was reached, but by the low reproductive rate of these folk, whose deficient cultural equipment could guarantee them little more than bare survival.

Their successful occupation of such large parts of the earth is all the more remarkable in view of the adaptation to the various natural regimes that had to be achieved both physiologically and psychically. The extremely high number of losses of life that constantly occurred brought about not only a sharp selection, which in conjunction with isolation fostered race formation, but also must have powerfully hindered cultural development. The old Stone Age inventory that has come down to us shows how the different techniques, once developed, were tenaciously retained for long periods of time.

The influence of these cultures on the landscape was surely modest and was probably limited to the modification of primitive settlement places, often taking advantage of natural shelters (caves, rock overhangs), and to their immediate surroundings through the use of firewood and

the effects of fire. C. O. Sauer rightly points out that man by nature is inclined to be sedentary, most of all because of the long period of helplessness of his children, and so must have been as sedentary as it was possible to be at this cultural stage.[6] We can hardly attribute to this stage a deliberate use of fire in the landscape, so there must have been tiny cultural islands in the midst of the ocean of the natural landscape.

STAGE OF SPECIALIZED COLLECTORS, HUNTERS AND FISHERMEN

Since the last Ice Age, particularly toward the end of it, archeology testifies to accelerating advances in many parts of the world — the Near East, North Africa, Europe, and also the New World—which indicate rationalization and specialization upon the foundations of the pre-existing ways of life. These are the phases known as Upper Paleolithic or Mesolithic. Certain wild animals take on great importance as game, depending on the various environments. Hunting techniques, artifacts, the whole manner of living, are built around them, so that tundra, taiga, deciduous forest, and steppe hunting cultures develop, which are geographically displaced along with the changes of the late glacial period. Fishing populations are formed along streams, lakes, and seacoasts, and also specialized collectors, who concentrate on certain grains (e.g., wild rice) or fruits (e.g., acorns).

Such transitions also take place still later in Neolithic or even historical times, but then already under the influence of higher cultures that have developed in the meantime, and with a partial adoption of their achievements. Examples are the East Siberian hunters of fur-bearing animals who learned, under influence from the south, to make use of the reindeer for draft and riding, or the mounted hunters of North

[4] Robert J. Braidwood and Charles A. Reed, "The Achievement and Early Consequences of Food Production: A Consideration of the Archaeological and Natural Historical Evidence," *Cold Springs Harbor Symposia on Quantitative Biology,* XXII (1957), 19–31.

[5] Edward S. Deevey, Jr., "The Human Crop: How Many Acres of Vegetation Does It Take To Raise a Man?" *Scientific American,* CXCIV (1956), 105–12.

[6] Carl O. Sauer, "The Agency of Man on the Earth," in William L. Thomas, Jr. (ed.), *Man's Role in Changing the Face of the Earth* (Chicago: University of Chicago Press, 1956), pp. 49–69 [reprinted in Part IV of this volume].

and South America who took over the horse from the Europeans. Both in the New World and in northern Asia, a certain amount of cultivation was also often adopted, without, however, becoming very prominent. Conclusions from late ethnological observation, therefore, are not reliable by themselves.

In any case, at this stage, the division of labor between the sexes becomes sharper as the women of the specialized hunters and fishermen, too, continue their collecting activity, in so far as they have not gone over to cultivation. An enrichment of the activities of each group occurs, though as yet not exactly a multiplication of the livelihood forms within each of these cultures.

Specialization is directed toward such products as are able to provide, at least seasonally, an especially rich return. Preservation and storage begin to play a role. The supply of food thus becomes more constant and certain, and we can trace mainly to this fact the increase in population density that is clearly to be observed. Among the fishermen population density rises especially high, for example, almost one person per square kilometer among the Haida of the Queen Charlotte Islands (British Columbia) while it reaches some five to ten times the gatherers' figure among hunters and specialized collectors.[7]

As a rule, therefore, the units of settlement, consisting of the more closely related groups, are larger, and besides there occurs the formation of "tribes" of the order of size of several thousand persons. Kinship relations, like the marriage rules, are often highly elaborated, and are supplemented by still other groupings such as age-classes and the like. This rich biosocial organization is supported and sanctioned in myth (totemism), and, as a cultural aim in itself, penetrates all of life. It is only partially favored or required by practical necessities, like the partly collective hunting and fishing, and also war, which presupposes a certain amount of discipline and authoritative direction. All authority within

the framework of these societies, however, is exclusively based upon age, wisdom, or virtue, and is therefore precarious.

The almost constant state of war, which seemingly exists at least among many hunter tribes, appears to be almost as much a result of the hunters' psychology, a social requirement, as it is a consequence of their slight territorial fixation which leads to perpetual movement of the tribes and changing of their camps, and so to ceaseless conflicts. The fishermen seem generally to be peaceful in character, and this may be why they attain greater population densities. At any rate the densities of population reached at this cultural stage, also, seem to be determined not so much by an upper limit on the carrying capacity of the environment as by other conditions of life.

It is decisive for the formation of the cultural landscape that settlement at this stage gradually frees itself altogether from natural shelters and begins to create a new and independent landscape element in the form of hide tents, earth huts, wooden huts, snow huts, and so on. As a result of the average increase in size of settlements, the more highly influenced surrounding zones must also have expanded, at least among the highly sedentary populations (fishermen, specialized collectors). In addition, much more profound and extensive changes of the natural landscape are attributed to these cultures: the extermination or heavy decimation of certain kinds of animals,[8] in which, in many cases, post glacial climatic changes also probably played their part; further, the trimming-out of many forests into park landscapes, as well as the extensive pushing back of the forest in favor of grass steppes and savanna-like formations

[7] Kroeber, *op. cit.*

[8] For example, the Folsom and Yuma cultures of southwestern North America (10,000–8,000 B.C.) are charged with the extermination of the mammoth, mastodon, camel, longhorned bison, muskox, cave bear, wild horse, and giant sloth. Cf. Fritz Kern, *Der Beginn der Weltgeschichte* (Munich: Lehnen, 1953), p. 65. According to Bird, the first immigrants to southeastern Patagonia killed off the wild horse and giant sloth between 5,400 and 3,000 years ago (*loc. cit.*).

through deliberate and regularly repeated mass burning, which must have served partly the purpose of the hunt, and partly the renewal and thinning-out of the vegetation to increase the supply of game or certain wild plants of which use was made.[9] No doubt such measures were not equally applicable or momentous in all geographic regions. On the whole, however, they must be counted among the very large interferences of man with the plant and animal world of nature.

STAGE OF CLAN-PEASANTRY

The next geographically significant step, naturally, is the transition to planned food production through cultivation and animal husbandry. Along with many intermediate types the peasantry in its different forms arises as the basis for all further development. Its appearance on the scene is linked archeologically with the "Neolithic," and earliest proved, apparently, for the Near East after the seventh millennium B.C.[10] Here we have to do with settled village farmers, at first without pottery, who raised wheat and barley, apparently with rainfall, near the lower limit of the dry forest in the foothills of the Zagros Mountains; they possessed in a domestic state at least the goat, and probably already had the sheep, the cow, the pig, and the half-ass as well.[11] It can hardly be doubted that the Near

East is the home of small-grain cultivation, since the wild forms of the principal grains are also native here. Many investigators, however,[12] cling to the opinion that the kind of plant cultivation today widespread chiefly in tropical areas, using the quite primitive planting stick that probably arose from the collectors' digging stick, should be regarded as the earliest and original form of all plant cultivation, and they put its origin into South Asia (India). This view is in no way supported archeologically, and much speaks against it, among other things the fact that the South Asian peninsulas in ancient times always constituted targets rather than points of departure for historical movements within the framework of the continent. Although the zones of this plant cultivation today lie marginally in relation to the probable center of origin of grain cultivation and its later spread, and so appear somewhat older on ethnological grounds, this refers primarily to technique and tools used and should not simply be carried over to the cultivated plants themselves. H. Kothe[13] has been able to show that in the area of small-grain cultivation, too, the planting stick, or rather its elaboration the furrowing stick [*Furchenstock*], originally predominated and was only replaced later (in the Bronze Age) by the plow that had arisen from it. There is accordingly nothing to prevent reversing H. V. Wissmann's recently developed view of the course of events,[14] and (taking account on the one hand of the archeological

[9] Sauer, *op. cit.*; Omer C. Stewart, "Fire as the First Great Force Employed by Man," in *Man's Role* . . . , pp. 115–33.

[10] The time estimate is still in dispute because of the contradictory radiocarbon dates. Although the earliest known farming settlement has until now been dated at *ca.* 4750 B.C., it apparently must henceforth be redated to about 6500 B.C., which agrees better with additional excavations of early settlements (Jericho, Matarrah, Mersin). See Robert J. Braidwood, "Near Eastern Prehistory," *Science*, CXCVII (1958), 1419–30.

[11] Robert J. Braidwood, *The Near East and the Foundations for Civilization* (Eugene: Oregon State System of Higher Education [Condon Lecture Publications], 1952). In the 1957 paper (Braidwood and Reed, *op. cit.*), the authors restrict the stock of domestic animals to the goat, because of the preponderant number of goat bones.

[12] Among others Emil Werth, *Grabstock, Hacke und Pflug: Versuch einer Entwicklungsgeschichte des Landbaues* (Ludwigsburg: E. Ulmer, 1954); and Carl O. Sauer, *Agricultural Origins and Dispersals* (New York: American Geographical Society, 1952).

[13] H. Kothe, "Entwicklung und Bedeutung des Getreidestockbaus," *Forschungen und Fortschritte*, XXV (1949), 147–50; *idem*, "Völkerkundliches zur Frage der neolithischen Anbautechnik," *Beiträge zur Frühgeschichte der Landwirtschaft*, I (Berlin, 1953), 7–38.

[14] Hermann von Wissmann, "Ursprungsherde und Ausbreitungswege von Pflanzen- und Tierzucht und ihre Abhängigkeit von der Klimageschichte," *Erdkunde*, XI (1957), 175–93.

material and on the other of the recognition by E. Werth of the probable homelands of most of the domestic plants and animals of the tropical and monsoonal horticultural and hoe-culture zone in India)[15] regarding this land as the chief intermediary in the transmission of advances received from the Near East into the rest of the tropical and part of the monsoon world. A reappraisal and reassessment of the manifold connections among cultivating tools, techniques of cultivation, and cultivated plants is necessary to overcome certain established oversimplifications.[16]

It may be taken as certain that the successful appearance of a fully developed peasantry was preceded by a long period of preliminary stages, in which many techniques and plants were tried out. It is also probable that this took place over a wide area and that the realization of the possibility of growing plants was gained over a long time, at many places, and with numerous plants. It was decisive that the attempts were kept up, that the corresponding plants proved useful for food, and above all that a society was ready to readapt on a large scale to this new manner of subsistence. The example of the North American Indians, beyond Mexico and the Pueblo cultures, shows that a group of societies could live for a long time in awareness of cultivation, and even to a certain degree adopt it, yet persist essentially in the old hunting way of life. Cultivation remained an auxiliary aid and to some degree a luxury,[17] for the Indians of the eastern

woodlands, while it had become a necessity to the Mexicans and the Pueblo tribes. Neither in the one case nor in the other are ecological reasons critical.[18]

We must therefore suppose a readiness for readaptation in the Near East, among the inhabitants of the "Fertile Crescent" around the Syrian Desert. Probably larger groups had taken up here the regular harvesting of the same wild grains that were later taken into cultivation. The flint sickles and grinding stones of the Natufian (early Postglacial) and later pre-farming settlements thereby take on an altogether special meaning.

It is interesting that the first farmers, as it seems, had only the goat as a domestic animal. This puts the acquisition of most of the later domestic animals only in the beginning of the farming phase.

The utilization of supplemental irrigation, whether natural or artificial, appears in the Near East already during the fifth millennium B.C., attested by the location of various farming settlements in full desert or desert steppe.[19] Likewise, the beginnings of tree cultivation may be set in a very early time. Otherwise the loss of the wild form of *Phoenix dactilifera*, for example, could probably hardly be explained.

But we cannot go further here into the questions of the origin of cultivation and farming, though this might also still throw much light on certain problems of the distribution of cultivating economy and of peasantry. In any case, a readiness to transfer to new ways of life, present in unequal degrees among the different pre-farming societies, must be taken into consideration along with other, chiefly ecological, conditions.

[15] Werth, *op. cit.*
[16] Thus plow culture is known to be connected with almost all known forms of cultivation technique, namely, broadcast seeding, row seeding, seed planting or insertion (pulses, maize), tuber planting (potatoes), seedling replanting (turnips, rice), etc. It can hardly be otherwise, basically, with the digging- and furrowing-stick, as well as hoe and spade culture. One must not forget that cultivated plants and the appropriate techniques of cultivation that go with them are ecologically bound, while techniques of working the ground, with the corresponding tools, are much more mobile geographically.
[17] Kroeber, *op. cit.*, p. 147.

[18] In view of the fact that the Indians of the American high cultures also worked with the digging stick under the most diverse natural conditions, its shortcomings can therefore not have been the reason for the secondary status of cultivation among the eastern woodland Indians.
[19] Hans Bobek, "Klima und Landschaft Irans in vor- und frühgeschichtlicher Zeit," *Geographischer Jahresbericht aus Oesterreich*, XXV (1955), 1–42, ref. to 28.

The definitive transition to a farming way of life (of any technical type)[20] must have brought with it first a practical and later necessarily a social depreciation of the other ways of life and their cultural concomitants.[21] It is generally considered —but also confirmed by much evidence— that women at this stage, because of their probably critical participation in the introduction and the early forms of the new economy, receive a great boost in prestige, expressed among other ways in the common matriarchal organization of the family and thus also of land tenure. One must nonetheless be cautious about simply referring back to the early stages of small grain culture the relations predominant recently in many areas of tropical horticulture. Fertility cults take the place of magic hunting rites. The appeasement of nature-spirits, whose rights one is conscious of violating through clearing and planting, becomes important. The notion of a sort of agreement concluded between the first settled ancestors and the local nature-spirits lends to these ancestors, to a heretofore unknown degree, the character of protector-overlords of the settled kinship group. The clan thus becomes the critical social group and at the same time the primordial unit of settlement.

The basis of subsistence is in the future susceptible of deliberate expansion, and at the same time assured to an extent previously unknown. Braidwood and Reed[22] point out the consequences that may have resulted for man's constitution from the

change of diet. But considering the animal husbandry and utilization of animals that almost everywhere appeared, and the continued, supplemental hunting and fishing, this change of diet does not seem so fundamentally important. However, a further increase of population density is possible in any case. Braidwood and Reed calculate, with various plausible assumptions, a density of population for the time of the existence of Jarmo (North Iraq, *ca.* 6500 B.C.) that is not far from the figure in the same area for the present day, namely, ten per square kilometer.[23] This is ten to sixty times the densities previously reached under favorable circumstances.[24]

In the pre-farming cultures a considerable part of the working effort in the individual households is devoted to the processing of raw materials and to the manufacture of different articles of use, and the number of these articles increases because of the increased flexibility of subsistence and heightened demand. However, they remain still predominantly within the framework of the households, which as extended-family households indeed command a plentiful labor supply, and they lead only in certain cases to the creation of specialized new livelihood forms that are often restricted to kinship groups, e.g., the smiths in Africa. Among these village or tribal industries, regional specialization, based on local raw materials or on tradition, also occurs in early times. A lively trade evolves in connection with it, carried on in the form of trading trips or in periodic bush or village markets. The distances over which certain much coveted goods are distributed in this way are astonishing. However, it should not be overlooked that, at least in later periods, specialized itinerant merchants from distant high cultures had a hand in this trade.

The relationship with the soil changes.

[20] The concept of the farming way of livelihood will not, as often happens, be restricted here to the realm of grain cultivation or the domain of the plow, since the sharp dichotomy between "farmer" [*Bauer*] (in this restricted sense) and "planter" [*Pflanzer*] rests on weak footing for the times before the rise of plow cultivation.
[21] Although hunting often enjoys a high social prestige in later periods, this does not necessarily contradict what is said here, since it may be a matter partly of a "sanctified encystment" exalted above the economic and everyday realm, and partly of a later superimposition by still strongly hunting-oriented groups.
[22] *Op. cit.* (see n. 4, above).

[23] *Loc. cit.*
[24] This only applies, of course, to the actual areas of settlement, although including extensive uncultivated areas. For the temporal setting of Jarmo, see Braidwood and Reed, *op. cit.*

It is no longer the wild plants and wild animals of a given district to which claim is laid, but the soil itself, since it is indispensable for the care of plants. It becomes the property of the occupant clan, but individual households, which are extended or "large households," have claim to its use in required measure. In cases of crowding land apportionment is by aliquot parts, which later grow into individual property.

The most primitive form of division of farmland must be that into more or less regular or irregular, squarish or also round loose blocks, such as arise first though the occupation of free land and gradually become denser. Only where the large plow, especially heavy and difficult to turn, was developed, that is, in northwest Europe, and at first probably within the framework of a field-grass rotation, do long strips first come into use, quite often individually laid out and separated by wide marginal ridges. Probably all other strip-divisions, which are widely distributed irrespective of the sort of tools used, must be of secondary origin, following the pattern of communally cleared, and perhaps originally also communally worked, large parcels divided in usufruct strips, and later into strip-properties, according to the number of claims on them. This may have been the case with traditional family groups as well as (later and probably oftener) with village communities influenced and regulated by overlords (see below). Where individual landownership becomes established early enough, as in the long-settled districts of the Near East, there remains—so far as regulations set by overlords do not work against it—the traditional division into square lots, which are further split up only in course of time so that miniature blocks or blockstrips arise.

The settlements of such free clan-peasant communities grow and multiply through filiation. They thrive in free adaptation to the land and create tribal areas of settlement. Alien groups seeking admission encounter difficulties. In more hemmed-in areas a chessboard pattern of different clans

may originate. In the long run, the territorial principle, which arises from common interest in the land, comes into competition with the tribal-family principle of the clans, without any clear decision between the one and the other being reached at this stage of a free peasantry.

Political cohesion is loose. In the settlements and on occasion in the tribal districts, family or clan heads meet to decide current business according to custom. All authority, even that of a religious leader or a war leader selected in given cases for purposes of common defense, is precarious, that is, it ultimately depends on the personality and its "charisma" [25] as well as on good will. Individual rights or interests can still be effectively protected only by the clan according to the ancient principle of reciprocity, or retaliation. Any conflict, and also any good fortune, calls forth or reveals deep partisan feelings and cleavages. The system of two competing parties is deeply rooted in such anarchic clan-peasant societies.

The intensively used farmland becomes markedly different from the pastoral land of the peasant cultures. The pastoral land undergoes degradation, to the point of elimination of vegetation from the vicinity of the village. The sod-fertilizing of the permanent field economy likewise makes for degradation of the natural forest. But certainly, apart from irrigated regions, in ancient times there prevailed systems of land rotation, so that large expanses were covered with secondary growth.

Surely, the peasant economy was the first one able to cut extensive breaches in the great mass of the natural forest. In many regions it finally came to the point that the forest was almost entirely destroyed. This process of penetration into the forest reflected again the established ecological pattern, since the farmers, according to their kinds of economy, sought either suitable types of forests for pasturing or particular soils favorable to cultiva-

[25] Max Weber, *Wirtschaft und Gesellschaft* (Tübingen: J. C. B. Mohr, 1922), p. 140.

Hans Bobek

tion. The quasi-natural grasslands, on the other hand, seem to have been hardly attackable for a long time by primitive farming tools. The character of the farmland itself was determined by the numerous communities of cultivated plants and the cultivation techniques. Originally, no doubt, mixed cultivation on incompletely cleared and worked surfaces prevailed also in extratropical areas, while the large and uniformly tilled fields become victorious only with progressing plow culture. The vegetable and kitchen gardens of our peasants, but above all the *cultura mista* of the Mediterranean area and certain eastern Asiatic forms of mixed cultures, may be regarded as late echoes or redevelopments of the older situation.

SUBSIDIARY BRANCH OF PASTORAL NOMADISM

Recent research is more and more inclined to the view that nomadic animal husbandry should be conceived of not as an independent cultural stage but as an ecologically conditioned offshoot of farming culture, and specifically of small-grain farming. Not only the lack of autonomy of this way of life, which always and everywhere is bound to acquire supplementary food materials from the farmers, but also the numerous transitional forms that occur between the small-grain farming and the nomadic groups, the high degree of coincidence of their respective areas of distribution, and finally the identity of their animals, are indications that can hardly be refuted. Pastoral nomadism has reached beyond the small-grain farming area in only two places: in North Asia, through the adoption of migratory reindeer herding in taiga and tundra, and in Africa, where it has in part pushed back or overlain tropical hoe-cultivation.

The transitional forms can be grouped around the two basic types of "partial nomadism" [26] (i.e., involving a part of the

[26] Kunz Dittmer, *Allgemeine Völkerkunde: Formen und Entwicklung der Kultur* (Brunswick: F. Vieweg, 1954), p. 257.

population only) as it shows up for example in the so-called "transhumance" and the half or "seasonal nomadism" of the mountains and steppe borderlands, in which the great majority of the population takes part, to be sure, but moves about with the herds for only one part of the year (summer or winter). The *Alpwirtschaft* [European mountain pasture economy] combines elements of both types. The seasonal shift between several fixed settlements is another widespread feature somehow related to nomadism. The development of pastoral nomadism is explainable on the one hand from the presence of widespread pasture areas usable only seasonally and not suitable for permanent occupation, and on the other hand from the doubling of the economic interests of small-grain farmers who possess cattle. The culture-historically important fact that such farmers, through a shift of their emphasis back and forth between cultivation and animal-raising, could easily and briefly change their livelihood form, rests upon these circumstances. The taking-up of nomadism or of settled ways by whole populations must have played a larger role in the history of the arid zone of the Old World than historians have until now realized.

If everything indicates that the elaboration of pastoral nomadism took place through a segregation out of the livestock-raising, small-grain farming cultures of the Near East, where the intimate neighborhood of ecologically very different areas must have been especially inviting, then this livelihood form, like grain-farming culture itself, spread into adjoining natural regions where it underwent characteristic transformations. It is probable that originally only the small animals (goats, sheep, and possibly the ass as a beast of burden), which still today play a large role in the Near East, were herded.[27] Later on in the

[27] For the view still largely held by ethnologists, that the bovine was the first herd animal of pastoral nomads (cf. Dittmer, *op. cit.*, p. 260), there is neither archeological support nor the least inherent likelihood in the nature of the case.

African savannas cattle, only exceptionally connected with pure pastoralism in the Near East, came into prominence, e.g., on year-round reedgrass pastures on lake margins. In the Eurasian steppe it was the horse, in the Asiatic North the reindeer, and in the hot deserts the camel. The cattle-herders of Africa are chiefly stationary (like the few who live in the Near East), without, however, going over to real sedentariness and cultivation.

The slight bond with the soil obviously contributed to the fact that among pastoral societies the family, clan, and tribal organizations became the predominant ones, and formed both the economic and political units. This, however, did not exclude the adoption of aliens on any level, so that the relatedness of many groups was often more fictitious than real. Furthermore, there were confederations of different tribes for political purposes.

The relation with the settled farmers derived from the fundamental need of the products of farming economy felt by the nomads, and from the mutual competition for the land, at least during specific seasons. In this regard, the two most important periods in the development of nomadism should be assessed rather differently.

This division into periods arises from the fact that about the end of the second millennium B.C. horse-riding first appeared in the Eurasian steppe, and spread with the greatest rapidity.[28] Very soon the camel (especially the dromedary) was also used for riding in the desert. The revolutionary character of this process lies in the military superiority that thus for long fell to the mounted nomads, and made them the scourge of the settled farming population, but also capable of wide conquests and empire-building. This was a superiority

that actually held until the threshold of the present. In the succeeding centuries nomadization seized hold of whole populations like a wild fire, in Central Asia as well as in the Near East and North Africa.[29] Only powerful states were able to resist, not infrequently under dynasties of nomad origin.[30] Another and more positive consequence was the opening-up of the great deserts for commercial traffic.

Compared with the world-wide historical manifestation of nomadism in the second period, its role in the preceding period looks pale. It is hard today to get a clear idea of the meaning of pastoralism in its early days, for conditions in the realm of the non-riding African cattle herders may not simply be generalized, on account of their peculiarities. The early pastoral groups were surely often economically dependent on the sedentary folk, to whom they were always reattracted. Full nomadism if developed at all must have been much more weakly evolved, because of the lack of efficient beasts of burden.[31] These tough folk, used to the hardships of a merciless nature, may well have developed early a subjective feeling of superiority. To this might have been added some objective advantages, like greater craft and organizational skill in their leaders and a stronger internal cohesion in the group. It is certain that aggressions against and domination of settled folk by nomad tribes were occurring long before the development of riding (for example, the Akkadians in Sumer; cf. also the ancient kings' titles as "Herder of Peoples"). But one must guard against attributing to the early herders the shock power of the later, highly militant mounted nomads.

[28] Franz Hančar, *Das Pferd in prähistorischer und früher historischer Zeit* (Vienna and Munich: Herold, 1956); K. Jettmar, "Les plus anciennes civilisations d'éleveurs des steppes d'Asie centrale," *Cahiers d'Histoire Mondiale*, I (1954), 760–83; F. Kussmaul, "Zur Frühgeschichte des innerasiatischen Reiternomadismus" (Ph.D. diss., Tübingen, 1953).

[29] Kussmaul, *op. cit.*; Bobek, *Klima und Landschaft Irans* . . . ; von Wissmann, *op. cit.*

[30] See also Owen Lattimore, *Inner Asian Frontiers of China* (New York: American Geographical Society, 1940).

[31] The domestication of the camel is surely much more recent than that of the smaller animals. The domestication of the horse took place first for the purpose of using the meat, in the remote northern steppes and broadleaf forests. Cf. Hančar, *op. cit.*

A parallel to the significant role of the mounted nomads, which can only be mentioned here, is formed by the warlike and mobile sailor tribes—also arisen from farmer elements—of the ancient Mediterranean, North Europe, and Oceania, who likewise founded or destroyed kingdoms.

STAGE OF FEUDALLY OR AUTOCRATICALLY ORGANIZED AGRARIAN SOCIETIES

Let us turn back from side developments in certain areas to the peasantry and its further evolution. It may be surprising that we cite the elaboration of overlordship as the most significant next step, but it was under this leadership that the peasant cultures grew beyond their inherent limitations. Dominion or overlordship [*Herrschaft*] actually only becomes possible at this stage upon the foundation of a peasantry, for only in this framework does it acquire meaning and stability. Overlordship means the power of command over men and their goods in various degrees, based on coercion. But only after men had entered into a stable relation with the soil, as peasants (and also pastoralists), and could produce goods regularly with its help, does overlordship gain substance, taking dominion over the land and thence exerting compulsion over men. Thus it becomes a source of power and riches, and so an institution of importance in world history, which created the state in its strict sense.[32] The warlike hunters likewise sometimes gain power over their fellows but cannot shape it into an enduring overlordship. They kill their prisoners or free them, for they do not know how to draw use from them. They do not subjugate, but annihilate or drive away their opponents, al-

though individual slavery is a feature with them.

Overlordship brings the division of the society into strata with different status and functions: privileged upper strata as bearers and usufructuaries of lordship, lower strata with lesser rights as objects of overlordship, which imposes certain duties on them. These consist of work, or surrender of some of the fruits of their work, or of both. Slavery appears only as an extreme of the diminution of rights and imposition of duties.

Overlordship thus arises through subjection of a population under coercive rule by an alien ethnic group, generally as the result of a conquest. Probably attention has been called too exclusively to the domination of peasants by pastoralists, for which many examples are at hand from later times, but which cannot be assumed to have played in the early days of pastoralism the general or even exclusive role ascribed to it by a theory much contested today. There was never any lack of warlike tribes among the cultivators who could achieve the same thing, and this is likewise true for acculturated hunters, as the development of the New World seems to show. It may be open to doubt whether real dominion arises also through a mere gradation of a clan-peasant society, as when charismatic clan chiefs claim an intermediary role between society and the gods or ancestors, and emerge as a kind of priest kings, or when war leaders elevate themselves as rulers. Presumably, the step from authority to rulership generally succeeds only in connection with conquests and superimposition.

Overlordship or dominion is organized in various ways that differ from each other notably in scope and character. There are two extreme developments, one of which is represented by a thoroughly decentralized feudalistic system, the other by a highly centralized monarchic-bureaucratic structure. These different developments also embody a geographic problem. The latter form is mostly thought to be connected—

[32] It seems unreasonable to water down the concept of the state, to the essence of which belong some minimum of official compulsion and firm institutions, into a collective notion simply for "political function," and then, as often happens in ethnology, to speak of a "state" even among gatherers. There is for instance no state among the ancient Germans before the conquests involved in the *Völkerwanderungen*.

no doubt with some reason, but hardly in an exclusive way—with the necessity (or possibility) of centralized organization of large-scale irrigation in great river lands. From our standpoint it seems important, first, that centralized dominion permits an assembling of goods, skill, and men on a hitherto unprecedented scale. The large households of the lords—from small dynasts to the godlike king of kings—stand out quantitatively and qualitatively high above the general level of peasant economies. New values, new goals, arise and instigate new efforts and achievements that leave everything previous behind. They also bring about the specialization of men in particular functions. In this way there grow up for the first time and on a large scale secondary and tertiary livelihood forms. They serve first and foremost the needs for conservation, symbolization, and exaltation of power, an elevated standard of life, and, not last, the worship of the divine. Priests, officers, civil servants, and holders of various offices appear, whose assignments are often rather irrationally established and defined. Handicraft, too, is able to develop into a distinct way of life only in the shadow of such lordly great households.

The influence of the lordly order upon population cannot be simply described. There is no doubt a better defense externally, and the peaceful conditions guarantee structure within the state and allow a considerable increase in the population. Braidwood and Reed have calculated for early dynastic Sumer, on certain more or less plausible assumptions, an average population density of twenty per square kilometer (including unworked land), which is twice the figure for pre-state peasant North Iraq.[33] But here the influence of irrigation must be taken into account as well as the fact that cities were already present. The influence of overlordship as against such factors is hard to isolate. A lower natural increase rate for the lower

population strata than for the upper ones must often be assumed, as a consequence of marriage restrictions imposed from above or by circumstances, and of decidedly poorer living conditions. War losses and devastation are also to be taken into account. In the Near East, mountain peasantries that have remained free often show higher densities than the populations of neighboring administrated districts, and are centers of population export. The rulers often deliberately bring about shifts of population, both in order to weaken defeated enemies and to extend settlement.

The cultural landscape effects of overlordship are notable, most of all in states of patrimonial or centralized bureaucratic organization, such as we find in the ancient East and its outliers, as well as in ancient America. We find here monumental buildings like temples, tombs, palaces, and large-scale fortifications, which occupied thousands of requisitioned laborers during many years. There are, furthermore, irrigation works and flood-control structures in grand style, which all require the mass application of labor. The organization of such works needs tight control, and it is no wonder that this control also covers other aspects of life, especially the supply of foods, so that such states almost take on the character of giant households of the overlords. Yet agricultural production, in such states too, remains mostly in the hands of the peasants, who are subject only to a more or less detailed regimentation (e.g., in Egypt and in the Inca State).

Of lesser magnitude is the influence upon the cultural landscape in those zones where overlordship has a decentralized character, and state building has a feudal basis. Modest courts and lordly manors, as well as castles, are the new element here. But other less striking effects are also to be observed in both cases.

The lordly order, with its positive, established law, competes with the customary law of the clan-peasantry, and an undercutting of the old type of family community is often the result. This affects clan

[33] *Op. cit.* (see n. 4, above).

groups above all,[34] while on the other hand village communities—with an increasingly fragmented population, to be sure—even gain in importance over large areas as the villages are made responsible by the authorities for taxation, compulsory labor, and the preservation of security and order. They must be seen therefore (contrary to a widespread older view), not so much as descendants of the traditional clan-peasant order but largely just as a product of a secondary democracy, which arises from the equal and common obligations of all toward superior authorities. Nevertheless, in the constitution of these village communities remainders of the old clan-peasant customary practices are also inextricably interwoven. In the Middle Ages of the West, the example of the free cities that had meanwhile grown up doubtless contributed to village formation.

This development, particularly, was of great importance for the formation of the rural landscape in manorial times, in so far as the village communities, collaborating with or even instigated by the landlords, largely took over the regulation of farming and other land use. The village lands were organized and regularized according to the principle that like obligations must correspond to like rights to cultivation and other uses. Plow-culture, especially, lends itself to such regulations which lead to the common-field system and culminate finally in the practice of periodical redistribution of the land. Such communal systems, with or without redivision, existed and still exist in many areas in both Western and Eastern Europe and widely in the Near East,[35] and less commonly, it seems, in the Mediter-

ranean area. Strip-fields, and fields regularized and equalized in other ways, as well as periodic redivision, are not unknown among tropical and extratropical planters. A yearly redivision of the cultivated land, supervised by the authorities, prevailed for instance in the old Inca State.[36]

In East Asia, too, field division underwent a regularization under the influence of the overlords, as the Chinese *tsing-tien* system attests; it was further developed in Japan as the "Jori" system.[37]

Today we cannot make general statements about the pieces of the lords' land that were not given over to the peasants, nor about the way they were utilized. They were probably worked mainly by the compulsory labor of subject peasants, bondsmen or serfs. Mixed forms of enterprise may have predominated.

The question arises whether overlordship or dominion spread from one source area or whether various places of origin must be supposed. It seems that we have to think here, as in the case of the appearance of cultivation, of various starting points within the peasant world, but that their definitive shaping (in the sense of state-building) took place in a restricted area and spread from there. In this process, the inevitable echo of the innovation beyond the particular boundaries of states and empires must play a role, so that social stratification in such border areas is accelerated. Trading relations, returning mercenaries, and finally the need for defense have special significance in this connection.

History teaches that the first organized dominions, and with them the first states, were created in the Near East, that is, in the area where farming has the longest history. It is surely significant that the

[34] To the least extent in eastern Asia, where the ancestor cult surviving until today has kept these groups alive and active longer than elsewhere.

[35] A. Latron, "La vie rurale en Syrie et au Liban," *Mémoires de l'Institut Français de Damas* (Beirut, 1936); Jacques Weullersse, *Les paysans de Syrie et du Proche Orient* (Paris: Gallimard, 1946); Hans Bobek, "Soziale Raumbildung am Beispiel des Vorderen Orients," *Deutscher Geographentag München 1948* (Landshut, 1950), pp. 193–206.

[36] J. H. Rowe, "Inca Culture at the Time of the Spanish Conquest," in Julian H. Steward (ed.), *Handbook of South American Indians* (Smithsonian Institution, Bureau of American Ethnology Bulletin 143 [6 vols.; Washington, D.C., 1946–50]), II, 183–330.

[37] T. Tanioka "Systèmes agraires: le Jori dans le Japon ancien," *Annales, Economies, Sociétés, Civilisations* (Paris, 1959) pp. 625–39.

peasant world in that area then already showed a marked differentiation. Here existed side by side neighboring groups of oasis farmers, dry-forest (steppe) farmers, partial and half nomads, and probably already full nomads, among whom there necessarily arose tension and friction, and who in addition showed notable differences in cultural level, population density, and warlike inclinations and capacities. The first known states grew up in the domain of Sumerian oasis farmers and may have been called into being by competition among neighboring groups as much as by the need for defense against pastoralists of different kinds (among them, perhaps, stationary cattle-raisers in the periodically flooded reed marshes). In any case, the strongly theocratic structure of these first states seems to me to indicate that they came about not so much through alien superimposition as by some endogenous elaboration of rulership among these oasis farmers. The circumstance that not military leaders, but ritual chiefs and senior priests of the clans, first were at the helm may be connected with the fact that the streams rising each year and the general dependence on the varying water volume must have powerfully enhanced the feeling of being at the mercy of supernatural forces, and thus also the influence of the priestly intermediaries.

The struggles for power between these originally small states, and their eventual fusion into the first "empire," were no doubt taken care of by war chiefs, and this necessarily brought superimpositions first of Sumerians over Sumerians, and at last also of aliens (Akkadians) who were very likely pastoralists. In the beginning they were probably just tolerated, then called for and forced to participate in the struggles. Thus there came about a secularization of power, but not completely, since the new kings probably laid stress on anchoring their power by taking over priestly functions in the traditional way. The gradual expansion of irrigation and all the services and constructions connected with

it, both more and more brought under central direction and executed by the compulsory labor of the lower classes, further contributed, in a secondary but still important way, to strengthening the kings' position, while stamping on the state organization a special mark of centralization.[38] Once formed, this system of rule of the god-king, with total state power as an institution, was able also to spread out farther into dissimilar areas.

STAGE OF EARLY URBANISM AND RENT CAPITALISM

The erection of dominion in the Near East is closely followed by the development of urban life, or to put it more correctly, government and city originate here in the same process. This was by no means the case everywhere, however. One more basis, and the decisive one, for the development of higher civilization has been won with the city.

By city we mean, in this regard, a larger settlement whose population consists to a considerable degree of representatives of secondary and tertiary livelihood forms, whose functions, therefore, are much more differentiated than those of peasant or nomad settlements. Thus, archeologically we recognize cities by their size as well as by differentiated buildings: temples, palaces, citadels, market places, dwellings of various sizes and forms, and usually an over-all fortification are characteristic.[39] We learn details about the differentiation of the population from the written sources that soon turn up: from ornamental representations, from the productions of a

[38] This was the creation of the "hydraulic civilization" according to Karl Wittfogel, "The Hydraulic Civilizations," in *Man's Role . . .* , pp. 152–64; and *Oriental Despotism: A Comparative Study of Total Power* (New Haven: Yale University Press, 1957). However, one must guard against overstressing this one factor in the creation of Oriental civilizations, just as much as against overemphasizing the role of the pastoralists.

[39] Large-scale cemeteries, in ancient Egypt, were mostly found outside, or marginal to, the towns.

highly elaborated handicraft, from the import goods of a lively trade.

The first signs of such differentiated building show up several thousand years after the first appearance of farming settlements. They are found in temples at Tepe Gawra (near Nineveh) and Abu Shahrain (Eridu, in the alluvial plain of the Euphrates), which appear during the Al-Ubaid period (after 3900 B.C.). A great "city wall" is found even in the pre-ceramic settlement of Jericho.[40] These are the oldest evidence to date for social gradation and organized warfare, that is for the elements that lead to the creation of dominion. Palaces appear in Sumer considerably later than temples. They are an outcome of the partial "secularization" of lordship already mentioned.

If we let our glance sweep over time and space, we find dominions that preserved—for some time, at least—an essentially rural character, or did not become identified with urban life to the same degrees as in the East. The Western and the Japanese feudal Middle Ages, and also in part tropical Africa, provide examples of this. There must therefore be good grounds for the almost complete identification of dominion and city in the Near East, which made great headway in any case and which characterizes almost all the ancient civilizations. I believe that we find such grounds in the same circumstances that favored the creation of dominion in this region. For the most ancient times, they lie in the rivalry between rather closely neighboring and rapidly growing populations (based on productive irrigation economies), which had to concentrate in agglomerated settlements, as large as possible, for self-protection and development of power. The strong attachment of oasis farmers to their land, in which they have invested so much, makes unfeasible any withdrawal of the sort that would be easier for dry-field farmers. Thus in pre-ceramic Jericho it was no doubt the

bountiful springs that compelled fortification. It was generally the strong tension between the very different livelihood forms that led to frictions in the East earlier than elsewhere, and later, after the rise of the militant mounted nomads, must have forced the imperiled settlements to consolidate. It is a fact that such "synoecism" can always be observed right up to the present time, especially in the oasis settlements of the whole dry belt of the Old World and on its borders.

Out of this close connection between dominion and city, there later emerged the peculiar economic form of the Oriental civilization, centered largely in its cities, which I have called "rent capitalism."[41] It is highly characteristic of all ancient urban life, and thus significant for world history. Its special character and its far-reaching consequences for ancient civilization in general and nearly all its later descendants, aside from a few attempts,[42] have heretofore been noticed too little and elaborated even less in economic history. Its decidedly "capitalist" character, especially (though differing basically from later "productive" capitalism), has been almost entirely overlooked. On the contrary, it is often completely obscured through mistaken designations such as "Oriental feudalism" and the like.

Rent capitalism arose through commercialization and the transformation, undertaken in a plain profit-seeking spirit, of the original lordly (or feudal) claims on income from the peasant and artisan under-strata.

Its elaboration was definitively promoted by the keeping of accounts and other forms of rationalization of rent drawing that were developed early in the large temple estates;[43] also by the fact that after the first

[40] K. M. Kenyon, "Jericho and Its Setting in Near Eastern History," *Antiquity*, XXX (1956), 184–95.

[41] Hans Bobek, "Aufriss einer Vergleichenden Sozialgeographie," *Mitteilungen der Geographischen Gesellschaft in Wien*, XCII (1950), 34–45.
[42] Such attempts were made above all by Karl Marx, Max Weber, L. Brentano, and a few others.
[43] By "rents" I mean here in general the totality of regular and effective claims on the production of farmers and craftsman, resting on the most various sorts of titles.

secularization of rulership, there followed an endless sequence of breaks in the continuity of the upper strata through conquest and other reversals. The absolute, self-interested, alien, inimical and certainly exploitative character of Oriental government, which generally is devoid of any feeling of duty beyond the religious, had thus been continually renewed and at last established. The role played in this latter development by militant nomadism, in the rapidly switching Oriental dynasties and large parts of the upper strata, needs no further elaboration. Ibn Khaldun, the statesman and cultural sociologist, exposed it as early as the 14th century. To this strong nomadic influence, the Oriental upper strata seem to owe their deeply rooted disdain of every sort of productive work, and especially of farming and of peasants in general, a disdain combined, however, with a brisk acquisitive interest.[44]

The essence of the commercialization of the originally overlordly claims on income consisted in partitioning them off and attaching titles to the single parts, which could be traded freely like goods. Thus the peasant productive economy became conceptually split into a system of production factors, for each of which a special and usually uniformly valued part in the gross proceeds in kind was calculated. The following were, and as a rule are still today, held to be important factors of production: water (which usually remains combined with land in areas of sufficient rainfall or ample water supplies from rivers), seed, work animals (and other inventory, which is scanty enough), and finally human labor. Separate rules control the obligations toward government and village functionaries. It is well known that the ideal of rent capitalism is attained when the share-cropping farmer does not touch more than

a meager share of the work of his hands. But it is even possible to split up farm work itself (as in plowing, harvesting, sometimes care of trees, etc.) and to pay for it with appropriate shares of the product. The concept of the "enterprise" or operating unit begins to dissolve, under such a system, into a series of individual titles, or rather tasks, and corresponding claims on income.[45] This dissolution has gone to different lengths in the various regions of the Near East in the course of time. Often, to be sure, it has receded in periods of true feudalization, but has always soon gone forward again.[46]

But since any sort of palpable property in the classic Oriental state at this stage is burdened with a factor of insecurity, because of the inherent arbitrariness of the system, early attempts can be recognized to transform easily seized property titles into intangible debt titles.[47] The opportunities to place the peasants in debt are very favorable in the Near East for two reasons: one is the lack of resources of most peasants that has its roots in the rent-capitalistic system. The other is the climatically conditioned frequency of crop failure. The peasant must quite often go into debt in order that he and his family can survive. It is an absolute ideal of the rent capitalist to get as many peasants as possible into debt so permanently that with

[44] One may trace the psychological contributions of the nomads to the creation and invariable maintenance of the rent-capitalistic spirit among the Oriental upper strata to the mentality of the pastoralist, whose herds produce a yearly "profit" without his having to do anything about it.

[45] Several farmers together often form joint enterprises, as I observed in Persia, in which the pooling of certain means of production is included. The resulting harvest is apportioned in a specified way to men and capital inputs. Such joint enterprises are called by the same name (*sherkat*) used for joint stock companies. Their purpose, besides getting together the necessary equipment, is easier management of the painstaking and manifold tasks.

[46] Such periods of feudalization occurred repeatedly, e.g., in ancient Egypt, before and after the foundation of the Sassanid Empire; after the Mongol and Ottoman conquests; and also at certain times in the Byzantine Empire. Among many mountain tribes (e.g., the Kurds), feudal traits still show today in the agrarian structure.

[47] These are difficult to seize, since debt-titles are bound to persons and quite often rest only on oral agreements.

all their yearly payments they can never liquidate the initial debt, which soon becomes legendary.

The practices used to get around the condemnation not only of usury but of any kind of interest, so notably present in all great religions of Oriental origin, are legion. The commonest, for example, is to estimate an advance of grain at the highest price before the harvest, then at the lowest when it is turned in after the harvest. Another is the fictitious purchase of a commodity (by the creditor) with the understanding that the partner (debtor) must buy it back at a higher price.

Rent capitalism was probably fully developed by the beginning of the second millennium B.C. at the latest, as we may conclude from the very detailed legal rules found in the Code of Hammurabi (*ca.* 1700 B.C.) which threaten the dilatory debtor with severe sanctions. It should also be noted that rent capitalism applies not only to the products of the farm economy, but in the same manner to those of all sorts of primary production and handicraft industries as well. The measures adopted are the same: appropriation of the means of production and the regular advancing of loans, i.e., the creation of indebtedness.[48]

[48] A similar procedure was developed for most of the other wealth-creating branches of the economy, for example, mining, fishing (especially pearl fishing), and pastoral husbandry. In commerce the investment of capital with a corresponding apportionment of returns (*commenda*) was usual, but it only fits the nature of the case, and contains no special flavor of rent capitalism as long as excessive claims are not connected with it. This rent-capitalist character, which (apart from the practice of creating debtors) obviously derives from allotting the owner of the means of production an exaggerated claim on gross returns, is not so strongly expressed in pastoral livestock raising as in agriculture and handicraft, since no other means of production besides land (and water) are required in addition to the animals themselves. Land and water, are, however, mostly held by the tribe under nomadic pastoralism, and can be appropriated by urban capitalists only under especially favorable conditions. Such conditions are present, to be sure, if the tribal leaders themselves turn into capitalists and appropriate the lands of their tribe. But the maintenance of such

It must be emphasized here that rent capitalism, as one of the characteristic and portentous achievements of Oriental and other civilizations derived from it, cannot be traced back simply to artificial irrigation, which since Karl Marx has been regarded as the most important factor in the growth of "Asiatic agrarian society," and has recently once again been so represented.[49]

The direct and indirect effects of the rent-capitalist system can be summarized as follows. In the first place, agricultural and industrial production, and also most of the extractive activities like mining, fishing, forestry, and so forth, remained in the hands of small enterprises, no matter how strongly the various property titles were concentrated, or dispersed, in the hands of a few large or many small "capitalists." The reason for this was not a lack of sufficient markets; the Oriental cities were for thousands of years the largest in the world. And it was also not primarily an underdeveloped technology; most of the great advances of agricultural technique in preindustrial times were worked out in the Near East or its immediate neighborhood, whether in plant cultivation, tillage (plowing), or irrigation. The reason lay on the one hand in the disdain and lack of interest of most members of the upper strata for productive work, and on the other in the threat to large enterprises from the arbitrariness of the rulers, but above all in the undoubted inferiority, from the standpoint of profits, of the self-owned and operated large enterprise, as against the yield

claims in the domains of freedom-loving tribes is always precarious.

It should be mentioned that within the rent-capitalist system more favorable forms of cooperation of capital and labor have also been elaborated, like the "planting contract" or the fixed lease. In the first case, a landowner allows and finances the planting of trees by a farmer, against a later division of the plantation according to a certain scheme; in the second case, the increased return due to greater effort goes entirely to the farmer. Both are as a rule confined to irrigated districts near cities or other favored areas.

[49] By Wittfogel (cf. n. 38, above).

of a larger number of small enterprises, exploited under rent capitalism. Other things being equal, with full concentration of all means of production in the hands of one capitalist, a number of free peasant families on the edge of subsistence will get more from the soil than the same number of free wage workers or slaves. Besides, the risks are shared in the first case, while in the second they all fall on the entrepreneur. Large slave enterprises are usually heavily burdened with fixed costs. Thus, as far as we can tell, they hardly ever played a role in the Near East, and only transitorily—in times of very low prices for slaves—in neighboring civilizations of a related economic type.[50] It is thus wrong from an economic standpoint to characterize these ancient civilizations as "slaveholding societies," as the Marxist-Leninist economic and social history does.

In the second place, the constant skimming-off of a substantial part of the proceeds of production under the rent-capitalist system, without a corresponding economic return, proves a detrimental practice, impeding progress. The deliberate reduction of the peasants and artisans to a naked minimum of existence deprives them of the necessary working capital so that they are compelled to practice destructive exploitation of themselves, the land, and the work animals. Thus it can be explained that this civilization, showing such mighty technical advances in its initial stages, became more and more nearly stationary in

technique after the full establishment of rent capitalism. Almost no more inventions that could improve agricultural, industrial, mineral, and other production can be recorded, and even if, as is probable, any such was made, it was brought to nothing by the uninterested attitude of the upper strata toward the process of production, and the extreme poverty and consequent indifference of the broad working masses. Neither racial reasons nor political-military events nor yet purely intellectual history, but only the quite unimpressive, and yet very effective, socioeconomic mechanism can satisfactorily account for the historical fact of the millennium-long "marching in place" of the originally highly creative ancient high culture.

Rent capitalism was a true capitalism in so far as it was characterized by a striving for unlimited gain and in so far as it adopted accounting practices and attained a high degree of accountancy and rationality—characteristics that are lacking in all the earlier stages of evolution of mankind, including the lordly order. Rent capitalism differed from the more recent "capitalism" (heretofore as a rule the only thing so called) in that it was not linked with production, but rather was satisfied with skimming off its proceeds. In regard to production it remained fundamentally sterile. For this reason it lent to ancient urbanism as a whole a definitely parasitical character, economically.

On the other hand, since it concentrated a good part of the products of agriculture, mining, and other primary branches of production in the cities and put them within reach of a rather broad and differentiated element of the population there, it gave these cities the possibility of an unheard of rise not only in the number of their inhabitants, but also in material and cultural level. Within the framework of this ancient urban life and its later offshoots, mankind was able to put forth its highest cultural flowering, at the cost, to be sure, of the broad rural masses. The absolute primacy of the city over the land is diagnostic for

---

[50] How strongly the rent-capitalist spirit itself has penetrated even into the preferential domain of slave enterprise—mining—is shown in the fact that Athenian state mines on the Laurion, where at times 20,000 slaves were working, were never run by the government itself—in spite of a proposal to this effect in the fourth century B.C.—but were always leased. The leased enterprises were surely small, according to all we know about ancient mining, and furthermore were worked in part not with owned but with rented slaves, who were thus put to profitable use by rich slave owners. See A. Aymard, *Les cités grecques à l'époque classique. La ville, 2ᵉ partie: Institutions économiques et sociales* (Brussels: Société Jean Bodin, 1955), pp. 78 ff.

this civilization; the land was pushed into a dependent and servile position in political, social, economic, and cultural matters. One may speak of a "fellahization" of the rural population in extreme cases of exploitation (according to certain Oriental examples), and signify thereby a degradation extending into both the physical and moral spheres.

The spread of ancient urbanism started from the Near East, which itself was only gradually, and never completely, permeated by it. It ran mostly toward west and east, following the track of the expansion of farming, and especially of plow farming (see map). The city was fully constituted in its area of origin by 3000 B.C. It appeared in northwestern India in the second half of the third millennium B.C., in the eastern Mediterranean region around the end of the third millennium, and in northwestern China only in the course of the second millennium B.C. During the first millennium B.C. it permeated the western half of the Mediterranean region as well as the remaining parts of India and China. Townlike agglomerations (*oppida*) soon appeared also in Atlantic Europe, in the course of its acculturation and colonization around the beginnings of our era. But only much later, after a severe regression, did there arise a new and more autonomous city life which was destined for a great future. On its further course, ancient urbanism pushed to southeastern and insular Asia and also reached Japan in the first millennium A.D. Finally, with the rise of the American Indian high cultures, it appeared also in the New World.[51]

[51] The direct influence of Southeast Asia on ancient American high cultures is gaining more and more in likelihood today. See, for example, Robert Heine-Geldern, "Das Problem vorkolumbianischer Beziehungen zwischen Alter und Neuer Welt und Seine Bedeutung für die allgemeine Kulturgeschichte," *Anzeiger der philosophischen und historischen Klasse der Oesterreichischen Akademie der Wissenschaften,* XCI (1954), 343–57; *idem,* "Die asiatische Herkunft der südamerikanischen Metalltechnik," *Paideuma: Mitteilungen zur Kulturkunde,* V (1954), 347–423; *idem,* "Herkunft und Ausbreitung der Hochkulturen," *Al-*

In this mighty expansion over so many different natural and cultural regions, urbansim experienced numerous modifications, without managing, however, to belie in its basic features its common origin. It is interesting to observe how the early temple-city type reappears chiefly in southern and insular Asia and also in America, while in the Old World dry zone and the Mediterranean area mostly the palace and castle, or citadel type of the warrior chiefs, took hold, and in East Asia both are mixed. It would lead too far if we went into any depth here to explain the regional modifications of ancient urbanism and their social geographic bases. Let us only mention one change that it underwent in the Mediterranean, which was very significant for later development.

Despite all its brilliant evolution in economy and culture, the city in the Near East, unlike the city in the Mediterranean region, did not succeed in working itself into an independent political body, and this failure was characteristic also for the whole Asiatic wing of its expansion. The main reason for the failure in the Near East must be sought in the special character of dominion in this area, to which allusion has already been made. It was the ever repeated rule of force based on conquest and superimposition, primarily by nomad groups, that caused all beginnings of the elaboration of self-government in the cities to collapse. These cities therefore remained, until the modern reforms, mere conglomerates of small and politically undeveloped communities working mainly on a personal (ethnic, religious, or craft) basis. They were, and remained, just as much subjected to the central or provincial authorities as the surrounding country. Nevertheless, while in the open country the organization of the population into respon-

manach der Oesterreichischen Akademie der Wissenschaften für das Jahr 1955 (Vienna, 1955), pp. 252–67; *idem;* "Kulturpflanzengeographie und das Problem vorkolumbianischer Kulturbeziehungen zwischen Alter und Neuer Welt." *Anthropos.* LIII (1958). 361–402.

sible village communities proceeded steadily, under the influence of overlordship and at the expense of the original clan or tribal groupings, the same process was denied any considerable results in the cities in so far as their consolidation into political entities is concerned.

However, in the Mediterranean cities, especially in the Greek *polis* but also in many Phoenician maritime cities, the corporate principle was able largely to replace the monarchial system, first affecting the landholding families who constituted the city in the beginning. The city thus became an autonomous political body of patricians enjoying equal rights. In due course, the right to an equal vote became extended, as we know, to ever wider circles of urban population, and thus the city developed into a democratic commune. In this way there came about an integration of customary original clan elements with features of overlordship and rule within the political framework of the city, a process of great historical significance, since it set the frame for later urban life and, along with it, civilization in the West. Economically, however, the Mediterranean city largely persisted on the course of rent capitalism, which was finally to be overthrown only by the economic spirit of the later northwestern European city.

If we ask ourselves why this political achievement was effected in the Mediterranean city but not in the Oriental one, we must point mainly to the continuity and relative homogeneity of the Greek upper classes since the conquest and settling of the country. If even here the tribal war chiefs raised themselves up as kings in the course of the conquest, nevertheless they remained, more than ever in the Near East, under obligation to their fellow tribesmen, particularly the nobility, and dependent upon them for their power. They lacked both the possibility and the tradition of elevating themselves to the rank of kings, and there was no repeated exchange of the upper classes. The happy shores of Greece were protected by the Mediterranean Sea

against those brutal hordes of conquerors from the desert who were always falling upon cities of the East, where every germ and starting point for a free civil development was finally annihilated.

A fundamentally new element, the city, was added to the cultural landscape at this stage of human development. In it the secondary and tertiary livelihood forms, previously latent or actually present but scattered, found a privileged place and setting for previously unknown development. A new pattern of life-relations appeared, as portions of land and people became associated with a specific city as their central place, that is, their gathering point and focus for the stimulation of their political, economic, and cultural life. This focusing expressed itself clearly enough in the rural landscape, too, as zones of diminishing intensity of land use, communication facilities, and all sorts of other urban-influenced features grew up around the cities. Among the cities themselves, one can recognize a rank order according to the size of dependent regions, which is somewhat broken only by cities of far-reaching trade or with export industries. In any case, court-cities and imperial capitals dominated. However, size and wealth of the associated regions usually set rather strict limits for the economic growth of such cities, which therefore, while exerting a great attractive force on the rural population, were almost always burdened with a genuine unemployment problem. This often reached very great proportions in the capitals. The rent-capitalist economy, together with all state intervention (which occurred, for example, in Hellenistic, Roman, and Byzantine times), could not do away with this unemployment, since, because of its structural qualities, it was just not able to intensify production in any considerable degree.

The scenery of the rent-capitalist city is characterized, then, by the splendid great buildings of the state or its rulers, municipalities (where present), and wealthy individuals (often in the form of foundations) on the one hand, and on the other hand through the colorful mass of small shops of merchants and artisans. Their concentration in bazaars, trading, and handicraft centers is an early achievement of the Near East that spread widely. They are built by the state or private individuals, and offer one more opportunity for bringing industry into the service of rent charges.

Population conditions undergo hardly any fundamental changes. The concentration of great masses of people in cities is new. In the Old World dry belt and in most of its border regions, a large part of the population is included within the towns, while in the village-bound rice-farming regions of southeast Asia they are often developed only as skeletons. It is significant that the excessive pressure on the rural populations often encourages their flight, and hence the depopulation of formerly rich settled lands. Thus it was in the Near East and in several parts of the Mediterranean region.

The expansion of ancient urbanism and of the rent capitalism which almost everywhere accompanied it did not take place without resistance from the peasant and pastoral populations. The nomads above all were almost always able to escape from the permanent grasp of state power, and hence of the townsmen, while the smaller groups of oases fell prey to overlordship and exploitation by the tribes. But the peasant population, too, was often able to escape this grasp permanently, if adequately protected by remoteness and difficult forest or mountain land. Thus within the great zone over which urbanism spread, enclaves of free and warlike peasantry, in which ancient clan-peasant ways are more or less well preserved (*Kabylias*), are often found.

STAGE OF PRODUCTIVE CAPITALISM, INDUSTRIAL SOCIETY, AND MODERN URBANISM

It has become the fashion to follow V. G. Childe's habit of speaking of "revolutions" when dealing with the great steps in the evolution of economy and society. Thus

Childe[52] speaks of the "food producing revolution" and means thereby the changeover from mere exploitative forms of economy based on food collecting to productive forms, through the taking-up of plant- and animal-raising with all the accompanying phenomena. There is hardly any doubt, though, that these advances must have had the character of "evolutions" rather than "revolutions." This revolutionary character can rightly be ascribed only to the last of these developments, so often designated as the "Industrial Revolution" of the eighteenth and early nineteenth centuries. The powerful, rapid, and fundamental way in which it transformed all previous arrangements and ways of life, and is altering them at an ever accelerating rate and bearing mankind away toward new and still unknown shores, fully justifies such a designation.

We are no longer entitled, after what has been said in the last section, to call the intellectual attitude with all its accompaniments that evoked this transformation simply "capitalism." I think I have showed that capitalism in the strict sense of the word has probably been in existence for 4,000 years, and that in the form of "rent capitalism," to which too little attention has been paid, it had already given a distinctive stamp to the preceding stage of human cultural evolution. Almost all ancient civilizations more or less of the urban type carry its imprint quite unmistakably.

What was new about the epoch of industrialism, facilitating its breakthrough, and today still supporting and impelling it, was the application of capital to *production*, and its creative linkage with production, which received a mighty stimulus. Because of these things we can call the present stage that of "productive capitalism" to make it plain and to separate it clearly from what has already been present. Likewise a broadening in meaning of the concept of "capitalism" is proposed, so that not only pri-

[52] V. Gordon Childe, *Social Evolution* (London: Watts, 1951); and *Man Makes Himself* (New York: Mentor Books, 1951).

vate and individual but also collective capitalism of any kind may be understood by it.

The course of the innovation, originating in northwestern Europe, can be clearly seen historically: in the 1760's, cotton processing in England and Scotland was stepped up by the introduction of labor-saving mechanical devices, first driven by water-mills, but after 1786 also by steam. The mechanization of the processes of manufacturing and industrial production kept spreading out uninterruptedly from there. The new era had begun.

The preconditions for this joining together of technical inventiveness and manufacturing processing, for the purpose of increasing the efficiency of the productive processes instead of just multiplying them, were extremely complex. The effective factors therein have often been treated by economic historians, and variously evaluated. The absolute state as the taskmaster and sponsor of heavy manufacturing production; the colonies as sources of capital, furnishers of raw materials, and markets for products; the spirit of Protestant dissidents and other groups directed especially toward economic activity; the freeing of labor force through changes in the agricultural situation; the development of the natural sciences and technology; and many other factors have rightly been pointed out. All played their part in the birth of the new way of doing things. On the whole, though, it was the civic spirit of northwestern Europe to which everything was due. The fact that this spirit succeeded in establishing itself against the traditional powers earlier and more definitively in many countries of that area, and above all in the British Isles, gave these countries a decisive head start and the pioneer role in the inception of the new kind of economy.

But the question arises, with this way of regarding things, why only northwestern Europe, among all the civilizations that were continuations and descendants of ancient urbanism and more or less marked by the rent capitalism linked with it, could free itself from that economic outlook and shove off for new shores. We can answer this question here only in a very generalized way, at the risk of arousing criticism among many historians.

The first urban colonization of Atlantic Europe, which took place under the auspices and by the civilizing means of the Roman Empire, can only be regarded as an offshoot of Mediterranean urbanism. With the breakup of that empire, it suffered the well-known retrogression that deprived the cities of a large part of their effectiveness and character in a new situation where civilization had lost ground. Only after about 1000 A.D. did the renaissance of urban life in this region become noticeable. Taken as a whole, it can be considered a renewed emanation from the revivified west Mediterranean center, and consequently it reflects many characteristic traits rooted there. But on the other hand it stands, in many respects, as an independent development of a culture region that had meanwhile come to economic and social maturity.

This new Occidental city took on its internal and external form in the years between 1000 and 1500 A.D. For the first time in human history it combined political effectiveness and commercial and industrial activities to a degree that henceforth marked the spirit of these cities and their citizens.[53] The background and main reason for this achievement was that these cities, profiting by their opportunity to make themselves into a third political force between the king and the already entrenched feudal powers, purposely excluded the representatives of the landholding feudal elite from their pledged associations and brotherhoods from the very start—in strong contrast with the contemporary cities of upper Italy and other parts of the

[53] In the late phases of the Greek *polis,* civil liberties were also extended to the handicraft workers of the city population, but they could not break through the deeply rooted rent-capitalist tradition, which long after still remained or re-emerged as a decisive factor in both Greek and western Mediterranean cities.

western Mediterranean which, in the course of their struggles for political and economic autonomy, actually compelled the numerous feudal lords to enter their communes and to swear the citizen's oath. In doing this they were, to be sure, backed by a deeply rooted tradition. Of course there existed transitional cases, above all in France, Burgundy, and South Germany. On the whole, however, the landholding feudal nobility in the north, outside the cities, remained a rural element, and at first and for a long time still there was no such fusion of it with the urban patrician group as there had been in the south.[54]

Thus there grew up in the north a type of city that, like the Mediterranean city, formed an autonomous political body in which, however, the productively enterprising citizens lent the tone. Although the merchant class that formed the patrician group here also tried to invest its capital in real estate and sought rural as well as urban income derived from rents, it remained at the core essentially bound up in the old psychology, for generally it could succeed in these efforts only in opposition to the feudal lords. It had more effect where, as in Flanders and the rest of the Netherlands, the cities were so strong that they managed early to break up the feudal order of the country. The most important economic foundation of the cities of the Occidental north continued, however, to be commerce and manufacture, above all, along with long-distance trading and the exchange of goods with the rural population. In this the various privileges were of much help in reserving these branches of economy to the cities.

The relative prosperity of the Occidental peasants helped not a little to bring about this state of things. It was, on the one hand, in itself a result of the "fossilization of the landed estate" and of the gradual devaluation of rents, but on the other also of the favorable ecological conditions in a constantly moist natural broadleaf forest

[54] Cf. Edith Ennen, *Frühgeschichte der europäischen Stadt* (Bonn: L. Röhrscheid, 1953).

region. Furthermore, this region long continued to possess reserves of land for settlement, which fact also contributed to the weakening of the pressure exerted by landlords. The regularly recurring crop failures that play so large a role in semiarid regions, and offer rent capitalism so much opportunity to apply its usurious practices, are wanting here.

When, in the time of princely absolutism many centuries later, the Occident also experienced a general urbanization of the landholding nobility, many traits of ancient urbanism and rent capitalism also made their appearance, such as the brilliant development of court-cities with palace luxury and display of splendor, but also tax-farming, backwardness, and impoverishment of the broad masses. However, the townsman's bourgeois spirit was already much too well established, and the commoners in the leading countries had already captured too many important positions, for the final victory to be wrested from them.

We can recognize a preliminary stage of productive capitalism in which capital was applied to the organization of large-scale production, but production got along mainly without mechanical aids and therefore still depended in great degree upon compulsory labor. The colonial plantation economies and the more developed manorial economies in England and other parts of the Occident belong to this type, as do the manufactories and various primary production industries, such as mining, in the mercantilist age.

The effects of the modern industrial economy on the structure of society and thereby on settlement and the population situation are quite well known. Only a few lines are needed here. But we should take notice of the different phases that are recognizable in the formation of industrial economy and society: an early phase in which the new ways spontaneously develop, and fumblingly and often hastily take on form; the classical phase of "coal and iron," when industry secures its powerful position and resulting social tensions dramatically deepen; and finally the new phase, since the First World War, in which it vigorously extends its material and energy bases, and, in the leading countries, thoroughly permeates and conditions the whole order of life, and in which, simultaneously, evolutionary solutions for many problems get under way.

In the first phase the new livelihood forms of the private entrepreneur and the industrial laborers arise. The plants are still small and not fully mechanized; they select locations adjoining old settlements where they are more tolerated than sought, or at new sites where waterpower is available. Together with the "master residence" of the entrepreneur and the still rustic huts of the workers, they form clusters that subsequently stretch out without any order. The conditions of work are hard, of a patriarchal type but emphasizing more the rights and arbitrary power of the entrepreneur than his obligations. The curve of population, despite high mortality, begins to climb, because the breakdown of the old order has abolished the old marriage restrictions and new job opportunities are opening up increasingly. Thus a considerable part of the excess population streams into the new industrial settlements, but is hardly noticed politically.

In the second phase, beginning about the middle of the nineteenth century, mechanized industry, technically much improved, attains a powerful position in the state and the economy, which is still continuously extended under the direction of private enterprise. The old ways of livelihood, resting on the principle of a traditional, status-oriented conduct of life, are in full retreat, but still defend themselves in the countryside and in the conservative circles of the upper classes. A new type of city has arisen, which permits mighty, previously unheard of concentrations of people, since the decisive factors for it are no longer those of a local or regional center with a surrounding rural area, but those of industrial location. The size of the plants has increased and a certain natural order has in part taken effect, as they group themselves by preference in or near coal basins or along canals and railroads connected with them; giant residential quarters of low or high buildings spring up, obeying a principle of arrangement that is more formal than reasonable. The layout is able to avoid the more flagrant sanitary hazards of the early period, but it cannot stop the evil outgrowths of speculative housing construction. Mortality, especially infant mortality, and deaths in epidemics, decrease thanks to advances in medicine. Natality figures remain high because of the great afflux from the country. Thus the increase of population is greater than ever before. The economic and social position of the tremendously swollen labor force continues to be poor, though slightly improved. There comes a sharp division of society along class lines, proceeding from the industrial sector, together with the rise of corresponding interest groups on the economic and political level, in which process the urban "middle class," because of the multiplicity of its interests, naturally tends more and more to fall behind.

On the international stage, too, powers confront one another mainly over economic interests, whose purposes and scale are largely taken over from the private capitalistic sphere. This does not prevent these nations from being clothed at the same time with a good part of the emotional values and the irrational nimbus that have been freed by the destruction or devaluation of now obsolete social structures.

In the third phase, as yet fully realized in only a few cases, but with tendencies clearly evident since about the time of World War I, the whole population seems already steeped in the spirit of industrialism. The old livelihood forms have lost their identity. They have become only job differences, while an ever larger part of personal life undergoes assimilation and homogenization. Occupations multiply in like degree, as tertiary activities increase in bulk and strictly productive employees fall numerically behind, in consequence of the mechanization still growing stronger and soon also of the automation of production processes. At present these people hardly constitute 50 per cent of all workers in most advanced countries. Since locational differences—urban or rural—are being smoothed out in their social effects, by the ever increasing opening-up of the rural districts to communication and traffic, at last there is left, as a socioeconomic differential in the population, almost no more than the difference of income, expressed in the scale and kind of consumption and degree of responsibility in the highly differentiated productive process.

Class conflicts have experienced a significant weakening in the crucible of the world wars and depressions and of the social processes that accompanied them. Productive capital has become largely anonymous, or collective, whether in corporate or state property. Everyone is a potential or actual shareholder, even if fictive as in the Communist system. The giant concerns or agglomerations of concerns are jointly managed by directors who are simultaneously employees. In public life the great interest groups, workers' unions, and professional organizations have become decisive, bringing their influence to bear on the political, economic, and even cultural level, so that the leadership in the finished industrial society lies in the hands of a many-membered hierarchy of managers with a completely fragmented responsibility that is often hard to comprehend.

The demand of the masses for a constant rise in, and simultaneous assurance of, standards of living, and the problem of the ever increasing industrial expansion compel the state, even where there is no revolutionary upheaval, to resort to massive intervention, and finally lead to a direct or socialistic economic and welfare policy.

In this phase, natural population increase slows down, since birth control now penetrates to the broad masses. But urban settlements continue to sprawl—less in the old than in the new industrial regions and around the great metropolises. This is mostly the result of the rise in the general living standard, which demands better housing and servicing than those offered by the antiquated and often run-down residential quarters of the inner parts of the cities. The degree of urbanization, already significant in the preceding phase, now attains tremendous proportions, around three-quarters of the whole population. Furthermore, the rural settlements increasingly take on an urban character, to the extent that differences in the way of life between city and country become obliterated.

The aspect of settlements—whether residential districts or business centers, industrial plants or traffic facilities—changes, since purely formal and representative principles are no longer followed as before, and one tries to build according to purpose and materials. A movement toward integral planning is growing, which takes in whole agglomerations and even whole regions and finally countries, and is supposed to arrange them according to their functional relations.

Like all great achievements of mankind the new industrial economy, barely born, immediately set out in its progress over the earth. The expansion first took place in spatial contiguity, covering continental Europe. But long before this was completed, it jumped over to North America, and later to Japan and other countries; today the whole globe is under its influence. Industrialization, having appeared in Western Europe with revolutionary force, was certainly bound to thrust all the other unprepared cultures into severe crises. The course and circumstances of industrialization and the penetration of industrial forms of society under such various natural and cultural conditions make up the essence of all subsequent world events and have called forth altogether different modifications of the various environments of the earth. Here, too, only some outlines can be drawn.

In Western Europe itself the stubborn survival of older ways in the cultural landscape, social order, and tradition considerably delayed and held back the full establishment of the industrial order in the form described. Until today, or at least up to the last world war, many of the values of the Europeans stemmed from craftsman, peasant, or even noble circles, and found their support in a cultural landscape rich in historical symbols. A good part of the creative power of the European spirit can be explained by this tension-laden atmosphere.

The tendencies of the new industrial civilization could assert themselves much more easily in North America and the other new lands of northwestern European, but not Mediterranean, colonization. This is understandable, for there existed by and large a cultural *tabula rasa,* or, rather, one was created by pushing away the natives; and in addition many immigrants, in search of freedom and success, embraced anything new more easily and strongly. Thus the third phase of the evolution came more rapidly and was more complete here. A strong agricultural sector is common to most of these new lands, but it reflects the rationalizing and mechanizing tendencies of the new age. As a consequence, the population of wide regions became stabilized at a stage of low density, while any further population growth is almost exclusively restricted to industrial districts and large cities. By no means minor problems arise from this "precocious" situation, which is probably what most sharply differentiates these new countries from Europe. The difficulty of exporting simultaneously both industrial and agricultural surpluses, familiar especially in North America, is just one of them.

The lands of old Mediterranean colonization, in which great masses of native or imported colored population have become more or less blended, behave toward industrialization like other old civilizations (including the Mediterranean one itself). They are heavily impregnated by rent capitalism—those of Spanish background more so than the Portuguese (especially Brazil) which were partly influenced by early productive capitalism—and the transformation is late and laborious. Those lands like Argentina, Uruguay, and others, which have experienced a recent and very mixed European immigration, hold a transitional position.

Scientifically, it is hardly justified to contrast the industrial economy and society of the Communist lands, primarily the Soviet Union, with "capitalist" industrialism as being fundamentally different in kind, as Pierre George does, for example.[55] Not only is the Marxist-Communist movement intellectually rooted in Western Europe, and its development intimately linked with the creation of industrial society, but also the goals and concrete results are essentially the same, at least for our purposes. Political means and with them certain forms of the collectivization of property, above all productive capital, are different, but on the whole they constitute only one case (though often an extreme one, indeed) in a many-graded series of manifestations that are all common and peculiar to industrial society and set it apart from older civilizations. There are some accessory traits, however, like the extensive use of compulsory labor (state-slavery), that recall more primitive stages in the development of mankind, but that also appears in a private, state-sanctioned form in certain early stages of productive capitalism. The severity inherent in the Soviet system, though it is democratic in form, can be explained partly from the special difficulties that faced the rapid building-up of an industrial society in an underdeveloped country, and also partly from the special traditions of the absolutism of the tsars, which was strongly influenced by the Orient. The doctrinaire rigidity of Marxism-Leninism makes it difficult to lead it onto the evolutionary path that has become characteristic for the more flexible systems of the Western industrial countries.

The situation of the great old civilizations, to whose self-conscious peoples the thoughtless designation "underdeveloped

[55] Pierre George, *Géographie sociale du monde* (Collection "Que sais-je?" [Paris: Presses Universitaires de France, 1952]).

countries" sounds unpleasant, is marked
by two great problems. On the one hand,
they have slipped into the "population
squeeze" situation[56] of the industrial world
under direct and indirect Western help,
without yet being industrialized, so that
their peasant masses go on multiplying beyond any bearable measure, and their living
standard, already low, drops critically. On
the other hand, the industrialization of
backward nations in a world dominated at
least economically by highly industrialized,
and still industrially expanding, powers becomes ever more difficult, even almost impossible by evolutionary means. Too many
problems, internal and external, must be
solved at one time. Any help from the outside runs the risk of being channeled
wrongly, and any internal measure needs
the support of many others presupposing
the greatest insight by the rulers and often
a readiness for considerable sacrifices on the
part of the ruling upper strata. The tradition of rent capitalism is not a favorable
foundation for this. It is understandable,
therefore, that the young generation is
often inclined toward revolutionary solutions.

We cannot take up the special problems
which are thrust upon the rest of the truly
underdeveloped societies by the impact of
industrialism.

Conclusion

Mankind has come a long way. This way
led it once—at a very low level of command
over nature, but endowed with the precious
gift of a unique capacity for adaptation—
to a scattering in small groups over almost
all the natural regions of the earth. This
was a long period of isolation and terrible
decimation of the little groups because of
their own ignorance and an often severe
nature. It led mankind to a differentiation
into the different races and primary cultures, but naturally did not favor the further development of their cultural patri-

[56] The population squeeze is due to the decline
of mortality while a high birth rate persists.

mony. Seen in the perspective of earth
history, more significant forward steps were
taken by man only recently. We have tried
to trace them and to sketch their significance from the geographic standpoint.

The basis of all higher evolution was
won by the conversion to food production
by plant cultivation and animal husbandry,
since a notable increase in the densities of
humans was made possible thereby. A free
clan-peasantry of various forms arose, in
the bosom of which, among relatively
crowded irrigation farmers, the beginnings
of lordly rule took place.

Overlordship took over a part of the
peasant's production in the forms of landlords' rent and made possible, through its
accumulation and the bringing together of
the work of dependent men, a raising of the
cultural level high above that of the peasant framework. Its achievements are the
state and the city as germ cells of all further development.

The ancient city is the birthplace of high
culture. It put the lordly rent system on a
commercial basis and thereby broke a path
for the spirit of acquiring wealth and for
rational thought, without seeking, however,
close connection with the productive process. Rent capitalism rose in this way. Ancient urbanism thus hampered seriously the
further development of its own economic
basis.

Up to that time, it seems, all the decisive
steps were made in the Near East, which
is revealed as the center of diffusion of the
older achievements.

In the ancient city of the Mediterranean
region, however, the basic and still valid
ideas of government and politics took form;
they can be regarded as a city-induced fusion of extremely ancient clan peasant ways
with the principle of lordly rule.

At last, there sprang up in the Occident,
on the basis of specific regional conditions,
productive capitalism, i.e., the deliberate
application of capital to raising productivity. Only on this foundation could the
modern industrial economy evolve which,
with all its accompanying features, has be-

come our fate. It was reserved to the Europeans to make into next-door neighbors the culture hearths of mankind so long largely wrapped up in themselves and turned away one from another, though indeed not out of contact—and thus to stir up problems and conflicts for the solution of which no way is yet in sight.

The span of civilization is too short for man's nature to have been able to change profoundly in the meantime; but we have to reckon with certain results of rapidly increasing domestication. The last phase revolutionized the cultural environment of man in a previously unheard of way, and clearly we stand today just at the beginning of further, still unheard of innovations. It seems that man is on the point of multiplying the reaction of his autonomously fashioned cultural environment upon his own nature, and subjecting to his will several life processes that heretofore were inaccessible to his influence. We may be awed before such possibilities of conquests and extensive dominance over nature. But nothing prevents our supposing that the life-instinct of our species, that has always carried on so far, will protect the species from being destroyed by its own unchained intelligence.

I. H. BURKILL

HABITS OF MAN AND THE
ORIGINS OF THE CULTIVATED
PLANTS OF THE OLD WORLD

I have been interested in the means of living that the jungle tribes of the East possess and in the Andamanese as among the lowest. They exist as neolithic relics and have survived because of the barrier that the ocean afforded, adjusting their numbers to their food supplies. Their antagonism to any who might intrude is so fierce that it has separated one tribe from another completely and led to the existence of several collateral languages within the islands. They hunt and they fish and are food-gatherers of all the vegetable stuff that they find edible. I have collected together the available information on this and find that the whole of it is derived from perennial plants, and that it comprises almost nothing which can be eaten without cooking—most of it not without cooking with wood ashes to make it such that even their inured digestions can digest it. One of their best foods is the tuber of *Dioscorea glabra* Roxb., for which they dig assiduously. Their improvidence is so great that if in past times the land held any tuber requir-

Reprinted, with permission of the author and publisher, from *Proceedings of the Linnean Society of London,* CLXIV (1951–1952), 12–42. The author is best known for his monumental *Dictionary of the Economic Products of the Malay Peninsula* (2 vols.; London: Crown Agents for the Colonies, 1955). The essay reprinted here was delivered as a "Hooker Lecture" on November 22, 1952. Mr. Burkill's work reflects several decades of research in southeast Asia. Now retired, he served for many years as director of the botanical gardens at Singapore and botanical secretary of the Linnean Society.

ing less digging, they must have destroyed it by over-exploitation. But today they make *D. glabra* a crop-plant to the small extent that the elders issue a taboo on the digging of the yams in the season of new growth, saying that the rain-god, Puluga, needs the yams at that season; and they issue a like taboo to protect the seed-crop of *Entada scandens* Benth. and the palm-cabbages of *Caryota*.[1]

Cousins of the Andamanese are the Semang of the northern forests of the Malay Peninsula. They are in a slightly worse position because they do not have access to the sea; but R. J. Wilkinson suggested that they had the resources of the shore until recent times.[2] They wander in family groups in the densest and most beast-infested forests, feeding on the tubers of wild yams and aroids, etc., and move forward at very short intervals as they exhaust the available food supplies. As with the Andamanese, their vegetable food is derived entirely from perennials. Now and then the fruiting of a wild durian tree or an unusual abundance of wild fruit introduces a halt of longer duration in which they clear the ground under the fruiting trees the better to get the falling fruit; but this is not tilling. If they venture to push a few sugar-

[1] Edward H. Man, *On the Aboriginal Inhabitants of the Andaman Islands* (London: Anthropological Institute of Great Britain and Ireland, 1932), p. 85.

[2] Richard J. Wilkinson, *A History of the Peninsular Malays with Chapters on Perak and Selangor* (2nd ed.; Singapore: Kelley & Walsh, 1920), p. 1.

canes into the soil, the wild elephants destroy them before their return.[3]

The Andamanese and the Semang are Negritos. There is no future for them; and their past has been millennial stagnation. The forest masters them; and in it they are in very truth agents with the wild pigs in the natural selection of the wild yams, maintaining to their' own disadvantage deep-rooting habits by destroying any variation towards surface-rooting and any diminution of protective nauseousness.

I would here point out that wild yams are basic among food plants of humid tropical forests; and that wherever such forests occur the genus *Dioscorea* is at home—a food in a raw state for such animals as can root for the yams, and a food after cooking, sometimes rather prolonged cooking and even tedious preparation, for Man, yet attractive enough for a score of species to have been taken into cultivation, some here, some there; but the Andamanese have been too witless. Yet I must put forward an excuse: *Dioscorea glabra* propagates itself by seed, which seed is certainly formed freely; but if it be sown, several years pass before there are tubers large enough for use; and it would indeed be asking much to ask one who has never tilled to conceive the idea that by tilling a harvest so remote could be of benefit. To the verdict—too witless—, extenuating circumstances may be admitted.

Perennials are collectively intractable. Tillage did not begin with them, but when intelligent men contacted annuals favorably prepared by Nature. This happened in several parts of the world, but undoubtedly earliest in southwestern Asia, where likewise was the first domestication of animals, the first urbanization, the invention of the wheel, and the first use of iron weapons.

[3] Father Paul Schebesta, who described these simple folk, sent me specimens of the wild Dioscoreas that they eat and I gather that it is every one available. [See his *Among the Forest Dwarfs of Malaya* (London: Hutchinson, 1929); first published as *Bei den Urwaldswergen von Malaya* (Leipzig: F. A. Brockhaus, 1927)].

It is generally agreed that Man, being at the time a food-gatherer, with hunting his most enterprising form of food-gathering, domesticated the dog as a companion in the hunt. After that there was a wandering to the New World which took the dog, but not habits of tilling. In the Old World Man proceeded to domesticate some of the animals that he hunted. They would be of similar size to his companion, the dog, and assuredly sheep or goats. Unfortunately the history of this event is difficult to piece together: but this fact is sure—that sheep never lived in forests but in open country where they sought security by agility on broken hillsides, upon mountains; but Man put an efficient protectiveness between them and any desire for mountains and grazed his flocks over hills and wide plains in southwestern Asia. Tillage dawned among these herdsmen of sheep at that time of the year when abundant spring pasture enabled them to dally and, dallying, to try to increase the supply of vegetation. The opportunity was created by Nature; she makes grass prairies where the summer rain is inadequate to maintain trees and creates conditions that favor annuals. It happened— I think no other verb than happen is appropriate—that Nature put in the way of these herdsmen annual grasses whose provision for survival lay (i) in the abundance of their output of seed, and (ii) which grew gregariously, so that when the seed was ripe and was plentiful it could be collectively harvested, and (iii) was edible. Moreover, the foliage before harvest time was good food for the sheep; and the seed after harvest was in an ideal condition for storage. It was impossible for Man to overlook the advantage of increasing the supplies of a grass so eminently desirable which, even if he were forced to move to other pasture too early for harvest, could be given over to the sheep. The double lien drew grasses into what I believe was the earliest sustained tillage in the world. The cultivation must have been slovenly in the extreme, as some is always. Gaedukevich describes Kirghiz of the Ust-Urt who, on finding a patch of bared silt, broadcast grain over it and then drive the sheep forward to trample it in.[4] The harvest must have been by plucking the individual spikes if large enough, or there might be found other ways; Pliny described the use of a comb for millet as customary in Gaul, and a famine-stricken native of India will harvest grass seed by sweeping with a winnowing basket or strip of cloth. Such ways of getting in the return are readily found. The habit of protecting the growing crop had to be acquired. That the tiller should be able to dally meant that he had to possess enough food on the hoof to be able to await his harvest. The all-compelling difference between him and the Andamanese lay in that he was a capitalist and secure.

It may be well to point out that there is a difference between a cultivated plant and a cultigen, that a cultigen carries in a heritable condition some character, qualitative or quantitative as we assess it, derived from cultivation, and that there is only one time in the life of a plant when a character can be impressed, namely the time when Man determines on his resowing. Therefore it matters greatly how often this time comes round—yearly or at wider intervals; and for two reasons, one, merely the arithmetic fact that in ten years an annual offers ten opportunities, but a perennial perhaps not more than one or even fewer; the other and overpowering reason, that Man, particularly early Man, might keep on one course if he had to repeat his sowing year by year, but was sure of losing direction when the occasions were more spaced. In fact Man drifted into establishing characters for his cultigens. What he did was to make a gift of free earth to a wild plant in the hope of a return; and with a good return he was induced to repeat; but on repetition the seed might come again from a wild source, so that he did no more than repeat the first experiment. It was only when he needed to keep seed from one generation

to another that a cultigen could be originated. That came with attempts to extend the range beyond the plant's natural limits, in which, really by accident, the essential isolation would be introduced. Acclimatization, the first property of a cultigen, could be induced according to the difference between the new and the natural habitat. It is always to be remembered in seeking for origins of cultigens how their chances of fixation are increased away from home.

A thought comes to mind here—a wild plant to be worth tillage straight from the wild stage had to be rather outstanding, or of a group of a few that were outstanding. Man must have worked on a narrow front.

As Man acclimatizes he selects unconsciously for simultaneous seed-bearing, for he tends not to harvest seed produced abnormally early and loses seed produced abnormally late. At the same time he unconsciously selects against shattering or scattering, for he loses the seed of plants which do this. By protecing his crop against birds which are deterred by awns, awns eventually cease to be important, and awned and awnless plants become equal contributors to his seed for resowing. The loose panicle, difficult for the bird to perch on, ceases to be an asset necessary for success. The process of acclimatization operated subconsciously.

The system of tillage now in mind began, as postulated, with cereals. Hehn, who became a great authority on the spreading of its plants into Europe, commented that when Man had established the habit of cultivating cereals, he would quickly pass on to cultivating pulses.[5] I agree. Meanwhile Man remained a food-gatherer of supplementary food, notably greens, which, when they were weeds, could be culled as well from tilled as untilled land, until they

[4] Henry Field and Kathleen Price, "Early History of Agriculture in Middle Asia," *Southwestern Journal of Anthropology*, VI (1950), 21–31.

[5] Victor Hehn, *Kulturpflanzen und Hausthiere in ihrem Übergang aus Asien nach Griechenland und Italien sowie in das übrige Europa* (7th ed.; Berlin: Gebrüder Bornträger, 1902), p. 210. [Published in English as *The Wanderings of Plants and Animals from Their First Home* (London: Swan Sonnenschein, 1888)].

became more easy to obtain from out of the crops than from elsewhere, whereafter they would be given a place of their own. Much has been made lately of "crops from weeds"; but every crop plant was a weed once. The interest is in discovering when they passed from weeds to crops. Of competition in the soil we know almost nothing,[6] but the experiments in competition of barley with weeds commenced by Dr. H. H. Mann and T. W. Barnes are a beginning.[7]

Plants accepted for cropping as greens would be such as matured among the cereals and pulses, and all the oldest would be short-lived. After the adoption of (i) cereals, (ii) pulses, and (iii) short-lived greens, it is by no means unreasonable to think that Man would grow (iv) oil-seeds such as the genus Brassica furnishes. But when he found it possible to live on the produce of one locality in a static way he would proceed to (v) what an agriculturist understands as "roots"; then (vi) herbaceous fruits, (vii) fibre and dye plants, and long afterwards (viii) woody plants, chiefly fruit trees, and (ix) various industrial plants. A large measure of urban development had to occur before the entry of group ix.

Immediately after the War of 1914–18 the Soviet Republics organized a great hunt for material for their domestic agriculture and put it under the direction of Professor N. I. Vavilov.[8] Vavilov wrote of it that it consisted of "numerous expeditions sent to different parts of the globe" and that they "collected an enormous amount of material." The seeds brought home were sown in experimental stations

[6] Sir Edward J. Russell, *Soil Conditions and Plant Growth* (8th ed.; London and New York: Longmans, Green, 1950), p. 492.

[7] H. H. Mann and T. W. Barns, "The Competition Between Barley and Certain Weeds Under Controlled Conditions," *Annals of Applied Biology*, XXXII (1945), 15–22, XXXIV (1947), 252–266.

[8] [For a convenient summary of his work, see "The Origin, Variation, Immunity and Breeding of Cultivated Plants: Selected Writings of N. I. Vavilov," translated from the Russian by K. Starr Chester, *Chronica Botanica*, XIII (1951), 1–366.]

through Russia and a vast herbarium built up for record and reference. There has never been and possibly may never be another effort of its kind on so large a scale. Its size prevented immediate fruition and some of the earlier published results bear the marks of preconceptions that invite criticism. Vavilov, who had travelled to gather material in Europe, Afghanistan, China, Abyssinia, North and South America, attended a congress in London in 1931 of the History of Science and Technology and read a paper entitled "The problems of the origin of the world's agriculture," wherein he stated that "there are seven fundamental independent world centers of origin of cultivated plants . . . chiefly confined to the tropical and subtropical mountain regions" and that these "have given rise to the whole world agriculture." Five of the centers are in the Old World and two in the New. He calls the five centers, Mediterranean, southwestern Asia, India (excluding from it the northwestern part), eastern and central mountainous China, and mountainous East Africa, chiefly Abyssinia. Four years after the Congress he varied his plan a little, dividing southwestern Asia into Near East and Central Asia, and cutting off from India a center which he called the Indo-Malayan center. (Fig. 1) His procedure for determining centers was to take a map, and to select the cultigens of importance, then to mark on the map where the recognizable races of these cultigens are found: where the marks lie thickest there is a center. The method he called the differential method. It has the fault of taking the whole of its evidence from the plants and disregarding the cultivator. The further claim that the centers are all in mountains embodies the fault. Every phytogeographer is aware that mountains are rich in species, richer than plains. This is explicable by the crowding of microclimates into mountains whereby the chances of survival of variants are multiplied. Useful and useless plants are subjected to the same opportunities; as they vary, so may their varieties be able to persist, but those

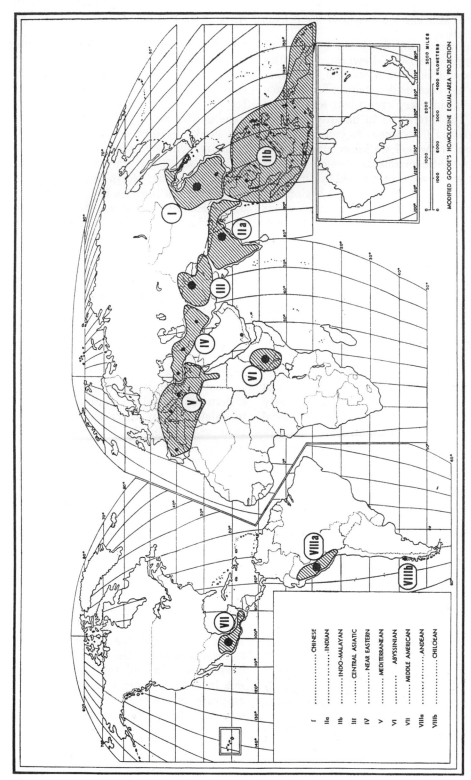

Fig. 1. World centers of origin of cultivated plants. [Redrawn from "The Origin, Variation, Immunity and Breeding of Cultivated Plants: Selected Writings of N. I. Vavilov," *Chronica Botanica*, XIII (1951), 22–23.]

of the useful plant do not become cultigens until man isolates them. And the persisting variability of cultivated plants in mountains is chiefly a consequence of incompetence in agriculture of the average mountaineer. Mountain chains are therefore a good field for the skilful plant-breeder to explore for new forms, but not a sure source for the world's cultigens.

The value of isolation is all-compelling. Natural geographic isolations have led to some of Man's greatest successes—cases in which Nature made the opening and Man succeeded. I illustrate this by a map of the distribution of the genus *Olea* with the area of the olive (*Olea europaea*) (Fig. 2). Man brought the olive forward in natural isolation, for as the map shows, its area is outside that of the rest of the genus. The date (*Phoenix dactylifera*) is extra-marginal to the inferior species of its genus. The fig (*Ficus carica*) is marginal within its great genus. The mango (*Mangifera indica*) has but one associated species of its genus in that part of India where it originated, inferior species being concentrated in Malaysia. The coconut palm (*Cocos nucifera*) developed far away from the rest of the genus *Cocos*. Man would not have spent millenniums in effecting so little ennoblement, if he had had greater isolation accompanying his effort. Man, as I see the problem, was more likely to succeed in making a cultigen on the margin of a mountainous area than within it: and the differential index is a pointer for the search of material for ennoblement.

I find it instructive to take the countries which Vavilov names as holding his "centers" and to make from them the map of Fig. 3. I have numbered the compartments so constructed from west to east, and their boundaries are political boundaries. It is axiomatic that if the political boundaries be firm, they represent cultural discontinuities, past or present, such as cannot but be barriers to the dispersal of cultigens. As Fig. 3 shows, the compartments make a belt across the map, the southern boundary of which is either sea or desert. A few words

on the recognition of the desert as a boundary are called for because there has been speculation on the degree in which a milder climate in the Sahara during the millenniums following the passing away of the Glacial Epoch would let economic plants migrate. Most particularly this speculation has turned on the value of the Nile Valley as a highway for migration. An increase in the severity of the desert must be admitted; and the problem becomes to ascertain conditions at a date when cultivated plants existed. Surely we may exclude any period before 8000 B.C. and almost as confidently any period before 7000 B.C. But certainly at 4000 B.C. the Nile Valley margin in Middle Egypt was not quite desert; hunters sought food on it, and that proves the presence of animals; and villagers made receptacles of ostrich eggs, which proves the presence of ostriches. But I can find no reason for thinking that cultivated plants passed from the Mediterranean margin to Guinea or from Guinea to the Mediterranean margin at any remote period. It may be pointed out that the northern sorghums were originated by tillers debarred from the Mediterranean by wide waterless country, who concentrated on them in the absence of cereals from beyond the sands. The Nile valley offers a more delicate problem; and the theory of some Egyptologists that the great reverence which Egypt showed for the land of Punt, i.e., the tropical south, rose from the rulers of historical Egypt having come thence, has been used in arguing that there was early contact. But Egypt's way thither was by sea: it left the Nile Valley near Thebes for the harbor of Kosseir, abreast of Thebes, and continued by coasting (see Fig. 6); by land great empty spaces separated Thebes from the mountains of Eritrea and Abyssinia. Petrie points to Kosseir as being on the way by which the ruling race would have come;[9] and if so, caution is certainly necessary in postulating prehistoric connec-

[9] Sir William M. Flinders Petrie, *A History of Egypt* . . . (6 vols.; London: Methuen, 1894–1901), I, 12.

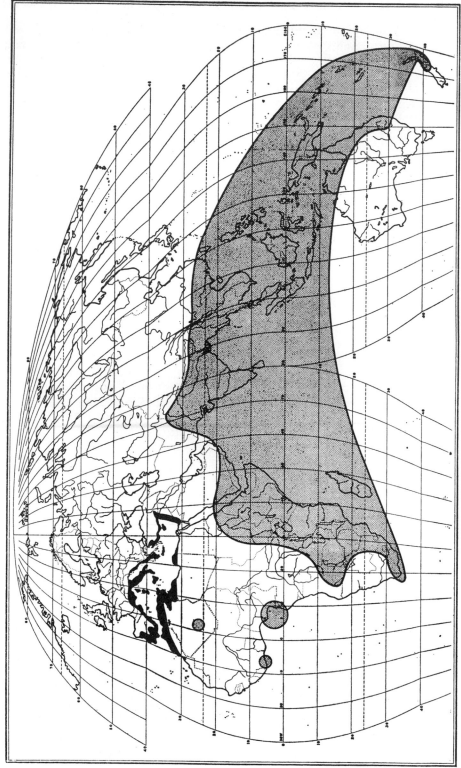

Fig. 2. Dispersal of the genus *Olea* in the world. *Olea europaea* in black; the rest of the genus within the shaded area. [Base map courtesy of Goode's Map Series, Department of Geography, University of Chicago.]

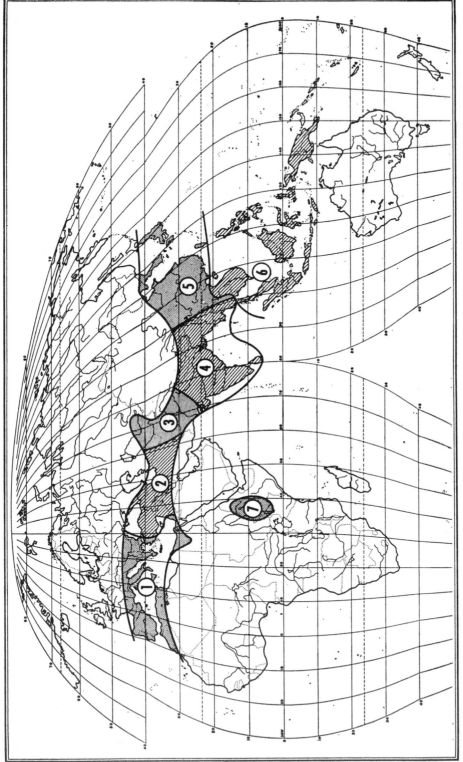

Fig. 3. Compartments of origination, being the political units named by Vavilov as holding his centers. [Base map courtesy of Goode's Map Series.]

tions up and down river. I shall later need to show that the way out of Africa for certain economic plants was across the southern end of the Red Sea to Arabia and not to Egypt.

I return to Fig. 3. The northern boundary of the belt is weaker than the southern by reason of gaps between the great moun-

whose revolutions in almost every period of history Egypt has humbly followed" can be applied to Egypt's crops, and Egypt must be assigned to the Near East instead of the Mediterranean. By a transfer of the partition there is left a more natural Mediterranean compartment. Vavilov's revision of 1936, whereby he recognized that the

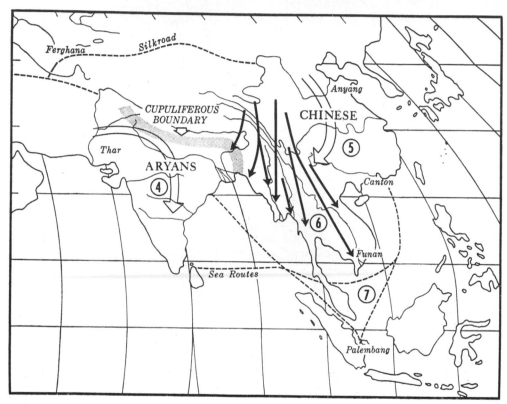

FIG. 4. A readjustment of Vavilov's compartments from India eastwards. The arrows show how the migration of semi-mongoloids separated the Aryans and the Chinese.

tains over which it passes. One gap, the wide gap between the Caucasus and the Himalaya, is partly blocked by deserts; that between the Alps and the Black Sea has been very penetrable, so that plants from the Near East could reach the uniform, fertile, easily tilled soils of the Danubian plains.

Of the north-to-south partitions, Vavilov lays down that between compartments 1 and 2 on the wrong side of Egypt. Gibbon's words "accessible only on the side of Asia

southwestern Asiatic center is appropriately divided into Near East and Central Asia or as I shall call it Inner Asia, is convenient. The two halves manifestly grew apart as Man became less nomadic. In an interesting contrast the components of the Mediterranean grew together as Man got control of the sea. Vavilov uses the Thar or Indian desert to delimit his Inner Asia towards India; it serves. His centers further east are unnatural and I have prepared a map (Fig. 4) to correct this. About

3000 B.C. there was a civilization in north-western India, the "Indus civilization," into which excavations at Mohenjo Daro and Harappa have given an insight. It was in touch with contemporary civilization at the head of the Persian Gulf. At the same period, according to the Chinese historians, nascent China was ruled by a king (2737–2705 B.C.) named Shennung—the name means divine laborer—who invented agricultural implements and taught tillage. The date is unreasonably late for a beginning of tillage in their part of the world, but could be a date for the introduction of metal tools, as copper and bronze were in contemporary use in the Indus civilization. The Chinese were able to keep their line of agriculture; but the Indus civilization went down. On its ruins came the Aryans. Carleton has written how greatly it would clarify history could we discover that Mohenjo-Daro was destroyed by the Aryans;[10] but all we know or surmise is that about 2000 B.C. and continuing later over a long time, pastoralists bringing their establishments with them wandered from the northwest into the Indus area and when they were numerous enough, being well led, say about 1500 B.C., they took possession of the land. It is surmised that they were led by a sort of knighthood, as were the Kassites, who took Babylon a little earlier. There is no indication that they brought new crops to India, but that they took over what was already there as they settled. In 1000 B.C. they were centered in the middle Indus Valley; then they overflowed around the north of the Thar into the Gangetic plains, perhaps having been strengthened, and if so by a more defined invasion than their original coming. By 250 B.C. their expansion had been so great that the emperor Asoka could set marks of his rule almost everywhere in India. I must define "India." I use the word for the whole triangle from the Cupuliferous boundary line (Fig. 4) to Ceylon. So delimited, it is very well charac-

terized both phytogeographically and ethnically. No species of the Cupuliferae nor of the Coniferae passes from the north and northeast into the triangle, nor does Mongolian blood, except by infiltration at the Bengal angle. Contemporary with the Aryan expansion there was expansion of the original China—a very gradual and massive expansion that swallowed up everything in front of it by taking possession of new plants and fitting them into a very sound form of agriculture.[11] By the time of Asoka the Chinese advance was approaching the present political limits of China and was shortly to break up the Shan kingdom of Yunnan; but that was not to close the gap between the Chinese and India, through which migrants came southwards at various times more or less as the arrows on the map indicate, and their invasions put buffers between the Aryans and Chinese which held their agricultural systems apart. The compartments that I recognize have accordingly been regrouped. India (4) is the triangle that I have defined; "China" (5) will be used for the area occupied by the Chinese; "Indochina" (6) for the land south of China and east of India; Malaysia and Polynesia (7) [not to be confused with the 7 on Fig. 3] complete the number of the compartments. A contrast of phytogeographic importance between India and China lies in that India receives its rain after its greatest heat, whereas China receives its rain with its greatest heat.

It has not escaped comment that the Mexican-Central American center (see Fig. 1) is on the same latitude as the belt across Asia; and the circumstance has been explained by suggesting that the latitude favored the energy of Man. The explanation is inadequate; forethought, rather than energy, was the outcome of the latitude. Fig. 3 shows that the latitude varies considerably; compartment numbers 1, 2 and 3 run together; and the others are

[10] Patrick Carleton, *Buried Empires: The Earliest Civilizations of the Middle East* (London: E. Arnold, 1939), p. 163.

[11] [See Owen Lattimore, *Inner Asian Frontiers of China* (New York: American Geographical Society, Research Series No. 21, 1940)].

scattered. This suggests that numbers 1, 2 and 3 possess something in common which the others do not possess. I explain the differences in this way: Man's greatest agricultural development began in numbers 2 and 3 when as yet they were not culturally diversified, and number 2 helped number 1 forward, it being easier for plants to spread east or west than north or south against the influences of heat and daylengths. China did much independent originating, the results of a struggle of a peculiar people against a peculiar climate; India and Indochina owed their differences to India coming under the influence of southwestern Asia, whereas Indochina was out of reach. Malaysia and the Pacific as laggards differ in degree from the last named. But the cornerstone everywhere was in what Nature gave for Man to use, and the first advance was made possible by pre-existing pastoralism. On realizing this, I was somewhat disturbed by the fact that there are pastoralists in Asia who refuse to till, for instance, Mongols whose complete refusal to add anything to their food of a vegetable nature seemed to deny that a pastoralist must start tilling when to do so is easy. There are abundant references in print to this Mongol habit; yet doubting their verbal accuracy, I consulted Dr. Joseph F. Rock who has travelled among the Mongols. I asked if his Mongols disregard the easy possibility of flavoring their mutton from the abundant wild species of the genus *Allium* on their lands, to which Dr. Rock said that they do not even use these. But again it is not the whole of the Mongols who refuse to cultivate. Riasanovsky records that among some of them provision is made for resuming possession of land tilled in the previous year.[12] I conclude that where riches are in the flocks, pride makes the richer ostentatious in not tilling.

There are no grounds on which it is possible to name one particular cereal as the first that Man adopted; but these as alternatives assuredly came through the first trials and were established early— the ancestry of the cultivated barley (*Hordeum vulgare*), the small spelt (*Triticum monococcum*), the line of the wheat beginning with emmer (*Triticum dicoccum*) or something like it, the common millet (*Panicum miliaceum*) and the ancestry of the foxtail millet (*Setoria italica*). Vavilov on his differential theory says that emmer took origin in Abyssinia and the two millets in the Far East. The statement is a declaration of their great variability in the places named; but it is easier to think that Abyssinia and the Far East received these crops than that they originated them.

Barley, when two-rowed, has an obvious parent in the wild *H. spontaneum* C. Koch, which grows in Palestine, Syria, Mesopotamia, Persia, Turkestan and Afghanistan, i.e. in the compartments of the Near East and Inner Asia. It is completely interfertile with *H. vulgare*. Barley, when six-rowed, could have come from *H. agriocrithon* Aberg, which apparently is not rare in Tibet and extends towards Turkestan, and may possibly be the six-rowed wild plant reported from Transcaucasia. Thus there is a home for barley where expected. When were the parents taken into cultivation?— the one or the other in time for the cultigen *H. vulgare* to have been made and spread before *c.* 6000 B.C., by which time it had become a crop of the Nile Valley and Mesopotamia. This date is more or less that of a burial at Silsile, which is a fair way up stream from Thebes[13] where it was found, as well as of ruins in Nippur in Babylonia. Written records show barley to have been the chief grain of Sumeria in the third millennium as it was of Upper Egypt. The grain was eaten either as porridge or as torrified groats.

[12] V. A. Riasanovsky, *Customary Law of the Mongol Tribes* (Harbin: "Artistic Printing House," 1929).

[13] G[eorg] Schweinfurth, "Über die Pflanzenreste," in Heinrich Schäfer, *Priestergräber und andere Grabfunde vom Ende des Alten Reiches bis zur Griechischen Zeit vom Totentempel des Ne-User-Rê* (Deutsche Orientgesellschaft, Berlin. Wissenschaftliche Veröffentlichung, VIII [1908]), 152–64.

Emmer (*Triticum dicoccum*) is sufficiently like *T. dicoccoides* Koernicke, to have been derived from it; and if so, would have been originated within the area—Palestine, Syria, Mesopotamia, Persia and Kurdistan, where *T. dicoccoides* is wild: this is contrary to Vavilov's theory of an Abyssinian origin. It was found with barley in the Silsile burial; and it became so much the leading cereal crop of Lower Egypt that the harvest month was named after it. Barley and emmer were possibly in equal demand in Egypt until the device of bread making towards 2000 B.C. threw barley into the background.

The small spelt (*Triticum monococcum*) occurs wild through Asia Minor as well as in the Crimea. Being second class, the better grains named above seem to have blocked its extension towards the south and southeast; but its cultivation spread north-westwards into Europe.

The foxtail millet (*Setaria italica*) is regarded as a cultigen derived from *S. viridis* Beauv., a grass of very wide dispersal from the Atlantic right across Europe and Asia. It would not be unnatural for Man to have taken the parent into cultivation in more than one part of the area, for he took into cultivation other species of Setaria in various places and ennobled them in a less measure; and origination in Inner Asia as one of the several is quite probable. Vavilov and Bukinich discovered that in Afghanistan today the grain of *Setaria viridis* is harvested.[14]

The common millet (*Panicum miliaceum*) has the same climatic requirements as the foxtail millet which, considered along with their very general companionship, suggests origination in the same part of the world; but no parental form has been proved. The nearest form is the Abyssinian *P. callosum* Hochst.; and this might

as easily be a derivative as otherwise. Vavilov is by no means the only botanist who has claimed an origination for it in the Far East; but origination in Inner Asia would afford a better center from which it could be dispersed. We know of it in cultivation in Europe and in China alike at early dates.

The millets are crops of shorter duration than the others. No one prefers them. Grain of millet is *arzan* in Persia where *arzani* means cheapness. Not long ago and possibly still, the grain was sold in Turkestan at only two-thirds of the price of wheat. The Russian soldier in Siberia is provided with it as rations because it is cheap. The poor in Peking abandon it as soon as they can afford a better grain. So from early days would Man tolerate it where the seasons or his habits demanded an early return; and I cannot but think that the opportunities of Inner Asia favored millets when those of Near Asia favored barley, emmer, and later the better wheats.

When in 250 B.C. the Babylonian priest Berosus wrote that barley grew wild in his country, he may have had *Hordeum spontaneum* in mind. When Pliny wrote that barley was the oldest (*antiquissimum*) of the cereals, he doubtless was echoing a popular belief. It was ancient anyhow; and to be already "barley" by 6000 B.C., the wild parents must have been taken by Man up to a millennium earlier.

It is easy to match pulses against the cereals named as the first of the Near East and Inner Asia; these come to the mind at once—the chick pea (*Cicer arietinum*), the garden pea (*Pisum sativum*), out of which the field pea (*P. arvense*) is a development, the broad bean (*Faba vulgaris*) and the lentil (*Lens culinaris* Med., or more familiarly *L. esculenta* Moench.). The chick pea had for its parent *Cicer pinnatifidum* Jaub. & Spach, which grows wild in Palestine, Syria and Asia Minor.[15] The origins of the others are not so straightforward.

[14] N. I. Vavilov and D. D. Bukinich, "Agricultural Afghanistan," Supplement 33 to *Bulletin of Applied Botany, Genetics, and Plant Breeding* [*Trudy po Prikladnoi Botanike, Genetike i Selektsii*] (Leningrad, 1929). In Russian with English summary.

[15] M. G. Popov, "The Genus *Cicer* and its Species," *ibid*, XXI (1928), 3–239. In Russian with English summary.

The lentil has been originated in more than one center. It is found wild in Asia with small seeds and wild in the Mediterranean with large seeds (the subsp. *L. macrosperma* of some writers). De Candolle regarded the latter as large seeded by ennoblement and wild by escape. On that view he could postulate a single center of origination, namely the Near East. Barulina in a very elaborate monograph gives as her view that the large seeded came into cultivation from a wild state in the Mediterranean.[16] The difference in size of seed can be remarkable: Vavilov took samples of 100 seeds from Spain, Algeria, and Italy which weighed respectively 9.0, 8.8 and 8.3 gm., whereas similar samples from Bokhara, Afghanistan, and India weighed respectively 2.6, 2.5, and 2.0 gm. The greater antiquity of tillage in Asia would indicate the first center to be in Asia; and Barulina suggests on Vavilov's differential method, northern Afghanistan for the center of origin, regarding which I would say that it is evidently very well suited to the climate and variable because it is carelessly cultivated. It is cultivated from the Atlantic to the Pacific, far beyond the area that can have been natural to it wild. Hehn shows on linguistic ground that the Lithuanians and Slavs received it from Italy and that in Asia it was passed northwards from Persia, for the Persians did not know it until they moved into Persia. Barulina points out that the plant shows many races in Greece, Italy, and Spain.

The garden pea originated in southwestern Asia; but its parentage still needs analysis. Govorov suggests three lines of ennoblement which he calls *Pisum sativum, P. arvense* and *P. asiaticum;*[17] but that this makes discussion of its origin easier or not is conjectural. He finds a differentiation center for all three in Afghanistan and a minor center in Abyssinia. As in the

lentil, so here the races of Asia are smaller seeded than the races of Europe.

The broad bean is the most intriguing of all the cultivated Leguminosae. De Candolle discussing it with great care was reduced to suggesting that a parent, at one time spread from the western Mediterranean to the Caucasus and northern Persia, had failed to hold its place save at the two extremities, so leading to a doubled ennobling.[18] Whether this suggestion be accepted or not, Man has been able to cause the Mediterranean line to have strikingly large seeds, while the Asiatic line has small seeds; and the seeds of the Mediterranean line are no longer pulse, but are eaten before maturity as greens. Vavilov gives these figures of the sizes of the seeds. 100 seeds from Spain, Tunis, and Italy weighed respectively 200, 171, and 130 gm. against the same number of seeds from Bokhara, Persia and India, 38, 30, and 20. He found his differentiation center in Afghanistan.[19]

I would mention yet two more pulses, the "Kesari" of India (*Lathyrus sativus*) and the French lentil (*Vicia ervilia*). The first is the cheapest pulse of India where it appears as a weed in barley crops in a way that seems to illustrate how pulse cultivation began. Vavilov suggests that its home is Afghanistan; De Candolle had suggested the country south of the Caucasus and Caspian. The other pulse, *Ervum ervilia*, is particularly a crop from the Caucasus to Afghanistan; and its use in Spain is a result of the Arab domination which began in A.D. 711. Campbell Thompson suggests that it was the *se-sis* of Sumeria.[20]

It is rather difficult to point with confidence to the plants that were in demand as greens among the first cultivators. This class, greens, covers all plants that supply

[16] Helena Barulina, "Lentils of the U.S.S.R. and of Other Countries," Supplement 40 (1930) to *ibid*. In Russian with English summary.

[17] L. I. Govorov, "The Peas of Afghanistan," *ibid*, XIX (1928). In Russian.

[18] Alphonse de Candolle, *Origin of Cultivated Plants* (New York: D. Appleton, 1885), p. 316.

[19] N. I. Vavilov, "Studies on the Origin of Cultivated Plants," *Bulletin of Applied Botany* . . . , XVI (1926), 5–248, ref. to 129. In Russian with English summary.

[20] R. Campbell Thompson, *A Dictionary of Assyrian Botany* (London: British Academy, 1949), p. 102.

from vegetative parts above ground, tender tissues, such as young leaves and stems, young fruits and immature seeds; and the sources are exceedingly numerous. Ochse enumerates 298 species whose leaves are eaten in Malaysia, chiefly in Java, mostly when very young.[21] When alternatives are so numerous, and supplies are available from wild plants, where is the inducement to cultivate? Early Man would be in no haste to extend his small plots if the open field satisfied his needs; but in a curious way suspicions are aroused that some of the greens of the Near East were not taken into cultivation as greens but as oil-seeds. Lettuce is among them. It is generally accepted that the cultivated lettuce (*Lactuca sativa*) had its origin in the Near East from *L. scariola* L. But no one cultivates the latter for the sake of its leaves; however, it is a subordinate oil-seed today in parts of Africa. If we infer, as is reasonable, that when the origination of lettuce began its parental form was already cultivated, then it was cultivated for its seeds.

The cress that we eat in mustard and cress is from an oil-seed plant (*Lepidium sativum*) of the same part of the world. Brassicas store oil in their seeds and the young leaves can be used as greens; the oil might well have been the cause of their cultivation. There is no natural connection between carrying oil in the seed and producing an abundance of leafage; but cultivation pointed in the two ways and the oils are edible oils.

Spinach (*Spinacea oleracea*) and the leafy beet (*Beta vulgaris* var. *cicla*, or near it) entered into Man's tilled plots in this part of Asia. High temperatures force beets to flower; lower temperatures lead to overwintering with a swollen root. Spinach and beets are sufficiently alike to have had their names confused when they were transmitted eastwards which would not have happened if the root-forming beet had been

transmitted.[22] Laufer thought that the leafy beet had been carried to China by Arabs,[23] and if so, they, sailing from Persian ports, would have the leafy beet. A leafy beet diffused into India where Roxburgh, finding it, called it *B. benghalensis*. Endive (*Cichorium endivia*) and chicory (*C. intybus*) were ennobled, the last partly, in the Near East; and endive seems to have furnished the "bitter herbs" of the Jewish Passover. The cucumber (*Cucumis sativus*) and the melon (*C. melo*) had ennoblement also: there would be a time when the melon had not become sweet.

I turn to the genus Brassica, great in the service of Man for its seeds, its leaves, and its swollen tuberous stems or roots; and again as the cauliflower for its inflorescences. This polymorphy is associated with chromosome dissimilarities; and the interspecific sterilities resulting, by means of the isolation of species that they produce, have been invaluable to Man in his work of ennobling.

Raphanus, without chromosome dissimilarities, serves Man like Brassica, yielding oil, greens and roots, but without the striking polymorphy. *Camelina* and *Eruca* yield oil and greens.

I think it significant that the two Brassicas which particularly supply greens are at home where they get sea winds, *B. oleracea* by the Atlantic and *B. chinensis* by the Pacific. The place of *B. juncea* is midway; and it is the most tropical; and as such is rather widespread in Africa. It is pungent in its wild states as a defence against herbivores; but a double boiling enables Man to remove enough of the pungency for use as food; and, submitting to that extra trouble, he has found it worth while to ennoble it in southwestern Asia. It has the chromosome number, $n = 18$, and meeting *B. chinensis* which has the chromosome number $n = 10$, the two could

[21] J. J. Ochse, *Vegetables of the Dutch East Indies* (Buitenzorg, Java: Archipel drukkerij, 1931).

[22] Berthold Laufer, *Sino-Iranica: Chinese Contributions to the History of Civilization in Ancient Iran* (Chicago: Field Museum of Natural History, Publication No. 201, 1919), p. 395.
[23] *Loc. cit.*

not cross; and *B. juncea*, diffusing eastwards into the country of *B. chinensis*, has
been accepted greedily by China and grown
without confusion with *B. chinensis*. *B.
chinensis* meanwhile has been broken (imperfectly) into the microspecies *B.* subsp.
chinensis, *B. pekinensis* and *B. nipposinica*
which so freely intercross that it is only by
Man's action that they are kept apart. On
the western side of *B. juncea* the arrangement of ten chromosomes is met with again,
the closely allied species, *B. campestris* and
B. rapa, having it. It is evident that they
had a common origin and that it was on the
less tropical side of *B. juncea*, for *B. campestris* extends as a wild plant into Siberia.

The early cultivators must have been
considerably favored by Nature's imposition of the isolation preventing crossing
with *B. juncea* and it has to be added, with
B. napus; for the chromosomes in *B. napus*
are $n = 18$, as in *B. juncea*. The separation of *B. rapa* from *B. campestris* must be
attributed to Man. De Candolle wrote
"when the root or lower part of the stem
is fleshy, the seed is not abundant." [24] I
am uncertain if that is so pronounced that
Man, finding his seed-crop diminished
when he ennobled for roots, would be led
into the channels dividing rape from turnips; but it might be so. The diverging
must have been started in southwestern
Asia and both lines found their way
through *B. juncea*, diffusing independently
towards the East and producing these two
parallels: (*a*) while the rapes were being
brought forward in the West and being
worked up into a line which today ends
in "Colza," working up in the East was
leading to the "Sarson" of India and its
like; (*b*) while the turnip was being
brought forward in the West—brought forward early and so effectively that Pliny
could write that it came third in importance in Italy after the vine and corn—in
Asia eastern turnips were getting character
and, thanks to their cold-resistance, a com-
parably important place; turnips, for instance, are today the winter vegetable of

[24] De Candolle, *op. cit.*, p. 36.

Tibet. When they reached China, it would
be found that they crossed with *B. chinensis*, but Chinese horticulture was on their
arrival efficient enough to see to that.

In Europe the possession of turnips did
not preclude ennoblement for tubers of *B.
napus*, nor did it in the East; for in the
West the Swede was extracted and in the
East the Pak-choi (Bhutia rai of the Himalaya). Southwestern Asia seems to have
been the eastward limit of the area over
which *B. oleracea* developed; but its chief
ennoblement must have been in the Mediterranean and within reach of the Atlantic
winds. Pliny wrote of cabbages heavy
enough to break a cottager's table: I should
like to know if the enormous cabbages reported from Manchuria[25] are produced by
the favoring of winds from the sea.

The radish (*Raphanus sativus* L. sensu
latissimo) is of so many forms that taxonomists easily devise subspecies and discover ways in which demands can be met
that parents should be forthcoming in lands
from the Atlantic to the Pacific. As in Brassica so in Raphanus, ennoblement has resulted in oil and tuber being alternative
objectives. Europe, at one time found the
oil worth producing, but does so no longer.
Europe at one time was interested in raising bulky radishes for food, but now uses
little radishes for their condiment value.
The bulky radishes hold their place firmly
in tropical Africa, India, and China; and
the leaves serve as greens. Such must have
been the radish which Khnema Khufu, the
Cheops of Herodotus, supplied to the workmen who built his pyramid, the greatest
pyramid in Egypt, *c.* 2780 B.C.[26] The record indicates an importance like that which
Pliny attributed to the turnip in Italy
nearly three millenniums later. The origination of this certainly bulky radish must
have been in the Near East and nearby
part of the Mediterranean; and the Latin
name *radix syria* was an appropriate one.

[25] Sir Alexander Hosie, *Manchuria: Its People,
Resources and Recent History* (London: Methuen,
1901), p. 196.
[26] Herodotus, *History* II, 125.

The Japanese microspecies *R. raphanistroides* Sinsk., has had its origin in a Japanese wild form.

The Near East and the Mediterranean together have provided four other related sources of oil, *Brassica nigra* Koch, *Sinapis alba* L., *Camelina sativa* Fries, and *Eruca sativa* Lamk. It is interesting that Man found Nature to provide all these in the one part of the world just as she provided him with a group of cereals in another part, but not really surprising that he should adopt for use a group at a time, and sort them out later in tillage.

The dwellers in the Near East came to demand oil in considerable quantities. The records of production-control by Assyrian and Babylonian kings and, later, of the maintenance of public baths in the cities and towns where all comers oiled themselves profusely, suggest that the land could not produce enough.

Sesame (*Sesamum indicum*) and the castor oil plant (*Ricinus communis*) seem to have been welcome when they reached the East. The latter was already in Egypt in the time of the Badarian civilization (between 4000 and 3200 B.C.) and three millenniums later Herodotus found its oil to be used as an unguent in the marshes of the Nile.[27] Sesame had reached Sumeria by the time of the third dynasty of Ur (say *c.* 2350 B.C.), and is recorded as *se-gis-mi*, after which date it becomes of frequent mention in the clay tablets that have been read.[28] The castor-oil plant, very variable in Africa, has either varied since arrival in Europe and Asia or there have been introductions of variety after variety. Persia holds a curious small seeded form.

The several valencies of the Brassicas— for greens, oil, tubers—have carried my narrative away from greens to oil-seeds, but I return to give a place to the onion (*Allium cepa*) which combines the qualities of greens and condiment and is the best of a group of greens with alliaceous flavor. The genus *Allium* extends from the Atlantic across Europe and Asia, south to Abyssinia, and is in America. Garlic, leek, and chives are all traced with ease to wild sources, but not the true onion, which seems to have been brought to the Near East from deep in Asia. A cold spell is good for it and flower-formation needs long daylight; its home moreover had droughts, for it guards itself against them. It would get these conditions in, say, Dahuria which is regarded as the home of chives (*A. fistulosum*); and we may assume that it was brought out of Inner Asia to the Near East where first we hear of it. Khnema Khufu supplied it to his laborers along with the radishes and garlic (*A. sativum*). The leek (*A. porrum*) has been proved in Assyria from about 1950 B.C.;[29] but all of these species had undoubtedly been already long in cultivation.

There is a little interest to be got regarding fibre plants by reading Herodotus' account of the way in which the contingents in Xerxes' vast army were clad when Greece was invaded by them in 480 B.C.[30] Nearly all of them were clad in skins; only the Assyrians were in linen and the Indians in cotton. The cotton bush had been brought to Assyria by Sennacherib about 694 B.C., but had not displaced linen.

The cotton bush is the first woody plant that I have had cause to name in this gathering together of the early assets of southwestern Asia. The Bible frequently refers to "the field," meaning the agricultural land which was not fenced, and then again to the orchard which was fenced. That conveys a distinction between the herb and the tree, and it, indeed, relates to two distinct cultivation techniques: in the field the plant was sown and the harvest was gathered en masse; in the orchard the individual was treated as such, was planted by itself and was propagated in a very large measure asexually. This had two results: Man learned much about the ways of life of his woody plants, but lost a large proportion of his opportunities for selection

[27] *Ibid,* II, 94.
[28] Thompson, *op. cit.,* pp. 98, 101.
[29] *Ibid,* p. 52.
[30] *History* II, 61–92.

through seed: his best chance of advance with trees was by search in the countryside for something that Nature had to give that was better than what he already had, and to take it into his care. Apart from the intensity of the search, he was in the position of advancing more slowly with the woody than with the herbaceous plants: we can extend beyond the word woody and say "more slowly with the perennials than with the annuals."

Possibly the fig (*Ficus carica*) was the first tree to be cultivated in the Near East and it is likely that Man obtained more horticultural skill by attention to it than by anything else. It was manifestly very well adapted for experiment; but it is useless to guess when he began with it.

While the Syrian was practising grafting fig trees, his neighbor to the south was multiplying the date palm by suckers from ground level and learning that they in time gave fruit exactly as the parent. Both Syrian and Arabian were making curious discoveries in pollination which I must pass by. Then wine-making was invented in southwestern Asia which brought the grapevine (*Vitis vinifera*) from the position of a forest fruit to be had in season to something to be raised in quantity; and it was amenable to multiplication by cuttings. It is significant that when the knowledge of wine-making came to the Greeks they said, "we have that plant and call it ampelos" and when it came to the Latins, the Latins made the same remark substituting *vitis*, with the same meaning as *ampelos*, "twiner".[31] And wine-making brought the grapevine within the orchard fence.

I have tried to show that Man owed the locality in which he initiated tillage of cereals to Nature's offer of proper materials; and I wish to show that the generosity of Nature led to the promotion of fruit-culture in the same quarter. Vavilov has written enthusiastically of the richness of the

forests in the Caucasus and the Kopet Dagh in woods wholly of wild pears and apples or of other trees that could be parents of most of the European fruit trees. These inviting regions are not remote from Mesopotamia. Sargon of Akkad, who reigned *c.* 2870, made an expedition over the Taurus and brought back desirable trees;[32] Queen Shub-ad of Ur was buried (before 2600 B.C.) in a bonnet adorned by models in gold of pears and pomegranates; and no doubt there was a lively interest in cultivating desirable fruit in the Euphrates plains in the third millennium B.C. from times before. Later, so we read, Menush, a king of Haldia (near Lake Van, Kurdistan) conducted water by a canal, planting its margins with fruit trees; and we are told of the tree plantings of great Assyrian despots of the 8th and 7th centuries B.C., Tiglath-Pilezer, Sennacherib, and Ashur-bani-pal; and there is a despatch in existence of Darius, son of Hystaspes, King of Persia 521–485 B.C., to an official named Gadates stationed among the Greek colonies in Asia Minor, congratulating him on his "care of the plants from beyond the Euphrates." Xerxes, the son of Darius, and Cyrus, the claimant of the Persian throne in 401, were also great tree planters. They could not have been if the material had not been handy in the country to their north. Nature had so worked there that many trees had water-storing tissue about their growing ovules; which, when the ovules had finished growing, could be used to promote seed-dispersal; and the trees with that purpose had given origin to fleshy fruits of which a rather striking assemblage was available. It rested for someone to explore it; and the kings about Mesopotamia were induced to do that.

Their fruit trees had become well distributed in the Near East when the Romans needed to send administrators to govern the lands surrendered to them on the overthrow of Mithridates (66 B.C.); and the administrators took a pride in bringing some of the

[31] W. T. Thiselton-Dyer, "Flora," in Leonard Whibley (ed.), *A Companion to Greek Studies* (3rd ed.; Cambridge: Cambridge University Press, 1916), p. 61.

[32] C. Leonard Woolley, *The Sumerians* (Oxford: Clarendon Press, 1929), p. 79.

fruits to Rome. At this time Varro said Italy had become an orchard. Though Darius was master of a part of India and Xerxes drew troops from India, no Indian fruit trees are known to have been brought by the Persian rulers to their own country.

In central Europe "we find everywhere evidence of the arrival towards 4000 B.C. from the East of a short-headed race and of human settling through the forest region on the sides of lakes and steppes which expose the first signs of agriculture and pastoralism."[33] All that the settler grew is not demonstrable; but very patient study of old inhabited sites in Switzerland and elsewhere enables us to name plants grown in the third and fourth millenniums by identification of their seeds from the mud.[34] Most of the identified seeds are of wild plants natural to the neighborhood; a minority were cultivated. Barley was grown in three forms; wheat in three forms, emmer and small spelt and the two millets, *Panicum miliaceum* and *Setaria italica,* the broad bean, the pea and the lentil. Of apples there were two sizes, and it has been suggested that one of them was cultivated, though that seems questionable. Excluding the apple all the cultivated plants were annuals.

It is somewhat astonishing how little we know of contemporaneous cultivation in the Mediterranean region. Agriculture there was, and trade which carried metal tools about. From Coon's *Races of Europe*[35] I have borrowed a map, which he zoned in half-millenniums, and I have ruled on it an arrow to indicate the migration of the round-headed folk who brought the first signs of agriculture. This line is beyond the area of contemporaneous use of metals. It is proved that emmer was the cereal of Italy in the second millennium B.C., and as just

mentioned, it was a cereal of the Swiss lake dwellings in the third millennium. The curved arrow on the map is the suggested course by which emmer reached the Swiss lakes, Greece being off it. Greece is a country poor in corn land and indeed imported corn in classical times, paying for it in wine and oil; and if Greece had emmer early, it was probably obtained from Thrace, where, as probably also in the Swiss lakes, it had been preceded by millets. At 400 B.C. the classical Greeks were very well aware of neighbors towards the north with a way of feeding unlike their own; they being the Scythians who fed on millet; and the habit seemed to the Greeks strange enough for comment. Xenophon, returning with "The ten-thousand," recorded falling in with it at the western end of the Black Sea. Herodotus, home from Babylon, told his countrymen that Scythians and their neighbors on the north of the Black Sea, though they had wheat (this would be emmer), ate millet. The attitude of the Romans towards the millets was like that of the Greeks; they looked down on millet-eaters and knew the Gauls to be such, but it happened to be a Greek who recorded this—Polybius, carried to Rome as a hostage in 167 B.C. and sent with the other hostages taken at the same time to the Etruscan frontier next to the Gauls, though later allowed to reside in Rome. He tells that with his own eyes he had seen an abundance of millet and that the transalpine Gauls grew it likewise. Julius Caesar sent a lieutenant, Tribonius, to besiege Massilia (Marseilles) in 49 B.C.; and it is recorded that the garrison was reduced to feeding on old millet and spoiled barley. Strabo, the geographer (56 B.C.– A.D. 24), recorded that the Iberians of France, living between the Garonne and the Pyrenees, raised millet as their universal grain. These references show that crops of it bordered the Mediterranean within which it was refused; but better grain was diffusing through the millet and Julius Caesar had no difficulty in getting in Britain on his first visit (55 B.C.) the corn that he demanded. Thereafter the Romans insisted on

---

[33] Fritz Kern, "Die Rassen in der Vorgeschichte," *Archiv für Rassen- und Gesellschafts- Biologie,* XXII (1929), 199–205.

[34] A convenient list of them appears in Elisabeth Schiemann, *Entstehung der Kuturpflanzen* (Berlin: Gebrüder Bornträger, 1932), pp. 22–23.

[35] Carleton S. Coon, *The Races of Europe* (New York: Macmillan, 1939).

Britain raising wheat and supplied it to their armies on the Rhine. I have mentioned earlier that no one eats millet in preference to wheat; but cultivators may be obliged by climate or their own habits to grow millet rather than wheat, and the soil of the Upper Danube is a sign that they brought it also. The garden pea, the broad bean, and the lentil, demonstrated to have been in the possession of the dwellers by the Swiss lakes, could have travelled as emmer probably did. Having reached the

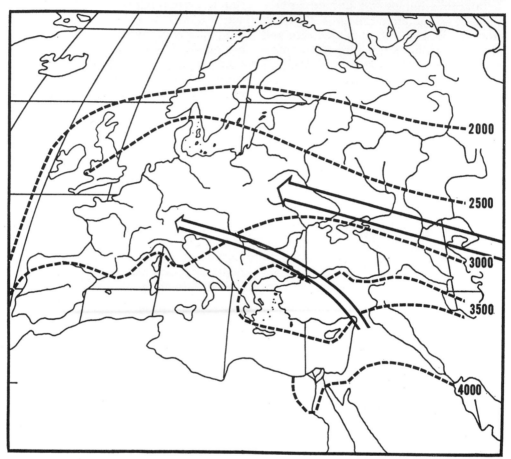

FIG. 5. Europe zoned in half-millenniums by the spread of metals, with one arrow to indicate the direction of the movement of round-headed migrants from Asia to central Europe, and a second arrow suggesting the diffusion of Emmer from Syria to central Europe. [The delimitation of the zones is derived from C. S. Coon's map of "Neolithic Movements and Chronology" in *The Races of Europe* (New York, 1939), 80–81.]

millet belt about the Mediterranean must have existed by the cultivator's will, say by his reaction to something in the climate, for the only part of Italy where millet growing ruled has the climate of central Europe.

If we allow that it was the migrants from the East who brought millet growing, then the presence very early of *Cannabis* in the edge of the Alps, these were in a position to descend Italy and do this long before there was shipping enough to annul the Adriatic as a barrier. This came about towards 750 B.C. A little earlier Carthage had been founded, and the Phoenicians in time took to the western Mediterranean the plants that Syria had. They took, for instance, the pomegranate which became *punica* in Latin because Italy received it via Carthage. Cato, trying to drive the Romans to make war on Carthage, held up in the senate a fresh fig with "see how near our enemy is that we can obtain this from him." And the grapevine was established in Morocco with great success. There was written a book on the agriculture of Carthage which is lost, and there is no knowing what more they took; and it was left to the Syrians serving under the Arabs after Spain was invaded in A.D. 711 to cultivate many eastern plants in Spain which they knew there under Arabic names.

The sugar cane was brought by them in A.D. 714, and probably *Colocasia esculentum*.[36] Both of these had had to travel from India to Syria and Egypt and had reached the eastern Mediterranean about the beginning of our era. The eggplant (*Solanum melongena*) and the carob (*Ceratonia siliqua*) were others.

Sir William Thiselton-Dyer did a great service for my subject when he made compendia of all the economic plants referred to in Greek and the Latin classics.[37] The frugality of the Greeks, as he comments, caused every possible native plant to be used as food, and an insipid herby diet demanded an abundance of condiments to help it down. The Greeks resorted to the onion firstly but, besides, to many labiates, cruciferae, and umbelliferae, such as were readily obtained from the fields, and if brought into cultivation were only slightly ennobled. In Italy there was likewise an extensive diet of greens. Horace mentions boiled mallows and boiled nettles. Other herbs supplying spinach-like dishes were *Valerianella olitoria*, purslane (*Portulaca oleracea*), alexanders (*Smyrnium olusa-*

trum), *Eruca sativa*, and species of *Rumex*, which have not or have scarcely been ennobled.

The Roman walled-in garden held greens that were better but had not come from far away;—leek, cabbage, sea kale, chicory, globe artichoke, etc. Thiselton-Dyer remarked that the Mediterranean had made its own greens.

The Roman occupation of Gaul brought about a head-on collision between the indifferent cultivation of the Germans with their millet, and the Roman cultivation. The Romans compelled the Germans to raise their own resources, taught them to eat cabbage and take to many southern herbs. It is only necessary to scan the following list of plants of German gardens with names in German from the Latin to see this: the garden pea, lentil, parsley, onion, beetroot, caraway, radish, horse-radish, mint, coriander, chervil, lovage, lavender, penny-royal, lettuce, fennel, aniseed, asparagus; and, says Hehn, after naming the above, with their origins, "there are many more." [38]

In so far as it is reasonable to believe that millet growing was brought from Inner Asia to central Europe, it is reasonable to ask if it could have been taken in like manner from Inner Asia to northern China. An early importance of millets in northern 'China is proved in various oblique ways. The reputed founder of the Chou dynasty (1122 B.C.) is given a name which is millet deified. The oracle bones excavated at Anyang (for its position see Fig. 4) ask if the millet crops will be good, the period being late in the second millennium B.C. The ancient ceremony, the origination of which is attributed to Shen-nung (2737–2705 B.C.), of sowing Five Grains is usually found to include the millets as two of the five; but apparently there was greater sanctity in the number being five than in their precise nature. A demonstration of the continuing in favor of millet lies in the great value put on the millets still by the thousands of Chinese who live from hand to mouth. The great millet or Kaoliang, a species of sor-

[36] I. H. Burkill, "The Contact of the Portuguese with African Food Plants," *Proceedings of the Linnean Society of London,* CL (1938), 84–95, ref. to 85.

[37] The first was published in Whibley's *Companion to Greek Studies,* pp. 42–68; the second in John E. Sandys (ed.), *A Companion to Latin Studies* (3rd ed.; Cambridge: Cambridge University Press, 1921), pp. 66–89.

[38] Hehn, *op. cit.,* p. 494.

ghum, was not in China then. I think that the original two millets reached China very early from Inner Asia and were extensively ennobled in China. I do not add the following as proving how they came, but call attention to Baron von Richthofen's theory that the Chinese had come into their country from Khotan, that is by the way in which the millets could have come.[39]

As the soil of An-yang has provided hemp seed; and as *Cannabis sativa* is a native of Inner Asia, so its presence along with millets suggests the millets' travelling.

When the Chinese started cultivating for cereals, there was an indigenous pulse, *Glycine hispida* Maxim, volunteering in their fields, ready for adoption as a crop which indeed it became and, ennobled to *G. soja,* proved so satisfying that its name in Chinese came to mean pulse.

The Chinese received other cereals and pulses from southwestern Asia before there is any record of their travel, for it cannot have been long before they had wheat and barley, the broad bean, garden pea, and lentil. It has been suggested that they received rice from the south at a very early date, the evidence being the pitting of the surface of an old piece of pottery;[40] but it is difficult to accept the dates put forward. Among the bones unearthed at An-yang are in small number those of the water buffalo which in domestication is the beast of heavy plowing as in water for rice; but it would be rash to insist on the possession of rice from the possession of the buffalo.

The center of Asia bred nomads; and they hemmed in the Chinese on the west and, moreover, preyed on them. The sea confined the Chinese on the east, and adventurers to Japan merely added Japan to the area of Chinese economy without making room for Chinese. They tried expansion northwards into Ordos, but could not

feed their colonists. The only opening for them was an overflow southwards. This considerable confinement resulted in the agriculturally very efficient Chinese developing autochthonously—not so much at the cereal or even the pulse level, as from the greens level of the sequence. The originality of the development was consequential on the very unkind climate of the northern spring, at which time very cold and very dry winds sweep down from the cold pole in eastern Siberia and prevent the renewal of growth in the vegetation, while an enduring grey dust-storm shuts the sun out. In 1000 B.C. the Chinese were fighting their way southwards. In 600 B.C. they had crossed the Yang-tze Kiang, having already the stamp of originality deeply impressed on their feeding. As they advanced southwards they absorbed the crops of a less unkind climate in a degree that makes 600 B.C. the end of an epoch.

The Chinese had taken to eating seedlings, as we in spring eat mustard and cress, chiefly those of their pulses. The soya bean is one; others that they eat today include the broad bean, *Vigna sinensis, Phaseolus aureus* and other species of that genus; then outside the pulses, seedlings of the Labiate *Perilla ocimoides,* of the Composite *Aster indicus,* and of the Polygonaceae of both species of *Fagopyrum;* there are others. I was astonished to observe in the central market in Shanghai how much of the Shepherd's purse (*Capsella bursapastoris*) and *Medicago denticulata* is consumed; but these are not cultivated plants: I introduce their names only to illustrate the intensity of the need in March for any form of edible growing stuff. Of cultivated plants they eat large quantities of the new shoots of *Chrysanthemum* as we eat Brussels sprouts; and bulbs of *Lilium tigrinum* and allied species.

In the springtime of the year before the Japanese spring festival has come, the Japanese make use of the petioles and new leaves of *Petasites japonica* and *Oenanthe stolonifera,* the tender shoots of *Aralia cordata,* which plants may be called semi-cul-

[39] Ferdinand von Richthofen, *China: Ergebnisse eigener Reisen und darauf gegründeter Studien,* (5 vols.; Berlin: D. Reimer, 1877–1912), I, 340 ff.
[40] Johan G. Andersson, *Children of the Yellow Earth: Studies in Prehistoric China* (London: K. Paul, Trench, Trübner, 1934), p. 186.

tigens, and of *Alliaria wasabi* (*Wasabia japonica*), a not unpleasantly pungent vegetable.

The East has done its utmost to make *Brassica chinensis* into the best of cultigens and split it into several microspecies only held apart by cultivation methods.

Nothing proclaims the originality of Chinese agriculture more than their resort to silk as a fibre. They possibly adopted *Abutilon avicennae* as their first fibre plant, and silk, a luxury fibre, not until long after, when they were already cultivating the mulberry and many fruit trees. The excellence, today, of certain of their fruits shows that they developed much horticultural skill, which they applied effectively to the persimmon (*Diospyros kaki*), the jujube (*Zizyphus jujuba* Lamk.), the peach (*Prunus persica*), the apricot (*Prunus armeniaca*), and the walnut (*Juglans regia*). The Chinese were fruit tree-minded before the Latins, but apparently not before the people of southwest Asia to which the peach and apricot may have extended naturally and in which these two were brought forward as well as in China. The earliest record of the cultivation of a Chinese fruit tree is Menicus' undoubtedly late mention of the Mulberry in "happy the peasant in possesion of a few mulberry trees about his dwelling that he may clothe his parents in silk"; for Menicus died in 289 B.C. We must allow to silk a long earlier development; and in 325 B.C. something was known of it in India which reached the ears of Nearchus, there with Alexander-the-Great. It seems that about this time silken robes were carried out of China as gifts to the great. In 134 B.C. the Chinese emperor sent his general Chang Kien westward to seek out the wandering Yue-chi Mongols and to make a treaty with them against a common enemy, the Hsiung-nu; and when the general came back after ten adventurous years with seeds of the grapevine and of alfalfa (*Medicago sativa*) it was to tell his master that a great trading nation could be reached in Inner Asia by taking the road by which he went. The emperor made use

of the grape stones to plant a vineyard about one of his palaces, and the coming of the grape to China added a borrowed word to Chinese, for their wild grape went nameless,[41] and was now named after the cultivated vine from the language of Ferghana. This recalls what happened in Greece and Italy on the coming of wine making. The bringing of the alfalfa seeds shows that it had been in the general's mind to improve the breed of horses that China had, for alfalfa had become the standard horse fodder and it actually reached Italy for the purpose in the time of Chang Kien. China must have been very ready to trade, as in the next few years after this caravans to the number of twelve a year went over the Silk Road, as the way came to be called, often ending the journey at the Ferghana annual horse fair. Herrmann suggests that though it is uncertain that from the very first they set out carrying silk, this very soon became their chief outward merchandise.[42]

About fifty years ago, I happened to need some transport animals close to the Burma–Siamese border and was able to hire them from Chinese traders making annually a journey from Yunnan to Tenasserim; they traded all the way but the only thing light enough for through carriage was silk. I mention this to call attention to its great suitability for the nascent China–Inner Asia trade.

A sequel to the honors which fell on Chang Kien was that the Chinese took to crediting to him the introduction into China of any western plants whose origin they did not know. Laufer in his *Sino-Iranica* set himself the task of disproving statements that Chang Kien had brought into China sesame, coriander, the pomegranate, a cucumber, chives, safflower, a fig, and a walnut. The direction, however, whence they came, except possibly the walnut, was cor-

[41] Laufer, *op. cit.*, p. 225.
[42] Albert Herrmann, *Die alten Seidenstrassen zwischen China und Syrien: Beiträge zur alten Geographie Asiens* (Berlin: Weidmann, 1910), p. 3.

rectly assumed as the Silk Road. It seems that the habit of attributing these to Chiang Kien grew about 400–500 years after his death, and the date of their coming, when the necessary allowance for loss of record is made, might be regarded as about the first century A.D. We then observe that a fruit tree such as the pomegranate soon had more than one race in China: we detect repeated introduction as indeed must have happened. The fruit of the pomegranate is perfected for transport. Did northern China receive sorghum over the Silk Road? This needs working out.

It suits me to return to southwestern Asia, for besides sorghum there are African plants such as sesame whose advent in China needs explanation. It has already been mentioned that the Near East seems to have welcomed the coming of sesame, being greedy for more and more oil-seeds, and that its name appears in Sumerian records about 2350 B.C. Though the way to Sumeria is not documented, Strabo (*c.* 54 B.C.–A.D. 24) states that it was the oil-seed of southern Arabia in his time, and proves its fitness for the climate. It is interesting to observe the length of time—nearly three millenniums—that it took to reach northern China. I wish that one could apportion that time between slowness of Man's progress, and the slowness demanded by acclimatizations.

The African genus *Vigna* supplied *V. sinensis* to Asia over the Sabaean lane, as Schweinfurth suggested.[43] Campbell Thompson has found its name as *lu-ub-sar* (the parent of the modern Arabic *lobia*) in Sumerian records of about the same date as sesame's.[44] The Greeks accepting this plant and, intrigued by the vexillum and keel of the flower, renamed it *phaselos*.

Sorghum certainly came along the Sabaean lane, not once, but many times, possibly incessantly in use as a viaticum.

Naturally the microspecies of sorghum produced in the near parts of Africa were those that came.[45]

Every new recipient seemed to call it straight away "millet" or "grain" in a way that suggests an almost certain traffic in the grain before the raising of the plant; and so it fails to be singled out in the records. Pliny is informative in regard to its coming to Italy: "within these last ten years," he says, writing in the middle of the first century A.D., "there has come from India, a millet black in color, generous of grain, like a reed in stem, reaching seven feet, and yielding more freely than all that fruits." I believe that this plant, holding on in Italy in an obscure way, became the Mediterranean broom-corn, of which we pick up traces when the Dark Ages closed.

The tamarind (*Tamarindus indica*) may or may not have been carried over the Sabaean lane: this depends on whether it is native in India as well as in Africa; if it is not a native of India then it was carried over. The cereal, *Eleusine coracana*, was carried over; so also cotton, *Gossypium herbaceum*, this from East to West,[46] and the banana (*Musa paradisiaca*), to become an exceedingly important food crop in Uganda. Late in time the sugar cane (*Saccharum officinarum*) and the aroid *Colocasia esculentum* travelled the same way. Our information that the sugar cane did so, rests on a statement that Dioscorides made towards the end of the first century A.D. that sugar was obtained from Arabia Felix; but the transfer of Colocasia cannot be nearly dated. The bulrush millet (*Pennisetum typhoideum*) and the tuberous *Coleus dysentericus* Baker, travelled to India over the lane.[47] I have found an unexpected illustration of apparent transfer from Asia to Africa in Vavilov's excellent account of

[43] G[eorg] Schweinfurth, "Abessinische Pflanzennamen," *Abhandlungen der königlichen Akademie der Wissenschaften zu Berlin aus dem Jahre 1893,* II, 1–84.

[44] Thompson, *op. cit.,* pp. 57, 94.

[45] I. H. Burkill, "The Races of Sorghum," *Kew Bulletin,* 1937, pp. 112–19, ref. to p. 116.

[46] J. B. Hutchinson, R. A. Silow, and S. G. Stephens, *The Evolution of Gossypium* (London: Oxford University Press, 1947), p. 83.

[47] For the latter see N. E. Brown, "Tuberous Labiatae," *Kew Bulletin,* 1894, pp. 10–14, where the synonym *Coleus tuberosus* Benth. is used.

the varieties and races of flax (*Linum usitatissimum*).[48] Vavilov collects a group of races together under the name "Microspermae"; they occur through Asia Minor and Persia to Afghanistan then south through India and reappear in Abyssinia, whither I think they must have been carried from Asia. They are not in Egypt where flax is in a form spread around the Mediterranean; and so the intriguing result of Vavilov's taxonomy is another doubt regarding Vavilov's own supposed close relationship of Abyssinia and Egypt. Helena Barulina in her account of the lentils remarks that the lentils of Abyssinia approach the lentils of Afghanistan and India.[49]

I feel that I should mention the calabash gourd (*Lagenaria vulgaris*) as a possible illustration of transfer from Africa to Asia over the lane. This interesting gourd is the best of all gourds for calabashes because its surface tissue hardens more than that of any other gourd. The natural wit of Man was bound to use it as a receptacle if he had it at hand; and he has had it in the New World as well as in the Old. A question thence arises—by what means did it get either to the Old from the New or to New from the Old. There are fantastic theories about demanding that unknown voyagers at a strangely early date carried it (and cotton also) across the Pacific. My own belief is that Nature made it common to the Guinea and Brazilian margins of the Atlantic and that it spread thence. Gordon Childe says that the Aryans had calabashes at 2000 B.C.,[50] and we know that Mediterranean folk in classical times had calabashes made from this gourd as well as from a few others and used them for wine bottles, even considerably, and splashed themselves in the baths with water from them. If the use of calabashes at 2000 B.C. be continuous with use by the Greeks and

Romans as is probable, then we need to account for the coming to southwestern Asia of *Lagenaria vulgaris* and a natural way would be by the Sabaean lane.

It has been pointed out by Sir David Prain and me that the African landfall of the Sabaean lane was inhospitable to such plants as the greater yam, being far too dry for its thrift.[51] So too for other plants, whose coming to Africa from the East was delayed until the Yemenite Arabs had so developed their colonies in Zanzibar as to make a home for them. This they did between the eighth and the eleventh centuries A.D. The route from Yemen to Zanzibar and also to the Majunga coast of Madagascar is indicated on the map (Fig. 6). The L-shaped shaded area in Africa marked on that map, the area where the sorghums were ennobled, comes to the coast at Zanzibar. Within the two limbs of this L is the humid equatorial forest area with its own cultigens; and the L-shaped area has cultigens of its own likewise. It is to be observed that the forests nearly cut Africa in two; and it is to be added that east of the end of the forest there lies land desert enough to take a part in the cutting, but leaving a channel in the lattitude of the Victoria Nyanza. I have pointed out that J. D. Snowden's excellent taxonomic study of the sorghums suggests that the gap serves as a recasting factory between the northern and the southern sorghums, all the species losing their identity in it.[52] Thus viewed the gap divides the L into two parts. The races of sorghum which were taken early to Asia were those of the eastern end of the northern limb of the L; and they had been evolved by selection on it. I take it as important to note how closely their development was hid from the Mediterranean, for we begin to understand by observing such to occur what a real barrier the Sahara was.

[48] *Bulletin of Applied Botany* . . . , vol. XVI (1926).

[49] *Op. cit.*

[50] V. Gordon Childe, *The Aryans: A Study of Indo-European Origins* (London: K. Paul, Trench, Trübner, 1926), p. 127.

[51] Sir David Prain and I. H. Burkill, "Dioscorea in the East" (2 vols., *Annals of the Royal Botanical Garden, Calcutta,* XIV [1936]), 318.

[52] See Burkill, "The Races of Sorghum," p. 115, and J. D. Snowden, *The Cultivated Races of Sorghum* (London: Adlard & Son, 1936).

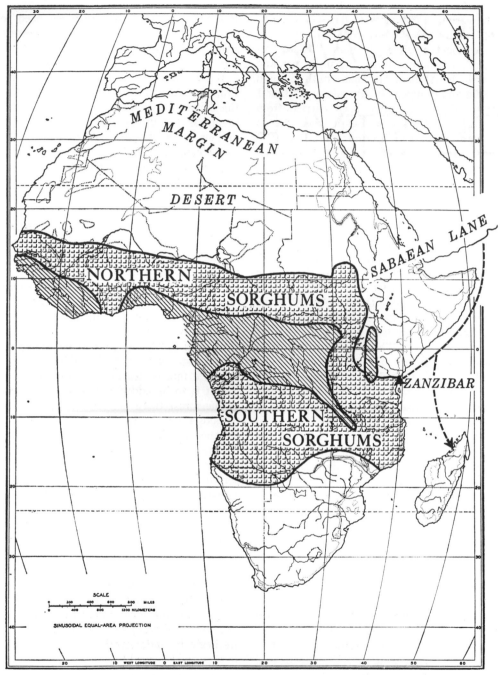

FIG. 6. Africa zoned culturally. The realm of the equatorial forest is cross-hatched. [Base map courtesy of Goode's Map Series.]

The way out was sideways by the Sabaean lane. It is recognized that Africa has been comparatively ineffective in plant ennoblement. Vavilov, counting up the cultigens of different parts of the world, stated that no continent among those that he had studied showed up so badly as Africa. However, on the northern limb of the L some curious ennoblements have been accomplished. There we find as a pulse the geocarpous Leguminosa, *Kerstingiella geocarpa,* and a source of oil one of the Polygalaceae, *Polygala butyracea,* and a small millet, *Digitaria exilis* Stapf. (I reduce *D. iburua* Stapf.) The angle of the L appears likely to have seen the ennoblement of *Coleus dystentericus* Baker, and *C. dazo* A. Chev. & Perrot, at least in part.

The cross-hatched area on the map is a country of yams, comparable therefore, with the humid forests of the Malay Peninsula where the Semang live; but less striking in results. The chief *Dioscorea* of the Guinea forests, *D. cayenensis,* when brought by the Portuguese into competition with the Asiatic *D. alata,* took second place. The Guinea palm which supplies oil (*Elaeis guineensis*) is not the equal of the eastern coconut palm; and the leading masticatory nut, the cola nut, though enormously prized by habitué, has not excited the cultivation that the areca nut has.

Because drier climates so effectively hem in this humid area, its ennobled plants were retained within it until shipping carried them across the Atlantic.

I proceed to India and commence with Fig. 7 giving the dispersal of wheat fields in India, and Fig. 8 of the dispersal of rice fields in India. The two maps should be compared. They represent what has happened, namely a borrowing of the one cereal from the West and of the other from the East. Then follows Fig. 9 which gives the dispersal of sorghum in India. This is grown in the season of rice where rice cannot be readily grown. It demands less water than wheat and therefore is grown where it is difficult to raise wheat. The actual intensity of wheat and rice has been

greatly altered by the irrigation engineer; but the antithesis of wheat and rice remains and powerfully affects the dietaries; for instance, a high-caste man can be a

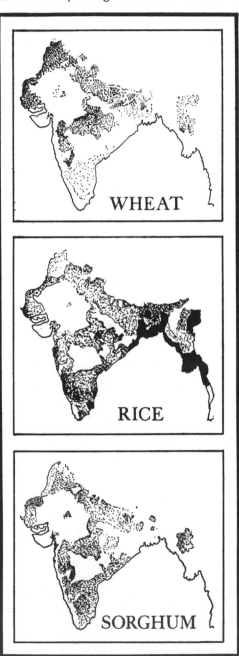

FIGS. 7, 8, 9. The dispersal of wheat, rice, and sorghum in India.

complete vegetarian on wheat and pulses, but with difficulty on rice without fish; therefore there are Brahmins who eat fish lest their race perish.

There is another West versus East contrast that is peculiarly interesting; it is in the sources of oil. From the direction of the Pacific at a remote time came the coconut palm (*Cocos nucifera*) finding the humidity necessary for its thrift easily so long as it grew near the sea and using as means of transport for its large fruits the ocean currents. It may have reached India naturally, if also with Man's help. It has been proved by Man's planting that it can be grown in the interior of Bengal even at 200 miles inland, but could not have got there without Man; on the Bombay side there is one place where it has been grown at 80 miles from the sea; but north of the Arabian Sea it will not grow—not even by the sea. Therefore there was a time when the Sind coast and the greater part of the interior of India were without the pleasant oil that it gives. The areas there without easy supplies now grow sesame, hemp, linseed, the castor oil plant, poppy, and certain *Brassicas*, and again, not to misrepresent the case, the Niger oil seed plant (*Guizotia abyssinica*) which has not had a long history in India, and towards the northeast *Perilla ocimoides* which has come round the corner of the Himalayas from the direction of China. Paying attention to the first six, we find that all of them are plants that have come from the West. When? I believe from the time of the Indus civilization, which is dated as around 3250–2750 B.C. The implication on observing the sources of oil to have come from the West, the known fact that there was a connection between the Indus and the Sumerian civilizations, the presumption that the founders of the Indus civilization were intruders into an India of Dravidians, is that India had been dependent on such forest trees as *Schleichera trijuga* Willd. for its oil, except where the coconut was available, until the Indus civilization was introduced.

I have laid out my observations in a way which permits me to suggest that the triangle which I have defined as India was the meeting ground of two spreading cultures, the one dominated by the history that I have been tracing, while the other originated in Indochina beyond the reach of the domination. Unfortunately it is very difficult to envisage the beginnings of this new culture. Indochina is more the land of the bamboo than any other part of the world; with the aid of the bamboo the building of a new house is delightfully easy, and kings would think nothing of compelling the complete removal of a capital. The face of the land changed as migrations blotted out the old physiographic characters. But if the Mon came into Indochina about 2000 B.C. they must have had a large part in shaping the culture.

Clay tablets exist showing shipping in the Persian Gulf in the days of Ur. Mohenjo Daro was not too far from the coast to benefit by an extension to it; but Harappa was by the river Ravi, far inland; and it was in Harappa that sesame seed was found. Presumedly, therefore, sesame was cultivated through the Indus civilization and possibly the agriculture of Sumeria had taken hold of a fairly large part of northern India. We do not as yet know the language used **then**. When the Aryans had taken the Punjab they left records in Vedic which one dates as of 1000 B.C. and the immediately following centuries; then the language changed to Bali and from Bali it became Sanskrit, which in turn began to break up into the current Indian Indo-Aryan vernaculars about A.D. 800, but lingered, like monkish Latin, to later than A.D. 1500. It used to be customary in botanical writings to welcome a Sanskrit name as a sign of ancient cultivation; it is obvious now that we have deeper sources and some reason for using the evidence of sanskrit names with care. Sanskrit is not older than Latin; Vedic is. A name for sesame appears in Vedic (*tila*), passes through Sanskrit and persists today. The seed, we know, was eaten as a porridge with pulse or cereal grain; and as a source of oil its importance was so great that its name meant oil, the metonomy being from oil to sesame; and in that case all the other oil seeds raised would be secondary to sesame at the time when sesame obtained its name among the Aryans.

There is evidence that the Aryans came into India using hempen ropes, with *bhanga* as a name for Cannabis fibre. They may have been users of hempseed oil before they contacted sesame oil and found it better.

There is a vedic name, *erand*, for the castor oil plant which likewise passed through Sanskrit to the modern Indo-Aryan vernaculars. It invaded Chinese as *i-lan* and exists in Pushtu, as *arhand*. Kittel has suggested that this name was originally Dravidian and borrowed by the Aryans, which supposition accepts the castor oil plant as in India before the Aryans came. A great abundance of additional names in Sanskrit attests to great familiarity with it; it was *chatravija* or painted seeds, *pancanguri* or five-fingered leaves, etc., as well as *erand* and *amanda;* and *amanda* links up with *amadam* in Telegu and *amanakkam* in Tamil. Kittel's supposition seems good; and the conclusion can be sustained that the castor oil plant was spread through India before the Aryans came. It would be a basic oil plant for illumination and for anointing the body as it had been earlier in Mesopotamia.[53]

There is a third oil-seed with a vedic name, *sarshapa*, a Brassica; but no vedic name has been detected for linseed and poppy. Yet linseed has a name in Bali and poppy in Sanskrit. Surely the absence of a name for linseed in vedic does not prove its absence; but it is easy to believe that the poppy came late.

I have used Duthie and Fuller's *Field and Garden Crops of the United Provinces*[54] as a guide to furnish an authoritative list

of what justifiably can be called the current important crops of the Upper Gangetic plains; and I have analyzed my list, extracting out of it in the first place the crops that are sown in October. They are wheat, barley, safflower, opium poppy (grown for oil), lentil, field pea, *Lathyrus sativus*, linseed, and three Brassicas. They are all crop-plants of southwestern Asia and the quantity of all of them that is grown decreases eastwards towards Bengal where they almost if not entirely disappear. It is obvious that they are crops brought to India as strangers from the West, requiring the "cold weather" for growth. Then I extracted from the work the crops sown in May. They are the grain crops, *Setaria italica, Paspalum scrobiculatum,* and *Eleusine coracana;* and the pulses *Phaseolus aureus* Roxb. (including *P. radiatus*), *P. mungo* L., *P. calcaratus* Roxb., and *P. aconitifolius* Jacq. They ripen in three months; and nothing that requires more time can be used, for the crop must be harvested to make way for the October sowings. They are of various origins, but the pulses are endemic to India; the first named being a very valuable plant. Prain suggested[55] that the wild *Phaseolus sublobatus* Wall., a weed of field margins and like places from the Bombay coast to the China Sea and to the Philippines, gave rise to it as well as to *P. mungo*, which is reasonable; but it may be that *P. aureus* had multiple origins, not all of them within India. That the other Phaseoli had their origination in India is incontestable. Over and on the eastern limits of India, *P. ricciardianus* Ten. takes a place in cultivation and in central China *P. chrysanthus* Savi. *P. aureus* has a vedic name. In India but not quite to the very north, *Panicum miliare* enters this group of crops and, to a small extent, *P. psilopodium*, which is believed to be parent of *P. miliare*. A cultivation of parent and extraction in the same country shows that state which I have called semi-ennoble-

[53] Thompson, *op. cit.*, p. 130.
[54] John F. Duthie and J. B. Fuller, *Field and Garden Crops of the United Provinces* . . . (3 vols. Roorkee, India: Thompson Civil Engineering College Press, 1882–93).

[55] See the report of Sir David Prain in *Journal of the Asiatic Society of Bengal*, LXVI (1897), 433.

ment, a state in which ennoblement is always liable to be frustrated by want of isolation. To the list of leguminous crops that India originated may be added *Dolichos lablab,* but ennobled for greens. India accepted two other Leguminosae, *Cajanus indicus* and *Vigna catiang.* India ennobled a series of cucurbits, also for use as greens, being such as do not have fruits too heavy for suspension—*Momordica charantia, Trichosanthes dioica, T. cucumerina,* and *Coccinia indica.* But all of these except the Momordica are only semi-ennobled, fruits of wild plants being brought to the table as sufficient without the ennobling. *Trichosanthes anguina* is completely ennobled, with *T. cucumerina* for parent.

The eggplant (*Solanum melongena*) seems to stand as a cultigen entirely to the credit of India. Like the cucurbits, it serves as greens, the fruit being cooked at a slightly immature stage. Its origin has been much disputed, but I believe that taxonomists will find within var. *insanum* a parental form. Originally the plant was round-fruited and would carry several fruits together. Selection was directed to getting a larger fruit and that became associated with fruits tending to be solitary. As a round fruit, the sanskrit name *varta* or *vartaka* was appropriate, for the word is traced to an adjective meaning "round." As round-fruited it reached China; and so it happened that a Chinese visiting Samarkand in A.D. 1221 expressed his surprise at finding there the fruit elongated.[56] The plant must have reached Malaysia with relatively small round fruits; otherwise the Malays would not have classified it as a *tĕrong* along with their several species of Solanum. *Varta* gave rise to *baigun* in India, *bedingan* in the Levant, then when the Arabs took it to Spain *berenjena,* and with the definite article prefixed *albergine* in French—an interesting sequence which embodies much history. Ennoblement seems not to have been very remote in time, but

rapid enough for different countries to contain new forms differing in a degree that enabled Filov to group them geographically.[57]

Alocasia indica is another plant ennobled in India for service as greens; but it became overshadowed when *Colocasia esculentum* was brought from the eastward. India would be greatly led towards ennobling greens because they were wanted for service with the rice.

India originated the cultivation of the mango (*Mangifera indica*) and the jack fruit (*Artocarpus integra* Merr. or *A. heterophylla* Lank.), some other species of *Artocarpus,* and various species of the genus *Citrus,* and borrowed from Indochina many plants for additional ennobling. There is no cleavage between botanists in regard to the part of the world within which rice originated, but much uncertainty in regard to the manner in which it originated within that part.[58] Rice undoubtedly came into cultivation in Indochina. It is just possible that the area extended into adjoining India. Thence it spread across India, apparently taking wild rice with it, for it is difficult to believe that the wild rice, now accompanying it, was there before. The vedic Aryans knew rice. It does not happen to be mentioned in their oldest book, but that does not prove its absence. Continuing to diffuse westwards from India it was in Mesopotamia in the 7th century B.C.[59]—a slow but not unusually slow progression. As it crossed India wheat would so to speak fight back and delay it; and still more so after the boundaries of India had been crossed.

The greater yam (*Dioscorea alata*) came into India out of Indochina. In its case we are able unusually narrowly to indicate

[56] E. V. Bretschneider, *Mediaeval Researches from Eastern Asiatic Sources* (2 vols.; London: K. Paul, Trench, Trübner, 1910), I, 89.

[57] See his report in *Proceedings of the Academy of Sciences of the U.S.S.R.* [Doklady Akademii nauk SSSR], XXVI (1940), 815.
[58] D. Chatterjee's "Note on the Origin and Distribution of Wild and Cultivated Rice," *Indian Journal of Genetics and Plant Breeding,* XI (1951), 18 ff. supplies a good starting point for understanding the position.
[59] Thompson, *op. cit.,* p. 105.

where its cultivation originated; it was just beyond the Cupuliferous boundary line.[60]

A home of *Musa balbisiana*, parent of the banana, is where the greater yam originated. Cheeseman recommends that *Musa paradisiaca* L. be accepted as a name for the cultivated banana, with *M. balbisiana* Colla as a name for the wild parent.[61] But *M. acuminata* Colla is part-parent of some races of the cultivated banana. This species also comes from beyond India. The sugar cane must have entered India by diffusion through Indochina, for it appears to have originated further east. The chief components of the betel quid came perhaps by the same way; but it is probable that the idea of the quid preceded them and that they were betterments. It is recorded of the betel nut that the Chinese emperor, Wu-ti, after he had annexed the state of Nan-yue (the coastal extreme south of modern China) in 111 B.C., insisted on its cultivation at his palace in Shen-si, along with various oranges, the litchi, and the lungnan; and, says Laufer, many gardeners lost their lives for failing.[62] The betel palm grows in Hai-nan and had probably reached that island by the time of Wu-ti.

Southwards the region of Indochina passes into Malaysia, which is the greatest humid region of the Old World. It is apparent that Malaysia was so to speak bombarded from the coasts of Indochina with migrants who are best called pre-proto-Malays. The date according to some was about 1000 B.C.; others would have it earlier. Blagden postulated a fringe of these folk on the whole coast from the Irrawaddy to Tong-king[63] which looks probable and would account for radiating invasions of

the islands such as certainly took place. As coastal, they lived undoubtedly in fishing villages; and what they took into the islands was the habit of living on fish with such additions as they could get from the land. Kern suggested that they invaded the islands in the possession of the working of iron, the control of the domestic buffalo, and a knowledge of how to grow irrigated rice. The idea that they had iron is now discounted and I think that we must abandon the supposition that they cultivated rice with the aid of irrigation, but admitting that they had what is called dry-land rice. It is quite certain that when they reached Java they came up against a considerable neolithic population. It is well demonstrated that metals came to the islands after these migrants; van Stein Callenfels suggests that metals came about 300 B.C.[64] Obviously before this, a migration eastwards had been started that after centuries reached the longitude of Samoa and then fanned out as Polynesians. These kept no tradition of rice, and worked no iron. In the last centuries B.C. India discovered how to cross the Bay of Bengal and began to make trading voyages to what was called Suvanabhumi or the coast of gold, where lived people who clothed themselves in bark cloth and were ready to buy Indian cottons. There is a story in Pali of a voyager who was nicknamed the bark cloth wearer, for, after the misfortune of shipwreck, he clad himself in what he could get; and another of a merchant who by marrying a naked princess got a kingdom. One venture led to another and ultimately to the establishment of powerful hinduized kingdoms in several parts of western Malaysia. These kingdoms brought the land forward greatly and there came about a marked contrast between western Malaysia where they were and eastern where they were not. The West grew rich in rice and the East kept poor. This contrast in the first degree depended on the climate, for large parts of the East are unsuited,

[60] For a summary of its history see I. H. Burkill, "The Rise and Decline of the Greater Yam in the Service of Man," *The Advancement of Science*, VII (1951), 443–48.

[61] E. E. Cheeseman, "The Classification of Bananas," *Kew Bulletin*, 1948, pp. 17–28, 145–55, 323–28, ref. to p. 148.

[62] *Sino-Iranica*, p. 262.

[63] See his report in the *Journal of the Royal Asiatic Society, Straits Branch*, vol. XXXVII (Singapore, 1902).

[64] *Bulletin of the Raffles Museum, Singapore*, XIII (1937), 150.

and those who live there turn to sago, yams, and other roots for starchy food; but the sinews of the western states were certainly in their rice fields.

This differentiation did not arise immediately; Coedès dates it as "from intense colonization in the second and third centuries, A.D. bearing fruit in the 4th and 5th." [65] Towards A.D. 600 the states in Malaysia began to shake themselves free of the influences from India. This having been the history, when we discover an economic plant to have names in Polynesia and Malaysia that show a common origin, we detect pre-hindu cultivation: when we observe a name in Malaysia to be sanskritic we suspect introduction from India at some date before A.D. 600 and probably A.D. 200–300. For instance, we find the Malay word for yam, *ubi,* to be used throughout the Pacific in one form or another, and deduce that Dioscoreas, chiefly *D. alata,* were a very important food at the date of the Polynesians' departure. We find the Malay word *tĕbu* for sugar cane, *tales* for *Colocasia esculentum,* *biah* for *Tacca pinnatifidā,* *nyior* for coconut to be repeated, and recognize that the names having travelled with the migrants, the plants had made a large cultivated element in the foods of the pre-proto-Malays out of whom the Polynesians sprang.

The sanskritic vernacular plant names that I have on record are met with in the following languages in this order: Malay, Javanese, Sundanese, and then in small numbers further afield on old shipping routes that the Malays used. Only a few refer to foods of importance, the onion being one of these, the water melon (*Citrullus colocynthis*) another. Sesame presents a third case, but invites further investigation. It has two widely spread names which appear in Malay as *bijan* and *lenga.* The first I believe is from the sanskrit word *biji,* a seed. Why call it seed?—the priests settled that, for it gave the sacrificial oil-

seed. They had not needed it in the kitchen with the coconut at hand. *Lenga* needs tracing. The immigrants were responsible for bringing in improved fruit-trees. The words most usual in Malaysia for the *Citrus* and *Eugenia* fruits are sanskritic and bear testimony to ennoblement in India within the genus *Citrus* and of *Eugenia jambolana.* Ennobled races of *Zizyplus jujuba* must have been brought. The jack fruit tree has two names; it is *nangka* very widely and the origin of that name awaits explanation; but it has the sanskritic name *panasa* used as *panas, pinasa, lamasa, benaso,* etc. in various Malaysian languages, and it is peculiar that *nangka* had not sufficed where they are. The tree was taken to China under the sanskritic name *panasa* (altered to po-no-sa) during the short period A.D. 502–557. Chau Ju-kua, inspector of maritime trade at Canton in *c.* 1225, recorded that his countrymen, understanding that it had come from the country of Po-lo, suspected a mistake and renamed it Po-lo-mi; and as such or as Po-lo-mat and Po-lo-mit it has remained; truncated to Mit (cay mit or tree mit) it has entered Anamese. Hirth and Rockhill suggested Fu-nan to be Po-lo and that was certainly right; the tree was passed forward to Canton from that hinduized kingdom.[66] *Cajanus indicus* and cucurbits of the genera *Luffa* and *Trichosanthes* have sanskritic names and may be adjudged introduced cultigens. But the majority of the sanskritic names do not indicate supplies for the kitchen so much as royal pomp or priestly observances. The rulers laid out parks after the Indian manner, planting what the ruler of one state called in 775 A.D. "lordly trees," [67] such as these: *Miche-*

---

[65] George Coedès, *Les états hindouisés d'Indochine et d'Indonésie* (Paris: E. de Roccard, 1948), p. 40.

[66] *Chau Ju-kua, His Work on the Chinese and Arab Trade in the Twelfth and Thirteenth Centuries,* translated from the Chinese by Friederich Hirth and W. W. Rockhill (St. Petersburg: Printing Office of the Imperial Academy of Sciences, 1911), p. 212.

[67] I. H. Burkill, "The Early Economic History of the Tree *Mesua Ferrea* (Guttiferae)," *Proceedings of the Linnean Society of London,* CLVI (1944), 85–91, ref. to 88.

lia champaca, *Mimusops elengi* (both natives of India brought for their scent), *Cassia fistula, Elaeocarpus ganitrus, Anthocephalus cadamba, Mesua ferrea, Albizzia lebbek, Schima noronhae,* and *Calophyllum inophyllum,* trees which might be found with trouble in Malaysia but with ease in India. The priests according to their observances, whether Brahmin or Buddhist, needed *Ficus religiosa* but *F. rumphii* was acceptable as sufficiently similar; needed *Saraca indica* but would accept *Ixora coccinea;* needed the Sacred lotus and multiplied the tanks in which it was grown; the worshippers of Shiv required his emblem of trifoliate leaves which they obtained in *Aegle marmelos* or *Feronia limonum* or *Butea monosperma.* Of these *Ficus rumphii,* the *Feronia,* and the *Butea* were available in parts of Malaysia; the others were brought as cultivated plants from India. The Malaysian *Ficus septica* was accepted for the Indian *F. glomerata. Calotropis gigantea* has a sanskritic name and religious use for which it was grown. As pleasant *Ocimum* was raised; for dyeing *Woodfordia floribunda* and *Carthamus tinctorius,* the latter certainly, the former probably brought from India. The castor oil plant was introduced. *Moringa oleifera* was brought in as a condiment. The two peppers, *Piper nigrum* and *P. longum,* were brought also. A love of intense scents led to the bringing of *Hedychium coronarium, Hibiscus abelmoschus,* and jasmines. I have not mentioned the mango (*Mangifera indica*) because its names are not actually sanskritic; *mempelam* is from one Dravidian language and *mangga* from another; but it had come from India. Nor have I mentioned *Paspalum scrobiculatum* because its name in Java, *kodoan,* is likely to have come from Gujarat in A.D. 611 with the fugitives whose arrival is depicted on the Borobodur temple. *Jelita* for *Corchorus capsularis* in eastern Malaysia possibly came by slaves brought from Chittagong by the Dutch.

I have sought for a return from Malaysia to India and find only two plants, neither beyond doubt. One is the sandalwood tree (*Santalum album*). Fischer pointed out its discontinuous distribution in India and indications that it is spreading as evidence of having being introduced.[68] The only contribution that I can make is to call attention to the double evidence of its arrival in Ahmednagar towards the reign of Akbar (A.D. 1560–1605). Abul Fazl states in his "Ain-i-Akbari" that it had been brought but does not precisely date its arrival. Garcia da Orta whose *Colloquies* were published in 1561, states that he had seen the tree at Ahmednagar; and it happened that Akbar besieged Ahmednagar in 1560. It is clear that it was a novelty at the town which is 120 miles due east of Bombay city and must have been brought thither from southern India a little before 1560. The other possible introduction from Malaysia is the patchouli, *Pogostemon heyneanus* Benth., brought first in an inferior race, then in ennoblements.

After the sanskritic influence had gone, Malaysia obtained a knowledge of many plants from the Arabs and Persians who came trading by ship with dry goods and lodged a few economic plants. At the same time and indeed earlier the Chinese were bringing their own plants to Malaysia, and by their names we know that they introduced *Acorus calamus, Aglaia odorata,* Chinese chives (*Allium odorum*), celery (*Apium graveolens*), wormwood (*Artemisia vulgaris*), the tea tree (*Camellia sinensis*), *Chrysanthemum coronarium, Lycium chinense,* and the litchi (*Litchi chinense*). Because the Chinese language is uncouth to Malay ears, there could have been an unwillingness to adopt names of various additional plants.

Carrying on with the help of Indochinese, Indian, Persian, and Chinese loans, Malaysia has done very little origination and ennobling of cultigens. A few years ago I was able to obtain from two friendly Ma-

[68] C. E. C. Fischer, "*Santalum album* in India," *Kew Bulletin,* 1927, pp. 200–2; see also his more recent statement in the *Journal of the Bombay Natural History Society,* XI (1938), 458.

lays of different villages near Telok Anson, Perak, lists of the substances that they ate with the daily rice, by name and by weight. A Malay likes two substantial meals a day and each consists of rice and of something eaten with the rice. My useful friends, under the direction of Mr. E. F. Allen of the Department of Agriculture, Malaya (to whom I am exceedingly grateful), kept up their returns from November 1946 to March 1948, during which time they resorted to over 100 different food-plants. I have analyzed the returns grouping the vegetables under (a) native plants such as a new Malay settlement might fall in with, seek, and use; (b) Indochinese plants, such as the pre-proto-Malays would be expected to know; (c) Indian and Chinese loan plants; (d) loan plants that came from further away through India or China, and (e) American plants not available until after A.D. 1500. By weight converted to percentages, my friends used: (a) 16; (b) 30; (c) 23; (d) 12 and (e) 18. It is interesting that even the American element came to table in greater quantity than the native. Colonization without support is difficult in proportion to the land's lack of resources and it is obvious that the first comings of the pre-proto-Malays, as the comings were not massive, must have been far too difficult for the bringing of rice irrigation. Irrigation came with the state-building activities of the Indian adventurers; and their settlement in western Malaysia and absence from eastern Malaysia were a major factor in creating the difference of which I have written. I would add that as showing the need of state-craft for irrigation: the Malay Peninsula continued to grow little but dry-land rice until British administration, about eighty years ago, created a secure land tenure that enabled irrigation to be undertaken.

The reader may be interested in knowing what were the most used components of the meal with the rice—in greatest quantity the terminal parts of banana inflorescences, something comparable to a cauliflower, consisting of male and sterile flowers; then (2) fruits of the eggplant (Solanum melongena) slightly immature; (3) cucumbers; (4) tubers and petioles of Colocasia esculentum; (5) fresh new leaves of the uncultivated fern Diplazium esculentum; (6) fruits of Musa in immature stages; (7) shoots and young fruits of the jack fruit tree; (8) pineapples; (9) Ipomea reptans, partly from wild sources and partly from Chinese cultivation; (10) legumes of Vigna sinensis; (11) tubers of the Sweet potato (Ipomea batatas); (12) seedlings of Vigna sinensis, three to four days old, as prepared by the Chinese; and so forward.

It seems clear that the pre-proto-Malays came with dry-land rice and the tubers that the Polynesians relied on, the Greater yam and Colocasia, the tubers of Tacca pinnatifida, probably the cereal Job's tears (Coix lachyrmajobi), and some ennobled Musas, and kept up the ennobling of these while relying on their fishing and what the uncultivated land provided, the resources of the cultivations to the west being unknown.

When we have dated the coming of the pre-proto-Malays as 1000 B.C. and the beginning of tillage in Inner Asia as perhaps 7000 B.C., the lateness of Malaysia is impressive, and then the smallness of achievement towards ennoblement is understood. It seems reasonable to surmise that beginnings in China and India might have been before 4000 B.C. and beginnings at the southern end of the Red Sea a little earlier; but in Africa at large very much later.

Man has taken an enormous time everywhere in effecting very little. The pattern has been cereals first if available, then pulses if available, then greens and roots, etc.; and the more humid parts of the world have been such that Man had to start without the advantage of cereals and pulses and with the disadvantage of the materials being perennial. Perennials are most intractable if they be tall trees with cross-pollinated flowers fertilized by uncontrolled pollen. Even the durian (Durio zibethinus) has had very little ennoblement; the jiring (*Pithecolobium jiringa* Prain) very little; the rambutan (*Nephelium lappaceum*) none. On the other hand, the breadfruit (*Artocarpus communis*) has had much in the Pacific islands, where the isolation of the islands has contributed and every tree has been under observation. In the ennobling of yams and Colocasia the Polynesians took a pride; it was a mark of distinction to possess a clone or race that a neighbour did not know; but such emulation is now passing away.

After A.D. 1500 American plants were spread with very great rapidity, particularly those that made a quick return such as maize. But with them I cannot deal.

HUGH C. CUTLER

FOOD SOURCES IN THE NEW WORLD

As soon as life arose there was a need for food. While a few simple living froms appear to subsist on inorganic materials alone, the use of other organisms as food for animals is probably as old as plants and animals themselves. As the kinds of life increased in number, food habits grew in complexity. Many lower forms of life die when deprived of a certain food, but animals which have used diverse food sources can subsist when some of these are absent. These animals also are more flexible in their utilization of substitutes and, as adaptable animals, are tolerant of changing environments or moves to other habitats. Man is an adaptable omnivore and has the widest range of any mammal.

There has been a tendency to think of man as an organism dropped, as man, into a strange environment to initiate his search and experimentation for food. In reality man is the end product of a long series of animals and has developed and survived by adapting himself to a changing environment. For food man has probably tried to use almost every kind of material he encountered, soils, salts, ants, cattle, mushrooms, beer, cress, and corn. In all cases man was limited to what raw materials were available. When in need man is, like

Reprinted, with permission of the author and editor, from *Agricultural History*, XXVIII (1954), 39–41 (Copyright, 1954, by the Agricultural History Society). The author is executive director of the Missouri Botanical Garden and associate professor of botany at Washington University, St. Louis.

other animals, less particular about the food he eats, and he uses a wide variety of materials. But of the wide variety of foods which can be called edible, long before the development of agriculture, gathering man found it profitable to collect only those foods which gave an adequate return for the time and labor he invested.

Several years ago I made a survey of possible food sources of the ancient inhabitants of the lower San Juan River basin of Utah and as part of this study I tried for several days to gather enough food to live. This turned out to be a struggle even during the most favorable season of the year and with good metal tools to aid me. I gathered barely enough to keep from being hungry and I could not accumulate a substantial surplus. Only a small population of hunters and gatherers could exist in that region for I had to utilize the plants from a large area. Most of my food came from a relatively few kinds of plants, at that season sego lily bulbs, rice grass seeds, cactus plants, yucca pods, greens of the pigweed relatives, and young underground stems of reed grass, rush, and cattail. Of all these foods, a grass gave the greatest returns for my labor. This is true in most regions for the grains have little water and a high food content and they can be gathered readily with primitive equipment. Cactus stems and spinach-like greens were tasty and easy to gather and prepare, but had little food value. I soon tired of the taste of yucca pods, and sego lily bulbs were scarce and difficult to dig. Young underground stems were relatively rare, although excellent in flavor, and I would have destroyed all the plants in a few days if I had not stopped gathering them. Mormon tea (*Ephedra Torreyana*) was an adequate beverage. With the solitary exception of Mormon tea, every one of the plants I found to be edible is used by the Navajos, Hopis, and Utes of the region and has been identified among the remains of the prehistoric Indians of the same region. Mormon tea is sometimes used as a medicine by the Indians but not as a daily drink. In the Southwest every kind of plant part is gathered for food: fruit, seeds, leaves, stems, and underground parts.

The only two plants which apparently were domesticated within the present United States are the sunflower and its relative, the Jerusalem artichoke, although there is some evidence for adding the tepary bean and the pumpkin (*Cucurbita pepo*) to this list. Many gathered food crops of this country would produce good yields and the occurrence of occasional wild plants with unusually large and abundant edible parts shows that the plant could have been improved for man's use. Of the seed crops the Indian rice grass, the wild vetch and the beach pea appear suited for domestication, while many tuber and root-bearing plants eaten by the American Indians can be easily grown. In the West numerous different relatives of the parsnip and carrot were gathered. Yampa, bitterroot and several others could easily have been domesticated. There were sunflowers with large tuberous roots, the sandroot of the Pima-Papago country, the bigroot morning glory of our Midwest, and the potato bean of the east and northeast. But the appearance in the Southwest of the already developed crops of corn, beans, and squash about the time of the introduction of agriculture probably made it unnecessary to domesticate new crops.

Far to the south, in the highlands of the Andes of Peru and Bolivia, the natives grow a peculiar assortment of crop plants. Their mainstays are the earth vegetables, foods like the underground stems or tubers of the nasturtium, oxalis, *Ullucus,* and the potato, all of them planted by burying pieces of the tubers from the last harvest. All of these cultivated plants have wild relatives growing in the same region, often as weeds in and about the tilled fields. The center of variation of the edible cultivated nasturtium and of its wild relatives lies in the Andes of Peru and Bolivia. There, too, is the greatest diversity of the tuberous forms of Oxalis, both cultivated and wild. *Ullucus,* an odd plant in a little known family, has many varieties in this region. *Ullucus* has not spread far and the apparently wild plants are very similar to the cultivated ones. The center of potato domestication is in these highlands. The cultivated species, varieties, and forms surpass in number and variability those found in any other place. In addition, the local farmers gather the tubers of several wild potato species which grow as weeds in and about their fields.

The potato was the mainstay of the highland civilizations, the most important food of Tiahuanaco and the higher parts of the Inca Empire, but it did not become a major crop in other regions. In most of the lowlands it could not compete with corn, sweet-potatoes, or mandioca, crops which enjoy a warm climate. We cannot take potatoes from Bolivia and Peru and grow them in the United States without giving them special treatment because they are intolerant of our longer summer days in our high latitudes. The potato we grow probably came from Chile and was brought to us via Europe, where long before it was grown as a food it was planted as a curiosity in botanical gardens. In volume and weight the potato is the world's greatest crop but 70 per cent of the tuber is water, so the calory content of the entire crops is far less than that of corn, rice, or wheat. About 90 per cent of the world's potato crop is grown in Europe, more than a third of it in Russia, and less than 8 per cent of the crop is grown in the New World.

Several other vegetatively propagated crops probably were domesticated in the Bolivia-Peru region. Some of these are so dependent upon vegetative propagation that they seldom produce seeds. Among these crops are the edible canna, arracacha, the yam bean, and *Polymnia*, a relative of the sunflower, and Jerusalem artichoke with dahlia-like tubers.

In the Lake Titicaca basin lies the center of origin of at least three locally important seed crops. A lupine, there called *tarhui*, is harvested at altitudes as high as the potato fields. Its seeds are bitter and slightly poisonous until thoroughly washed, so after the Conquest the lupine was replaced in many places by the European horse-bean, or fava. The most important seed crop of the highlands is quinoa, an herbaceous plant related to pigweed and not to be confused with the entirely distinct quinine trees native to the eastern Andean slopes. There is an amazing number of quinoa varieties and considerable variation within each variety. One usually finds related weed forms growing in cultivated fields of quinoa and it appears that a major part of the variability of the cultivated varieties springs from crosses with these weeds. The best cultivated varieties of quinoa are erect and little branched, with dull white lenticular seeds with so little soapy taste that they scarcely need to be washed to be palatable. Less desirable and weed-like varieties are low and branched, with dark-colored, shiny, nearly globular, small seeds which are bitter and soapy and must be washed well to be edible. Quinoa seeds are high in protein and attempts have been made to grow the plant in Europe and the United States, usually without success because the plant does not often fruit in the long days of our summers. The quinoa and oxalis occasionally found growing in Mexico were introduced there after the Conquest, but in prehistoric times were grown from Chile and the Argentine to Colombia. Another member of the same

genus, *kañhua*, is found only in parts of Bolivia and Peru, and has a small number of varieties centered a short distance south of Lake Titicaca.

The several beans grown in Bolivia and Peru were important only in the lowlands. On the Pacific coast the Indians grew varieties of common and lima beans second in number only to those of Mexico and Guatemala as well as the jack bean, *Canavalia*. This genus of beans is found in both the Old and New Worlds but the species of each hemisphere are distinct. The cultivated *Canavalias* of Peru and most of those from late sites of southern Arizona fall within the species called *Canavalia ensiformis*, but some of the seeds from a late level of Tonto ruin, a Pueblo III site in central Arizona, may belong to another species.

All squashes and pumpkins and all the wild species of the genus to which they belong are natives of the New World alone. The Hubbard types of squash may have originated in Bolivia; the turban forms of the same species (*Cucurbita maxima*) appear to come from farther east. Our knowledge of the early distribution of squash species has been greatly extended by the discovery of seeds and stems of the perennial horse-squash, *Cucurbita ficifolia*, and of *C. moschata* in early levels of a site in North Coastal Peru excavated by Dr. Junius Bird.[1]

In this high Andean region centered about Lake Titicaca there is an agriculture based on plants propagated vegetatively *and* plants propagated by seeds. All of the species were domesticated in the region and, to judge by the archeological remains, the many native names, and the numerous varieties of each species, both groups of plants are ancient. It is likely that when man began to farm in this region, he used the tuber and seed bearing food plants which he previously gathered. In this same

[1] T. W. Whitaker and J. B. Bird, "Identification and Significance of the Cucurbit Materials from Huaca Prieta, Peru," *American Museum Novitates*, No. 1426 (New York, 1949).

Lake Titicaca region the alpaca and llama were domesticated.[2]

The llama is the best known of the four American camel relatives. It, and the alpaca, are known as domesticated animals. Its primary use is in transporting cargo. Llama dung, gathered, dried, and used for fuel, is probably more valuable than the animal's meat, hide, or wool. The llama is thought to represent a domesticated form of the guanaco. The guanaco is the most tolerant of environment of the American cameloids and formerly was an important source of food and clothing, especially in Argentina, but has been exterminated over most of its former range until only a few semidomesticated herds still persist. All four of the American cameloids will interbreed and produce fertile offspring. The alpaca has characteristics which suggest that it is a hybrid, the result of crossing of llama and vicuña. The alpaca is not used for transportation but is valued for its wool, hides, dung, and meat. The vicuña is the only one of the four cameloids which has never been domesticated but it was systematically rounded up in drives organized under the Incas. When caught, some animals were killed but most were only clipped for their hair and then released to breed and increase.

Near Lake Titicaca the guinea pig probably originated and here it is still found as a household pet and food animal, running about the house and subsisting mainly on table scraps and some greens gathered for it.

Herd animals, like the alpaca and llama, are usually associated with seed agriculture; household animals like the guinea pig are considered associates of vegetative crop planting.[3] In the highlands we do not know which, llama or guinea pig, was domesti-

cated first, so this throws no light on which one of the two groups of food plants is older.

Many wild animals are caught, kept as pets, and utilized as food, but these cannot be considered as truly domesticated. They are not kept to breed and increase about the house although they are to be considered as semidomesticates or potential domesticates. The only other truly domesticated animals native to the New World are the turkey of North America and the Muscovy duck of northern South America. Some breeds of dogs may have originated in the New World by crosses of the Old World dogs with their relatives the wolves of this hemisphere, but there is little evidence for this. An odd breed of dogs, which disappeared soon after the Conquest, was kept for food in the region about the Caribbean. Some of the early records contain descriptions of these dogs and there are old pottery figurines from the Tarascan area of Mexico, some of them showing a dog with an ear of corn in its mouth. The ceremonial feeding of dog effigies by the Lacandones of the Mexican Rio Lacanjá region probably is a survival of the use of corn to fatten these meat animals.

Corn is the greatest crop of the New World and probably one of the oldest. The best evidence available indicates that corn originiated on the eastern slopes of the Andes in Colombia, Ecuador, Peru, or Bolivia. I favor the last two countries for there, in a region where the last steep slopes of the mountains meet the savannas and forests of the upper Amazon, the natives grow a kind of corn which possesses many characteristics which are considered primitive.[4] In this corn the plants are slender and branched at the base, the leaves long and slender, the ears long, slender, flexible, and not greatly compacted and condensed in length. The cobs are brownish in color, the brownish grains borne on pedicels, the pollen grains small. All of these are characteristics of

[2] R. M. Gilmore, "Fauna and Ethnozoology of South America," in J. H. Steward (ed.), *Handbook of South American Indians* (Bureau of American Ethnology Bulletin No. 143, 6 vols., 1946–50), VI, 423–62.

[3] Carl O. Sauer, *Agricultural Origins and Dispersals* (New York: American Geographical Society, 1952), p. 84.

[4] Hugh C. Cutler, "Races of Maize in South America" (Harvard University, *Botanical Museum Leaflets*, XII [1946]), 278.

wild-growing grasses rather than those of highly developed corn varieties. No one has ever seen wild corn but, with a few changes, none of which is greater than ones we already know in corn, a wild species of gama grass growing in the same region as this primitive corn of Bolivia and Peru could become a corn-like plant.[5]

After its domestication, corn was carried northwards and up the slopes of the Andes. In Guatemala corn encountered another species of Tripsacum and probably crossed with it to produce the plant known as teosinte.[6] Enough of the characteristics of the new grass entered corn to give it added vigor and variability and to this we owe the great number and diversity of the races of corn in Guatemala, Mexico, and the United States.[7]

The hypothesis of a South American origin, a crossing of maize with Tripsacum to produce teosinte, and the consequent introduction of new germ plasm and variability into maize fits all the known facts more accurately than any other hypothesis. Although this tripartite hypothesis was proposed in detail fourteen years ago, no better one has been needed or suggested. It is unlikely that we will ever find archeological material of corn from the eastern Andean slopes because they are moist and vegetable material soon decays, but the presence of a primitive kind of corn, of a variable relative of corn, and of many dominant characters of corn in this area support a belief in this as the place of origin. The fact that no corn has been uncovered in some early sites of dry coastal Peru while from sites of the same age and older in our Southwest we have excavated forms of pod corn, a

primitive kind of corn, does not invalidate this hypothesis of a South American origin. Corn varieties are very rigid in their cultural requirements and it is likely that corn was able to travel faster, with the aid of man, along the eastern slopes of the Andes and through Central America than it could be brought over the cold heights of the Andes to the Pacific Coast. But this is purely hypothesis and must be tested when new evidence is uncovered.

There is good support for the belief that Tripsacum introduced new variability into maize of Central and North America. The recent thorough study of races of maize of Mexico by Wellhausen and others delimits four ancient indigenous races, races which have been in Mexico so long that their source is unknown, and four pre-Columbian exotic races, races which probably arose in other regions and were brought to Mexico long ago. All of the twenty-four other races of corn in Mexico are considered to have developed by crossing within the basic eight races and teosinte, the hybrid of Tripsacum and maize. Certain of the derived races reached the United States and the great corn industry of our Corn Belt owes its origin to the crossing of a descendant of one of these Mexican races with Northern Flint corn to produce the vigorous and high yielding modern dents.[8]

As a result we grow more than half of the world's corn crop and the high yields we obtain have made it possible for one man on the farm to produce enough food and raw materials to support nine people off the land. Our industrial civilization is founded on corn just as much as were the earlier civilizations of the Aztecs, Mayas, and Incas.

Far to the east of the Andes, in that part of Brazil which stretches out towards Africa, is a region of scrub desert covered mainly by thorny shrubs, cacti, and other drought resistant plants. There grow many species of *Manihot*, a genus of woody

[5] Hugh C. Cutler, "A Comparative Study of Tripsacum Australe and Its Relatives," *Lloydia*, XX (1947), 233.

[6] Paul C. Mangelsdorf and R. G. Reeves, *The Origin of Indian Corn and Its Relatives* (Texas Agricultural Experiment Station, Bulletin 574 [1939]).

[7] E. J. Wellhausen, *et al, Races of Maize in Mexico, Their Origin, Characteristics and Distribution* (Cambridge, Mass.: Bussey Institution of Harvard University, 1952), pp. 199–205.

[8] W. L. Brown and Edgar Anderson, "The Southern Dent Corns" (*Annals of the Missouri Botanical Garden*, XXXV [1948]), 255–68.

plants, some of which bear starchy water-storing roots. The roots of several of the wild-growing species are gathered by the inhabitants in times of food scarcity. In this northeastern region of Brazil, where the largest number of varieties and the greatest range of variation within the species is found, the mandioca, or cassava, plant was domesticated. There are two groups of mandoca varieties, the bitter and the sweet. The roots of the bitter forms must be treated to remove a poisonous juice while those of the sweet forms can be used as food without such treatment. The bitter varieties produce better crops under the conditions of northeastern Brazil, but they have not spread far. A few sweet varieties are grown from Argentina to Mexico. Brazil is still the principal producer of mandioca, although most of it is used at home and the total production for export of Africa and the East Indies is far greater.

Mandioca is propagated, like sugar cane, with sections of the stems. Some varieties are ready to harvest in six months while others may take as long as three years to mature a good harvest of roots. Before the harvest a farmer's wife may dig up a single root from a plant for the next meal, then refill the hole so the plant continues to grow, a practice similar to that of the Maine farmwife who gathers a few early potatoes. Corn is a secondary crop over much of Brazil and mandioca is the mainstay. Sweet varieties of mandioca are eaten boiled, but most mandioca is prepared as a dry meal by peeling the roots, grating them, squeezing out the poisonous juice, and then drying the meal on a flat plate of stone, pottery, or metal over a slow fire. This meal can be kept for a long time and eaten dry without any further preparation, or mixed with shredded meat.

An alcoholic beverage is sometimes prepared from the sweet forms of mandioca by boiling the roots, masticating them slightly to add saliva, and putting them in a pot with water. The saliva contains an enzyme which changes starches to sugar and the sugar is acted upon by yeasts to produce alcohol. This process is relatively simple and can be applied to seed as well as root and tuber crops. It is an old process, widely spread throughout most of South and Central America, although strict controls on alcoholic beverages and the acculturation of the Indians have almost eliminated native beers in Central America. The process reaches its greatest refinement in the highland valleys of Peru and Bolivia.[9] There corn is ground, mixed with saliva, added to water and, after a day, heated to stop the enzyme action. The liquid is placed in other pots to ferment for three to eight days, depending on the temperature, and then is ready to be drunk. Shops selling *chicha,* as the native beers are usually called in American Spanish, display varied signs to advertise their wares. Tassels, usually considered a symbol of nobility in Inca areas, are widely used just as we employ a crown or shield to suggest noble lineage. Flowers added to signs suggest that the brew is freshly prepared and suitable for a holiday.

There is another source, besides saliva, for the starch-converting enzyme, and that is sprouted, or malted grain. Grains are soaked in water and allowed to germinate until the young shoot is nearly as long as the seed. This is the method employed with barley in the beer industry. It is well known in the Andes where seed crops are common but unknown to the east, where the roots and tubers are the main foods. I think malting was practiced in the Andes before the Conquest for it is mentioned in early reports and several native languages have names for all the steps in the process. The complexity of the process makes me doubt that it can be as ancient as the chewing method of preparing the mash for brewing.

Corn beer is an important food in much of highland South America. In some places it is the major means of consuming corn and the average inhabitant may drink more than a liter of *chicha* per day. It is likely

[9] Hugh C. Cutler, "*Chicha,* A Native South American Beer," Harvard University, *Botanical Museum Leaflets,* XIII (1947), 33–53.

that the yeasts provide substances essential to the diet but otherwise unobtainable in foods of the region.

The use of coca leaves is another one of those complex methods which, like the extraction of the poison from mandioca roots and the preparation of corn mash, probably arose after considerable thought and experimentation. Shrubby tea-like plants of coca are grown by planting seed in beds and transplanting the seedlings to specially prepared terraces on the moist eastern slopes of the Andes of Peru and Bolivia. The young leaves are picked and dried and transported to the highlands where most of them are chewed or, more accurately, soaked and sucked, with a small piece of a bar of the ashes of the quinoa plant mixed with clay to hold the ashes together. The use of an alkali with a drug plant resembles the pan or betel nut chewing of the Far East. Coca was used by only a small part of the Indians at the time of the Inca Empire but the coca habit has spread so far over Bolivia and Peru that the development of these countries is seriously hindered.

There are many other seed-grown plants on the same slopes where the seed-sown coca plant was domesticated. Among them are the tree tomato, several kinds of papaya and passion fruits, and the pepino (*Solanum muricatum,* a relative of the potato with a fruit tasting like a cross between a cucumber and a melon). The many kinds of cacao, or chocolate, fruits of the eastern Andean slopes are gathered for the sweet pulp surrounding the seeds and in pre-Conquest times it is unlikely that the seeds or chocolate beans were used as they were in Mexico. The plants are often grown from seed.

Peru and Bolivia constitute the greatest center for New World cultivated plant origins but they are closely followed by the highlands of Guatemala and Mexico, where the lima bean, scarlet runner, and the tepary bean originated and where the center of the common or kidney bean may lie. In the Guatemala-Mexico plant center the husk tomato was domesticated long ago and when weed wild tomatoes reached Mexico from the center of the tomato species on west coastal South America, the very similar tasting tomato was domesticated.[10] Some varieties of peppers were domesticated as well as two species of squash, *Cucurbita pepo* and *C. mixta.* The importance of Mexico and Guatemala as a center of origin of maize varieties has already been mentioned.

Only one of the two plants domesticated within the United States and only one of the ten wild edible plants which were selected as possible domesticates can be propagated vegetatively with ease. All of the plants listed for Mexico are grown from seed, none propagated vegetatively. In the Peru-Bolivia center about half of the plants, and many of the most important ones, are usually propagated vegetatively while, to the east in Brazil and the countries of the Amazon, Orinoco and Paraguay watersheds, most plants, like mandioca, the arrowroots, cannas, and pineapples, are propagated from pieces of stems or roots. In all these areas it appears that man used whatever was available in his neighborhood. I do not believe that agriculture began with root and tuber crops and that these earth crops are more ancient domesticates than the seed crops.

Nor do I believe that we have as yet any valid evidence for a single center of origin of agriculture. Certainly there is little in the cultivated plants to suggest that this is true. Of all the hundreds of species man plants, only the bottle gourd, *Lagenaria,* is generally accepted as having been grown on both the Old and New World continents prior to Columbus, and even in this, the varieties grown in the Old and New Worlds appear to be distinct. While Polynesians are usually considered to have cultivated the sweet potato before white men arrived in the islands, the fact that several wild and cultivated species of the same genus, found in both hemispheres, have edible

---

[10] J. A. Jenkins, "The Origin of the Cultivated Tomato," *Economic Botany,* II (1948), 255–68.

roots, makes it desirable to seek better proof than the sketchy reports of the early explorers that the species native to the Americas is identical to the prehistoric ones of the islanders.

There is good evidence for very early post-Columbian contacts between Peru and Asia both across the Pacific and through the Mediterranean. Natives of the interior of Assam who grow corn which resembles that of Peru, also grow squash, bean, peanut, Cyclanthera, and amaranth varieties typical of Peru. It should be possible, by a study of the varieties grown in Asia and a comparison with ones still grown in Peru, to define clearly the area from which the migrants came and perhaps to identify the route and even the travelers who carried them to Asia. The many cultural similarities which have been assembled by proponents of theories involving trans-Pacific movements are impressive, but so far there is no positive evidence which can be pointed to in the cultivated plants.

H. EPSTEIN

DOMESTICATION FEATURES IN ANIMALS AS FUNCTIONS OF HUMAN SOCIETY

The creation of domesticated animals and cultivated plants is the oldest and grandest example of experimental biological activity of man. It is an example of the transformation and adaptation of nature by labor to the satisfaction of the needs of human society. Cultivation and domestication were the first steps in the economic and scientific revolution of the New Stone Age that ended the impasse of savagery and ushered in the age of neolithic barbarism.[1]

Domestication changed the life of the beast, the character of the animal, and its anatomy and physiology. The domesticated animal in its turn profoundly affected the life of human society, the character of man, and his physical development.

Apart from the domestication of the wolf, which may have been as much due to the animal's voluntary attachment to the offal and warmth of human habitation (a phenomenon that has been observed among foxes in the Arctic) as to the human desire for companionship,[2] the domestication of the remaining domestic animals seems to

have had economic reasons: the provision of a reserve of animals for sacrificial purposes in the environment of settled cultivators that became progressively depleted of game (cattle); the substitution of wild species (reindeer) for domestic stock that could not be propagated in a new and unsuitable environment; and the provision of additional food reserves (rabbit) or beasts of burden (dromedary).[3] In close symbiosis with his domesticated animals, man soon learned to develop for his own benefit certain features—domestication features—that do not occur, or are excluded from propagation, in the wild animal.

Color.—The first changes in domestication affect the size and color of the stock. Already in the wild state, leucism and albinism sporadically occur among species normally of a dark coloration. Wolves, in which the prevailing color is zonar-grey, may develop a more or less marked grey or red tinge, while in some cases the fur is much paler than usual, even pure white, and in others nearly or quite black.[4] Among birds, wild boar, and wild deer, white specimens are not uncommon, while among deer kept in parks, albinism frequently spreads throughout the herd within a few generations.[5] In the wild state, albinistic individ-

Reprinted, with permission of the author and editor, from *Agricultural History*, XXIX (1955), 137–46 (copyright, 1955, by the Agricultural History Society). The author is professor of animal husbandry in the Faculty of Agriculture of the Hebrew University, Jerusalem, Israel.

[1] V. Gordon Childe, *What Happened in History* (Harmondsworth: Penguin Books, 1950), p. 48.
[2] A. Pedersen, "Eine Entdeckungsreise nach Nordost-Groenland," *Wild und Hund*, XLVIII (Berlin, 1926); Karl Kronacher, *Allgemeine Tierzucht* (6 vols.; Berlin: P. Parey, 1921–27), I, 56–73.

[3] C. Daryll Forde, *Habitat, Economy and Society: A Geographical Introduction to Ethnology* (New York: Dutton, 1934), p. 455.
[4] N. A. Iljin, "Wolf-Dog Genetics," *Journal of Genetics*, XLII (1941), 359–414.
[5] Max Hilzheimer, *Natürliche Rassengeschichte der Haussäugetiere* (Berlin: W. de Gruyter, 1926), p. 32.

uals of otherwise dark species are commonly eliminated by the process of natural selection. In arctic and subarctic regions, the reverse has taken place in several species.

In domesticated animals, artificial selection of color variations has been practiced since early times. White used to be especially valued, and selection of breeding stock was directed accordingly. The Hottentots of the Cape of Good Hope selected their cattle according to color in order to facilitate distinction between the stock of different owners that was pastured in common. Every stock owner kept and bred only animals of his selected color, exchanging those that differed for animals of the desired pattern. However, none of the Hottentots ever exchanged a white ox or cow, which they looked upon as an invaluable leader of the herd. This preference for white cattle the Hottentots seem to have brought with them on their migration from their earlier home in East Africa.[6] The ancient Egyptians worshipped Isis in the likeness of a white cow, and used to pray that the deity send them a white ox. The half-Hamites of East and East Central Africa slaughter a white bullock at the great ceremony of handing over the country from one age-grade to the other.[7] In Cadzow Forest, Lanarkshire, Scotland, two white bulls were slaughtered in the Druid temple every year, on the sixth day after the first full moon following March 6. Among the German tribes, as among the Persians, Scyths, and Venetes, white horses were particularly esteemed. When Xerxes arrived at the Struma river, his magi sacrificed white horses in honor of the river. The Slavs held a white horse sacred to the sun god Svatovit, and a black one to Triglav, the god of darkness and evil.[8]

Many primitive pastoralists regard certain color patterns as the most desirable from an economic or social point of view. The Arabs of Najd breed their hairy sheep in a single color pattern—black, with the head, tip of tail, and lower part of the legs white. The sheep of Hijaz, on the other hand, are white with fawn-colored ears, while the goat of Hijaz, which furnishes the material for the tents of the Bedouin, is black.[9] In Ruanda-Urundi, East Africa, wealthy tribal chiefs keep herds of cattle of a uniform coloration—red, white, or variegated.[10] This custom is traceable to Ethiopia, where it may have originated. The custom of selecting cattle with a view to certain color patterns has extended also into southern Africa in the train of the Bantu migrations. Chief Lewanika of the Barotse people of Northern Rhodesia maintained a herd of pure white cattle with black points. These were all slaughtered when Lewanika died in the year 1916.[11] The Zulu have among their cattle a type with white body, black muzzle, black inside to the ears, and a few black spots near the tail setting. At one time these animals were regarded as royal cattle and treated with great respect; in fact, it is thought that to some extent they were held sacred.

Selection of domestic stock according to color is practiced even among modern breeders. Originally the cattle of the Netherlands were commonly red or red-and-white. Black-and-white colored cattle were imported from Jutland after rinderpest had

---

[6] H. Epstein, "Animal Husbandry of the Hottentots," *Onderstepoort Journal of Veterinary Science and Animal Industry*, IX (1937), 653.

[7] Charles Seligman, *Races of Africa* (London: T. Butterworth, 1930 [2nd ed., London and New York: Oxford University Press, 1957]), p. 165.

[8] Victor Hehn, *Kulturpflanzen und Haustiere in ihrem Uebergang aus Asien nach Griechenland*

und Italien sowie in das übrige Europa (7th ed.; Berlin: Gebrüder Bornträger, 1902), 44. [Published in English as *The Wanderings of Plants and Animals from their First Home* (London: Swan Sonnenschein, 1888).]

[9] H. Epstein, "The Fat-tailed Sheep of Arabia," *Zeitschrift für Tierzüchtung und Züchtungsbiologie*, LXIII (1954), 381–96; *idem*, "The Hejas Dwarf Goat," *Journal of Heredity*, XXXVII (1946), 345–52.

[10] H. Kroll, "Die Haustiere der Bantu," *Zeitschrift für Ethnologie*, LX (1928), 241.

[11] H. H. Curson and R. W. Thornton, "A Contribution to the Study of African Native Cattle," *Onderstepoort Journal of Veterinary Science and Animal Industry*, VII (1936), 661.

destroyed many Dutch herds. However, this color pattern became predominant in Holland and other countries where Friesian cattle were bred only after U.S.A. breeders imported about 10,000 head of Dutch cattle during the decade 1875–1885, the importers insisting on the black-and-white pattern.[12] Similarly, Aberdeen-Angus cattle were originally found in several shades of color. The black color of the modern standard came to the fore during the seventies and eighties of the nineteenth century, owing to the demand of American importers for dark-colored specimens.[13]

Although color plays an important role in the breeding of cattle, it has commonly but a fictitious economic value. Occasionally the importance attributed to color markings may even be to the detriment of the breed if valuable breeding stock is culled owing to some minor color deviation from the established standard. An exception forms the absence of pigment which causes constitutional weakness of the skin, especially detrimental in tropical and subtropical climates with intense solar radiation. For this reason, breeders in subtropical countries show a justified reluctance to import white Shorthorn cattle. For a similar reason, dairy farmers in South-West Africa used to show preference for Friesian bulls excluded from registration in European herd books because of a black-colored scrotum. That even taxation may influence color in livestock is illustrated by a peculiar tax on black cattle which the Dutch India Company introduced in several districts of Cape Colony. This tax contributed to the culling of black animals from the herds of the Boers.[14]

In early times, sheep breeders paid little attention to the color of their flocks, which comprised white, tan, grey, black, and variegated specimens. The purple dyeing industry, first developed by the Phoenicians on a large scale, provided the impetus for the gradual elimination of colored sheep from improved flocks; for none but a black dye can be used on wool that is black, tan, or grey. As the murex fishery started the Phoenicians on their maritime career, purple dyeing spread throughout the Mediterranean region, and with the dyeing industry extended the demand for white wool.[15] With the modern industrialization of weaving and dyeing, the elimination of colored sheep has spread so rapidly that all improved wool-bearing breeds now carry white wool; and there are only a few left in which some difficulty is still experienced in preventing a light scattering of dark fibers in the fleece.

A further illustration of the extent to which color in several domestic animals represents a function of modern society is provided by the large financial interests involved in the breeding of numerous color fads in dogs, cats, rabbits, poultry, pigeons, and fish. Even in the horse, kept singularly free from capricious color fancies, the white-colored Apeloosa breed speckled with black in the manner of a leopard has been evolved for the purpose of furnishing a showy circus horse.

Horns.—Among primitive pastoralists, it is a frequent practice to bend the horns of cattle, sheep, and goats into various shapes, or to increase their number by splitting the buds. Certain Nilotic tribes such as the Dinka and Nuer deform the horns of their cattle artificially—a custom believed to be of ancient Egyptian origin. Among the Dinka, the usual deformity is with the one horn forwards, the other back. Among the Nuer, one horn is trained to grow upwards.

[12] Dirk L. Bakker, *Studien über die Geschichte den heutigen Zustand und die Zukunft des Rindes und seiner Zucht in den Niederlanden* (Maastricht: Druck Leiter-Nypels, 1909).

[13] James MacDonald and James Sinclair, *History of Aberdeen-Angus Cattle* (London: Vinton, 1910).

[14] Eric A. Walker, *A History of South Africa* (London: Longmans, Green, 1928 [3rd ed., 1957]).

[15] Lucien Febvre and Lionel Bataillon, *A Geographical Introduction to History* (New York: Knopf, 1925), p. 259 [First published as *La terre et l'évolution humaine: introduction géographique à l'histoire* (Paris: La Renaissance du Livre, 1922.)]

the other brought in a curve forwards across the beast's forehead. Cattle with artificially or naturally deformed horns have a social and emotional value, and the interest in such animals extends far beyond the Nile region into Kenya.[16] In South Africa, artificial deformation of the horns used to be practiced by several Bantu peoples; while in Northern Rhodesia, horns that hang down and swing owing to the lack of cores, or that are otherwise distorted, still excite high admiration.[17]

In several parts of Africa, horn gigantism in cattle has a high social value. Originally this feature was developed by Hamitic mountain dwellers in the western desert of Egypt. With the introduction of humped zebu cattle into Africa, horn gigantism passed into several hybrid (sanga) breeds derived from the crossing of the original straight-backed cattle of the Hamites with humped zebus. Single horns may attain a length of over 80 inches, and a basal circumference of 33 inches.[18] The reasons for the selection of giant-horned cattle are social and ceremonial rather than economic. Among the Masai and many other pastoral tribes throughout the savanna belts of Africa, animals with very large horns are held in high esteem. The cattle of the Masai are very mixed in type; for as a result of numerous predatory raids on their neighbors, nearly every variety of cattle in East Africa has found its way into the Masai kraals. All of these are humped, and two main types may be distinguished: a rather small, lightly built sanga strain with very long and splendidly curving lyre-shaped horns, and a thickset short-horned zebu strain which yields nearly twice as much milk; nevertheless the sanga strain is more highly valued. Comparative study of other social traits of the Masai has suggested that their cattle complex developed farther north among the Hamitic Galla of Ethiopia and has been carried south by the advances of the Nilo-Hamitic pastoralists, of whom the Masai are the largest and most powerful group.[19]

In Uganda, the short-horned zebu is hardier and possesses greater power of resistance to rinderpest, tuberculosis, and other diseases, as well as to such adverse conditions as poor grazing or fly infestation, than the long-horned sanga cattle. In spite of this economic advantage of the zebu, the long-horned sanga cattle are more highly valued. In Tanganyika Territory, short-horned zebus are encountered in addition to giant-horned Ankole cattle. Economically, the zebu is definitely the more useful animal: hardier, maturing earlier, milking better, working better, and furnishing a superior carcass. It maintains its condition when food is scarce and innutritious, and water available only every other day. But the owner of an Ankole beast thinks altogether differently. He will not exchange a long-horned Ankole cow of poor conformation and production for a better but shorter-horned zebu.[20]

However, in some instances economic reasons operate against social forces. Among the Kivu cattle of the Congo, there are occasionally encountered horns of so huge a size that the animals suffer serious incommodation. The Warundi and Wawira consider such horns beautiful, but the Wanyabongo do not hold them in favor because the cows of the giant-horned variety are poor milkers and the breed is hard to fatten.[21] In general, the breeders of the giant-horned cattle are fighting a losing battle; for natural selection outweighs their preference for giant-horned stock. In the course of a few centuries, the short-horned zebu, introduced into East Africa by Indian and

[16] Charles G. Seligman, "Egyptian Influence in Negro Africa," in S. R. K. Glanvill (ed.), *Studies Presented to F. L. Griffith* (London: Oxford University Press, 1932).

[17] Edwin W. Smith and A. M. Dale, *The Ila-Speaking Peoples of Northern Rhodesia* (London: Macmillan, 1920), I, 128.

[18] Richard Lydekker, *The Ox and Its Kindred* (London: Methuen, 1912).

[19] Forde, *Habitat, Economy and Society*, p. 303.

[20] Curson and Thornton, "A Contribution to the Study of African Native Cattle," p. 658.

[21] F. Carlier, "L'Elevage au Kivu," *Bulletin Agricole du Congo Belge*, vol. III (1912).

Arab traders, has superseded the longhorn cattle in nearly all low-lying areas and restricted their habitat to well-watered mountain grassland.

Under modern range conditions, horns in beef breeds of cattle are not only superfluous but an obvious disadvantage. Polled cattle are quieter and easier to handle and fatten. In general, their hides and carcasses are also more valuable, as polled cattle do not hurt each other on pasture or during shipment. Ranchers in the United States have therefore developed hornless types of the most popular beef breeds, Shorthorn and Hereford. Such cattle have been imported into Australia and the Argentine; and it is reasonable to assume that in the more advanced ranching countries the poled types will gradually gain on the horned.

Dwarfism.—During the early stages of domestication, environmental conditions are generally less favorable to the development of the tamed animals than is the normal life of the wild beast. The beginnings of domestication are therefore frequently accompanied by a reduction in the body size of the domesticated stock, owing to natural selection in relation to the adverse conditions. The vast majority of these primitive dwarf breeds are pituitary dwarfs characterized by a hereditary underdevelopment affecting all parts and organs of the body alike so that the entire skeleton is well proportioned.

The number of achondroplastic breeds of domesticated animals is far smaller, and the reason for their evolution differs from that of the pituitary dwarfs. Achondroplasia is characterized by a marked difference in bodily proportions. There is an average size trunk coupled with abnormally stunted extremities.[22] The earliest record of an achondroplastic animal, dated to about 1900 B.C., is represented by the painting of a bitch from Beni Hassan, Egypt, where this type seems to have been evolved, because of its grotesque appearance. Judging

from the care the Egyptians bestowed on the import of human dwarfs from Negroland, dwarfism was highly valued. Prior to the conquest of Peru by the Spaniards, the Incas had also developed an achondroplastic breed of dog that vanished with the Inca civilization.[23] Among the Huancas and several other tribes of Peru, these dogs were regarded as sacred and some were mummified. The modern dachshund, extreme representative of achondroplasia in dogs, has been evolved for badger hunting from short-legged hounds similar to those still occurring among spaniels and bassets. However, the original purpose has now almost completely given way to the breeding of the type for fashion, as in the case of the Dandie Dinmont and Skye terriers, the pug, Pekinese, and other dwarfs of less pronounced achondroplasia, as well as in the numerous pituitary dwarf breeds of dogs.

In equatorial Africa, several achondroplastic breeds of goats are encountered in the general breeding area of pituitary dwarf goats.[24] In Busoga and eastern Uganda, an achondroplastic goat is bred that is prized for its unusual appearance. The hair grows extremely long over the back and sides and on the top of the head; it falls over the eyes like the hair of a Skye terrier. The Bongo, a true Negro people of the eastern Sudan, and the Mittu, of the high Nilotic group of inter-Congo-Nile tribes, have two different goat breeds, one of which is dwarfed and characterized by the heavy body and short legs.[25] A similar small and plump breed, distinguished by the heavy belly reaching nearly to the ground, is ecountered among the Hausa in the region from Zaria to Katsina and Sokoto. In the most pronounced form, achondroplasia is met with in the dwarf goats of the Cameroons, which are distinguished by the heavy compact

[22] Epstein, "The Hejas Dwarf Goat," 345–52.

[23] Hilzheimer, *Natürliche Rassengeschichte der Haussäugetiere*, p. 63.

[24] H. Epstein, "The Dwarf Goats of Africa," *East African Agricultural Journal*, XVIII (1953), 123–32.

[25] Georg Schweinfurth, *Im Herzen von Afrika* (Leipzig: F. A. Brockhaus, 1918).

body on very short thick legs.[26] All these breeds, which are highly valued by their owners, have been developed solely for their strange appearance, in an environment that favors dwarf goats of any type —pituitary, achondroplastic, or mixed.

Among cattle, only a single achondroplastic breed is known—a humped zebu with a long deep body on tiny crooked legs.[27] This breed, which is held sacred, is kept in several Indian temples for the attraction of visitors.

The only achondroplastic breed of livestock developed for a purely economic, rather than an aesthetic purpose, was the Ancon sheep that traced its origin to a male achondroplastic lamb born in a small flock of normal sheep in Massachusetts, in 1791. The Ancon breed, no longer extant, was characterized by the long body and the short, crooked legs which prevented it from jumping fences—the reason for its propagation.[28]

Weight and Speed in Horses.—An increase in size and weight of domesticated animals has been brought about solely as a consequence of changes in human social relations. In the horse, increase in size and weight has proceeded in two different directions: one has led to the evolution of the heavy breeds of draft horses, the other to the Thoroughbred and its derivatives.

Horses of large size were first evolved during Roman times in response to the demand of the legions for a strong cavalry horse such as is represented in the equestrian statue of Marc Aurel. The foremost breeding center of heavy horses was Spain, where the ancestral stock, as illustrated by numerous iron age sculptures and rock drawings, seems to have been heavier than in other parts of Europe, Asia, or northern Africa. From Spain the Romans introduced these horses into several of their colonies,

including Britain. The Roman importations altered the stock of western Europe to such an extent that by the middle of the second century A.D., the original small twelve-hand ponies were no longer easily obtainable along the routes traversed by the Roman legions and their auxiliaries.[29]

During feudal times, the increasing weight in armor made the breeding of a still larger horse essential. Horsemen commenced to wear some form of defensive armor during the early centuries A.D., but especially during the close of the twelfth century, when the use of the crossbow and the experience of the Crusades initiated a great development of European armor. The hauberk gave way to armor of interwoven chain, while the latter in its turn, from the year 1300 onwards, was gradually superseded by plates of metal until, at the beginning of the fifteenth century, the knight was sheathed in a complete panoply of plate armor. This ever increasing weight of mail demanded horses of increased size and strength, and induced the development of the large breeds of horses in those countries where knighthood flourished most, that is, in Spain, France, and Flanders. By the sixteenth century, a charger was capable of carrying a rider weighing, with his own armor and that of his steed, about 425 pounds.[30]

The horses of Britain gained considerably in size when the Saxons and Danes imported larger breeds from the Continent, and especially when the Normans introduced that large and heavy breed of horses which had been steadily developed for twelve centuries in northwestern Europe.

The origin of the recent breeds of heavy draft horses in France, Belgium, and Britain, goes back to the seventeenth century when, after the introduction of firearms,

[26] Adolf Staffe, "Die Haustiere der Kosi," *Zeitschrift für Tierzüchtung und Züchtingsbiologie,* XL (1938), 252–85, 301–42.

[27] J. Ulrich Duerst, *Grundlagen der Rinderzucht* (Berlin: J. Springer, 1931), p. 238.

[28] Kronacher, *Allgemeine Tierzucht,* II, 71.

[29] J. Cossar Ewart, "On Skulls of Horses from the Roman Fort at Newstead near Melrose," *Transactions of the Royal Society of Edinburgh,* XLV (1907), 555–87.

[30] William Ridgeway, *The Origin and Influence of the Thoroughbred Horse* (Cambridge: Cambridge University Press, 1905), p. 336.

the heavy armor of the feudal knights fell into disuse, and the powerful charger, no longer required for war, was made into an animal of draft. A heavy draft horse became necessary for several purposes: industrialization, by creating large urban centers with increasing demand for agricultural products, induced farmers to plow up heavy lands, so far used only as pastures, for the production of feeding crops, wheat, and sugar beets. Work on such land required a heavy type of horse which is now gradually being replaced by the tractor. Further, in Britain, Belgium, and northern France, the industrial revolution called for a suitable draft animal for the short-distance transport of heavy loads in urban areas. It took several decades until this task was taken over by motorized transport. Similarly, the ever increasing weight of cannons called for a progressive increase in the weight of horses until, in the course of the First World War, mechanization of transport became general in the armies at the western front.

The evolution of the racing type in horses is traceable to the second millenium B.C., when the peoples of the northern grassland zone, after the development of the light two-wheeled war chariot from the heavy ox-cart, carried their campaigns of conquest into China, India, western Asia, Egypt, and southern and western Europe. Chariot races for a long time remained a characteristic feature of all horse breeding peoples settling beyond the fringes of the grassland zone.[31] But the true racing type was evolved only after the horse was freed from the chariot. The peoples of northeastern Asia were the first to bring riding to the highest and most one-sided perfection, so that even the anatomy of the horsemen became adapted to their mode of life on horseback. We learn from Chinese sources that the Huns taught their children to ride on the backs of sheep at the age when other infants learn to walk. The most

far-reaching development of the racing type was accomplished by the Arabs, who experienced the value of a horse of great speed and endurance in their intertribal raids characteristic of Bedouin society, as well as in the campaigns of Mohammed and his successors.

The Thoroughbred race horse, which has had such a profound influence on nearly every breed of riding horses throughout the world, was founded on oriental blood. It is significant that the development of the English race horse at the beginning of the seventeenth century followed the revolutionary changes in the art of warfare brought about by the introduction of firearms.[32] Instead of the knight's heavy charger, a light cavalry horse bred for speed, staying power, and maneuverability, became an essental part of nearly all European armies. And it is only since the introduction of the machine gun that the importance of the remount has begun to fade. Parallel with this recent development, the breeding of Thoroughbred horses has become largely the prerogative of a leisured class of society, the basis of an industry built on racing and betting.

With the reduced demand for remounts, racing itself has undergone significant changes. The importance of long distance races has declined in favor of short distances. The resulting neglect of the stayer families in Thoroughbred breeding, and the coming to the fore of the sprinters, has been accompanied by genetic changes in the racing stock, both anatomically and physiologically; anatomically mainly in the skeleton of the shoulder and croup; physiologically in the capacity of the organism to incur a high "oxygen debt."

Meat and Fat.—Since the beginning of domestication, all animals, with the exception of the cat, have furnished human society with meat. Even the flesh of the common pariah dog is still valued by several African native peoples. But until rel-

[31] Joseph Wiesner, "Fahren und Reiten in Alteuropa und im Alten Orient," *Der Alte Orient,* vol. XXXVIII (1939).

[32] Matthew H. Hayes, *Points of the Horse* (5th ed., London: Hurst and Blackett, 1930), pp. 359–60.

atively recent times, the especial development of a meat-producing type was only occasionally accomplished. The ancient Egyptians evolved a beef type from their longhorn cattle when the wealth, amassed during the dynastic period in the palaces of the rulers and the temples of the priesthood, encouraged the demand for beef of a superior quality. However, it was only in the course of the industrial revolution that the concentration of large populations in towns and cities and the increasing accumulation of wealth created an unprecedented and persistent demand for animal products, particularly meat. Remunerative prices encouraged breeders to develop suitable breeds of livestock; and it is no coincidence that the second half of the eighteenth century witnessed Robert Bakewell's pioneer work in improved methods of breeding for beef and mutton, and that nearly all the more important breeds of beef cattle, mutton sheep, porkers, and bacon swine were developed in Britain, then industrially the most advanced country.[33]

In 1710, at the Smithfield Market, center of British meat trade, beefs averaged 370 pounds, and sheep 28 pounds in weight; whereas in 1795 average weights were 800 and 80 pounds, respectively.[34] In the course of the nineteenth century, the weights of cattle and swine in western and central Europe were more than doubled. In Bavaria, during the period 1816–67, the weight of cattle increased by 40 per cent and of swine by 71 per cent; during the following 50 years, the weight of cattle by another 170 per cent and of swine by 70 per cent.[35]

During the period of development of the modern breeds, the value of fat and tallow greatly exceeded the value of lean meat. For prior to the introduction of petroleum, tallow was the principal material for lighting. In accordance with paragraph 35 of

the "Capitulae de villis" of Charles the Great, the fattening of oxen was directed solely to the production of tallow, which was rendered at the place of slaughter. During the two decades, 1826–45, the average prices of beef and tallow in Austria were 6.9 and 16.8 kreuzers per one pound, respectively. Kidney fat during the same period cost twice as much as beef, and a large proportion of fattened cattle and sheep were sold direct to candle and soap factories.[36] For this reason, Bakewell was not worried when a customer complained that his sheep were so fat a gentleman could not eat them.

As soon as petroleum, gas, and electricity took over the role of the candle, the relative value of fat and meat changed in favor of the latter, and breeding and fattening methods were altered accordingly. While in France, 150 years ago oxen used to be fattened at the age of 10 to 15 years, since young beasts were merely growing and putting on flesh during the fattening process instead of large masses of valuable fat, the present demand in nearly all industrialized countries is for beef from early maturing cattle not older than 30 months at the time of slaughter. A contributory factor to this development is the growing percentage of married women employed in modern commerce and industry. While in a family in which the husband was the sole breadwinner, it was of little account if beef derived from old beasts had to be cooked for the formerly normal time of five hours; nowadays, with many married women having to add their income to that of their husbands in order to make ends meet, the demand is for tender cuts of young animals suitable for quick steaks and roasts. In consequence, the breeding for baby beef and fat lamb to meet these requirements is changing the breeding policy and thereby the anatomical and physiological character of many breeds of livestock in several countries such as Britain, the United States, New Zealand, Australia, and the Argentine, to an increasing extent.

[33] Laurence M. Winters, *Animal Breeding* (4th ed.; New York: Wiley, 1948), p. 18.

[34] Victor A. Rice, *Breeding and Improvement of Farm Animals* (3rd ed.; New York: McGraw-Hill, 1942), p. 21.

[35] Kronacher, *Allgemeine Tierzucht*, IV, 144–45.

[36] Duerst, *Grundlagen der Rinderzucht*, p. 516.

In semiarid regions, the breeding of sheep and cattle with a view to fat-production has taken a different direction. In western Asia, cattle and sheep with store reserves of fat in various parts of their bodies were evolved about 5,000 years ago. In cattle, accumulations of fat are deposited in the hump, which may be either cervico-thoracic or thoracic in situation.[37] Such humped cattle, known as zebu, have since spread over a large part of southern Asia and throughout Africa south of the Sahara. They excel other types of cattle in hardiness and resistance to drought. The original zebu type had a cervico-thoracic flesh hump, not given to complete adipose deterioration, although in times of plenty a certain amount of fat may be deposited in layers, at first subcutaneous, then between Musculus trapezius and Musculus rhomboideus, and finally beneath the latter. The endeavor of pastoralists to increase the quantity of fat in the hump has led by way of selection to an overdevelopment of the thoracic part of M. rhomboideus, capable of considerable adipose development. Thereby the situation of the hump passed from the cervico-thoracic to the thoracic, M. trapezius simultaneously undergoing certain secondary structural and functional changes.

In sheep, the accumulation of fat is concentrated either in the rump or the tail. Fat-rumped breeds may have very short tails or be completely devoid of caudal vertebrae, while in fat-tailed breeds, the tail displays a marked variability in size and conformation, in some breeds attaining so great a length as to sweep the ground. Fat-tailed breeds extend over a large part of southern Asia, a small area in southeastern Europe, and the whole of Africa, excluding Somaliland and the tropical forest belt. Fat-rumped sheep are bred in the Horn of Africa, southern Arabia, and Iran, extending from the Black Sea through Turkestan,

Mongolia, and Manchuria to China, and including the greater part of Siberia.

The development of store reserves of energy in the tail or rump, on which the animal draws during periods of nutritional scarcity, is explainable through the agency of artificial selection. This implies that fat deposits on the tail and rump of sheep may sporadically occur among any breed but that it was only in steppe and desert regions and among peoples lacking other fat-producing animals that these features were considered of sufficient economic importance to induce breeders to select specimens with adipose deposits for breeding purposes. Among ordinary sheep, the occurrence of both fat-rumped and fat-tailed animals has been recorded. The Cotswold and Romney Marsh breeds exhibit a marked tendency to accumulate fat on the rump almost to the degree of producing a deformity.[38] In some Border-Leicester rams there is a considerable amount of fat at the root of the tail or on the buttocks.[39] Since there exists no economic necessity in Britain to produce a fat-rumped or fat-tailed breed, such animals are not selected for breeding purposes; on the contrary, they are culled, as the fat deposits in the rump and tail are considered undesirable. Fat-tailed and fat-rumped sheep were developed in steppe and desert regions where such animals proved more resistant during periods of drought than the bulk of the ordinary stock, and where the fat-producing swine was lacking for religious reasons or because the nature of swine is unsuited to the roaming life of nomads.

Milk.—The first development of a dairy type in cattle took place during the period of the urban revolution in Sumer and Elam, where the fertility of the soil and the cooperative effort of a planned society enabled farmers to produce a surplus of foodstuffs.

[37] H. H. Curson and J. H. R. Bisschop, "Some Comments on the Hump of African Cattle," *Onderstepoort Journal of Veterinary Science and Animal Industry*, V (1935), 621–44.

[38] Richard Lydekker, *The Sheep and Its Cousins* (London: G. Allen, 1912), p. 118.

[39] J. Cossar Ewart, "Domesticated Sheep and Their Wild Ancestors: Wild Sheep of the Argali Type," *Transactions of the Highland and Agricultural Society of Scotland*, XXVI (1914), p. 90.

Villages expanded into cities, surrounded by gardens, fields, and pastures. Artisans, laborers, transport workers, and traders were withdrawn from direct food production. The temples of the priesthood, where the wealth was concentrated, provided breeding stock, farm equipment, boats, and tools.[40] The demand of urban society for a regular supply of milk and dairy products called for a type of cattle adapted for this purpose. From Mesopotamia, this new type spread in three main directions: (1) eastwards, north of the zebu belt, to the shores of the Pacific; (2) along the eastern and southern coast belt of the Mediterranean, down the west coast of Africa as far as Nigeria; and (3) along the northern littoral of the Mediterranean through Switzerland and the coastlands of the North Sea to the Channel Islands and Britain (Celtic shorthorn).

When the industrialization of western Europe created a market for milk and dairy products, several breeds of cattle were developed to meet these requirements. Outstanding among these are the cattle of the Netherlands, the Jerseys and Guernseys, and the Brown Swiss, all of them either entirely or predominantly of the shorthorn type originally evolved for the purpose of supplying milk and dairy products to the urban populations of ancient Mesopotamia.

No other domestic animal, with the exception of the goat, has been developed for the purpose of milk production to the same extent as have cattle. Even the goat is not milked so universally. And the milk of the buffalo, camel, horse, and reindeer is used only in a few restricted areas; no special dairy breeds have been evolved from them. In certain conditions, the sheep approaches the goat as a milk producer. After the Thirty Years' War, milking of sheep became a general practice in central Europe, owing to the lack of cattle, the tremendous loss of population, and the reduced demand for wool. At that time several dairy breeds of sheep were evolved, a remnant of which is still found in the marsh sheep of East

Friesland. The dairy properties of sheep have been developed also in some other conditions. Before the Hottentots of South-West Africa came in contact with goat-breeding Bantu peoples, they had no goats and used to milk their fat-tailed sheep and teach their infants to suck the milk straight from the udders.[41] In Southern France, where the true Roquefort cheese commands a high price, sheep are kept for their milk as well as their wool. In the more remote parts of the Balkans, western Asia, and North Africa dairy breeds of sheep are retained in agriculturally and industrially backward regions. But with the growing impact of industrialization on economic and social conditions, dairy sheep breeding is losing its importance even in these countries.

Wool.—In the first stage of their exploitation by man, most domestic animals are of no use until they are killed. The sheep was domesticated in order to make human society independent of the vagaries of the hunt for meat and skins. In both the wild and primitive domesticated sheep, the body is covered with a coat of short hair, extending into a mane in mature rams. But already in wild sheep the hair in its structure is definitely wool although it is coarse, stiff, and nearly straight. It possesses the essential character of wool in the finely intricate arrangement of its serrated and imbricated scaly surface that gives to wool the remarkable felting property upon which its peculiar utility depends. Under domestication, the hair has become longer, finer, and wavier, chiefly through selection of suitable breeding stock that appeared either spontaneously or upon the crossing of various strains of domesticated sheep. And as the woolly fleece could repeatedly be plucked or shorn from the live animal, the sheep entered a higher stage of exploitation by man—the stage of its usefulness for its wool while alive, and for mutton and skin after exhaustion of its usefulness as a source of wool. Only in countries with

[40] Childe, *What Happened in History*, p. 95.

[41] Epstein, "Animal Husbandry of the Hottentots," p. 660.

a warm climate where people have no need for wool, as in southern Asia and in Africa south of the Sahara, primitive breeds of woolless sheep have survived to this day.

In goats, the hair has not developed the peculiar quality of felting. For this reason mohair and cashmere, although valuable textile fibers on account of their luster, length, fineness, and strength, have but a restricted use: mohair in the manufacture of upholstery and lining materials, rugs, summer suits, draperies, and decorative trimmings, and cashmere in the manufacture of shawls. And, unlike wool, which has been bred into every improved breed of sheep, mohair and cashmere have remained the respective properties of only two breeds of goat, the Angora and Cashmere.

Improvement of wool in sheep has taken two main directions: the elimination of colored wool and breeding for white fleeces as a prerequisite of dyeing, and the improvement in the weight and quality of fleeces, more especially the elimination of kemp.

With the gradual shift of economic power from western Asia to Greece, and from Greece to Rome, the wool industry migrated to the western Mediterranean region. Breeding stock was imported from Asia Minor by way of Samos to Attica and Epirus. From Greece, fine-wooled sheep were brought to Sicily and lower Italy, and to the ancient Greek colony of Massilia at the mouth of the Rhone, whence they reached the Iberian peninsula. During the 450 years of their rule, the Romans imported large numbers of fine-wooled sheep into Spain in order to improve the local breeds. Gades and Cordoba became the marketing centers that furnished Rome with the finest woolen cloth. The setback to the Spanish wool industry, caused by the Visigoth invasion in 456, was of short duration as the newcomers soon settled down to an agricultural existence. When the Moors conquered Spain in 712, they found a flourishing agriculture and soon developed an extensive weaving industry which became famous throughout the medieval world. As soon as the Moors were driven out, the Catholic church and nobility got hold of the merino flocks which produced the best type of wool then known anywhere.

During the latter part of the eighteenth century there was an ever growing demand for wool of an extremely fine fiber suitable for the manufacture of soft fabrics such as broadcloth. To meet this demand, merino flocks of Spanish origin, established in Saxony, Silesia, Prussia, Austria, and Italy, were bred for the single purpose of producing such fine wool. The flocks of Saxony in particular became world famous for the most marvelous fleeces ever known—wool of gemlike luster, so beautifully fine and even and of such exquisite downiness of touch that all other wools seemed base by the side of it.[42]

Social development in England favored the growing of wool, since the great plague of 1348 had reduced the number of laborers to such an extent that landowners were obliged to turn their lands into pastures. Wool became the sheet anchor of English farming. During the reign of Edward III (1327–1377), Flemish weavers, dyers, and fullers, skilled in the then most advanced methods of cloth making, were induced to settle in England by a grant of special protection. They were joined by others of their countrymen who came to England as refugees in the reign of Elizabeth.[43] However, climatic conditions did not encourage English farmers to produce so fine a wool as that of the Spanish merino; and at the time when the merino craze swept over Europe, the enormous industrial expansion and growth of urban populations caused such a rapid advance in land values that it no longer paid the English farmer to keep sheep for their wool alone. After the Napoleonic wars, England's export wool trade was cut away at its roots and English wool could not even hold its own in the

[42] Robert H. Burns and E. L. Moody, "The Trek of the Golden Fleece," *Journal of Heredity,* XXVI (1935), 433–43.

[43] Walter C. Coffey, *Productive Sheep Husbandry* (3rd ed.; rev. by William G. Kammlade, Chicago, Philadelphia, etc.: Lippincott, 1937), pp. 6–7.

home markets. By 1824, it had become un-salable in the face of competition by cheap Silesian and other German wools, and du-ties were unable to protect the local indus-try. The merino, therefore, could not gain a foothold in Britain and it is no coinci-dence that Robert Bakewell made a mut-ton breed of the Leicester sheep, with com-plete disregard for its wool, and that all the breeds of sheep subsequently evolved in Britain were of the mutton type. Wool could be grown more cheaply and profit-ably on the wide pastures of the colonies.

While this development started in Brit-ain, then industrially the most advanced country, it did not end there. With the rise of industrialization, a similar development took place in central and western Europe. In Germany, within the nineteenth century the value of mutton increased five times in relation to the value of wool and the type of sheep bred in western Europe changed accordingly.

Even in Australia, New Zealand, and the Argentine, where the bulk of the wool was formerly produced by pure merinos, the rise in the importance of mutton, since the introduction of refrigerating plants in cargo vessels, has resulted in a large amount of cross-breeding and coarsening of the wool. The days have passed when in the more remote districts of Australia the value of a shorn sheep was approximately one shil-ling, that is, one fifth of the value of its annual yield of wool.[44] With the invention of combs that will comb comparatively short wool, long fine wool has become rela-tively less valuable than formerly. Manu-facturers can now combine quality, length, and strength more cheaply and speedily than the wool grower can through breeding. Hence, sheep farmers no longer attempt to get into the fleece the maximum of fineness, length, and weight; and a different type of sheep producing a coarser wool and su-perior mutton, has gradually replaced the fine-wooled merino type all over the world.

[44] Friedrich Aereboe, *Allgemeine landwirtschaft-liche Betriebslehre* (6th ed.; Berlin: P. Parey, 1923), p. 379.

MORTON H. FRIED

LAND TENURE, GEOGRAPHY AND ECOLOGY IN THE CONTACT OF CULTURES

But if it so be that the multitude throughout the hole llande passe and excede the dew numbre, then they chewse out of euery citie certeyn cytezens, and buylde vp a towne vnder their owne lawes in the nexte lande where the inhabitauntes haue muche waste and vnoccupied grounde, receauinge also of the inhabitauntes to them, if they wil ioyne and dwel with them . . . But if the inhabitauntes of that lande wyll not dwell with them, to be ordered by their lawes, then they dryue them out of those boundes, which they haue limited and apointed out for themselues . . . For they counte this the moste iust cause of warre, when any people holdeth a piece of grounde voyde and vacaunt to no good nor profitable vse, kepying other from the vse and possession of it, whiche notwithstanding by the lawe of nature ought thereof to be nowryshed and relieued.[1]

Even in Sir Thomas More's description of Utopia, contacts between societies of different degrees of complexity depended on three primary factors: land tenure, geography, and ecology. Since the sixteenth century, however, the mountainous accumulation of data and the persistent quest in social science for details have often totally obscured the large and basic patterns of acculturation. It is now time to utilize the growing stockpile of ethnological

Reprinted, with permission of the author and publisher, from *American Journal of Economics and Sociology,* XI (1952), 391–412. The author is associate professor of anthropology at Columbia University, New York.

[1] *Sir Thomas More's Utopia,* ed. J. C. Collins (Oxford: Clarendon Press, 1904), 66–67.

fact to construct broad hypotheses which may serve as tools in the study of the evolution of culture. There is no more promising area in which such studies may begin than that relating to the contact of societies.

The thesis that geography has played, and continues to play, a significant role in the determination of the times and localities of cultural contact, hardly needs demonstration. Perhaps equally obvious is the part which geography has played in deterring interaction or the ways in which it has been used by specific societies as a shield and defense against alien penetration.

Ecology, which might be called the action aspect of geography, combines indigenous resources with a specific cultural inventory of exploitative techniques, making possible a certain distribution of human population over a particular region. Any specified interaction of a population with its natural environment is only one of a number of the possible solutions of the exploitative problems of a given area since the ecological process of the moment is the result of the unique history of cultural events. When a society with intensive exploitative demands enters an area in which the population pursues less promising modes of production, certain broad categories of events and certain types of sociocultural relationships are unavoidable.

The exploitative system of a culture, however, is only in part a question of the environment divided by the technology. It is also necessary to consider the organization of human resources. Within this field, which is usually known as "social organization," the student encounters a welter of institutions and associations, families, clans, phratries, moieties, tribes, communities and nations, which often, because of their intrinsic interest, obscure the approach to larger questions. But, underlying each of these groups is a relationship of individuals or a cluster of individuals to the means of production—ultimately, in non-industrial societies, to the arable or hunting land. Thus, land tenure stands out as a diagnostic criterion of social organization. Indeed, it is in the struggle over systems of tenure or ownership that the contest between social systems for the control of an area is to be understood.

This paper is an attempt to point out the similarities in the processes involved in the contact of cultures in two widely separated portions of the world. In each case the invading culture was of far greater economic complexity than the indigene. Where such a disparity exists and there is an aggressive meeting of societies the result tends to fall within one of three large categories: total destruction of the native culture, transformation of the native culture, or incorporation of the native culture.[2] This hypothesis will be illustrated with data drawn from the contact of expanding European culture and the aboriginal population of the New World north of the Rio Grande, and with evidence selected from the meeting of expanding Chinese civilization and aboriginal culture in southwest China.

Which of the three large scale alternatives becomes the precise fate of a specific people, the "fate" within which occurs the detailed acculturation usually studied by anthropologists,[3] depends on the combina-

tion of factors summed up as land tenure, geography, and ecology. The first factor, the nature of the indigenous social organization as it is revealed in the system of land tenure, is of special interest, since it, alone of the three, seemingly presents great opportunities to individuals in directing the development of culture. Thus, the settling of our own West and the subsequent expropriation of the Indians is often viewed in terms of individual pioneers who bravely and *personally* carried forward the frontier. It is not the intent here to reopen the case against the great man theory of history, but one can hardly help noting that on the shifting historical stage it is often impossible to distinguish a hero from a scoundrel. According to John Collier:

The Indians of the whole country lost 90,-000,000 acres to whites through the direct and indirect workings of land allotment in the years from 1887 to 1933; but in addition, they lost to whites the *use* of most of the allotted land still Indian-owned.[4]

If one looks for the perpetrator of this frequently denounced system of expropriation, no single villainous hand may be isolated. But the investigator may be chagrined when he discovers that one of the key roles in pressing the adoption of the allotment system was filled by none other than Carl Schurz, to whose liberalism many a park and statue have been dedicated.

Reading further in Collier, one discovers that:

When Albert B. Fall passed from office, to be indicted, tried and imprisoned, all his pira-

---

[2] Ruth Benedict, "Two Patterns of Indian Acculturation," *American Anthropologist*, XLV (1943), 207–12. The present view bears few resemblances to Benedict's analysis and is in some respects totally disparate.

[3] For anthropological treatment of the theory of acculturation see Bronislaw Malinowski, *The*

Dynamics of Culture Change: An Inquiry into Race Relations in Africa (New Haven: Yale University Press, 1945); Ralph Linton (ed.), *Acculturation in Seven Indian Tribes* (New York: Appleton-Century, 1940); Melville J. Herskovits, *Acculturation: The Study of Culture Contact* (New York: J. J. Augustin, 1938); Robert Redfield, Ralph Linton, and Melville J. Herskovits, "A Memorandum for the Study of Acculturation," *American Anthropologist*, XXXVIII (1936), 149–52.

[4] John Collier, *The Indians of the Americas* (New York: Mentor Books, 1947), p. 134 (italics his).

cies had been smashed; he had filled the role of the indispensable villain in the drama, needful at the beginning. But the Indian Bureau moved automatically, implacably on.[5]

In such a fashion does the necessity of history play tricks on us all.

Emphasis upon geography as an important factor in the shaping of acculturative processes is not novel. Students treating of the contact between American Indian tribes and the expanding European civilization frequently stress the physical retreat of the aborigines. One anthropologist, for example, dealing with the problems of Fox Indian acculturation noted that for these people, "it was not feasible to achieve the desired sanctuary, as was done by many tribes of the North American Southwest, by virtue of geographical position. . . ."[6] Likewise, treating of cultures on the other side of the world, Owen Lattimore decides that those individuals with the deepest stake in a primitive culture must retire into the wilderness before the onslaught of a more highly organized society.[7]

Ecological factors in acculturation have also gained frequent mention. Though as early as 1518 More pointed to the importance of differences of technique and degree of exploitation of the natural environment in his Utopia, an authority on American Indian land planning has stated much more recently that:

The Indian had to go. Unable, unwilling to use more than 1 per cent of the continental resources, he had to yield to the race which was willing and able to exploit, consume, waste or dissipate, in two centuries, the accretion of the historic and geologic past. . . .

The Indian lost two-thirds of his reservation lands largely because he could not adapt his culture and economy fast enough to conform to the white methods of exploiting the continental natural resources. Where he made the

adaptation, where he proceeded to exploit the natural resources in his possession commercially by and for himself, there he retained possession of his lands.[8]

Finally, we may cite at least one previous statement that makes explicit the need for the destruction of early communalistic types of land tenure when societies with great exploitative demands encounter, in their expansion, tribes of simpler socioeconomic structure.

The tribal title was an indefensible title, considering the spirit of the age. Nineteenth century America was absorbed by its faith and hope in the future—or rather, its belief in infinite free land and untrammelled free enterprise. The tribal title found few friends in that age of individualism. To smash the Indian's communalism, and to get rid of his obnoxious tribalism, came naturally to be a leading motive in Indian policy. And nothing was conceived as of greater efficacy in bringing about the dismemberment of the tribes than the forcing upon each Indian man, woman, and child of a piece of his or her reservation.[9]

Though each major point to be found in this paper is thus shown to appear clearly in the literature, what none of these citations, or others the writer might assemble, indicates is that any given situation depends on a delicate and intricate balance of all three factors. And, beyond this, none of them demonstrates that the total process in question has wider reference than merely to the history of our own country.

The three factors of land tenure, geog-

[5] *Ibid*, 149–50.
[6] Natalie Joffe, "The Fox of Iowa," in Ralph Linton (ed.), *Acculturation in Seven American Indian Tribes*, p. 260.
[7] Owen Lattimore, *Inner Asian Frontiers of China* (New York: American Geographical Society, 1940), pp. 209 ff.

[8] Walter V. Woelke, "Indian Land Tenure, Economic Status and Population Trends," *Report on Land Planning*, Part X (Washington, D.C.: U.S. Government Printing Office, 1935), p. 2. We must dissent from Mr. Woelke's unfortunate and misleading use of the term "race." The process involved, as we hope to demonstrate, is a cultural one: racial differences, when they coincide, are merely a fortuitous complication. In the Asian material the process will be demonstrated to take place within a single major conventional racial grouping.
[9] Allan G. Harper, "Salvaging the Wreckage of Indian Land Allotment," in Oliver La Farge (ed.), *The Changing Indian* (Norman: University of Oklahoma Press, 1943), p. 86.

raphy, and ecology have played similar roles wherever an aggressive and expanding economy based upon complex exploitation of natural resources has contested the occupation and dominance of a given area with a less highly developed culture. The expanding economies are not always associated with European cultures, Caucasoid populations, or Indo-European languages. In northern Southeast Asia the expanding Chinese society, without tutorial assistance from the West, developed techniques for dealing with aborigines which show many startling parallels to those which appeared during the violent expansion of our own frontier. Indeed, the Chinese example, since it is associated with an ideology which had few resemblances to the value system of nineteenth century American capitalism, offers further evidence of the preponderance of material conditions in shaping the destinies of peoples, as opposed to ethical or psychological conceptions of ideal states of being.

DEVELOPMENTS IN AMERICA

The amount of reservation land available to Indians, including allotted lands, unallotted (tribal) lands, and reserves for schools and agencies, is about fifty-five million acres. This is perhaps three times the amount of land devoted to our national parks and monuments and may be compared with the roughly one million acres of generally fine land which is devoted in the United States to the game of golf.

At that, the figure given for Indian lands is misleading. A considerable portion of this land is swamp, desert, or barren rock and therefore totally useless. As Ward Shepard has pointed out:

The overwhelming bulk, about 90 per cent, of the whole Indian estate is composed of grazing range and timberland, and most of the grazing land is in the semiarid West.[10]

The same authority also points out that the total amount of arable land owned by

the Indians is about four million acres, less than 8 per cent of their total holdings.[11]

About two-thirds of the fifty-five million acres of Indian-owned lands are in tribal tenure. Once again the statistic distorts social reality since the overwhelming part of this tribal land is concentrated in three unallotted reservations in Arizona and New Mexico. This condition lends support to our theory. The American Southwest, particularly the arid and rugged sections near the Grand Canyon, represents one of the least developed portions of our national estate. The area is so marginal to our economy that the government used the area during the recent war as the site of its most extensive Japanese relocation centers, prisoners-of-war camps, and desert training areas. At present, of course, it is the site of considerable testing of new and dangerous weapons.

The southwestern area represents the last stronghold of aboriginal culture in the United States and therefore deserves priority of treatment. We must look for the explanation of this situation in terms of the factors proposed above.

Despite their location in an area marginal to our national economy, some Pueblo Indians, characteristic native residents of this area, enjoyed what was probably the most productive agricultural system in aboriginal United States. There is archeological evidence that canal irrigation was utilized and some of the ditches reached considerable size.[12] The native systems, however, fell far short of the demands of the encroaching white culture, demands which, almost from the time of earliest white settlement, were geared to national and international markets. It is hardly surprising then to find many basic changes in the nature of post-contact Pueblo agriculture. New crops have been cultivated,

[10] Ward Shepard, "Land Problems of an Expanding Indian Population," in La Farge, *op. cit.,* p. 79.

[11] *Ibid,* p. 77.

[12] Paul S. Martin, George I. Quimby, and Donald Collier, *Indians Before Columbus: Twenty Thousand Years of North American History Revealed by Archeology* (Chicago: University of Chicago Press, 1947), p. 192.

domesticated animals of great economic importance have been introduced, and new techniques, such as plowing, have supplemented or replaced earlier methods. These changes, resulting in partial restructuring of the native societies, have brought some grave dislocations in their wake, dislocations which are sometimes poorly understood or misinterpreted.[13] Many difficulties in the adaptive process are reflected in the various degrees of conflict between the Indians and the white invaders. The struggle, however, has often derived from a competition, not for land but rather for rights to the sparse and valuable water resources.[14]

The remarkable cultural strength of the Pueblos in maintaining ancient customs as well as a large degree of communal cooperation has recently been explained in terms of the vigor of Pueblo culture.[15] Such tautological "explanations," unfortunately, are frequent in social science. It is our contention, however, that an explanation of greater utility and broader application may be sought in an investigation of the relatively advanced aboriginal productivity which was capable of offering a base upon which natives could sustain mild competition with the whites. Even in this area the Pueblo Indians have sometimes adopted white commercial techniques in order to survive. Thus, certain groups of Indians have abandoned the worthless territories of their reservations and purchased good land elsewhere.[16]

The Pueblos represent one of our three broad acculturative types. Because of their location in a peripheral geographic area,

and because of the marginal ecological value of the region to the nation at large, the aboriginal society of the Pueblos has remained a cul-de-sac within a larger, more complex social body. But there have been many tokens of surrender: limitations of area, alterations in custom, presumptive increases in personal insecurity, and a growth of witchcraft. The Pueblos, retreating into secrecy to preserve their cultural legacy, have also found it necessary in some cases to camouflage their political organization, adopting virtual façade governments to answer demands of the invading society. Under the cover of puppet officials, the old men strive with growing difficulty to preserve a culture that already shows advanced symptoms of atrophy and imminent disaster.[17]

It should be noted at this point that the Pueblos represent a variation of the pattern of incorporation. The major importance of the factors of geographic and economic marginality in their survival, as opposed to the lesser significance of factors of political and social organization, lead to obvious dissimilarities when the Pueblos are compared with certain examples drawn from southwest China. A better comparative picture would be gained from the utilization of data drawn from the Andean area, Central America, or Mexico.[18] But Pueblo examples are useful because they give an opportunity to demonstrate the differences of total pattern that may derive from alternative relative weights of the three major factors.

There are many examples in aboriginal

---

[13] For a recent elaboration of this critical theme see Robert A. Manners, "Anthropology and 'Culture in Crisis,'" *American Anthropologist,* LIV (1952), 126–34.

[14] William Whitman, "The San Ildefonso of New Mexico," in Linton (ed.), *Acculturation in Seven American Indian Tribes,* p. 400.

[15] Laura Thompson, *Culture in Crisis: A Study of the Hopi Indians* (New York: Harper, 1950).

[16] Leslie White, "The Pueblo of Santa Ana, New Mexico," *Memoirs of the American Anthropological Association,* LX (1942), 39–40.

[17] I am indebted to Prof. W. D. Strong for the insight into Pueblo façade government. The effects of atrophy show clearly in many recent discussions and description of Pueblo culture. Cf. Leslie White, "The Pueblo of Santo Domingo," *Memoirs of the American Anthropological Association,* XLIII (1935), esp. 22; Bernard Siegel, "Pueblo Patterns at Taos," *American Anthropologist,* LI (1949), esp. 567–74.

[18] A stimulating analysis of data drawn from this area is available in Julian H. Steward, "Levels of Sociocultural Integration: An Operational Concept," *Southwestern Journal of Anthropology,* VII (1951), 374–90.

America of cultures which were exterminated as the result of the invasion of European civilization. For our purposes we may consider the native inhabitants of the northeastern sections of the United States and adjacent parts of Canada. Contact proved so devastating for these people that, "the native life having long since been crushed, we know comparatively little of the Atlantic seaboard cultures." [19]

We do have a picture, however, of a certain range of exploitative activity. Certain tribes in the area, such as the Delaware and the Tuscarora, were horticulturalists. Other tribes, farther north, depended on hunting and gathering and grew few or no crops. Short distances from the coast the celebrated Iroquoian tribes were dependent on harvests of maize, beans and, squash. In sections of Canada bordering Maine, Algonkian-speaking Indians relied upon the hunt. With but two categories of exceptions all of these cultures have been swept away. The northernmost parts of the area remain marginal to the demands of the invading society and here there are still hunters who maintain cultures with certain resemblances to their earlier state, among them the Naskapi. [20] Some of the old horticulturalists still survive but in this case survival has been biological rather than cultural. In their house types, farming, and intensive participation in white culture, such people as the Onondaga are hard to distinguish from the white farmers in their midst. Though they have a certain group identity, stimulated by access to a reservation, their aboriginal culture persists only in tiny and fragmented details. The title of James Fenimore Cooper's novel, *The Last of the Mohicans,* is an obituary to these vanished cultures. Today such biological survivors of this general cultural area as the Mohawk are best known as structural steel workers and sometime denizens of Brooklyn.

[19] Alfred L. Kroeber, "Cultural and Natural Areas in Native North America," *University of California Publications in Archaeology and Ethnology,* XXXVIII (1939), 92.

[20] Frank G. Speck, *Naskapi* (Norman: University of Oklahoma Press, 1935).

All of our factors, geography, ecology, and land tenure, operated to the detriment of the original inhabitants of the northeast area. They came into early contact with Europeans and this contact remained continuous, and constantly increasing in tempo. [21] Ecologically, the Indians of this area hardly scratched the surface of their resources in terms of European demands. Oddly enough, though the horticultural Indians were of great importance to the original colonists, presenting the newcomers with a galaxy of crops unknown in the Old World, the most important economic function which the eastern Indians could fulfill in contact economy was hunting. The fur trade flourished in this area and, though it did much to maintain certain elements of aboriginal social organization, albeit temporarily, the new economic importance of furs seems to have made sharp inroads in the domain of native land tenure. Broadly speaking, a pre-Columbian system in which little or no stress was placed upon concepts of land title was transformed into a network of familial and individual claims of ownership. [22]

Some anthropologists stress the diversity of land tenure systems which were opera-

[21] European contact with the Pueblos was equally early but, except for missionary pressures, was discontinuous; intensive and constant contact is much more recent in the Southwest than in the Northeast.

[22] We do not wish to enter here into the controversy over the precise forms of tenure of hunting grounds in the pre-Columbian Northeast. The reader is directed to Frank G. Speck and Loren C. Eiseley, "Significance of Hunting Territory Systems of the Algonkian in Social Theory," *American Anthropologist,* Vol. XLI (1939); Frank G. Speck, "Family Hunting Territories and Social Life of the Various Algonkian Bands of the Ottawa Valley," *Memoirs of the Geological Survey of Canada,* LXX (Anthropological Series No. 8 [1915]); John Cooper, "Is the Algonquian Family Hunting Ground System Pre-Columbian?" *American Anthropologist,* XLI (1939), 66–90. We would take the position advanced by Julian H. Steward, "Economic and Social Basis of Primitive Bands," in Robert H. Lowie (ed.), *Essays in Honor of A. L. Kroeber* (Berkeley: University of California Press, 1936).

tive in native North America,[23] but we would see greater significance in the fact that no American Indian tribe, in the absence of pressures emanating from expanding European capitalism, developed a system of land tenure based upon and combining the concepts of restricted individual usufruct with only partial limitations on abuse, free alienation, the use of political bodies to insure ownership, and the use of land as capital through pawn, mortgage, rent, or collateral. Concomitantly, no tribe developed systems of either tenancy or wage labor in agriculture, nor are there any cases in which classes of slaves carried the brunt of agricultural toil.

Between the nearly extinguished eastern Indian and the relatively flourishing Pueblo Indian there is an intermediate type. The Plains Indians are an interesting example of this category of "transformed" Indians. We cannot be concerned here with the age or typicality of Plains culture; by the time of prolonged white contact the Plains tribes displayed in varying degrees most of those patterns which endear the area to Hollywood scenarists. In brief, this was a culture of horse-riding buffalo hunters some of whom maintained peripheral contacts with river bank cultivators.

As in the East at an earlier date, certain Plains tribes which could be relied upon for continuing supplies of furs and skins received encouragement. Among these tribes were the Blackfoot who enjoyed a longer period of prosperity and cultural autonomy in Canada than in the United States. This stemmed from the continued importance of the fur trade in central Canada at a time when such trade was being replaced by agriculture or grazing in the United States. From another point of view, it may be said that non-Indian populations moved

more slowly into the less desirable Canadian plains.[24] Later, however, as white exploitation of the area increased and the focus shifted from hunting to agriculture in the east and grazing in the west, the social forms of the indigenes, so conducive to the earlier productive system, failed to lend themselves to the new demands. Even the marginal river bank cultivators gave way before the pressure of white settlers. One of these tribes, the Fox, was pushed from pillar to post in the eighteenth and early nineteenth centuries. Caught between the expansionisms of France and England, plunged into continual warfare by the necessity of securing larger and larger hunting territories to supply the demands of the fur trade, the Fox were several times on the verge of extinction. The nadir was reached when the Fox, originally from Michigan and Wisconsin, arrived in Kansas in 1846.[25] From that point they rallied by adopting a basic institution and technique of the culture that was dispossessing them. They purchased land. The white society which steadfastly refused to recognize, except in haphazard fashion, Indian tenure based upon occupation, and which, over the years, observed the terms of its own charters and treaties only when adherence proved expedient, was now faced with deeds and titles covering specific tracts of land. The question was now one of the defense and sanctity of private property. In the eyes of the law the Fox were no longer savages but citizens and they were accorded the protection of the state government under which they lived.

The Fox salvaged their bodies by sacrificing their culture and hit upon the basic vulnerability of the invading society in the process. Not all Plains Indian tribes fared so well. Many were destroyed as completely as the tribes of the East, losing not only culture but life as well. At best,

---

[23] "Different tribes developed different solutions for the land problem, and by the time that the Europeans arrived these had achieved a bewildering variety. Any generalization that will fit North American landholding as a whole will also fit landholding anywhere in the world." Ralph Linton, "Land Tenure in Aboriginal America," in La Farge, *op. cit.*, p. 42.

[24] Oscar Lewis, *The Effects of White Contact upon Blackfoot Culture* ("Monographs of the American Ethnological Society," VI [1942]), 63, 66.

[25] Natalie Joffe, "The Fox of Iowa," p. 288.

some of the tribes were reduced severely in numbers and relocated on reservations. Here they suffered quick cultural strangulation and, by the turn of the present century anthropologists investigating these tribes did so only by probing the memories of the old people. The Northern Arapaho, for example, suffered terrible diminution and ended as wards of the government, poverty stricken, culturally distressed, and thoroughly bewildered. The government has induced these people, who live in cattle country, to cultivate relatively barren soil so that they are continually dependent on further aid. Northern Arapaho culture, already vastly transformed, will soon become less than a memory.

CHINA: THE HISTORICAL BACKGROUND

In the preceding analysis there has been a tacit assumption that the general historical and cultural background is familiar to the reader. Unfortunately, such an assumption may not be made about the history of southwest China and it is necessary to devote some space to a resume of pertinent events in that area.

Southwest China comprises two provinces, Yunnan and Kweichow, and the southern parts of Szechuan and Sikang. In general, the area was not originally Chinese either in language or culture but Chinese pressures began quite early and continue to the present day. The earliest external political influences in Yunnan, according to legend, came not from the Chinese in the north but from the southwest, from India. Thus, Indian princes were said to have been the rulers of petty States in western Yunnan about 2,500 years ago.[26] The earliest Chinese interest in Yunnan of which there is reliable record is reported in the *Ch'ien Han Shu* and concerns the establishment of a kingdom called Tien,[27]

the character used for this name still being employed in Chinese writings to refer to this province. We know very little about Tien. Its people, "bound up their hair in a knot, cultivated the ground, and congregated in towns."[28] But the Chinese connection with Tien is explicitly reported:

At first in the time of Wei the king of Ts'oo, the General Chwang Keaou was sent up the Keang with troops to settle the boundaries of the several tribes from Pa and Tëen-chung westward. Chwang Keaou was a descendant of Chwang, the king of Ts'oo. When returning to report his success, he found the king of Ts'in. On reaching the Tëen Marsh, he found it 300 *le* square, bordered by rich-soil level land for some thousands of *le;* the inhabitants of which he overawed by his military strength, and attached them to the kingdom of Ts'oo. The highway being thus rendered impassable, Chwang Keaou remained with his followers, and established himself as king of Tëen. Assuming the garb of the barbarians, and adopting their customs, he was accepted as their chief.[29]

The date of this invasion of Yunnan by Chuang Ch'iao was about 300 B.C.[30] For our purposes, the significance of the statement lies in its description of Chinese adopting native customs, rather than the reverse.

By the time of Han Wu Ti (r. 140–87 B.C.) the nominal sovereignty of Tien was lost to Han, the event probably occurring in 109 B.C.[31]. That the actual processes of government remained in local hands may be read, however, in the statement that, "the King of Tëen was invested with the royal seal; the people being still entrusted to his rule."[32]

At this time Chinese interest in Yunnan was largely based upon a desire to secure the passages to India as well as to insure the military security of Szechuan. The lack of interest in exploiting Yunnan as an agricultural region is reflected in the relative

[26] Joseph Rock, *The Ancient Na-Khi Kingdom of South China* (2 vols.; Cambridge, Mass.: Harvard University Press, 1947), I, 7.

[27] *Ibid*, pp. 5–6. Cf. A. Wylie (trans.), "History of the Southwest Barbarians and Chaou-seen," *Journal of the Royal Anthropological Institute,* IX (1879–80), 53–65.

[28] Wylie, *op. cit.,* p. 55.

[29] *Ibid,* p. 56.

[30] Rock, *op. cit.,* p. 6 (note).

[31] *Ibid,* p. 8.

[32] Wylie, *op. cit.,* p. 61.

absence of irrigation projects in the area during this period.[33]

The general obscurity which shrouds the early history of Yunnan is lifted briefly during the period of Three Kingdoms. It was during San Kuo times that the famous Chu-ko Liang conducted several military campaigns in southwest China. Chu-ko Liang reported that he had found the throne of Tien occupied by the fifteenth lineal descendant of the ruler who had been invested by Han Wu Ti. It was not until 649 A.D. that this ruling line was replaced. The new kings bore the family name of Meng and claimed descent from the early Indian princes. With the accession of the Meng line came the establishment of the kingdom of Nan Chao, which lasted from 649 to 1253, during which time Yunnan was independent of the Chinese Empire.[34]

Until 1253 the interaction of Chinese and aboriginals in Yunnan was characterized by infrequent contact and little exchange of population. This is not to say that the fluorescent Chinese civilization of the Han, T'ang, and Sung periods contributed nothing to the local cultures. With the exception of spasmodic and nominal political suzerainty, however, the elements which moved from China into Yunnan are better characterized as part of a slow process of diffusion rather than acculturation. It was not until the Ming dynasty that the Chinese, capitalizing on the military successes of the Mongols, began to move into Yunnan in significant numbers, thus precipitating constant and mass contacts and new demands on local resources and economic organization.

It was from Ming times (1369–1644) that Chinese migration into Yunnan assumed proportions which might be compared with the pressure of white settlers on the American frontier. Even as late as

1516, however, it seems likely that Chinese political controls were hardly more direct than they had been in the time of Han. A Ming document draws this picture:

Owing to bad communications and natural barriers, this land (Li-chiang) is separated far from Imperial rule. Thus it is advisable to make the native leader of these people their ruler. He is given an official seal by the emperor and also the hereditary right to control the land and its people. Such privileges are not accorded simply as a reward for merit acquired, but from part of a special policy of the government applied to suit the circumstances of the people. This means that their manners and customs are so different from ours that the emperor is obliged to allow the native rulers to maintain their hereditary right.[35]

Inadequate census data makes difficult the estimation of the rate of influx of Chinese into Yunnan. It is generally accepted, however, that the number of Chinese was small prior to Ming times. By the beginning of our own century Major H. R. Davies submitted a population estimate based upon impressions gained during many years of travel in Yunnan. Davies believed that there were ten million Chinese in the province, the bulk of them concentrated in certain level areas where they formed 80 to 90 per cent of the population. The aborigines, in 1900 as at present, were largely to be found on the hills or in the low valleys.[36] According to Lin Yueh-hwa, a contemporary Chinese anthropologist who has done field work in Yunnan, the total population of present day Yunnan is twelve million, of which nine million are Chinese.[37] Lin agrees with Davies in finding the Chinese collected in the arable plains, but his calculations, if correct, seem to make Davies' estimate too high, there being no room for natural population increase or the

[33] Chi Ch'ao-ting, *Key Economic Areas in Chinese History, as Revealed in the Development of Public Works for Water-Control* (London: Allen & Unwin, 1936), p. 36.
[34] Rock, *op. cit.*, p. 9.

[35] *Ibid*, p. 67.
[36] H. R. Davies, *Yunnan: the Link between India and the Yangtze* (Cambridge: Cambridge University Press, 1909), p. 307.
[37] Lin Yueh-hwa, "Social Life of the Aboriginal Groups in and Around Yunnan," *Journal of the West China Border Research Society*, Vol. VIII (1936).

significant enlargements of the population that must have resulted from the Japanese invasion of eastern China. It should be noted that at least one authority believes that Yunnan still has more aboriginal inhabitants than Chinese. The same source agrees, however, that the plains are dominated by the Chinese.[38]

DEVELOPMENTS IN CHINA

We may now pursue the investigation of the contact of cultures in southwest China in the manner of our analysis of similar events in America.

First, we must recall a difficulty. The Pueblos, presented as a demonstration of the incorporation of a culture, owe their peculiar status primarily to a confluence of geographic and ecological factors. It is true that these societies also enjoyed the most complex and developed mode of production in native America north of the Rio Grande, but in their lack of a state apparatus, the absence of socioeconomic classes, the embryonic nature of their division of labor, and their emphasis upon a social structure oriented about kinship, they furnish an atypical example of this incorporating type of culture contact. Likewise, in southwest China there is a difficulty; oddly enough the reverse one. Here there are excellent examples of incorporation in which the expanding Chinese society took over the basic social structure, replaced the top bureaucracy and political superstructure, but paid little or no heed to the majority of traits which comprised the way of life of the invaded culture.

A number of cases of cultural transformation may also be found. In these instances the indigenes were driven from their home areas and suffered violent alterations in their fundamental modes of behavior, yet they were not destroyed. These peoples were made, through the unrelenting pressures of military action, economic exploitation, and political sanction,

to alter many of their traditional lifeways. Not the least alteration sustained was a reorganization of their social structure in terms of differential status, rather than egalitarian kinship. But, of the third category of acculturative possibility, the liquidation of both populations and their culture, examples are lacking. Unlike the conditions in Columbian America, there were no peoples in southwest China which, as groups, depended for their subsistence upon hunting or gathering. That such groups existed in this area in the remote past is virtually certain, but the time since their disappearance may well be in excess of 1500 or 2000 years.[39]

Here now is the difficulty: southwest China and the New World north of the Rio Grande do not have total congruence in the present comparison. However, in view of the tremendous distaste in American social science for "unilinear" theories of cultural development, this feature may be regarded perhaps as an intellectual, if not an analytical advantage. It is also obvious that the two regions have a substantial degree of developmental overlap. It is this large sector of similarity to which we are calling attention.

The Min Chia, people who live around Ear Lake in northwest Yunnan, furnish an example of cultural incorporation following prolonged contact. The Min Chia still differ from the Chinese who have infiltrated their area in many ways. So subtle are some of these differences that of the two most recent chroniclers of the Min Chia, one, C. P. Fitzgerald, treats the group as non-Chinese with many Chinese traits,[40] while the other, Francis L. K. Hsu, treats these

[38] Georges Cordier, *La province du Yunnan* (Hanoi, 1928), p. 342.

[39] Cf. Wolfram Eberhard, *A History of China* (London: Routledge & K. Paul, 1950), pp. 6–9; *idem*, "Early Chinese Cultures and Their Development: A New Working Hypothesis," *Annual Report of the Smithsonian Institution for 1937* (Washington, D.C., 1938) [translated by C. W. Bishop from *Tagungsbericht der Gesellschaft für Völkerkunde*, II, Leipzig, 1936].

[40] Charles P. Fitzgerald, *The Tower of Five Glories: A Study of the Min Chia of Ta Li, Yunnan* (London: Cresset Press, 1941).

people as Han, although admitting their non-Chinese origin.[41]

Actually, the Min Chia are descended from a population involved in the old kingdom of Nan Chao, mentioned above. So powerful was Nan Chao in the first century of its existence that, first with Tibetan assistance and then alone, it stood off Chinese armies bent on its conquest.[42] Nan Chao had a productive agriculture which was by no means primitive, as may be read from a Chinese account written during the T'ang period:

Agriculture was conducted under a latifundia situation, with farms as large as ten miles each way. Harvests were supervised by officials who distributed the necessary amount of unhusked rice each peasant family would need for subsistence, and took the rest of the harvest for the State. All peasants had to fight at the order of the State or the Chieftain, and such soldiers were not paid. For every hundred families there was a police officer to maintain peace and order.[43]

Chinese culture, including Chinese social and political structure, seeped slowly into the Nan Chao region. The quickest and most decisive changes which followed the Mongol conquest of the area were those which replaced the former political bureaucracy with Chinese overlords and a new group of lesser native officials. Other rapid changes were effected in the tax and fiscal systems. Previously, the class exploitation in Nan Chao had largely been confined within a limited area, but now the economy took on "ultramontane" aspects as a considerable portion of the wealth produced went into Chinese coffers far from

[41] Francis L. K. Hsu, *Under the Ancestors' Shadow: Chinese Culture and Personality* (New York: Columbia University Press, 1948).

[42] Wilhelm Credner, *Cultural and Geographical Observations made in the Tali (Yunnan) Region with Special Regard to the Nan-Chao Problem,* trans. Erik Seidenfaden (Bangkok: Siam Society, 1935), pp. 5–6.

[43] Chen Han-seng, *Frontier Land Systems in Southernmost China* (New York: International Secretariat, Institute of Pacific Relations, 1949), p. 8. This is Chen's summary of material drawn from the *Man Shu* of Fan Tso.

Yunnan. But other cultural elements changed much more slowly. The old language, a non-Chinese one, persisted, although the number of Chinese loan words was high. There was an acceptance of the guild system of commercial organization, changes in housing type, and clothing, as well as many others. Most of these shifts seemed to have occurred with a minimum of conflict. Since the time of Kublai Khan, the major troubles in the area have been between Chinese and Moslems;[44] the Min Chia have taken only minor roles in the disturbances. Indeed, Min Chia men who were literate in Chinese could progress through the Imperial examination system and might govern distant Chinese places, achieving honor and high position.

A similar picture might be drawn from the people of Likiang, a semiautonomous non-Chinese kingdom located to the northwest of the Min Chia. However, it is in the south, in the land of Sip Soong Paa Na, that certain interesting variations appear. Sip Soong Paa Na, as a state, never achieved the political centralization of Nan Chao. Furthermore, it seems likely that its economy represented not one level of productivity but several, with an effective articulation of the varying modes of production conspicuously absent. As Chen Hanseng has shown, the nature of the contact relationships which followed the expansion of the Chinese into Sip Soong Paa Na depended largely on the degree to which the sub-area being invaded was previously integrated into the political structure of the whole.[45]

In Sip Soong Paa Na, as in Nan Chao, the first major contacts with the Chinese came with the invasion of the Mongols who established a system of tribute payments. Under the succeeding Ming, the tribute was regularized and labor requisitions were introduced. Though the population in the

[44] A major legacy of the Mongols in this area is the Moslem population much of which is descended from the Moslem mercenaries who settled or were settled here during the Yuan dynasty.

[45] Chen, *op. cit.,* p. 8.

area of previously complex political organization seemed to take to the new system easily, the efficiency of Chinese control was guaranteed by relacing "hereditary succession of Chieftains . . . by approved succession granted by the Imperial Court in Peking." [46] During the Ch'ing (Manchu) dynasty, the economic exploitation of Sip Soong Paa Na by the Chinese was intensified. The actual functions of draining wealth from the area, however, were performed by merchants and tax collectors.

The most highly organized areas of Sip Soong Paa Na in both political and economic structure were in the north. Here, localities merged easily with Chinese administration and economy. Already class divided, they were accustomed to tax and tribute, *corvée* and draft, hierarchy and bureaucracy. As a matter of fact, the change was hardest on the old ruling class —the basic farming population had simply changed masters. A much more difficult time and universal dislocation was had in the more southernly districts which had never been more than nominally associated with the political and economic structures of the north. In the south, the precontact forms of land tenure were largely communal in nature. Though individual families worked definite plots, there was little point in the question of ultimate ownership since the periodic reallocation of fields to fit altered needs was a function of chieftainship.[47]

The system by which the Chinese exploited these areas was a relatively inefficient one. Local chieftains, themselves bound by ties of kinship to many of their tribesmen, were entrusted with the collection of tribute. Since their own interests were opposed to such collections, the payments were small and irregular. The Chinese struck back in 1726 by adopting a policy of removing hereditary chieftains.[48]

When the Chinese then tried to collect taxes directly and when back taxes were demanded on the penalty of land confiscation, revolt broke out. The abortive rebellion was crushed and the new system was extended, but the Chinese ran into new and even more grave administrative difficulties. With their consolidation of the areas of the north behind them, they had pushed deeper and deeper into the marginal areas of the south, areas that were increasingly peripheral to their economic interests, technology, and methods, and which were strange to their concepts of sociopolitical organization. In addition, and closer to home, the normal cyclical defects in Chinese bureaucracy began to multiply and the whole system was threatened by internal corruption and self-seeking. Finally, a new policy was instituted. The compromise, under which Chinese magistrates administered native areas side by side with hereditary native chiefs, restored the area to a semblance of peace.

The failure of the Chinese program for the area was a dual one. The Chinese superstructure, on the one hand, failed to fit the native political base and, instead of a relatively simple and clear-cut war with a ruling class, the Chinese were faced with a general rebellion of the population. Second, the productive techniques and the standards of native agriculture differed from and remained at variance with Chinese methods and demands. That this situation is a reflection of our ecological hypothesis is to be seen in the extreme reluctance of Chinese farmers to migrate into these areas. The normal process in recent Yunnanese history has been for Chinese peasant cultivators to swamp those aborigines who occupied favorable stretches of arable land but who exploited these territorial resources in ways deemed inefficient in traditional Chinese economy. Under these conditions the "inefficient," or as it might read in Chinese, "barbaric," producers were pushed either into the mountains or into the low, malarial valleys.[49] This

[46] *Ibid*, p. 9.

[47] In *The Peoples of the Southwest Border Region* (Canton, 1948), Chiang Ying-liang describes a similar system in an area of Yunnan northeast of the one under discussion.

[48] Chen, *op. cit.*, p. 12.

[49] Chiang, *op. cit.*, pp. 14–15.

analysis is confirmed in the area of Sip Soong Paa Na, where we find the valleys left to the Pai Yi, the relatively unincorporated tribespeople.[50]

What has been represented in this paper as a clear ecological (e.g., cultural-environmental) point is frequently presented as a racial or biological one. The argument is that Chinese cannot live in those Yunnan valleys which dip below 4000 feet elevation because they are Chinese. This means that they tend to get malaria or other diseases more readily than the aborigines, or that they succumb to tropical lassitude, or that they have an inbred horror of such places. Of course, such explanations are not explanations at all. We do not have the kind of statistical data that would enable us to say whether one group is more prone to disease than another under similar circumstances—furthermore, the hazard of malaria seems at least as great in parts of east-central China as in the low Yunnan valleys. Actually, where agricultural conditions are promising the Chinese enter in great numbers without regard to the elevation.[51] But, the geography of Yunnan is such that the low areas tend to be marginal in terms of traditional Chinese crops and farming methods. Furthermore, if Yunnan would be imagined as a plane, its southeastern corner, the sector having the smallest Chinese population, would be lower than the others. That there is a correlation between elevation and Chinese settlement in Yunnan we do not deny. That the relationship depends on racial rather than cultural factors is an unwarranted deduction.

One of the most populous ethnic groups in southwest China is the Miao. People of this linguistic and cultural designation live not only in Yunnan, but may be found in Kweichow, Szechuan, and elsewhere. A large number of Miao, passing through Chinese acculturative pressures in the past,

have achieved acceptance and peace within a traditional Chinese social framework.[52] This, however, has involved the sacrifice of many typical Miao traits. Those Miao who have adhered to their former ways and who have resisted involvement in Chinese exploitative economy have suffered the familiar fate of military punishment and loss of original locales.[53]

The Miao, who say of themselves, "As fish are to water and birds are to the air, so the Miao are to the mountains,"[54] practice an agriculture which falls far short of Chinese demands. They are geared to subsistence farming and grow diversified crops instead of applying themselves to the production of chosen grains which are associated with marketable and taxable surpluses. Furthermore, in the absence of crop rotation and in their failure to use fertilizers, particularly night soil, in an intensive way, the Miao cannot rely too long on any given fields but must move to new lands when the old acres are exhausted.[55] Such a use of land is confined, in traditional China, to soils of low arability or general inaccessibility.[56] It is a system culturally abhorrent to peasants long accustomed to the most intensive application of labor to the soil. Such a method of agriculture, however, characterizes not only the Miao, but other aboriginal groups as well, most of them also having suffered Chinese encroachments which pushed them into more and more marginal terrains. Thus, of the aboriginal tribes dwelling along the difficult banks of the Salween River, a Chinese has written:

[50] Chen, op. cit., p. 15.

[51] Cf. Davis, op. cit., p. 56.

[52] Margaret P. Mickey, "The Cowrie Shell Miao of Kweichow," Papers of the Peabody Museum of Archaeology and Ethnology, Harvard University, Vol. XXXII, No. 1 (1947).

[53] Joseph M. Amiot, Mémoires concernant l'histoire, les arts, les moeurs, les usages, &c. des Chinois (15 vols.; Paris: Nyon, 1776–91), III, 387–422; F. M. Savina, Histoire des Miao (Hongkong: Société des missions-étrangères, 1924), pp. 143–53.

[54] Savina, op. cit., p. 173.

[55] Ibid, p. 214.

[56] Field observations of the author, 1947–48.

Among the people of the Salween there are only cultivators who, almost without exception, cultivate their own fields. Their tools are rudimentary: a small digging stick . . . and a small plough made out of a single piece of wood with which they work in dry fields and in the rice fields only to a depth of 4 or 5 inches. They have no other tools. . . .

They do not know how to use fertilizer. In the rice fields, after the harvest, they burn the stalks and the ashes take the place of fertilizer for the next year. . . . How, under such conditions, can they have a flourishing agriculture? [57]

This may be compared with a description of the agriculture of the Ch'ü-tzu, another tribal society in this area:

Since the Ch'ü-tzu lack agricultural tools, their return from farming is rudimentary. They never use the hoe in preparing the earth. They cut down the trees and brush which is dried then burned. They spread the ashes thus obtained to a depth of several inches, then, with the aid of a bamboo digging stick, they dig small holes in which they put grains of maize. To sow buckwheat, false rice, and millet, they simply throw the grain on the ground. Then, with the aid of a bamboo broom, they level the surface of the planted ground. After this they await the harvest which is almost always abundant. . . . One year they cultivate one piece of land, the next year another. When they have finished cultivating the land about their houses, they go off to live someplace else where new lands may be found. Thus, in effect, after having been so used, a piece of land is stripped of productive force. It is necessary to wait eight to ten years for the shrubs and trees to grow back in sufficient quantity to give the ashes necessary for a new planting. [58]

The Chinese responded to the problem of aboriginal occupation of desirable areas in the fashion familiar in our country dur-

ing the past few centuries—they fell upon such groups as the Miao with as much military force as could be mustered in difficult areas. The major period of Miao conquest fell between the years 1763 to 1776. [59] Today, the Miao are largely Han in culture. Some Chinese sources report this as if it were a strange and inexplicable phenomenon, failing to associate the acculturation with the bloody campaigns of the eighteenth century. [60]

CONCLUSION

Three factors are of vital importance in the determination of the nature of cultural contacts between two societies which are of unequal sociopolitical complexity. These factors are geography, ecology, and social organization; they do not work singly but always in tandem. Geography, the spatial distribution of natural environmental features about the earth, plays a significant role in setting the place and time of contact. It also conditions the continuity and intensity of subsequent contacts and eventually may offer a source of refuge for the conservative elements of a culture threatened by change from the outside. Ecology, the interaction of man as a cultural animal with his environment through the medium of technology, plays an even more direct part in deciding the broad nature of acculturation. Finally, the forms of social organization especially as they are expressed in systems of land tenure are invariably decisive. The critical diagnostic clue is the difference between the ways in which exploitative rights to strategic resources are distributed in the two societies. In a certain sense, as we have attempted to indicate, the focus of conflict between invader and invaded lies in this arena.

The broad possibilities of acculturative process which attend the expansion of com-

[57] Chang Chia-pin, "Vie des peuplades riveraines de la Saloen," in J. Siguret (ed. and tr.), *Territoires et populations des confins du Yunnan* (Peiping: H. Vetch, 1937), I, 229.

[58] Li Sheng-chuang, "Etude sur les races du premier district des marches coloniales yunnanaises," in Siguret, *op. cit.*, pp. 177–78.

[59] Savina, *op. cit.*, p. 143.

[60] Niao Ch'ü-lung (ed.), *Report on the Miao Research*, 1935, p. 259 (in Chinese); Liu Chiai, *The Miao*, 1934, pp. 14–15 (in Chinese).

plex societies into areas inhabited by simpler peoples may be reduced to three. The most extreme solution of the conflict between an expanding society and an invaded one lies in the utter annihilation of the indigenes. This is often a rapid process which combines the swift reduction of the native population, sometimes abetted by the spread of disease and the introduction of poverty, and the equally hasty destruction of the native way of life. This alternative has actually operated, among other places, along the Atlantic seaboard of the United States and adjacent Canada.

The interaction of the three factors involved in the acculturative situation, however, may lead to a condition of greatly reduced pressure. Relative isolation, a lack of crucial minerals, or a temporary confluence of economies are some of the special elements which may give more time for adaptation. Under these circumstances what occurs is a gradual transformation of the indigenous culture, not into an image of the invaders but to a condition which approximately fits the needs of the invaders. Such developments will necessarily vary with the region and with the demands of the expanding culture. Thus, though there are numerous and often profound differences in detail between the acculturation of the Miao and Pai Yi in China and the Plains Indians in America, both fall within this broad category of transformation.

The final possibility is incorporation. Here the two societies have tremendous basic similarity before contact though the cultural superstructures may show great diversities. Thus, though both societies employ advanced techniques of farming, are class-divided, employ the state as an instrument of polity, have priesthoods, etc., they may vary in crops, gods, artistic productions, literature, and many other ways. Contact may be initiated with violent wars which, with their associated plagues, reduce the population. Later, however, though numbers of persons succumb to ac-

celerated exploitation, the population stabilizes at a point still to be reckoned high, and may actually go on to increase. Meanwhile, in the socioeconomic sphere, the invaders do not oust the vanquished but merely take over the upper ranks of the hierarchy. Taxes and *corvées* formerly owed the native ruling class are now demanded by the invaders who often take care to maintain the peasantry, thereby perpetuating older relationships. Meanwhile, a more temperate process of diffusion may be at work which very slowly chips away at certain features of the older local culture which have grown anomalous. Thus there may be an influx of strange words into the vocabulary, new gods into the pantheon, or novel elements into native art.

Though our illustrative materials have been drawn from only two areas of the world, we have implied that both the acculturative types and determinants have universal application. For this reason, our two areas lie at the antipodes; it is hardly necessary to state that the events which transpired in one area were not inspired by happenings in the other. Since this is the case and since our emphasis has been comparative, it must be admitted that, to the degree that we have described similar conditions and events, a parallel process has been taking place in America and in southwestern China. This development, in its broadest forms, has been parallel despite the tremendous differences in the ideologies of the United States and China. As such it gives a striking example of the way in which practical necessity overrides ethical or idealistic desires in the shaping of culture.

We must conclude, however, on a note of warning and expectation. In the stress laid upon similarities, little attention has been paid to the differences between events in the two areas. It is not our intention to claim that the detailed types of colonial administration associated with a nineteenth century capitalistic economy are identical with those developed by a well-integrated "Oriental" economy.[61] To seek out and explain those differences will be the task of a future paper.[62]

[61] The standard reference to the analysis of China as an Oriental society is the work of Karl A. Wittfogel, *Wirtschaft und gesellschaft Chinas* (Leipzig: C. L. Hirschfeld, 1931), and "Die Theorie der orientalischen Gesellschaft," *Zeitschrift für Sozialforschung*, VII (1938), 90–122. See also his more comprehensive *Oriental Despotism: A Comparative Study of Total Power* (New Haven: Yale University Press, 1957). Brief summaries of the theory are available in John K. Fairbank, *The United States and China* (Cambridge, Mass.: Harvard University Press, 1948 [rev. ed., 1958]), and a recent and very sketchy criticism by Wu Ta-k'un, "An Interpretation of Chinese Economic History," *Past and Present*, Vol. I (1952).

[62] [The paper referred to has not yet been published, but many of the ideas in the present article are elaborated in David Kaplan's "The Law of Cultural Dominance," in Marshall D. Sahlins and Elman R. Service (eds.), *Evolution and Culture* (Ann Arbor: University of Michigan Press, 1960), chap. 4. See also Morton H. Fried, *The Fabric of Chinese Society* (London: Atlantic Press, 1956)].

DAN STANISLAWSKI

THE ORIGIN AND SPREAD
OF THE GRID-PATTERN TOWN

Many geographers have concerned themselves with the study of towns, their distribution, position, site, function, and anatomy, and yet, of the innumerable articles
and books written on this subject, none, to
my knowledge, has been devoted to the
origin and spread of the design that is now
standard throughout much of the world—
the grid pattern with straight streets (parallel or normal to one another) and rectangular blocks. It is true that some writers
have casually considered this pattern, con-
cluding that it spontaneously recommended
itself to the town builder whoever or wherever he might be. I likewise made this
assumption at first. But the obviousness of
the grid is more apparent than real. In the
record of its use it seems to have been no
more obvious than, for example, the wheel.

My interest started in the Spanish towns
of the New World, where I soon found that
not only did native towns fail to exhibit
such a pattern but during the earliest period of Spanish settlement it was lacking
also,[1] and subsequent Spanish cities, except when constructed under direct orders,
were likely to vary greatly from the simple

rectangular design.[2] It was this that indicated the need for further inquiry into the
background of grid towns. My investigation led me into the Middle East and into
the third millennium before Christ. That
the grid may have an even longer history
awaits further archeologic investigation. It
may have been a one-time invention which
has spread from its source region until at
present it encompasses the globe.

ARGUMENTS FOR AND AGAINST THE GRID

The casual assumption that the grid almost automatically becomes the pattern of
a new settlement cannot hold up in the
light of the history of its distribution. Only
those regions directly associated with, or
accessible to, areas of earlier use have
shown evidence of its existence. I know of
no region in the world that will clearly
contradict this thesis. But when once
known and recognized and fitted into the
culture pattern, the grid has both obvious
advantages and some disadvantages. Let
us consider the disadvantages first. From
the point of view of the individual there are
many reasons for a man to place his building, whether it be dwelling or workshop or
temple, at an angle with buildings near by
and at some distance from them rather
than directly in line and adjoining. Such
placement offers advantages in terms of
circulation of air and exposure to sunlight,

Reprinted, with permission of the author and
editor, from the *Geographical Review,* XXXVI
(1946), 105–20 (copyright, 1946, by the American
Geographical Society of New York). The author
is professor of geography at the University of
Texas, Austin.

[1] There is no record of the use of the grid pattern for a generation and a half after the Spaniards arrived in the New World. They founded
many new towns during this period, but the grid
did not appear until the third decade of the sixteenth century.

[2] After the restrictions were weakened—for example, in the eighteenth century—many towns
came into being, but, with examples of the grid
all around them, they grew with hardly a suggestion of that pattern.

as well as accessibility of the various parts, whereas in the grid efficiency is largely lost without the alignment and juxtaposition of buildings. Second, again as regards the individual, there are other plans that would have greater utility. For example, the radial plan with streets leading out from a center like spokes from the hub of a wheel offers certain advantages over the gird in communication from the periphery to the center. Third, the topography very frequently indicates easier street planning than the insistence upon straight lines mounting hills and falling steeply into valleys.

To consider the advantages of the grid plan is to consider a longer, and from many points of view, a superior list. Perhaps its greatest single virtue is the fact that as a generic plan for disparate sites it is eminently serviceable, and if an equitable distribution of property is desirable, there is hardly any other plan conceivable. It can be extended indefinitely without altering the fundamental pattern or the organic unity of the city. Property can be apportioned in rectangular plots fitting neatly into a predetermined scheme of streets and plazas. It can be sketched on the drawing board and, within certain obvious limitations, made serviceable. It is also far the easiest plan to lay out with crude instruments of measurement. For a *compact* settlement of rectangular buildings this scheme is the only one that lends itself to the efficient use of space. Moreover, a distinct advantage for the grid-plan town under certain political conditions is that of military control. This would apply in the case of subject towns to be held under control; for it has been clearly recognized, not only by the Spaniards in the New World [3] but by Romans and early Greeks before

them,[4] that a tortuous street facilitates defense by individuals and a straight street lends itself to control from without.[5]

THEORIES OF ORIGIN

One theory as to the origin of the grid is based on its obvious efficiency in the use of space where rectangular buildings are involved. The reasoning is seductive but not borne out by facts. Examples of strict rectangularity of buildings with a highly irregular street pattern are far too common. They long predate the first use of the grid and continue to the present in large areas of the world.[6]

Another point of interest with regard to theories of the origin of the grid-pattern town concerns the straight processional street. Another far too casual assumption was likewise made here that such a street would suggest the advisability of others

[3] "Fundación de pueblos en el siglo XVI," *Bol. Archivo Generál de la Nación,* VI (1935), 350. In these orders of Philip II it is suggested that where horses are available the wide street is better for defense. Obviously "defense" meant defense of Spaniards, not of natives, for the former were the possessors of horses (*caballeros*). A narrow, tortuous street would have meant the doom of Spanish horsemen in a native revolt.

[4] Rex Martienssen, "Greek Cities," *South African Architectual Record* (Johannesburg), Jan. 1941, p. 25 (quoting Aristotle); Vitruvius, *The Ten Books on Architecture,* trans. M. H. Morgan (Cambridge, Mass.: Harvard University Press, 1914), p. 22.

[5] It is sometimes assumed that the grid was the product of military thought. That it recommended itself to military thinking is not, however, proof that it was originated by soldiers. Polybius (*The History of Polybius,* trans. E. S. Shuckburgh, from the text of F. Hultsch, 2 vols. [London and New York: Macmillan, 1889], I, 484) says: "The whole camp [Roman] is a square, with streets and other constructions regularly planned like a town." Note the last words. The prior existence of the non-military organization is implied.

[6] Throughout the long early history of Mesopotamia the rectangular building was common (see S. H. Langdon, "Early Babylonia and Its Cities," in *The Cambridge Ancient History,* I [London: Cambridge University Press, 1923], 356–401, ref. to 374, 392, 395). Nevertheless, irregularity of streets is also typical (see E. A. Speiser, *Excavations at Tepe Gawra* [Philadelphia: University of Pennsylvania Press, 1935], I, 13, 20, 24, and plates 7, 9). Egypt, for an even longer time than Mesopotamia, showed, with one exception, this combination of rectangular buildings and irregular streets (see G. C. C. Maspero, *Life in Ancient Egypt and Assyria* [New York: Appleton, 1892], p. 17; and Armin von Gerkan, *Griechische Städteanlagen* [Berlin and Leipzig: W. de Gruyter, 1924], p. 31; and Martienssen, *op. cit.,* p. 5).

parallel or at right angles to it. This also fails to be borne out, both in Egypt and through the long history of early Mesopotamia.[7]

The theory that the grid stemmed from an orientation toward the points of the compass, probably based on religion, has proved equally inadequate. In Mesopotamia, Egypt, and early Greece the orientation of a building and even a street was common, but it did not lead to the laying out of other streets in accordance.[8] On the other hand, in Mohenjo-Daro, in northwestern India, there was obvious orientation of all the streets and rectangularity of blocks, yet excavation has shown no temple, and there may have been none.[9] It seems, then, that religious significance as basic to the grid can likewise be written off as inapplicable.

In weighing these advantages and disadvantages of the grid pattern certain things seem clear.

1. It is possible only in either a totally new urban unit or a newly added subdivision. This pattern is not conceivable except as an organic whole. If the planner thinks in terms of single buildings, separate functions, or casual growth, the grid will not come into being; for with each structure considered separately the advantage lies with irregularity. History is replete with examples of the patternless, ill-formed town that has been the product of growth in response to the desires of individual builders. Nor is it simple to rectify an older city. The difficulty, and probably the impossibility, of this has been demonstrated by Von Gerkan.[10]

2. Some form of centralized control, political, religious, or military, is certainly indicated for all known grid-plan towns. When centralized power disintegrates, even if the grid pattern has been established it disappears. This is indicated clearly by medieval Europe as compared with Europe under Roman rule.

3. It may indicate colonial status, not necessarily a situation in which the younger settlement is bled by the older, but more frequently an amiable association for mutual benefit between mother and daughter settlements.

4. Desire for measured apportionment of land.

But none of the foregoing can be said to indicate that a strongly organized political group desirous of founding a colony will, because of its obvious virtues, set up a grid town. The virtues are obvious only when demonstrated. This is confirmed by history. According to the evidence, only those exposed to the idea will utilize this pattern. Hence another requirement must be added:

5. Knowledge of the grid.

THE CITY OF MOHENJO-DARO

The earliest record we have of this street pattern is that of Mohenjo-Daro, a city which flourished in the first half of the third millennium before Christ.[11] This city was not casually built. The precision of its plan could not have been accidental. It was a well rounded concept designed to fit the needs of a highly organized, highly urbanized people. The streets were straight and either parallel or at right angles to one another, as far as the inaccurate instruments

[7] Von Gerkan, *ibid;* T. H. Hughes and E. A. G. Lamborn, *Towns and Town Planning, Ancient and Modern* (Oxford: Clarendon Press, 1932), p. 2.

[8] Maspero, *op. cit.*, p. 196; Langdon, *op. cit.*, p. 374; Speiser, *op. cit.*, p. 24; von Gerkan, *op. cit.*, pp. 31, 78.

[9] Sir John H. Marshall (ed.), *Mohenjo-Daro and the Indus Civilization* (2 vols.; London: A. Probsthain, 1931), I, 22, 283.

[10] Von Gerkan, *op. cit.*, pp. 114, 115. This fact was recognized by the Spanish king in his instructions to Cortes (see "Collección de documentos inéditos relativos al descubrimiento, conquista y organización de la antigua posesiones españolas de ultramar," Ser. 2, 17 vols. [Madrid, 1885–1925], IX, 177).

[11] E. J. H. Mackay, *Further Excavations at Mohenjo-Daro* (New Delhi: Manager of Publications, 1938), p. 7. The dates here given—2800–2500 B.C.—correct an earlier assumption. But these dates do not indicate the earliest establishment or the end of the city. It may be far older than these dates suggest and may have continued its existence for many centuries after 2500 B.C.

of the time permitted. This was not a placing of buildings merely with the idea of the
individual in mind. The concept was that
of an organic city in which all parts were
designed to function within the whole.

Trade was of enormous importance to
the people of the city.[12] The very high
quality of the manufactures makes evident
that it was indubitably the home of men of
skill with a long background of training and
organization. That Mohenjo-Daro does not
represent the earliest settlement of this
people may be indicated by the fact suggested above, that the grid city is completely planned and established as a new
unit. We can, therefore, postulate that the
ancestors of the people inhabiting Mohenjo-Daro had a long history of social
organization in this region or elsewhere.[13]

For the next known example we must
seek much later times,[14] although there

may be Oriental material that will, when
known, alter opinion with regard to this
intervening period. There is at present no
reason to suppose that any Oriental settlement with anything suggesting a grid pattern could rival Mohenjo-Daro in antiquity.
However, Creel [15] has some interesting
though inconclusive statements on early
Chinese planned buildings and streets. The
next record of the grid is found at the eastern Mediterranean in the eighth century
before Christ. Sargon of Assyria, tiring of
his old capital, decided to perpetuate his
glory by the establishment of a new one,
Dur-Sarginu. For its site he chose the unimportant and formless little village of
Magganuba, where he laid out his new
capital precisely in terms of the grid. This
was not destined to last, but the gap in
time was not to be long until Hippodamus,
and undoubtedly his predecessors, would
take up the idea in Greece and Greek lands
and establish it in such fashion that it was
not again to be lost to the record.[16]

A CONTINUING TRADITION IN INDIA?

The question may be raised why one
should attribute to a single invention a plan
that has appeared in places far distant from
one another with a gap of long centuries

[12] Ernest Mackay, *The Indus Civilization* (Lon-
don: Dickson & Thompson, 1935), pp. 75, 199–
200; Dorothy Mackay, "Mohenjo-Daro and the
Ancient Civilization of the Indus Valley," *Annual
Report of the Smithsonian Institution, 1932*
(Washington, D.C., 1933), pp. 429–44.

[13] This idea is likewise suggested by Marshall,
op.. cit., pp. 103, 106, 282, 283.

[14] Had this paper been written somewhat earlier,
there would have been included the terremare settlements of Italy that were originally described
by L. Pigorini (see various publications in the
Bulletino di Paletnologia Italiana) and accepted
and further developed by many serious writers.
The description of how a Bronze Age people
crossed the Alps to the Italian plain and beyond
and took with them, even to Taranto, their pile
construction, using it in precisely planned towns,
makes a fascinating story, but unfortunately it
holds little truth. This has been demonstrated by
the exhaustive work of Gösta Säflund: *Le terremare delle Provincie di Modena, Reggio Emilia,
Parma, Piacenza* (Lund: C. W. K. Gleerup, 1939);
reviewed by C. F. C. Hawkes and Edith Stiassny
in the *Journal of Roman Studies*, XXX (1940),
89–97. There is no proof of systematic planning of
the town pattern or of most of the other features
attributed by Pigorini to the settlers of the second
millennium B.C. No migration from the lake
country is proved, or any connection of Hungarian and South Italian settlements with those
of North Italy. David Randall-MacIver refers to
the uneasy feeling he had concerning the terremare
theories and writes in praise of Säflund's conclu-

sions (see his "Modern Views on the Italian Terremare," *Antiquity*, XIII [1939], 320–23; and his
review of Säflund's volume, *ibid*, 489–90).

[15] H. G. Creel, *The Birth of China* (London:
J. Cape, 1936). Creel says that buildings in a
settlement of the fourteenth century B.C. (p. 57)
were carefully oriented but that their arrangement
otherwise has not yet been determined (p. 68).
He quotes a poet of a later period who, in describing the city, said that land was distributed
in predetermined plots and that, under central
supervision, houses were planned along streets
that presumably were straight (p. 64).

[16] Babylon and its form are a matter of question. Herodotus credited it with a grid form—or
at least so he seems to imply. Robert Koldeway
(*The Excavation of Babylon*, trans. A. S. Johns
[London: Macmillan, 1914], p. 242) says: "The
streets, though not entirely regular, show an obvious attempt to run them as much in straight
lines as possible, so that Herodotus was able to
describe them as straight. They show a tendency
to cross at right angles."

between. The question is not an unreasonable one. A further inquiry into Indian
sources might yield the answer. The data
that we have at hand, although inaccurate
as to dating, seem to indicate a strong possibility that the tradition of Mohenjo-Daro
has been continued in India, perhaps un-
brokenly. If one were to accept the claims
of recent Indian writers with regard to
town planning in their country, one would
need to seek no further; for it is their contention that town planning existed in India
long centuries before the Christian Era.[17]
The brilliance and completeness of Indian
town planning indicated in the Śilpa Śastra
is not an overnight creation.[18] It is the outcome of the thought of many men and must
have evolved through many centuries. The
casual assumption that Indian town planning derives from Alexander's generals, the
Greek Bactrian kings, or Vitruvius and the
Romans may not be a fair one, in view of

the great elaboration of Indian thought,
and in view of the indicated contribution
of architectural types from the Iranian plateau as well as of the possible development
of town planning, even among the Dravidians.[19] India may have carried the tradition
of this town pattern for all later ages to
accept at their leisure.

One regrets that Sargon, in the eighth
century before Christ, did not record why
he chose the grid or where he found his
sources for such a plan, but again, eyes
may have been turned to the East. The
trade from Mesopotamia through Persia
and even into India cannot be questioned.[20]
That the East was contributing ideas, specifically in architecture, which might suggest a contribution to broader planning is
shown by Herzfeld's demonstration that
even the Ionic pillar was a product of lands
to the east of Greece.[21]

To those who question the assumption of
Indian derivation it can be asked: "Where
has the pattern of the grid town appeared
without possible connections with India?"
No part of Europe or Asia except those regions that had contact with this area of
oldest appearance has given evidence of the
grid pattern.[22] Nor did any part of Africa

---

[17] There is no doubt of the fact that the Greek Magasthenes wrote glowingly in the third century of the city of Pataliputra. It was described by him as an elongated rectangle. See Linton Bogle, *Town Planning in India Today*, IX (London, 1929), 14; and J. W. McCrindle, *Ancient India as Described by Megasthenes and Arrian* (London: Trübner, 1877), p. 66. This was after the invasion of Alexander, but hardly a long enough time had intervened for the construction of the city by order of the Greeks. Indian writers, how-ever, would push their dates even further back on the basis of their evidence. It is unfortunate that there is a certain "timeless" quality to Indian scholarship that casts some doubt upon its use-fulness. The dating of the records is far from conclusive. See the following: Ram Raz, *Essay on the Architecture of the Hindus* (London: J. W. Parker, 1834); C. P. Venkatarama Ayyar, *Town Planning in Ancient Dekkan* (Madras, 1916); W. W. Tarn, *The Greeks in Bactria and India* (Cambridge: Cambridge University Press, 1938), especially p. 419; "The Question of King Milinda," trans. from the Pali by T. W. Rhys Davids, in Max Müller (ed.), *The Sacred Books of the East*, XXVI, Part 2 (Oxford: Clarendon Press, 1894), 208.

[18] Concerning this and collateral subjects see *Architecture of Manasara*, trans. from the origi-nal Sanskrit by P. K. Acharya (London: Oxford University Press, 1933). Śilpa Śastra is a collec-tive term for numerous old treatises on the man-ual arts of the Hindus.

[19] Venkatarama Ayyar, *op. cit.*

[20] Trade between these two countries was well established at the time of Mohenjo-Daro and probably even before then. See Langdon, *op. cit.*, p. 362; Ernest Mackay, "Summerian Connections with Ancient India," *Journal of the Royal Society of Great Britain and Ireland*, Oct., 1925; René Grousset, *Les civilisations de l'Orient* (4 vols.; Paris: G. Crès, 1929-30), I, 13; H. R. Hall and C. L. Woolley, *Ur Excavations, I: Al-Ubaid* (Lon-don: Oxford University Press, 1927), p. 397; Sir M. Aurel Stein, "The Indo-Iranian Borderlands: Their Prehistory in the Light of Geography and of Recent Explorations," *Journal of the Royal Anthropological Institute*, LXIV (1934), 179-202; and Sir Percy Sykes, *A History of Exploration from the Earliest Times to the Present Day* (2nd ed.; New York: Macmillan, 1936), p. 2.

[21] E. E. Herzfeld, *Archaeological History of Iran* (London: Oxford University Press, 1935), p. 15.

[22] It has been mentioned above that new mate-rial on the Orient may yet alter conclusions. But note the irregularity of Khotan, a settlement of Central Asia earlier than the Christian Era (Sir M. Aurel Stein, *Ancient Khotan*, 2 vols. [Oxford:

exhibit this pattern until Alexander introduced it as derived from eastern Mediterranean lands.[23]

No Proven New World Examples

Nowhere did this plan appear in the New World, statements to the contrary notwithstanding. The Chimu city of Chan Chan on the Peruvian coast certainly was, it is true, one of straight lines and right angles.[24] Some of these lines were maintained for a notable length, but they did not carry on through; the organic quality of the grid plan was broken by irregularities. It was rather a series of blocks, many rectangular, but not communicating with other blocks in the functional way necessary to the grid.

Many contentions have been made concerning the use of the grid in Mexican towns, but here again the evidence does not support it. The famous "Plano en Papel de Maguey," despite some theories to the

contrary,[25] is obviously a post-Conquest design drawn to the order of Europeans.[26] The theory that Tenochtitlán had rectangular blocks because of the rectangularity of its temples and temple squares does not stand up, in view of the fact that so many places in the Old World had square temples and corresponding courtyards, with the remainder of the settlement clearly at variance. Certainly Cortes and Bernal Díaz remarked about the straightness of the passageways leading into Mexico, but nowhere did they suggest more than the straightness of single streets.[27] It might also be indicated that in their apparent surprise at first sight of this straight passageway these Spaniards, who were used to the tortuous streets of sixteenth-century Spain, surely should have been even more struck with the rectangularity of blocks. Failure to mention such a condition may well be taken to indicate that it did not exist.[28]

According to present evidence, the rectangular grid was nowhere a casual, spontaneous thing. In spite of its apparent ob-

Clarendon Press, 1907], plan 23). Neither the cities of Phoenicia nor her colonies exhibited the pattern. See von Gerkan, *op. cit.,* p. 30; and J. I. S. Whitaker, *Motya: A Phoenician Colony in Sicily* (London: G. Bell & Sons, 1921). The grid was not known in Minoan Crete (Martienssen, *op. cit.,* 7) or in Greece during its early centuries. Pre-Roman Spain lacked it (see *Excavaciones de Numancia: Memoria presentada al Ministerio de Instrucción Publica y Bellas Artes por la Comisión Ejecutivo* [Madrid, 1912], p. 11), as did pre-Roman France (Joseph Gantner, *Grundformen der europäischen Stadt* [Vienna: A. Schroll, 1928], p. 44).

[28] There is one exception to be noted here, the little settlement of Kahun in Egypt, which was planned and set up as a unit by the Pharaoh Usertesen II as a settlement for the workmen on the pyramid being constructed at that time. See W. M. Flinders Petrie, *Kahun, Gurob, and Hawara* (London: K. Paul, Trench, Trübner, 1890), pp. 21, 23. However, this settlement was established some centuries after the establishment of Mohenjo-Daro, when the connections of Egypt with Sumeria and those of Sumeria and Mohenjo-Daro were clear. Moreover, Kahun was not an organic unit but rather like a barracks.

[24] J. L. Rich, *The Face of South America: An Aerial Traverse* (New York: American Geographical Society, 1942), photograph 277; Otto Holstein, "Chan-Chan: Capital of the Great Chimu," *Geographical Review,* XVII (1927), 36–61, fig. 26.

[25] George Kubler, "Mexican Urbanism in the Sixteenth Century," *Art Bulletin,* XXIV (1942), 160–71, footnotes 3 and 59.

[26] Manuel Toussaint, F. Gómez de Orozco, and Justino Fernández, *Planos de la ciudad de México* (Mexico City: Editorial "Cultura," 1938), p. 36.

[27] Hernán Cortés, *Cartas de relación de la conquista de Méjico . . .* (2 vols.; Madrid: España-Calpe, 1932), I, 98 (Map 2): "Son las calles della [referring to Temixtitan—site of present Mexico City], digo las principales, muy anchas y muy derechas." By his limiting phrase he specifically excludes all but the main streets as being wide or straight. Also Bernal Díaz del Castillo, *Historia verdadera de la conquista de la Nueva España* (3 vols.; Mexico City: P. Robredo, 1939), I, 309 ff.

[28] Note also in "Narrative of Some Things of New Spain" by the Anonymous Conqueror, trans. M. H. Saville (*Documents and Narratives concerning the Discovery and Conquest of Latin America,* No. 1 [New York: Cortes Society, 1917]), the failure to indicate anything resembling a grid and also the comparison of various cities of Mexico with cities of Spain. This may not be proof that the pattern of streets in Mexican cities was as amorphous as those of sixteenth-century Spain, but it certainly does not suggest the striking difference that would immediately be apparent to a Spaniard if they were straight.

viousness, it would seem that it was not put into practice by any except those who had known it previously or who had access to regions of its occurrence.

THE GREEK RECORD

The continuous record starts in the sixth century before Christ, in Greek lands.[29] Before this time the regular pattern was clearly not a typical feature of Greek settlement.[30] There are many examples of earlier Greek cities showing anything but the regularity of the grid plan, and a definite record of cities settled at least as late as the middle of the seventh century before Christ shows that irregularity was typical. In fact, according to von Gerkan, as late as the early part of the fifth century some cities were settled without a standard pattern. Hippodamus, a Milesian, is credited by Aristotle with being the planner of the grid-pattern harbor of Athens, the Piraeus,[31] but even earlier than the Piraeus—probably also of the fifth century—was the grid design of Hippodamus' own birthplace, Miletus. There can be no doubt that the plans of Hippodamus were not born in his brain but derived from earlier times—there is at least one clear example, Olbia—and perhaps distant places. It is interesting to note that the earliest plans are associated with Ionic Asia Minor and settlements by Ionians on the Black Sea, and not nuclear Greece. So the first appearance among Greeks was in the western extension of

Asia, where it could have been based on earlier knowledge and use.

Long before the time of Hippodamus, the Greeks had been expanding their knowledge of the world through their growing trade connections. For several centuries these connections were those of "tramp" traders, who either settled among "barbarian" peoples, taking more and more control of the region by reason of their superior training, or merely came temporarily to these regions to exchange merchandise. This did not involve planning. It was simple contact for the purposes of exchange and profit.

The Greeks pursued their course westward through the Mediterranean, making contacts with the present Italian mainland and islands. Many different groups were involved in this trade until the latter part of the eighth century, when Corinth was infected with the virus of what might be termed precocious imperialism. Whereas before the founding of Syracuse all Greeks, so far as can be determined, traded with the west, after 734 B.C. Corinthian goods became dominant in the market and eventually were far more important than the materials from all other Greek traders combined.[32]

Corinth was operating according to a plan. Whereas theretofore settlements had, presumably, been made rather casually, Syracuse was founded under authority from the mother city and by settlers who were dispatched to the place with orders based on careful planning. These orders included instructions for the division of land for use by the settlers. Here was a clear indication of the growth of centralized control. It was likewise an indication of increasing importance of trade as well as of a possible pressure of population at home.

To the east the Greeks were making other contacts. Miletus sent out secondary

[29] D. M. Robinson and J. W. Graham, *Excavations at Olynthus* (Baltimore: Johns Hopkins University Press, 1938), Part 8, p. 35.

[30] Martienssen, *op. cit.*, pp. 19, 33; Gantner, *op. cit.*, p. 37; H. V. Lanchester, *The Art of Town Planning* (London: Chapman & Hall, 1925), p. 9; Hetty Goldman, *Excavations at Eutresis in Boeotia* (Cambridge, Mass.: Harvard University Press, 1931), p. 50.

[31] "A Treatise on Government," trans. from the Greek of Aristotle by William Ellis (New York, 1912); Percy Garner, "The Planning of Hellenistic Cities," *Transactions of the Town Planning Conference, London, October 10–15, 1910* (London: Royal Institute of British Architects, 1911), p. 113.

[32] Alan Blakeway, "Prolegomena to the Study of Greek Commerce with Italy, Sicily and France in the Eighth and Seventh Centuries B.C.," *British School at Athens Annual No. 33*, Session 1932–33 (London, 1935), pp. 170–208, ref. to p. 202.

colonies, particularly after the middle of the eighth century, to take over the trade of the Black Sea. The "great Asiatic mother of colonies," like Corinth, was not averse to the use of force to maintain trade supremacy. She was, however, the greatest center of Oriental influence, and the attainments of these Asiatic Greeks are thought by some to have been far superior to those of the European homeland. Their contacts with the interior of Asia Minor and the countries of high civilization to the east of the Mediterranean were a liberal education.[33]

The drive of colonization both in the Mediterranean and in the Black Sea was temporarily reduced during the period of the Tyrants.[34] During their regime, however, there was an even greater centralization of control, and part of this remained to contribute to the colonization that increased again after their decline. After the epoch of the Tyrants, the trade of the Asiatic Greeks spread greatly through the lands of the friendly Lydian king Alyattes. This monarch controlled a considerable part of the interior of Asia Minor and had alliances with Mesopotamia, Egypt, and others. His son, Croesus, likewise a Hellenophile, offered continuing opportunities for Greek traders, which were only partly broken by his defeat at the hands of the Persians just after the first half of the sixth century.

The planning that is called Hippodamic was a product of the period following that of the concentration of power in the hands of the Tyrants, and also following the period of greatly expanded trade through Lydian country into Mesopotamia and other eastern lands where examples of the grid were to be seen. Olbia was laid out in grid form at the end of the sixth century, Miletus not long afterward, in the fifth

century, after the destruction of the old city by Cyrus of Persia.

By this time all of the factors favoring the grid had come into being: (1) There was centralized control, and a background of town planning. (2) Totally new units were being founded, with dependent— "colonial"—status. (3) Knowledge of the grid was available from the East. (4) Desirability of the grid as a general plan would have been apparent, especially with regard to the distribution of land, which was important to the land-hungry Greeks.

It is likewise interesting to note, and perhaps it is the explanation of the Greek acceptance of this plan, that its methodical regularity and orderly quality well suited the Greek philosophic view of worldly order created out of variety. The idea of a corporate whole is typical of Greek thought of the period.[35] During this period the settlement of towns was widespread, and the grid was used by Greeks not only in their homeland but in western places as well. For example, there is Thurii in southern Italy, commonly attributed to Hippodamus; there is Selinus in Sicily, and Naples on the peninsula. These undoubtedly made their contribution to, and saw their continuance in, Roman planning of a somewhat later date.

EFFECTS OF ALEXANDER'S CONQUESTS

After the period of Hippodamus the next striking development of the use of the grid plan is in the Alexandrian age, when it was spread so widely by the conqueror and his heirs. Again it is of interest to speculate whether the strengthening of interest in the plan at this time was not a product both of the background in Greek lands and of further knowledge acquired in eastern lands. Alexander brought in his entourage not only fighting men but men of intellectual attainment who might easily have been struck by urban developments in the lands they visited.

[33] D. G. Hogarth, "Hellenic Settlement in Asia Minor," in *The Cambridge Ancient History*, II (New York: Cambridge University Press, 1924), 543–62, ref. to 550–51.

[34] *Idem,* "Lydia and Ionia," *ibid,* III (1925), 501–26, ref. to 515.

[35] A. L. Kroeber, *Configurations of Culture Growth* (Berkeley: University of California Press, 1944), p. 100.

The cities that remain from the time of Alexander or his successors present us with excellent examples of the planning of the period. Many were founded in Anatolia. Priene, the best known, through the work of Wiegand and his associates,[36] is a perfect example of the grid pattern, its buildings precisely oriented and carefully aligned with the streets. In the more distant lands are the cities of the Greek Bactrian kings and those of India proper, which, although commonly accepted to be of Alexandrian age or later, may indeed show an earlier history.

The transfer of knowledge along the Mediterranean by Greeks, however, was a matter of early centuries—long preceding the Alexandrian age—and the technique of town planning was carried into lands that were to become Roman. Here it became basic to later Italian settlement form. Greek traders were in Italy centuries before the rise of Rome. During this early period the Etruscans arrived from the east and settled in the peninsula.[37]

The early Etruscan settlements were certainly not neatly plotted grids, though, within the exigencies of the hill locations which they chose for their settlements, they may have striven for greater regularity than appears at first glance.

Greek influence was felt throughout Etruria from the outset. After the middle of the seventh century, however, the influence became more strongly Ionic.[38] This was the period of the first definite Etruscan grid town, Marzabotto, built at the end of the sixth century, and perhaps the first real grid town in Italy. Here the *cardo* and *de-*

cumanus of later Roman cities clearly appear.[39]

It is to be recalled that Ionic influence in Italy coincides not only with Marzabotto but with Olbia, and roughly with Miletus, all of which used the grid plan that had had earlier exemplification in parts of western Asia. It is to be recalled likewise that Ionian Greeks had wide experience and knowledge of these regions of western Asia.

In the early period of Roman development there is little, if any, evidence of awareness of the grid—or of town planning at all. It was the late Republic and the early Empire that saw the rapid development of the form. Then it spread through Roman colonies to near and distant points in the Empire.

THE ROMAN GRID

The grid plan as used by the Romans was not precisely that of the Greeks. It was an adjustment of the plan used by Greek traders to the demands of a Roman order, perhaps with influences derived from Etruscan practices, with an interesting association of the Roman block and the *jugerium*, the rural unit of surveying.[40] The town block was clearly rooted in history, and linked with the distribution of agricultural plots.

This rigorous, clear pattern lent itself smoothly to the necessities and point of view of the Roman state. Here was an intense centralization of power in the hands of men faced with the pressure of population and the necessity of protecting exposed frontiers of the Empire. For both these problems daughter colonies were an obvious solution. Particularly after the civil wars of Sulla, Caesar, and Octavian, who had amassed great armies to support their causes, there was a pressing necessity for the absorption of these soldiers into a peacetime economy. This was largely

[36] Theodore Wiegand and Hans Schrader, *Priene* (Berlin: G. Reimer, 1904).

[37] Probably in the eighth century. See E. H. Dohan, *Italic Tomb-Groups in the University Museum* (Philadelphia: University of Pennsylvania Press, 1942), pp. 105–9.

[38] Hans Mühlestein, *Die Kunst der Etrusker* (Berlin: Frankfurter Verlags-Anstalt, 1929). One of the major divisions of this book is "Epoche des Uberganges vom orientalisierenden zum ionisierenden Stil: ca. 650–550."

[39] Pericle Ducati, *Storia del' Arte Etrusca* (Florence: Rinascimento del Libro, 1927), I, 372–74.

[40] R. C. Bosanquet, "Greek and Roman Towns," *Town Planning Review*, V (1915), 286–93, 321.

achieved through the establishment of newly planned urban units in various parts of the Empire. Given the necessities of the Roman state, the psychology of its rulers, the background of its history, what was more logical than to establish the grid wherever new urban units were planned?

Following the downfall of the Western Empire the era of city planning came to a close, and, more important, even those cities that were completely planned and built before the dissolution of the Empire fell into other ways and forms, so that the end of the medieval period saw hardly an example of Roman planning in the cities that she had established.[41]

THE MEDIEVAL COLLAPSE

Following upon the organized control and planning of the Romans, the early medieval period saw a degree of collapse in which the factors militating against the serviceability of the grid pattern town became dominant. Centralized power, basic to its establishment, no longer existed. Division of power and localization of authority came into being. No longer was the broad power present which tends to maintain a single pattern. Second, as has been indicated, defense of the local unit was facilitated by tortuous lanes; straight thoroughfares lent themselves to control by centralized power. Third, with local control each unit used its topography as individuals saw fit. There was no necessity for following the rigorous grid plan. Indeed, for many topographic situations it would have been costly and excessively difficult, and it served no real purpose in this feudal period. Fourth, this was a period in which trade was greatly restricted, and the grid plan, which had functioned well for a trading center, was no longer needed for that pur-

pose. Perhaps more important than all others is the fact that there was no longer the idea of equitably distributed plots of ground. This was not a period of small holders asserting their rights over definite recognized portions of territory. The feudal order operated on an entirely different basis.

However, in spite of all these tendencies toward breakdown, the pattern was never completely lost in the former Roman lands. Several examples remain in northern Italy —Turin, for example. Traces remain in such places as Braga in Portugal, Chester in England, Tarragona and Mérida in Spain, and Cologne and Trier in Germany. Some would place Oxford in this category, though this now seems dubious.[42] It has been fortunate for the planners of later centuries that these examples remain.

THE RENAISSANCE

If the early part of the Middle Ages saw the decline and almost the obliteration of this pattern, the later Middle Ages saw its adumbration again, and the Renaissance its establishment. Again political conditions had changed so that central power, planning, and trade re-emerged and local units existing in the feudal structure began to lose their dominance—in short, the trend again contributed to the utility of the grid.[43]

Particularly was there a striking advance in the use of the pattern in the thirteenth century. In this century at least one urban unit using the grid was made by Italians in Sicily. The Germans, in establishing cities on the Slavic frontiers and beyond, such as some of those in Prussia, Breslau, and Kraków, used this plan as their basis.

THE GRID IN FRANCE AND ENGLAND

But most important during this period was the establishment in France of the

[41] Oskar Jürgens, "Spanische Städte: Ihre bauliche Entwicklung und Ausgestaltung," *Hamburgische Universität Abhandlungen aus dem Gebiet der Auslandskunde*, XXIII, Ser. B, 13 (1926), p. 1; Ramón Menéndez Pidal, *Historia de España*, II: "España Romana" (Madrid: España-Calpe, 1935), 607.

[42] Hughes and Lamborn, *op. cit.*, p. 73.
[43] A. E. Brinckmann, "The Evolution of the Ideal in Town Planning since the Renaissance," trans. from the German, *Transactions of the Town Planning Conference* (see footnote 31), p. 171.

bastides, the *villes-neuves*. The record is clear. The site was plotted into rectangular blocks, divided by streets parallel to one another or at right angles, in which the main roads running from the gates led to a large square or market place at the center. Around this square were the homes of the more important residents, with arcades giving shade to the walk.[44]

The most important founders of the French bastides were St. Louis and his brother, Alfonse of Poitiers. Kings of England who possessed French territory at this time also built towns of a similar order in France.

Again the function and desirability of the pattern are apparent with the change in the political and social order. Again power was centralized, and it was those individuals that exerted power over a large area of land who were responsible for the establishment of the towns. Again it is to be noted that it was not the replotting of existing towns. This is virtually impossible. These were completely new units founded under the direction of centralized power, and all at one time. They were under military control and functioned as military centers. Also, the plots in town were distributed on the basis of standardized units, and again it is to be noted that the agricultural plots beyond the city were likewise distributed in terms of standard units.

The situation in England is probably not as clear as that in France, but perhaps it is even more interesting. Although English settlement of this period was clearly influenced more strongly by France than by any other source, there are still the yet undetermined possibilities of an earlier development within England itself. As was mentioned above, Oxford is thought by some to be a Roman foundation. This seems a dubious postulate. It appears now that Oxford was clearly later than Roman

[44] Félix de Verneilh, "Architecture civile au Moyen Age," *Annales Archéologiques*, VI (1847), 71–88, ref. to 74–75.

times, but almost as clearly it seems indicated that it may have been earlier than the period of the French bastides, and may perhaps have reached back into Saxon times. Ludlow is another example of a town that was clearly earlier than the period of the bastide. It is a foundation of early Norman time, settled during the twelfth century, and probably using the grid plan. This, of course, suggests knowledge brought in from the continent. It may well have served as a partial inspiration for later models.

The real development of towns in England, mostly in the pattern of the grid, began with Edward I. It should be noted that Edward possessed territories in France, his training was French, his language was French. He knew well the town planning of thirteenth-century France, and it is clear that this was the model he had in mind in setting up the so-called Welsh bastides and other towns in England. Again the factors contributed to the utility of this plan; for now England with a centralized authority felt itself in need of totally new units and had the experience of France before it.

With one exception nothing more need be said regarding the grid in Western Europe. Its serviceability in the period of expanding settlement both within Europe and in European colonies was obvious. Never has it been lost since the time of its redevelopment toward the end of the medieval period.

SPAIN AND THE NEW WORLD

The exception to be noted is Spain. Isolated from the rest of Europe during the long period when she was involved in internecine warfare, she failed for the most part to take part in developments of neighboring countries. It is unfortunate that she lacked their experience with Renaissance planning; for it was she that conquered the New World and established thousands of completely new settlements there. As she was uninitiated in the methods of town planning, her settlements were amorphous for about three decades after the beginning of her control. Finally she realized the necessity for a plan, and for this she turned to her neighbors, and beyond them to the Roman and Greek sources from which they had profited. But this is a subject in itself and must be treated in a separate paper.[45]

[45] [See Dan Stanislawski, "Early Spanish Town-Planning in the New World," *Geographical Review*, XXXVII (1947), 94–105].

RHOADS MURPHEY

THE CITY AS A CENTER
OF CHANGE: WESTERN
EUROPE AND CHINA

Every sedentary society has built cities, for even in a subsistence economy essential functions of exchange and of organization (both functions dealing with minds and ideas as much as with goods or with institutions) are most conveniently performed in a central location on behalf of a wider countryside. The industrial revolution has emphasized the economic advantages of concentration and centrality. But is it true to say that change, revolutionary change, has found an advantage in urbanization; in concentration and in numbers? The city has instigated or led most of the great changes in Western society, and has been the center of its violent and non-violent revolutions. In Western Europe the city has been the base of an independent entrepreneur group which has successfully challenged and broken the authority of the traditional order. In China, while cities with the same universal economic functions arose, they tended until recently to have the opposite effect on the pattern of change. China has consistently reasserted itself as a single political unit, but it is otherwise the appropriate qualitative and quantitative counterpart of Europe, and provides a reasonable basis for comparison. China and Europe have been the two great poles of world civilization, and an examination of the different roles which their cities played

Reprinted, with permission of the author and editor, from *Annals of the Association of American Geographers*, XLIV (1954), 349–62. The author is associate professor of geography at the University of Washington, Seattle.

may help to elucidate other differences between them.

The following generalized and capsulized discussion aims only to suggest this difference, as an example of what might be made of an approach to the study of society through an analysis of the city's role in the process of change.[1] By cutting a familiar

[1] This is not a new idea. Other and older applications of it would include Giovanni Botero, *A Treatise Concerning the Causes of the Magnificence and Greatness of Cities,* Trans. Robert Peterson (London, 1606); Georg Simmel, "Die Grossstädt und das Geistesleben," in Theodore Peterman (ed.), *Die Grosstadt: Vorträge und Aufsätze zur Städteausstellung* (Dresden: Zahn & Jaensch, 1903); N. S. B. Gras, "The Development of the Metropolitan Economy in Europe and America," *American Historical Review,* Vol. XXVII (1921–22); Michael Rostovtzeff, "Cities in the Ancient World," in Richard T. Ely (ed.), *Urban Land Economics* (Ann Arbor: Edwards Brothers, 1922); Ernest W. Burgess, *et al, The City* (Chicago: University of Chicago Press, 1925); Henri Pirenne, *Medieval Cities: Their Origins and the Revival of Trade* (Princeton: Princeton University Press, 1925); Max Weber, *Wirtschaft und Gesellschaft* (Tübingen: J. C. B. Mohr, 1922), Part 1, chap. 8; Louis Wirth, "Urbanism as a Way of Life," *American Journal of Sociology,* Vol. XLIV (1938); A. M. Schlesinger, "The City in American History," *Mississippi Valley Historical Review,* Vol. XXVII (1948); William Diamond, "On the Dangers of an Urban Interpretation in History," chap. 4 in Eric F. Goldman (ed.), *Historiography and Urbanization* (Baltimore: Johns Hopkins University Press, 1941); Sylvia L. Thrupp, *The Merchant Class of Medieval London* (Chicago: University of Chicago Press, 1948); Pierre George, *La ville: le fait urbain à travers le monde* (Paris: Presses Universitaires de France, 1952).

pie in another way we may arrive at useful insights. In doing so in the short space of an article the writer realizes that he must raise or beg more questions than he answers, and may in particular be guilty of oversimplification or distortion. But the virtue of such an attempt may lie in its disturbing or even irritating nature; it aims less to prove than to provoke. To quote from Karl Marx with this in mind, ". . . the whole economical history of society is summed up in the movement of this . . . separation between town and country."[2] In distinguishing between European and Chinese civilization, we must of course assume a complex multiplicity of causes, many of which may elude us, and many of which may have little or nothing to do with geography. The distinctions and the arguments which follow do not imply that this basic fact is disregarded, but they pursue the matter from a point of view which has frequently been neglected and which may be suggestive of important factors.

The cities of western Europe have been, at least since the high middle ages, centers of intellectual ferment; of economic change; and thus, in time, of opposition to the central authority. They became rebels in nearly every aspect of their institutional life. It was trade (and to a somewhat lesser extent specialized manufacturing) which made them strong enough to maintain their challenge to the established order. Their spirit of ferment was the spirit of a new group, urban merchant-manufacturers, which could operate from a base large and rich enough to establish increasingly its own rules. This setting tended to ensure that the universities, which grew up in cities originally for convenience and centrality, would frequently nourish skepticism, heresy, and freedom of enquiry.[3]

[2] Karl Marx, *Capital* (2 vols.; Chicago: C. H. Kerr, 1906–9), I, 387.

[3] Oxford and Cambridge, as rural universities, help to enforce this point. They were proverbially conservative, and their most important job was the training of students for the ministry. Spain's distinction from Western Europe on this and

Even where they did not overtly do so, the concentration of literacy and learning in the cities was a stimulus to dissent.

Most of the cities which rose out of the cultural and social chaos following the destruction of Roman unity and preceding the development of a new national unity grew in answer to new conditions, for northwest Europe was ideally situated for trade. Most of them were in their origins much older than this, and had begun as administrative, military, or ecclesiastical centers. But a score of major rivers, navigable and free from floods, silting, or ice throughout the year in this mild maritime climate, led across the great European plain to the open sea; the peninsular, indented nature of the coast critically heightened mobility. The invitation which this presented to inter-European trade furthered the ascendancy of the commercial function. The shift of commerce and associated urbanism from the Mediterranean to northwest Europe seems to have begun before the Age of the Discoveries, notably in the Hansa towns and in Flanders. This may be in part a reflection of the mobility inherent in the lands around the Baltic and North Seas, once they had learned from the Mediterranean the lessons of commerce and absorbed the civilizing influences of this earlier developed area. In any case, these northern cities came to be dominated by trader-manufacturers. Trade was a heady diet, and enabled urban merchants to command cities which had originally been administrative creations. While the cities did not alone destroy feudalism, they owed much of their prosperity and independence to its decline: freer trade, wider exchange, and failing power of the landed nobility. And their very growth as rival power bases accelerated the collapse of the old feudal order.

As the growth of national unity progressed, under the institutional and emotional leadership of monarchy, an alliance of convenience between king and city arose

nearly every other point raised is merely a reminder of the old aphorism "Africa begins at the Pyrenees."

which met the crown's demands for funds and the city's demand for representation. Urban merchants had the money to support the king in his foreign wars and in his struggle with the divisive domestic ambitions of the nobility and the church. In return the city received an increasing voice in the affairs of state, through representation in parliaments, and indirectly through the making of policy in which the throne was obliged to follow. But while this alliance of revenue in exchange for concessions was one of mutual interest, its ultimate result was the strengthening of the urban commercial sector until it overthrew or emasculated the monarchy, and with it the traditional order as a whole. Having helped the king to power over the nobility, the city achieved a modus vivendi with him which left it in control of the affairs vital to it. As a current reminder of the development of urban independence, "the city" of London retains its originally hard-won privilege of excluding the reigning monarch, who is also excluded from the House of Commons, in part the city's creation and in part its weapon. To a certain extent the king, and even the nobility, were willing to go along with the process of economic change instigated by the city since they profited from it as the principal source of wealth in which they were often investors as well as tax collectors. But the new values which the city emphasized, and their institutional expression, were in direct conflict with the traditional society based on land; the city repeatedly bred overt revolutionary movements designed to establish its new order as the national way of life.

As centers of trade, the cities were free of the land and of its social and political limitations embodied in the institutions of post-Roman society. They developed their own law which was in differing degrees independent of the traditional, rural law. Their institutions were self-made, and they were not beholden to the traditional system which they challenged. The companies and corporations which the merchants organized went far beyond the scope of guilds in their successful attempt to order most of the social and economic fabric (instead of being limited to a trade-union function, as the guilds of China predominantly were). Traditional guilds were overlaid with new merchant organizations, or were clothed with new functions and powers, although some of the older guilds remained as conservative or retarding influences. The economic institutions which arose concurrently were also new-made sources of strength: banking, letters of credit, private property, interest, speculation and investment, representing needs and ideas which were almost wholly foreign to the traditional society of the countryside, and which were the accompaniment of an ever-widening trade. For the invitation to commercial expansion overseas was as strong in Europe's geography as the earlier invitation to trade among the lands surrounding the Baltic, Mediterranean, and North Seas. A leading agent of this process was necessarily the city, where trade flowed through break-in-bulk points such as the mouths of the Rhine or the English ports facing the Channel. Merchant corporations for overseas trade became the strongest and most progressive, or revolutionary, of the city's agents. Interestingly, the original charter of the British East India Company stated that "gentlemen" (by which was meant the landed gentry) "shall be excluded" from membership.

The city was the natural center of political change as it had been of economic change. The growth of modern Europe may be regarded as the steady progress of a new class of urban traders and manufacturers toward a position of control in a society and economy which their own enterprise had largely created. It was they who had realized the potential of Europe's location for world trade, and they who had developed and applied the technological and economic tools which made Europe the center of the world. The destruction of the old pattern was implicit in this process, and also implicit was the revolutionary expression, by the cities, of their claim to political power. City-country alliances were formed, and the dissident groups from the country often bore the brunt of the effort, since they were the more numerous, as well as sharing in the spoils. But the city was in the van, and even diverted or perverted rural dissent and rural force to its own ends; leadership and money were frequently more decisive than numbers. It is of course true that at least in England this city-country alliance left and perhaps still leaves the landed gentry with prestige and thus with considerable power, while it left wealth with the urbanites. Characteristically this wealth was used to acquire land and gentry status. This balance of advantage was particularly pertinent in the matter of parliamentary representation.

Revolutionary changes are nearly always the work of an alliance of groups, but the history of modern Europe is suggestive of the city's key role, despite the recurrent blurring of city-country distinctions. The first great modern revolution, in seventeenth-century England, was the work of a city-country alliance, but London was mainly Puritan, and the outcome might be regarded as the victory of urban merchants and their country confreres over the traditional authoritarian alliance of cavalier and peasant based on the land.[4] Two centuries later Manchester and Birmingham had joined London in the final stages of the contest between urban "radicalism" and country "conservatism," epitomized in the struggle over the Corn Laws, the Reform Bills, free trade, and the Manchester School. By this time cotton textiles had well supplanted woolen textiles as the chief manufacturing industry; since it came relatively late it was not greatly hampered by guild restrictions, as wool had been; it established itself in Manchester, which as a then unincorporated town lacked formal-

ized controls. It may irritate many readers as a loose generalization, but still seems worth stating for argument, that representative government and the industrial revolution, perhaps modern Europe's two most significant products, were created by the city. The Low Countries provide as good an illustration of this as does England.

In France the picture was less clear since urban merchant-manufacturers were less prominent in the national economy. Even so, it was Paris which created and carried the revolution. Paris used peasant distress and rebellion, but was never dethroned by it. One may say that Paris later destroyed Charles X and Louis Philippe. By this time, however, the Napoleonic land reform had given the peasant a stake in the status quo and helped to keep him a conservative counter-influence to the city, after his revolutionary ardor of the 1790's had served its purpose and cooled. Thus, in part, is derived the country's role in the destruction of the Second Republic and the Paris Commune, "radical city movements." Across the Rhine these distinctions become increasingly blurred, as for example in the Peasant War in early Reformation Swabia and Franconia. In Eastern Europe it is difficult to draw distinctions between city and country, or to find an independent urban-based group living on trade and challenging the existing order. Nevertheless even in twentieth-century Russia, while the Soviet revolution was in part carried by peasant groups, leadership remained in the urban intellectual group which had instigated the change.

In northwest Europe, which is our concern here, the city has been a consistent seat of radicalism. This is not to overlook the recurrent Jacqueries which in every society have been the desperate recourse of an oppressed peasantry. But in the West these have often been closer to reaction than to revolution—the peasants were demanding the restoration of the *status quo ante,* not the establishment of a new order. Where they did attack the old order it was characteristically on specific points, such

[4] Generalization on matters such as this is particularly hazardous. A recent study has cast serious doubt on these commonly accepted alignments. See Douglas Brunton and Donald H. Pennington, *Members of the Long Parliament* (London: Allen & Unwin, 1954).

as Wat Tyler's demand in fourteenth-century England for the disendowment of the church. The same pattern is apparent in rural opposition in America, in uprisings like the Whiskey Rebellion or in political parties like the Populists. The removal of abuses does not necessarily mean revolutionary change, despite the violence or the "leveling" sentiments which usually characterized rural dissidence.

In China, while the peasant and the countryside were in some respects like the West, the city's role was fundamentally different. Chinese cities were administrative centers. With few exceptions this function dominated their lives whatever their other bases in trade or manufacturing. Their remarkably consistent, uniform plan, square or rectangular walls surrounding a great cross with gates at each of the four arms, suggests their common administrative creation and their continued expression of this function. Local defensive terrain, such as at Chungking, occasionally made this common plan unsuitable, but the stamp of governmental uniformity is nonetheless apparent. This was true for cities which had originally risen as trade centers, or which became more important commercially than they were administratively. It is possible to find a clear separation in many provinces between administrative and commercial cities, where the capital is not the most important commercial base: Chungking and Chengtu in Szechwan, Chengchow and Kaifeng in Honan, Hankow and Wuchang in Hupeh, Siangtan and Changsha in Hunan, Soochow and Nanking in Kiangsu, Wuhu and Anking in Anhwei, Tientsin and Peking in Hopeh, and other less clear cases.[5] But despite this degree of functional specificity, little urban independence or urban-based revolutionary change appeared until the traditional fabric was rent by the growth of Western-inspired treaty-ports, Even in the exceptional cases where trade

or manufacturing was the sole or predominant basis of the city: Chingtechen, the site of the Imperial Potteries, or Canton, the consistent focus of foreign trade, there never developed a merchant-controlled urban base free in any significant sense of the traditional state order.

A case in point is Shanghai. Long before the city became a treaty-port under foreign domination, it was the leading commercial hub of the Yangtze Valley and may even have exceeded Canton in the volume of its trade. A British visitor in 1832 maintained that it did, and his count of junk traffic suggests that Shanghai was then among the leading ports of the world.[6] It nevertheless remained well down on the list of delta cities by size despite its lion's share of the trade. Another British visitor in 1843, the year in which Shanghai was opened to foreign trade as a treaty-port, estimated its population at 270,000, Hangchow at one million, Soochow, Ningpo, and Nanking at half a million each, and six other delta cities at figures equal to or greater than Shanghai's.[7] Shanghai has never performed any administrative functions outside its own metropolitan limits, and it may be for this reason that it did not dominate the delta until Western entrepreneurs largely took over its development. In bureaucratic China, trade alone could not rival administration as an urban foundation. Outstanding locations for trade, such as Hankow (or Shanghai), as advantageous as Amsterdam or London, were frequently not put to full use until European traders built major cities there. Wuchang, opposite the mouth of the Han, was an almost exclusively administrative city before 1850, while Hankow itself was only a moderate sized town.

Large cities seem to have been proportionately more numerous in China than in

---

[5] Compare for instance the original development of London as two cities separated by open country: Westminster as the administrative center and "the city" as the center of business.

[6] Rhoads Murphey, *Shanghai: Key to Modern China* (Cambridge, Mass.: Harvard University Press, 1953), p. 59.

[7] Robert Fortune, *A Journey to the Tea Countries of China and India* (London: J. Murray, 1852), I, 97–98.

Europe until the nineteenth century, and until the eighteenth-century urbanism may have been higher. Perhaps a quarter or more of the population lived in towns and cities of more than 2500 population, and perhaps 10 or 15 per cent in cities over 10,000. The big cities of the East as a whole were huge by European standards; this was a consistent feature of what has been called "Oriental society." [8] In China most cities or towns of 5,000 or more had well-defined commercial or manufacturing districts, and special areas for each important enterprise: banking, metal goods, food markets, textiles, woodwork, and so on. This pattern remains in most contemporary Chinese cities. But the cities were not decisive centers of change in a commercialized economy. They served as imperial or provincial capitals, seats for garrison troops, and residences for governors, viceroys, and the ubiquitous cloud of officials and quasi-officials with their "service-providers." Their business was administration, and exploitation, of the countryside. Marco Polo, in describing the magnificence of Peking, accounts for it as follows:

. . . and this happens because everyone from everywhere brings there for the lord who lives there and for his court and for the city which is so great and for the ladies and barons and knights of whom there are so many and for the great abundance of the multitude of the people of the armies of the lord, which stay round about as well for the court as for the city, and of other people who come there by reason of the court which the great lord holds there, and for one and for another . . . and because the city is in too good a position and in the middle of many provinces.[9]

Here is a clear picture of a city based on administration from a central location, where trade flows in largely in response to the existing structure of officials, troops, court, hangers-on, and the host of people necessary to support them, from secretaries and servants to bakers and dancers. Six hundred years later at the end of the nineteenth century European travellers in China reported the same phenomenon, on a smaller regional scale: large cities whose sole function appeared to be administration, or important trading cities at key locations which were nevertheless dominated by officials and the magistrate's *yamen* (office). Thus Archibald Little, describing the city of Kweichow in Szechwan where the manufacture of salt brine and coal dust balls, and trade on the Yangtze River were the apparent sources of its prosperity, writes that the city was a main station for the collection of *likin* (internal customs tax) and "the town is studded with the numerous mansions of the wealthy officials and their dependents." [10] With the opening of Chungking as a treaty-port, *likin* was collected at Kweichow only on local hauls and the city rapidly decayed despite its apparently strong economic base in manufacturing and trade.

The trade process appears to have lacked the dynamic quality by means of which Europe's cities rose to power. Pre-eighteenth century China had a trade as great as or greater than pre-eighteenth century Europe, but Europe's subsequent commercial expansion left China far behind. Why this happened, and why China never produced the revolutionary economic and political changes which re-made Europe into an arbiter for the rest of the world is a vital question. An analysis of the city's role may help to suggest some relevant factors. Why was the Chinese city not a European-style center of change?

China is geographically isolated by a formidable assemblage of barriers. To landward lies the greatest mountain mass in the world, with its extensions from the Pamir

[8] See esp. Karl A. Wittfogel, *Oriental Despotism: A Comparative Study of Total Power* (New Haven: Yale University Press, 1957). For example, ancient Alexandria had a population of about one million in a country (Egypt) with a total population of only seven million.

[9] Marco Polo, *The Description of the World*, trans. A. C. Moule and Paul Pelliot (4 vols.; London: G. Routledge & Sons, 1938), I, 236–37.

[10] Archibald J. Little, *Through the Yangtze Gorges* (London: S. Low, Marston & Co., 1898), pp. 87 ff.

Knot, reinforced on the south by rain forests and spectacular river gorges, on the north by the barren wastes of Siberia, and on the west and northwest by a vast sweep of desert. Seaward a coast deficient in harbors faces a huge and until recently commercially underdeveloped ocean, by European standards. Chinese trade with Japan was at several periods considerable, and with southeast Asia even larger, but it did not approach eighteenth or nineteenth-century European levels. It tended to be characterized by luxury goods, strategic goods (such as copper for coinage), or specialties such as Chinese porcelain. With these exceptions, especially the highly developed and diversified trade between southeast coastal China[11] and southeast Asia, China did not greatly extend herself commercially, and was for the most part content to send specialized goods, like silk, to the rest of the world through middlemen intermediaries: the Arabs by sea and the Turkish peoples of central Asia by land. Significantly, the largest concerted Chinese attempt in foreign trade was an imperial government project (the famous Ming expeditions of the fifteenth century), which lasted only some thirty years and apparently found no solid base in the Chinese economy or in its merchant group.

Internally, trade moved largely on the great river systems, running fortunately east and west, but there was no such close interconnection between these river basins as in Europe, by sea or across plains. Physically China is built on a grander scale, but the landscape presents no such invitation to exchange as has sparked the development of Europe. Europe is multipeninsular, each peninsula tending toward

economic distinctiveness and political independence, but joined by cheap sea and river routes. This plethora of complementary areas and their transport links magnified the basis and the means of exchange. Although its early trade development was not larger than China's, by the middle of the eighteenth-century commercial expansion overseas had joined and accelerated commercialization at home, and Europe stood in a class by itself. The cities of western Europe were both the creators and inheritors of this development. But in China the cities remained centers of the unitary national state and of the traditional order rather than its attackers, epitomes of the status quo. As direct links in the official hierarchy, they were the props of the empire. The universities were urban, for convenience as in Europe, but they stimulated no dissent. Their accepted function was to train scholars who could staff the imperial civil service, and they fed their graduates into the imperial examination system. This, and the better economic and social position of scholars generally in China than in Europe, encouraged the universities and the literati to support the status quo; European intellectuals may have taken a vow of poverty, but they remained a dissident or discontented group.

Physically, China lacked Europe's outstanding advantages for trade, and on the other hand presented a base for highly productive agriculture, through irrigation. Wittfogel's revealing work on the organic connection between the need for mass organized water control and the growth of a monolithic bureaucratic state in China lends insight into the origins and pattern of the institutional structure.[12] With China's

---

[11] Southeast China has many fine harbors and overseas trade has been prominent there for centuries. But it is effectively isolated from the main body of China by mountains, including those which help to make its harbors, and trade there has thus made much less impact on the rest of the country. The distinctiveness of the southeast is also clear in its many regional ethnic and linguistic elements.

[12] K. A. Wittfogel, "Foundations and Stages of Chinese Economic History," *Zeitschrift für Sozialforschung,* IV (1935), 26–58; "Die Theorie der orientalischen Gesellschaft," *ibid,* VII (1938), 90–123 (this article clearly states the administrative basis of the Chinese city, and discusses the reasons and implications); *Wirtschaft und Gesellschaft Chinas* (Leipzig: C. L. Hirschfeld, 1931); and *Oriental Despotism.*

environmental advantages, water control made agriculture the massive core of the economy, and at the same time left the bureaucracy in a position of ramified command. It was not possible for urban merchants to win independence from this system. They had less economic leverage than the rising European merchants because, with the preponderant position of agriculture, they never occupied proportionately as large a place in the economy.

The state of course did its part to prevent the development of a rival group, and by taxation, requisition, and monopoly ensured that the merchants would be kept relatively impotent. This was a job which European states and monarchs, though equally determined, failed to accomplish; their merchants were in a stronger position, and the state was weaker: it was merely *primus inter pares*. Land hunger in China, as a reflection of a population too large for the available arable land (increasingly serious during the past 200 years, but even in Han times worse than in most other parts of the world, including Europe), also acted to restrict commercial development, since it meant high land rents. Capital could almost always be invested with greater profit and safety in land, or in rural loans, than in productive or capital-generating enterprises outside the agrarian sphere.

Where extra-agricultural opportunities for investment did exist, the individual entrepreneur was at the mercy of the bureaucratic state. Many of the major trade goods were government monopolies. Elsewhere the essentially Western concepts of private property and due process of law, in a word, of the entrepreneur, were lacking in a society dominated by agriculture and officials. Extortion, forced levies, confiscation, and simple financial failure as the result of arbitrary government policies were the daily risk of the merchant. Some individuals did indeed become very rich, for example the famous *hong* merchants of Canton, but their wealth came necessarily through official connection: by possession of gentry status, by office holding or official favour, or by trading as part of a government monopoly (such as foreign trade under the Canton system and at most other periods was). Even so their gains were never secure. The greatest and richest of the *hong* merchants died in poverty, having lost official favour. While this also happened to many of the pre-eighteenth-century European capitalists, it did not prevent the survival and growth of individual capitalist families or firms or of a moneyed group. The famous Ch'ing dynasty billionaire Ho Shen, said to have been worth the equivalent of nearly a billion and a half U.S. dollars, was not a merchant at all but a favourite minister of the emperor Ch'ien Lung, which demonstrates the real source of wealth in traditional China. Yet he too died in poverty and disgrace (by suicide in place of a suspended death sentence in 1799) at the hands of Ch'ien Lung's successor.

In China merchant-capitalists did not use their money to establish their independence, as did the merchants of London or Antwerp, or to stimulate the growth of a new economic pattern. Unfortunately for the Chinese merchants, the imperial revenue was at most periods derived largely from the land tax and from the government trade monopolies. Agriculture was proportionately more productive than in Europe, and revenue from trade less necessary. Peking thus did not need the merchants as the king had needed them in Europe to finance the ascendancy of the national state, to pay for its wars with rival states, or to meet its normal bills. No concessions were necessary; the merchants could be squeezed dry, and were, with no harm to the state. The commanding position of the bureaucracy, and the fact of the bureaucratic state, are perhaps explainable by a similar process of default. Merchants were necessary or useful to perform essential (and, to the state, profitable) commercial functions; they were tolerated, but kept under strict control, and this was simpler and cheaper than for the state to manage all commercial dealings itself.[13]

But the merchants were also identified with the state as well as being stifled by it. Their numbers were recruited largely from the gentry class, who had the capital and the official connections essential to commercial success. Gentry merchants worked willingly with gentry officials in the management of the state monopolies, including foreign trade. Outside the monopolies, the same partnership operated, as a matter of mutual interest. In addition, most gentry members, whether or not they were engaged in trade, also performed other semi-official functions, comparable in some degree to the British landed gentry. These "services" represented a considerable part of their income; they were not likely to attack the system which nourished them. In a more general sense, the tradition of revolt in this hierarchical society did not include the reordering of social or economic groups, but concentrated on the removal of bad government. Individual or group improvement was not to be won by destroying the fabric, but by making optimum use of one's position within it.

Finally, China had maintained since Han times and with few breaks a remarkable degree of unity[14] and a central power which no single European state achieved until quite late in its modern development. In China even towns of the *chen* (market town) rank (population *ca.* 3000–5000) were seats of garrison troops, whatever their prominence in trade. In Europe in the course of the crown's contest with the nobles, and of the international rivalries which also developed among the plethora of separate national states, urban merchants found an opportunity which contrasted sharply with

the rooted monolithic nature of the Chinese state.

The cities of China were consequently microcosms of the empire, not deviants. They were not backwaters, for necessarily, learning, art, and the trappings of cosmopolis were concentrated in them. Yet, each was a symbol of the imperial system, operating not only under the direct thumb of Peking, but according to its precepts. Obvious considerations of convenience made them central places, market towns, transport termini or break-in-bulk points, and exchange centers of varying degrees of sophistication. But these universal urban functions do not automatically bring with them the character of rebellion or innovation which we have rightly come to associate with cities in the West. The main distinction of the Chinese city was concentration, as the node of the traditional society and as its power base. Imperial authority filtered down more slowly into the countryside, becoming more dilute with every level. Every government with ambitions of central power attempted to control the peasant. In a largely pre-commercial and pre-industrialist society of a basically molecular character, this could never be perfect control. China lacked not only the tools of control for its huge area, such as communications and literacy, but the bond of common interest and attitude which a completely commercialized economy tends to create, often by sublimating or suppressing conflicting interests. In the absence of such tools or conditions to implement rural control in China, the importance of the city as a center of political and military power on the side of authority was magnified.

Change in China, as elsewhere, has been the work of a city-country alliance, with the leadership coming usually from the gentry based in cities or towns. But the origins of dissent and the main force of attacks on the status quo have been far less urban in China than in the West. While the rebellions were in many cases closer to the usually unsuccessful *Jacqueries* of the West than to the really revolutionary changes

---

[13] In *Oriental Despotism,* pp. 109–10, Wittfogel speaks of this arrangement as being based on "the law of diminishing administrative returns."

[14] The persistent unity of China despite wide regional diversity is something of a puzzle, but may be related to China's dramatic isolation and to the unitary rather than peninsular nature of her continental base.

generated in Western cities, they were the predominant agents of what change did take place. They were successful where their Western analogues failed because there was no more potent agent of change, no other group (if we except the several nomadic invasions and conquests) and no other economic base by which change might even superficially be forced. The similarity with the *Jacqueries* lies in the fact that Chinese rebellions rarely challenged the basic nature of the existing order, but only its administration. The new dynasty which resulted might mean new blood, but seldom new institutions.

Given a largely closed, agrarian system, it is understandable that each dynasty, as it lost its momentum, lacked the means of maintaining a high productivity and effective distribution as population increased, and that it eventually declined into corruption. This was especially so in the rural sphere, easy prey to tax and rent manipulation (and the source of most of the national revenue and income), but marginal enough to be sensitive to oppression. At the same time, the lack of large extra-agricultural economic bases for an independent group prevented the growth of new ideas or new institutions to challenge the old, even while the old lay in ruins. The city-country alliance which in Europe made revolution made only a change of administration in China. The city was too dependent on the traditional order to attempt its destruction.

The accelerated impact of the West on China during the nineteenth century has by the twentieth century set in train profound changes, and it is natural to find that these are reflected also in the city's role. The Kuo Min Tang was a largely urban-based movement, and though its revolutionary aspects became less and less prominent under the more compelling problems of security against Communists and Japanese, it was far more than a change of administration. It was in fact the political vehicle of a new group, nurtured not only in Western thought, but in the essentially

Western milieu of the treaty-ports. Negatively also the cities have made a new impression. The present Communist regime had prominent rural roots, and came to power with an announced resentment and distrust of cities, calling them the centers of reaction (and also of degeneracy, softness, and vice), though its venom was directed particularly against the foreign-created treaty-ports.

It was basically the impact of the West, including the Soviet Union, which ensured that this latest of rebellions would for the first time successfully destroy the existing fabric. In the treaty-ports themselves development had been too brief, and too much limited by the inertia of the agrarian economy, to produce an effective base for change to rival Communism in its originally rural base. Nevertheless these urban centers, many of them new as large cities dependent on trade, played much the same role as the cities of late medieval Europe. They were rebels against the traditional order because for the first time in the history of China they provided opportunity for the merchant. Money could not only be made, but invested, in trade or manufacturing, with safety, profit, and prestige. Private property, and all of the values of R. H. Tawney's "Acquisitive Society" had been enthroned in the treaty-ports by the West, and to the Chinese businessman Shanghai or Tientsin were all that traditional China was not. He was prepared to work for the establishment of a government and society which would make a respectable place for a commercial industrial bourgeoisie, based, as the term implies, in cities.

This new group was shaped by the West and largely created the Kuo Min Tang. They formed an alliance with some of the landed gentry, for example Chiang Kai-shek, who was both landed and bourgeois, but they were never in any sense a peasant party, and their ties with the land were feeble. While they answered, or promised to answer, many of the needs of the new class of treaty-port Chinese, and kept peace with the gentry, they did not seriously attempt to answer the questions and strivings of the Peking intellectuals, nor the more compelling needs of the peasants. Communism ultimately rode to power in part as a crusade against the "merchant capitalists" of Shanghai on the one hand and the Western-inspired intellectuals of Peking on the other.[15]

To be sure, the Chinese Communist Party and its leaders are urban-trained Marxists operating intellectually and practically in an urban framework, and dedicated to an industrialization program which necessarily centers in the cities. Their political control also depends substantially on their control of city populations and city enterprises. In so far as they thus push the city toward the middle of the stage as a recognized base at least for economic and technological change, they continue the about-face in the city's role which the Western impact began in the treaty-ports. In any case, active urban agency for change is a recent phenomenon in China, perhaps one may say a direct transmittal from the West.

This analysis, in attempting to particularize the city's role in the two great centers of world civilization, has necessarily dealt with institutions as much as with place. The urban differences were expressions of distinct societies. It was broadly speaking the bureaucratic state in China which stifled the growth of European-type cities despite the volume of trade or the

regional specialization of commerce and manufacturing which existed. In Europe, too, wherever bureaucratic and/or persistently authoritarian governments ruled, commercialization and industrialization were late and/or little, and the urban-based entrepreneur usually exerted small influence. Some other common ground may exist between these bureaucracies, and the suggestions that physical conditions required or invited central control, and that geographic factors helped to minimize the opportunity of the merchant, are perhaps as applicable to easten Europe, or to Spain, as to China. The imprint of Roman Law and of Mediterranean urban traditions may also help to account for the east-west distinction in Europe. In any case, maritime western Europe followed a course whose urban direction lay at the root of its wealth, its power, and its distinctiveness.

Sir George Sansom, in a characteristic series of lectures given at Tokyo University in 1950 and published in 1951 under the title *Japan in World History,* typifies the modern European attitude and contrasts it with the Tokugawa Japanese by quoting as follows from Alexander Pope's "Windsor Forest," written about 1712:

The time shall come when free as seas or wind
Unbounded Thames shall flow for all mankind,
Whole nations enter with each flowing tide
And seas but join the regions they divide.

This is so revealingly and typically English, and so untypically Chinese, because it shows the world through the eyes of the London merchant. Ironically, merchant towns of a European type had begun to develop in Japan by the sixteenth century around the Inland Sea (perhaps an oriental Mediterranean?), including self-governing Sakai, living on the trade with China and southeast Asia. Sakai, with its own army and its council of merchants, was so close to the European pattern that contemporary Jesuit observers compared it with Venice. This promising development was crushed, despite its apparently strong eco-

[15] As the capital and as the seat of the largest Western-founded universities, Peking was a center of intellectual ferment by the end of the nineteenth century since intellectual contact with the West was easiest there. Traditional, imperial China had by then lost enough prestige that dissension flourished in Peking itself. While many of the intellectuals rejected China's traditional civilization in whole or part, their struggles in this scholar's community made little impact on the nation as a whole. The Chinese Communist Party was founded in Peking in 1921, but largely deserted it for a rural base. Student and intellectual ferment in Peking was revolutionary in thought, but ineffective in action. Both the treaty-ports and the countryside proved in the end to be much more effective bases for change or for rebellion.

nomic base, by the feudal revival of the Togukawa and its superior armies reacting to the political threat which they felt was posed by the existence of even quasi-independent merchant cities. Here we may perhaps see an expression of Japan's insularity and strategic commercial location, and perhaps *inter alia* of the weight of influence from China. The latter was earlier expressed in the great period of Japanese borrowing from T'ang China when Nara, Japan's first real city, was built on the Yamoto plain as a smaller scale copy of Ch'ang An, the T'ang capital. Nara omitted Ch'ang An's massive walls, and walled towns as such have never existed in Japan at any period, one reflection of a basically different set of geographic and social conditions.

But our purpose here has been only to suggest. The city has been a center of change in western Europe, while it has been the reverse in traditional China, despite the broad similarity in urban economic functions in both areas. Urban character and urban roles may be useful indicators of the nature and dynamics of the diverse entities of society.

EDGAR KANT

CLASSIFICATION AND
PROBLEMS OF MIGRATIONS

Man wanders in all parts of the world without exception, often in some areas, in others more seldom. He has wandered alone or in families, in groups or in tribes—sometimes a whole people together—from the dawn of history until our days. As regards migrations in the widest sense, can anyone express their meaning in the life of mankind in a more striking or concise way than Count Paul Teleki in his philosophical statement: "Migrations are not isolated events. They are accompaniments of human life, which arise from the nature of life. They are as diverse, compounded of as many factors, and as changeable as life itself. They are natural and constant, and not unusual events in the history of the human species." [1]

It is therefore natural that cultural geographers, parallel with the study of the more static features of the human race, are more and more occupied with the dynamics of population. Its processes were already strongly emphasized by Friedrich Ratzel in his pioneering *Anthropogeographie*.[2] Characteristically, he dedicated that work to the founder of migration theory, Moritz Wagner. As a matter of fact the roots of Ratzel's work go back to the time when the theory of the geographical distribution of organisms animated a whole set of biological and anthropological scientists. Single plans and ideas which found a place or were further developed in Ratzel's work originated in the years 1872–73, when he had a chance to go over with Wagner the latter's theory of migration and its application to human life.

In fact Ratzel began with the principle that mobility is an essential trait of any people, even the seemingly firmly settled ones, and that the prominence of some more obvious movements as well as the unimpressiveness of other less evident ones lead to wrong conclusions in both ethnography and history. When Jean Brunhes and Camille Vallaux said that Ratzel's division into *Beharrungsgebiete* and *Bewegungsgebiete* had once more given proof of a tendency to unfruitful classification, their reproach was not well founded.[3]

Between the inclination to systematize and classify on the one hand, and the hesitancy to do so on the other, we see a disparity that is characteristic between general (systematic) geography and regional geography and also between theory and empiricism. Regional geographers have a more pronounced liking for the empirical—and at the same time a unique ability to get lost in regional details, as historians do in unique events—and often hesitantly stand

Translated, with permission of the author and editor, from 'Migrationernas klassifikation och problematik," *Svensk Geografisk Årsbok,* 1953, pp. 180–209. The author is professor of geography at the Royal University of Lund, Sweden.

[1] Paul Teleki, "Népvándorlások," *Földrajzi Közlemények,* Vol. LXIII (1935).

[2] Friedrich Ratzel, *Anthropogeographie* (2 vols.; 2nd ed.; Stuttgart: J. Engelhorn, 1899–1912).

[3] Jean Brunhes and Camille Vallaux, *La géographie de l'histoire* (Paris: Félix Alcan, 1921), p. 202. Cf. Ratzel, *Anthropogeographie,* I. 113–208.

in need of squeezing reality into their system. The researcher oriented toward general geography, on the contrary, stresses the importance of the larger overview, comparisons, and general regularities. He also needs a more developed system of concepts with which reality can be surveyed and the multitude of phenomena can be classified in the most purposeful way.

The whole of the difference of opinion between the French and German schools of anthropogeography mentioned earlier is based to a large degree, it seems, on the insufficiently developed distinction between diverse nomadic wanderings, ethnic penetrations, invasions and intrusions on the one hand, and the rest of migratory phenomena, such as out- and in-migration among one and the same sedentary people on the other hand. With his division into *Beharrungsgebiete* and *Bewegungsgebeite*—even if the names are not particularly fortunate, from a terminological viewpoint—Ratzel strove after a certain generalization. He thereby drew attention to the differences in peoples and regions of different degrees of mobility, and distinguished forms of mobility. The occasional stability of population he himself summarized as the "result of population mobility." Thus we can state that in certain cardinal questions, concerning for instance the sedentariness or wanderings of peoples, in fact there does not exist any deeper chasm between fundamentally different points of view.

It cannot be denied that the geographers of the 1800's had a certain predilection for past times and more primitive and naturebound phenomena of movement and traffic. Contemporary problems were set aside when it was found that pure geographical causality worked better in the aforementioned cases. For example, even in the beginning of the 1900's, Ferdinand von Richthofen asserted: "We like to plunge into studies of the geography of traffic dealing with past times or underdeveloped countries; but the first railroads spoil our results, and the traffic geography of western culture stands essentially in an extremely remote relationship to physical geography. It is continually becoming more a branch of economics and international economics." [4]

The foregoing is also true to a certain degree of a part of the geographer's attitude toward the study of migration. The geographer who asserts that human dependence upon natural conditions is the central theme of geography, or leans on ethnology, often enters by preference and with great perception into the study of the movements of pastoral or agricultural nomads, or of different kinds of transitional forms between nomadic life and permanent settlement such as transhumance, and the chalet pattern of the northern European countries (*fäbod—sätervösen* in Sweden, *seterliv* in Norway, and *karjamajatalous* in Finland, respectively). Geographers have likewise made excursions into the discipline that includes prehistory and the history of the migrations of peoples, and up to or into human races, i.e., eo- or protomigrations.

In contrast, there has been considerably more of an attitude of waiting or avoidance with respect to modern migrations in technically and economically advanced countries. Some geographers seem to think that such movements are so complicated and so tied up with contemporary social relations or with economic processes that their investigation belongs rather to the fields of sociology, economics or statistics. Only in the last decades has a change in their attitude been noticeable. In this connection it should be pointed out that current migration problems already had a prominent place at the Amsterdam Geographical Congress in 1938.

I shall not go any further into the problems and attempts at classification of prehistoric and historic migrations. In my view they belong more to the subject matter of anthropology, archeology, or history. It is certainly true that many geographers,

[4] Ferdinand von Richthofen, "Chinas Binnenverkehr in seinen Beziehungen zur Natur des Landes," *Mitteilungen des Ferdinand von Reichthofen Tages zu Berlin,* 1912.

for example Ellsworth Huntington and Griffith Taylor, have tried to solve large problems in connection with eo- or proto-migrations and historical wanderings of peoples.[5] Their zealous research and flights of imagination have not always been accompanied, however, by equal skill at criticism and knowledge of the subject. For this reason they have more than once taken refuge in a one-sided geographic monism or climatic determinism. According to their interpretation, almost the whole course of migration history can be characterized, as a humorous critic put it, as the enterprise of erratic nomads who, with the help of a hygrometer fastened to their saddles, look out to the far horizons to find new pastures in place of those that have suddenly disappeared.

It cannot be denied, however, that representatives of the geographical sciences, namely geologically or climatologically trained paleogeographers and historically competent geographers, can give worthwhile help to the anthropologists, archeologists, ethnologists and historians where investigation of the history of the dispersal of the human race, or the determination of the routes of folk wanderings in past times are concerned. In this connection I can only touch on a few major questions about which different opinions seem always to be held.

Thus certain writers, for example Quiring,[6] consider that the migrations after the Stone Age—such as the migrations of the lake dwelling folk out of the west in the Copper Age, the Indo-German invasions of the Balkan Peninsula, the Near East, and India in the Bronze Age, the Germanic wanderings to the south and west

in Roman times, the Arabs' and Turks' medieval expansion to the west, and so on —were not controlled by natural events. On the other side, there have been attempts to show that the great folk movements of the Stone Age, like the Chellean, Acheulean and Neanderthal, Aurignac, Solutré, Magdalenian or rather Capsian and Campignian migrations, cannot be explained by the lust for conquest of hunting folk unless they took place on the basis of geologic and geoclimatic changes.[7] There are some scholars, however, who assert that even the more recent wanderings of peoples have climatic factors as their cause. For example, the Finnish geographer Leo Aario[8] connects the Viking voyages with the warm dry period of A.D. 800–1200. According to John Frödin,[9] certain of the Viking trips were linked to monsoon changes in northwest Europe.

Among the mass migrations within recent times that can give us an approximate picture of the folk wanderings from A.D. 200 to 1300, geographers are certainly most interested in the exodus of the Boers from the Cape, the so-called Great Trek or migrations to Natal and Transvaal. This interest includes a number of important problems, not only sociological-ethnological and historical ones, but also geographical-ecological. The Boers had been for the most part Dutch farmers and sailors. Their transformation into a pastoral people who

---

[5] Ellsworth Huntington, *The Pulse of Asia* (Boston and New York: Houghton Mifflin, 1907); Griffith Taylor, "Climatic Cycles and Evolution," *Geographical Review*, VIII (1919), 289–328, and *Environment and Race* (London: Oxford University Press, 1927).

[6] H. Quiring, "Küstenverschiebungen, Klimawechsel und Völkerwanderungen der Steinzeit," *Prähistorische Zeitschrift,* Vols. XXXII–XXXIII (1941–42).

[7] Albrecht Penck, "Völkerbewegungen in Deutschland in paläolithischer Zeit," *Sitzungsberichte der Preussischen Akademie der Wissenschaften*, Mathematische Klasse, Vol. XIV (1936). For a closer examination of prehistoric migrations see, for instance, Louis-René Nougier, *Géographie humaine préhistorique* (Paris: Gallimard, 1959), and Max. Sorre, "Les migrations des peuples," in *Bibilothèque de Philosophie scientifique* (Paris, 1955).

[8] Leo Aario, "Uber die Wald- und Klimaentwicklung an der lapländischen Eismeerküste in Petsamo, mit einem Beitrag zur nord- und mitteleuropäischen Klimageschichte," *Annales Botanici Societatis Zoologicae-Botanicae Fenniae Vanamo*, Vol. XIX (Helsinki, 1943).

[9] John Frödin: "Overgångsformer melan nomadliv och fast bosättning i Mellan- och Sydeuropa," *Ymer*, 1941, No. 3, 190–224.

in almost all respects adapted themselves to the dry conditions of the South African veld, was simultaneously a transformation of the life-form, which the late Leo Waibel, applying the terminology of plant ecology, called "the transformation of a hygrophile people into a xerophile people." [10] This example, extremely interesting from the standpoint of ecological and genetic social geography, also plainly shows to what very promising problem situations the study of migration is linked.

No thorough ecologic-geographical investigation has taken place, either, concerning a much more recent migration phenomenon, namely the exchanges of peoples that followed the peace of Lausanne, and which brought about the exchange of a million persons, Greeks from Turkey and Moslems from Western Thrace and Macedonia. In addition, the merciless and dismal bequest of World War II—forced migrations and transplantings of many peoples, dreadful mass deportations, enormous masses of political refugees and displaced persons—gave us countless problems concerning both temporary and permanent migrations. Associated with these movements are sociologically interesting processes concerning vertical social mobility, social adaptation, declassing, and so forth. Until now, sociological, social-geographic, and demographic research has only been able to give provisional and hasty overviews and quick sketches.

An entire chapter in anthropogeography should be devoted to the study of nomadic life, a problem complex to which many scholars have devoted loving care and which to a large extent is crowned with extraordinarily comprehensive results. On this foundation the typology of nomadic and seminomadic migrations stands before us as an almost complete structure.

Nomadism in the broad sense is a fairly indefinite term. It takes in a whole range of different ways of life and kinds of migration. The well-known African scholar

E.-F. Gautier[11] certainly made the nomads into the starring actors in the great drama of the Dark Ages, but he did not go much further in his typology than a division between *erg* and mountain nomads. There is nothing in his work that gives any intimation of the great diversity in nomad life. The only authors at this early stage who have a more comprehensive overview of the various types of nomadism are A. Bernard and N. Lacroix.[12] They first set up five different types,[13] which later were reduced to three: half nomads, steppe nomads, and desert nomads. To these P.-G. Merner[14] later added as a fourth category mountain nomads, with many transitional forms from full nomadism to agriculture, transhumance, and also to so-called *Alpwirtschaft* (old mountain economy), which corresponds to the Scandinavian *fäbod* or *säter* pattern. Bernard's division is based chiefly on the extent of migrations. Merner's, on the contrary, takes into account the regularity of movements and the places between which they take place.

Many important contributions to the typology and classification of pastoral migrations have been made by Philippe Arbos, Jules Blache, and John Frödin. In his critical commentary on Blache's "L'Homme et la montagne" Arbos[15] proposed a highly in-

[10] Leo Waibel, *Probleme der Landwirtschaftsgeographie* (Breslau: F. Hirt, 1933).

[11] E.-F. Gautier, *Le passé de l'Afrique du Nord: les siècles obscurs* (Paris: Payot, 1937).

[12] Augustin Bernard and N. Lacroix, *L'Evolution du nomadisme en Algérie* (Paris: A. Challamel, 1906).

[13] The five types are: (1) Quasi-sedentary natives who migrate only within the *douar* or tribal territory; (2) nomads with a limited zone of movement (20–50 km.), who oscillate between the Tell-Atlas and the steppe without fixed routes of migration; (3) nomads with separate winter and summer camps; (4) nomads with summer pastures in the Tell area and winter camps in the Sahara; and (5) true Saharan nomads. See Bernard and Lacroix, *op. cit.,* pp. 65–108.

[14] P. G. Merner, "Das Nomadentum im nordwestlichen Afrika," *Berliner Geographische Arbeiten,* Vol. XII (1937).

[15] Jules Blache, *L'Homme et la montague* (Paris: Gallimard, 1934); *idem,* "Les types de migrations pastorales montagnardes: Essai de classification," *Revue de Géographie Alpine,* XXII

teresting dichotomous division of pastoral life:

They also consider more recent developments—the crisis of nomadism, the increas-

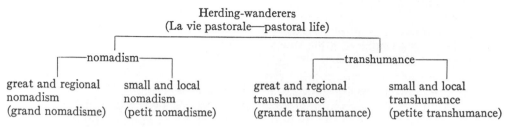

Herding-wanderers
(La vie pastorale—pastoral life)

nomadism		transhumance	
great and regional nomadism (grand nomadisme)	small and local nomadism (petit nomadisme)	great and regional transhumance (grande transhumance)	small and local transhumance (petite transhumance)

At the Geographical Congress in Amsterdam in 1938, Faucher presented a synthetic overview of migrations, which was supposed to include all known forms of pastoral nomadism and transhumance, at least within Europe.[16] John Frödin's fundamental work on alpine migrations in central Europe, which was issued at the beginning of the 1940's, like his studies of the Scandinavian *fäbod* and *säter* patterns and transitional forms between nomadic and completely sedentary life in central and southern Europe, laid the foundation for an almost complete classification of all the named kinds of periodic migration of oscillatory type.[17]

R. Capot Rey, Jean Despois, and René Raynal, in their studies on North Africa, have made important contributions to the present typology of pastoral migrations.[18]

ing chaos of individual migrations, and the processes of sedentarization. In addition they differentiate between temporary and total or definitive sedentarization.

It has been pointed out by many scholars that for several hundred years now an obvious case of overpopulation has been noticeable in the mountainous areas of Europe, especially in the Alps. Among other expressions of overpopulation is the fact that permanent settlements have climbed to notable altitudes, for instance to 2050 meters in the French Alps, to 2076 meters in the eastern Alps, and all the way up to 2133 meters above sea level in the Swiss Alps. In a related development, the cultivation of grains has been pushed to higher and higher levels, so that it now reaches 1945 meters in the Otztaler Alps, 2035 meters in the French Alps, and 2100 meters in the Swiss Alps.[19]

The upward movement of the extreme limits of settlement and cultivation signifies a notable expansion of the *oikoumene* at the expense of unused mountain land. This movement continues as long as highland villages are relatively isolated and remote from modern economic life, far away from routes of rapid traffic, industrialization, price-economies, and the growing attraction and rising standards of living in the lowlands and the cities.

(1934), 525–31. See also Philippe Arbos, *La vie pastorale dans les Alpes françaises* (Paris: A. Colin, 1922), and "L'Homme et la montagne, d'après J. Blache," *Revue de Géographie Alpine*, XXII (1934), 851–60.

[16] D. Faucher, "Les mouvements migratoires actuels et les influences agissant sur leur caractère," *Comptes Rendus du Congrès International de Géographie, Amsterdam, 1938*, II, Rapports (Leiden, 1938), 83–93.

[17] John Frödin, "Om fäbodbebyggelsens utbredning och olika typer i Europa," *Svensk Geografisk Årsbok*, 1929, pp. 176–94. A good survey of the great variety of livestock raising on alpine pastures is given in Frödin's fundamental work "Zentraleuropas Alpwirtschaft," *Instituttet for sammenlignende Kulturforskning*, Serie B, XXXVIII, 1–2 (Oslo, 1940–41).

[18] Robert Capot-Rey, "Le nomadisme pastoral dans le Sahara français," *Trauvaux de l'Institut de Recherches Sahariennes*, Vol. 1 (1942); Jean Despois, *L'Afrique du Nord* (Paris: Presses Uni-

versitaires de France, 1949); René Raynal, "Déplacements récents et actuels des populations du bassin de la Moulouya (Maroc Oriental)," *Comptes Rendus du Congrès International de Géographie, Lisbonne, 1949*, IX (Lisbon, 1952), 67–80.

[19] Frödin, "Zentraleuropas Alpwirtschaft."

The growing excess of population on the one hand, and the easier means of communication and increasingly close contacts with the outer world on the other have brought a great many changes. In the first place, an ever-larger emigration of the menfolk to the lowlands and cities in winter to earn supplementary incomes has taken place. These seasonal migrations formerly went on in association with a strong emigration, and in certain mountain districts led to actual depopulation, a descent of the upper limits of settlement, cultivation, and pastureland, and, accordingly, to a reduction of the total extent of the *oikoumene*.

As a result of these processes, almost all the western, central and southern European mountain areas have lost inhabitants. In many cases the decline of population has been considerable. It has been greatest in the French and Italian Alps, the Pyrenees, the Massif Central, and the Apennines, but occurs also in Wales and Scotland. Abandoned farms are also found in the Norwegian mountains.[20] The density of population in the Chablais Alps (Haute-Loire) decreased from 45 per square kilometer in 1846 to only 26 a hundred years later. According to Bernard, the altitudinal limit of pasture in Vallemaggia (Canton Ticino) sank 100 to 200 meters in the course of 50 years.[21]

The depopulation of highland areas can certainly be compared, or to some extent equated, with the general "flight from the countryside" to the cities and industrial districts, but there is a quantitative difference, in that mountain areas have become relatively more depopulated than valleys and lowlands. The characteristic form of emigration, connected with the shrinkage of the *oikoumene*, has therefore received a special name, "the flight from the mountain settlements" (*Höhenflucht, l'exode montagnard, Gebirgsentvölkerung, spopolamento montano, depopulation of the mountains, folketapning av fjellbygdene*, etc.). A whole group of highly interesting studies has been made on the flight from the mountain settlements, especially with reference to the Alps and Apennines. But we still lack a synthesizing work that would take account of the whole phenomenon of downhill migration, at least for Europe.

Simultaneously with the shrinkage of the *oikoumene* as a consequence of the flight from the mountains, there has taken place elsewhere an intensification of the *oikoumene* in the form of internal colonization, and accompanying redistribution of population. *Veen* colonies (peat colonies), the drying and colonization of Haarlemmermeer, Wieringermeer, northeast and eastern Flevoland polders in the Netherlands, the diking of the Pontine Marshes in the Roman Campagna, and land improvements and new colonization in many countries are pertinent examples of this trend. These developments have attracted the attention of all economic and agricultural geographers.

In many parts of the world the foreseeable advance of the limits of settlement and cultivation, of new settlement and pioneer belts, and the more or less rapid opening up of large sparsely settled or uncultivated lands, have become problems of first rank. Among the more prominent examples of successive population shifts, special mention should be made of the "westward movement" in North America, the "marcha para oeste" in Brazil, the "dvizhenie na vostok" in Russia, and the explosive waves of Chinese immigration and colonization in Manchuria in the 1900's. At the begin-

---

[20] Aadel Brun Tschudi, "Avfolkningen i Vest-Agder og nedleggingen av heiegårdene, saerlig i Sør-Audnedal og Spangereid," *Norsk Geografisk Tidsskrift*, V (1934–35), 207–48. See also Øivind Rødevand, *Nordmen på flyttefot: Studier over den geografiske mobilitet innen Norges befolkning i vårt århundre* (Oslo, 1959), *passim*.

[21] H. Bernhard, "Die Wirtschaftsprobleme des Vallemaggia (Tessin) als typisches Gebirgsentvölkerungsgebiets," *Schriften der Schweizerischen Vereinigung für Innenkolonisation und industrielle Landwirtschaft*, Vol. XXXVI (1928). See also A. Koller, *Geographische Grundlagen der Entvölkerung in den Alpen* (Bern, 1945); and Yves Bravard, "Le dépeuplement des hautes vallées des Alpes-Maritimes," *Revue de Géographie Alpine*, XLIX (1961), 1–127.

ning of the 1930's, Isaiah Bowman took the initiative in calling for a more comprehensive study of new areas of settlement—the so-called "pioneer fringe"—and of the possibilities of colonization and emigration on the borders of the *oikoumene*.[22] But there is no need to deal with this problem here, for Helge Nelson has already discussed it at some length.[23]

In consequence of the profound changes and the expulsions of peoples that took place during and after both world wars, and the great economic crisis at the beginning of the 1930's, the interest of scholars has been focused on problems of so-called economically depressed areas (*Notstandsgebiete*). Moreover, very serious problems have arisen, especially after World War II, in connection with the resettlement and re-employment of large groups of refugees. In addition, there has arisen the question of backward or retarded areas (*régions arriérées*) and underdeveloped countries.

A dozen years ago the geographer Norbert Krebs, of Berlin, published a tentative map and rough classification of migratory movements in Europe.[24] He made a special effort to differentiate between regions with greater or lesser emigration and districts characterized by areally dispersed or sharply focused immigration. In addition he took account of territorial boundary changes followed by voluntary emigration or forced evacuation, as well as shifts in population that took place during the depression among industrial folk in distressed areas, and the return movement to the countryside from industrial centers and cities.

The influence of depressions and economic conditions on migrations has been noted especially in studies of international movements. In contrast, little attention has been paid to variations caused by economic conditions in the internal migration field. The question, to what extent do out-migrations caused by an economic crisis in a given area correspond to a return migration after the crisis has been overcome, has not yet been carefully analyzed. It would seem that part of the presumed temporary migrants are thus gradually changed into permanent in-migrants. It would certainly be an interesting contribution to migration study to investigate more closely the chronological and chorological migrational processes between depressed or undeveloped areas and prosperous or boom regions, respectively.

The expression "depressed area" dates from the 1930's, when it was introduced as a designation for regions that suffered especially from the world economic crises or were most heavily afflicted with unemployment. As an older figurative expression, the term "distressed country" has been applied in Ireland. But the concepts "depression area" and "underdeveloped country" are by no means irreproachably defined. A clarification of these expressions is needed, since the preparation of maps, along with migrational and labor market studies, regional planning and rehabilitation activities, as well as regional stabilization and flexibility policies must be based on firm and clear foundations. Unfortunately, predictions that can be applied in practical national and international labor policy are very hard to make. The strength, direction, persistence, and variability of migrational movements are without doubt much more involved than what can be arrived at through the help of uncomplicated theoretical formulas.[25]

[22] Isaiah Bowman, *The Pioneer Fringe,* American Geographical Society, Special Publication No. 13 (New York, 1931).
[23] Helge Nelson, "Nybyggar- och kolonisationszonen på norra halvklotet," *Svensk Geografisk Årsbok,* 1932, pp. 201–24.
[24] Norbert Krebs, "Wanderbewegungen als Ursachen von Bevölkerungsverlagerungen in Europa," in K. H. Dietzel, O. Schmieder, and H. Schmitthener (eds.); *Lebensraumfragen europäischer Völker* (Leipzig: Quelle & Meyer, 1941), pp. 58–88; idem, "Typen europäischer Wanderbewegung," *Forschungen und Fortschritte,* XVIII (1942), No. 11–12, 105–8.

[25] For instance, D. Jaranow's study "Preselničeski dviženija, populacionen kapacitet i koefficient na naselnost" (*Stopanska Misál,* III, No. 1, 1932) is this kind of theoretical attempt to formulate a general law.

The most acceptable distinctions among economically depressed areas yet made for economic and social geographers have recently been presented by Erich Egner, professor at Göttingen.[26] According to Egner, two types of depressed areas (*Notstandsgebiete*) can be distinguished, viz. (1) stranded areas (*gestrandete Gebiete*) and (2) retarded or underdeveloped areas (*unterentwickelte Gebiete*). Stranded areas occur as a result of structural modifications in the bases of economic life. They are caused most often by non-economic factors, for example as a result of exhaustion of natural resources, the loss of a locational advantage due to technological developments, or through deprivation of *umland* or hinterland. Such areas are characterized by acute economic distress, pronounced unemployment, reduction in total income, reduced buying power, low per capita volume of trade, and severe social problems. In contrast, retarded or backward areas in which natural resources lie fallow or are conspicuously underused are usually found in parts of the world with arrested economic development, often characterized by relative inaccessibility, by low levels of living, and/or by a significant flight from rural villages. The population excess of such areas must be leveled off, above all through emigration to other areas or to foreign countries.

In connection with depressed areas and migrations associated with them, an opposite case may be cited: so-called boom areas and boom-migration. A boom—i.e., a feverish and often unforeseen economic event—can be regional or occur at single points, for example through the discovery of rich new gold veins or oil fields. Many examples could be cited of boom areas, boom towns, and boom migrations.[27] In

1851 there began a tremendous immigration into the newly discovered Victoria Gold Field from other districts in Australia. Out-migration from these districts was very great—greater, for example, than took place after the drought of 1883. Johannesburg, the large "Golden City" in the Witwatersrand mining district, which now delivers almost half of the Transvaal's gold, was just a little village of mud huts in 1884.

Active interest of social and economic scientists in questions of population dynamics became especially noticeable in the latter half of the nineteenth century, when internal migrations in the older industrial countries were accelerated and in many cases exceeded or partly replaced emigration. At the same time, population capacity for expansion was lacking in many agricultural districts. Progressive differences in salaries, income, living standards and profits, that is, the more or less pronounced development of regional economic differences, and social or economic gradients between city and country brought about an acceleration of older migratory flows and the initiation of new ones. On the other hand, transformations in agriculture, which was gradually turned from a subsistence household to a profit-making orientation, also played a part. Moreover, work was rationalized and mechanized, and permanent agricultural laborers were steadily replaced by occasional or seasonal workers.

Theories designed to explain the causes of migration and to predict their consequences, as well as estimates of future population growth, began to emerge at the close of the last century. These theories, and the relatively impressionistic "migration laws" that were proposed, were later briskly discussed, criticized, and corrected in many respects.[28]

Meanwhile, the typology of migrations has become richer in content, and new contributions have been made to a more

[26] Erich Egner, "Zur Problematik wirtschaftlicher Notstandsgebiete," *Wirtschaftsdienst,* 1951, No. 1.

[27] Cf. W. T. Chambers, "Kilgore, Texas: An Oil Boom Town," *Economic Geography,* IX (1933), 72–84; and R. T. McMillan, "Boom Migration: Incidence and Aftermath," *Rural Sociology,* vol. VII (1942), No. 2.

[28] See quotation and discussion in Edgar Kant, "Etüüde siserännete ruumiküsimusist—Études concernant les questions d'espace pour les migrations intérieures," *Tartu,* VI (Tartu, 1938), 220–77.

complete classification. Despite many attempts at classification by different authors —statisticians, economists and sociologists as well as geographers—we still lack a generally used or recognized classification of migrational processes which would incorporate all forms of so-called horizontal migration within modern society and provide a foundation for systematic study and description.

The American sociologist T. Lynn Smith recently proposed that for analytical purposes it is most illuminating to divide migrations first of all into international movements (emigration and immigration) and internal movements within the United States. However, he asserts that international migrations are not differentiated further into significant categories or types. On the contrary, he finds that internal migrations can be divided readily into clearly marked types, viz.: (1) migrations from country to cities (rural–to–urban), (2) migrations from cities to country (urban–to–rural), (3) migrations from province to province (state–to–state), and (4) migrations from one country place to another (farm–to–farm).

In addition, Lynn Smith attempts to treat modern labor nomadism or "ambulantism," i.e., the migrations of workers who constantly wander from place to place following the crops and are employed only during busy periods. He also gives some thought to the new "seminomadism" which results from highly developed specialization within certain ambulatory enterprises —e.g., bridgebuilding, railroad, highway, and tunnel construction, and work associated with flood control and storage dams. In spite of its merits, the classification scheme proposed by Smith is too closely tied to conditions in the United States; it is neither complete nor sufficiently grounded in principle.[29]

One more example of migration classification may be cited. Since about the year 1950 the official West German migration statistics differentiate among the following types on a regional basis:

(1) Migrations across the frontiers of the Bundesrepublik (*Bundesauswanderungen*), i.e., movements between the Soviet Zone, Berlin, and the Bundesrepublik, as well as migrations between the Bundesrepublik and foreign countries.

(2) Migrations across provincial boundaries (*Landesauswanderungen*), i.e., migrations that cross provincial boundaries, both within the Bundesrepublik and beyond its borders.

(3) Migrations from one province to another within the Bundesrepublik's territory (*Bundesbinnenwanderungen*).

(4) Migrations within a province (*Landesbinnenwanderungen*).

Apparently there are gaps even in the official typology, because internal migrations from one district (*Kreis*) to another have not been fully noted.[30] It should be possible to follow in- and out-migrations affecting each district with respect to *Landesauswanderungen* and *Landesbinnenwanderungen*, but there is no way to compare the actual internal migrations according to district.

The typology and systematics of migration, especially internal migration, have been further elucidated in different ways in several investigations undertaken in Sweden. First of all it can be mentioned that in the last decade a distinction has been made among migrations of the types $L \rightarrow S$, $S \rightarrow L$, $L \leftrightarrow L$, and $S \leftrightarrow S$, or $L \rightarrow$

[29] T. Lynn Smith, *Population Analysis* (New York: McGraw-Hill, 1948). See also "Statistics of Migration: Definitions-Methods-Classifications" (*International Labour Office, Studies and Reports,* Series N [Statistics], No. 18 [Geneva, 1932]). An

attempt to develop a few concepts of basic "ideal" types which are differentiated by sociologically significant criteria is given in a paper by Rudolf Heberle, "Types of Migration," *The Southwestern Social Science Quarterly,* June 1955, pp. 65–70.

[30] G. Müller, "Wanderungsstatistik," *Raumforschung und Raumordnung,* XI (1953), 45–47.

T, T → L, L ↔ L and T ↔ T, where L =
"country" [*landsbygd*], S = "cities" [*stä-
der*], and T = "urbanlike agglomerations"
[*tätorter*].

Thus Torsten Hägerstrand divides internal migrations into the following categories, depending upon the environment of
the place of origin and the goal of migration: (a) country place to/from country
place, (b) country place to/from urbanlike
agglomeration, and (c) urbanlike agglomeration to/from urbanlike agglomeration.[31]

Starting with the primary tables of the
Central Statistical Bureau, G. Ahlberg has
recently erected a still more detailed tableau having to do with migrations among
A, B, C, and D communes as well as with
smaller or larger towns.[32] In addition, this
tableau gives expression to an apparent
tendency for migrations to great cities to
increase at the expense of migrations to
communes of A-type as the degree of urbanization increases in the commune in
which the migration originates.

The question of the systematic investigation of migrational movements was also
raised by the geographical group at the
social science organizing conference at
Uppsala in 1950. In the discussion of problems concerning central places and *umlands,* in various connections with internal
migrations, Professor D. Hannerberg emphasized among other things that it would
be necessary to deal with total migration,
that is, all types of migration, and not

[31] Torsten Hägerstrand, "Innovationsförloppet ur
korologisk synpunkt," *Meddelanden Från Lunds
Universitets Geografiska Institution,* XXV (1953),
174 ff.

[32] G. Ahlberg, *Befolkningsutvecklingen och ur-
baniseringen i Sverige, 1911–1950* (Stockholm,
1953). *Idem,* "Population Trends and Urbanization in Sweden, 1911–1950," *Lund Studies in
Geography,* Series B (Human Geography), XVI
(1956). The rural communities (parishes) have
been classified as follows, depending upon the
percentage of the population that is agricultural:
A communities: 75–100 per cent, B communities:
50–75 per cent, C and D communities: 0–50 per
cent. The D communities differ from the C communities in that more than two-thirds of the
population live in urbanlike agglomerations.

merely with some selected types. The purpose of the exposition given in the following paragraphs is to contribute further to
the elucidation and perfection of a usable
classification of migrations, especially of
internal population movements.

A classification of migrations can undoubtedly be made in different ways, depending on the criteria emphasized. However, among the most important distinguishing characteristics, special mention
should be made of duration (chronological
criterion) and spatial course or extent
(chorological criterion).

From the chronological standpoint, both
internal and external migrations have often
been divided into the following categories:
(a) accidental or temporary, (b) permanent or periodic (seasonal), and (c) definitive migrations. Divisions into long-lasting
(long-term) migrations and short-lasting
(short-term) migrations have also been
made. As for seasonal migrations, they can
be internal, international, intercontinental,
and sometimes even transoceanic (for example the so-called "swallow migrations"
between Spain and Argentina). Parenthetically, there occurs in both sociological and
geographical literature a peculiar category
of periodic migrations, which has received
the name of alternating migrations (*Pen-
delwanderungen, migrations alternantes,
commuting*). A very large literature now
exists on such migrational movements of
alternating type between residence and
working place. It is especially applicable
to industrialized regions where a high percentage of the economically active population is employed outside of the residential
communes, as in Belgium, where as much
as two-fifths of the working population
belongs to the alternating group. In my
view, this form of movement should be
described under the ordinary traffic concept, according to which traffic can take
place within the boundaries of one and the
same town or commune (so-called pseudo-
commuting), between different central
places, or between country and town. This
is true particularly of the daily alternating

traffic (*Tagespendler,* "daily commuters"). Only "non-daily commuters," that is, weekly or seasonal commuters, should be described as periodic migrants. There is unanimity on one point: "frontier workers" (*travailleurs frontaliers, Grenzgänger*) or interstate commuters are temporary migrants. The designation "frontier workers" is used to denote workers residing near a frontier, who work in the neighboring state, and usually have to cross the frontier to go to their work and to return home. These alternating movements take place within the limits of "minor frontier traffic" and by means of simple frontier cards. But it may happen that frontier workers go a greater distance from their home and return home only once a week or even less often (intercountry or interstate periodic migrants).

But it is the chorological classification of migrations, especially of internal migrations, that is most interesting. The geographical element of migration problems is most conspicuous in chorological questions.

We speak today of intercontinental as well as intracontinental migrations. In fact, these concepts are inexact. Intercontinental or, more traditionally, transoceanic migrations (overseas migrations) comprise all migrations from one to another of the five great continental divisions of the world, as well as migrations between South and North America. Migrations between Europe and Asia—within the territory of the Soviet Union—have likewise been characterized as intercontinental.[33]

In contrast, continental migrations are those that take place over land or water within the same continent—excluding the Americas—and inside the European or Asiatic boundaries of the Soviet Union. Migrations from one metropolitan or mother country to a colony and vice versa, and from one colonial territory to another are sometimes described as emigration and immigration, and sometimes as international migration. Movements between different colonial territories have also been described as intercolonial migrations.[34]

There has long been a desire to differentiate between international and national migration. These two main categories are in general use, but the terms are misleading. If one wishes to distinguish between migrations occurring (a) between the territories of two states, i.e., between two different economic labor markets, or (b) between different administrative or geographic areas within the same state territory, i.e., between two different sub-labor markets within the same national economic region, then one may speak of intercountry and intracountry migration.

It is well at this point to pause for some observations on a classification of intracountry or internal migrations. Based on an earlier attempt to make this distinction,[35] and on recent literature, the following comprehensive classification is proposed:

    I. *Intralocal or intraregional migrations,* i.e., migrations that take place within a more or less uniform area, a particular landscape, a village, an agricultural commune, a city or a sub-labor market. These movements include:

        A. *Intra-urban migrations* (intra-city migrations),[36] including internal migrations within cities, urbanlike agglomerations or conurbations; and

        B. *Intrarural migrations* (rural intra-community migrations), including

---

[33] E. H. Thörnberg, *Från det moderna samhället* (Stockholm, 1935).

[34] P. B. de la Brosse, "Le surpeuplement du delta Tonkinois et l'immigration intercoloniale," *L'Asie Française,* vol. XXXIX (1939). See also "Statistics of Migration" cited in Note 29 above (pp. 101–6). The term "colony" is used in the generic sense of dominions, possessions, protectorates, dependencies, mandated territories, etc.

[35] Edgar Kant, "Etudes concernant les questions d'espace . . ."

[36] B. Tableman, *Intra-Community Migration in the Flint Metropolitan District* (Ann Arbor: Institute for Human Adjustment, University of Michigan, 1948).

migrations in the countryside which has its course within a commune, an agricultural area, etc.

II. *Interlocal or interregional migrations.* These movements include:

A. *Migrations by change of environment or milieu,* i.e., movement between geographically or economically different parts of a country, landscapes, tracts, administrative units, lands, provinces, or regional labor markets. Here belong also migrations from countryside to cities and vice versa, migrations between agricultural and industrial districts, between depressed and prosperous areas, downslope migration in mountainous areas, etc.

B. *Migrations between similar parts of a country,* i.e., movement between landscapes, tracts, and sub-labor markets, or migrations between places of the same or similar type. According to Heberle and Meyer, this category includes (1) interurban migrations (intercity migrations), and (2) interrural migrations.[87]

Interlocal or interregional migrations are without doubt the most fascinating and problematical of all forms of internal migration, particularly in the case of migrations between different regions or tracts. Such migrations constitute the most important form of social metabolism; they also reflect the division of labor and cooperation obtained between city and countryside. Finally, they also play a role in the transmission or infusion of city culture into the countryside ("rurbanization" or urbanization of the countryside) and vice versa ("countrification" of the towns). In this respect, the question of central places, and especially of the mutual relations of central places with their *umlands* is worthy of special consideration. Fortunately, notable advances have recently been made in studies of in- and out-migration and of place of birth. This advance is strikingly evident if one compares older and newer works.[38]

As was mentioned above, most attention has been paid in regional geographic studies of migration to the flight from the countryside. In this connection, return movements that take place between cities (interurban) and outside of central places have been relatively neglected. Circulation within the countryside is least well known.

Finally, we should not overlook migrations that take place within cities (intraurban) and conurbations. Corresponding studies, primarily of the frequency of change of residence in large cities, have been carried out in connection with urban sociological analyses. City organization and the depopulation of the urban core have often been studied, but we still lack a detailed investigation of the population succession within urban areas. Since investigation of this sort would have great meaning for the local growth of a city, among other things, it deserves fuller development.

One more remark should be made concerning labor or social migration. When E. Willeke, in his articles on the spatial aspects of human labor (also full of meaning for geography!), treats the question of "job changes" (changes of occupation) by workers, he designates such transfers as "professional migration" (*berufliche Wanderungen*), and finds that as soon as such "professional migrations" are accompanied by an upward or downward movement on the social ladder, we are dealing with a special kind of migration, the so-called "social migration" (*soziale Wanderungen*).[39] Other writers, for instance Nothaas[40] and Thörnberg,[41] have also devoted attention

[87] R. Heberle and F. Meyer, *Die Grossstädte im Strome der Binnenwanderungen* (Leipzig: S. Hirzel, 1937).

[38] K.-E. Bergsten, "Sydsvenska födelseortsfält," *Meddelanden Från Lunds Universitets Geografiska Institution,* XX (1951); *idem,* "Variability in Intensity of Urban Fields as Illustrated by Birthplaces," *Lund Studies in Geography,* Series B (Human Geography), III (1951), 25–32.

[39] Edu. Willeke, *Von der raumgebundenen menschlichen Arbeitskraft* (Jena: Fischer, 1937).

[40] J. Nothaas, "Soziale Wanderungen," *Allg. Statist. Arch.,* vol. XXIII (1933–34).

to the so-called vertical social mobility under the rubric of "social migration."

However, on the basis of my conceptions
of social space and social mobility,[42] I
cannot go along with either Willeke's division of migrations or Nothaas' nomenclature; moreover, I am convinced that these
authors introduce a confusion of concepts
in both terminology and the apportionment of work among sociologists and social
geographers. As for "professional migration" in the purely sociological sense, it
should be advantageous to label this whole
process as simply a "change of job" (*yrkes-
växling, Berufswechsel*). In contrast, professional migration in the sense of horizontal mobility should be reserved to mean the
movement of surplus workers from one geographical area to another. Different kinds
of work have significantly different fields
of migration, as has been shown in many
studies and cartographic investigations.[43]

[41] E. H. Thörnberg, *Från det moderna samhället.*
[42] Edgar Kant, "Den sociologiska regionen, den
sociala tiden och det sociala rummet," *Svensk
Geografisk Årsbok,* 1948, pp. 109–29 [Summary
in English, 130–32].
[43] Heberle and Meyer, *op. cit.;* Edgar Kant,
"Études concernant les questions d'espace . . . ,"
and "Den inre omflyttningen i Estland," *Svensk
Geografisk Årsbok,* 1946, pp. 83–116 [Summary
in English, pp. 116–24]; V. Leban, "Doseljevanje
v Ljubljane," *Geogr. Vestnik,* vol. XVIII (1947);
J. Wallander, *Flykten från skogsbygden* (Stockholm, 1948); Sven Dahl, "De olika yrkesgrup-
pernas flyttningar," in Gerd Enequest (ed.),
Tätorter och Omland (Uppsala, 1951), pp. 87–99;
K.-E. Bergsten, "Sydsvenska födelseortsfält," *op.
cit.*

Last but not least, the study of different
kinds of migration phenomena should stimulate new methods of cartographic analysis
and of description. Ratzel, as we know, was
very skeptical about the mapping of migrational phenomena. He believed that it was
contrary to the nature of cartography to
analyze or describe mobility, something
that can only be described in words.

I cannot share this view. The technique
of migration cartography has in the course
of time made notable advances. In our
day the student of migration has available
a wealth of methods and symbols. Here can
be cited as examples arrow or flow-line
methods, map-series, isochronic and isarithmic techniques, star diagrams, and so on.[44]
The method of cartography is not complete, but is now in full development. Thus
we hope that it too will correspond to the
judgment of the geography of population
given by Jean Brunhes and Camille Vallaux: "To study and define fully settled
groups is nothing else than to formulate an
abstraction; to grasp and describe groups
in movement, in so far as possible, means
to describe life itself." [45]

[44] [In the original version of his article, Professor Kant reproduces nine figures from previous
studies to illustrate the cartographic techniques
mentioned here. In addition to these figures, the
interested reader will profit from study of the
relevant illustrations in F. J. Monkhouse and
H. R. Wilkinson, *Maps and Diagrams: Their
Compilation and Construction* (New York: Dutton, 1952)].
[45] *La géographie de l'histoire,* p. 201.

TORSTEN HÄGERSTRAND

THE PROPAGATION
OF INNOVATION WAVES

In a previous number of the Lund Studies in Geography I gave a brief report of an investigation concerning the introduction of motorcars in Scania, the southernmost part of Sweden.[1] The following is a more complete account of the same topic. In addition, some comparisons are now drawn with the diffusion of radios. This paper is a link in a more extensive research into the present-day diffusion of culture elements.

The process of diffusion is carefully described by ethnologists and folklorists with reference to ancient times. Present-day instances are rare. They are put forward mainly in the United States by Pemberton,[2] McVoy,[3] Kniffen,[4] and a few others.

Reprinted, with permission of the author, from *Lund Studies in Geography,* Series B (Human Geography), IV (1952). The author is professor of geography at the Royal University of Lund, Sweden.

[1] Torsten Hägerstrand, "Migration and the Growth of Culture Regions," *Lund Studies in Geography,* Series B (Human Geography), III (1951), 33–36.

[2] H. E. Pemberton, "Culture Diffusion Gradients," *American Journal of Sociology,* XLII (1936), 226–33; idem, "The Curve of Culture Diffusion Rate," *American Sociological Review,* I (1936), 547–66; idem, "The Spatial Order of Culture Diffusion," *Sociology and Social Research,* XXII (1938), 246–51.

[3] E. C. McVoy, "Patterns of Diffusion in the United States," *American Sociological Review,* V (1940), 219–27.

[4] Fred B. Kniffen, "Geography and the Past," *Journal of Geography,* L (1951), 126–29; idem, "The American Agricultural Fair: Time and Place," *Annals of the Association of American Geographers,* XLI (1951), 42–57; idem, "The American Covered Bridge," *Geographical Review,* XLI (1951), 114–23.

Kniffen strongly emphasizes the importance of a cultural approach to questions of distribution in geography.

There are many Swedish works concerning more primitive stages, and the ways of thinking are lucidly summarized by Svensson.[5] His conclusions seem to be useful also in connection with modern problems.

Historical facts, however, only exceptionally admit a statistical treatment. Only in certain favorable cases may changes in the distribution of culture elements in past centuries be studied with perfect precision. Excellent examples are the essays of Margaret Hodgen on the diffusion of windmills in England,[6] and of lace, glass, silk and paper making, cloth fulling and coal mining from 1100 to 1900.[7] Usually it is feasible only to determine where a certain culture trait was to be found, but not to what degree. The changes in spatial distribution with time have to be expressed by means of displacements of culture boundaries.

If mere boundary lines are to give an adequate cartographic picture of the distribution of culture elements, then these elements should appear in mutually exclusive regions. But on the contrary, we find all

[5] S. Svensson, "Skånes folkdräkter: en dräkthistorisk undersökning 1500–1900," *Nordiska Museets Handl.,* vol. III (1935); idem, "Bygd och yttervärld: Studier över förhållandet mellan nyheter och tradition," *ibid,* vol. XV (1942).

[6] Margaret T. Hodgen, "Geographical Diffusion as a Criterion of Age," *American Anthropologist,* XLIV (1942), 345–68.

[7] Margaret T. Hodgen, "Similarities and Dated Distributions," *American Anthropologist,* LII (1950), 445–68.

ranges of transition between centers where the element occurs in high density, and peripheral areas where it is rare. When studying changes we cannot draw boundary lines and observe their displacements without very crude simplifications. Instead, we must ascertain the spatial distribution of ratios. Changes in distribution are to be treated as changes of ratios and gradients.

I maintain that changes in spatial distribution (i.e., changes in ratios and gradients) of culture elements occur in conformity to certain undiscovered principles. In searching for these principles, it is of no importance that the phenomena considered have a traditional place in geography. In fact the objects themselves are not the center of observation. They are used as indicators of people's ways of behaving with regard to the relative location of dwelling places. This study has less reference to the geography of specific culture elements than to a "geography of cultural behavior."

The first claim for an indicator is not that it is of "geographical importance" but that the data are complete and capable of quantitative analysis. To that end one must put up with those objects which happen to have been recorded. Further, the data must be complete for more than one moment in time. We have to map the situation at several different moments. Moreover, the conditions of this study require that these moments should succeed each other within short intervals. When we are going to observe changes in ratios and gradients instead of mobile boundaries, it is necessary to be complete. Short intervals give an idea of the degree of order and continuity in the process.

The diffusion of an innovation propagates in two dimensions, the spatial and the social. We are going to examine only the spatial dimension.

SOURCE MATERIAL

The motorcar.—The automotive development in Scania since World War I is most conveniently traced by means of a running

series of printed lists of vehicles compulsorily registered with the country administration. These contain specification of the owners' names, occupations, and postal addresses. Hence they permit both social and spatial observations.

Indeed, some observations should be made on the subject of the lists up to 1923. Because of the regulations for registration, the lists include a number of heavy motorcycles among the cars. I did not find it necessary to separate these, since, as innovations, they are closely related to the cars.

Again, the lists contain vehicles which have been registered as of a certain time. This does not necessarily mean that they all are still in use at the time in question. This inconsistency disappeared in 1923 when the car tax was imposed. The increment from year to year is real, however, which is the point in question.

The tabulation of motorcars per post office was carried out biannually from 1918 to 1930, and included more than 62,000 items. A relatively small number of cars, which were registered in Scania but had addresses referring to other parts of Sweden, have been omitted.

The radio.—Unfortunately, one cannot follow the development of radio so closely. Only statistical data concerning districts of 500 to 1,500 square kilometers in size survive of its history. The figures used are from official statistics.[8]

CARTOGRAPHIC METHOD

The purpose of the method is to comprehend the data concerning motorcars in isarithmic maps showing the density in relation to population in thousands.

The areal subdivision.—When making ratio maps one must usually rely on figures referring to civil divisions. In Sweden such districts are very unequal in size and irregular in shape. Hence ratios cannot be fairly compared. When one part of the investigated region is made up of small units

[8] *Sveriges officiella Statistik: Telefon och Telegraf,* 1926–48.

and another part of large ones, the ratio map will be more detailed in the former part than in the latter. Irregularities within the large divisions will be eliminated and a false idea of regional contrasts may arise.

In our case the data refer to a relatively dense distribution of points—the post offices. This fact has induced us to reject the

for two reasons: (1) the hexagon approximates the circle and therefore the actual orientation of the network will bias the figures only moderately; (2) interpolation of isarithms between hexagonal points is less arbitrary. We thus escape those contradictions between pairs of diagonal points which are common in a square system.

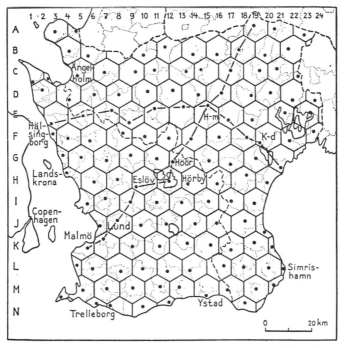

Fig. 1. Hexagonal unit areas. The dots show the position of the median point in every cell. The broken lines from K 5 to A 19 and from E 3 to G 21 refer to the course of the profiles shown on Figures 8 and 9.

above method and instead to try to compute the ratios on the basis of geometrically defined areas. Thanks to two dot maps of population, showing the state in 1917 and in 1940, the number of inhabitants is easily estimated within whatever boundaries we wish to draw.[9]

In choosing between a square and a hexagonal pattern the latter was preferred

The network used is shown in Figure 1. The unit area corresponds to 100 square kilometers. No urban settlements were divided among several cells.

Location of spot-heights.—If only the central points were chosen as "spot-heights,"[10] the finished map would be distorted in some places like the ordinary topographic map. The population clusters often form peaks on the ratio map. If a

[9] Sten De Geer, *Befolkningens fördelning i Sverige* (Stockholm, 1919); W. William-Olsson, *Befolkningens fördelning i Sverige år 1940. Karta* (Stockholm, 1946).

[10] For this concept see B. C. Wallis, "Distribution of Nationalities in Hungary," *Geographical Journal*, XLVII (1916), 177–88, ref. to 178.

cell contains an eccentric cluster it is desirable that the accompanying peak run up and over and not beside it. To that end, the spot-heights were displaced from the geometric centers of the cells to centers of population.[11]

There are several ways to define a center of population.[12] We chose the median point as the most readily obtained (Fig. 2). A

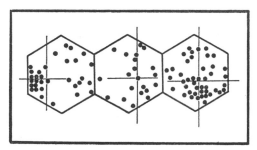

FIG. 2. Median points.

meridian line was fitted to bisect the cluster of population dots (each dot representing 100 inhabitants). The same procedure was repeated with a parallel. The intersection of the lines gave the point required. The position of the median point in every cell is denoted in Figure 1.

The Isarithmic interval.—The isarithmic values selected increase in a geometric progression with ratio 2 (0.25, 0.5, 1, 2, 4, 8, 16 . . .). This implies a constant interval in the logarithmic scale. This fact is taken advantage of in the course of interpolation, which is performed graphically on logarithmic paper. A transformation to the natural vertical scale will give nonlinear profiles, increasing in steepness with nearness to the peaks. To avoid the insoluble interpolation toward zero, empty cells are left open. Generally the 1-isarithm is the lower limit. Areas with minor ratios are only shaded.

[11] See J. W. Alexander and A. Zahorchak, "Population Density Maps of the United States: Techniques and Patterns," *Geographical Review,* XXXIII (1943), 457–66.

[12] E. E. Sviatlovsky and W. G. Eells, "The Centrographical Method and Regional Analysis," *Geographical Review,* XXVII (1937), 240–54.

DIFFUSION OF THE MOTORCAR (1918–30) AND THE RADIO (1925–47)

The distribution of motorcars (cf. Fig. 3 *a-b*) is constantly variable during the period considered. The series of maps clearly shows that we should avoid speaking of a culture boundary in transition. At the beginning there is a scattered distribution which becomes more condensed. With regard to our hexagonal area units the development manifests itself as a change of ratios. With the following short description of the development it will be illustrative to use the map of the urban hierarchy (Fig. 4) as a common background.

By 1918 the introductory phase has continued for about fourteen years. Acceleration does not commence until the end of World War I. At the beginning certain centers run over their surrounding areas. In 1918 we notice Ystad (M 15), Malmö (K 5), and Hälsingborg (E 3) on the coast, and Höör (G 13) in the interior of the region (cf. Fig. 1). In 1920 Trelleborg (N 8), Landskrona (H 4), Ängelholm (C 5), Lund (J 8), Eslöv (H 10), Kristianstad (F 20), and some smaller towns constitute peaks. All those remain as such for a long time (cf. the profiles shown in Figs. 8 and 9).

The transition occurs mainly from west to east with one exception. The Kristianstad area (around F 20) forms a separate center which widens to the north and west, where it meets the main field.

The urban hierarchy channels the course of diffusion. In addition to the influence from a center on the neighboring districts, we find short circuits to the more important places at a greater distance. Subordinate centers arise. These details in the mechanism are most evident on the median maps of my previous paper.[13]

In 1918 there are three main clusters: (1) southern Scania, north and west of Ystad, (2) western Scania, a triangle

[13] See "Migration and the Growth of Culture Regions," p. 35.

formed by Malmö, Hörby, and Hälsing-borg, and (3) the Kristianstad district. In western Scania we find several clusters of the second order. A considerable part of the region is empty.

east and north of the region. The general large increase between 1920 and 1922 depends upon the introduction of cheap "Fords."

In 1924 there are only a few empty cells

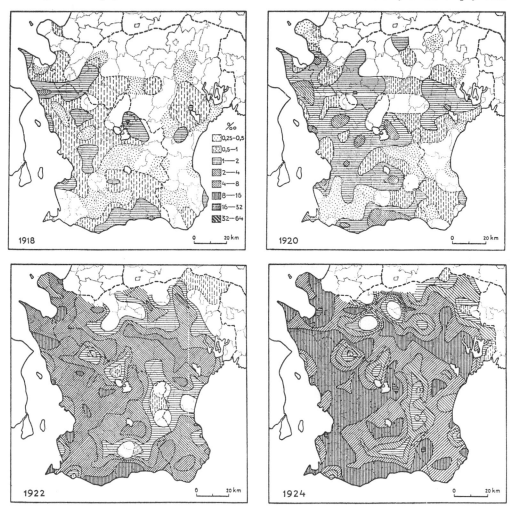

Fig. 3 *a-b*. Motorcars per 1,000 inhabitants biannually from 1918 to 1930. Maps for 1926–30 shown on page 360. These maps should be compared with the configuration of the urban hierarchy as shown in Fig. 4.

In 1920 the areas with up to two cars per 1,000 inhabitants are widened but not brought together. The low density south of Malmö is noteworthy.

In 1922 there are no separate clusters left. The ratios in the areas first permeated continue to increase. Empty spaces now appear only in the center and toward the

left. The predominance of western Scania, however, is constantly evident.

In 1926 the western predominance begins to lessen.

In 1928 peaks appear in the interior, surpassing even those of the western coastal districts.

In 1930 the distribution is evenly spread

out over the region. Yet there are blank spots with a retarded development. We should observe that it was a rather long time before the car appeared at all in some of those cells.

mark and the European continent exercises a strong influence on the above-mentioned parts of Scania. As Lägnert showed in his study of wheat cultivation, a similar west-east movement was evident even in that

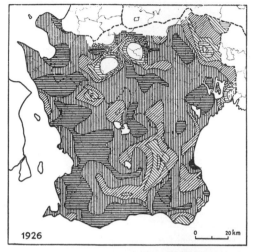

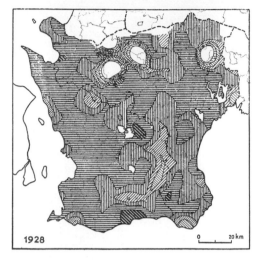

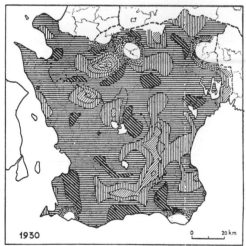

FIG. 3 *a-b Continued*

The fact that the development started in southern and western Scania presents a special problem. I take the same view as Godlund in his paper on the development of bus service.[14] The proximity to Den-

case, if one makes proper allowance for the soil conditions.[15]

There is of course no constant rule that innovation will unfold only in this way. In ancient times we find other patterns.[16] We have to take into account the sources of

[14] Sven Godlund, "Bus Services, Hinterlands, and the Location of Urban Settlements in Sweden, especially in Scania," *Lund Studies in Geography*, Series B (Human Geography), III (1951), 14–32.

[15] Folke Lägnert, *Veteodlingen i södra och mellersta Sverige* (Lund, 1949).

[16] See Svensson, "Skånes folkdräkter."

impulses and the susceptibility in different districts.

The mean isarithms, "Pleions."—It is impractical to try to obtain a deeper idea of the progress by mere inspection of the

year by the number of inhabitants in the region as a whole we get a mean ratio. With the aid of mean ratio isarithms we may divide all maps into two types of areas, one showing where ratios are greater than the

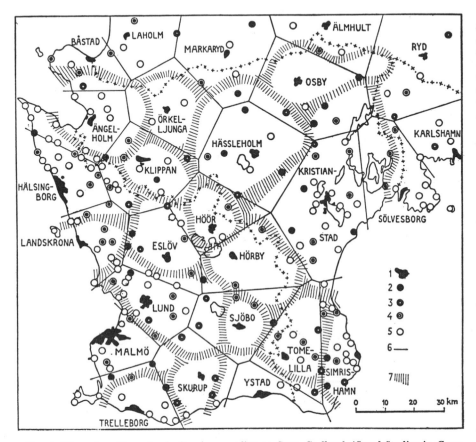

Fig. 4. The urban hierarchy in Scania according to Sven Godlund (*Lund Studies in Geography*, Series B, III, 1951). 1–4 represent centers in order of rank: (1) Regional centers, (2) townlet center, (3) township center, (4) market center, (5) special urban settlement (e.g., industrial villages, fishing and watering places), (6) extent of the hinterlands of regional centers, (7) boundary zones of bus traffic hinterlands. Among the regional centers Malmö (pop. 128,000 in 1930), Hälsingborg (pop. 56,000 in 1930), and Kristianstad (pop. 14,000 in 1930) possess superior positions.

series of maps. We have to comprehend them and analyze the underlying figures.

The isarithm system selected is an arbitrary sample of the infinite number of possible contours. Of these, however, there is one with a singular position because it can be defined from given data. If we divide the sum total of items for a certain

mean and another showing where they are less. In comparing the original maps we must pay attention to two courses, the transition outward from centers and also the general increases in ratios. By means of the mean ratio isarithm we eliminate the latter. The mean ratios for Scania have been computed as follows:

TABLE 1

REGISTERED MOTORCARS AND POPULATION OF
SCANIA, 1918–30

Year	Registered Automobiles (M)	Population in thousands (P)	Mean Ratio (M/P)
1918.......	706	719.2	1.0
1920.......	1,320	720.1	1.8
1922.......	4,614	733.3	6.3
1924.......	7,717	740.3	10.4
1926.......	11,847	746.5	15.9
1928.......	16,249	751.7	21.6
1930.......	19,830	754.8	26.3

On Figure 5 *a,b* areas encircled by the mean ratio isarithms are hatched. These areas have a positive anomaly. We will call them "pleions," a concept borrowed from climatology.[17]

Changes in number and positions of

[17] See V. Conrad and L. Pollak, *Methods in Climatology* (Cambridge, Mass.: Harvard University Press, 1950), p. 280. According to these authors the concept was introduced in 1909 by H. Arctowski and referred to regions with positive temperature anomaly; it seems to be useful in the cartographic analysis of many variable elements.

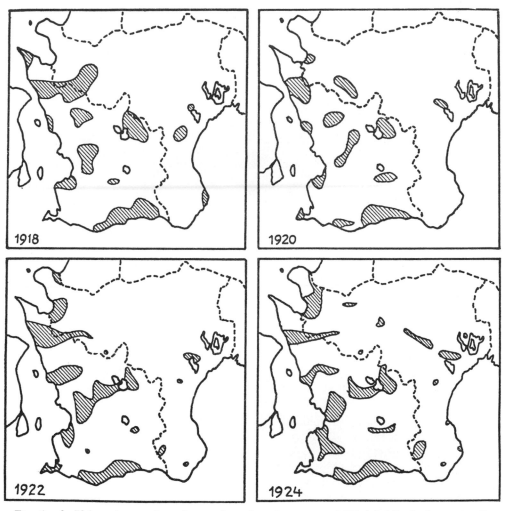

FIG. 5 *a-b*. Pleions (areas where the number of motorcars per 1,000 inhabitants is greater than the mean ratio).

pleions are quite inconsiderable from 1918 to 1922. Yet a tendency toward fusion into larger flakes is perceptible between 1920 and 1922. With the single exception of the Kristianstad center, the northeastern part of the region lacks pleions. In 1924 minor

siderably increased number of cars (Table 1).

The superficial content of pleions grows with time. This fact indicates a broadening of the distribution.

The firmness of the pattern is striking.

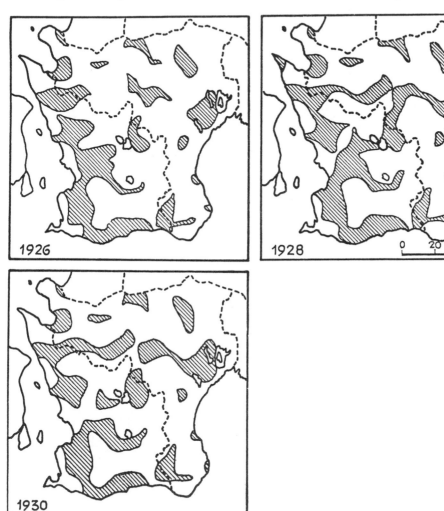

FIG. 5 *a-b Continued*

pleions begin to appear in the northeast. By 1926 they have increased in size, and, at the same time, the southern and western pleions run into each other. In 1928 we get a pair of ribbons joining western and eastern Scania. The situation by 1930 is practically identical, in spite of the con-

It is clear that cities and towns will keep the lead. But certain country districts, too, tend to persist as pleions.

The time lags.—The automotive development evidently shows a permanent time lag between different areas. Every cell has its own curve of growth. There is no use plotting all these curves on a map. Instead, we are going to select a few examples.

In Figure 6 *a* the increase in ratio of the region as a whole is represented by a dashed line. Along with this mean curve three selected cell curves from southwestern (K 5), central (I 11), and northeastern (A 21) Scania are grouped as examples. All of these curves are more or less equal

From 1931 and forwards up to 1939 we can estimate it to about five years.

In my opinion we cannot interpret this time lag only in terms of the different economic conditions in different areas. Economic conditions—for example the distribution of incomes—do not change very fast. In general we have to assume that in a given cell, at least as many persons owned

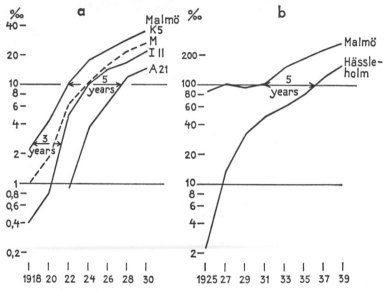

Fig. 6 *a-b*. *a* = Motorcars per 1,000 inhabitants 1918–1930 in Scania (the dashed line M) and in the cells K 5 (Malmö), I 11, and A 21. *b* = Radios per 1,000 inhabitants 1925–1939 in the Malmö and Hässleholm districts.

to one another and fairly parallel to the mean curve. The main difference is a time lag. This amounts to two or three years between K 5 and I 11 and five years between K 5 and A 21.

By way of comparison let us consider the diffusion of radios from 1925 to 1939. Here the source material is less detailed, unfortunately. From the statistics available we select figures referring to southwestern Scania (the Malmö district) and northern Scania (the Hässleholm district) (Fig. 6 *b*). Until 1931 the Malmö district remains stationary with a relatively high ratio of radios per 1,000 inhabitants. Meanwhile, the ratio of the Hässleholm district rapidly increases. Here, too, we find a time lag.

a motorcar or a radio in 1930, for example, as might have afforded to buy these things five years earlier. If economic conditions alone were active, there is no reason why every cell without time lag should not closely follow the general increase in ratio up to saturation limits at different heights. However, a uniform raising of the "ratio surface" requires an even distribution of information about the new item from the very beginning. In fact, the information seems to extend only to restricted distances around the places where the novelty already exists. The information seems to flow mainly in the network of social contacts.

Change profiles.—Now we need a closer idea of how the "ratio surface" really behaves when rising. The most simple way is to cut out a series of profiles.

Behind the displacements of isarithms outwards from the centers several kinds of changes may be concealed. We can consider different possibilities theoretically (Fig. 7) in advance.

Along the ordinate the ratio (F) is marked off in logarithmic scale. It is the relative rather than absolute changes which are essential. The abscissa represents distance (D).

The median points of the three districts *a*, *b*, and *c*, are intersected by the profile. Of these *a* is a center of innovation. We

(K 5) and proceeds in a northeasterly direction. The other starts in Hälsingborg (E 3) and proceeds eastward. They cross in Hässleholm (E 15). The profiles are not straight but have moderate bends in order to pass through cells that are important centers.

Profile K 5–A 19 Motorcars (Fig. 8).— We find a change of type I (according to Fig. 7) between 1918 and 1920 in K 5 and H 10, and between 1922 and 1924 in C 7. If we consider the trend as a whole of the curves from 1922 and later, taking no account of the zigzag details, the successive changes correspond to type II. K 5

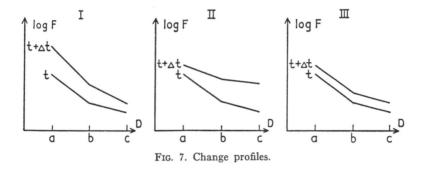

FIG. 7. Change profiles.

disregard the fact that in real life we have a whole hierarchy of such centers. The lower curve indicates the situation at a given time (*t*). This situation is the same in alternatives I, II, and III.

Now a short time (Δ*t*) passes. At the time *t* + Δ*t* three different tendencies may be traced:

I. The relative increase is greatest in *a* and diminishes outward.

II. The relative increase is smallest in *a* and grows outward.

III. The relative increase is equal in *a*, *b*, and *c*.

All these possibilities involve an outward displacement of isarithms, however varied.

We are now going to examine to what extent the above types of changes will be recovered in the empirical gradients. The courses of the profiles are shown in Fig. 1 as regards motorcars. One starts in Malmö

(Malmö) remains with only a small relative increase like a hinge around which the bundle of curves revolves until the upper parts reach the level of K 5. In the details we find that the "valleys" more and more approximate the peaks according to type II. In the final stages the changes approach type III. The change between 1928 and 1930 agrees closely with this type. Now the development has gone so far that the ratios in the central cells G 13 and E 15 surmount the primary center K 5.

Profile E 3–G 21. Motorcars (Fig. 9).— Change of type I occurs in 1918–20 in E 3 and F 20. With these peaks as hinges, an elevation of the intermediate parts follows according to type II. In 1930 those parts surpassed the starting point E 3. Again the general change between 1928 and 1930 lies very close to type III. An impulse to recurrence of type I is found in E 15 and F 20.

The prevalent evolution is the same as in profile K 5 A 19 (Fig. 8).

The number of inhabitants in every cell is marked off along the abscissa in both profiles. In the beginning there is an obvious positive correlation between ratio and number of inhabitants. As time goes on this correlation becomes less and less pronounced.

14). This improved the receiving conditions. At the same time the radio interest was stimulated. We find a new innovation center with a peak at Hörby according to type I. With two peaks now as hinges, an equalization of type II follows. Soon Malmö recaptured the predominance. The change was not distinctly of type III until 1944. We thus find certain similarities in

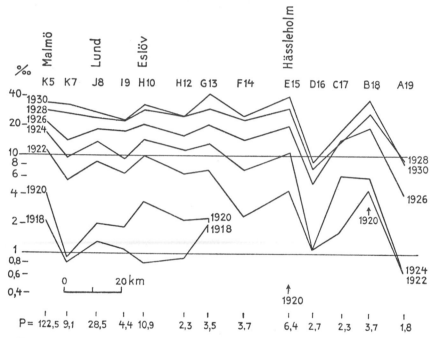

Fig. 8. Profile K 5—A 19. Motorcars per 1,000 inhabitants 1918–1930 in logarithmic scale. In 1918 the cells F 14—A 19 contain no motorcars. In 1920 isolated peaks (the arrows) appear in E 15 and B 18. Not until 1922 is the profile continuous. P denotes the population in thousands in 1930.

Profile Malmö–Hässleholm. Radio (Fig. 10).—This profile coincides as far as possible with K 5–A 19, but as the figures refer to larger districts the curves will be much smoother.

In 1925 a wireless station was situated in Malmö. Thus stage I in the above scheme of changes had already been passed. Until 1928 the changes proceeded according to type II. In 1929 there was a modification in the general circumstances. A new radio transmitter was built at Hörby (H

the sequence of stages between the diffusion of radios and motorcars.

On the basis of the previous observations we may attempt to interpret the different types of changes.

Type I belongs to the *primary stage* of a diffusion process. Centers hastily grow up.

Type II brings a retardation in the primary centers. Instead there is a centrifugal increase in other areas trying to overtake these centers. New centers will appear. This

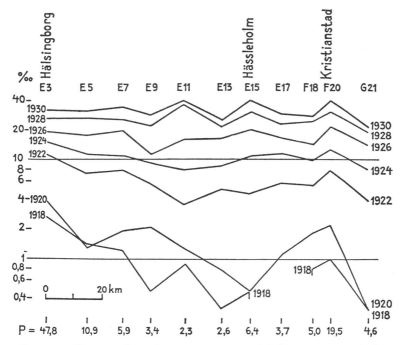

FIG. 9. Profile E 3—G 21. Motorcars per 1,000 inhabitants 1918–30 in logarithmic scale. P denotes the population in thousands in 1930.

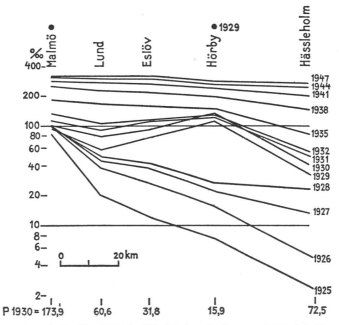

FIG. 10. Profile Malmö—Hässleholm. Radios per 1,000 inhabitants 1925–1947. The two dots at the top indicate the location of the radio station. P denotes the population in thousands in 1930.

is the proper *diffusion stage,* when the more considerable regional contrasts become leveled.

Type III is the *condensing stage.* The phenomenon in question is now commonly known.

Another characteristic feature is a general retardation in the course of time. We have to suppose that the ratio surface asymptotically approaches a *saturation stage* when further increase is impossible in the given conditions. The distribution of the radio in 1947 was very close to that stage.

If we imagine the stages I, II and III passing in succession as in a motion picture, at the same time as the curve rises with retarding velocity, we will obtain some idea of the way the innovation wave propagates within a population.

Of course we have to make quantitative observations of many culture elements in their diffusion before the outlines drawn here can be stated as principles.

In conclusion we shall contemplate the importance of the observations which have been made.

Reaching stage III was a relatively rapid affair in the cases studied above.

Many culture elements might make much slower progress, especially when they do not start in the top of the urban hierarchy but in some peripheral areas.

Moreover a diffusion may die off long before stage III, leaving behind a distribution which is inexplicable by means of our usual equipment of factors. When making a statement concerning some distribution we often risk supposing a phenomenon in stage I or II to be determined by favorable conditions with about the same distribution. Instead a better explanation may be that a start was made in some place by mere chance, after which the diffusion mechanism began to operate through the network of social contacts, thus forming a distribution ("region") which could have been located otherwise, all things being equal. This view is perhaps applicable to many industrial regions with a puzzling localization.[18]

A careful study of the diffusion mechanism by means of all such indicators as we can find may help us to treat these problems.

[18] Cf. Hodgen, "Similarities and Dated Distributions," maps 1–6.

PART 4

LANDSCAPE AND ECOLOGY

The ten articles in this section deal with some features of cultural landscapes and some problems of cultural ecology. Both themes imply interest in the relation of nature and culture, but it is difficult to distinguish between forces that are clearly within and clearly beyond human control. The results of several decades of patient study have taught us that man acts in and upon nature, and not merely in response to the demands of nature. To understand the cultural connotations of habits and habitats we must proceed cautiously and inductively, first by examining some of man's works and then by considering his modification of the works of nature.

In this consideration no issue is more important than relative mobility. A sedentary society blessed with abundant labor or powerful tools can build cities, terrace hillsides, and drastically alter vegetation and soil. In contrast, the habitats of wandering hunters and gatherers show relatively little evidence of human agency. To be effective ecologically, man's efforts must be focused and sustained.

In the first article in this section Richard K. Beardsley and his co-authors give some indications of when, where, and how this concentration of effort was achieved. The first of their evolutionary stages, "Free Wandering," is entirely hypothetical, and it may not be a necessary postulate.[1] "Restricted Wandering" and "Central-based Wandering" imply storage facilities, dwellings, and other features of a recognizable cultural landscape. The rest of the classification implies increased activity at some one place, which becomes a site of semipermanent occupation, then a nucleus for a fully sedentary society, and, finally, a settlement within a hierarchy of settlements. Ultimately, the organization of space is strictly defined, and the activities of man and his landscapes display increasing specialization and complexity.

For our purposes this discussion can be summarized in a single statement: fixity of settlement or sedentariness is directly related to the degree of complexity of a culture or a landscape. This simple correlation is of course not the sole contribution of the discussion, and we have already learned from Edgar Kant that migration is a prominent feature of modern industrial and commercial societies. Nevertheless, it is clear that community mobility can be used in

[1] Cf. Hans Bobek's comments in Part III and Carl O. Sauer's discussion in the final selection of this volume, pp. 222 and 540 respectively.

369

combination with other features of culture to define a progressive trend. The essential validity of this classification is attested by archeological and ethnological evidence of all but the free wandering stage.

In Max. Sorre's essay on *genre de vie* mobility is treated as but one of many significant cultural variables. As an integrating theme, *genre de vie* (which we translate imperfectly and awkwardly as "way of life") brings together many problems that are of interest to students of landscape and ecology. Sorre's immediate objective is to provide examples that clarify the meaning of the concept. The topics he considers—livelihood, diet, technology, settlement patterns, social organization, population, and so on—range over most of the field of cultural geography. The key topic is livelihood or, more generally, activity, although Sorre does not suggest that *genre de vie* can be reduced to this alone. For example, the most meaningful thing we can say about the Masai is that they are pastoralists, but this does not mean that their livelihood, or even their treatment of livestock, is common to all pastoralists. Little is gained by demonstrating that the Masai resemble Arab bedouins more closely than they resemble Eskimos or even Bantus, for each group has its peculiar *genre de vie*.

Sorre's discussion of the problems of generic classification leads to consideration of some problems of genesis. Again, we are presented with the alternatives of independent invention versus borrowing or diffusion, single origin versus multiple origins, and inertia versus rapid innovation or accommodation. The last problem invites consideration of why particular cultures tend to encourage or frustrate change. Sorre's discussion of circulation and exchange paves the way for a study of routes and their foci, and hence of urbanization. His closing remarks suggest that distinctive ways of life are rapidly disappearing under the impact of specialization, standardization, and accelerated diffusion. It is difficult to apply the concept of *genre de vie* to highly urbanized and industrialized societies.[2]

From this study of a wide range of cultural features, we turn to Derwent Whittlesey's classification of major agricultural regions. Agriculture is of special interest to the geographer, for it covers more area than any other mode of land use and is readily observed in the field. This article represents the culmination of innumerable studies by geographers interested in the classification and delimitation of regions. The map summarizes the results of studies on a continental scale, which had evolved from detailed surveys within particular countries or realms.

These remarks give some indication of the importance of the article and our reasons for including it here. As an expression of cultural geography, it has major shortcomings, primarily because the classification shows little regard for process or genesis. Agricultural systems involve much more than crops and

---

[2] For extended discussion of the problems outlined in this essay see Sorre's *Les fondements de la géographie humaine* (3 vols., Paris: Colin, 1947–52).

their combinations. Dietary preferences, inherent physical contrasts, different historical backgrounds, diverse government policies, contrasting systems of land tenure, and varying rates of diffusion also influence patterns of rural activity and the spatial arrangement of agriculture. The chief merit of this study is its consideration of differing degrees of intensity and the balance between subsistence and exchange. Whittlesey's map depicts some important aspects of cultural differentiation at a particular period of history. As a pioneer work of classification and synthesis it deserves more critical attention than it has received, and we may at least hope that attempts will be made to bridge the gap between this cartographic effort and Bobek's map of cultural patterns on the eve of the European expansion overseas.[3]

In the fourth article in this section Max. Sorre discusses another problem of manifest interest in cultural geography: nutrition and its relation to human welfare. In effect he asks for consideration of some patterns that are implicit in Whittlesey's regions. Diet is a sensitive indicator of cultural differences, and many ingredients of diet have importance as symbols of cultural identity. Every society has a distinctive combination of preferences and avoidances, and peoples in advanced stages of acculturation may cling to traditional dietary habits long after they have abandoned other features of their cultures.[4] Moreover, in this consideration cultural geographers have a rare opportunity to express value judgments, for from the standpoint of human health and welfare diets may be described as sufficient or insufficient, good or bad.[5] The relation of famine to migration is well known,[6] and, as Sorre indicates, diet must be included in any evaluation of Malthusian or neo-Malthusian theories. Perhaps the main reason for relative neglect of this important subject is the fact that few geographers (or social scientists in general) have intimate knowledge of the diets of non-Western societies.[7] As an expression of ecological imbalance, hunger is a problem of manifest interest to cultural geographers.

The preceding discussion could be prolonged indefinitely for there is no limit to the number of case studies that might be offered to illustrate each point. In

[3] For discussion of the trends and movements during this interval see Alfred Hettner, *Der Gang der Kultur über die Erde* (Leipzig and Berlin: Teubner, 1923); A. Grenfell Price, *White Settlers and Native Peoples* (Cambridge: Cambridge University Press, 1949); and the several studies of "pioneer settlement" initiated by Isaiah Bowman, e.g., *The Pioneer Fringe* (New York: American Geographical Society, 1931); *Pioneer Settlement* (New York: American Geographical Society, 1932), and *Limits of Land Settlement* (New York: Council on Foreign Relations, 1937).

[4] Numerous examples of persistent food prejudices are given in Frederick J. Simoons, *Eat Not This Flesh* (Madison: University of Wisconsin Press, 1961).

[5] See Jacques M. May, "The Mapping of Human Starvation," *Geographical Review*, XLIII (1953), 253–55, 403–4, and Plates 8 ("Sources of Selected Foods") and 9 ("Diets and Deficiency Diseases") in *Atlas of Diseases* (New York: American Geographical Society, 1953).

[6] See, for example, Walter H. Mallory, *China: Land of Famine* (New York: American Geographical Society, 1926), and the discussion of the causes of Irish emigration in Redcliffe N. Salaman, *The History and Social Influence of the Potato* (London: Cambridge University Press, 1949).

[7] A good indication of what is known and what needs to be known is given in the list of sources that accompanies Plates 8 and 9 of the *Atlas of Diseases*. See also David Gottlieb and Peter H. Rossi, *A Bibliography and Bibliographic Review of Food and Food Habit Research* (Quartermaster Food and Container Institute, Library Bulletin No. 4 [Chicago, 1961]).

lieu of this unattractive prospect, we have added one study that provides concrete illustrations of some of the problems outlined above. The subject is engrossing, for shifting cultivation is practiced by diverse peoples in a large part of the intertropical realm. It is a primitive system in the sense that it requires minimal equipment and is practiced by peoples who have little interest in commerce or exchange. But in his study of the Hanunóo of Mindoro, Harold Conklin demonstrates that shifting cultivation is far too complex and variable to be described as something devoid of pattern. As in any major system of land use, the distinction between local peculiarities and regional similarities is difficult to define. In this case understanding has also been hindered by biased notions of what is desirable or attainable. By careful field observation and studied avoidance of value judgments, Conklin is able to describe the agricultural system of the Hanunóo in precise cultural and ecological terms. It is not unlikely that studies of this sort will reveal that shifting cultivation ranges along a vast continuum, bounded on one side by completely sedentary habits and on the other side by highly mobile non-agricultural ways of life.[8]

In the articles reviewed thus far attention is directed to man's creative activity. Edgar Anderson's article extends the discussion to include consideration of accomplishments that are incidental and accidental. In a related work he describes weeds as "camp followers." [9] This vivid designation suggests that plants may follow man and even depend upon him without being carried or cultivated. In addition to useful and ornamental species, every cultural landscape is characterized by weeds and their animal equivalents, both microscopic and macroscopic. Some weeds eventually evolve into crops (e.g., rye), some crops become weeds (e.g., bamboos), and hybridization may take place between crop plants and weeds (e.g., wheat). The importance of these processes in cultural ecology is demonstrated when we realize that combinations and colonizations of this sort result not only from the mingling of native and alien species, but also from man's creation of new habitats. In the long view of history fire has been man's most important tool, and it has altered the composition of vegetation in vast realms.[10] Anderson's essay adds new dimensions to cultural ecology, and it invites us to explore the margins, corners, and byways of cultural landscapes. In addition, his discussion helps us to appreciate the difficulties that accompany any attempt to distinguish between natural and artificial environments.

Many studies in cultural geography have been designed to elucidate man's conquest of the habitable world. But "conquest" conveys a false impression,

[8] See also Conklin's "The Study of Shifting Cultivation," *Current Anthropology*, II (1961), 27–61, which includes an appended bibliography of more than a thousand works.
[9] Edgar Anderson, *Plants, Man and Life* (Boston: Little, Brown, 1952).
[10] Cf. G. Kuhnholtz-Lordat, *La terre incendiée: essai d'agronomie comparée* (Nimes: Maison Carrée, 1939); and the articles of Omer C. Stewart ("Fire as the First Great Force Employed by Man") and H. H. Bartlett ("Fire, Primitive Agriculture, and Grazing in the Tropics") in William L. Thomas, Jr. (ed.), *Man's Role in Changing the Face of the Earth* (Chicago: University of Chicago Press, 1956).

for culture history offers many examples of regression and contraction as well as progression and expansion. We have already profited from Edgar Kant's description of some striking examples of emigration and depopulation, and from the discussion of diminishing mobility in the evolutionary classification of Beardsley and his co-authors. These themes are developed more fully in Aldo Sestini's study of regressive phases in the development of cultural landscapes.

It is not necessary to remind ourselves that the causes and consequences of the decline of civilizations have been debated at length. It is sufficient to recall that such well known figures as Ibn Khaldun, Edward Gibbon, Oswald Spengler, Michael Rostovtseff, Henri Pirenne, Arnold Toynbee, and Ellsworth Huntington have tried, with greater or lesser success, to account for these major historical trends.[11] The examples given by Sestini are of smaller scale, but they demonstrate that the conquest of the *oikoumene* has never been complete. Throughout history, and even in modern times, progress in one area has been offset by retrogression elsewhere. For example, irrigation developments have encouraged abandonment of grazing land, and economic progress in valleys has drawn population away from adjacent highlands. Fortune, misfortune, and the normal ebb and flow of human activity have caused settlements, landscapes, and entire civilizations to rise, flourish, decline, and disappear. In the Occident one modern trend is clear, for urbanization and industrialization have been accompanied by massive rural depopulation. It is not correct to say that the *oikoumene* has shrunk, but foci of activity have shifted and each generation has left a new pattern of "ghost towns" and abandoned land.[12]

The next three essays deal with the cultural geography of settlements, and each is devoted to a similar problem. The essay of H. J. Fleure is designed to facilitate understanding of the processes of settlement accretion and growth. Albert Demangeon tries to identify factors that influence the concentration or dispersion of rural settlements. And Glenn Trewartha presents a case study from the colonial period of American history that complements and clarifies some of the points stressed by Fleure and Demangeon.

Fleure's article is a good illustration of the merit of combined historical and comparative study. He is mainly interested in the evolution of towns and cities in Europe, but his consideration of that development is preceded by analysis of factors that have encouraged or discouraged urbanization in other parts of the world. From Africa, where a complex of natural and cultural factors inhibited urban growth, he turns to the urban civilizations that evolved in the great flood plans of the Near East. The prerequisites and local contingencies of this development are compared with the less promising conditions in India,

[11] This theme is developed from the viewpoint of the cultural geographer in two articles by Rhoads Murphey, "The Decline of North Africa Since the Roman Occupation: Climatic or Human?" *Annals of the Association of American Geographers*, XLI (1951), 116–32, and "The Ruin of Ancient Ceylon," *Journal of Asian Studies*, XVI (1957), 181–200.

[12] A discussion of the geographic consequences of major economic fluctuations appears in Erich Otremba, "Die Flexibilität des Wirtschaftsraumes," *Erdkunde*, XV (1961), 45–53.

and the Indian situation, in turn, is compared with the more elaborate and durable development in China. With these surveys to guide him, Fleure moves to the Mediterranean region, and reviews the political, economic, and environmental aspects of Greek and Roman urbanization. Following the general course of evolution and diffusion he arrives in northwestern Europe, and attempts to account for the meager development of urban life in the Middle Ages and the factors that led to acceleration of urbanization in later centuries.[13] Viewed together, the several studies in this essay demonstrate that urban development is conditioned by processes of centralization and specialization that run through the whole fabric of cultures.[14]

Demangeon's consideration of the causes of settlement concentration or dispersion has such a marked negative tone that it is tempting to describe it as nihilistic. But he is not content to refute theories; his main purpose is to demonstrate that they should be combined. The question under consideration is easy to pose: why are settlements clustered in some areas and widely scattered in other areas? Environmental considerations clarify the problem without solving it, for similar settlement patterns may be found in different environments, and different settlement patterns may be found in similar environments. The problem suggested by this comparison is resolved in part if attention is directed to the influence of social conditions, particularly inheritance regulations and land tenure, but Demangeon can find little evidence to support the thesis that distinctive settlement patterns coincide with particular ethnic groups. The questions left unanswered by these considerations invite study of differences in agrarian economy. In short, Demangeon eliminates the prospect of any simple or "obvious" explanation and shows that we cannot hope to understand the form or arrangement of settlements unless we take account of natural influences and the complex of social and economic conditions that define a *genre de vie*.[15]

Glenn Trewartha's study of rural settlement in colonial America is also devoted to the problem of contrasting functions and forms. The distinction between the community spirit of New England and the more individualistic and

[13] This theme is developed more fully in several works of Henri Pirenne, e.g., *Medieval Cities: Their Origins and the Revival of Trade* (Princeton: Princeton University Press, 1925 [Doubleday Anchor Books, 1956]), and "Northern Towns and their Commerce," *Cambridge Medieval History,* VI (1932) 505–27. See also H. J. Fleure, "Some Types of Cities in Temperate Europe," *Geographical Review,* X (1920), 357–74, and Robert E. Dickinson, *The West European City* (London: Routledge & Kegan Paul, 1951).

[14] For further discussion see V. Gordon Childe, *Man Makes Himself* (New York: Mentor Books, 1951), pp. 114–42; Robert M. Adams, "The Origin of Cities," *Scientific American,* CCIII, No. 3 (Sept., 1960), 153–72; Carl H. Kraeling and Robert M. Adams (eds.), *City Invincible: A Symposium on Urbanization and Cultural Development in the Ancient Near East* (Chicago: University of Chicago Press, 1960); and Lewis Mumford, *The City in History* (New York: Harcourt Brace, 1961).

[15] Only the second part of the original article is translated here. In the first part Demangeon surveys the distribution of concentrated and dispersed settlement in the entire world; in the third part he presents a more refined classification of settlement types. For further discussion and bibliography see Gabriele Schwarz, *Allgemeine Siedlungsgeographie* (Berlin: Walter de Gruyter, 1959).

speculative spirit of the Southern and Middle colonies is explained in large part by different institutional and legal backgrounds. In New England, village settlement was encouraged by concern for defense, religious uniformity, and the prevalence and persistence of town grants that favored community rather than personal interests. In contrast, settlements outside New England were conditioned by the strong commercial and speculative interests that accompanied the rise of the plantation system and the advance of the frontier. The conclusions of this study have relevance to problems in cultural geography that go far beyond the issue of contrasting settlement patterns in colonial America.

Carl Sauer's essay on the agency of man is a fitting conclusion to the discussions presented in this volume. As in most of the studies we have examined, the approach is historical and comparative, and its purpose is to clarify processes that have been initiated and carried forward by man. Sauer's essay contains no explicit methodological or programmatic statements, but it includes a recommendation that cultural geographers should accept the challenge of dealing with all of human time. Read as a conclusion to thirty-three related studies, it contains few surprises and develops many familiar themes. The association of culture change and climatic change is new, but the emphasis on movement, diffusion, and differentiation characterizes most of the preceding studies. One theme is developed more fully than before—the capacity of man to alter his natural environment—and the evidence presented to illustrate it reminds us that the record of man's accomplishments includes destruction as well as construction. "Wherever men live, they have operated to alter the aspect of the earth, both animate and inanimate, be it to their boon or bane." Eroded hillsides and impoverished floras are as intimately associated with particular cultures as settlement patterns and cultivated fields. This anthology began with a suggestion that the methods perfected by physical geographers could be applied to the works of man. It concludes with a suggestion that we retrace our steps and use knowledge acquired in the study of culture to understand the modification of nature by man.[16]

[16] It is not possible here to give even a selected list of works that provide concrete evidence of modified environments, but it should be noted that this theme is ably developed by several authors in *Man's Role in Changing the Face of the Earth*. The history of thought of this theme is outlined in Clarence J. Glacken, "Changing Ideas of the Habitable World," *ibid*, pp. 70–92; J. R. Whitaker, "World View of Destruction and Conservation of Natural Resources," *Annals of the Association of American Geographers*, XXX (1940), 143–62; and Franz Tichy, "Die vom Menschen gestaltete Erde: Auffassung und Darstellung im 19. Jahrhundert," *Die Erde*, XCI (1960), 214–57. The subject of "conservation" includes problems that fall within and beyond the flexible limits of geography. For some indication of its scope and challenges see Edward T. Price, "Values and Concepts in Conservation," *Annals of the Association of American Geographers*, XLV (1955), 64–84, and Walter Firey, *Man, Mind, and Land: A Theory of Resource Use* (Glencoe, Ill.: Fress Press, 1960).

RICHARD K. BEARDSLEY, ET AL.

FUNCTIONAL AND EVOLU-
TIONARY IMPLICATIONS OF
COMMUNITY PATTERNING

INTRODUCTION

The classification of cultures into a workable number of types for descriptive or interpretative ends has occupied anthropologists since the science was born. Many kinds of data have been selected. Within the last decade Coon's[1] subdivision of human societies into six levels on the basis of complexity of institutions, and the attempts by Strong,[2] Armillas,[3] Steward,[4] Willey and Phillips[5] to distinguish devel-

Reprinted, with permission of the authors and editor, from *Memoirs of the Society for American Archaeology,* XI (1956), 129–57. The members of the seminar that produced this report and their affiliations are as follows: Richard K. Beardsley (*chairman*), professor of anthropology, University of Michigan; Preston Holder, associate professor of anthropology, University of Nebraska; Alex D. Krieger, lecturer in anthropology, University of Washington; Betty J. Meggers (*editor*), research associate, Smithsonian Institution; John B. Rinaldo, assistant curator of archeology, Chicago Natural History Museum; Paul Kutsche (*recorder*), assistant professor of anthropology, Colorado College.

[1] Carleton S. Coon, *A Reader in General Anthropology* (New York: Henry Holt, 1948).

[2] William D. Strong, "Cultural Epochs and Refuse Stratigraphy in Peruvian Archaeology," in *A Reappraisal of Peruvian Archaeology* (assembled by Wendell C. Bennett, "Memoirs of the Society for American Archaeology," IV [1948]), 93–102.

[3] Pedro Armillas, "A Sequence of Cultural Development in Meso-America," *ibid,* pp. 105–11.

[4] Julian H. Steward, "Cultural Causality and Law: A Trial Formulation of the Development of Early Civilizations," *American Anthropologist,* LI (1949), 1–27.

[5] Gordon R. Willey and Philip Phillips, "Method and Theory in American Archaeology, II: His-

opmental periods in the Mesoamerican and Andean archeological sequences may be cited. Our excuse for attempting yet another formulation is that the current schemes emphasize either ethnographic criteria that are difficult or impossible to detect archeologically, or unique features of particular cultural configurations rather than general criteria defining more universal patterns. Starting from a point of view different from those heretofore employed, we have tried to develop a classification of cultures that is usable with both ethnographical and archeological data and that has functional and evolutionary as well as historical and descriptive significance.

Our point of departure was community mobility. We visualized human communities as ranged along a spectrum, from unrestricted wandering at one end to complete sedentariness at the other, and examined many cultures to see whether clusterings could be detected along this spectrum. It seems to us that reasonably distinct divisions can be made, and that there are relatively few borderline cultures whose classification is difficult.[6] Furthermore, different degrees of community mobility are reflected in different kinds of

torical-Developmental Interpretation," *American Anthropologist,* LVII (1955), 723–819.

[6] Most prominent are "mixed economies," such as the Toda, who constitute communities from one point of view but from another form specialized segments of larger interdependent groups. Time did not permit an adequate examination of such cases.

archeological remains, so that identification is not limited to living groups.

The fitting of all cultures of the world, living and extinct, into a single scheme means that the definitions must be in general terms, although it is remarkable how detailed they can be and still remain widely applicable. The details are not those that characterize and contrast distinct historic traditions, but those that distinguish culture types. Hence, although one of our categories, simple nuclear centered, has many of the same characteristics as the "Formative" of Nuclear America, our definition does not include traits that are unique to this particular New World manifestation and set it apart from other forms of simple nuclear centered communities elsewhere. This is in accord with our desire to produce a classification that can be used to describe and interpret types of culture rather than particular configurations.

As a preliminary to a discussion of the categories of community patterning several other points should be made clear, some terminological and others philosophical. Most important in the category of terminology is our use of "community," defined as the largest grouping of persons in any particular culture whose normal activities bind them together into a self-conscious, corporate unit, which is economically self-sufficient and politically independent. At its simplest, this is a band or horde; at its most complex, a nation or empire. In between, it may be a village or town and its environs. A tribe or culture would normally be composed of several communities in our sense, sharing common language and culture but independent in the conduct of normal daily life. The community was chosen as the focal point because it can be identified on all levels of cultural complexity and because the term carries no other connotations than those included in the definition. Similarly, we have preferred "wandering" to "nomad" for hunting and gathering groups, reserving the latter term for domesticated animal users, which it connotes in many people's minds. A "com-

munity pattern" is the organization of economic, socio-political, and ceremonial interrelationships within a community, and is largely synonymous with "cultural complex." However, when a fine line is drawn, our use of "community pattern" includes a special kind of community mobility, while we sometimes refer to a similar cultural complex as being associated with different degrees of community mobility. We are not trying to draw a sharp distinction between these terms, but have used the one most appropriate when a distinction was to be made. In naming our types of community patterning, we have tried to find labels that are brief but descriptive, and that have not been used in a conflicting sense before. To define them we have selected traits that are typical and distinctive.

Certain points of view implicit in our description and analysis of community patterning should be made explicit here. We have assumed that archeological cultures are comparable to living cultures, and with the aid of certain deductions can be classified in the same way. We have further assumed that the primary factor in the dynamics of cultural advance from one category to another is an improvement in subsistence, although we recognize that on some occasions socio-political organization may be an important consideration in accelerating or retarding this advance. We have taken it for granted that in general sedentary life has more survival value than wandering life to the human race, and that, other things being equal, whenever there is an opportunity to make the transition, it will be made. Although people sometimes complain of the drawbacks to urban life and the increasing fragmentation of occupation and knowledge, the superior survival value of the supra-nuclear integrated community pattern is clearly shown by the increased life expectancy that goes with it.

The comments made thus far, as well as the discussion that follows, are generalized and somewhat simplified. We are aware that there is more to be said on almost every point, and that we have glossed over certain aspects more than some of our readers may like. However, rather than pursue all the nooks and crannies along our path, we prefer to point out its direction and some of the mileposts. Since some of the periods and parts of the world mentioned are outside our first-hand familiarity, we may have misinterpreted their characteristics. We hope that any gaps or errors will not cause readers to discard the framework, but will stimulate them to correct and improve it.

Primary Types of Community Patterning

The seven primary types of community patterning we have distinguished are: Free Wandering, Restricted Wandering, Central-based Wandering, Semi-permanent Sedentary, Simple Nuclear Centered, Advanced Nuclear Centered and Supra-Nuclear Integrated. These form a sequence from extreme community mobility to complete sedentariness, as well as from simplicity to complexity of culture. It will be noted that these types are not necessarily mutually exclusive in the present world political organization. A supra-nuclear integration like the nation of Peru may contain within its boundaries simple nuclear centered and even semi-permanent sedentary groups who pursue their aboriginal way of life with little or no knowledge of the larger unit, or interference from it. In our sense, these inclusions are not a real part of the supra-nuclear integrated community because they do not conform to the definition of community as we use the concept. On the other hand, if one ignores the criterion of economic and political self-sufficiency, one may look upon the effective components (cities, towns, villages) of a supra-nuclear integration as having functions equivalent to simple or advanced nuclear centered communities, providing goods, services and social outlets for their members. The ethnographic and archeological examples are those we think con-

form best to the specifications of our definitions.

FREE WANDERING

Definition.—A community that moves frequently and without restriction, the direction and continuousness of wandering and the amount of territory covered being conditioned only by the movement of large game and the local abundance of food resources.

Dynamics producing.—Although this was first postulated as the initial type of human community patterning, further consideration suggests that it need not have been. Territoriality exists among non-human primates, and man could have evolved with such a concept. This being the case, as long as he remained in the area of his origin, territorial restrictions would probably have been observed. However, it seems likely that such restrictions were temporarily waived when increasing numbers, increased human adaptability, or environmental changes such as retreat of glaciers made man's geographical expansion possible. Such reasoning indicates that this was at most a temporary stage, transcended when population in the new area became well distributed and sufficiently dense, but it seems to be the best explanation for the rapid dispersal of the human species at certain periods.[7]

A second dynamic producing free wandering is the depletion of the population so that density is low compared with the productivity of the food resources. A few groups (perhaps all originally restricted wanderers) that have suffered decimation under European contact appear to have temporarily regressed to a kind of free wandering community patterning.

Ethnographic criteria.—A free wandering community pattern is not characteristic of any intact culture today. However,

[7] Loren C. Eiseley, "The Paleo Indians: Their Survival and Diffusion," in *New Interpretations of Aboriginal American Culture History* (Washington, D.C.: Anthropological Society of Washington, 1954), pp. 1–11.

one group that approaches it is the Ala-caluf, who are described as divided into small family units that move about continuously and without any territorial considerations. Food storage is absent, ruled out by the humidity that spoils everything by mildew. Material equipment is minimal, and except for a canoe, fire, poles for dislodging shellfish, spear, harpoon and line, bark bucket, skins for covering huts, axes, and knives, it is made as needed and discarded after use. There is no social organization beyond the family, and families come together only on rare and brief occasions when a stranded whale provides unusually abundant and concentrated food. Religion is unformalized and ceremonies are few and sporadic.[8] Much of this description is similar to that of restricted wandering, except for the lack of territoriality. Whether Alacaluf culture may be taken as representative of free wandering is uncertain, although it is adapted to similar conditions of mobility.

Ethnographic examples.—The Alacaluf approximate a free wandering pattern as a result of depletion of their population under European contact.

Archeological criteria. — Ideally, free wandering should be attested by a very wide distribution of artifact types that are simple in nature and limited in variety. In general, such remains should represent the initial occupation of any given region, or the resumption of occupation after interruption in the case of areas glaciated during the Pleistocene. Since camps were moved frequently, evidence of occupation may be undetectable or at best scanty, consisting of ash or charcoal, split or burned animal bones, and a few artifacts.

Archeological examples.—While it is difficult with our present knowledge of early cultures to distinguish the effects of diffusion from the actual unrestricted movements of people, certain simple industries

of Paleolithic age in the Old World may be associated with free wandering. The "hand ax," "choppers or chopping tools," "pebble tools," "Levalloisian flake-tools," "Mousterian disc-core tools," and "microlithic tools" all have a tremendous distribution in Europe, Africa, and Asia. Probably all such basic techniques were slowly spread over great lengths of time, both by diffusion and by freely or intermittently unrestricted wandering groups of people. In the New World, the distribution of Clovis points over the greater part of North America may provide a comparable example, whereas Folsom points, being of much more restricted distribution, may represent a transition in the direction of the next community type: restricted wandering. In South America, too little is known of early complexes to make even a qualified identification.[9]

[8] Junius Bird, "The Alacaluf," in J. H. Steward (ed.), *Handbook of South American Indians* (Washington, D.C.: Bureau of American Ethnology, Bulletin 143), I (1946), 55–79.

[9] Corresponding terminology in other schemes: Julian H. Steward's "Pre-Agricultural" ("A Functional-Developmental Classification of American High Cultures," in *A Reappraisal of Peruvian Archaeology* ["Memoirs of the Society for American Archaeology," IV (1948), 103–04] includes this and our two following stages. Alex D. Krieger's "Paleo-Indian" ("Basic Stages of Cultural Evolution," in Sol Tax (ed.), *An Appraisal of Anthropology Today* [Chicago: University of Chicago Press, 1953]), and the "Early Lithic" of Willey and Phillips (*op. cit.*) include both free wandering and restricted wandering community patterns. Kalervo Oberg's "Homogeneous Tribes" ("Types of Social Structure among the Lowland Tribes of South and Central America," *American Anthropologist,* LVII [1955], 472–87) presumably is characteristic of free wandering as well as restricted wandering, and some semi-permanent sedentary groups.

(Note: Krieger desires to place on record the fact that the four-stage outline of New World culture growth be presented during one of the discussion sessions at the International Symposium in Anthropology held in 1952 (Krieger, *op. cit.*) was a grossly oversimplified treatment, prepared at the request of the program chairman for that day in an hour or two, and not published in full. He thus considers it inadequate for serious consideration in this or other publications (e.g., Willey and Phillips, *op. cit.*). At the same time, it must be regarded as a reflection on American anthropologists that, in spite of the tremendous output of literature in the last decades, no more than a half dozen attempts have ever been made to

RESTRICTED WANDERING

Definition.—Communities that wander about within a territory that they define as theirs and defend against trespass, or on which they have exclusive rights to food resources of certain kinds. Movement within the territory may be erratic or may follow a seasonal round, depending on the kind of wild food resources ultilized.

Dynamics producing.—Restricted wandering is a community pattern older than man, and more widespread than primates. It appears to represent a satisfactory adjustment of population density to food resources, with the guarantee of exclusive or prior rights to some foods for the members of each community. On the human level, this may lead to some degree of conservation with benefits to those practicing it because they can expect to inhabit the same region in future years. Hence, restricted wandering can be looked upon as a community pattern that sets the stage for more than totally exploitative relations with plants and animals. In this role it is a significant stage in the evolution of food-producing. As a community pattern adapted to sparse, scattered, or seasonally available food resources, it is an ancient form that has survived in certain parts of the world until recent times.

Community characteristics.—Population density is low and the maximum size of the permanent community is relatively small. Bands of less than 100 individuals are typical. Members of a band may travel together or in nuclear or extended family groups for all or part of the year. In either case, the community defends its territory against unauthorized, exploitative trespass, but may permit the entry of other individ-

___
generalize on cultural stages for the New World as a whole. Dee Ann Suhm, Alex D. Krieger, and Edward B. Jelks ("An Introductory Handbook of Texas Archeology," *Texas Archeological Society, Bulletin 25* [Austin, 1954]) have used the term "Paleo-American stage" in place of "Paleo-Indian" in order to avoid the implication that the earliest inhabitants of the New World were Indians or even Mongoloids in the racial sense.)

uals or groups under special circumstances.

Economic aspects.—Hunting, fishing, and gathering techniques exploit the food sources. Community mobility is required by the seasonal nature of the food supply, or by the small productivity of the territory in any one place. The bulk of an adult's property is composed of food-getting utensils—bow and arrow, spear, basket, digging stick, ax, etc. Most edible resources of the environment are exploited and rules of sharing operate so that unusual skill or luck of an individual benefits the group as a whole. Most restricted wanderers practice little if any food storage.

Social organization.—The largest social unit is the local group or band, which owns the territory. It may be composed of related and/or friendly families or a single extended family. If there is a chief, he is primarily an advisor and has no coercive power. One spouse at a time is typical. Status differences are minimal or absent. Personal property is rarely inherited; instead it is frequently destroyed at the death of the owner.

Ceremonialism.—Religious beliefs are often vaguely defined. Magic may be used to bring luck in hunting and for curing. Shamanism is frequently present. Puberty rites or other group ceremonies may be absent, sporadic or well developed.

Ethnographic examples.—South American groups whose community pattern is restricted wandering include the Ona, Yahgan, and Guayakí; in North America, the sub-Arctic Athabaskans, Chippewa, Shoshone, Paiute, Apache, and Coahuiltecans belong to this type. Among Old World examples are most Australian aborigines, the Semang, and the Kalahari Bushmen.

Archeological criteria.—Sites left by restricted wandering groups are not essentially different from those of free wandering groups, both community patterns being characterized by an almost constant mobility that prevents extensive accumulation of camp refuse in any one place. Theoretically, the more confined movements of restricted wanderers should be reflected in more limited distribution of characteristic artifact types than in the case of free wanderers; and the more intensive exploitation of particular habitat areas should be reflected in more specialized tools. Food-grinding implements and stone-lined hearths appear to be more characteristic here than among free wanderers. Awls and needles reflect the basketry making and skin working known on the ethnographic level.

Archeological examples.—Most of the sites and cultures identified as "Paleo-Indian" belong here, such as Frontier, Red Smoke, Plainview, Sulphur Springs, Chiricahua, Eden, and Cody. Others should be included which are transitional between "Paleo-Indian" and "Archaic" (both poorly defined terms at present), such as: Falcón focus in Southwestern Texas and possibly Huancayo in Peru. Certain European Mesolithic assemblages that may reflect restricted wandering include Tardenoisian, Swiderian, Aterian, and the bulk of the Finnish dwelling place sites.[10]

CENTRAL-BASED WANDERING

Definition.—A community that spends part of each year wandering and the rest at a settlement or "central base," to which it may or may not consistently return in subsequent years.

Dynamics producing.—A half-wandering, half-sedentary community pattern represents an adjustment to one of three different types of subsistence resources: 1) a storable or preservable wild food harvest, such as acorns or mesquite beans; 2) a locally abundant food, such as shellfish; and 3) incipient agriculture producing a small harvest. These have in common the provision of a food supply that enables the community to remain in one place for weeks or months. It is probable that except in the case of a natural resource like fish

[10] Corresponding periods in other schemes: Steward's "Preagricultural" (*op. cit.,* 1948); Krieger's "Paleo-Indian" (*op. cit.*); Willey and Phillips' "Early Lithic" (*op. cit.*). Oberg's "Homogeneous Tribes" (*op. cit.*) includes free wandering, central-based wandering, and some semipermanent sedentary groups.

or shellfish, which furnishes an inexhaustible local fresh food supply, this community pattern depends on one of two kinds of advance in subsistence techniques: domestication of plants or methods of food preparation (e.g., acorn leaching, salmon smoking). It is an "on the fence" compromise between wandering and sedentary life which, when based on incipient agriculture, appears to have been an important step preceding full dependence on agriculture and completely sedentary life in many parts of the world. In other places, it is an adjustment to special conditions where wild foods are unusually productive or can be converted to storable surpluses. Whatever the subsistence basis, the central-based wandering type of community adjustment produces a general similarity in cultural features.

Community characteristics.—Population density probably shows about the same variation as among restricted wanderers, but the average size of the local group is somewhat greater. In its sedentary aspect, the community is fairly cohesive, but when the season for wandering begins it frequently breaks into smaller segments composed of individual extended or even nuclear families, which become economically self-sufficient. These may gather the next year at the same or at a new base camp, or may individually align themselves with other families at different bases. From the viewpoint of family mobility, territoriality may thus be less strictly observed than among restricted wanderers, but community rights of prior or exclusive access to certain food resources are generally recognized.

Economic aspects.—During its sedentary phase, the community functions in a manner comparable to that of wholly sedentary groups. Subsistence is derived principally from the harvest, perhaps supplemented by hunting or fishing. During its wandering phase, activities parallel those of restricted wanderers, taking advantage of seasonally available wild foods. Food surpluses accumulated for winter or rainy season use are not exclusive to any individual or family, and do not constitute a basis for status or wealth distinctions. Occupational division of labor is absent, although certain families may have hereditary pre-eminence in crafts that are practiced in some degree by all.

Social organization.—The community, composed of a group of nuclear or extended families, may have less cohesion than among restricted wanderers. Sense of solidarity is broken down by self-sufficiency of smaller units during part of the year, and in some instances by failure of the community to have the same members during its sedentary phase in successive years. This atomistic orientation is reflected in the absence of coercive power in the hands of the chief, who serves as a symbol of the community. Differences in social status among adults are minor or absent, in conformity with the communal access to food supplies and their total consumption for survival.

Ceremonialism.—Concern for the dead seems to be more marked than among restricted wanderers, perhaps because of a lesser necessity for abandoning aged or ill persons. Shamans employ magic for curing. Group ceremonies may be regularly recurrent, occasional, or absent.

Ethnographic examples. — The South American tribes characterized by a central-based wandering pattern all seem to be incipient agriculturists, whose environment or food growing technology is inadequate to make domestic plants a year-round food source. Such tribes are sedentary in the rainy season and wandering in the dry season. Examples include the Sirionó, Timbira, and Caingang. North American groups, among them the northern and central California tribes, interior Salishan tribes, and the Eskimo, make use of wild food resources. Special wild foods also support central-based wandering in the Old World, as among the Kamchadal, Goldi, Gilyak, Maritime Koryak, and Maritime Chukchee of northern Asia and tribes of the Upper Nilotic Sudan in Africa.

Archeological criteria.—A site occupied by central-based wanderers should ideally provide indications of seasonal occupation. However, the thinness of the deposit left by each visit and the perishable nature of food remains, which provide the best evidence of seasonal use, make this detectable only rarely. In general, these sites have thicker midden accumulations than are associated with restricted wandering or semi-permanent sedentary community patterns, and the main source of confusion lies with sites of the simple nuclear centered type, which are also frequently of considerable depth.

Shell middens are probably the most numerous and widespread type of site identifiable with central-based wandering. Although a seasonal occupation is not always observable, it has been suggested in several cases.[11] Cave deposits reflect another typical kind of "central base." House pits or structures and storage pits may be distinguishable. Burials occur in cemetery areas, middens, or caves, attesting to better care of the dead than in free or restricted wandering. Grave offerings are absent or simple; if occasional graves are unusually rich, they may be attributable to an individual who achieved unusual status, perhaps because of abilities as a shaman. Vegetable remains indicative of incipient agriculture in the Americas include primitive maize, amaranth, Jerusalem artichoke, Job's tears, and bulbs or tubers of types that did not later become staple starches. In addition to chipping and grinding, stone polishing is associated with central-based wandering in many parts of the New World; where it is absent, cut and polished bone or shell may be a technological equivalent. Stone bowls, stone mortars, and milling stones may occur. Pottery is sometimes

[11] See Gordon R. Willey and Charles R. McGimsey, "The Monagrillo Culture of Panama," *Papers of the Peabody Museum of Archaeology and Ethnology,* Harvard University, XLIX (1954), No. 2; and Adam and Elfriede Orssich, "Stratigraphic Excavations in the Sambaqui of Araujo II, Paraná, Brazil," *American Antiquity,* XXI (1956), 357–69.

present in small amounts and in the southeastern United States is mainly a fiber-tempered ware.

Archeological examples.—In South and Central America, shell middens or sambaquis are frequent along the coast and on major rivers and none need be specifically mentioned. Cultures in North America include Faulkner, Baumer, and Indian Knoll in the Middle West; Lamoka and Laurentian in the Northeast; Savannah and Stallings Island in the Southeast; Pecos River and Edwards Plateau in Texas; San Pedro and Basket Maker II in the Southwest; Santa Barbara and central California on the West Coast. In Europe, Mesolithic cultures such as the Maglemose in the Baltic Sea area appear to represent central-based wandering.[12]

SEMI-PERMANENT SEDENTARY

Definition.—A community, which can be identified with a village, that establishes itself in successive locations, occupying each for a period of years. The population is stable and continuously sedentary, but able to be so only by moving the village periodically.

Dynamics producing.—With one exception (northwest coast), all groups exhibiting this type of community mobility practice simple, exploitive agriculture in areas of average to poor natural soil fertility. In the absence of restorative techniques to maintain productivity, or because of the perishable nature of crops, no surplus can be relied upon indefinitely from the same fields or held against future need. The large area required to support each

[12] Corresponding periods in other schemes: Steward's "Preagricultural" and "Basic Agricultural Beginnings" (*op. cit.*, 1948) both overlap central-based wandering, since our primary criterion is not presence or absence of agriculture. Krieger's "Food Gathering" (*op. cit.*) embraces restricted wandering as well as central-based wandering, as does Willey and Phillips' "Archaic" (*op. cit.*). Oberg's "Homogeneous Tribes" (*op. cit.*) includes restricted wanderers and some semi-permanent sedentary groups.

person prevents great population concentration as well as permanent settlement.

Community characteristics.—Population density is low because of the large amount of land required to maintain agricultural subsistence. However, it is more concentrated than among wandering groups, with villages of 500–1000 individuals not unusual. Local ecological conditions extend the range both below and above these figures. Each village is independent and self-sufficient, although it may maintain cordial relations with other villages. Ethnographic accounts rarely mention a concept of territoriality such as exists among restricted wanderers. Rights of prior access are usually respected in relation to gardens, which are held frequently by smaller units than the community.

Economic aspects.—Sexual division of labor in the acquisition of food is well defined. Men clear the fields and hunt, alone or assisted by other male members of the community. Women harvest and prepare the food. Meat and fish are frequently shared, and perishable agricultural surpluses are disposed of in community ceremonies or festivities (e.g., Melanesian potlatch, Plains village feasts, Amazonian dance "fiestas"). Prestige accrues from the distribution or destruction of surplus food or other property, rather than from its accumulation, although sharing is frequently an obligation that is not socially rewarded. Village or tribal specialization in the manufacture of ceramics, basketry, manioc graters, or similar products occurs, with consequent regularization of trade relations. Within a community some individuals may be recognized as superior craftsmen, but their creations are rarely considered preferable for daily use. The basic skills employed in weaving, pottery making, and other crafts are known to all.

Social organization.—Clans and/or moieties are typical of semi-permanent sedentary groups, although extended family organization is also relatively frequent at this level. Some individual is usually designated as the headman or chief, but his

powers depend more upon his personal
qualities than upon status vested in the
office. He acts as agent for the community
rather than in his own interest. Temporary
intervillage confederation may occur in
time of crisis. Social differentiation ranges
from incipient to well developed, with warfare and shamanism the primary means of
acquiring prestige. Polygyny is usually permissible, although frequently it is practiced
only by a few men, principally chiefs or
shamans. Puberty rites signal the transition to adult status of one or both sexes.

Ceremonialism.—Concepts of the supernatural are comparable to those among
wandering groups, including belief in forest
spirits and ghosts of the dead, but a sharper
definition results in more formalized techniques of influence. Group ceremonies,
featuring masked dances and "folk drama,"
are held to promote success in agriculture
and other food quests important to the
community as well as at puberty and other
events in the life cycle. Shamans are characteristic, and sometimes wield considerable
power by virtue of their connections with
the spirit world. Their main function is
curative rather than priestly. The dead are
frequently buried in the house floor, although cemeteries sometimes occur, and
grave offerings are simple. The house is
frequently abandoned on the death of an
adult resident.

Ethnographic examples. — Semi-permanent sedentary communities are characteristic of the tropical forest area of South
America, of which the Mundurucú, Jivaro,
Witoto, Tenetehara, and Wai Wai may be
considered typical examples. In North
America, the Plains horticulturists, historic
Pawnee-Arikara, Algonkin and Iroquoian
tribes of the eastern woodlands, and historic groups in the Mississippi Valley and
Southeast can be cited. Elsewhere, this
pattern is characteristic of Melanesia and
of the Congo agriculturists.

Archeological criteria.—Refuse deposits
are relatively thin, and in the New World
potsherds are one of their regular constituents. Although it may be varied, pottery

is simple and utilitarian. House structures
are patterned in their relationship to one
another, and this patterning is repeated
from site to site. Isolated graves may be
encountered in the village or burial may
be in cemeteries. Evidence of ceremonial
activity may be discernible and storage or
cache pits are often encountered.

Archeological examples. — In South
America, sites of the Aruá phase at the
mouth of the Amazon and of the Taruma
phase of British Guiana are typical examples of semi-permanent sedentary culture in the tropical forest. Upper Republi-
can, Lower Loup, Great Bend, and sites
on the Upper Missouri and in the middle
Atlantic states are North American examples. In the Old World, this pattern is
represented from the early Neolithic to considerably later times in central and northern Europe.[13]

SIMPLE NUCLEAR CENTERED

Definition.—A permanent[14] center, with
or without satellites. The center may be
a self-supporting town, or a market or ceremonial place that serves as a focus for surrounding villages or hamlets. The center
is not strikingly differentiated in content
from its satellites except when its character
is primarily ceremonial.

Dynamics producing.—The principal factor making maintenance of a permanent
center possible is the introduction of agricultural techniques adapted to the local
environment, so that the effect is conservational. Cultivated plants become the primary food source, reducing the per capita
area needed for subsistence maintenance

---

[13] Corresponding periods in other schemes:
Steward's "Basic Agricultural Beginnings" (*op.
cit.*, 1948) embraces both central-based wandering
and semi-permanent sedentary. Krieger's "Food
Producing" (*op. cit.*), Willey and Phillips' "Pre-
formative" (*op. cit.*), and Oberg's "Segmented
Tribes" (*op. cit.*) all include both semi-permanent
sedentary and simple nuclear centered.

[14] The term "permanent" denotes potentiality
rather than realization, since a center may be
destroyed or abandoned because of conquest, epidemic, or other non-subsistence failures.

or providing a dependable surplus sufficient to release a portion of the community from the role of primary producers. This newly available resource can be exploited in two different ways, the choice probably depending on the manner in which the agriculture is conducted. In one type of simple nuclear center, the village becomes permanently sedentary and the community is independent and self-sufficient. In the other, several population aggregates join forces to support a center, which links them together and provides market and ceremonial services. The satellite communities are inhabited by primary producers and the nucleus is not self-sufficient. The former may be referred to as an undifferentiated simple nuclear center, and the latter as a differentiated one.

Community characteristics.—In addition to allowing greater permanency of settlement, improved agricultural techniques multiply the number of individuals who can be supported on a given amount of land, with the result that population density makes a notable advance with the inception of simple nuclear centered community life. Although undifferentiated centers tend to concentrate the population in relatively isolated clusters comparable to the patterning of semi-permanent sedentary villages, most simple nuclear centers have satellites (farmhouses, hamlets, villages, etc.) that tend to eliminate unoccupied intervening regions. The physical arrangement of the center is patterned or partly planned. The number of individuals composing a community begins about at the upper limits of the previous stage and may reach several thousand. This increased community size is reflected in changes in the means of social integration.

Economic aspects. — Full-time occupational specialization is characteristic of some part of the population, either in administration, ceremonialism, or technology. These specialties typically are hereditary. Diversification of production and acquisition of surplus in food or manufactured goods are correlated with increased intracommunity trade as opposed to communal distribution, although in a crisis individual wealth is normally sacrificed to community welfare, and leveling mechanisms that prevent excessive aggrandizement in real property are common. The diversification of material goods in quantity and quality becomes a basis for social stratification in terms of property rather than personality attributes and for the increasing of status by inheritance. Except in the New World, real estate begins to come under private ownership at this stage, and land holdings constitute a basis for social differentiation. Intercommunity exchange of manufactured goods becomes more formalized, but distributes mostly luxury goods to chiefs and members of the upper class rather than utility items for daily use.

Social organization.—Kinship-based organization continues to be important, but is overlaid to some extent by differential status within or between families. Incipient to well-developed social stratification is correlated with an increase of ascribed over achieved status. The chief acts to some extent in his own interest or the interest of his class, and usually has power to coerce subjects, particularly as individuals or as members of the lower class. His power is related to the size and distinctness of the upper class, however, and where the social stratification is minimal, the chief's role is little different from what it is in semi-permanent sedentary communities. Individuals or families of high status tend to live in preferential locations or better houses in an undifferentiated community, or in the permanent center in a differentiated one.

Ceremonialism.—Religion is formalized and externalized in temples, ritual, prayers, and offerings. Sacrifice becomes a means of influencing the gods. A ceremonial calendar determines the time of ceremonies. Both increase in community size and specialization of religious ritual seem to be responsible for the allocation of part of the community to an audience role rather than the participation characteristic in semi-permanent sedentary and in wandering groups.

Public ceremonies directed toward community goals (successful harvest, rainfall, victory over enemies, etc.) predominate over those commemorating birth, puberty, and death. Gods become differentiated from ghosts and spirits, and priests from shamans. Ceremonial paraphernalia are elaborated.

Ethnographic examples.—Highland Indian communities in Peru and Ecuador, and Indian communities in Mexico and Central America exemplify the differentiated type of simple nuclear center. The market and ceremonial functions of these towns or villages as a focus for rural inhabitants in the surrounding area are well known. In North America, Creek, Natchez, and Caddo communities were similarly organized. The southwestern Pueblos, by contrast, represent the undifferentiated type, each pueblo being an independent and self-sufficient town, in which all members of the community live most of the time. Many aboriginal communities in India and the Middle East also retain the characteristics of simple nuclear centered. As in Latin America, these communities are incorporated under larger political units today, but function independently and with little interest in or understanding of their national affiliation.

Archeological criteria.—Ceremonial structures, especially earthworks, and deposits of habitation refuse suggesting long-term occupation are diagnostic. Pottery is differentiated into utilitarian and ceremonial wares, the latter decorated and predominating at ceremonial sites and as grave offerings. Cemeteries often contain a few unusually elaborate graves representing individuals of higher social status. Luxury objects of local manufacture include stone sculpture, mosaic, engraved shell, etc., for ceremonial use. In some areas (e.g., Europe), copper and iron weapons are associated with graves of the upper class, and provide evidence of both social stratification and intercommunity trade. House structures of adobe or stone have a patterned arrangement, and the ceremonial area may show evidence of planning rather than simple accretion.

Archeological examples.—A large number of sites are identifiable with simple nuclear centered community patterning, partly because they are actually relatively abundant and partly because they are conspicuous. The ceremonial type of simple nuclear center appears in many local archeological sequences and the earthworks that are frequently a feature of this stage have been the object of considerable investigation in many parts of the world. Chavín in Peru, Marajoara at the mouth of the Amazon, Formative sites of Mexico and Middle America, and Adena, Hopewell, and Mississippi cultures in the eastern United States are a few of the New World examples of differentiated simple nuclear centers. The undifferentiated type, or village center, is best represented by the Colonial, Sedentary, and Classical Hohokam and by Pueblo III in the Southwest. In Europe, a great many late Neolithic and Bronze Age communities probably belong in this stage.[15]

ADVANCED NUCLEAR CENTERED

Definition.—A community of homogenous tradition differentiated into an administrative center and satellites consisting of villages, hamlets, and scattered homesteads.

Dynamics producing.—As indicated by the similarity in terms, this type of community differs more in degree than in kind from the preceding one. It probably develops from the simple nuclear center as

[15] Corresponding periods in other schemes: Simple Nuclear Centered equates rather well with what Armillas (*op. cit.*), Steward (*op. cit., 1948*), Willey and Phillips (*op. cit.*), and others have called "Formative" culture in Nuclear America. Most of Krieger's "Food Producing" (*op. cit.*) belongs here, although his category also includes semi-permanent sedentary. Oberg's "Politically Organized Chiefdoms" and "Feudal Type States" (*op. cit.*) both correspond to some extent with simple nuclear centered, but emphasize political developments that are not essential to this type of community, where integration may alternatively be of a commercial or religious nature.

agricultural techniques improve and are able to provide larger surpluses. These increasingly come under the control of the upper class. As the elite becomes stabilized and strengthened, it is less affected by public opinion and the main deterrent to private accumulation of wealth is removed. What was an essentially voluntary integration on the simple level becomes more administrative and coercive on the advanced level.

Community characteristics.—The administrative center is the largest population concentration, although it may not be the residence of the majority of the people belonging to the community. The tendency toward a somewhat scattered settlement pattern is like that of the differentiated simple nuclear centered community, although the satellites may be larger here. The number of people in the community and the population density are greater than in any of the preceding types.

Economic aspects.—Surplus production, especially of food, may be acquired by the ruling class in the form of taxes, which seem to make their appearance at this stage. Well-developed occupational specialization decreases family self-sufficiency, and to the degree that goods must be acquired from others, distinctions in wealth and property are more pronounced. "Earning" a living becomes possible for occupational specialists, and ability to devote full time to learning a craft results in proficiency and technological improvement. Public or temple granaries, filled by taxes, permit the priests or rulers to support labor for large-scale construction and to maintain a large body of retainers. Standardization of time and space concepts permits uniformity of measurement, which is reflected in more uniform products in architecture and manufactures.

Social organization.—Administration is carried out by a hierarchy of officials typically headed by a chief or king. Government assumes the tasks of social integration, law and politics supplanting kinship

as the dominant regulator of interpersonal relations. Social classes are distinguished by dress and have different rights and privileges. Although achieved status is possible in special conditions, the transition from lower to upper class status is difficult to make and class affiliation tends to be hereditary. Education is confined to members of the upper class, and typically dispensed in the temples. Law is formalized and even codified, with punishments specified for crimes.

Ceremonialism.—Hierarchical ranking of priests parallels the civil administrative hierarchy. The relatively spectacular appearance of the center is largely because of the presence of impressive temples, frequently of stone. A recorded calendar forms the basis for planning and holding ceremonies. A pantheon of gods represents significant aspects of the natural and human world, and the most important of these have special temples. Idols are characteristic, and human sacrifice may be made to influence a powerful deity. The priesthood is a depository of wealth and power.

Ethnographic examples.—Although some transitional groups can be found between any of the community patterns so far described, the greater relative fluidity of the gradation between simple and advanced nuclear centered makes it difficult to decide in many cases whether the group should be put in the upper range of simple or the lower range of advanced. The choice will depend on the relative weighting of various traits. Typical examples of advanced nuclear centered are easily recognized in Dahomey and Ashanti of West Africa, but New World cultures were mostly above or below this stage at the time of European contact. A few, like the Chibcha of Colombia, are not well enough known to make a positive identification.

Archeological criteria.—There is a major contrast between the richness of the remains at the "capital" and the relative simplicity of the satellite communities. Public buildings show evidence of planned construction and uniformity of architecture. Ceramics are well made and ceremonial wares are typically elaborately decorated. Textiles, stone work, wood carving, and other crafts are competently executed and indicate specialization of occupation. Large scale differential treatment of the dead makes it possible to recognize from the grave goods not only class differences, but frequently occupational specialists as well. Head deformation, tooth mutilation, and similar practices often distinguish members of the upper class from commoners.

Archeological examples.—New World examples of advanced nuclear centered communities are found only in Mesoamerica and Peru. Among them are Gallinazo and Nazca cultures in Peru, Tikal and other Maya centers, Teotihuacan and Tula in the Valley of Mexico. In the Old World, early "city-states" of Mesopotamia, Crete, and early classical Greece, and possibly Mohenjo Daro and Harappa in the Indus Valley, are examples of this stage.[16]

SUPRA-NUCLEAR INTEGRATED

Definition.—A community that integrates nuclear centers and other formerly independent units of heterogeneous tradition, typically by conquest and subjugation.[17]

[16] Corresponding periods in other schemes: Advanced nuclear centered coincides rather well with Steward's "Florescent" (*op. cit.*, 1948), and Willey and Phillips' "Classic" (*op. cit.*) Krieger's "Urban" (*op. cit.*) includes this and the following stage. Oberg's "City States" (*op. cit.*) equates with advanced nuclear centered in terms of his description, although his example (Chan Chan) is classified here in the following community pattern.

[17] This category includes a wide range of cultures, and it may be necessary to subdivide it into simple and advanced as was the case with nuclear centered. Our type description applies primarily to the pre-industrial form, which might be characterized as simple. With industrialization and the growth of scientific method, certain changes take place in the community integration, some of which are mentioned in the description. In the brief time at our disposal, we were not able to pursue the question of whether these can be considered simply as more intensive develop-

Dynamics producing.—The relatively few examples of advanced nuclear centered communities extant, and the short period occupied by this type in the archeological sequence of most parts of the world, suggest that it is relatively transitory and readily moves ahead to expansion, conquest, and supra-nuclear integration. This may take longer where several advanced nuclear centers are in competition than where expansion conflicts only with the interests of less advanced types of communities. Conquest may be promoted by the increasing requirements of food, commodities, or raw materials for maintenance of the administrative or ceremonial superstructure or the economic system in excess of what the members of the expanding advanced nuclear centered community can supply; by the desirability of strengthening morale, or community or upper class prestige by demonstrating superiority in warfare; or by some other social requirement, such as the need for additional manpower, slaves, or sacrificial victims. Or, the ability to maintain the enlarged administrative and military structures required for territorial expansion may be considered as an expression of more intensive food production, which places the burden of subsistence provision on a smaller percentage of the population and frees large numbers of people for other tasks. Whatever the original impetus, the advantages of welding different peoples and different environments into a single political unit are such that cultural momentum has carried communities time and again into supra-nuclear integration, each expansion proceeding as far as the then available means of transportation, communication, distribution, and coercion permitted, and each decline and fall followed by another attempt at unification. This pattern of expansion and conquest, defeat and realignment of boundaries has continued up to the present day.

ments of pre-industrial trends or whether they should be separated and such cultures be called advanced supra-nuclear integrated.

Community characteristics.—The capitals of supra-nuclear integrated communities are typically the largest cities of their time, although some advanced nuclear centers may overlap their lower range. Population distribution within the community is variable, dependent on geographical differentiation in the occupied area, the type of conquered groups, and their capacity to retain their traditional pattern. Manipulation of the population by the government may be practiced, including resettlement, colonization, and the founding of communities for special purposes like mining, commerce, or border defense.

Economic aspects.—Large scale circulation of goods is accomplished by the levying of taxes and tribute in produce as well as by commerce facilitated by the use of a medium of exchange. Commercial attitudes are prevalent, and indebtedness may be punished by slavery. Wealth is accumulated in goods, land, or slaves. Starvation in the midst of plenty is made possible by the existence of large urban populations who do not produce their own food and by the channeling of food surpluses to the hands of the few. Goods, lands, services, and even people are bought and sold. Accounts, deeds, bills of sale, and other records are part of the "paperwork" accompanying transactions.

Social organization.—Administrative procedure is similar to that developed in advanced nuclear centered communities. The major addition is military organization, frequently including a standing army, for internal policing as well as external expansion. The ruler may be identified with the gods and wield absolute power with divine sanction. At the opposite extreme in the social hierarchy is a large lower class with a minimum of prerogatives, if not actually reduced to slavery or serfdom.

Ceremonialism.—The religion of the conqueror frequently becomes the state religion and is imposed upon conquered groups. In addition to the divine sanction that reinforces the ruler's power, the religious organization itself frequently holds

considerable political power, which may be exercised to forward or oppose the plans of the ruler or noble class. However, with the growth of scientific knowledge, supernaturalism tends to change from a coercive force to an ethical standard and ceases to be a major mechanism of social control.

Ethnographic examples.—Since the primary criterion here is community pattern rather than technological accomplishment, some groups classified as supra-nuclear integrated may have less spectacular material cultures than others classified as advanced nuclear centered. The best known aboriginal New World examples of supra-nuclear integration are the Inca and Aztec Empires. In the Old World may be named the aboriginal African kingdoms of the Congo and Nigeria. All modern nations fall into this class, although the effective community as we define it does not always coincide with accepted political boundaries and our type description is oriented toward the pre-industrial form, which has been the traditional concern of anthropologists.

Archeological criteria.—This community type has relatively few overt archeological manifestations. These include the presence of roads between centers, extensive irrigation works, and evidence of conquest provided by the stratigraphic superposition of features identifiable with the conqueror over those of the conquered. The construction of forts in the architectural style of the conqueror at strategic places is another criterion.

Archeological examples.—In the New World, the Chimu, Mochica, and Tiahuanaco empires of Peru can be cited. Abundant Old World examples are found in the classical empires of the Mediterranean, Near East, India, and the Far East.[18]

[18] Corresponding periods in other schemes: Steward's "Empire and Conquest" (*op. cit.*, 1948), and Willey and Phillips' "Post Classic" (*op. cit.*) refer to supra-nuclear integration. Krieger's "Urban" (*op. cit.*) embraces advanced nuclear as well. Oberg's "Theocratic Empire" (*op. cit.*) corresponds mainly to an early form of supra-nuclear integration.

COMMUNITY PATTERNS AMONG PASTORAL NOMADS

In the categories just described, a certain type of community mobility is related on the one hand to a certain level of subsistence economy and on the other hand to a certain constellation of material, socio-political and religious traits. These three aspects seem to be functionally linked, resulting in distinct community patterns. The functional character of the patterns can be tested by examining groups whose subsistence economy utilizes domesticated animals. From the standpoint of mobility, such communities could be included in restricted wandering. However, an examination of socio-political and religious features indicates that three complexes can be distinguished, which closely parallel three of the community patterns based on domesticated plant foods.

INCIPIENT PASTORAL NOMADIC

Definition.—A community whose pattern of wandering is established by the herds that provide the food supply. The animals may not be completely domesticated, but they at least tolerate the presence of human beings.

Dynamics producing.—A very diffuse distribution of pasturage (reflecting hostile climate) seems to be the primary determinant of the almost continuous wandering characteristic of animals upon which incipient pastoral nomads depend. The instinctive behavior of the animals themselves determines a pattern of mobility which effects a utilization of available forage as good as or better than that which human beings are able to achieve by organizing and controlling the movements of the herd. However, even partial or incipient domestication of this sort makes it possible to support a socio-political organization that is one step above that of restricted wanderers, who live by wild foods alone.

Ethnographic criteria.—Among the types distinguished in the sequence from wild food to agriculture, central-based wanderers equate best with incipient pastoral nomads. Similarities include a community composed of related families under a headman with limited authority, intermittent fragmentation into smaller wandering groups, general lack of occupational specialization, and absence of a pattern of warfare or aggression against other groups. The incipient form of animal domestication also equates with the incipient agriculture of central-based wandering. Some of the traits that conflict with this comparison are the presence of ironsmiths as full-time occupational specialists among certain Asiatic pastoralists and the accumulation of wealth as a basis for social status differentiation among some of the same groups.

Ethnographic examples.—This type of community patterning was never developed in the New World. Old World examples include Asiatic reindeer herders (Lapp, Samoyed, Koryak, Chukchee, Tungus) and the cattle herding Hottentot.

Archeological criteria and examples.—It is probable that the limited and perishable nature of the material culture and the almost constant mobility of the community make incipient pastoral nomadism impossible to detect archeologically. At least, we cannot think of any archeological sites that would suggest this community patterning.

EQUESTRIAN HUNTING

Definition.—Hunters and gatherers who possess the horse as a domestic animal, but use it primarily as a tool for hunting rather than as a food source.

Dynamics producing.—The introduction of the horse as a new and efficient hunting tool in a grassland or parkland environment increases the capacity both to acquire food and to transport it. The ability to exploit a larger radius for daily subsistence and to accumulate food in quantity permits a larger population concentration than in the same environment when the horse is absent. Consequently, although community mobility remains high, it is possible to maintain a level of socio-political and religious development similar to that associated with greater sedentariness among agriculturalists.

Ethnographic criteria.—Equestiran Hunting communities resemble semi-permanent sedentary groups in a number of respects. Both are characterized by well-defined sexual division of labor in the acquisition and preparation of food; distribution or destruction of property as a means of acquiring prestige; clan or moiety organization; a chief whose power and prestige depends primarily upon his personality; warfare and rivalry as means of improving social status; temporary confederation in time of crisis; and in the realm of religion, group ceremonies and well-developed shamanism, for success in warfare and for curing.

Ethnographic examples.—This community pattern developed out of restricted wandering and semi-permanent sedentary in the New World after the introduction of the domesticated horse. Examples are the bison-hunting tribes of the North American Plains (Blackfoot, Assiniboin, Crow, Plains Cree, Kiowa, Comanche, Arapaho, Cheyenne, Dakota) and the guanaco-hunting Tehuelche of the Argentine pampas.

Archeological criteria and examples.—This community pattern is difficult to detect archeologically because of its high degree of mobility and the perishable nature of most of the material culture. There is a possibility that the introduction of the horse in antiquity in some parts of the Old World may have produced an equestrian hunting community type, but we know of no archeological evidence.

DIVERSIFIED PASTORAL NOMADIC

Definition.—Nomadic pastoralists whose subsistence is derived from a variety of domesticated animals, each of which has an important role in the economy. These communities characteristically follow a regular seasonal pattern of movement.

Dynamics producing.—One requirement for this type of community patterning is a stable pastoral economy with diversified herds utilized in a variety of ways, both for food and for transport. This provides not only a reliable food supply and a preservable surplus, but also the means of moving large amounts of goods so that material wealth may be accumulated. It is probable that the interrelation with nuclear centered groups characteristic of this kind of culture is a requirement for the maintenance of its advanced features rather than a convenience. The ability to draw upon the resources of a nuclear center appears to compensate partly for the difficulties inherent in community mobility and to permit a more highly developed sociopolitical organization than would be possible if it had to be totally supported by the resources of pastoral nomadism.

Ethnographic criteria.—Except for the difference in community mobility, this type of pastoralism has much in common with simple nuclear centered groups. Both are characterized by full-time occupational specialization by part of the population, social stratification based on wealth, kinship-based social organization, and a chief who acts to some extent in his own interest and has power of coercion. Pastoralists have more highly developed patterns of warfare than do agriculturists of the simple nuclear centered level, and have managed to achieve spectacular supra-nuclear integrations by conquering and exploiting sedentary nuclear centered groups. Such empires, balanced precariously between separate loci of military and economic power, were transitory and readily disrupted.

Ethnographic examples.—No communities of this type appear to have existed in the New World. Old World examples are the Kazak, Mongol, Kalmuk, Kirghiz, Bedouin, and Tuareg.

Archeological criteria and examples.—Although camp sites are not likely to be evident archeologically, such monuments as the mound (Kurgan) tombs distributed from South Russia (Three Brothers Tomb) to Pazyryk and Shiba in Mongolia undoubtedly relate to Diversified Pastoral

Nomads like the Scythians, Sarmatians, and Huns. The pattern has existed at least since early in the first millennium B.C. in dry-land Asia and Africa.

SIGNIFICANCE OF COMMUNITY MOBILITY AND PATTERNING

This comparison of domestic animal-using communities whose food supply is mobile (and who themselves are forced to be mobile) with those of plant users whose food supply is in a fixed location makes it possible to evaluate the effect of community mobility on cultural development. Within the sequence extending from wild food gathering to intensive agriculture, increased cultural complexity is correlated with increased sedentariness, while in the domesticated animal-using scale, increased cultural complexity is achieved even though community mobility is preserved. Diversified pastoral nomads are even able to attain a kind of supra-nuclear integration possessing most of the essential features of this stage as represented among sedentary groups. However, the fact cannot be escaped that the upper levels of cultural development are characteristically associated with sedentary communities. Settled life has a definite advantage, and communities that are able to progress beyond the restricted wandering level without settling down do so because special circumstances partly offset the handicaps inherent in community mobility.

Our preliminary classification of community patterns was based on the degree of mobility characteristic of the community. We then considered the subsistence economy and the socio-political and religious features associated with each degree of mobility. Analysis showed the recurrent appearance of similar combinations of characteristics, strengthening the postulate that the community pattern approach provides a workable classification for the description of human societies. The next question is: Do these categories also have

functional, evolutionary, or historical significance?

FUNCTIONAL BASIS OF COMMUNITY PATTERNING

A comparison of the community patterns of agriculturists with those of pastoral nomads (including equestrian hunters) reveals a general similarity of socio-political and religious features, and certain comparabilities in economic organization when not specialized to deal with the particular subsistence resource. The fact that these constellations of traits recur not only among unrelated groups with the same subsistence base, but also among those with different subsistence bases (plants vs. animals), suggests that there is a functional explanation. Since on the lower levels essentially the same community pattern can be developed by groups with differing degrees of mobility, the ability to settle down would not seem to be a critical factor until cultural development is pushed to the advanced nuclear centered level and beyond. This leaves the productivity of the subsistence resource as the major determinant. In view of the fact that the productivity of any subsistence pattern depends upon at least three variables—the food resources, the potentiality of the environment, and the techniques of exploitation—it seems remarkable that the cultural adjustments align themselves into so few basic types. The fact that they do so emphasizes the existence of functional determinants, which do not allow free variation in basic cultural features.

The functional nature of these community patterns is illustrated in the case of the Northwest Coast. Although this culture area has frequently been cited for its exceptional characteristics, the community pattern has much in common with our semi-permanent sedentary category. This can be explained by the fact that the wild food resources were sufficiently abundant, reliable, and amenable to techniques of preservation to achieve a subsistence potential that in other cases was accomplished only with the aid of domestication. The results were similar to those produced in other areas by the adoption of slash and burn agriculture.

The reason for these equivalences of cultural complexes associated with different degrees of mobility and different domesticated food sources can be seen in Figure 1. Community patterns based on

culture pattern among groups with different subsistence bases emerges. Central-based wandering and incipient pastoral nomadic resemble each other in economic (food distribution), socio-political, and religious features because both have a subsistence characterized by incipient domestication. Semi-permanent sedentary and equestrian hunting are similar in that both depend upon an exploitive type of plant or

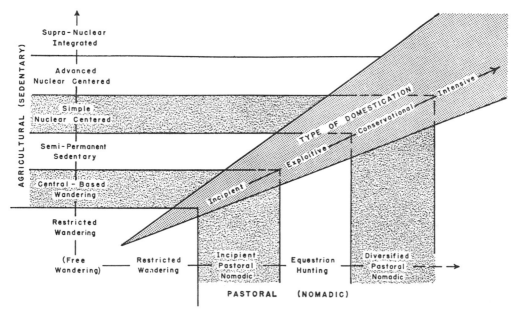

FIG. 1. Correlation of types of community patterning with types of domesticated subsistence technology. The seven primary community patterns are shown at the left and the secondary types associated with reliance on domestic animals are along the bottom. Those with similar general cultural features are designated by intersecting bands. The technology of domestication characteristic of the comparable community types, and explaining their cultural similarities, is indicated in the diagonal wedge across the center. The apex of this wedge extends backward from the region identified with incipient domestication to take account of the fact that when the incipient form is recognizable, the roots of domestication are already buried in the past. Furthermore, the dog is possessed by restricted wanderers today and probably was tamed if not domesticated at that level in the evolutionary scheme.

wild foods and on agriculture are listed on the left, those utilizing domesticated animals along the bottom. The bands connect comparable community patterns in the two scales. At their junction, we have characterized the degree of development of techniques of domestication. When this is added, the explanation for the similarity in

animal use, which exhausts local food resources and keeps the community from settling permanently in one place. Diversified pastoral nomadic groups have developed intensive and conservational techniques of utilizing domestic animals that make it possible for them to support some of the more complex socio-political and religious features found among simple nuclear centered and advanced nuclear centered agriculturists, whose techniques are also conservational and intensive. The recurrence of similar culture types, community patterns, or levels of cultural development—whatever one may wish to call them—can thus be explained not only on the basis of functional integration of cultural traits with each other, but also by the fact that there is a functional relationship between the cultural complex as a whole and subsistence resources of certain degrees of productivity. This being the case, cultures that do not fit well into the categories we have described should be explicable in terms of specific, local differences in environment or technique of food getting that pushes the subsistence potential away from the norm for the category, but not over the borderline into the next category.

EVOLUTIONARY ASPECTS OF COMMUNITY PATTERNING

This brings us to the observation that our categories constitute stages or levels of development in an evolutionary sequence. Each clearly grows out of a previous one and into a following one. In the discussion of dynamics producing each type, we have described what we feel to be the major differences in subsistence potential to account for changes in community mobility and in socio-political and religious features of the culture. In the simpler, wandering groups these differences do not seem great, but a close examination suggests that, although small, they played an important role in the discovery of plant domestication.

Restricted wandering is the simplest and most mobile type of community pattern represented among intact human societies today, yet among many restricted wandering groups activities that might lead to the invention of agriculture can be discerned. The necessity of permanently maintaining the community on a certain prescribed amount of land offers incentives toward conservation of the plant food re-

sources for future yield. Since the territory is held against trespass, the group can reap any rewards of conservation practices. With the right plants, this could lead to a harvest sufficient to allow the group to remain in one spot for part of the year. In any event, some living central-based wandering communities practice incipient agriculture, and a number of archeological sites identified with this community pattern also present evidence of agricultural beginnings. Certain naturally abundant wild food sources can also support this partially settled type of life, and cultures specialized toward their exploitation may be sidetracked from discovering or appreciating the benefits of domestication.

The development of staple food plants moves the community from central-based wandering to semi-permanent sedentary. Supplemented by hunting and fishing (New World) and animal domestication (Old World), agriculture produces sufficient food from a circumscribed area to maintain the population in a sedentary condition. However, the lack of understanding of soils and their conservation means that agriculture will maintain the population indefinitely only if the village is moved periodically as the old fields cease to produce. The next step is the development of a technique that will maintain fields in permanent production, such as fertilization, crop rotation, or irrigation. When this is done, the community becomes simple nuclear centered. Whether the village is permanent as in the southwestern Pueblos and in Peru, or whether there is a permanent ceremonial center supported by scattered farms or hamlets, may depend on the kind of agricultural techniques employed and the problems of the local soils and environment. Once agriculture is really conservational and intensive, technical knowledge grows, and with its application subsistence potential increases. The tremendous advances that are being made today suggest that the limits to agricultural productivity are not even yet in sight.

The source of the impetus for increasing

cultural complexity at the advanced nuclear centered and supra-nuclear integrated levels is difficult to discern. Effect follows cause so closely that with our unrefined methods of analysis they often are not clearly separated. It can be argued that social factors are uppermost and that the nature of the political organization is of critical significance. However, as one proceeds from restricted wandering through central-based wandering, semi-permanent sedentary, and simple nuclear centered to advanced nuclear centered, the socio-political advances can be recognized as consequences of increased population concentration, resulting in turn from improved subsistence resources. The more complex the culture becomes, the more features develop that may promote or inhibit fullest or most efficient utilization of the available resources. These can be considered causal in a sense. However, the dynamics producing the various community types strongly suggest that although social organization may propel the culture in a certain direction, it can only do so within the limits set by the subsistence resources at its disposal. This is equivalent to saying that a certain population threshold is a prerequisite to the maintenance of certain socio-political structures, and that to cross this threshold a certain level of food production is essential.

In contrast to the community patterns in the wild food to agriculture sequence, which may be looked upon as levels of development in an evolutionary scale, the types of community pattern found among domestic animal users do not seem to have this relationship to each other. Incipient pastoral nomadic and equestrian hunting communities appear to be adaptations to special ecological situations, and neither seems logically precedent to diversified pastoral nomadism. The cultural configurations are sufficiently comparable to central-based wandering, semi-permanent sedentary, and simple nuclear centered in the domesticated plant subsistence sequence, however, to suggest that these community patterns can be understood as the consequence of differing levels of productivity in the domesticated animal subsistence base.

HISTORICAL SEQUENCES OF COMMUNITY PATTERNING

Although our categories seem to be logical stages in the evolution of culture, all are not represented in every local historical sequence. For example, in parts of the Southwest, central-based wandering seems to have led directly into simple nuclear centered communities; on the coast of Peru, there seems to have been a jump from restricted wandering to simple nuclear centered; and in parts of the tropical forest the sequence was from restricted wandering to semi-permanent sedentary.

These alternative local situations can be explained by the form in which improvements in subsistence resources were acquired by each community. It can be assumed that techniques of agriculture were more often acquired by diffusion than by invention. Differences in environment between the source and recipient communities would be reflected in differences in the productivity of the agriculture, with consequent effects on the culture. In Figure 2 the types are placed in their evolutionary order and the alternative local sequences are shown by arrows. By holding environment as if it were a constant and assuming acquisition of plants and techniques of cultivation by diffusion, the factors responsible for jumps of one or more levels can be readily isolated. A restricted wandering community will become central-based wandering if the evolutionary sequence is followed. However, if plant domestication is introduced, but without conservational techniques of cultivation required by the local environment, it will jump to semi-permanent sedentary. This situation must have occurred many times, when agriculture diffused from river valleys or irrigation centers into forested regions. The climate would frequently allow the plants to grow, but lack of knowledge of fertilizers and other conservational measures would result in soil depletion and prohibit the type

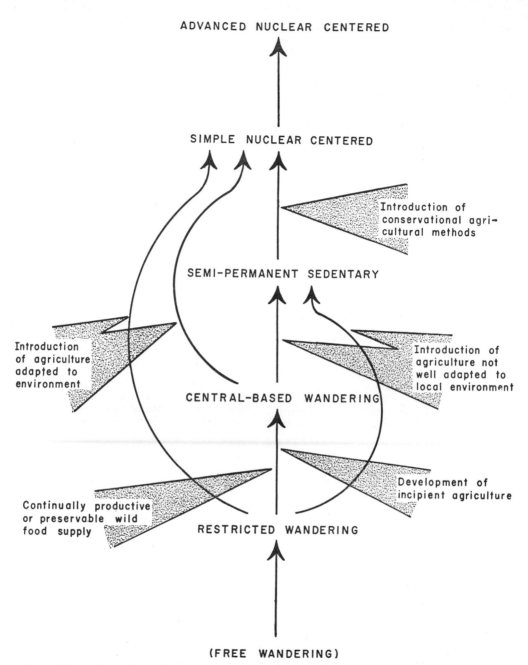

ADVANCED NUCLEAR CENTERED

SIMPLE NUCLEAR CENTERED

Introduction of
conservational agri-
cultural methods

SEMI-PERMANENT SEDENTARY

Introduction
of agriculture
adapted to
environment

Introduction of
agriculture not
well adapted to
local environment

CENTRAL-BASED WANDERING

Development of
incipient agriculture

Continually productive
or preservable wild
food supply

RESTRICTED WANDERING

(FREE WANDERING)

FIG. 2. Dynamics of alternative local sequences of community patterning. The primary community types are arranged in evolutionary order, as indicated by the series of straight arrows up the center of the diagram. The steps that may be skipped under certain conditions are shown by the curved arrows and the conditions favorable to each jump are briefly stated. Since there appear to be no alternative paths above the simple nuclear centered level, the upper end of the sequence has been omitted.

of permanent settlement associated with agriculture at the source of the diffusion. If, on the other hand, the restricted wandering community received both domesticated plants and conservational techniques of cultivation adapted to the local environment, it might move directly to the simple nuclear centered level. The acquisition of the same kind of conservational agricultural complex by a central-based wandering group would also allow it to move directly to simple nuclear centered. One has only to recognize the advantages of such shortcuts to understand why the difficult, experimental stages of agricultural technology were so often skipped when it was possible to profit by discoveries made elsewhere.

SUMMARY AND CONCLUSION

Examination of human cultures from the point of view of community mobility has resulted in the definition of seven primary types characterized by differences not only in mobility but also in other aspects of the culture. These categories are: Free Wandering, Restricted Wandering, Central-based Wandering, Semi-permanent Sedentary, Simple Nuclear Centered, Advanced Nuclear Centered, and Supra-Nuclear Integrated. These types have functional, evolutionary, and historical as well as descriptive validity. They can be identified with considerable accuracy archeologically as well as ethnologically, and so provide a framework for relating the past and the present.

In addition to these seven primary categories, defined initially on the basis of differential community mobility, we have recognized three secondary categories of communities, whose dependence upon domesticated animals keeps them in almost constant movement. They are: Incipient Pastoral Nomadic, Equestrian Hunting, and Diversified Pastoral Nomadic. Except in their degree of mobility, these communities have many of the characteristics of central-based wandering, semi-permanent sedentary, and nuclear centered communities respectively.

It is our feeling that the examination of cultures from the point of view employed in this paper has shed some light on the evolutionary and functional aspects of community patterning. There is a great deal more to be said, however, than we have touched upon here. We have, for example, not attempted to discuss cultural diffusion versus parallelism in accounting for similarities in economic, social, and religious customs among people in widely separated parts of the earth who belong to the same community type. Perhaps it may be said that the chances for parallel development and independent invention increase when similar prior conditions prevail, such as natural resources and population pressure, which can encourage or even force a society to improve its subsistence techniques. Then, with plant and animal domestication and further population increase, societies may automatically become more complex and similar institutions arise without specific diffusions. However, this line of investigation cannot be adequately pursued here.

The whole question of stability in the various levels of development has barely been raised. One might examine to what extent atypical and particularly more advanced traits can be assimilated by each community type without disturbing its functional integration, or how well the different forms of community patterning are able to resist disintegration when confronted with a crisis imposed by sudden contact with an alien culture. Perhaps typical cultures are more viable than those with deviant features. In studies of culture contact, a classification based on community pattern may provide a useful orientation for analysis.

Although other theoretical considerations might be mentioned, we conclude this discussion by pointing out that the analysis of culture in terms of community patterning also has a practical aspect. It is an approach to the understanding of culture that permits the incorporation of archeological data to a greater extent than do other over-all classifications. For the archeologist, it not only makes possible the elaboration and extension of inferences from fragmentary evidence, but it also facilitates comparisons through time and space. More importantly, however, the community pattern approach gives archeologists and ethnologists a means of correlating their data and removes some of the bonds that tie one to the past and the other to the present.

MAX. SORRE

THE CONCEPT OF
GENRE DE VIE

Thirty-seven years have passed since Vidal de la Blache introduced us to the fundamental notion of *genre de vie*,[1] which had already been exposed as a topic of geographic interest by Friedrich Ratzel. It is surprising that the concept has not yet been the subject of a critical elaboration, for ethnographers have accumulated information on *genre de vie* in all parts of the world, and geographers, above all in Western Europe, have made a great contribution to its description in their regional monographs. A kind of impediment persists, for some think that the concept is too vague and prefer to ignore it, while others experience uneasiness when trying to use it, and still others believe that it is applicable only to more or less archaic groups and has little value in an account of the modern world. Besides, we can find no systematic development of the concept in the relics of Vidal's writings edited by Emmanuel de Martonne.[2] It is difficult to be-

Translated, with permission of the author and publisher, from "La notion de genre de vie et sa valeur actuelle," *Annales de Géographie*, LVII (1948), 97–108, 193–204. The author is professor emeritus of geography at the Sorbonne.
[1] Paul Vidal de la Blache, "Les genres de vie dans la géographie humaine," *Annales de Géographie*, XX (1911), 193–212, 289–304. I have also made extensive use of C. Daryll Forde, *Habitat, Economy and Society: A Geographical Introduction to Ethnology* (New York: Dutton, 1934).
[2] Paul Vidal de la Blache, *Principes de géographie humaine, publiés d'après les manuscrits de l'auteur par Emmanuel de Martonne* (Paris: A. Colin, 1922). [Translated by Millicent Todd Bingham as *Principles of Human Geography* (New York: Henry Holt, 1926).]

lieve, however, that a definition of *genre de vie* would not have been incorporated into a definitive version of this work, for the concept is implicit at all stages of its evolution. Nothing prevents us from trying to resume the discussion, or from trying to clarify the concept by drawing upon recent studies in ethnology and sociology.

CONTENTS OF THE CONCEPT

I propose to analyze the complex of habitual activities, which characterizes a human group and provides the foundation for its existence, by adding some modern examples to those given by Vidal.

Elements of genre de vie.—The concept is extremely rich because it embraces most, if not all, of the activities of a group and even of individuals. It is necessary to arrive at an advanced stage of cultural evolution to find evidence of emancipation from its bonds. The material and spiritual elements of culture are techniques in the largest sense of the word, i.e., habits transmitted by tradition that enable men to live in particular environments. The persistence of a group is assured not only by the institutions that maintain its cohesion, but also by techniques and implements for the utilization of energy sources and raw materials. Human genius is stimulated and oriented by environmental pressures, but it also has its own creative power. Consider, for example, the state of cultural advancement in three areas of similar environment: British Columbia, the southern littoral of Chile, and Tasmania. Only in the first of these areas did rich and varied culture evolve [e.g., the Nootka, Haida, Kwakiutl]. The Alacaluf and Yahgan of southern Chile represent miserable remnants of the most backward groups of humanity, and the Tasmanians were at an even more primitive level of culture. According to Forde, "The mental indolence and lack of foresight so often attributed to the Fuegians would appear to be a still more marked characteristic of the Tasmanians."[3] The essential issue is the original or acquired (and sometimes lost) ability of a group to utilize the possibilities of its environment.

It is not unreasonable, at least at the outset, to describe a *genre de vie* as a combination of techniques. In addition to knowledge of animal husbandry, including castration, and the use of livestock for food, the practice of pastoral nomadism may entail milking and the manufacture of milk products, the use of riding and pack saddles, various methods of harnessing, and the making of garments and tents. Pastoral practices vary according to climate, type of livestock, topography, and the magnitude of displacements caused by differentiation in the quality and quantity of pastures. In my opinion, which differs from long established notions, the efficiency of pastoral practices rests on knowledge, acquired empirically, of the properties of environments and the requirements of livestock. The ability to make a distinction, so familiar to us, between the natural and supernatural is not a very old accomplishment. Moreover, each material technique has a counterpart in religious or magical practices, and no great importance needs to be attached to the choice between these two words. Primitive man kills his prey with arrows, stones, or hunting sticks; but he also counts on assistance from incantations and symbolic drawings, in which we see the crude beginnings of art. At another stage of civilization, all the rites of fertility, of which water rites are a part, are just as relevant in a description of *genre de vie* as

the use of digging sticks, hoes, or plows.[4] The native American practice of burying fishheads with grains of maize has been interpreted as the origin of the use of nitrate fertilizer; but the practice must have another meaning. Shepherds and farmers have both performed water rites, and rock inscriptions show that they were known in the depths of the Sahara. If we describe certain customs associated with the delicate practices of grafting as "obscene" this is because we are no longer aware of the sacred meaning of the customs, which reached us from the ancient Orient through the intermediary of the Carthaginian agronomists and their Arab copyists.[5] In this connection, we should also mention the rites, processions, and prayers by which the Catholic peasant seeks to obtain heavenly rains for his thirsty fields. These practices should be included under the same heading in a description of *genre de vie*. Therefore, when we define the concept, we must take care not to mutilate it. In addition to visible material elements, we must include non-material or spiritual elements, and we must of course also consider social elements, for the development of a *genre de vie* is inconceivable apart from the atmosphere of an organized society.

The Role of elements of genres de vie. —The observation of complex *genres de vie* reveals some distinctions that are already evident when we consider more simple forms. All traits do not have the same functional or temporal significance. Some are at the very foundation of a *genre de vie* and act as forces of creation or organization, while others carry on functions of conservation and fixation. In addition we

---

[3] Forde, *op. cit.*, p. 100.

[4] In *L'Homme et les plantes cultivées* (Paris: Gallimard, 1943), André-G. Haudricourt and Louis Hédin have assembled some data on fertility rites.

[5] In his "Book of Agriculture," Ibn al-Awam, a Moorish scholar inspired by accounts of ancient Nabataean agriculture, mentions an analogous fertility rite associated with grafting. See *Le livre de l'agriculture d'Ibn al-Awam*, translated from the Arabic by J.-J. Clément-Mullet (2 vols.; Paris: A. Franck, 1864–67).

can describe elements that play roles of restriction or limitation. Finally, we find relict elements that are not readily identified as being useful. These distinctions do not have decisive or absolute values, but they clarify the functions of a *genre de vie*.

The most ancient agricultural societies may be defined in terms of their creative or organizing traits. The selection of crops, the manufacture and use of implements, and the procedures for sowing or planting are fundamental techniques around which all of the *genre de vie* is organized. In some extensive climatic realms such associations are remarkably stable: e.g., the association of tubers or a cereal with large grains like maize with the planting stick in the tropical forests; the association of small grains of the millet type with the hoe on the light soils of the Sudan or the Deccan; the association of flooded fields and transplanted rice in Monsoon Asia; and the triad of wheat, the ox, and the plow in the rural landscapes of the temperate areas of Eurasia.

Other elements, such as social structure and economic organization, often act as agents of fixation. To understand their character and role it is necessary to look at very advanced forms, such as the *genres de vie* founded on a combination of cereal cultivation and sedentary pastoral economy in social milieus based upon a strong village structure with collective restraints. In such cases, the settlement pattern, agrarian structure, system of land tenure, and mode of exploitation provide material evidence of the functions of the *genre de vie*. The distribution of soil tends to immobilize the habits of the agricultural group. We are well aware of the extent to which land fragmentation and dispersion can impede the substitution of a modern system of exploitation for an archaic one.

After having functioned as fixing agents, traits of this sort may persist as inhibiting elements in a new *genre de vie*. Comparable examples can be found in cultures based upon a pastoral livelihood. The great nomadic tribes of the steppes and deserts of Eurasia derive maximum profit from their animals, but many of the peoples who combine sedentary or nomadic pastoralism with farming (e.g., in India, and southern or eastern Africa) make poor use of their livestock. Religious prescriptions restrain them; and as soon as the prohibitions disappear, they make fuller use of their herds (e.g., the Hottentots). In this case, religion has played a negative or restrictive role.

Rituals and practices that were once tied to certain modes of activity may persist after the forms of livelihood that they supported have disappeared. For example, after the Yakut adopted reindeer breeding they retained some of the materials that had been used with the horse, e.g., the saddle. The excavations of Russian archeologists in the Eastern Altai have exposed funeral objects—reindeer masks of plated gold on horse skulls—that perpetuate the memory of the change of domestic animals. Until recently, popular traditions in the French countryside evoked very ancient states of civilization. As the traditions of our own rural civilization are erased, these relic traits also disappear.

Ultimately, an equilibrium between elements of different orders is established, an equilibrium which assures the internal cohesion of the *genre de vie* and symbolizes the durability that is one of its essential characteristics.

Genre de vie and natural environment. —Let us recall here only a few consequences of the general relations described by Vidal de la Blache. As assemblages of techniques, *genres de vie* are active expressions of the adaptation of human groups to their natural settings. The specialization and stability of this adaptation depends upon the specialization, stability, and durability of the *genre de vie*. And local changes of the former are expressed by variations in the latter.

Among peoples subjected to the pressures of a highly specialized desert or arctic environment that does not vary markedly from year to year, the direction indicated by the external influences does not change, and *genres de vie* are always oriented in the same way. But there are marginal environments, less well defined, where first one and then another group of conditions prevails: e.g., the arid or sub-humid margins of the steppes. To such marginal conditions belong marginal *genres de vie*. A prolonged period of severe drought may transform a group of pastoral nomads into a band of gatherers, reduced by the loss of their herds to the lowest level of life; or it may transform sedentary pastoralists into nomads, at least for a time. Before their livelihood was enhanced by irrigation works, the inhabitants of Ceará, in northeastern Brazil, were well aware of the effects of droughts. Similarly, it has long been known that settlers on the edge of the Thar desert abandon their villages during severe droughts.

The culture of the Eskimos—the strange people who have elected to live amidst almost perpetual snow and ice—offers the best examples of a faithful reflection of environmental conditions in a *genre de vie*. The culture of the Eskimos is one of the most extensive and at the same time one of the most specialized in the entire world. There is nothing comparable in the Old World. However, as Daryll Forde[6] suggests, the basic uniformity of Eskimo culture does not mask its variability. A certain number of traits are found throughout the Eskimo realm and are lacking in the territories occupied by the nomadic caribou hunters. The harpoon and the skin covered canoe (kayak) are missing only in the extreme northwest, but the dog sledge, the snow house (igloo), and ice hunting methods disappear as one moves toward the southeast and southwest. On the subarctic margins of the Eskimo realm, one sees specialized forms of kayak, large wooden canoes (umiak), and all the equipment necessary for the hunting of whales in the open sea. Finally, on the Barren Grounds, travelers have described "Caribou Eskimo,"

whose way of life differs markedly from the rest of the group. All of these changes of material culture and habits express variations of the *genre de vie* in connection with what might be described as the progressive deterioration of the arctic environment.[7]

We may be satisfied with these remarks, for the other aspect of the relationship between a *genre de vie* and its milieu—that of the modifying power of man—does not have to be emphasized here. It will be noted in its proper place.

The mark of genre de vie on mankind. —The imprint of a *genre de vie* on groups and individuals is another factor that encourages its preservation. It is able in large degree to shape man's physical appearance and mental structure. As Vidal remarked, "*genres de vie* have an autonomy that is attached to the human being and follows him. It is not only the Bedouin and the Fellah who are thus set apart, but also the Vlach shepherd and the Bulgarian farmer, and the sailor and peasant as far as our own shores. The soul of some peoples seems to be formed of a different metal than that of others."[8] These oppositions burst forth when different peoples must struggle for the conquest of space. The conflict of the sedentary farmer and the pastoral nomad is one of the common themes of history and geography.

The list of such examples could be extended almost indefinitely. The important idea is that of the persistence of the imprint. It is perceptible when groups are juxtaposed and perhaps even more striking when they are superimposed. On the plateau of East Africa, the Bakitara, Banyankole, and Masai live in the midst of

---

[6] Forde, *op. cit.*, chap. 14, and bibliog. on p. 483.

[7] The most recent general accounts by geographers are those of Maurice Zimmermann, *Etats scandinaves—Régions polaires boréales* (Paris: A. Colin, 1933) [Vol. III of *Géographie Universelle*]; Forde, *op. cit.*, chap. 8 and bibliog. on p. 478; and Pierre George, *Les régions polaires* (Paris: A. Colin, 1946), pp. 139–56.

[8] Vidal de la Blache, "Les genres de vie dans la géographie humaine," p. 304.

sedentary farmers, but they maintain the individuality of their *genre de vie*.[9] They have deliberately rejected the economic possibilities offered to them in order to devote themselves to the wanderings of their cattle. Their livelihood shows to what extent a traditional *genre de vie* can restrict the use of a territory that has greater potentialities. The opposition of the Fulani to the Sudanese agriculturalists who completely surround them is no less striking. Indeed, the preservation of their ethnic type over such a vast area is one of the most impressive aspects of the cultural geography of Africa.

The action of the *genre de vie* is also exerted on the somatic type. If we object that the racial characteristics of the Masai or the Fulani reflect their distant origins— for they are invaders and we know something of their journey—, we merely postpone the solution of the problem. In the operation of the *genre de vie* there are forces that influence human physiology: e.g., dietary practices and the nature and extent of physical exertion. But we are unaware of how these influences are reflected in heredity or how individual characteristics become group characteristics.

On the other hand, the formation of a psychic patrimony, created by language, traditions, and rituals, is indisputable. The individual is a prisoner of his group, and of its interdicts, antipathies, and hatreds. The most complex facts are the easiest to ascertain and explain in the light of the distinction between the roles of the different elements of a *genre de vie*.

Can *genres de vie*, as thus defined, be classified? We usually begin by grouping them according to dominant activities. Since we no longer accept the dogma of an immanent progression of cultural stages, it would not be prudent to attempt a genetic classification. I believe we must be satisfied with current usage, without concern for further precision.

THE EVOLUTION OF GENRES DE VIE

A definition of *genre de vie* like the one that has been outlined gives only an incomplete and distorted view. In order to have geographic interest, this complex of habits must have a minimum of durability and stability. Otherwise, we would not be able to grasp it. A *genre de vie* is born, grows, and flowers—and it is when it has reached this degree of maturity that we characterize it. Hence, the necessity to evoke a complementary, and not at all contradictory aspect, that of evolution. This consideration enables us to improve our understanding of *genre de vie*. Vidal de la Blache has identified the combinations that promote fertilization, birth, and growth. Without repeating what he has written, which must be regarded as definitive, we can attempt to extend the analysis.

The example of the Eskimo.—Let us return to the Eskimo, who have been the subject of several decades of ethnographic and archeologic research.[10] The origin and transformation of their culture pose difficult problems, but the available information is full of geographic interest. The archeologists have discovered vestiges of three ancient cultures, which are difficult to place in chronological order: that of Thule, that of Cape Dorset, and that of the islands and shores of the Bering Sea. The Thule culture occupies a central position, and the superimposition in this district

[9] For accounts of the pastoral peoples of East Africa see Forde, *op. cit.*, pp. 287–307; for the Fulani see Jules Blache, "La question pastorale en Afrique occidentale," *Annales de Géographie,* LI (1942), 26–44.

[10] In addition to the accounts of Forde (*op. cit.*) and Vidal de la Blache, "Les genres de vie . . . ," see the following articles in W. L. G. Joerg (ed.), *Problems of Polar Research* (American Geographical Society Publication No. 7 [New York, 1928]): Diamond Jenness, "Ethnological Problems of Arctic America," pp. 167–76; Knud Rasmussen, "Tasks for Future Research in Eskimo Culture," pp. 177–88; and Waldemar Bogoras, "Ethnologic Problems of the Eurasian Arctic," pp. 189–208. See also T. Matthiasen, "The Archeology of the Thule District," *Geografisk Tidsskrift,* XLVII (1944–1945), 43–72.

seems to be arranged as follows: Dorset (tenth century), Thule (marine hunters spread over the entire Arctic shore of Canada from the tenth to the twelfth centuries), Ruin Island connected with Alaska (fourteenth century), and, finally, the modern Eskimo. The Thule district seems to have been a hearth of radiation, and the Thule culture appears to have succeeded an earlier culture. The Eskimos of the Barren Grounds seem to be a people in course of retrogression, and not survivors of a group that had not been able to complete its adaptation to the arctic environment. Swept away by their pursuit of the caribou, they turned their back to the sea and lost the elements of their culture that were tied to littoral conditions. It is an incontestable fact, as the older authors knew, that the Eskimos have been in the course of a migration for more than ten centuries. But the direction of their travels along the northern shores of Canada remains in dispute. The connection between the southwestern and southeastern wings of Eskimo culture are established by the common possession of the umiak. But how can we explain the disappearance of once common subarctic characteristics in the domain of the Thule culture? And what is the exact nature of the connections between the Thule and Bering Sea cultures? Did movement take place from east to west or in the reverse direction? It is certain that the *genres de vie* of the Eskimo result from an evolution of near millennial proportions, with modifications caused by changes of climate. The major lines of this evolution are still indistinct.

We should remember these themes that appear in the discussions of the archeologists: the influence of different environments, the importance of implements, the possible role of diffusion, the contamination of one culture by another, and the vast scale of adaptation, ranging from the maritime vocation of the coastal fishermen to the nomadic habits of the caribou hunters. These themes are encountered repeatedly

in any systematic study of the evolution of *genres de vie*.

Evolution of internal origin.—To what extent are *genres de vie* capable of evolving independently without benefit of external pressures? This question does not seem arbitrary if we reflect on what has already been said about elements of fixation and conservation, and if we recall that Vidal often mentioned the effects of forces of inertia. It seems clear that *genres de vie* may evolve spontaneously.

Technological innovations, such as the invention of the plow or the outrigger canoe, may have far-reaching effects, regardless of the state of advancement of the culture in which they are placed. The evolution of the first civilizations was based upon improvements in technology that permitted better use of man power and other sources of energy. Since it is an offense to violate established rules, innovations have not always been accepted with alacrity. But we cannot explain the transformation of the most ancient societies if we refuse to recognize the cumulative effects of local inventions. Two other factors of early transformation were demographic growth and the development of a social organization that favored division of labor. The first trend was a perpetual menace, because it upset the balance between resources and needs. Primitive peoples, especially those in harsh environments, have tried more often than is generally realized to solve their population problems by birth control. They have also been compelled to look for new resources. As soon as it was extended beyond individual families, the division of labor tended to promote specialized castes and a separation of agriculture and industry.[11] We find evidence of the differentiation of two great categories of *genres de vie,* but at the initial stage of their evolution the separation was sociolog-

[11] For a full discussion of the effects of division of labor see Richard C. Thurnwald, *Economics in Primitive Communities* (London: Oxford University Press, 1932).

ical rather than geographical. Subsistence activities continued to be paramount.

With the passage of time the separation of agricultural and industrial occupations became more conspicuous. The latter assumed a growing importance and absorbed a larger and larger share of human energy. As their products ceased to be consumed locally, the autonomy of industrial enterprises tended to increase. New *genres de vie* of heterogeneous character began to break away from the undifferentiated primitive forms. Wherever agriculture could not absorb all of the activity of a group or sustain it, a balance of energy was available, either permanently or seasonally, that could be used to increase industrial production. The Western love of rigid distinctions encourages us to overlook the assistance that was offered to the rural world by small workshops scattered through the countryside. The peasant was employed, according to hours and seasons, as a farmer or a craftsman. This option is no longer available to him, but our regional monographs give a clear picture of the former pattern of farms associated with small workshops. In the villages of Picardie, Vimeu and Champagne and in the Jura, Massif Central, and Pyrenees, such industries as lace work, weaving, knitting, and also metal and wood working were successful for a long time. Industrial concentration has altered this symbiotic relationship.[12]

We must attempt to discover how *genres de vie* that incorporate such diverse modes of activity were formed. It is not difficult to identify the forces that favored separation, but this development did not always lead to segregation, for a factory could be built on the foundation of a workshop and remain in the midst of cultivated fields.

Some consequences of this evolution.—
With the progress of industrialization (and

also urbanization), modes of livelihood based solely upon manufacturing cut their ties with agriculture and were located according to their own needs. In their formation and in their progress, technological advancements, governed during the last century and a half by the progress of science, have played a dominant role. After three-quarters of a century of experimentation, the perfection of the steam engine by James Watt inaugurated a new era in the history of *genres de vie*. It was a triumph of the human spirit that shattered the old framework of industrial technology.

The characteristics of these new modes of livelihood, differing markedly from those that have already been described, will be discussed later. For the moment, let us remember only that in the older *genres de vie* the activity of the group satisfied all of its needs, including food supply, tools, shelter, and clothing. A long time has passed since French countrywomen have spun their own linen or wool, or even baked their own bread. A period began when functional specialization caused the differentiation— one might say dismemberment—of *genres de vie*, and reduced the activities of the group as such. At the same time, the community lost part of its autonomy, for it was more dependent on the complementary activities of other communities.

*Evolution by adaptation to a new environment.—*Since this problem has already been considered in the discussion of the Eskimo, it does not have to be examined in detail. When a group leaves its territory, whether voluntarily or by necessity, it transports its *genre de vie*. If the new setting is similar to the old one, traditional habits will be retained. But habits and environments may not be compatible. In this case, new ways are imposed. Why should an Eskimo migrating toward the southeast retain the elaborate methods that he had perfected for hunting seals on the Arctic ice? The environment does not always necessarily affect the group, for it may refuse to adapt itself to a new setting

[12] It is not possible here to give a bibliography on these mixed *genres de vie*, which have often been the object of detailed descriptions in geographic monographs.

and accept the prospect of decline. Nevertheless, the environment exerts a compelling force, and it presents us with some very general problems.

We have just considered the displacements and migrations that lead a people from one bio-climatic milieu to another. Since the appearance of *Homo sapiens*, the distribution of climates, and hence of vegetation, has changed. The chronology, cyclic character, and amplitude of these variations are disputed, but there is no doubt of their reality. Our species saw the great pluvio-thermic changes of the Ice Age, and the primordial *genres de vie* were conditioned by these events. Prehistoric archeology throws some light on this subject but cannot answer all of its questions. In any case, if we can accept the premise that a human group may have been able to remain in a territory subject to such changes by modifying its *genre de vie*, then we can also believe that it might have been able to adapt itself to conditions in different latitudes. To an earlier generation of scholars, the similarity between the material culture of the ancient inhabitants of our latitudes and that of the modern Arctic peoples suggested an hypothesis, which we have been obliged to reject, of uninterrupted continuity.

Introduction of new elements.—In addition to changes of the physical milieu other external influences may exert pressure on human groups. Invaders sufficiently numerous to impose their ways can introduce new habits without destroying an old cultural foundation. The historical development of the *genres de vie* of Western Europe is revealed by a superimposition of horizontal strata broken by some penetration in depth. The substratum of our rural life goes back to very remote times, but Celts, Germans, and Latins rearranged this primordial foundation, and new elements, such as techniques of harnessing, caused ferment. The resulting pattern conveys the misleading impression of a syncretism where each element seems to be determined by all other elements.

The introduction of an innovation may be sufficient to upset a *genre de vie* and give it a new dynamism. In pre-Columbian times the Indians of the prairies were bison hunters. In the sixteenth century the Europeans introduced the horse, which was promptly naturalized, and the people of the plains became equestrian nomads. They kept their *genre de vie*, but with a new aspect produced by increased mobility, and opportunities to exploit larger territories and transport heavier and richer loads. The horse became a symbol of wealth and an object of rivalry. Its possession bestowed on the Blackfeet and other hunting tribes a decisive superiority over the agricultural peoples who had pushed the frontier of cultivation several hundred miles beyond the Mississippi, and who were now obliged to retreat toward the east.[13]

In addition, innovations may spread as a result of contact between neighboring groups. In the Far East, Europeans were surprised by the familiarity of some of the products brought to local markets by the native peoples. The latter had learned to cultivate alien plants, introduced through the European plantations, in addition to their traditional subsistence crops.[14] Elsewhere in this essay, evidence will be given of the enrichment of the Sudanese farmer by his adoption of American plants. For the moment, let us note only that in some districts of the Guinean zone one observes an evolution similar to that of Southeast Asia.

The process of assimilation may go as far as the adoption *in toto* of a new *genre de vie*. This is true of some Paleo-Asiatic peoples who have adopted the customs of the Eskimo.

Single origin versus multiple origins.—At this point, the geographer begins to wonder if it is possible to establish the origin or dispersal of the elements of a

[13] See Clark Wissler, "The Influence of the Horse in the Development of Plains Culture," *American Anthropologist*, XVI (1914), 1–25.

[14] Ch. Robequain, "Problèmes de colonisation dans les Indes néerlandaises," *Annales de Géographie*, L (1941), 37–57, 114–36.

genre de vie. He turns to the ethnographer, who possesses proven methods and whose discipline has enjoyed the fruits of impressive accomplishments. But in many cases the ethnographer is also stopped by this question: can a given culture trait evolve spontaneously in distant places as a result of similar needs, or must one explain such resemblance by diffusion? The answers offered vary according to individual convictions and the dogmas of particular schools.[15]

In my view, it is imprudent to give a general answer and deny the possibility of specific explanation. When we find irrigation techniques that are entirely comparable in the two extremities of the immense cultivated area of Eurasia (China and the eastern Mediterranean), may we suppose that lifting devices of the same type and similar institutions have evolved independently? [16] The irrigation system of pre-Columbian America is surely independent of all imitation. The possibility of diffusion in Eurasia remains open, but it is not absolutely necessary to invoke it.

Problems of limitation.—In some cases evolution is arrested and human groups, crystallized in their ways of living, accept the prospect of extinction rather than the challenge of change.

Nomads often show a surprising lack of flexibility. In this case we refer to true nomads, not to the peoples of marginal zones who practice marginal *genres de vie.* The problem of their sedentarization has often been posed to colonial administrators. In the Kazakh and Kirghiz territories of the Soviet Union, nomadism was quickly suppressed, but not without a change of the *genre de vie* and profound modifications of habits that extended even to the

vital equilibrium of the Kazakh tribes.[17] The demise of native peoples has often been traced to their inability to modify traditional habits during periods of contact with Europeans. The survival of the Eskimo on the east coast of Greenland is a triumph of the enlightened policy of the Danish government. Lack of evolutionary aptitude can be found even among agricultural peoples, but they have been able to transform their *genres de vie* by adopting new crops.

Inertia and inflexibility result from the specialization and tight cohesion of a human group in its adaptation to a particular environment. The critical issue is its ability or inability to discard outmoded ways of life.

CIRCULATION AND GENRES DE VIE

If it is true that the formation of a *genre de vie* demands a certain stability necessary for the adjustment of components and the establishment of roots, then all of its changes, even when they are caused by external pressures, must be tied in some way to circulation. This facility enables the human group to participate in a more general pattern of life and introduces germs of renewal that invigorate old modes of livelihood. It also promotes the development of new customs, stamped with a new imprint and organized according to new demands. No region, however isolated it may seem, is sheltered forever.

Circulation and traditional genres de vie in the Old World.—There is abundant evidence of the bond that united the formation and evolution of our agricultural civilization and the elementary forms of circulation entailed in prehistoric migrations. Our rural *genre de vie,* at least as it appeared at the end of the eighteenth century in northern France, included influences transmitted from the Neolithic Age. Modern research on the origin of cultivated plants has illuminated this subject. We are able to distinguish the hearths

[15] Ragnar Numelin gives a bibliography and summary of these discussions in "Diffusionsproblemet i kulturforskningen," *Terra: Geografiska sällskapet i Finland Tidskrift,* LVII (1945). [French summary on p. 35.]

[16] This problem is posed by Jules Sion in *Asie des Moussons,* I: *Généralités, Chine, Japon* (Paris: A. Colin, 1928). [Vol. IX of *Géographie Universelle.*]

[17] Pierre George, *U.R.S.S.* (Paris: Collection, Orbis, 1947), p. 474.

whence our great cereals (wheat and barley) and the vegetables associated with them were diffused. We are also able to retrace the course of the dispersal, from the Mediterranean and Indo-Iranian lands to the Danube Valley and the zone of loess deposits, and then along the great routes running generally toward the north.[18] We are not always able to identify carriers or determine if there were secondary centers of radiation, but we know that we possess fundamental data on migrations during the Neolithic and Bronze Ages. The history of circulation in prehistoric Europe demonstrates that the elements of our rural *genres de vie* spread within constantly expanding circles. The characteristics common to the rural civilizations of northern China and the Occident cannot be explained unless we consider the ancient diffusions through the gateways of Kashgar and Dzungaria, and across the high plateaus of Central Asia.

At each period of history circulation carries elements that renew *genres de vie*. In the Middle Ages and in modern times, Lombardy and especially Flanders have been centers for the dispersal of new implements, and new methods of farming, water utilization, and soil conservation. In his description of the muddy plateau of Picardy, Albert Demangeon says: "This softening of the earth, which is the true mark of human effort, was accomplished in Flanders long before it was attempted in France." And he adds that the diffusion between the two areas demanded easy communication.[19]

The expansion of the oikoumene.— With the great discoveries of the fifteenth and sixteenth centuries, the diffusions that had brought a *genre de vie* born in more southerly countries to middle and northern Europe, were extended until they encom-

passed the globe. The entire world became accessible. This development had vast consequences, and it paved the way for another revolution.

Wherever possible European colonists transplanted the essential elements of their *genre de vie*. During the centuries that followed its initial expansion, European culture spread beyond the realm of temperate climate. Since conditions of environment and settlement were different, European colonists not only reproduced Old World patterns but also created extensive and in part transitory new ones, which nevertheless showed unmistakable signs of their ancestry. In South Africa, the descendants of Dutch immigrants (the Boers) were able to blend old and new elements into a stable *genre de vie*. European immigrants were able to reproduce their way of life in New England, but they were obliged to perfect a new combination in the Middle West. In the tropical zone the Europeans developed a unique livelihood based upon introduced luxury crops for the European markets (e.g., sugar cane, coffee, cacao) that were cultivated by transported slave laborers. In this case, the dependence on circulation involved a triple tie. The plantation system was profoundly disturbed by the suppression of slavery and the expansion of capitalism, but its original characteristics were not entirely destroyed.

What happened to the native *genres de vie?* The most archaic forms were condemned to disappear, sometimes with the peoples who practiced them. In this connection we think especially of the North American Indians. In other cases, indigenous cultures were transformed by the absorption of new elements. For example, Sudanese agriculture kept its rather archaic character until the sixteenth century, although a few elements had been introduced from the East (Egypt and India). It was a poor complex, but after the discovery of the New World, it was enriched by some American crops. The circumstances of the introduction are remarkable, for it entailed the substitution of new

[18] See Paul Vidal de la Blache, *Tableau de la géographie de la France,* Vol. 1, part 1 of Ernest Lavisse (ed.), *Histoire de France* (Paris: Hachette, 1903).

[19] Albert Demangeon, *La Picardie et les régions voisines* (Paris: A. Colin, 1905), chap. 12.

crops of higher yield for old crops of similar aptitude: e.g., manioc for the yam, the sweet potato for the Kafir potato (*Coleus dazo*), and especially the peanut for the Bambara groundnut (*Voandzeia subterranea*).[20] These modifications seem to have obeyed a law of least change, and the traditional rotations were not changed. The enrichment of European agriculture by the introductions of maize and the potato is well known. These two plants now occupy such a prominent place in our culture that it is hard to imagine the situation when they were unknown.

All the agricultural zones of the world have been affected by this immense upheaval. The examples given here are sufficient to clarify its general significance. Crop introductions have reduced differences within each zone, and circulation has thus contributed to the uniformization of the world.

Circulation as an essential condition of genres de vie.—The action of circulation is not limited to the transportation of the elements of *genres de vie* or their modification; it is an essential condition of their existence and an agent, in some degree, of their stabilization.

Among the most original and most highly specialized *genres de vie* are those that have been described in the mountainous areas of Europe. They are based on a combination of subsistence farming and pastoral practices that are highly varied but always entail exploitation of the higher slopes of mountains during the summer months. The pastoral economy obeys the seasonal rhythm of the vertical succession of ecological zones. Other important tasks are reserved for the leisure period during the long winter. Since this pattern of life develops in a closed frame—except where a valley provides access to numerous passes and functions as an axis of communication routes—it seems to be protected from the general movement of peoples and goods. In fact, the *genres de vie* of the European highlands show great stability and marks

[20] Haudricourt and Hédin, *op. cit.*, p. 138.

of archaism. So we see once more that stability does not necessarily mean immobility. The livelihood of many highlanders is based on the practice of transhumance, which entails the feeding of animals in stables during the winter season and driving them to mountain pastures for the summer months. The surplus of labor is scattered over the neighboring plains, and the opportunities for supplementary employment, sometimes at great distances, have brought relief to a precarious economy that could persist only with difficulty on its own funds. Thanks to the perpetual movement of men and animals, a kind of equilibrium was established.[21]

In this case, the *genres de vie* practiced in neighboring regions — mountains and plains—are complementary, and their preservation is tied to the mechanisms of exchange. Vidal de la Blache often spoke of the combination of rich and poor areas in France. We should also speak of an association of *genres de vie,* and the exchange that is established between them. And we should not overlook the frequency of distant migrations.

Commerce as an agent of destruction and differentiation.—The effects of circulation are extremely complex. In addition to carrying useful and even indispensable elements, circulation opens possibilities in all directions.

As a bearer of promises or illusions, it facilitates the escape from our rural areas of all who dream of an easier or more prosperous life. The railroad has been an active agent in the acceleration of the rural exodus: it did not create it, but it has certainly facilitated it. The railroad upset the demographic balance in the peasant milieu, and contributed, therefore, to the drastic alteration of our rural *genres de vie.*

On the other hand, the improvement of transportation facilitates the disposal of farms products in a wider market and stimulates production. Specialized forms of

[21] It is sufficient to reiterate the thesis presented by Philippe Arbos in *La vie pastorale dans les alpes françaises* (Paris: A. Colin, 1922).

agriculture, oriented by the requirements of a particular type of production, have replaced modes of livelihood based on a polyculture designed to satisfy local needs. The highly productive viticulture of southern France exists in its modern form only because of efficient transportation which has forged an original human type: a wine producer markedly different from his predecessor, who developed practices that set him apart from the surrounding peasantry. In this connection, we might have mentioned the gardeners of our urban suburbs or the farmers of the irrigated districts in southern France.

We have already described the internal forces that favored the development of mixed *genres de vie* combining industrial and agricultural activities. Their persistence is tied to the maintenance of a local balance: industrial activity carried on in rural workshops or small factories established in the open countryside. This balance is upset if the local economy cannot absorb large seasonal surpluses of labor. In this case, the small industries succumb to competition, workers emigrate toward the centers of heavy industry, and the rural *genre de vie* persists in pure form. Sion demonstrated this process in comparing the fate of the rural industries of eastern Normandy, a land of pasturage with limited need of labor, to those of Picardy, a land of sugar beet cultivation where agricultural activity is more intense.[22] Regardless of the importance of these internal forces, how can we explain a mixed *genre de vie* such as that of Vimeu, where the locksmith's trade is based upon the initiative of rural laborers and imported materials, unless we think of the commercial activity that scattered its products as far as Argentina?

At another stage of evolution, economic segregation occurred as a result of complex causes. It is not our purpose to examine the problem of industrial location. Let us note only that the major industrial regions are

[22] Demangeon (*op. cit.*) and Jules Sion, *Les paysans de la Normandie orientale* (Paris: A. Colin, 1909).

served by elaborate networks of communication. Facilities for the supply of raw materials or fuels and the disposal of finished products are prerequisites of their existence.

Creative circulation and urban genres de vie.—Circulation not only develops, transforms, and specializes already existing *genres de vie,* but it also encourages the formation of new ones. The appearance of transportation specialists permits us to speak of the creative role of circulation.

Commerce has played an important role in the livelihood of the pastoral peoples of the arid zone. In Arabia and the Sahara it has provided them with an important source of income. Their *genres de vie* have been drastically altered by modern transformations of commerce, which have caused an almost complete collapse of the caravan trade.

In our culture, groups devoted to circulation are often scattered in the mass of the population, and it is difficult at first sight to recognize the originality of their mode of life. Moreover, they are often concentrated in specific places, e.g., around harbors, railroad stations, and airports. One even finds settlements of several hundred people composed entirely of railroad workers. In such communities, one gains a clearer understanding of the uniqueness of their *genre de vie.*

Let us consider a typical case, that of railroad mechanics or engineers. Dedicated to machinery that never stops, their way of life develops according to a rhythm that isolates them in some sense from other men. They are virtually tied to the machines that they are obliged to operate or service in all kinds of weather. A heavy responsibility rests on them, as on sailors or aviators, for the slightest mishap can endanger their own lives and the lives of the travelers in their charge. They are united by tight bonds to all who participate in one way or another in the maintenance and operation of transportation facilities. Curiously, even the agents of exploitation—those whose occupations have a commercial character but are also regulated by the rhythm of circulation—share this feeling of fraternity. Heavy burdens are imposed on the families of such specialists, and their vocation is often hereditary, as among men of the sea.

Our understanding of the creative power of circulation is still fragmentary. To measure this force, we must consider patterns of urban livelihood. Some towns founded on roads or at crossroads, survive only because of the commercial activity that is encouraged by a dense network of routes. These agglomerations derive little profit from agriculture, and they may not be able to maintain their population by natural growth. Food supplies, industrial materials, and even man power are imported from elsewhere. The period of great urban expansion, initiated by the industrial revolution, has not yet ended, and it has also been a period of improvement in communication, when transportation has mobilized increasing masses of heavy material and growing human crowds. Such is the nature of the intimate connection between circulation and urbanization.

In the eyes of a geographer, towns are more than accidents of the landscape, characterized by continuous occupation of the soil, compactness of buildings, and an extraordinary density of population. These physiognomic traits are the concrete and durable expression of the urban *genre de vie* as opposed to the rural *genre de vie,* although the latter is also dominated by the forces of circulation.[23] We must go beyond the realm of professional or individual specialization, which varies in any case according to the predominance of particular urban functions. Commerce, industry, and administrative activity may be paramount, and give a particular color to the life of entire groups. Above this diversity is a community of interest that defines a global *genre de vie.* The localization of urban functions is conditioned by physical geog-

raphy, but urban life is largely independent of the seasons. Even today, when tourism seems to introduce a kind of rhythm to urban life, the cycle runs counter to that of rural districts. Freed from the dependence on climate, the urban *genre de vie* is more closely tied to a social organization and economic complex. Towns could not survive without these links, because from an economic point of view they are consumers. The simple fact of human concentration demands a co-ordination that is not required when population is dispersed. Finally, participation in a pattern of extended relationships creates the atmosphere for which we have coined the words civility and urbanity. These traits provide a final touch to our description of the relations between circulation and *genres de vie.*

The Concept of Genre de Vie and the Modern World

With the completion of this sketch of urban *genres de vie,* we have moved far away from our point of departure. Indeed, we may wonder whether the same word should be used to designate the behavior of a tribe of shepherds and that of the citizens of a giant city. At the very least, the concept has been transformed while being enlarged. This development is not uncommon in disciplines that cannot have the rigor of mathematics. Our discipline is in a process of evolution, and its vocabulary is constantly being enriched. A critical revision of basic concepts would be useful. In order to proceed on this course, we must return to the two articles of Vidal de la Blache and reiterate the classical conception of *genres de vie.*

The extent and original meaning of the concept.—In its general sense, the expression is applied both to individual behavior, determined by personality, social status, and professional mores, and the habits of groups. The geographer prefers at the outset to restrict its application to groups, and his consideration is thus limited to collective *genres de vie.* Regardless of the changing meanings of the expression, it must al-

[23] For further discussion see Georges Chabot, *Les villes: aperçu de géographie humaine* (Paris: A. Colin, 1948), esp. p. 170.

ways satisfy this fundamental condition; and, as has been stressed from the beginning of this essay, it must also incorporate consideration of the cohesion of its elements. It was not without reason that Vidal qualified the concept by referring to a complex of *cemented* customs—in other words, the permanent traits which the geographer always recognizes as manifestations of *genres de vie*.

It is clear that the expression may be applied to diverse modes of livelihood, all based on direct exploitation of a biotic environment by means of gathering, hunting, animal husbandry, or farming. Vidal de la Blache referred to all of these modes, but for the purpose of his analysis did not utilize the most archaic of them, in spite of the useful information that might have drawn from a study of the activities of such peoples as the Eskimo. Most of the groups who practice hunting or gathering seem to be affected by some kind of evolutionary impediment, and this means that they cannot serve as appropriate examples. The livelihood of pastoralists and farmers inspires more fruitful reflection on this ensemble of "*organized* and *systematic* habits, of ever deepening impression, that are imposed by acquired force on succeeding generations, and provide an orientation for the forces of progress." [24] The last phrase implies both encouragement and limitation of evolution, a problem we have already discussed. If we restrict our attention to the *genres de vie* of pastoral nomads or sedentary farmers, we still possess a wide range of material, without even considering the mixed forms. These categories constitute two extremely rich series, in which specific types are differentiated according to the pressure of the environment, as well as the choice of crops or livestock and the ingenuity of techniques. The most characteristic of these forms have the added advantage of being sharply opposed. It is not extravagant to assert that four centuries ago they not only shared the greatest part

[24] "Les genres de vie . . . ," p. 194 (italics added).

of the continents, but also encompassed the largest segment of humanity.

In their purest forms, these modes of livelihood are complexes of autonomous habits designed to perpetuate the groups that practice them—at least in theory, for they rarely enjoy absolute independence. For example, artisans travel with the wandering tribes of Central Asia, and rural villages in the Sudan have castes of blacksmiths. This is the meaning of self-sufficiency. It also happens that the nomadic shepherd depends to some extent upon the sedentary peoples of the oases. Nevertheless, at various epochs the agricultural colonization of Europe seems to have been accomplished by self-sufficient cells. As autonomous units, these *genres de vie* clearly reflect both the animate and inanimate aspects of their environments. Similarly, one cannot separate the climate, soil, and natural vegetation of the Mediterranean lands from an account of a pattern of land use that may include horticulture, dry farming, irrigation farming, and transhumance. A type of progressive agriculture, developed in central and northern Europe, is linked in our minds with the distribution of loess deposits and alluvium. A *genre de vie* can be defined only with reference to its physical setting. Finally, it represents some degree of stability. These highly evolved forms—the results of efforts that are now crystallized—are products of durability. The first traces of them are of millennial age and they have profited from a progressive enrichment. They have had time to digest the elements that have gradually transformed them, and this explains their durability in vast areas, at least until the time of European expansion overseas. We have already given a more precise indication of the nature of this stability. Such are the essential attributes of the classic *genre de vie*.

Alteration of the concept in the rural framework.—In the tableau of modern rural life in Western Europe, we are no longer able to find the classic forms in all of their rigor. Moreover, new traits have been introduced. In many cases the concept has suffered appreciable alteration. This change is observed in two cases, which are produced by processes that have already been described, that of specialized forms of production and that of mixed modes of livelihood.

Specalization appears in two forms. In the first place, it evolves with the transition from a closed estate or village economy to an open economy. The non-agricultural occupations are gradually eliminated from rural life, and the countryside depends upon imports for the satisfaction of needs other than food supply. Artisans become more and more rare in the villages. In France, this evolution has been accelerated during the last generation or two, but its origins are very old. The other form of specialization is tied to the increasing commercialization of the products of farming or animal husbandry. Exploitation is oriented toward the highest returns, i.e., agricultural activity is more sharply differentiated. Monoculture is a typical expression of this trend, as are certain forms of diversified cultivation that are also designed for maximum yields (e.g., market gardening). In both cases increased productivity is facilitated by rigorous techniques and nearly continuous use of the soil. In these examples, the rural group no longer attempts to satisfy all of its own nutritional requirements. It is compelled to import part of the plant and animal substances that are required for its subsistence. In the wine-producing districts of southern France, the villages have even abandoned their garden belts; vegetables are purchased in Comtat or Rivieral. Until recently the Danish peasant exported his butter and consumed imported margarine. All of this means that two important attributes of the concept of *genre de vie*—autonomy and stability— have been attenuated. As a consequence of its commercialization, rural livelihood has lost its security. But at least in the second case—specialization of production— the relation to the physical environment has become more intimate, since the modes

of exploitation and the species or varieties used are selected for their suitability in a given climate with the aim of obtaining the highest possible yields.

As for the mixed *genres de vie,* in many cases it is quite possible that they were able to find all the raw materials for their activity—bone, wood, ore, textile fibers—in local environments. But their industries had long been accustomed to obtain supplies from the outside. The stability of these mixed forms was tied to a close coordination of the rhythm of agricultural and industrial activity. This solidarity is now threatened by external forces. For example, the cultivation of the beet in Vimeu depends upon all of the fluctuations of the sugar market, and the locksmith's trade is influenced by the trend toward concentration that affects all metallurgical industries. The internal cohesion of the mixed *genres de vie* is threatened. We do not want to say that they must disappear, but they are menaced according to the extent of their dependence on external factors.

In these examples we see that the notion of *genre de vie* tends to be altered even in the midst of the rural world. We can summarize the trend by saying that instead of being defined, as in the past, in terms of an environmental relationship, the concept is now defined in terms of the influence of a socioeconomic complex. The concept is altered with the changing dependencies of men.

Application of the concept outside the rural world.—It is safe to say that the concept can still find a vast field of application, both in its classical form and with the modifications introduced by the notion of mixed *genres de vie.* We think of the great crowds of peasants in Monsoon Asia, and the hundreds of millions of people who depend upon cereal cultivation (wheat, millets, rice). Indigenous forms of agriculture have been contaminated, as in Southeast Asia, by elements of plantation agriculture. We also know that small-scale village industries in the Tonkinese delta offer assistance to the rice-growing peasant. These patterns fit into the frameworks that have already been described. In spite of the great cultural revolution that has upset the ancient foundation of our rural societies, the notion of *genre de vie* can still be applied, if we take the precaution to make a few corrections, in some of the European cantons. The same can be said for the Americas, although new patterns of life were born in the United States with the triumph of mechanization and automation.

Nevertheless, we are less impressed by this persistence than by the increasing number of people who have been able to escape, as a result of the expansion of European civilization, from the domination of *genres de vie* based on exploitation of the soil. The most archaic types—hunting and fishing—are on the way to extinction. In our time, pastoral nomadism has suffered major reverses in the steppes of the Old World. While the production of food is increasing, the proportion of rural population to total population is decreasing among all the Occidental peoples. The absolute strength of the rural population is also waning, in spite of the general demographic growth. Non-agricultural occupations absorb an ever larger share of human activity. By 1939, there were even great countries where agricultural labor was accomplished by a small minority, and industrialization had spread through all layers of society. This change of occupation generally implies the abandonment of soil, and the formation of new groupings and powerful new centers of attraction in which the uprooted peoples are incorporated. The immigrant acquires new habits, or, to put it more concisely, he participates in a new *genre de vie,* for we have no other word to characterize the well organized complex of customs that is peculiar to a human group. We have outlined the formative processes, both for towns and *genres de vie* linked with circulation, and the use of the expression has seemed legitimate. The geographer must now attempt to define *genres de vie* different from those that have held his attention. They are not entirely new, for the expansion of civilization has been expressed for millennia by a flourishing of cities. But in our time urbanization is more highly developed and plays a more prominent role in human destiny.

All cities do not show the wealth and complexity that urban life implies. A workers' settlement near a factory in the open countryside, where the rhythm of life obeys the call of the workshops, a city of railroad workers with a single focus of activity, or a group of miners' dwellings in the neighborhood of a pit in the coal mining districts of northeastern France is perhaps not aptly described as "urban." The mode of life practiced in such settlements is governed exclusively by the requirements of the co-ordinating profession. It is not, however, of the same species as the mixed *genres de vie.* It is well advanced toward what we have described as an urban *genre de vie.* The urban forms also comprise a vast series, diversified by natural conditions—towns that have developed in the middle latitudes do not look like those of the tropics—by size, by dominant occupation, and by geographic function. We are conscious of how easy it would be to describe some varieties. Yet even in an analysis of the urban monsters that are so characteristic of our age, the specialization of certain quarters in the interior of the agglomeration encourages us to examine secondary *genres de vie* and their relation to the standard of living of particular groups and professions, for we must always come back to the profession and its imprint.

Remembering what has been said about circulation, we can summarize, in a few words, the traits of these *genres de vie.* They are no longer autonomous, but depend for their operation on larger areas, which vary in size according to the extent of the agglomeration. They can function only with the help of a double co-ordination: an internal co-ordination among various urban activities, and an external co-ordination between such activities and those of the urban hinterland. In the definition of these secondary *genres de vie,* the physical elements of the geographic complex are less important than purely human elements. Finally, if they have great powers of attraction, they also have great mobility, because a perpetual adaptation to changing circumstances is their law. The history of the past two centuries has been marked by the growth of cities. It remains to be seen whether this development will endure.

The standardization of genres de vie.—We have tried to demonstrate that if its meaning is adjusted to fit the general evolution of our societies, then the geographer can apply the concept with profit in an explanatory description of the modern world. *Genres de vie* are dissolving under our eyes. Others are organizing, expanding, and being imposed on men. It is enough to recognize the latter forms; but sometimes we hesitate. Is this because we are in the midst of the current and cannot distinguish its banks? Or does the acceleration of change in all forms of life, because of the extensive penetration of science, impede the consolidation of habits, feelings, and ideas? Actually, both of these inhibiting factors are effective at the same time. Finally, there is abundant evidence that all of the contrasts, formerly so marked, between human groups that practice different *genres de vie* have been blurred.

Already at the time when Vidal de la Blache wrote, this blurring had been mentioned by European observers of life on the other side of the Atlantic. In his studies of the economic evolution, Erich Zimmermann has often stressed the trend toward standardization in the modern world.[25] In France our generation has been able to make prog-

<hr/>

[25] [See Erich W. Zimmermann, *World Resources and Industries,* revised edition (New York: Harper and Brothers, 1951.]

ress in an old country of marked conservatism. Two series of forces are at work everywhere to reduce differences, although in inequal degree. In the first place, there is the trend toward mechanization and automation that is evident in all domains of creative activity. Manual labor is replaced by the machine, and man becomes an observer. The professional bent has become less appreciable in the *habitus corporis* and even in mental structure. The sentence quoted at the beginning of this essay— "The soul of some peoples seems to be formed of a different metal from that of others"—no longer seems so true. In the second place, there has been an equalization of standards of living, the basic type being the urban level. At the beginning of the industrial revolution, when Robert Peel spoke of the new race of men that was being formed in cities, the comparison was not favorable. After three quarters of a century the situation has changed. In the twentieth century the dietary and clothing habits in rural districts—the habits that define a standard of living—are falling in line with those of the cities. And the rest of the elements of the *genre de vie* follow the general trend. Thus, as if regulated by a pendulum, the movement of life reduces the differences that it creates.

The world seems to be losing some of its wealth and variety, and from our vantage point it seems that man has perhaps also suffered a profound loss. If we look closely, we see that the necessity of adaptation has been transferred from man to technology. In the latter, the geographer rediscovers the variety of local combinations that is the object of his inquiry. If he wishes to continue to use the fruitful concept of *genre de vie,* he must take account of what has been gained and lost.

DERWENT WHITTLESEY

MAJOR AGRICULTURAL
REGIONS OF THE EARTH

THE PROBLEM OF CLASSIFYING
AGRICULTURAL REGIONS

Of all the modes of using land, raising
crops and livestock covers the most space
and is the most easily observed in the field.
It therefore lends itself better than the
others to geographic classification—that is
to say areal analysis and synthesis.

Tillage of the soil and pasturage of animals are postulated on indefinite anticipated continuance of collaboration between
man and the ground, a relation embodied
in the term husbandry. In this respect these
occupations differ from the extractive industries, which take from the earth nature's
bounty with no provision for replenishment,[1] and also from manufacturing, trade,
and the professions, which use the earth
chiefly or solely as a localized site for their
operations. Oddly, the English language has
no term to cover both plant and animal

husbandry. For lack of a more fitting word,
"agriculture" is used in these pages.[2]

A good deal of information about agricultural geography is available. Descriptions of many regions in different parts of
the earth are scattered through the literature of travel, exploration, agriculture, and
anthropology, and there are a few studies
from the viewpoint of modern geography.
For a number of political areas a considerable body of statistics has been collected.
By employing these resources to extend and
check field observations, it should now be
possible for geographers to recognize the
principal agricultural systems of the earth
and to distribute their component regions
on a map. For the present most of this must
be done on a qualitative, empirical basis,
although some regions may be checked by
statistical measurements. Both sorts of
analysis have been made, but of particular
areas only. The widely different standards
taken as bases of recognition and measurement prevent comparison of these sporadic
studies. A prime objective of the classification here presented is to range all agriculture into regions of the same order of magnitude.

There exist, to be sure, worldwide classi-

Reprinted, with permission of the editor, from
*Annals of the Association of American Geogra-
phers,* XXVI (1936), 199–240. During most of
his academic career, Derwent S. Whittlesey (1890–
1956) was professor of geography at Harvard
University, Cambridge, Mass.

[1] The existence of farmed forests, shellfish plantations, and closed seasons on game and fish are
examples of provision for replenishment among
industries usually extractive. Similarly, indulgence
in overgrazing and in "soil mining" is plundering
in a realm customarily agricultural. The shadowy
border between extraction and husbandry illustrates the basic weakness of any definition or
classification—its oversimplification of complex
nature. The fluid merging of regions and types
is replaced by static lines indicating clean cleavage.

[2] Some may feel that it is unfortunate to use
agriculture, literally "field cultivation," to include
pasturage of livestock on natural grassland, but
there is ample precedent for doing so. Recent
dictionaries even extend the term to include forestry, and most national governments place the
supervision of pastoral occupations under the
jurisdiction of their bureaus of "agriculture."

fications of agriculture. Without exception they bear the imprint of climatic regions. So valued a contributor to the geography of agriculture as Engelbrecht could publish in 1930 a map entitled "The Agricultural Zones of the Earth," which merely restates the map of climatic regions in terms of crops, which explicitly quotes Köppen in delimiting "desert realms," and which, as a final obfuscation, distinguishes a type phrased in climatic terms, but actually based on landforms: "Continental Plateau-climate."[3] This map groups regions in which the agricultural systems are utterly unlike. For example the "Subtropical Cotton Zone" is made to include the United States Cotton Belt, northern China, southern Japan, a small district in Queensland, a bit of South Africa comprising both high and low Veld, and a belt in South America reaching from the coast of southern Brazil into the Chaco and embracing part of Uruguay. The boundaries of these and other regions bear no discoverable relation to agricultural boundaries as reported by observers in the field. Engelbrecht and others, by forcing agricultural regions into the alien pattern of climatic distribution, stress the late start of analytic studies of agricultural land occupance as compared with several other aspects of geography.

In the classification here presented regions are recognized and grouped into types on the exclusive basis of the inherent properties of the agriculture practiced. This is analogous to classifications of climate, all of which are founded on inherent characteristics—temperature, moisture, and air currents. It is so obviously sound procedure that it might go without mention but for the surprising fact that classifications of several elements of geography have been repeatedly attempted on a basis of extraneous conditions as well as inherent elements. This has been notably true of soils. It is still true of agriculture, as the classification cited proves.

[3] Hinrich Engelbrecht: "Die Landbauzonen der Erde," *Petermanns Geographische Mitteilungen, Ergänzungsheft*, XLV (1930), 286–97.

In this paper an attempt is made to further comparative study of agricultural regions by ranging on a single map all the agricultural systems of the first degree of magnitude, and to clarify classification by restricting it to properties inherent in the agriculture itself. In addition it undertakes an enquiry into the kinds of data needed for sound and adequate classification of major types of agricultural land occupance. In so far as it succeeds, the *schema* presented may serve as a framework within which further refinements of method and more exact statistical criteria can evolve.

CLASSIFICATION IN GEOGRAPHY

Basic among the scientific functions of geography is the regional distribution of the phenomena with which it deals. Recognition and distribution of the totality of landscape, natural and cultural, is indeed the first step in regional geography. This step has proved as difficult as the first step of an infant, because it involves analysis and synthesis of every element in the landscape, tasks not yet accomplished. It is a simpler undertaking to recognize regional differentiation of each separate element of the geographic landscape. This work stands uncompleted, and its status respecting agricultural regions is the occasion for preparing the classification here presented.

Most of the elements of the natural environment have been analyzed, and the distribution of regional syntheses has been mapped over the whole earth or the better-known parts of it. Although there are disheartening exceptions, these studies disclose a sound trend from empirical, qualitative classification toward statistical, quantitative classification. Recognizing regions and grouping them into types on a basis exclusively empirical and qualitative has at least two weaknesses. The procedure is based largely on personal judgment, a fruitful source of disagreement. It lacks objective elements out of which comparable studies of different regions may be built by independent workers. These crippling handicaps are eliminated by substituting for personal judgments, measurable criteria. These are the product of repeated observations in the field. In some cases they can be compiled into statistical form; in all cases they are expressed in uniform, standard terms. Thus personal judgments are tested and chastened by measured quantities.

Quantitative classification of climate has advanced further than that of any other element of the natural environment, thanks to the abundant data furnished by the weather bureaus of modern nations. The widely accepted scheme of Köppen is an excellent example. Tested in the field, this classification has required modification, but the refinements are based on measured data.[4] The other elements of the natural environment lag behind climate, but promising beginnings have been made. Landform types have been synthesized in such regional subdivisions as that worked out for the United States by a committee of the Association of American Geographers. The measuring of relative relief [5] is a tentative but perhaps a long step toward quantitative classification. Soils classifications combine qualitative and quantitative ingredients. The most recent and comprehensive is that of the United States Bureau of Soils.[6] Somewhat more tentative, and restricted to lesser areas, are regional distributions of surface waters, ground water, and minerals.

Plant ecologists have served geographers a good turn by distributing the major groups of plant associations. The regional allocation of animals is less advanced, particularly in respect to insects, the animal life most significant to geography of the present day. Herbertson was a pioneer in essaying a classification of the natural environment as a whole. His map bears an embarrassing resemblance to a map of climatic regions.[7] Possibly a more successful classification of "natural regions" can be made when all the elements on which it must rest have been more exactly distributed than is now the case.

Compared to the regional classification of elements of the natural environment, analysis of the cultural elements in geography is in its infancy. Human geography is less advanced than physical geography, and in its less easily observed aspects, such as social landscapes, has scarcely been broached, much less classified. In large measure regional classification of political and social landscapes lies in the future. For certain modes of economic occupance it has already been essayed. In no aspect of economic life do existing data permit earthwide classification on a statistical basis. Quantitative studies have perforce been confined to regions where government censuses afford the needed accumulation of information, or to very small districts worked single-handed in the field by individual geographers.

ANTECEDENTS OF THE
PRESENT CLASSIFICATION

Among the great groups of economic occupations, the regional distribution of agricultural land occupance has been carried furthest. The analysis of land use, and its corollary, the synthesis of agricultural regions, are rooted in an interest in commodities of commerce. In this study British

[4] V. Köppen, "Klassifikation der Klimate nach Temperatur, Niederschlag und Jahreslauf," *Petermanns Geographische Mitteilungen,* LXIV (1918), 193–203, 243–48. Revised in V. Köppen and R. Geiger, *Klimakarte der Erde,* 1:20,000,000 (Gotha: Perthes, 1928). C. Warren Thornthwaite, "The Climates of North America," *Geographical Review,* XXI (1931), 633–55, and subsequent revisions by this and other authors.
[5] N. M. Fenneman *et al,* "Physiographic Regions of the United States," *Annals of the Association of American Geographers,* XVIII (1928), 261–353; Guy-Harold Smith, "The Relative Relief of Ohio," *Geographical Review,* XXV (1935), 272–84.
[6] C. F. Marbut, *Atlas of American Agriculture: Part III, Soils Regions of the United States* (Washington, D.C.: U.S. Dept. of Agriculture, 1935).
[7] A. J. Herbertson, *Natural Regions of the Earth* (Wall Map) (Oxford: Clarendon Press, 1912).

geographers naturally[8] took the lead, and the work of Chisholm[9] may be singled out because of its wide influence. A little later German geographers began the attack on the regional distribution of agricultural zones, analogous to climatic zones.[10] In these two streams of thought may be discerned, somewhat obscurely, germs of the later classifications in which types of agricultural land occupance and the regional distribution thereof are recognized.

Until recently the British approach was dominant in the United States. The single most influential American work, while rounding out discussions of commodities, adhered to those commercially pre-eminent.[11] The first long step forward was the publication by the United States Department of Agriculture of an atlas which distributed on maps the principal plant and animal elements of commercial agriculture.[12] In this work the areal spread is introduced, and intensities of production are shown by means of dots. Whether wittingly or not, these concepts derive in part from German sources. This atlas, the first worldwide distribution of agricultural phenomena based on statistics, inevitably omitted production in areas where statistics had never

been compiled. This threw it out of balance as a complete study of agricultural crops and livestock, a fact which occasioned no disturbance in the English-speaking world, where commercial crops dominated the study of agricultural geography.

Following the atlas, the Department of Agriculture confined its attention to the United States, but evolved a quantitative classification of the agricultural regions within that vast and diverse area. In establishing agricultural regions, as distinct from commodity-production regions, the sea-change which British commercial geography had suffered in crossing to America became apparent. The interest in the United States had insensibly shifted to economic geography, i.e., from preoccupation with the commodities of commerce to recognition of all commodities. This marks the final step in synthesizing the elements analyzed in the atlas.[13] It should be noted, however, that the elements involved are the associated crops and livestock within each region. These are the items most readily subjected to statistical control; they are not the whole of agriculture.[14]

In 1924 Sapper revived Hahn's approach by directing attention to the significance of agriculture not commercial, but vital for the sustenance of large populations.[15] Just

[8] "Naturally," because of the preoccupation of Great Britain with commerce which culminated in the free-trade century in which the pioneers worked. Cf. Derwent Whittlesey, "Environment and the Student of Human Geography," *Scientific Monthly*, XXXV (1932), 265–67.

[9] George G. Chisholm, *Handbook of Commercial Geography* (London: Longmans Green, 1889, and numerous subsequent editions).

[10] Eduard Hahn, "Die Wirtschaftsformen der Erde," *Petermanns Geographische Mitteilungen*, XXXVIII (1892), 8–12, and map of "Die Kulturformen der Erde." Hinrich Engelbrecht, *Die Landbauzonen der aussertropischen Länder* (2 vols. and atlas; Berlin, 1899), *idem, Die Feldfrüchte Indiens in ihrer geographischen Verbreitung* (Hamburg: Friederichsen, 1914). This work, based on the census of India, influenced the classification presented in this paper as much as any single publication.

[11] J. Russell Smith, *Industrial and Commercial Geography* (New York: Holt, 1913).

[12] V. C. Finch and O. E. Baker, *Geography of the World's Agriculture* (Washington, D.C.: Government Printing Office, 1917).

[13] O. E. Baker, "A Graphic Summary of American Agriculture Based Largely on the Census," *U.S. Department of Agriculture, Yearbook, 1921*. The same, with data for 1930, *U.S. Dept. of Agriculture Miscellaneous Publicaton No. 105* (Washington, D.C.: Government Printing Office, 1922 and 1931, respectively). *Idem*, "Agricultural Regions of North America," *Economic Geography*, II (1926), 459, and subsequent issues. *Idem, Type-of-Farming Areas in the United States, 1930* (U.S. Bureau of the Census in co-operation with the Bureau of Agricultural Economics: U.S. Government Printing Office, 1933). The accompanying text is by Elliott F. Foster.

[14] See Foster, *op. cit.*, pp. 71–75 for statement of the basis of the classification. Baker recognizes other aspects of the rural scene in his "Agricultural Regions of North America," but does not analyze them.

[15] Karl Sapper, *Allgemeine Wirtschafts- und Verkehrsgeographie* (Leipzig and Berlin: Teubner, 1924).

as the study of commodities eventuated in maps of the distribution of stock and crop associations, so the German interest in agricultural (pseudoclimatic) zones produced maps of world distributions dealing with several aspects of agricultural life. The most significant of these distributes methods of production—plow culture, hoe culture, horticulture, and so on.[16]

Before the American workers had refined their classification beyond the first "Graphic Summary" (mentioned above) the classification proffered in this paper was well under way. It derives from fifteen years of collaboration between the author and Wellington D. Jones. By 1926 a crude world map of agricultural regions had been drawn and brief sketches of the several types recognized had been written. In January, 1931, photostat copies of their world map were issued; in 1932 a revised map was published.[17] In 1934 the author issued in mimeographed form a textual commentary on the agricultural types. The map published herewith is a revision of the preliminary work. The text is new. For both the author assumes full responsibility, while pointing out the large share of W. D. Jones in whatever merit the classification has.

Since the appearance of the preliminary studies by Jones and Whittlesey, others have made important contributions to an understanding of the character and distribution of agricultural types, and toward a world classification of agricultural areas. Among these, two cartographic studies have refined the definition of types and the delineation of regions in areas where statistics are available. The map, "Type-of-Farming Areas in the United States" (see note 13) recognizes more than 800 agricultural districts, differentiated almost wholly by items in the stock and crop association. This wealth of detail far exceeds available knowledge for other parts of the earth. Therefore any balanced world map of agricultural regions made at this time can use the information only in generalized form. Richard Hartshorne and Samuel N. Dicken's "A Classification of the Agricultural Regions of Europe and North America on a Uniform Statistical Basis"[18] recognizes eight types in the two continents named. Their work, like that of Jones and Whittlesey, proceeds along lines laid down by Wellington D. Jones in his "Ratios and Isopleth Maps in Regional Investigation of Agricultural Land Occupance."[19] It marks an advance in applying uniform statistical criteria to the areas analyzed. Like the Foster map, its statistical base is confined to aspects of the crop and livestock association.

Three German works based upon careful cartographic distributions deserve mention in this connection. They do not, however, display the close statistical argument which is apparent in the studies by Americans. Indeed, that would scarcely be possible, since they were published before the authors could have seen Jones's "Ratios and Isopleth Maps." One of these studies covers Europe, another Argentina, the third South Africa.[20]

The most comprehensive presentation of agricultural geography ever made is the series of articles which have been appearing in nearly every number of the periodical *Economic Geography*, beginning with volume II (1926).[21] In these studies each

[16] *Ibid,* p. 133.

[17] Respectively these were entitled as follows: W. D. Jones and D. S. Whittlesey, "Types of Agricultural Land Occupance," preliminary draft, Jan., 1931, on Goode's Homolosine Equal Area Projection. *Idem,* "Types of Agricultural Land Occupance," Fig. B in "Syllabus for Geography 102" (University of Chicago). The text of this syllabus and the remaining maps are the work of W. D. Jones.

[18] *Annals of the Association of American Geographers,* XXV (1935), 99–120.

[19] *Ibid,* XX (1930), 177–95.

[20] Carl Troll, "Die Landbauzonen Europas in ihrer Beziehung zur natürlichen Vegetation," *Geographische Zeitschrift,* XXXI (1925), 265–68. Franz Kühn, "Eine neue Wirtschaftskarte von Argentinien," *Petermanns Geographische Mitteilungen,* LXXIII (1927), 65–69. Joachim H. Schultze, "Eine neue Wirtschaftskarte von Südafrika," *ibid,* LXXVII (1931), 22–23.

[21] The authors engaged in this project are: O. E. Baker (North America), Clarence F. Jones (South

continent is divided into agricultural regions. Numerous maps of production, based on statistics, as well as maps delineating the synthesized regions, have been valuable in checking boundaries of the world map herewith presented, particularly where statistics are wanting. The information presented in this notable series has done much to confirm the subdivision into thirteen major agricultural types (Fig. 1), made by Jones and Whittlesey, which has remained unchanged since the original map was drawn in the very year the first of the *Economic Geography* articles appeared. The series does not in itself constitute a uniform classification of agricultural regions, partly because of the varied authorship, and partly because of advancing comprehension of the subject during the decade in which the articles have been coming out.

Covering a narrower field and adopting a more restricted viewpoint, the symposium on pioneer settlement published by the American Geographical Society contains the only, or the most recent, information about many frontier agricultural regions.[22]

Besides the publications cited many of the numerous treatises on agriculture contain valuable geography. Books and articles treating the regional geography of particular areas in which agriculture is one mode of land occupance are also valuable; the more important the agriculture of the region, the larger it looms in the regional handling. Both these sources have furnished many facts incorporated in the classification here presented.

More than half of volume L of the *Geographisches Jahrbuch* is devoted to a critical bibliography of economic geography.[23]

Two thousand and forty-five titles are listed, a large proportion of them on agriculture. The annual volumes of the *Bibliographie Géographique* furnish more nearly complete coverage of French and English works, as the *Jahrbuch* does of German and Scandinavian. Some unpublished doctoral dissertations are noted in the *Jahrbuch*. There is a bibliography of dissertations, published and unpublished, submitted in universities in the United States.[24] Several of the titles deal more or less exclusively with agricultural geography.

In view of the overwhelming flood of books and papers on the subject and the bibliographical aids mentioned, no attempt is here made to append a comprehensive bibliography. In the foregoing discussion of the classification, reference has been made to titles which have had direct bearing. Appended to the brief characterization of each type of agriculture which follows are lists of papers which illustrate that mode of land occupance and describe varied practices in the different component regions. Some of these studies have agricultural geography as their theme; others are regional investigations of areas in which agriculture monopolizes the scene. In selecting the titles, two groups with some claim to admission have been excluded. (1) Those which stress a viewpoint other than agricultural occupance of the land—matters such as settlement forms, habitat, historical evolution, prediction. (2) Those which confine their treatment to commercial products. An exception is made in favor of plantation crops and specialized horticulture, wherever in these two agricultural systems the individual crops embody the whole agricultural geography of the small districts which they occupy. In agricultural systems having diversity of output, to focus the attention on commercial crops masks the reality of agricultural geography be-

---

America), Olof Jonasson (Europe), Samuel Van Valkenburg (South Asia and archipelagoes), George B. Cressey (China), Robert B. Hall (Japan), Griffith Taylor (Australia), H. L. Shantz (Africa).

[22] *Pioneer Settlement: American Geographical Society Special Publication No. 14* (New York, 1932).

[23] Rudolf Lütgens, "Wirtschaftsgeographie einschliesslich Verkehrsgeographie (1908–34)," *Geographisches Jahrbuch,* L (1935), 135–318.

[24] "Dissertations in Geography Accepted by Universities in the United States for the Degree of Ph.D. as of May, 1935," *Annals of the Association of American Geographers,* XXV (1935), 211–37.

neath the pseudomorph of agricultural economics.

In compiling these lists the principal geographic periodicals have been combed. Several of them yielded no items. North American publications are more fruitful than those from other parts of the world. This is not surprising, because the trend of thought in the United States has followed agriculture more tenaciously than in other lands. If the number of articles published may be taken as an index of interest, there was only sporadic attention to agriculture during the early 1920's, followed by growing absorption up to the latest date. Before 1919 so few articles appeared that no systematic search for them has been made. That postwar date may stand to mark the awakening of interest in human geography which has made possible the classification discussed in the following pages.

FORCES AND ELEMENTS IN THE CLASSIFICATION

No world-wide classification of agricultural land occupance made today can be more than an essay—a target for criticism. The one here presented attempts to recognize agricultural regions of the first order of magnitude. Therefore it inevitably lumps regions which differ in details of their agricultural pattern, structure, and procedures. For the purpose of earth-wide survey, these differences are believed to *be* details. If desired, each major agricultural region can be subdivided into lesser units on the basis of these differences. That is an intended refinement envisioned within the frame here outlined.

Classification is a device for correlating facts in such a way as to bring them into focus from a particular viewpoint. An ideal geographic classification might well begin with arranging the facts into a regional pattern. Within each region, its structure is built up of observable items in the landscape.[25] Not all the landscape forms are

used. Only those are selected which disclose the collaboration of man and environment in agriculture.

In this classification of the geographic aspects of agriculture, the regional pattern is basically determined by two concurrent forces. One of these is the combination of environmental conditions which sets the limits of range for any crop or domestic animal and provides, within those limits, optimum habitats. The pertinent elements of the natural environment are climate, soil, and slope. (It is assumed that drainage and exposure are concomitants of the three dominant elements, and that altitude expresses itself in climate.) The other force is the combination of human circumstance which applies the habitat possibilities of plants and animals to human needs. The chief elements of the cultural circumstance are density of population, stage of technology, and inherited tradition. (Here again an assumption is made—that standard of living, fashion, and regulation by law are concomitants of the dominant elements.)

Climatic classifications have figured so crucially in the evolution of agricultural classifications that the areal correspondence of the two calls for particular consideration. Climate directly affects the number and character of plants that can be grown and the distribution of mature soils. From the map (Fig. 1) three groups of agricultural regions are seen to conform roughly to the climatic mold—dryland types, wetland types of the low latitudes, and wetland types of the middle latitudes. The most extreme climates—driest deserts, coldest high latitudes and altitudes—forbid agriculture. The more extensive areas thus handicapped are shown on the map, Figure 1. Climate somewhat less adverse, if coupled with other handicaps, such as infertile soil, ruggedness, slow drainage, or excessive exposure, creates unfarmable spots, most of

[25] By "observable items" is meant all those which are susceptible of being observed directly and also through some device, such as an instrument or a calculation based on enumeration. They are incomplete unless they include diurnal, seasonal, and cyclic variations.

which are too small to be mapped on the scale of Figure 1.

Almost as obvious as the broad resemblance between maps of climate and agriculture, are the marked discrepancies. Dry interior Asia-Africa has not the same agricultural system as dry interior Americas and Australia. The types covering wide acreage in the humid middle latitudes of the northern hemisphere are not extensively spread in the southern. Most conspicuous of all, the agriculture of eastern and southern Asia, notably China and India, does not parallel counterpart climates in the other continents. Differences spreading over such broad areas can not be attributed to variations in soil or slope, which are minuscule in comparison. They do correspond to what may be loosely defined as Occidental versus Oriental society and progressive versus backward cultures. Some of them correspond also to marked contrasts in density of population.

The major variables in differentiating regions of agricultural land occupance may be summarized, without regard to order of importance, as climate, soil, slope, density of population, stage of technology, and tradition. Their interaction produces the forms of the cultural landscape which facilitate and at the same time express its functioning.

The functioning forms which appear to dominate every type of agriculture may be listed under five heads:

1. The crop and livestock association.
2. The methods used to grow the crops and produce the stock.
3. The intensity of application to the land of labor, capital, and organization, and the outturn of product which results.
4. The disposal of the products for consumption (i.e., whether used for subsistence on the farm or sold off for cash or other goods).
5. The ensemble of structures used to house and facilitate the farming operations.

Each of these five items is susceptible of measurement, and therefore may ultimately be used in a quantitative classification of agricultural regions and types of land occupance. As yet the data on most regions are insufficient in one particular or another, and for large areas any sort of statistics is lacking. At present a classification based on these five criteria seems sound. Increasing information about farming ought to prove or disprove their validity.

Every crop and livestock association appears to have its ultimate range fixed by climate. Within these limits certain areas are ruled out by unfavorable soil, drainage, or exposure. Optimum natural conditions cover only a part of the total possible range.[26] Until recent centuries many plants and animals were restricted to the continent or subcontinent of their origin. Since Chinese, Polynesians, Arabs, and Europeans began to transfer useful species from one realm to another, too little time has elapsed for general adoption of the novelties, although all are now found in appropriate environments in every continent. That optimum growing conditions and the dominance of particular species do not correspond is due to the momentum of traditional competitors and the inertia of farmers, everywhere a conservative class. The producer, reluctant to try a novel crop or breed of stock, is only expressing the age-old remoteness which so long kept him in ignorance of other regions having natural conditions similar to his own but different flora and fauna. Some plants and animals may be raised in regions below optimum as to natural environment, but well disposed to economic profit by virtue of location near market, or by adherence to a favoring political unit. Conversely some are grown in only a small part of their optimum range, because no market exists for larger production.

When the crop and livestock associations of all the agricultural regions are appraised, they appear to fall into four great groups:

[26] For a succinct discussion of climatic limits and optima see Ellsworth Huntington and Frank E. Williams, *Business Geography* (New York: Wiley, 1926), pp. 15–31. Huntington has done much work on this subject, which is touched upon in several of his books.

1. Dominant animal rearing in regions too arid, rugged, or remote for successful crop raising.
2. Dominant production of crops, with animals minor or absent, but with crops varied because of a growing season never checked by cold.
3. Dominant production of crops, with animals minor, and with the number of crops strictly limited either by natural environment or by market.
4. Roughly equal production of crops and animals.

For use this classification is too coarse-meshed. It would throw together such different agricultural groups as the Kirghiz of Central Asia and the Argentine ranches; or the Yorubas of Nigeria with the Cantonese and the Imperial Valley farmers. These comparisons suggest that the methods of production can sharply differentiate regions which have essentially the same crop and livestock association. Tillage may be accomplished by means of elaborate machines, by hand labor using efficient tools, and by hand labor limited to sticks and other crude implements. Cows may be milked by machines or by the calves. The amount of care used in selecting seeds and improving breeds is of comparable importance.

The essential thing about successful method is that it shall be organized to fit the circumstances. It must take account of the relative abundance of land, labor, and capital. Since land is the one factor in farming which can not be markedly varied, the best method is the one which uses the available land most wisely. For example, it has been found that in regions where sparse population makes large machinery a necessity for grain farming, market gardens should be operated mainly with hand tools.

Closely associated with methods, but not strictly parallel, is the intensiveness with which the land is worked, and the outturn of products. The application of fertilizer improves different soils in differing degrees, and is subject to diminishing returns on any given soil. Output can also be increased by increasing the application of labor, but with diminishing returns once optimum tilth is achieved. Most Americans take for granted that outturn rises in direct ratio to the amount of high-grade machinery employed. This is true only where the proportion of labor to land is low. A small number of men can work more land with machines than with hand tools—in some operations many times as much. But if abundant labor is available and land scarce, a higher outturn per acre of most crops or animals can be obtained by using well-made hand tools, than by the best machinery. Intensiveness of application and quantity of return points to a fundamental cleavage between (1) the occidental world which uses machinery, (2) the oriental world which uses much hand labor and obtains high outturn, and (3) backward regions such as interior Asia and much of Africa, where hand tools, often crude, produce small return.

One more primary conditioning element in the agricultural system must be taken into consideration: the destination of the farm products. They may be consumed on the farm by the household, or they may be sold off the place in exchange for other goods or for cash. No farming region lives wholly without exchange of surplus, but the percentage of goods exchanged in the total produced ranges from almost nothing to very nearly everything. The critical difference is the intention of the farmer. If he grows his crops or raises his animals with the object of selling, he is a commercial farmer; if he merely sells what he happens to have left over, or what he is forced to part with by emergencies, he is a subsistence farmer. This distinction more or less parallels the division between the progressive agriculture initiated by Western Europeans and their descendants and imitators, and peoples lightly or not at all touched by the occidental mode of life. Many districts within these vast tracts of subsistence agriculture have been made to produce cash products, especially plantation crops, and so belong with the Europeanized world in respect to this item in the classification scheme.

The four heads of the classification thus far discussed are subject to statistical determination in regions where agricultural censuses and trade figures are collected. It would be desirable to establish statistical norms for each of these major conditioning elements of the world's agriculture. Complete statistics are lacking, but even if they were available, it would be hazardous to entrust the geographic welfare to them. Statistics often mask landscape differences which are fundamental and critical, and as often imply distinctions which have little or no geographic validity when checked on the ground. For example, Baker differentiates between a Corn Belt and a Corn and Winter Wheat Belt, in central United States.[27] This distinction Hartshorne and Dicken denounce: "Since the only elements which the different parts of [the Corn and Winter Wheat Belt] have in common are also found in the . . . Corn Belt, no logical reason is seen for separating them."[28] Then, on a basis of ratios between tilled crops and hay-and-pasture, these authors lump in a single agricultural region the more fertile half of Denmark and the wheatlands of Old Castile, while differentiating the Massif Central of France. According to the statistical basis they have ordained, their regions are doubtless correctly drawn, but their reliance on statistics entraps them into a failure to differentiate between dairy and mixed farming, while distinguishing between maize and small grains, a cleavage of a lesser order of magnitude. This astonishing departure from geographic reality does not invalidate the use of statistics, but it does point the need to provide for checking in the field. Provision should be made for a procedure which will impose choice of the most significant statistical ratios. It is chimerical to assume

[27] O. E. Baker, "Agricultural Regions of North America," pp. 447–65; *idem, Graphic Summary of American Agriculture*, p. 4.
[28] Richard Hartshorne and Samuel N. Dicken, "A Classification of the Agricultural Regions of Europe and North America on a Uniform Statistical Basis," *Annals of the Association of American Geographers*, XXV (1935), 99–120, ref. to 106.

that statistics can safely be used to displace the practiced eye of the field observer. Sound craft will employ both.

Quantitative field sampling of typical and critical districts provides one useful field check. This is nothing else than the "microscopic geography" which has been assailed by critics who prefer to perform their field labor in automobile seats. The common parlance of the countryside is a trustworthy guide; the local people generally designate their business by a name which is the touchstone of its significance. Another check is set up under the fifth head of the functioning forms of agricultural land occupance: the ensemble of structures used to house and facilitate farming operations. No experienced field geographer could mistake the layout of a dairy farmstead for that of a mixed farm, nor could he observe persistent differences in farm buildings between the American Corn Belt and the adjacent "Corn and Winter Wheat Belt." In some places the individuality of a farming region is so characterful that accurate outlines of it can be drawn from field observation without statistics; e.g., a district of plantation crop tillage in the midst of subsistence agriculture.

Statistics are useful adjuncts to the study of geography. They cannot be substituted for field study, because the areal reality which exists may not be accurately portrayed by statistical representations of it. In spite of the apparent reliance of the field observer on that unreliable quality, personal judgment, experience proves that observers who have agreed upon the items to be noted can classify farmstead types with almost complete accord. This is an important discovery, since the ensemble of structures used in farming operations constitute functioning forms of agricultural land occupance illuminating to the student and yet beyond the reach of statistics usually collected.

THE CLASSIFICATION

At the present time, before agricultural types have become crystallized on the basis of studies of one or two continents, or according to statistical formulas which leave out of account one or another basic item, it seems worthwhile to attempt a subdivision of the whole earth into agricultural regions and to group them into major types. The classification is largely empirical and qualitative, but it is based uniformly on the five criteria listed above. Wherever possible, statistics are used to analyze more sharply the elements of the classification, and available field reports are employed as a check on the statistics. The field studies of the author and of W. D. Jones between them embrace every continent except Australia, and have played a dominant role in working out the classification.

Thirteen types of agricultural occupance of the land are recognized, to which may be added a fourteenth head—land totally unused for agriculture. These are believed to comprise the major systems in vogue on the earth today. This is not the place for detailed consideration of the several regions which are allotted to each type. The classification itself is the topic under consideration.

The map (Fig. 1) distributes the thirteen types over the earth's surface. No map can give the total concept of reality, and the smaller its scale the less exact the picture. In using this small-scale world map of agricultural regions it must be clearly borne in mind that every region contains areas devoted wholly or in part to other occupations. This is obviously true of cities and towns, which, however, occupy little space. In contrast, forests are widespread, and in some large areas occupy more of the ground than does agriculture. The wooded mountain country between San Francisco Bay and the outlet of Puget Sound is a case in point. This map makes no attempt to portray the intensity of agricultural use. Areas of low productivity are grouped with districts of high productivity. Interspersion of widely different intensities is typical; e.g., rugged hill and mountain country, where small valleys and basins generally dominate

the farming of the whole. In contrast, small oases scattered about deserts and semiarid lands are not shown because they do not dominate their surroundings. Intensities can readily be worked out for regions covered by appropriate statistics, by applying the isopleth method in the requisite detail. Examples may be found in the work of O. E. Baker, and more particularly in the maps and discussions of dairying in the United States by Wellington D. Jones and by Richard Hartshorne.[29] Intensities, like all other quantitative studies, are important, but they can perhaps be more intelligently fitted in after geographers have come to tentative agreement as to what are the major types of agricultural land occupance.

NOMADIC HERDING

The vast spaces of the earth too dry to produce crops, yet not utterly barren deserts, are utilized for rearing livestock. Methods are much the same the world over, but intensiveness, care in breeding, and consequent outturn differ widely. This difference is related without exception to the disposal. Where the animals or their products are sold, methods are progressive; where products provide subsistence only, methods are backward. This contrast is expressed in the two terms livestock ranching and nomadic herding (Fig. 1).

Nomadic herding might be called the aboriginal form of the livestock business. Its climatic range runs the gamut, if the Lapp and Eskimo herders of reindeer are included. No landform excludes itself from the migrations of the nomads, and in many cases the seasonal range of climate at differ-

[29] W. D. Jones, "Ratios and Isopleth Maps in Regional Investigation of Agricultural Land Occupance," *Annals of the Association of American Geographers*, XX (1930), 177–95, ref. to Figs. 6, 7, 8. Richard Hartshorne, "A New Map of the Dairy Areas of the United States," *Economic Geography*, XI (1935), 347–55. European geographers appear to have discussed intensities without having mapped them. Cf. P. H. Schmidt, "Intensitätszonen des Landbaus [of Europe only]," *Geographische Zeitschrift*, XXXIII (1927), 34–38.

ent altitudes figures prominently in tribal itineraries. Two elements of the natural environment fix the length of stay in a place and determine the direction of migration: the amount and quality of drinking water and of forage (natural grassland). Of these the water is generally decisive, because it is the scarcer.

This simple agricultural existence is intimately dependent on the natural environment and subject to dire misfortunes brought on by the unreliability of rainfall in dry regions. It evolved in the Eurasian-African land mass, where all the domestic animals except the llama were first put to man's use. The stock which supports the agricultural system may be sheep, cattle, goats, or even camels or reindeer. Along with them a few work animals are kept—horses, asses, camels, or reindeer—to aid in herding, in roundups, and in moving camp. The animals provide nearly everything their owners have. Diet is based on milk, clothing and shelter on skins or on cloth woven from animal hair, utensils and implements are of skin, bone, or horn, if possible. Paraphernalia is reduced to the minimum by the necessity of frequent moving days. The habitation is a tent, a cave, or a snow hut, easily transported or replaced. The temporary settlements are widely scattered, and at unfavorable seasons vast areas are evacuated.

Nomads include physical types of great variety, but all alike cohere into tribal groups based on the family, and not on territory. Religious beliefs differ, but monotheism is widespread. Its principal form is Islam, born and bred in the heart of the nomadic country, and eminently suited to the spiritual needs of its people.

Nomadic herding regions are being encroached upon by livestock ranching, the commercial double of nomadism. In South Africa considerable land has been occupied by Europeans, and a little on the East African highland. In Soviet Russia the government aims to settle the nomads upon fixed centers, either collective or state stock

ranches. Some reindeer meat and hides are sold from Alaska and Lappland.[30]

LIVESTOCK RANCHING

Livestock ranching everywhere has been instituted by sedentary folk of European descent who have settled in dry country. They have taken with them habits, attitudes, and beliefs of humid regions, and with few and temporary exceptions, they have kept in contact with the outside world. Many of their inherited ways of life have become modified in the harsh and unsympathetic environment of their adopted lands. In extreme cases, as the Boers of South Africa, the pioneers had to turn nomadic, but succeeding generations were generally able to live a life more nearly in accord with their humid-country traditions. This is largely owing to the improved transportation of the past 150 years, which has brought the livestock ranching regions progressively closer to the outside world—their market and their supply store.

Ranching postdates the discoveries of the New World by Europeans, because until cattle, sheep, goats, and horses were introduced to America and Australia-New Zealand, the basic elements of the business were lacking in the new continents. In the Americas some imported animals, turned

[30] No reliable statistics exist for nomadic herding regions. In addition to the appropriate sections of the series "Agricultural Regions" in *Economic Geography*, further details of the agricultural life may be found in the following articles: Wellington D. Jones and Derwent Whittlesey, "Nomadic Herding Regions," *Economic Geography*, VIII (1932), 378–85; C. Daryll Forde, "The Habitat and Economy of the Northern Arabian Bedouin," *Geography*, XVIII (1933), 205–19; Gordon P. Merriam, "The Regional Geography of Anatolia," *Economic Geography*, II (1926), 86–95, 101–5; John Frödin, "Quelques traits de l'habitat pastoral de la Turquie du nord," *Geografiska Annaler*, XIV (1932), 229–42; E. Dardel, "Une région Malgache: le Boina," *Annales de Géographie*, XXXVII (1928), 527–83; K. B. Wiklund, "The Lapps in Sweden," *Geographical Review*, XIII (1923), 223–42; J. W. Hoover, "Navajo Nomadism," *Geographical Review*, XXI (1931), 429–45.

loose, became progenitors of a half-wild race. The Indians promptly caught them and spontaneously became nomadic herders as an advance over their traditional practice of collecting what they could from the natural environment. This system was extirpated, along with the plains Indians, when a world market for wool, hides, and meat developed. This market is the creature of the Industrial Revolution and the consequent rise of cities full of people who raise no animal products for themselves. The regions of the new continents akin in natural environment to the nomadic herding regions of the Old World are remote, but they have been tied to these growing city populations by instruments of the Industrial Revolution itself—the steamship and the railroad, the telegraph, and the refrigerator.

The livestock ranch is semi-sedentary. The ranch house forms a permanent center, where a good deal of capital is fixed in the shape of dipping vats, shearing sheds, and paddocks—facilities calculated to maintain the high quality of the products and to expedite their shipment. Usually the ranch is fenced, a refinement over the pioneer days of the open range. Some land may be tilled to raise forage for winter feeding in cool regions, or against the day of drouth. Wells or ponds distributed over the ranch supply the herds with water, which usually outlasts the forage. Ordinary movements of the herds are confined to the ranch, although in mountainous regions transhumance follows the seasons to remote pastures—often rented. During years of extreme drouth enforced nomadism drives stock from ruined grazing lands to less afflicted pastures. In all these movements "cowboys" attached to the ranch move with the herds, but at roundup and occasionally at other times they live briefly at the ranch house.

Great care is taken to improve the breed, and the rancher is a business operator on a large scale. Each region tends to specialize on the animal and the product for which it is best fitted. This is in line with the technical proficiency of the business.

Although all the leading ranching regions are in the new continents, inroads are being made on nomadic herding regions wherever railroads have tapped them. Stimulated by outside markets, European methods or settlers are intruding themselves, notably in Russian Turkestan, in the Atlas Mountains, and in the East and South African highlands.

Statistics are available for the chief livestock ranching regions. In the stock and crop association the ratio of browsing animals—cattle, sheep, goats—to total area is very low, and the ratio of cropland—mostly hay—to the total area is even lower. The percentage of draft animal units in the total animal population is likewise very low. Careful methods result in a high return per animal. The land is used extensively, since it requires several acres to feed an animal. This means huge holdings and a small and scattered farm population. Isolation urges absentee ownership; some holdings are organized as stock companies.

Livestock ranching is likely to be the mode of occupying an expanding frontier. The number of both people and animals just beyond the settlement may be negligible. This is notably the case in the southern part of the Amazon Basin, and scarcely less so in interior Australia.[31]

In summary comparison of the two types of agricultural occupance based on livestock and occupying the drylands of the earth, contrasts appear. One is a subsistence business, the other commercial. This

[31] This and each succeeding list of illustrative material is assumed to be an addition to the appropriate installments of the "Types of Agriculture" series in *Economic Geography:* William T. Chambers, "Edwards Plateau: A Combination Ranching Region," *Economic Geography*, VIII (1932), 67–80; Ralph H. Brown, "Belle Fourche Valleys and Uplands," *Annals of the Association of American Geographers*, XXIII (1933), 128–56; Leslie Hewes, "Huepac: An Agricultural Village of Sonora, Mexico," *Economic Geography*, XI (1935), 284–92; L. H. Halverson, "The Great Karoo of South Africa," *Journal of Geography*, XXIX (1930), 287–300.

results in a different cultural landscape and a widely divergent return for effort. It is a neat example of the utilization of essentially the same natural landscape in contrasting ways, the distinction being based on different stages of technology.

SHIFTING CULTIVATION

Within the humid low latitudes another pair of agricultural types may be recognized. Their character and regional distribution are less clean-cut, because the climate and interrelated vegetation and soils range from rain forest on laterite to park-savanna on friable soil, and from oceanic deltas to mountain basins at 14,000 feet elevation. Besides, there are large areas in almost identical natural environments which do not practice either agricultural system. Some historical relation between them can, however, be traced.

Shifting cultivation, the archetype, is widespread in the rain forest and on its borders. There lateritic soil, infertile at best, leaches and erodes rapidly when removal of the natural vegetation exposes it to sun and rain. This has led all primitive peoples inhabiting such lands to move their farmed plots every few years (usually from one to three, depending on local conditions), and to seek new land in the adjacent forest. After some years (five to a dozen), the plots being tilled are inconveniently remote from the village, and the tribe removes to a site in the deep forest, a new center from which another block of land is gradually cleared. The absence of domestic animals in aboriginal America restricted the farm products to crops, except for llama hair, while the presence of the tsetse fly in Africa prevented animal raising, save for poultry, pigs, and goats. In the true rain forest the large domestic animals languish, but in somewhat drier regions hardy strains survive, outside tsetse infected regions. Crops were few and monotonous until outsiders, especially Europeans, began moving from continent to continent, carrying seeds and slips, as well as livestock.

The forest dwellers live in small tribes,

segregated from their neighbors by abandoned and jungly clearings or by virgin forest. They build huts of thatch, sometimes thatch over mud, and have no more paraphernalia than they can move when the old home has to be abandoned. They are likely to be animists, and no major religion has ever affected most of them.

Tillage is crude, and fire is used to clear the ground, with some assistance from hand tools. Many tribes make sticks to serve as plows and root up the plants to harvest them. The return is inevitably very low, and food shortage is common toward the end of the growing period, after the old crop is consumed, and before the new one is ready for gathering. Little clothing is needed, and materials for housing are to be found everywhere.

Shifting cultivation extends beyond the rain forest, into several of the combinations of small trees and coarse grasses commonly called "bush." In this environment it lacks some characteristic features, and has to compete with nomadic herding or livestock ranching. Only in Africa, where the tsetse is the enemy of animal husbandry, does shifting cultivation spread far beyond the margins of the rain forest.

As in the case of nomadic herding, no statistics are available on the migrant tillers of the soil. Descriptions of their life and landscape are few, most of them being incidental notes tucked away in anthropological discussions, and incomplete from the geographic viewpoint.[32]

RUDIMENTAL SEDENTARY TILLAGE

Here and there in regions of shifting cultivation are areas where the inhabitants remain permanently, unless some catastrophe sets them wandering. Some of these districts of rudimental sedentary tillage have become rather densely populated because of special environmental conditions. Such

[32] Derwent Whittlesey, "Shifting Cultivation," *Economic Geography,* XIII (1937), 35–52; *idem,* "Fixation of Shifting Cultivation," *ibid,* 139–54. Georg Hörner, "Die Waldvölker," *Petermanns Geographische Mitteilungen, Ergänzungsheft,* XLII (1927), 23–29.

places are likely to be small islands, mountain valleys, and districts where the soil and the climate are favorable above the average. Either because the people inhabiting these districts have not the means to migrate, or because they refuse to leave a fertile spot for one less favored, they are compelled to re-use their fallow, abandoned clearings before the climax vegetation has had time to reclaim them. In forested areas, such land is jungly and requires much more labor for clearing than does the virgin bush. In open woodland the grasses have to be extirpated plant by plant, the native tools being too primitive to do the work as a plow would. Labor to perform this extra work is available, because the population is relatively dense. Because of crude tools and little or no knowledge of the value of fertilizing the soil, and because even the most fertile soils of low latitudes are not first-class, fields have to be left fallow for a few years between each two cultivations. Stock can graze on the fallow, unless domestic animals are unknown or the tsetse keeps them out. In effect, the tilled plots shift, but within an area that can be worked from a fixed village center. Adjacent villages are likely to be in contact with each other, and they may amalgamate into considerable units — social and political. Such were the pre-Conquest empires of the American highlands and the Maya lowlands. Similar although less extensive groupings were numerous in Africa and in many islands.

How far infiltrations of outsiders, singly or successively, may have aided in the fixation of migrant tribes is unknown. Certainly the intrusion of outsiders in historical time has tended to turn shifting cultivation into sedentary forms. With the coming of Europeans this tendency has been accelerated. The newcomers are eager to buy certain products, originally derived from forest or bush, but often easily grown continuously by the aborigines in districts accessible to market. Most of these are tree crops, which remain on the land for years, and which exhaust the soil less rapidly than

do annuals. Cacao, oilpalm, cocopalm, abaca, hevea rubber, and tree cotton are leading crop trees. With the introduction of improved methods, especially the animal-drawn plow and fertilizer, annuals also may be grown for sale. Peanuts, a self-fertilizing crop, and annual cotton are chief among these.

The primitive farmer who sells for export must grow food for himself, as he never gets enough cash to buy all his supplies. The crops he requires for subsistence he grows among his cash-producing trees or on other plots which he fallows and tills by turns. In a few places the agriculture is so advanced as to resemble the still more highly developed oriental types of agriculture rather than the ancestral shifting cultivation. This suggests that land occupance in all regions of shifting and rudimental sedentary cultivation may continue to move toward more efficient use of the land.

On the map (Fig. 1) the separation of sedentary from shifting agriculture is incomplete. There are unmapped belts a few miles wide along many railways and well established roads, where tillage has become somewhat fixed, as well as districts near the larger cities. These can not be shown on the scale of the map. Others, in transition from shifting to sedentary, cannot be identified with certainty.

The dwelling of the rudimental sedentary farmer may be like that of his migrant ancestors, but it is more likely to wear a sophisticated roof of corrugated iron, or a homemade imitation fashioned from gasoline tins. Household equipment, while simple, includes imported articles, particularly tinware, enameled ware, and coarse crockery. Cloths of European manufacture supplement or replace the native clothing, except where local native tradition is advanced and strong, as on the highland of Latin America.

As in the case of other primitive agriculture, statistics are few. Differentiation from shifting cultivation has not clearly been made, even by students in the field. A very few descriptions disclose the variety of regions which have in common a tentative settling down upon a fixed piece of terrain.[33]

INTENSIVE SUBSISTENCE TILLAGE WITH RICE DOMINANT

In the humid regions of South and East Asia and adjacent islands, another pair of agricultural types is found, very different from all the rest, but distinguished from each other chiefly by the presence or absence of rice in the crop association.

Where the season is long enough for paddy rice to mature, the highly intensive agricultural system supports the densest rural population found over large areas anywhere on earth. Although three sorts of crops are associated with three types of farmland, the key to this mode of land occupance is the paddy—irrigable deltas, floodplains, coastal plains, and terraces planted to rice. Two crops a year are garnered where the climate is hot, one where water fails or a cool season intervenes. Rice yields more grain per acre than any other crop. Land out of reach of irrigation, but not too rough, is devoted to varied crops, chiefly grains, oil-seeds, and cotton. Hillslopes too steep to till are planted to trees —mulberry, tea, pepper, and others.

Waters as well as all types of lands are compelled to furnish a share of the food supply. Fish are taken from the rivers and backwaters, and cultivated in artificial ponds. Aquatic plants yield a living to numerous ducks, or are pulled to spread on the fields as green fertilizer.

All the work is performed by hand, except plowing the paddies. Plows are pulled by carabaos, animals which are at home in watery mud. Hand tools are moderately ef-

fective, being made of iron or steel, but plows and irrigation pumps are primitive. Some of the tasks are incredibly arduous. Grain must be hung up to dry after being cut, tea and mulberry leaves must be carefully gathered, and the rice plants must be transferred one by one from seed plots to fields. Besides the routine jobs water must be pumped on to the paddies, and irrigation works must be kept in repair.

Natural flooding, annually or occasionally, helps maintain fertility in the paddy silts. On unirrigable lands two or more crops may be planted in the same field to minimize drain on the soil. The seeds may be mixed or planted in alternate rows. Rotation is likewise a well understood principle. In these regions of few animals the land is fed by every available sort of fertilizer, including nightsoil.

Because of the careful methods in vogue and the excellent tilth maintained by hand weeding, it is doubtful if the introduction of farm machinery would increase production. More likely the yield would be less. Certainly the rice paddies would produce less per acre if transplanting should be abandoned.

In spite of indefatigable labor, per capita production is not high and the people are abjectly poor. They live in close-set and close-packed villages crowded upon the smallest possible acreage, to preserve the precious land for tillage, or standing, sometimes inconveniently remote from the fields, on sand spits, tongues of unirrigable land, or other inferior soils. In delta districts whole populations may dwell on houseboats. The furnishings of homes are meager.

Few statistics are published for China, but Japan and especially India are covered by numerous reports. Where an all-year growing season permits, two crops a year are grown on the same land. This results in more than 100% of the total cropped area being in crops in the course of the year. Rice occupies the ground during the favored season, when nearly the total tilled area may be under this one crop. Studies

[33] Whittlesey, "Fixation of Shifting Cultivation"; Robert S. Platt, "Six Farms in the Central Andes," *Geographical Review*, XXII (1932), 245–59; O. F. Cook, "Milpa Agriculture," *Smithsonian Institution, Annual Report 1919* (Washington, D.C., 1921), pp. 307–26; *idem*, "Foot-Plow Agriculture in Peru," *ibid* (1920), pp. 487–91; Clement Gillman, "A Population Map of Tanganyika Territory," *Geographical Review*, XXVI (1936), 353–73.

of particular regions are more detailed, if not more numerous, than for the agricultural types previously discussed.[34]

INTENSIVE SUBSISTENCE TILLAGE WITHOUT PADDY RICE

In regions which neighbor the rice country, that crop is ruled out by either lack of moisture or a short growing season, and a good deal of land is out of service during part of the year. These handicaps modify the agricultural system in subtle but profound ways. For the dominant rice, several cereals are substituted, none of them so productive of grain. The climatic limitations bespeak continental conditions, and the farming regions are more generally inland, where readily irrigable delta, floodplain, and coastal plain are absent or small. Hence irrigation, although practiced wherever possible, is on a smaller scale. If it were not for large expanses of fertile soils —derived from loess and lava—the area in crops would be considerably less than it is. Apart from rice, the crops are much the same. The same threefold subdivision into irrigated plots, unirrigated fields, and slopes in tree crops is the rule. Hand methods and intensive application of labor to the land differ little from those in use in the paddy country. The people live in the same congestion as their rice-growing neighbors, and they suffer the additional burden of frequent famines, because of drouth or flood, both of which are characteristic of these lands of erratic rainfall. Occidental

[34] Ethel Simkins, "The Coast Plains of South India," *Economic Geography,* IX (1933), 19–50, 136–59; J. Riley Staats, "India East Coast," *Journal of Geography,* XXXI (1932), 93–111; George B. Cressey, "The Fenghsien Landscape: A Fragment of the Yangtze Delta," *Geographical Review,* XXVI (1936), 396–413; Robert B. Hall, "The Yamato Basin, Japan," *Annals of the Association of American Geographers,* XXII (1932), 243–74; Glenn T. Trewartha, "A Geographic Study in Shizuoka Prefecture, Japan," *ibid,* XVIII (1928), 127–259; *idem,* "The Iwaki Basin: Reconnaissance Field Study of a Specialized Apple District in Northern Honshu, Japan," *Annals of the Association of American Geographers,* XX (1930), 196–223.

technology has been of service in alleviating famine. Railroads quickly transfer food from favored districts to afflicted ones, and large-scale irrigation works insure a minimum output in regions where they have been constructed. Except for regions notably favored by fertile soil the population is somewhat less dense than in the more productive rice country.

The two oriental types of agriculture neatly illustrate contrasts arising from a single basic difference in the crop association, a difference due to climate. The borderlines between the two sorts of regions can be drawn on a statistical basis. On the margins are zones where paddy rice is grown, but not dominantly. On the map (Fig. 1) the lines mark the limit of *heavy* rice production. In many studies these two agricultural types are discussed together. Articles in periodicals cover marginal regions, the major areas of neither type being treated.

Akin to this mode of agricultural land occupance, in crop association, in intensiveness, in quantity of hand labor, and in outturn, is the agriculture of low latitude oases scattered across the desert of Inner Asia and North Africa. Of these Egypt is the most extensive and may be regarded as a large but otherwise typical example.

Irrigation alone permits the growing of crops in these oases, a fact which rules out dryland tillage, although some tree crops are grown in infertile soils. Despite this difference, the agricultural life is so nearly identical as to warrant grouping with cold China and dry India, except for the few oases which have turned to the production of some commercial crop, generally dates or cotton.

There is an arresting similarity in crops grown and in methods of growing them between the non-rice agriculture of the orient and places like the Kano District of the Sudan and the Mexican highland. Both these regions practice irrigation, both depend primarily on unirrigated fields, and both have some tree crops. Methods are much less intensive, however, the outturn per acre is correspondingly low, and the population light. It would not do to press the parallelism too far. True "oriental" agriculture does not extend westward and southward beyond the Sahara.[35]

COMMERCIAL PLANTATION CROP TILLAGE

In a few districts where intensive subsistence tillage dominated by rice has been the immemorial farm system, and in many places where shifting cultivation or rudimental sedentary tillage formerly held sway, Europeans have superimposed a distinct mode of land occupance—commercial "plantation crop" tillage. Not even livestock ranching is so dependent upon the outside world. Nearly every bit of the cash crop is sold outside the region of production, and most of it moves to the middle latitudes. The capital required to develop the business comes from Europe or North America. The staff, both administrative and technical, is recruited from the same regions, and the machinery is made there. Even the fertilizer which feeds the fields, and the flour, dried codfish, canned goods, and other staples which feed the officers and workmen, are imported. Occasionally, although not usually, the crop is indigenous. More commonly the field hands are local, although in many places they too must be imported.

The plantation is a device to procure in desired quantities and of a standard quality, commodities which cannot be produced in middle latitudes and which the low latitude inhabitants either do not grow (hevea rubber), or turn out in insufficient quantities (sugar), or of unreliable quality (tea). Commercial plantations were started as products of the newly discovered low latitudes ceased to be novelties and became regular items of consumption in the middle

latitudes. Plantings were rapidly extended, and new crops were added as cities throve on trade, on mining, and on manufacturing, and their redoubling populations created new markets. Inventions accelerated transportation. Refrigeration added perishables, like bananas, to the list of plantation crops. Improved machinery revolutionized processing, within the plantation district, of sugar, rubber, and other crops. Products not hitherto grown on plantations were discovered to possess value for a mechanized society—rubber, sisal, copra. New uses in industry were found for cacao, cotton, and vegetable oils. Sanitation improved the lot of the middle latitude staff by decreasing the risk of disease.

In a plantation crop region the most efficient machinery of production and the latest gadgets for comfortable material living are juxtaposed to, but not combined with, the primitive life and labor of the aboriginal dwellers. No contrast could be more bald. In other respects also the commercial plantation business is paradoxical. Its normal state is chronic overproduction, and yet decreasing fractions of most products come from plantations. This results from the fact that nearly every plantation crop is grown on a very small part of the total area to which it is environmentally suited and from which it can profitably be marketed. Hence new land is constantly being cleared and abandoned plantations are often converted to new uses. More serious still, nearly all plantation crops can be grown by natives, particularly if they can be sold from the field without processing. These conditions combine to glut the market unless the demand happens to be rising strongly. Today the banana is the only crop grown exclusively on plantations, although sisal is a close second. Tea, coffee, and sugar reach the market through the hands of planters, because natives cannot manage the careful and expensive processing required. But a large fraction of these crops is grown on small holdings of the local inhabitants.

A good deal of one-time plantation land

[35] D. H. Davis, "Agricultural Occupation of Hokkaido," *Economic Geography*, X (1934), 348–67; John R. Stewart, "Manchuria: The Land and Its Economy," *ibid*, VIII (1932), 134–46; Paul F. Gemmill, "Egypt is the Nile," *ibid*, IV (1928), 295–312; J. E. Guardia, "The Agricultural Nile Delta," *Bulletin of the Geographical Society of Philadelphia*, XXV (1927), 163–86.

has lost its distinctive character. In some West India islands, Hawaii, and the oases of coastal Peru and northern Argentina, generations of planters have lived on or near their holdings and administer the business personally or through overseers. There irrigated districts closely resemble irrigation agriculture in places where plantations never did exist. For this reason the Peruvian and Argentine oases are mapped as belonging to specialized horticulture, even though the leading crops are neither fruits nor vegetables.

In the humid subtropical climate of the United States South and the Brazilian highland, the two largest plantation regions, infertile lands have never been worked on a strictly plantation crop basis, and more and more plantations are being broken up, either by sale in small units, or by renting to share-crop farmers who work their few acres independently.

Commercial plantation crop tillage occupies in the aggregate a very small acreage, compared to any of the other types of agricultural land occupance which have been outlined. It has been stressed in geographic study, perhaps disproportionately, because of its commercial value to the middle latitudes and its nice expression of interacting natural and cultural forces.

The regions of production are too scattered and disparate to be readily brought into statistical focus. Plenty of data are available concerning each cash crop, but these do not suffice to picture clearly the regions of production, because some subsistence crops are grown by plantation laborers or by other indigenes. With the blurring of the lines between plantation production and production on small holdings, statistical comparison becomes even more difficult. Most accounts of plantation agriculture are stories of the individual cash crops. Because the one crop is so overwhelmingly dominant, some of these accounts are listed below.[36]

[36] Alice Foster, "Sisal Production in Semiarid Karst Country of Yucatan," *Journal of Geography*, XXIX (1930), 16–25; R. H. Whitbeck,

SUMMARY AND PROSPECTUS

In contrast with the two dryland types of agricultural land occupance, the five systems of the humid low latitudes are seen in review to depend largely on tillage. Livestock is excluded, wholly or with minor exceptions. Subsistence is the primary objective of the farmer except in the scattered spots where commercial plantation crops are grown by invaders from the middle latitudes, or where indigenes have been encouraged to produce a surplus of some of their crops and to grow plants hitherto unfamiliar, for sale to these same middle latitude consumers.

The seven types of agriculture thus far discussed cover a large part of the earth's tilled and grazed land, and they support nearly 70 per cent of the world's population. The remaining six types occupy for dwellers in humid middle latitudes of the occident a position of importance dispro-

"Geographical Relations in the Development of Cuban Agriculture," *Geographical Review*, XII (1922), 223–40; Robert S. Platt, "Geography of a Sugar District: Mariel, Cuba," *ibid*, XIX (1929), 603–12; A. Kopp, "L'Agriculture à la Guadeloupe," *Annales de Géographie*, XXXVIII (1939), 480–500; Earl B. Shaw, "St. Croix: A Marginal Sugar-Producing Island," *Geographical Review*, XXIII (1933), 414–22; John W. Coulter, "The Oahu Sugar Plantation, Waipahu," *Economic Geography*, IX (1933), 60–71; S. Van Valkenburg, "Java: The Economic Geography of a Tropical Island," *Geographical Review*, XV (1925), 563–83; John W. Coulter, "Small Farming on Kauai: Hawaiian Islands," *Economic Geography*, XI (1935), 401–9; Lucia C. Harrison, "Dominica: A Wet Tropical Human Habitat," *ibid*, XI (1935), 62–76; R. H. Whitbeck, "The Agricultural Geography of Jamaica," *Annals of the Association of American Geographers*, XXII (1932), 13–27; Robert S. Platt, "Coffee Plantations of Brazil," *Geographical Review*, XXV (1935), 231–39; William T. Chambers, "Life in a Cotton Farming Community," *Journal of Geography*, XXVIII (1929), 141–47; Sam T. Bratton, "Land Utilization in the St. Francis Basin," *Economic Geography* VI (1930), 374–88; W. A. Browne, "Grand Prairie: A Progressive Rice Region," *Journal of Geography*, XXI (1932), 138–47; Preston E. James, "A Specialized Rice District in the Middle Parahyba Valley of Brazil," *Michigan Papers in Geography*, IV (1934), 349–58.

portionate to their size. They include the principal commercial systems. Some of these are of recent origin—experiments in agricultural land occupance. From these lands of agricultural progress has come the impetus that reaches out to transform dryland husbandry (in livestock ranching regions) and to modify low latitude and oriental agriculture (in regions of commercial plantation crop tillage and rudimental sedentary tillage).

MEDITERRANEAN AGRICULTURE

From the geographic standpoint, Mediterranean agriculture is the most satisfactory of all the types. Probably because it represents an ancient and stable collaboration between man and the land. So vital has this proved that it stoutly maintains its character in the region of its origin, despite buffetings of the world-wide shift from isolation to interdependent economics. The settlement by Europeans in the new continents has only emphasized the integrity of the type, by developing in each continent a region approximating its prototype in the Old World.

To begin with, the unique Mediterranean climate and its intimate association with mountains and hills has created a distinctive stock and crop association of four interrelated functioning forms: winter crops grown with rain, all-year crops grown with rain, all-year or summer crops grown with irrigation, and livestock—mainly small animals—grazed on highlands in winter and on lowlands in summer. Natural environment coincides areally with crop and livestock association. The only possible exception is the doubtful case of southern Australia, where Mediterranean climate, *without the mountains* and suffering from newness and remoteness, has not bred all the characteristic forms of Mediterranean agriculture. In the Los Angeles basin of southern California the very recent settlers from humid regions (mainly people with money to spend), insist on cows' milk and dooryard lawns. These are ephemeral holdovers, sure to disappear with increasing pressure on natural resources, particularly the water supply. They were never features of the landscape in parts of California settled by people who went there to make a living.

Both subsistence and cash crops figure in the economy of every region of Mediterranean agriculture, although not of every farm. The relative emphasis on the several products varies with the rainfall. Thus North Africa produces more barley and goatskins, southern Europe more wheat and sheepskins. Tradition, market, and government favor may sway attention to this or that crop, but the elements remain constant. Southern France, Italy, and Chile stress wine, California and Spain stress oranges. More wheat is grown in Italy, where it is supported by tradition and tariff, than in California, which must compete with commercial wheat raising of interior United States. California markets its citrus and deciduous fruits fresh, and has an active canning industry for the perishable deciduous group; South Africa makes jams and preserves for the English market. Turkey grows cotton on the Adana Plain, and Russia is creating a truck farming district at the east end of the Black Sea.

Methods vary somewhat, but again the differences are details. Italy, Chile, and the Cape region employ little but hand labor. In California, where farmers can afford any machinery they care to use, all irrigating, most harvesting and planting, and much weeding must be done by hand. This leaves only plowing (on lands not too steep), and some weeding to be done by tractor-drawn implements. Small factories for processing surpluses are ancient in origin and widespread in all regions of Mediterranean agriculture. The California co-operative achieves economic results not very different from the latifundia in Spain, Italy, or Chile.

The business is intensive except where large landowners are able to hold estates for pasturing animals (as for example ring bulls in Spain) or for growing wheat. This is an ephemeral phenomenon, the sort of discordance between natural and cultural

forces familiar to the geographer but bound
to be resolved by time. Not all the land
is used with equal intensity, because its
adaptability varies widely — inevitable
where mountains alternate with plains and
where rainfall and available ground water
range from almost nothing to moderately
abundant. As a rule each district is used
to its maximum capacity. The return from
lowlands is high, and some of the horticultural land has a very high valuation. The
presence of much land of low grade, rugged
or unirrigable, brings down the total aggregate outturn.

The cultural landscape is much the same
everywhere. In times of insecurity folk live
on defense points, and when no danger
threatens they take to more accessible lowland sites. The new continents, peaceful
ever since their seizure by Europeans, all
have their farm villages on the lowlands,
whereas on many Mediterranean shores
people continue to dwell in their hilltop
houses because they can't afford to abandon
them and build new ones. Whether on hill
or plain, nucleated settlements are the rule,
because the horticultural character of the
business enables a family to live on the income from a small plot, and because unit
value is too high to warrant wasting garden
land as a site for farmsteads. Few structures are needed, and houses are small in
these lands of bright sunshine. Yet even
the poorer peasants possess household goods
more numerous and more valuable than the
low-latitude or the oriental farmer can
boast.

The transition zone to adjacent agricultural types is narrow and corresponds
closely with mountain ranges which limit
the climate on which the farming is based.
The olive has long been recognized as the
indicator of the spread of both Mediterranean agriculture and Mediterranean climate in the Old World. Hartshorne and
Dicken have used it, along with other orchard crops, in ratio to total cropland other
than hay. This criterion works admirably
in Europe, but in the new countries where
olives are not much grown and marginal

land is used only a little, it leaves a deal
of lightly farmed country in a limbo. This
they group under the head "Forests and
Unused." In the classification here presented the mountain boundaries are preferred, because there is some tillage and a
good deal of transhumant stock-grazing in
all the wooded borders of the intensively
tilled lowlands.[37]

COMMERCIAL GRAIN FARMING

More than any other type of agriculture,
commercial grain farming is the creature of
the Industrial Revolution. It has no proto-
types and does not antedate the day of the
self-scouring steel plow and harvesting machinery, inventions of the 1830's. It depends slavishly on these inventions, as well
as on the steamship (first successful in
1807) and the railroad (1825). The regions
now devoted to commercial grain farming
were previously used, if for any sort of
husbandry, by nomadic herders or livestock
ranchers. They lie on the border between
humid and semiarid climate, and the summers are short, the winters cold. Most such
regions are well inland.

The crop and stock association is simple
and standardized. Wheat is the cash crop,
with flax or barley subsidiary at times and
in places. Oats and hay feed the draft animals, of which there are a good many, unless tractors have supplanted them. Other
animals are kept for local supplies. No
other association has been found which will
provide a livelihood, except where standards of living are so low and population so
dense that oriental agriculture can be
adopted. This has taken place in Manchuria, the one region having subhumid con-

[37] Two of the following articles on this agriculture describe the commercial aspect of its horticulture: E. W. Gilbert, "The Human Geography
of Mallorca," *Scottish Geographical Magazine*, L
(1934), 129–46; John W. Coulter, "Land Utilization in the Santa Lucia Region," *Geographical
Review*, XX (1930), 469–79; Edward N. Torbert,
"The Specialized Commercial Agriculture of the
Northern Santa Clara Valley," *ibid*, XXVI (1936),
247–63; E. Halpern, "La Huerta de Valence,"
Annales de Géographie, XLIII (1934), 146–67.

tinental climate with short summers where commercial grain farming is not the dominant system.

The percentage of cropland in the total area is very high in favored districts. Some is left fallow, and partial or total crop failure is so common that it has to be expected once in a few years. The percentage of wheatland is likewise very high, comprising as much as half the total farmland in some places. The ratio of livestock to cropland is very low, and nearly half the total number of livestock units is draft animals.

Methods are progressive but not intensive. By using much large machinery, much low-value land, and little labor, the outturn suffices to maintain a sparse population. The return per acre is low compared to regions where more intensive tillage is practiced. Fertilizer is unknown, and only recently has the straw been plowed into the fields.

Like his neighbor the livestock rancher, the commercial wheat farmer is at the mercy of unreliable rainfall and in competition with many other regions, the outturn of which bears no predictable relation to his own. But his immobile grainfields cannot be moved to avoid drouth. Therefore his fortunes fluctuate wildly, and he is the most politically-minded farmer on earth. From the commercial grain regions come chronic or epidemic demands for the government to regulate common carriers (of the cash crop, the machines, the extra hands, and the long list of clothing, luxuries, and even food imported), and to reduce or cancel indebtedness (incurred in a venture requiring large capital and ruinous after a few successive seasons of low prices).

Huge acreage separates each farmer from his neighbors and from town. Towns have a smaller ratio of residences to commercial buildings than in any other landscape. In all the new continents the farmstead and its equipment is first-class, except on marginal lands which ought never to have been plowed.

Some observers have supposed that commercial grain farming is merely a pioneer, destined to give way to some other type. This was the case with bonanza wheat farming of such regions as the Corn Belt, the central valley of California, and the maize region of the Pampa. But in the humid continental climate with short summers, attempts to introduce other stock and crop associations have failed signally, with the sole exception of intensive subsistence agriculture without rice. The current Russian experiments in co-operative and state farming therefore hold special interest as perhaps paving the way for modifications of this very new and highly unstable system of agriculture.

The maps of Jones and Whittlesey and Hartshorne and Dicken agree on the outlines of these regions in North America. The border toward the North Pole has slowly expanded, thanks to the scientific propagation of hardier types of wheat. At times the dryland margins of all regions expand similarly, only to retreat during the succeeding spell of drouth years. The exact outlines of any region therefore fluctuate with the period for which statistics are chosen.

Although there are no notable variations in this standardized farming, nice distinctions from region to region demonstrate the delicacy of the balance between natural and cultural forces which prevails on this kaleidoscopic earth.[38]

COMMERCIAL LIVESTOCK AND CROP FARMING

This mode of agriculture, often called "mixed farming," displays maximum diver-

[38] Robert S. Platt, "Pirovano: Items in the Argentine Pattern of Terrene Occupancy," *Annals of the Association of American Geographers*, XXI (1931), 215–37; J. Sullivan Gibson, "Agriculture of the Southern High Plains," *Economic Geography*, VIII (1932), 245–61; John H. Garland, "The Columbia Plateau Region of Commercial Grain Farming," *Geographical Review*, XXIV (1934), 371–79; John Andrews, "The Present Situation in the Wheat-Growing Industry in Southeastern Australia," *ibid*, XII (1936), 109–35; N. M. Tuliakov, "Agriculture in the Dry Region of the U.S.S.R.," *ibid*, VI (1930), 54–80.

sity in detail amid essential uniformity in outline. It is one of three lineal descendants of the medieval agriculture of northern Europe, all of which feature both crops and livestock in different associations and in varying ratios. Today it is found not only in Europe, but also in the humid middle latitudes of all the other continents except Asia.

Where the climate is warm enough, wheat, maize, and oats are the principal grains. Wheat is consumed by people, oats by stock, and maize by both. Where summers are cool or wet, or where soil is infertile, rye and barley take the place of corn and wheat. Root crops are grown everywhere, but more especially in the rye-barley regions. There, potatoes for man, turnips and other roots for beast, and sugar beets are important. Hay is always present, often in the form of a legume. Surpluses of any crop may be sold, but the main cash products come from animals. Hogs and cattle and poultry predominate, with horses, mules, or oxen for draft. These diverse plants and animals suit the varied environment, which includes a wide range of soils, and the market, which is dominated by the nearby trading and manufacturing cities, with their multifarious demands. Vegetables and other minor crops add further to the variegated appearance of the farmed landscape. In the immediate vicinity of large cities spots of market gardening should be distinguished, and in the United States dairy districts likewise. On the scale of the map (Fig. 1) these areas are too small to show.

Methods include the employment of much machinery, careful attention to breeding and plant selection, a well established rotation in which legumes and hay play a part, and generous fertilization of the soil made possible by the considerable livestock density. Nowhere is the farmer more progressive than in these regions. He lives in the midst of the impedimenta of the machine age, and his objective is maximum mechanical efficiency on his farm.

The return is relatively high, being very high in some densely peopled countries of Europe where extra hand labor from families of factory workers may be had cheap at hoeing and picking seasons. In Europe national tariffs, subsidies, and other political devices go far to determine just which commodities are produced. Indirectly this affects the return per acre. Some crops, notably wheat, are grown on inferior land; some crops produce higher yields because subsidized sugar beets in the rotation maintain tilth at maximum efficiency.

The close interdependence between this farm system and centers of trade and manufacturing is disclosed by its weak development in eastern Europe and in the southern continents, even where the natural environment is satisfactory, and its absence in eastern Asia where intensive hand tillage held sway long before Europe outgrew the medieval three-field system of farming.

Nearly everywhere in North America the farmer lives on the acres he works, and this is likewise true of many regions in Europe and the southern continents. Since the farms are of medium size this does not impose severe isolation. Marketing towns are numerous, because in a cash system there is much trade. Parts of Europe have inherited the nucleated farm village from the distant past. It tends to persist because no one wants to abandon home and neighbors. The standard of living varies, but in every country it is relatively high, except in rugged or infertile districts where it is hard to produce enough from the niggardly ground to pile up a surplus for sale.

The percentage of cropland to total farmland is about the same as in regions of commercial grain farming, but the ratio of animal units to crops is much higher. Of the livestock, more than two-thirds are meat producers, chiefly cattle and hogs. Regions are distinguished from their neighbors (Fig. 1) by a combination of both products and methods, rather than by a simple statistical rule of thumb. Something of the variety which prevails from region to region is portrayed in the articles listed below.[39]

SUBSISTENCE CROP AND STOCK FARMING

The second of the three types of agricultural land occupance originating in northern Europe is outwardly much like the first. The one prime difference is profound—the farmer produces for his own sustenance and sells little or nothing. Having no cash income he cannot buy expensive machinery nor can he save the best seed from his fields or buy breeding stock. His return is correspondingly low, and he cannot market his rare surpluses in competition with the high-grade and reliable output of commercial regions. Lacking the stimulus of a competitive market, methods are crude. Thus the vicious circle continues to roll round and round.

Wheat almost never is found in the crop association. Apparently if land can produce wheat, it can support a cash system of farming. Rye or maize is the chief grain

food of the people, with potatoes and barley as other staples. Each self-dependent farm tries to produce all the varied commodities needed. For some of these the environment is unsuited and the outturn very low.

As a rule farmers are laborers on estates and they live in farm villages, relics of serfdom not many decades gone. For most of them living conditions are miserable. The breakup of estates which has been going on in most of these regions since the end of World War I should profoundly modify the system. As Germany and Sweden have proved, similar natural environment can be administered on a cash basis. The efforts to improve farming in Russia are especially worth watching. As yet the results are not plain. Along railroads, commercial livestock and crop farming is replacing its prototype devoted to subsistence. Near cities market gardens and dairy farms appear to be evolving. It seems likely that in so far as the Russian agrarian reform tends toward large-scale operation, it will not be successful in regions of subsistence crop and stock farming. Nowhere has this environment been effectively organized except by individual farmers working their several holdings and rearing their own animals.

In the countries fringing Russia on the west a transformation in land occupance is occurring, although less urgently pushed by the governments, all of which are devoted to private capitalism, as distinguished from state capitalism. Turkey has experienced more changes than any other of these states. A recent map of agricultural systems in Poland indicates the persistence of the three-field system in the region under Russian domination before World War I, in sharp contrast with commercial stock and crop farming in the parts formerly ruled by Germany, and even by Austria.[40]

[39] Stanley D. Dodge, "Bureau and the Princeton Community," *Annals of the Association of American Geographers,* XXII (1932), 159–209; Henry F. James, "The Agricultural Industry of Southeastern Pennsylvania," *Bulletin of the Geographical Society of Philadelphia,* XXVI (1929), 87–126, 167–92; A. Perpillou, "L'Evolution économique du Limousin méridional," *Annales de Géographie,* XXXVI (1927), 509–27; Earl B. Shaw, "Land Use in the Upper Ardeche River Valley of France," *Economic Geography,* XI (1935), 356–67; Richard Marcelle, "L'Evolution agricole du Plateau de Langres," *Annales de Géographie,* XXXVIII (1929), 133–437; Robert Capot-Rey, "L'Agriculture dans le territoire de la Sarre," *Annales de Géographie,* XXXII (1932), 97–118; K. C. Edwards, N. V. Scarfe, and A. E. Moodie, "The Nowy Targ Basin of the Polish Tatra," *Scottish Geographical Magazine,* LI (1935), 215–27; Roderick Peattie, "The Conflent: A Study in Mountain Geography," *Geographical Review,* XX (1930), 245–57; Joseph S. Roucek, "Romanian Peasant and Agriculture," *Journal of Geography,* XXXI (1932), 279–87; Andrew C. O'Dell, "Geographical Controls of Agriculture in Orkney and Shetland," *Economic Geography,* XI (1935), 1–19; H. Clifford Darby, "Settlement in Northern Rhodesia," *Geographical Review,* XXI (1931), 559–73.

[40] Wilhelm Müller, "Wirtschaftsgeographische Gliederung von Polen," *Geographischer Anzeiger,* XXXV (1934), 264–72; Richard Hartshorne, "Geographical and Political Boundaries in Upper

As in all regions of subsistence agriculture, statistics are lacking or unreliable. Few detailed field studies have been made. The boundaries between the commercial and the subsistence aspect of mixed farming in east central Europe are based on studies made in the critical zones.

Inclusion of the Mexican highland in this type of agricultural land occupance is based on undeniable similarities, in spite of wholly different histories. The likenesses appear to derive in part from the aggregation of the land into huge estates, worked by a landless class of peasants. "Peon" is a close equivalent of "serf." As in many parts of Eastern Europe, the Mexican estates are now in process of subdivision as a result of the revolution in politics and society of the past quarter century. Whether the system of agriculture to be built upon small holdings will resemble commercial stock and crop farming or some other type it is too early to say. One clear result has been the elimination of plantation crop tillage, formerly paramount in some districts.[41]

COMMERCIAL DAIRY FARMING

The third form of agriculture to evolve from the medieval system of northern Europe is dairying. Except where induced by an exceptional market, as in the vicinity of large cities in central and western United States, dairying makes its appearance where summers are too cool and moist for either maize or wheat, and where hay is the most satisfactory crop, year in and year out. Leguminous forage, root crops, oats, and two-row barley supplement the hayfeed of the cows, and rye or six-row barley and potatoes are grown for human consumption. In short, the members of the crop and livestock association are just about the same as in the two historically related

types, but the emphasis is very different.

Commercial dairying pays only where the products can be sold to an urban market. By far the largest buyers of dairy products are the city populations of the northern European type. The radius for shipping fresh milk is, roughly, overnight; for cream twice as far; for butter in refrigerators, across a continent on rails and from the antipodes in ships; for cheese, periods up to three or four years, depending on the kind. These facts explain the worldwide distribution of Danish and New Zealand butter, the special trade-mark value of many cheeses, chiefly of European origin, and the abundant supplies of milk and cream in the cities adjacent to the major dairy regions (Fig. 1).

Without careful preparation, perishable dairy products would spoil in long-distance shipment. Every step in feeding, milking, and processing is critical. The painstaking attention accorded cattle and milk is extended to the farmland. Manure fertilizer is abundant, but the infertile soils typical of dairy regions need all they can get. To supplement local forage, mixed grains and oilseeds are commonly imported. The dairy business is elaborately mechanized, and the capital investment in housing and equipment on high-grade dairy farms exceeds that in any other type of agriculture.

The dairyfarm landscape is noted for roomy barns—to house the cows and to store winter feed. This is true even of the mild winter climate along the coasts of northwest Europe. Holdings average larger than in adjacent stock and crop farm regions because hay is an extensive crop and there is a good deal of pasture besides, some of it wooded and of low carrying capacity.

This business, featuring animals, requires rather more labor than the crop farms, and there is no off-season during the year. The percentage of tenantry is low. Apparently the personal stake which keeps the owner on the job is a cornerstone of prosperity in this system of agriculture.

The return on successful dairy farming is high. Improvement of herds is a prime

Silesia," *Annals of the Association of American Geographers,* XXIII (1933), 202–3; Eugene Romer, *Atlas of Poland* (New York: A. Jechalski, 1916).

[41] Robert S. Platt, "Magdalena Atlipac, A Study of Terrene Occupancy in Mexico," *Bulletin No. 9, Geographical Society of Chicago* (Chicago, 1933).

means of increasing income. Most "gentleman farms" run by city men for a hobby are dairy farms where pure-bred stock is featured. These estates in new countries, like entailed properties in the Old World, have often taken the lead in the advancement of a region to ever higher levels of efficiency.

Statistically dairy regions are differentiated from neighboring crop and livestock husbandry by high ratio of hay to grain, high percentage of dairy cows in the livestock total, and a higher density of farm population. The percentage of land in crops is about the same, and the number of animal units per square mile runs close to that in commercial livestock and crop farming. Local variations are considerable.[42]

SPECIALIZED HORTICULTURE

Production of fruits and vegetables in kitchen gardens and home orchards is the rule in most agriculture of humid regions. Among the occidental systems of middle latitudes horticulture as an important phase of the business occurs only in Mediterranean agriculture. Elsewhere fruit and vegetable growing, if on a large scale, is specialized in exceptionally favored spots. Most of these areas are too small to be shown on

[42] Daniel R. Bergsmark, "Agricultural Land Utilization in Denmark," *Economic Geography,* XI (1935), 206–14; E. Cajander, "Die agrargeographische Lage und die Landbauzonen Finnlands," *Geographische Zeitschrift*, XXXIV (1928), 220–27; Henry M. Leppard, "Scottish Carse Agriculture: The Carse of Gowrie," *Economic Geography*, X (1934), 217–38; M. Le Lannou, "Le Trégorois: étude de géographie agricole," *Annales de Géographie*, XL (1931), 24–38; Philippe Arbos, "The Geography of Pastoral Life [French Alps]," *Geographical Review*, XIII (1923), 559–75; Hermann von Wissmann, "Die bäuerliche Besiedlung und Verödung des mittleren Ennstales," *Petermanns Geographische Mitteilungen*, LXXIII (1927), 65–69; Richard Hartshorne, "A New Map of the Dairy Areas of the United States," *Economic Geography*, XI (1935), 247–355; Axel S. Anderson and Florence M. Woodward, "Agricultural Vermont," *Economic Geography*, VIII (1932), 12–42; J. MacDonald Holmes, "Geographical Factors in the Foundation of New Zealand's Wealth," *Australian Geographer*, II (1934), 24–36.

the map (Fig. 1); the larger ones do appear, however. Each district concentrates on one or a very few crops, which it sells to a market as particularized as the producing area itself.

Perhaps the most ancient districts of specialized horticulture are the vineyards of Europe outside the Mediterranean climate. Some of them were instituted in Roman times, although they were put on a cash basis in the modern sense only two or three centuries ago. The most famous are the *côtes* of the eastern Paris basin, where southeast slopes and limestone soils offset the cool, dark climate and produce the prized light wines known under generic place names, such as Burgundy, Champagne, and Moselle. Similarly situated, and only a little less famous, are wines from slopes overlooking the Rhine, the Loire, the Swiss lakes, and the plain of northern Hungary. Near Bordeaux special soils and a quasi-Mediterranean climate produce wines ranking with Burgundies. In a very different climate and under irrigation, Argentina supplies itself with wine from the specialized oases, Mendoza and San Juan.

Other aspects of intensive fruit and vegetable growing had to await the market created by city populations which live by manufacturing, mining, and trading. Producing little or no food themselves, they purchase large quantities of horticultural crops.

This demand is satisfied in part by market gardens within a few hours trucking of populous cities. There, on the types of land which favor early harvest, intensive labor and consummate skill are devoted to raising the maximum of crops on the minimum of acres. Warm soils bring into bearing successive crops, each a bit earlier than in ordinary nearby gardens. Lavish application of purchased fertilizers enrich the light soil and produce high yields and quality. The value of market garden land averages higher per acre than that devoted to any other sort of farming. The crops are vegetables and bush fruits.

No outlay for housing is required, apart

from a residence, unless the business has progressed to the stage of growing crops in winter or starting seeds under glass. In such cases greenhouses are built over the gardens to utilize the same prized soil. During peak periods the farmer and his family must work almost incessantly. Therefore they usually live on the place in a small house, well-kept like the garden itself. This gives the market garden district the aspect of a scattered residential village.

Farther from the city market, in belts progressing into warmer climates, extend districts of truck farming. Lacking the market garden's advantage of nearness to market, truck farms make up for it by exceptionally favorable soil and by the climate, which matures the desired crops earlier than in their competitors' suburban gardens. Only in Europe and North America does the urban population induce truck farming. Districts in Europe lie in three regions. (1) Along the Channel coast of Brittany and the Netherlands, to supply the markets of Britain, Germany, and North France. In the Low Countries the business is conducted under glass as well as outdoors, and is favored less by climate than by soil, and by cheap labor with a long-standing tradition of meticulous tillage. (2) The narrow Rhône Valley, the bit of Mediterranean climate nearest to northwest Europe, is a continuous ribbon of truck farm. The superposition of truck farming on the original Mediterranean agriculture entails merely a different group of crops and not a marked change in the character of agricultural land occupance. At the head of the Rhône Delta this belt changes direction and runs along the Riviera into Italy. (3) Similar districts, which market their vegetables and fruits still earlier in the season, are the Algerian and Tunisian coast of North Africa, the plains of Morocco, and the nearer oases in the Sahara.

In North America two zones extend southward from the major urban region. The larger follows the sandy soils of the Atlantic coastal plain. In Florida it merges into low latitude climate. The smaller follows the Mississippi Valley and the Gulf Coast, but only intermittently. In the Rio Grande Valley it occupies irrigated land which has some of the qualities of a low latitude desert oasis. A quite distinct area in which truck farming occurs is the dry country west of the 100th meridian. Scattered through it from southern Canada to northern Mexico are irrigated patches producing a wide climatic range of fruits and a number of vegetables. The climax of this region is the low latitude desert of the lower Colorado basin and the Mediterranean climate of California. These areas are functional counterparts of the truck farms in the Sahara and on the shores of the Mediterranean Sea.

Commercial fruit orchards are found in many of the truck farming regions. All but hardy fruits, such as apples, cherries, and pears, are confined to climates milder than the urban regions of either Europe or North America can boast. Irrigation has evolved the large and handsome fruits common in the United States. In humid regions there are orchard districts in favored belts and spots within the areas mapped (Fig. 1) as producing commercial crops, livestock, and dairy products. Islands of more favorable climate are created in the sea of continental conditions by water bodies, which retard blossoms in spring and frosts in autumn, and by hills which set up air drainage. Examples are the apple district of southwestern Germany, and the fruit zones of Nova Scotia, the lower Great Lakes, the Middle Appalachians, and the Ozarks. The wine districts of northern Europe also belong in this category.

The landscape of the truck farm district or fruit belt looks much like a market garden area. Small houses, each on its own land, crops very carefully tended, and no livestock, except perhaps a horse or mule for plowing and hauling.

Besides fruits and vegetables a number of other crops are produced as specialties, at least in some districts. Many a crop of this sort is only one item in several produced by every farmer of the neighborhood.

Always it is sold for cash, and it may provide the principal income of the farm, even though the acreage occupied by it is but a small fraction of the tilled land. Sugar beets in humid regions, tobacco in the middle latitudes, flax and hemp for fiber, and many less widely distributed crops belong to this group. In the classification of major agricultural regions, these crops may properly be thought of as variants of the cash crops more usually characteristic of the association in which they are found.

Much the same sort of crop is cotton in humid climates. It is being grown increasingly as a specialty crop in regions which otherwise bear many of the earmarks of commercial livestock and crop farming.

In dry regions where irrigation must be practiced, cotton may dominate the business of small districts. Oases within Russian Turkestan, spots in the Levant, a district in the Argentine Chaco, coastal oases of Peru, and places in the lower Colorado basin are examples. Sugar beets in the Platte and Salt Lake oases of western United States, and sugar cane in irrigated districts of coastal Peru and northern Argentina are in similar case. On the map (Fig. 1) these irrigated spots are designated as specialized horticulture, because the agricultural system is much the same as in vegetable and fruit growing of nearby oases.

Specialized poultry production is a minor business, carried on chiefly in the United States, which resembles market gardening wherever it is found near large cities, and truck farming in the two large producing districts of California.

The small districts devoted to commercial horticulture and the other crop specialties rarely coincide with administrative divisions for which statistics are collected. In the field they are easily observed, because the break between horticulture and surrounding, extensive land utilization is sharp, adhering strictly to frost lines and changes in soil or slope. Some truck farms of the Atlantic and Gulf coastal plains, carved out of deep forest, are as strikingly

set off as are irrigated oases in deserts. Perhaps because they are clean-cut, many garden and orchard regions have been carefully studied. From these studies a composite picture of this manifold agricultural system can be seen.[43]

COMMERCIAL AGRICULTURE

With single exceptions everywhere on the wane, all the agricultural systems of the occidental middle latitudes are on a cash basis. The dependence of all this farming on the urbanized world created by the Industrial Revolution stands out clearly. The change-over from crude medieval agriculture began with the commercial Revolution of the sixteenth century, but came into its own only with the advent of invention and science on a grand scale. From almost exclusive dependence on agriculture, human existence broadened its material base to include trade, and then mining and manufacturing. Agriculture felt the repercussions of these mighty alterations of economic life. The market for its products was increased many fold, and the mechanism for intensi-

[43] Paul F. Gemmill, "The Agriculture of the Eastern Shore Country," *Economic Geography,* II (1926), 197–212; John L. Wann, "Where Florida Truck Crops are Grown," *ibid,* IX (1933), 85–103; Samuel N. Dicken, "Central Florida Farm Landscape," *Economic Geography,* XI (1935), 173–82; William T. Chambers, "Lower Rio Grande Valley of Texas," *ibid,* VI (1930), 364–73; Edwin J. Foscue, "Land Utilization in the Lower Rio Grande Valley of Texas," *ibid,* VIII (1932), 1–11; *idem,* "The Mesilla Valley of New Mexico: A Study in Aridity and Irrigation," *ibid,* VII (1931), 1–27; Otis Freeman, "Apple Industry of the Wenatchee Area," *ibid,* X (1934), 160–71; Charles C. Colby, "The California Raisin Industry—A Study in Geographic Interpretation," *Annals of the Association of American Geographers,* XIV (1924), 49–108; Clifford M. Zierer, "Utilization of Indiana Muck Lands for Specialty Crops," *Journal of Geography,* XXXI (1932), 313–23; Ella M. Wilson, "The Aroostock Valley: A Study in Potatoes," *Geographical Review,* XVI (1926), 196–205; E. G. H. Dobby, "Economic Geography of the Port Wine Region," *Economic Geography,* XII (1936), 311–23; Edward A. Ackerman: "An Algerian Oasis Community," *ibid,* XII (1936), 250–58; Harley P. Milstead, "Distribution of Crops in Peru," *ibid,* IV (1928), 88–96.

fying production was provided in the shape of machinery, transportation, fertilizer, refrigeration, and scientific farm management, including plant and animal breeding. For the first time in history agriculture became specialized so that today commodities are generally produced where the natural environment is favorable. Exceptions to this rule usually have a political explanation, and not the least significant portent of the current rise of exclusive nationalism is its tendency to set back the hands of the agricultural clock, by restricting commodity production within national boundaries.

OUTLOOK

While efforts are being made to produce more variety of crops at home, the forces of the Industrial Revolution are being increasingly applied to expand commercial agriculture in the low latitudes and to a lesser degree in the Orient. In these two apparently conflicting tendencies lies a prime challenge to society. Can economic distribution and social control be so organized by political means as to commercialize the remaining agricultural regions of the earth? If so, will the accomplishment wreck the unstable structure of commercial agriculture already in existence?

Agriculture is the broad base on which economic society rests. Its future is one of the most critical problems of the next generation. Geography ought to hold some of the keys to its solution. A refinement of the classification of agricultural types here outlined, or the substitution of a more realistic classification than this one proposed, may be a means of discovering at least one of those keys, by clarifying man's comprehension of the limitations and opportunities which Nature poses as incentives and restraints to human ingenuity.

MAX. SORRE

THE GEOGRAPHY OF DIET

The food shortage caused by the last war has encouraged geographers to re-examine an important chapter of their discipline, that of diet.[1] It would have been sufficient for them to follow the advice of Vidal de la Blache when he wrote: "Among the connections that tie man to a certain environment, one of the most tenacious is food supply; clothing and weapons are more subject to modification than the dietary regime, which experience has shown to be best suited to human needs in a given

Translated, with permission of the author and publisher, from "La géographie de l'alimentation," *Annales de Géographie*, LXI (1952), 184–99. The author is professor emeritus of geography at the Sorbonne.
[1] I have already given some essential information on this subject in *Les fondements de la géographie humaine*, I: *Les fondements biologiques* (Paris: Colin, 1943). Geographers will find a useful bibliography in Josue de Castro, *The Geography of Hunger* (Boston: Little, Brown, 1952) [first published as *Geografia da Fome, A fome no Brasil* (Rio de Janeiro, 1946)]. Among official sources see the works of the Health Commission of the League of Nations for the period prior to 1939. More recent information is given in two publications of the Food and Agricultural Organization of the United Nations, *World Food Survey* (Rome, 1946), and *The State of Food and Agriculture: A Survey of World Conditions and Prospects* (Washington, D.C., 1948). In addition, see the reports of the II° Congrès Scientifique International de l'Alimentation published by the Société Scientifique d'Hygiène Alimentaire et Rationelle de l'Homme (Paris, 1937). Finally, under the auspices of UNESCO a series of pamphlets was published in 1950 under the general title *Man and His Food* (New York: Educational Film Library Association, 1950). See especially the pamphlet of André Mayer entitled *Nutrition and Social Progress*.

climate."[2] These lines suggested a promising orientation and recent events, which have thrown a harsh light on the subject, have exposed other aspects of its importance.

Geographers were of course aware that hunger and its accompanying evils had always influenced the actions of men. History has preserved the memory of famines, and geographers need not go back more than a few generations to discover the stark terror caused by the threat of hunger. Moreover, newspapers provided reports of the suffering inflicted by poor harvests on vast areas. Nevertheless, for a large part of Western humanity these misfortunes seemed vague and remote, like a disappearing bad dream. Then, suddenly, these misfortunes were vivid and near, because we were hungry, because we saw strange diseases previsouly known only through medical descriptions, and because whole groups bore the marks of undernourishment. The magnitude of the hardship moved scholars and statesmen, and the problem of nutrition was recognized as something vital and urgent. Major international agencies, like the Food and Agricultural Organization of the United Nations (F.A.O.), made attempts to study the problem and suggest solutions. At the same time physiologists began to lay the foundation of a new discipline, the

[2] Paul Vidal de la Blache, *Principes de géographie humaine, publiés d'après les manuscrits de l'auteur par Emmanuel de Martonne* (Paris: Colin, 1922), p. 133. [Translated by Millicent Todd Bingham as *Principles of Human Geography* (New York: Holt, 1926).]

science of nutrition, which had been made possible by advances in biophysics and biochemistry. An immense field was opened to their investigations, and economists and biologists understood at last that human problems are defined by a consideration of needs and not solely in terms of production, exchange, or even consumption. The social sciences were becoming human again.

Human geographers participated in this general movement, for how could they hope to gain an intelligible image of the *oikoumene* without adequate knowledge of what men eat and their relative success in satisfying dietary needs? The productive capability of human groups and even their resistance to infectious diseases depend in large part upon this satisfaction. Without such information economic studies have no foundation. We must, therefore, treat the geography of diet as an essential chapter of human geography, and make use of the growing body of literature. Investigations conducted by government agencies, like the French Institut National d'Hygiène, or gathered by international organizations are available for our consideration. I will refrain from any direct attempt to summarize the contents of such a study, and try instead to define some of its essential concepts and outline its present and potential scope.

I

I have suggested elsewhere that the pathogenic complex should be regarded as the central concept in the geography of infectious diseases.[3] Now we must find a similar notion for the geography of diet, something concrete and capable of providing orientation in geographic analysis, either because it implies attachment to localized human groups or relation with other geographic concepts. The notion of the dietary regime responds to these needs. Let us define it precisely. We begin by disregarding the medical sense of the term. When we speak of the dietary regime of a human group we refer to the ensemble of foods and their

[3] *Les fondements biologiques*, pp. 291–362.

preparations that sustains it throughout the year. A combination of this sort is sometimes designated by the name of the food that serves as its core (e.g., meat or milk regimes). The concept is concrete rather than theoretical and, like all other geographic concepts, is revealed by direct observation.

Vidal de la Blache points out that the Greeks were strongly impressed by the differences that they observed among various peoples in dietary habits.[4] These Mediterraneans—consumers of wheat, olive oil, and wine, and sedentary farmers—had made contact at the confines of their domain with nomads who lived on the milk of their mares (*galactophagi*), with fishermen for whom fish were the main food (*ichthyophagi*), and their legends spoke of lotus eaters (*lotophagi*). Even more than skin color or stature, these habits, connected with natural resources and ways of life, seem to have impressed the Greek geographers as important ethnic characteristics. The use of milk and butter by men beyond the Alps made an equally strong impression on the Roman writers, from Pliny to the Gallo-Roman chronicles of the period of the great invasions. The latter spoke with repugnance or fright of tall barbarians with disgusting mustaches of butter and fierce horsemen who devoured putrid flesh hardened between the leather of their saddles and the skin of their mounts. In the Occident during the course of centuries, each region has developed or consolidated its dietary habits, which have become elements of national character. Goethe describes the preference for black or white bread as a shibboleth. Peoples often speak with astonishment or derision of their neighbors' cooking. Even in the same country, provincial differences inspire gibes, which are transmitted from generation to generation.

The discovery of the world, beginning with the sixteenth century, enlarged the experiences of Europeans. From the Pacific Islands and the glades of the equatorial

[4] *Principes de géographie humaine*, p. 133.

forests to the icy shores where Eskimos stuffed themselves with the grease of marine animals, travelers met peoples with menus that were in harmony with natural resources or climatic exigencies. The description of diet entered into geographic lore along with accounts of clothing, dwellings, and implements. Philosophers speculated on whether the fecundity of maritime peoples was derived from their consumption of fish. The intuition of the Greek geographers had become more and more scientific.

In order for the notion of dietary regime to assume its full significance, the stage of simple qualitative description had to give way to one of quantitative definition, and this occurred only with the progress of physical and natural sciences, during the era initiated by Lavoisier's works on combustion. We arrived at a time when it was possible to identify the conditions that must be satisfied in a scientific definition of diet. Descriptions ceased to be mere collections of curiosities or contributions to folklore.

For a geographer, dietary regime refers not to individuals but to precisely defined and localized human groups. As long as we deal with peoples of poorly developed social stratification, we encounter no initial difficulties. Each village and each tribe forms a homogeneous group of uniform dietary habits. Yet it is necessary to determine whether the subdivisions of these societies (which may be more complicated than we suspect) have had, at least at certain epochs, special regimes. The complexity of the problem increases in societies with pronounced stratification, and even at the level of relative uniformity differences between urban and rural diets may be observed. Inequalities between classes in standard of living may introduce strong contrasts between the diets of the rich and of the poor. For example, from a qualitative standpoint, we are able to gain a clear understanding of traditional habits common to Frenchmen as opposed to Englishmen. But for this comparison to be significant,

we must differentiate between social groups of equivalent level on either side of the channel. To avoid superficiality and error, the geographer must examine the data of the sociologists, and in any case he must circumscribe and delimit social groups.

It follows that the definition of diet must include consideration of all solid and liquid foods, whether animal, vegetable, or mineral. Such a definition allows enumeration and indication of quantities. Then a new classification may be made that distinguishes among the three great food categories: protein, carbohydrate, and fat. Each of these categories possesses its special value. By applying the principle of equivalent energy potential [*isodynamie*], it is easy to calculate the energy value of particular diets. International tables give the composition of a great number of foods and indicate the numbers of calories that they provide. International agreements have also established the energy requirements necessary to sustain both sexes according to age and activity (i.e., rest, moderate exercise, strenuous exercise). I will overlook the difficulties that arise from different interpretations of the variation in basal metabolism according to latitude. Comparison of the determinations of normal energy requirements allows an estimate of the energy value of particular diets. Given knowledge of the way of life or a particular group, such comparison allows us to judge if it is or is not properly nourished. With information on the weight of a crop and its caloric equivalent, we can also compare animal and vegetable resources with established needs. These methods are not yet well known to geographers; it would be in their interest to become familiar with them.

The principle of equivalent energy potential should not be strictly applied. The three categories of dietary components are not interchangeable, and common knowledge, confirmed by the works of physiologists, indicates that each must be present in diets in adequate amounts. Here again, there are norms. Geographers know the unfortunate consequences of the deficiency of some diets in animal proteins (e.g., in China, India, and the equatorial forests). Dietary imbalance is still more common than absolute insufficiency.

Moreover, the diets of all human groups also contain organic compounds and mineral or organo-mineral substances. Some are needed to build or renew tissue, while others have more complex and in part poorly known functions, either because they contribute to the maintenance of the chemical composition of the blood and body fluids, or because they function as catalysts. The effects of calcium or phosphorus deficiency are clear. Haven't cattle-raisers long been aware of racial differences between animals of granitic and limestone areas? The application of iodine as a treatment for such diseases as goiter has long been practiced among peoples of the plains. The physiologists are just beginning to understand the action of trace minerals that are present in the organism in infinitesimal proportions. Special mention should be made of sodium chloride, which seems to have played a key role in determining currents of movement and trade. Long before the dawn of history, salt deposits served as foci of trade routes, and until recently salt bars have had a value comparable to that of precious metals in the African trade. It is possible that some of the strange practices recorded in remote places, such as *geophagy* and perhaps even *coprophagy*, are related to salt deficiencies in diets. The geographer must concern himself with the question of how the groups he studies obtain the minerals that are required to maintain balanced diets.

Finally, there are the essential amino acids and vitamins, which are being assigned increasingly important roles. During the last war we saw how their deficiency produced, in addition to the horrors of famine, such diseases as pellagra with its acute and often terrifying forms. All the functions of the body, from growth to reproduction, are tied to the presence of vitamins, and the list of them continues to grow. Certain dietary peculiarities, such as the consumption of caterpillars by some forest dwellers, have long seemed strange and even repulsive to us. We also are impressed by the frequent recurrence of some culinary practices, such as the sauces that go with the consumption of rice in Monsoon Asia and improve the flatness of millet in Black Africa. These similar practices can hardly be attributed in general to the need of a complementary source of energy or to any necessity to stimulate appetites, although the last explanation may have some merit. We must turn to the vitamins themselves to find the reasons for practices that seem unexplainable. The instincts of primitive people have provided them with a safe guide. The description of dietary regimes thus requires enumeration of the vitamins that are associated with staple foods.

The mention of vitamins calls attention to procedures adopted in the preparation of raw foods. These substances are unequally distributed in animal or vegetable organisms. To polish a grain of rice or wheat or to peel a fruit is to deprive such foods of a part of their nutritional value. Beriberi, which is so widespread in the Far East, is associated with the practice of polishing rice. Thanks to the experiments of Eijkmann, we are no longer uncertain of the nature of this disease; we know that it is non-contagious and that it is an illness of dietary deficiency common in countries where polished rice is the staple food. Excessive milling also diminishes the nutritional value of wheat. Moreover, cooking destroys the active properties of certain substances even when it makes them more digestible. A normal diet includes a suitable proportion of raw foods. The study of diet must include more than an analysis of food sources; it must also include consideration of how they are prepared. A superior cuisine is a mark of cultural refinement not only for the wealthy classes, but also for the mass of a nation. These remarks should be enough to command the attention of geographers, and it is clear that the geography of cuisine may aspire to a more scientific status.

Finally, the definition of dietary regimes should include consideration of all foods consumed during the year, i.e., during a complete cycle of seasons. For most human groups, food supply is very unequally distributed during the year. Indeed, the inequality may be so marked that one is tempted to speak of a succession of diets. Among many hunters and fishermen, the year consists of a long period of restriction interrupted by occasional feasts. Regularity is greater among most primitive agriculturalists, but the reserve stored in granaries is rarely sufficient to compensate for periods of scarcity. Between successive crops, and especially in the weeks immediately preceding a harvest, there is often a period of dearth. In the most impoverished regions of France at the end of the eighteenth century, only the practice of mutual assistance among the peasants prevented starvation during such periods of dearth. In compensation, there are the days of plenty and feasts, when, after a fast of variable length, one is able to gorge oneself without restraint. Days of good fortune and festivals alternate with days of hard labor when abundant menus are necessary to sustain the work of the harvest. It is a temptation to describe such occasions as exceptions that should not be taken into account. But the visible evidence of the importance attached to storage and provision demonstrate that such an interpretation would be incorrect. In Java, Dutch sociologists have noticed that feast days celebrated by great meals are much too frequent to be overlooked in any account of persistent diets. However, in all such cases of heavy consumption associated with hard labor, we must take account of the increase in nutritional needs.

My intention has not been to offer a classification or map of dietary regimes, for such are available in *Les fondements biologiques de la géographie humaine.* I have tried instead to describe some techniques employed in nutritional studies that might be useful to geographers. With knowledge of these techniques, geographers may aspire through their regional studies to contribute to the common effort. This discussion is designed primarily to help geographers to use the data gathered by nutritional specialists, and it also offers some reflections on the geographic interest of dietary regimes.

II

When we examine diets from a geographic viewpoint, they appear in a dual guise as expressions of the environment, for climate sets nutritional requirements, and ecological conditions determine the composition and abundance of foods. Since these two relationships are quite obvious, they do not require demonstration.

The diets of the peoples of Oceania reflect the richness of the biotic resources of the archipelagos and the fecundity of the surrounding seas. Coconuts, breadfruit, and taro supply the base of their vegetable diet, and these foods convey an image of an entire natural landscape. Each of the great cereals of civilization (wheat, maize, and rice) covers a vast area of the world, but their primitive forms were tied to much more localized conditions. We are perhaps best able to see how certain elements of diet can symbolize a landscape when we examine sources of animal and vegetable fats.[5] The consumption of fats among the peoples of the Arctic zone demonstrates the bond that exists between diet and thermogenetic needs. Finally, the nature and quantity of animal proteins also reflect environmental conditions, but we must add that resources may not be sufficient to meet needs. Indeed, the balance of the diets of many forest dwellers in the equatorial zone is upset by insufficiency of animal proteins. Consequently, we cannot regard diet as an expression of perfect environ-

[5] Max. Sorre, "La géographie des matières grasses," *Annales de Géographie,* LIX (1950), 93–108.

mental adaptation. Primitive peoples and even those at a higher level of culture live at the margin of possibilities more often than is generally realized. On the other hand, in a single climatic province pastoralists and farmers may live side by side and practice different dietary regimes (e.g., the Fulani in the midst of the agricultural populations of western Sudan). In marginal steppe regions there are generally various dietary possibilities and also various types of dietary regimes. Such diversity warns the observer to be suspicious of simple interpretations. When the diet of primitive peoples seems to reveal direct or indirect environmental influences, other factors soon come into view, and this is of course even more likely to happen in a study of the diet of civilized peoples. Diet, like settlement, is one of the most characteristic and least simple expressions of culture, for it absorbs all the other elements that enter into the definition of a *genre de vie*.

In the first place, diet reflects the totality of the beliefs of a group, both negative and positive. Men very often do not utilize all the food that nature places at their disposal. They may abstain from certain products or ration themselves at certain times of the year. Such avoidance or restriction is not explained by reduction of needs, or because particular foods are not suited to a warm climate. Rational explanations of this sort were once abused. Any agreement between such habits and utility is fortuitous, because today, some of the ideas associated with the origin of food avoidance are no longer intelligible.

The relation of dietary habits and religion represents a well known chapter of ethnology, and one to which geographic interest is especially sensitive.[6] The notion of a mystical connection between an animal or plant and a human group is at the base of numerous dietary prohibitions, and food taboos may persist long after the memory of their motives has disappeared. On a

higher plane, the belief in reincarnation and the respect for all forms of life have similar consequences. The Brahman abstains from eating méat, even though he raises cattle and consumes milk and milk products. In this case, the poverty of animal proteins in diets has an adverse effect on human vigor. The list of foods regarded as impure, either by small groups or by vast religious communities (e.g., pork among the Moslems) could be extended indefinitely. Similar ideas may recommend the consumption of certain animal organs that are regarded as noble. Ritual cannibalism, otherwise so difficult to explain, probably corresponds to conceptions of this sort.

Most religions impose upon their followers periods of purification accompanied by fasting or abstinence. This is true of the Lenten period of the Catholic Church, with forty days of fasting, and avoidance of meat on Fridays and during times of vigil. With the passage of the centuries religious prescriptions of this sort have tended to become more flexible in the Catholic Church, but enforcement has been more rigorous in the Orthodox Church. In the Balkans until recently the interdiction against the eating of meat was spread over 206 days of the year. One cannot speak of the Christian Lent without also thinking of the Great Fast of the Jews and the Ramadan of the Moslems. In Christendom the corollary of these prohibitions has been a marked increase in fish consumption and the development of conserving, drying, and smoking industries. River fishing has also contributed to the general dietary trend. The role of fresh-water fish in the constitution of diets would be an exciting subject to study. We are reasonably well informed on the practices of the primitive populations of the equatorial forests, the riparian peoples of the Far East, and even Eastern Europeans, but we still have much to learn on this subject in Western Europe.

In regions of highly specialized diet, neglect of important possibilities of the environment may be caused by religious conceptions. After observing that the Chinese

[6] Pierre Deffontaines has given a useful inventory of these relations in *Géographie et religions* (Paris: Gallimard, 1948), pp. 367 ff.

make little use of their fauna, Sion notes that they eat only the meat of their pigs and poultry and that no milk or milk products enter into their diet.[7] This is especially surprising, since the Chinese nation was formed in the plains of the Yellow Earth, where pastoral vocations are often practiced. Sion believes that Chinese agriculture was formed by a concentration of effort in the plains. One expression of this narrow specialization is a diet radically different from that of the neighboring pastoral nomads. In this case, not without parallel elsewhere, it is not religion alone, but the cumulative weight of ancient traditions that determines food preferences and the related patterns of life.

The fact that diet is not always in agreement with the potentialities of environment is explained not only by the traditional productive techniques of a human group, but also by its social and economic structure. During the interval between the two world wars the countries of Danubian Europe specialized in the production of wheat and maize. They were in need of Western Europe's manufactured goods and in payment offered the best part of their crop. They exported wheat and consumed maize, and we know the nutritional consequences of too exclusive reliance on maize. Again, for a long time in most of the French countryside the secondary products of farms and the products of poultry yards were not effectively utilized. Except at harvest time, they were sold in neighboring urban markets, and the income derived from such sales usually did not enter into the general bookkeeping of the farm but went instead into the farmer's wife's cash box. Consequently, products of high nutritional value, such as eggs, did not enter into the producer's diet.

It is understandable, therefore, that the notion of the dietary regime is contingent on other conceptions, for it varies according to all the characteristics of the groups to

[7] J. Sion, *Asie des Moussons* (2 vols.; Paris: Colin, 1928), I, 47–52. [Vol. IX of *Géographie universelle.*]

which it is attached. Change in the standard of living in rural France during the last fifty years has had a profound effect on diets. During the 1880's the nourishment of the French peasant was basically the same as that of his ancestors. The introduction of the potato in the eighteenth century removed the menace of famine from the poorest lands. But meat and sugar were no more conspicuous in menus than they had been in the past. It was still the common practice for everything marketable (i.e., the quality products) to be sold outside. The pace of evolution was increased after the end of the First World War. Transportation difficulties between 1940 and 1945 caused further acceleration, and also transformed the psychology of the French peasantry. Rural menus were enriched by foods that had previously been directed to urban markets. The revolution has been profound. Planners speak of the increase in agricultural returns and make estimates of the amount of farm production that will be available for export. But these calculations must not neglect increases in local consumption over which we have so little control. The latter trend means an ascent of the rural world to a higher standard of living.

Urban diets have also been transformed, and this change has been reflected, by imitation, in rural diets. If we overlook religious considerations, one of the causes of this transformation resides in the ideas that men acquire about the efficiency of their diets. In the United States a kind of scientific superstition has tended to supersede religious concepts. Almost everywhere rising standards of living are expressed first by increased consumption of white bread, and then by increased consumption of meat and sugar. At a later stage, the consumption of rich cereals and then meat tends to decrease, and milk products and fruit play a larger role. Other causes are found in changing modes of living. The rhythm of life in industrial environments offers little encouragement to the meticulous and skilled culinary preparations that were the pride of the old countries. Canned foods invade menus, and as such food is poor in vitamins, the value of fruit is enhanced. Ultimately, nutritional deficiencies may be corrected by industrially prepared vitamins, made possible by the improvement of transportation and the development of the refrigeration industry; but modern man does not perceive the paradox. The entire world contributes to garnish the tables of the inhabitants of New York, London, and Paris. In French suburbs clusters of bananas crowd the carts of fruit and vegetable vendors all year around, and fresh fish can be found on all tables.

The geographical significance of diet is now revealed in a clear light, and we can see that it is linked with all the other chapters of human geography.

III

The study of dietary regimes, whether by correlation or factual analysis, demands extensive inquiries based upon full use of available statistics. An exhaustive and critical inventory of the literature in this field has not yet been made, and it is often difficult for geographers to discover what has been done. There is, however, a rather impressive mass of data on nutrition in different climatic zones. This information is of unequal value, but the research now under way responds in general to the requirements of modern nutritional science. We may hope that these efforts will lead to a re-examination of dietary norms for different latitudes, i.e., that they will solve the problem of basal metabolism. Competent authorities realize the need for a summary and synthesis of the findings that are either scattered in obscure publications or remain unpublished and virtually unknown. It is not possible here to offer even a rough outline of what such an effort might reveal. The discussion to follow is limited to a brief survey of work that has been accomplished in France within recent years.

The nutrition department of the Institut National d'Hygiène has been sponsoring studies of diet since 1946, and data on major cities (Paris, Lyons, Marseilles, St. Étienne, Strasbourg) and rural districts have been published in its *Bulletin*. In general, these studies reveal that food consumption is somewhat higher than the norms, but that it varies from time to time according to fluctuations in the cost of living and the influence of social and economic factors. These human factors are evidently of most interest to the health specialist. But a careful examination of the published tables reveals qualitative and quantitative differences among cities as well as rural districts that are of obvious geographic significance. This is especially true of rural diets, which reflect the peculiarities of different ways of life. Twelve elementary regions have been established: Dinan-Fougères, eastern Brittany, Mayenne, western Normandy, the Vendée *bocage,* the marshes of Brittany and Poitou, Nantes, Anjou, the Lyons highlands, the massif of Pilat, and the plains of Burgundy. Almost everywhere, the consumption of calories and total proteins is close to the norms, but dietary types can be identified on the basis of marked variations in the supply of animal proteins and other dietary constituents. These variations appear especially in the consumption of meat, milk, and dairy products. An attempt has been made to correlate types of diet with modes of livelihood, but the results are deceptive. Cartographic comparison does not reveal satisfactory correlations—a consequence, at least in part, of inadequate production figures and the arbitrary territorial framework of the *départements*. Moreover, allowance must be made for the influence of local traditions and familial habits. I suspect that dietary habits do not evolve at the same rate as the economy—an hypothesis suggested to me by the authors of these studies.

In any case, these studies indicate the desirability of further research under the sponsorship of the same agency. The authors did not fail to emphasize the preliminary character of their findings. Other types of diets are probably represented in France. The geographical basis of the studies appears to have been too narrow to permit delimitation of dietary regions, which would have been our aim. On the other hand, improvements will have to be made in cartographic techniques, which have not progressed beyond the stage of analytic representation.

IV

The belated appearance of these studies has not delayed attempts to attack the problem of nutrition by other means. When the League of Nations directed attention to this subject in 1928 the first investigations of its Health Organization revealed a frightening fact: more than two-thirds of humanity was suffering from chronic undernourishment. The peoples thus designated were either menaced by famine, had badly imbalanced diets or caloric intakes below the norms that barely allowed them to live, or suffered from mineral and, above all, protein deficiency. In short, those who were not condemned to death outright suffered from deficiency diseases that often have fatal consequences, or were unable to resist the assaults of infectious diseases. We have tended to think of hunger in terms of famine, its most dramatic form, but in the final analysis the less obvious masked forms probably claim more victims.

The studies undertaken since 1946 by F.A.O. have verified this balance sheet, and they have also provided evidence of inequalities in the distribution of food supplies. Deficiency is widespread, for only one-third of mankind consumes more than 2750 calories per day, and the daily ration of half of mankind is less than 2250 calories. Inequality of diets can also be described as a global phenomenon, for one-third of the world's population, in Europe and North America, consumes three-quarters of its food. The daily consumption of animal proteins varies from 12 grams in Japan to 61 grams in New Zealand. In Great Britain the consumption of meat and fish varies according to social groups at

the rate of 1 to 2, and the consumption of milk varies at the rate of 1 to 6. André Meyer who supplied these figures concludes that inequality in the presence of death depends initially upon inequality in the presence of illness, and then upon inequality in the presence of hunger and malnutrition.

Surprised by the long indifference to these problems, Josue de Castro[8] has looked for an explanation of the neglect. He attributes it to the moral bias, combined with all powerful economic prejudices, of a rationalist civilization that covers its face in the presence of any manifestation of primary instincts. Freed from its complex of guilt, the world now accepts the reality of hunger. I support Josue de Castro's claim that geography provides the best method for the study of such a complex and universal phenomenon. Indeed, if what I have said of dietary regimes is correct, geographical analysis alone can explain their local conditions and connections. The statistician indicates an approach, but the geographer goes to the heart of the matter. Hunger is an ecological phenomenon; a manifestation of disequilibrium between human groups and their physical and social milieus. But it also has remote connections. Famine is a regional occurrence with universal, and hence geographic, implications.

It is a surprising fact that the western hemisphere appears to be one of the world's great realms of malnutrition. And the calamity is not narrowly localized; it is widespread, although its intensity and causes are highly variable. In Latin America two-thirds of the population lives in perpetual fear of famine. According to Josue de Castro's estimate, diets are insufficient, imbalanced, and more or less deficient in proteins, minerals, and vitamins in three-quarters of the area, i.e., in Venezuela,

[8] Josue de Castro, *op. cit.* The author is both a physician and a geographer, and at present [1952] is serving as head of F.A.O. His book is a vigorous indictment of neo-Malthusian theses. The details of his argument should be received with some reserve, but the information he presents is indispensable.

Colombia, Peru, Bolivia, Ecuador, Chile, the north and extreme south of Argentina, the eastern half of Paraguay, and the northern half of Brazil. In the sugar-cane country of northeastern Brazil daily rations fall below 1700 calories, and in Bolivia they fall below 1200 calories. It is possible that these figures should be adjusted to compensate for a reduction in basic metabolism, but the poor composition of rations is more serious than their deficiency in energy value. Disequilibrium is also evident in the more favored countries. The state of chronic famine cannot be attributed to natural causes, nor to population pressure, for South America is still a sparsely settled continent. It is a legacy of the colonial past, and the commercial exploitation of the American soil. Exploitative cycles centered on gold, sugar, precious stones, coffee, rubber, and petroleum have superimposed their effects during four and a half centuries. But in Central America and the Antilles, the pre-Columbian history also must be taken into account. May we suppose that the apathy and melancholy so often witnessed among the maize-eating Indians of the high plateaus are not results of the altitude but rather of the cumulative effects of hunger among peoples who were subjected to harsh feudalism long before the arrival of Cortes? In the Caribbean region each island has its own cycle of evolution. At first sight North America seems to be free of hunger, but nutritional deficiencies are not lacking, for investigations reveal dietary insufficiency in the urban milieu. Real famine is rare, since it appears in true form only in the English Antilles and on the plantations of the southeastern part of the United States. In the latter region at the beginning of the present century pellagra caused 4,000 deaths per year. In 1938 the number of cases reached 100,000, and 2,113 fatalities were recorded as recently as 1940. There is a remarkably close correlation between mortality from pellagra and fluctuations of the cotton market.

With a heavier population burden than any other continent, Asia is the land of famine par excellence. In China, the world's most intense agricultural concentration is crowded into valleys on 10 to 15 per cent of the total area of the country, the deforested slopes having been abandoned to erosion. In addition to chronic famine, the population has suffered from rickets, anemia, and the debilitating effects of intestinal parasites. The utilization of human excreta as the unique source of fertilizer promotes the infestation, but if it were not used men would die of hunger instead of disease. Beriberi and pellagra are persistent among the consumers of polished rice. In China life expectancy does not exceed thirty-four years. According to the chroniclers, 203 serious famines occurred in one province or another during the period from 620 to 1620, and at least 15 of these were accompanied by outbreaks of cannibalism. Drought, which encourages plague, may be followed by floods, locust invasions, and sometimes by earthquakes and typhoons. But the effects of these calamities would be less terrifying if arable land were more abundant and technology were more advanced. Josue de Castro concludes that population pressure is not a cause but an effect, i.e., that the exasperating physiological effects of misery stimulate sexual urges and increase birth rates. This argument is questionable.

In a large part of India the quantitative insufficiency of diets is aggravated by a qualitative insufficiency caused by religious interdicts. Does this situation explain the difference in stature between most Hindus and the Moslems of the Punjab? Infant mortality is perhaps even more pronounced than in China, in spite of the fact that milk consumption is somewhat higher. Here again, the evil is very ancient and continues to grow. Josue de Castro, who refuses to emphasize the absence of birth control, charges the British administration with a list of serious failings: it made no effort to change a social structure that would have encouraged famine even without natural calamities; it was concerned primarily with attempts to increase profits and paid little attention to the problems of the indigenous peoples; and its grandiose irrigation schemes were designed solely for the increase of export products. In these charges we detect the familiar denunciations of colonialism and plantation economy of the capitalist type. This style of historical writing is of course excessively naïve. It is clear, however, that India lives under a persistent threat of famine, and that poor nutrition makes its peoples more susceptible to the ravages of malaria. The situation of Japan, which is almost as dramatic, is explained adequately by the chain of political circumstances during the last century.

Famine is also an ancient African scourge. Two thousand years before Abraham, a Pharaoh lamented the misfortune of his people because during seven years the Nile had not risen to flood. The menace, always present, assumes a variety of forms. Even if famine is caused by natural forces, men have always had a large share of the responsibility. Since the belated suppression of the slave trade, the colonial exploitation has not always been mindful, as it should have in its own interest, of the needs of the African peoples. When a clearer appreciation has been acquired of correct relations between subsistence and industrial societies, the problem has too often been expressed solely in terms of quantities. This is true everywhere, not only in Africa. But it seems misleading when we know the true nature of the dependence of pastoral peoples upon sedentary cultivators, to follow the example of Josue de Castro and relate the handsomeness of the Masai or the Saharan nomads to their diets. When this correction is made, one may conclude that dietary defects, regardless of their causes, weigh heavily on the African peoples. The propagation of pellagra in southern Africa provides a harsh confirmation of these defects. Europe seems to have realized at last that the revitalization of the African people is a problem of nutrition.

In addition, Europe must resolve its own problems of hunger. We understood the urgency of these problems before the last war, for the picture of the food situation prior to 1939 was somber indeed. A part of Mediterranean Europe seemed to be condemned to chronic dearth. In the *secano* lands of the Iberian Peninsula, where the deficient diet of the latifundia added its effects to those of natural calamities, and the Civil War aggravated both problems, 30,000 cases of pellagra were recorded in a single year. Dearth was also evident on the estates of southern Italy, where agrarian crises are perpetual, and in Eastern Europe, where the regime of large landholdings had disastrous results, and where a miserable rural proletariat was prey to pellagra, xerophthalmia, and rickets. In the latter region, composed of rural countries that had to export their crops to obtain industrial goods, the crises that shocked the world between the two wars had serious repercussions. During the immediate prewar years Germany took advantage of this situation to improve its own dietary regime. The only favored lands were France, Great Britain, and the Scandinavian countries. Yet, among the latter, Denmark, having commercialized its butter production to an excessive degree, witnessed the multiplication of ocular diseases. In 1936 Lord Boyd Orr concluded that 50 per cent of the British population was suffering from dietary defects—10 per cent because of insufficient money to buy adequate amounts of food, 20 per cent because of menus deficient in protein, and another 20 per cent because of vitamin and mineral deficiencies. These findings, received at first with incredulity, were confirmed by investigations in the following years. Since 1940, war has spread its scourge. Only the soldiers in the combat zones were preserved from malnutrition, for another death awaited them. Famine reappeared in its most acute forms and deficiency diseases appeared among peoples who classified themselves as civilized. This situation was ameliorated slowly and unequally after the liberation, but progress was threatened by climatic adversities.

Famine is really a very general phenomenon, but its regional manifestations obey complex rules. The play of natural forces is often the cause, but they always operate in a human setting. Climatic adversities may destroy crops in vast areas. There are the inevitable cold waves, and the inevitable sequences of wet and dry years. Then famine follows, for the expansion and contraction of the cultivated area is never synchronized exactly with the oscillations of the grain market. It is fatal if troubles prevent compensating shipments to an area of insufficient or exhausted supplies. In countries that are thus compelled to be self-sufficient, the interruption of commerce also promotes soil deterioration, and so paves the way for future famines. To suppress the menace it would be necessary to have a permanent surplus, produced by extension of subsistence farming and improvement of farming techniques. Regional self-sufficiency is discouraged by commercialization of basic foods (e.g., meat or cereals) or the substitution of foods of inferior nutritional value (e.g., maize instead of wheat). It is also discouraged by the use of arable land for industrial crops, by insufficiency of fertile soil, by inferior methods or implements, and finally by lack of co-ordination between supply and demand. It is certain that the latifundia and capitalist plantation systems have helped to erect one or more of these obstacles. But they are also found in lands of *minifundia,* and they were present in the New World before the Europeans arrived. Moreover, it is clear that the state of demographic congestion

maintained in some prolific countries by emigration barriers has aggravated their dietary situation to an insufferable degree. Finally, famine cannot be eliminated without a more humane organization of the market system.

V

Any study of this nature tends to exceed its limits, for the obvious reason that demographic conditions must be included among the variables. Will population growth upset the dietary equilibrium realized by improvement of the general conditions of agricultural production?[9] And will the anticipated limitation of food supplies eventually impose a limit to the size of mankind? The formula of Malthus may no longer be accepted, but his ideas are rephrased in modern terms. The neo-Malthusians clash with those who express unlimited faith in technological progress, in spite of the effects (which may be irreversible) of previous waste. Speculation on these problems has been offered without restraint. It is difficult to refute the idea of a limit, but I prefer to think, with the experts of F.A.O., that it is still rather far away. In spite of the wounds that ignorance, lack of foresight, and greediness have inflicted upon it, the earth could provide adequate support for its present inhabitants, and even more, if all men had free access to its wealth. It is through recognition of regional equilibriums that geographers can offer precious assistance to those who must plan for man's future needs.

[9] I have not tried to elaborate the controversies about the growth of human population, but have adopted a modest view in the spirit of Josue de Castro, André Mayer, and Lord Boyd Orr [the latter are authors of prefaces to the French and English versions of de Castro's book].

HAROLD C. CONKLIN

AN ETHNOECOLOGICAL
APPROACH TO SHIFTING
AGRICULTURE

Methods of shifting cultivation, while unfamiliar to many of us living in temperate latitudes, are typical of vast areas in the tropics. Such methods account for approximately one-third of the total land area used for agricultural purposes in Southeast Asia today.[1] In some countries, including the Philippines, it has been estimated that shifting cultivation produces food for up to 10 per cent of the total population.[2] In these regions the economy of large segments of the upland population is based solely on such means. Nevertheless, shifting agriculture is still only inadequately understood. It is often categorically condemned as primitive, wasteful, or illegal, with little or no regard for such pertinent local variables as population density, available land area, climate, or native agricultural knowledge. For most areas, detailed field reports against which such statements might be tested are totally lacking. There is a definite need for ascertaining what are the real facts about shifting agriculture.

In this paper, I shall attempt to throw some light on the nature of such methods

of upland farming and to draw our attention to certain important problems in this area of research. First we shall review some of the more frequent statements made by writers on the subject. Then we shall examine the pertinent ethnographic data for a specific culture, emphasizing not only the local environmental conditions and their apparent modification, but especially the determination of how these conditions and modifications are culturally interpreted.

For our purposes we may consider shifting cultivation, also known by such designations as field-forest rotation[3] or slash-and-burn agriculture, as always involving the impermanent agricultural use of pots produced by the cutting back and burning off of vegetative cover. We shall call such a field a *swidden*. This term, like its by-forms *swithen* or *swivven*, is an old dialect word from northern England (Northumberland, Yorkshire, Lancashire, and elsewhere) meaning "burned clearing" or "to burn, sweal, or singe, as heather."[4] It has been revived recently, and in an ethnographic description, by a Swedish anthropologist.[5] There are many vernacular terms for *swidden*, but few are widely known or used in the literature except in reference to

Reprinted, with permission of the author and editor, from *Transactions of the New York Academy of Sciences*, Series 2, XVII (1954), 133–42 (copyright, 1954, by the New York Academy of Sciences). The author is associate professor of anthropology at Columbia University, New York.

[1] E. G. H. Dobby, *Southeast Asia* (London: University of London Press, 1950), p. 349.

[2] K. J. Pelzer, *Pioneer Settlement in the Asiatic Tropics* (Special Publication of the American Geographical Society No. 29 [New York: Institute of Pacific Relations, 1945]), p. 29.

[3] Pelzer, *op. cit.*, p. 17.

[4] J. O. Hallowell, *A Dictionary of Archaic and Provincial Words . . . from the Fourteenth Century* (London, 1847), p. 838; J. Wright, *The English Dialect Dictionary* (London, 1904), V, 881–82.

[5] K. G. Izikowitz, "Lamet: Hill Peasants in French Indochina," *Etnologiska Studier*, XVII (1951), 7.

limited geographical regions: *kaingin* (*caiñ-gin*) in the Philippines, *ladang* in Indonesia, *taungya* in Burma, and terms[6] such as *djum* in India, *chitemene* in parts of Africa, and *milpa* in Central America.

Swidden agriculture, of course, involves more than is stated in our minimal definition, but before we attempt greater precision, let us examine some of the characteristics which various authors have attributed to it. The following list is not intended to be complete, but does include the most frequent and problematic statements and assumptions I have encountered.

(1) *Swidden* farming is a haphazard procedure involving an almost negligible minimum of labor output. It is basically simple and uncomplicated.

(2) Usually, and preferably, *swiddens* are cleared in virgin forest (rather than in areas of secondary growth). Tremendous loss of valuable timber results.

(3) *Swidden* fires escape beyond cutover plots and destroy vast forest areas. One author states that from 20 to more than 100 times the *swidden* area itself are often gutted by such fires.[7]

(4) *Swidden* techniques are everywhere the same. Such features as the lack of weeding and the use of a single inventory of tools are practically universal.

(5) Stoloniferous grasses such as "notorious *Imperata*"[8] are abhorred as totally useless pests by all groups whose basic economy is swidden agriculture.

(6) *Swiddens* are planted with a single (predominant) crop. Any given *swidden* can thus be said to be a rice or a maize or a millet field or the like. Hence, it is possible to gauge the productivity of a *swidden* by ascertaining the harvest yield of a single crop.

(7) Furthermore, it is possible to gauge the efficiency (i.e., relative to some other method of agriculture) of a given *swidden* economy in terms of its one-crop yield per unit of area cultivated.[9]

(8) *Swiddens* are abandoned when the main crop is in. "The harvest ends the series of agricultural operations."[10]

(9) There is no crop rotation in *swidden* agriculture. Instead, soil fertility is maintained only by the rotational use of the plots themselves. The duration of the rotational cycles can be determined by the time interval between successive clearings of the same plot.

(10) Not only is fertility lost, but destructive erosion and permanent loss of forest cover result from reclearing a once-used *swidden* after less than a universally specifiable minimum number of years of fallowing (set by some authors at twenty-five years).[11] It is claimed that "dangerous" consequences of more rapid rotation often result from native ignorance.

On these and many other points there is frequently an over-all assumption that the standards of efficiency in terms of agricultural economy in the United States or Western Europe are attainable and desirable among any group of *swidden* farmers.

FIELD OBSERVATIONS

From November 1952 until January 1954 I lived with the Yāgaw Hanunóo of southeastern Mindoro Island in the Philippines. The Hanunóo, numbering approximately 6,000, are pagan mountaineers who occupy about 800 square kilometers of forest and grass-covered hinterland, and whose primary economic activity is *swidden* agriculture.[12] I was able to observe and par-

[6] See Pelzer, *op. cit.*, p. 16.
[7] O. F. Cook, "Milpa Agriculture: A Primitive Tropical System," *Annual Report of the Smithsonian Institution, 1919* (Washington, D.C., 1921), p. 313.
[8] Pierre Gourou, *The Tropical World: Its Social and Economic Conditions and Its Future Status* (New York: Longmans, Green, 1953), p. 18.
[9] J. H. Hutton, "A Brief Comparison Between the Economics of Dry and Irrigated Cultivation in the Naga and Some Effects of a Change from the Former to the Latter," *Advancement of Science*, VI (1949), 26.
[10] Gourou, *op. cit.*, p. 28.
[11] Gourou, *op. cit.*, p. 31.
[12] H. C. Conklin, *Hanunóo-English Vocabulary* ("University of California Publications in Linguistics," IX [1953]), 1–3.

ticipate in more than a full annual cycle of agricultural activities. Since most of my efforts during this time were directed toward an ethnographic analysis of the relation between Hanunóo culture and the natural environment,[13] I was drawn toward an increasingly closer examination of Hanunóo concepts of the ecology of the Yāgaw area and of Hanunóo methods of *swidden* farming.

The following brief statements summarize the preliminary results of my investigation of Hanunóo *swidden* agriculture. Except where otherwise noted, these remarks apply specifically to the Hanunóo on the upper eastern slopes of Mt. Yāgaw (Fig. 1). The six settlements in this area comprise an unstratified, unsegmented, neighborhood-like community, which has a total of 128 inhabitants. The average population density for the entire Hanunóo territory is ten per square kilometer, but in the more heavily settled areas, such as Yāgaw, there are from twenty-five to thirty-five persons per square kilometer.

The Hanunóo do not have a general term for *swidden* or for *swidden* cultivation, but do employ a set of terms distinguishing developmental stages of potential, actual, or used *swidden* areas. These are based on changes—natural or artificial—in the vegetational cover. *Swidden* activities are best outlined by taking these stages in sequence, indicating the significant human activities and plant changes occurring at each:

First year.—(1) Activities resulting in a slashed clearing, a *gāmasun* (January–February): Possible *swidden* locations are discussed within the settlement group. Final decision depends on location augury, dreams, the local omens, as well as an intimate knowledge of the local forms of vegetation. The cultivator marks his plot with bamboo stakes and, using a large bolo, cuts down the underbrush and small saplings. Men and women participate in this

[13] H. C. Conklin, "The Relations of Hanunóo Culture to the Plant World" (Ph.D. diss. in Anthropology, Yale University, New Haven, Conn., 1954).

initial clearing, family units making up the usual work teams. The average size of a Hanunóo *swidden* is two-fifths of a hectare. This area averages about one hectare of cultivated *swidden* cleared each year for every eight people. The total area of productive *swidden* land in a given area, however, is always several times that of the most recently cleared fields, because of intercropping. As shown in Fig. 1, 48 new *swiddens* (numbered serially for each settlement) were cleared in the Yāgaw area in 1953. Of these only four were cut partly from virgin forest (amounting to less than 10 per cent of the total area cleared). Second-growth forest areas are preferred because the clearing of primary forest requires much more manpower for a given area, and demands a longer drying period before burning can take place than can profitably be allotted to such tasks.

(2) Activities resulting in a cut clearing, a *buklid* (February–March): Using the same bolos and a few single-bladed axes, men begin the more arduous task of felling large trees. Women continue to clear undergrowth and begin planting root crops (such as taro) which can survive the intense heat of *swidden* burning. Instead of being felled, a number of larger trees are pollarded, not only to remove unwanted shade branches, but also to provide firewood and promote seeding of other trees in the first fallow year. Smaller branches and cut underbrush are spread over the whole area so that complete burning will occur and exposed patches of earth will be protected from the dry season sun. These cutting, trimming, and drying activities may take more than a month, especially in a primary forest clearing. Group labor parties, repaid with feasts of rice, are usually needed to finish this stage.

(3) Activities resulting in a burned clearing, a *tūtud* (March–April–May): While the field dries, the Hanunóo farmer removes cut timber suitable for fence building or other construction purposes and clears a 4-meter-wide safety path around the entire clearing to prevent the fire from

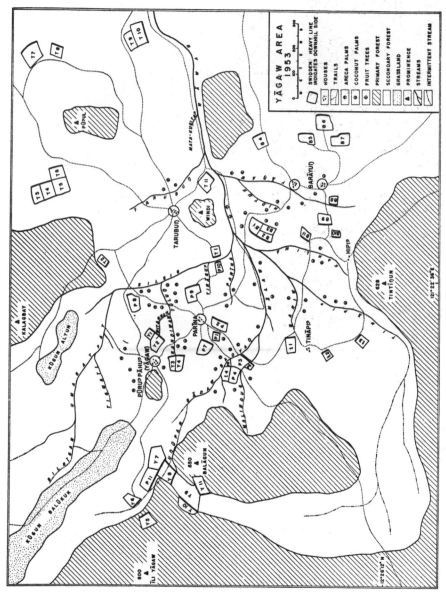

Fig. 1. Yagaw Area, Mindoro. Source: Field data, and U.S. Coast and Geodetic Survey, 1935.

escaping into surrounding forest or fallow *swidden* areas. Firing starts at the upward and windward margins. A steep hectare of dry, second-growth vegetation will burn up in an hour or less, depending on the wind. While secondary burning is being completed, men begin fencing the entire *swidden* to prevent wild and domestic mammals (especially the zebu) from getting at young crop plants. Constant guarding against daytime animal marauders is facilitated by the construction of scarecrows of straw, windblown dangling objects, and small field houses from which children can jerk lines leading to distant parts of the *swidden*.

(4) Activities resulting in, and necessary for the maintenance of, a planted *swidden*, a *tanman* (May through October): Maize is planted soon after the *swidden* is burned. The main rice planting comes at the end of the dry season, in May or early June. It is an important social and religious event and involves special spirit offerings, large work parties in gala attire, feasting, and the participation of men, women, and children. Men make the seed holes (*ca.* 5 cm. deep and 25 cm. apart) with two-meter long, pointed dibbles. Women and children follow, dropping a small handful of prepared seed (often from a mixture containing small quantities of pigeon pea, cucumber, melon, and sorghum seeds as well as rice). The Yāgaw average for planted rice seed is 40 gantas (1 3/5 cavans) per hectare. Other important *swidden* crops are planted less ceremoniously (e.g., sweet potatoes, in August), as are many secondary (i.e., non-staple) crops. During the rice growing season, other *swidden* activities include: completion of fences, continued guarding against destructive animals and birds, constant thinning and weeding (the entire *swidden* area being cleaned of weeds, shoots, and non-cultivated vines at least three times), building of granaries, and the almost continuous planting and harvesting of other crops in both new and old *swiddens* (see discussion of intercropping below).

(5) Activities resulting in a riceless field,

a *dayamihan* (October–November): The most important harvest in a new *swidden* is that of short–growing-season maize (in July and August). This is usually performed (including minor magical rites) by the cultivator himself, with only one or two helpers. The main rice harvest, in late October and early November, involves elaborate arrangements for group labor, feasts, magical rites, and religious offerings. It is the most important agricultural event of the year. Harvesting rice is done by hand (usually without knives) by men, women, and older children. The normal yield in rice ranges from 25 to 40 times the volume of the seed planted. One hectare of *swidden* land may give more than 30 cavans of unhusked rice. After threshing, drying, hulling, cooking, and other preparations, a settlement-wide celebration is held, after which the rigid observance of many rice-connected taboos, such as that which forbids one to eat new rice from another's *swidden*, are removed.

(6) Activities resulting in a cleaned *swidden*, a *lūmun bagʔūhan* (November–December): After gleaning, all rice stalks are cut, piled, and burned. Group labor, with compensatory rice feasts, are necessary to finish this task in less than two months. Other cultigens, especially leguminous crops and sweet potatoes, are now the focus of attention.

Dry season *swiddens*, always cut in second-growth areas, are cleared in September and October, planted in early November, and harvested unceremoniously in February, March, and April. They are usually small and are planted with corn and root crops only, never with rice. Some dry-season crops (including maize, certain beans, and sugar cane) are planted in main *swiddens* a few weeks before the rice harvest.

After the first year.—(7) Activities resulting in a recleaned (used, but still productive) *swidden*, a *lūmun dāʔan:* Fruit trees, and other perennial cultivates planted in new *swiddens* continue to provide edible food products if the plot is systematically

weeded and cleaned. By interplanting cultigens other than the principal grain staples,
the Hanunóo practice a kind of limited crop
rotation. Such intercropping results in successive harvests of different primary and
secondary crops for at least two years, frequently extended to five or six years, especially where the cultivation of banana
plants is continued. The many leguminous
crops so interplanted incidentally return
significant amounts of nitrogen to the soil.[14]
Single-crop *swiddens* are non-existent. Up
to 40 separate crops have been observed
growing in one Hanunóo *swidden* at the
same time.[15] One informant drew a map of
an "ideal" *swidden* containing 48 basic
kinds of plants (over 250 subsumed specific
types) including: forty-one cultigen crop
foods (including varieties of rice, sweet
potatoes, yams, taro, maize, squash, sugar
cane, and beans); one non-cultigen food
plant (papaya); and six non-food cultigens,
namely: tobacco, for chewing with betel,
areca, and lime; betel vine, for leaves used
in the betel chew; cotton, for spinning and
weaving into garments; indigo, for dyeing
cotton yarn; derris, for its fish-stupefying
roots; and vetiver, for its scented roots
(sachet).

Once productive cultivates give out—
but usually not for two or three years after
the main rice harvest—fallowing begins.
After five years, fallow second-growth forest (*talun*) types are readily distinguishable by their predominant plant forms.
The most common types are either some
kind of tree or bamboo. Bamboo second
growth is preferred for *swidden* making, be-

cause it dries uniformly and burns quickly
and completely. If not recleared, of course,
talun eventually reverts to primary forest
(*pūru?*). *Swidden* areas are not recut before at least five years of fallowing—after
the last cultigens give out—and this period
is extended preferably to more than ten. In
1953, most Yāgaw *swiddens* had been fallowed for more than eight years. The
Yāgaw area is in a rain belt and thus fallowing usually means the growth of replacement forest and a continuing natural re-
fertilization of the land. In areas where
there is a long dry season—aided by frequent burning for hunting purposes—tough
grasses tend to dominate the replacement
vegetation. Without artificial manuring and
draft animals, productive *swidden* cultivation then becomes difficult. Damper areas
seem more suited to continued *swidden*
making. Despite an apparently long history
of occupation by *swidden* farmers—there
are more than a dozen groves of coconut
palms in the area (see Fig. 1)—the Yāgaw
region today includes very little grassland.
And *kūgun* (*Imperata* spp.), the predominant grass, is highly valued for livestock
pasturage and especially for roof thatching.
It is a persistent weed, but in other respects
it is an important economic necessity.

Swidden activities require from 500 to
1000+ hours of work per year on the part
of the average adult Hanunóo. In addition
to *swiddens*, houseyard gardens are kept
for experimentation with new cultigens, and
for the individual cultivation of medicinal,
ritual, aromatic, and ornamental plants.

The Hanunóo recognize innumerable
natural and artificial factors as variables
affecting *swidden* agriculture. Ecologically
speaking, climatic factors, while closely
observed, can be modified least by the
Hanunóo. Edaphic factors, though not
practically amenable to artificial change,
can be dealt with in a more concrete manner. A study of Hanunóo soil classification
and associated ideas regarding suitability
for various crops—other variables being
equal—checked well with the results of a
chemical analysis of soil samples. Ten basic

[14] F. L. Wernstedt, "The Role of Corn in the
Agricultural Economy of Negros Oriental," *Silli-
man Journal*, I (1954), 59–67, ref. to 65.

[15] Cf. Edgar Anderson, *Plants, Man and Life*
(Boston: Little Brown, 1952), p. 84; E. D. Mer-
rill, "The Ascent of Mount Halcon, Mindoro,"
Philippine Journal of Science, II (1907), 179–
203, ref. to 179–80; J. A. Hester, Jr., "Agriculture,
Economy, and Population Densities of the Maya,"
Carnegie Institute, Yearbook No. 52 (Washing-
ton, D.C., 1953), pp. 288–92, ref. to p. 290; K.
Segawa, "The Means of Subsistence Among the
Formosan Aborigines," *Japanese Journal of Eth-
nology*, XVIII (1953), 49–66.

and thirty derivative soil and mineral categories are distinguished by the Hanunóo farmer. He may not know of the minute degree of lime disintegration and low pH value of *nápunápu?*, but he does know that certain beans and sugar cane (considered "high lime" crops, technically) will not thrive in such soil as they will in *barag?aη* (which has a higher lime content and pH value). Effects on soil quality of erosion, exposure, and over-*swiddening* are well understood. They are topics of frequent discussion, and preventive measures are often taken. Biotic factors are most subject to control and experimentation by the Hanunóo, and are of the greatest concern to them. More than 450 animal types and over 1,600 plant types are distinguished. The floral component is the more significant, especially in regard to swidden agriculture. Of some 1,500 "useful" plant types over 430 are cultigens (most of which are *swidden*-grown), existing only by virtue of the conscious domestication of the Hanunóo. Partly as a result of this intensified interest in plant domestication and detailed knowledge of minute differences in vegetative structures, Hanunóo plant categories outnumber, by more than 400 types, the taxonomic species into which the same local flora is grouped by systematic botanists.[16]

CONCLUSIONS

Much of the foregoing is fragmentary and perhaps more suggestive than conclusive. There is certainly a need for continued research in other areas[17] and for field observations covering greater periods of time. However, by using what recent ethnographic materials are available, we may tentatively rephrase the statements made earlier, so that a more accurate picture of *swidden* agriculture will emerge. Most of the changes we shall make indicate

that the *swidden* farmer sometimes knows more about the interrelations of local cultural and natural phenomena than ethnocentric temperate zone writers realize.

(1) *Swidden* farming follows a locally-determined, well-defined pattern and requires constant attention throughout most of the year. Hard physical labor is involved, but a large labor force is not required.

(2) Where possible, *swidden* making in second-growth forest areas (rather than in primary forests) is usually preferred.

(3) *Swidden* fires are often controlled by firebreaks surrounding the plot to be burned. Accidents happen, but greater damage may result from hunting methods employing fire in an area having a long dry season than from *swidden* clearing per se.

(4) Many details of *swidden* technique differ from area to area, and with changing conditions. Weeding is assiduously accomplished in some regions. Fencing is considered requisite if domestic cattle are kept, less so where such animals are rare. Wooden hand implements are very simple and are used only once. Metal cutting implements and harvesting equipment, however, vary greatly from region to region.

(5) Even the most noxious weeds, in one context, may serve the local economy admirably in another. *Imperata,* if dominant, restricts *swidden* opportunities, but its total loss causes similar hardships for those depending on it for pasture and thatch.

(6) *Swiddens* are rarely planted with single or even with only a few crops. Hence, the productivity of a *swidden* can be determined only partially by an estimate of the harvest yield of any one crop.

(7) It appears that the efficiency of *swidden* farming can be ascertained—relative to some other type of economy—only by taking into account the total yield per unit of labor, not per unit of area.[18]

(8) Because of intercropping, the harvest of one main *swidden* crop may serve only to allow one or more other crops to mature in turn. Plantings and harvests overlap us-

---

[16] For full details see Conklin, "The Relations of Hanunóo Culture to the Plant World."

[17] See, for example, E. R. Leach, "Some Aspects of Dry Rice Cultivation in North Burma and British Borneo," *Advancement of Science,* VI (1949), 26–28.

[18] Hutton, *op. cit.;* Leach, *op. cit.*

ually for more than a full year, and frequently continue for several years.

(9) *Swidden* intercropping, especially if wet season cereals are alternated with dry season leguminous crops, amounts to a type of crop rotation, even if on a limited scale. Cycles of field "rotation" cannot be meaningfully assessed by merely determining the number of years which lapse between dates of successive clearings. The agricultural use of the *swidden* plot following initial clear-

ing may have continued for one, several, or many years.

(10) It is difficult to set a minimum period of fallowing as necessary for the continued, productive use of *swidden* land by reclearing. Many variables are at work. A reasonable limit seems to be somewhere between eight and fifteen years, depending on the total ecology of the local situation. *Swidden* farmers are usually well aware of these limitations.

EDGAR ANDERSON

MAN AS A MAKER OF NEW PLANTS AND NEW PLANT COMMUNITIES

That man changes the face of nature may be noted by any casual observer; not even the ablest and most experienced scholar can yet estimate just how far this has reclothed the world. Whole landscapes are now occupied by man-dominated (and in part by man-created) faunas and floras. This process began so long ago (its beginnings being certainly as old as *Homo sapiens*) and has produced results of such complexity that its accurate interpretation must await research as yet scarcely begun. Though answers to many basic questions remain unknown, they are by no means unknowable.

The average thoughtful person has little inkling of this reclothing of the world; even professional biologists have been tardy in recognizing that in the last analysis a significant portion of the plants and animals which accompany man is directly or indirectly of his own making. The ordinary American supposes that Kentucky bluegrass is native to Kentucky and Canada bluegrass native to Canada. A few historians and biologists know that these grasses (along with much of our meadow and pasture vegetation) came to us from Europe. The research scholar inquiring

Reprinted, with permission of the author and publisher, from *Man's Role in Changing the Face of the Earth*, ed. William L. Thomas, Jr. (Chicago: University of Chicago Press, 1956), pp. 763–77 (copyright, 1956, by the University of Chicago). The author is curator of useful plants at the Missouri Botanical Garden and professor of botany at Washington University, St. Louis.

critically into the question realizes that some of this vegetation was as much a Neolithic immigration into Europe as it was a later immigration into the New World. Like Kentucky mountaineers, this vegetation has its ultimate roots in Asia and spread into central and Western Europe at times which, biologically speaking, were not very long ago.

It is obvious that landscapes such as the American Corn Belt have been transformed by man. Other man-dominated landscapes do not betray their origin to the casual observer. Take the grasslands of California, the rolling hills back from the coast, the oak-dotted savannas of the Great Valley. Here are stretches of what look like indigenous vegetation. Much of this mantle is not obviously tended by man; it has the look of something that has been in California as long as the oaks it grows among, yet the bulk of it came, all uninvited, from the Old World along with the Spaniards. Most of it had a long history of association with man when it made the trip. Wild oats, wild mustards, wild radishes, wild fennel—all of these spread in from the Mediterranean, yet over much of the California cattle country they dominate the landscape. Native plants are there, even some native grasses, but it takes a well-informed botanist going over the vegetation item by item to show how small a percentage of the range is made up of indigenous California plants.

For those parts of the tropics where plants grow rapidly it will take careful re-

465

search before we can have an informed opinion about such questions. Thorn scrub, savannas, bamboo thickets, weedy tangles of quick-growing trees and shrubs are known to have covered vast areas in the last two or three millenniums. Yet Standley, our greatest authority on the vegetation of Central America, digging up a small tree in what appeared to him to be a truly indigenous forest in the Lancetilla Valley, came upon a layer of potsherds.[1] What is the relation between the supposedly wild avocados of such a forest and the avocados eaten in the village that once covered that site? We now have various techniques (pollen profiles, carbon-14 datings, chromosome analysis, extrapolated correlates) which can give critical answers, but they are time-consuming, and their application to such problems has just begun.

The total number of plants and animals that have moved in with man to any one spot on the earth's surface is way beyond what even a biologist would estimate until he looked into the problem. There are the cultivated plants both for use and for display, the domesticated animals, the weeds, and their animal equivalents such as houseflies, clothes moths, rats, and mice. A much larger class of organisms is those not purposely introduced by man, which are neither eyesores nor plagues, but which, like weeds, have the capacity to get along in man's vicinity. Such are the daisies and yarrows and buttercups of our meadows. Such in a sense are even those native species that spread under man's influence. Take, for example, the sunflowers of Wyoming. They are certainly native to North America and may possibly in part be prehuman in Wyoming. They line the roadways yet seldom are elsewhere prominent in the native landscape. They appeared along the road, even though they may have moved in from not so far away. But how did they get into the spot from which they spread, and did pioneers or primitive man have anything to do with making this previous niche? This is the sort of question we are now making the subject of decisive experiments; we do not yet have enough results for decisive answers.

For micro-organisms the problem of the species which travel about with man staggers the imagination. Micro-organisms seemingly fall into the same general categories as macro-organisms. Brewers' yeasts are as much cultivated plants as the barleys and wheats with which they have so long been associated for brewing and baking. The germs of typhoid and cholera are quite as much weeds as are dandelions or Canada thistles. The micro-organisms of our garden soil are apparently the same mixture of mongrel immigrants and adapted natives as our meadow and pasture plants. Soils are good or bad quite as much because of the microcommunities they contain as because of their composition. Man's unconscious creation of new kinds of micro-organisms is an important part of his total effect on the landscapes of the world. Think, then, of this total composite mantle of living things which accompanies man: the crops, the weeds, the domesticated animals, the garden escapes such as Japanese honeysuckle and orange day lily, the thorn scrub, the bamboo thickets, the English sparrows, the starlings, the insect pests. Think of the great clouds of algae, protozoa, bacteria, and fungi—complex communities of microorganisms that inhabit our soils, our beverages, our crops, our domesticated animals, and our very bodies.

If we turn to the scientific literature for an orderly summary of where these species came from and how, there is a depressing lack of information. The crop plants and domesticated animals have been somewhat studied, the ornamentals and the weeds scarcely investigated. Even for the crop plants one notes that for those which have been the most carefully studied—wheat,[2]

---

[1] P. C. Standley, *Flora of the Lancetilla Valley, Honduras* (Chicago: Field Museum of Natural History, Botanical Series, Vol. X, 1931).

[2] Hannah C. Aase, "Cytology of Cereals, II," *Botanical Review*, XII (1946), 255–334.

cotton,[3] maize —there is now general recognition that their origins, relationships,
and exact histories are much more complex
problems than they were thought to be a
generation ago. In spite of these wide gaps
in our knowledge, I believe the following
generalizations will stand:

1. All the major crops and most of the
minor ones were domesticated in prehistoric
times. *Modern agriculture, classified solely
by the plants it uses, is Neolithic agriculture.*

2. For none of the major crops can we
point with certainty to the exact species (or
combination of species) from which it was
derived: for some we can make guesses;
for a number we can point to closely related
weeds. This merely complicates the problem. We then have to determine the origin
of the crop, the origin of the weed, and the
history of their relationships.

The world's knowledge of crop plants, in
other words, does not tell us very much. All
we know is that we are dealing with man's
effects on certain plants in the Neolithic
or before. Yet for weeds and ornamental
plants even less is known. A few general
observations may be offered, parenthetically, about their origins.

1. We can now point to crops which are
definitely known to have been derived from
weeds. For instance, rye as a crop originated from a grainfield weed.[5] As barley and
wheat spread farther north onto the sandy
Baltic plain, the weed gradually replaced
the crop. The origin of rye as a weed is a
far older and more complex problem. Stebbins and his students are far enough into
it to tell us that it is a story with several

chapters, most of them unsuspected until
recently.

2. We can point to weeds which originated from crop plants. The bamboo thickets that cover whole mountainsides in the
Caribbean came from cultivated bamboos.
It now seems much more probable that teosinte the weed was derived from maize the
crop than that maize was derived from
teosinte.

3. Crop plants and their related weeds
frequently have a continuing effect upon
each other. We have documented evidence
of weeds increasing their variability by hybridizing with crop plants and of crop
plants consciously or unconsciously improved through hybridization with weeds.
These processes recur repeatedly in the histories of weeds and crop plants. For wheat
it is clear that a minor grain was in very
early times built up into one of the world's
great cereals through the unconscious incorporation of several weeds from its own
fields.[6]

As a whole, ornamentals (though little
studied as yet) provide the simplest keys
and the clearest insights into the basic
problems of domestication of any class of
plants or animals. Some, the African violet,
for instance, have been domesticated within
the last century, but are already distinct
from the species from which they arose.
Such recent domesticates provide unparal-
leled experimental material for determining
what happens to the germ plasm of an organism when it is domesticated. Others of
our garden flowers originated in prehistoric
times. They seem to have been associated
with magic and ceremony; some of them
may have been with us for as long or even
longer than our crop plants. Take woad,
Isatis tinctoria, now known only as a garden flower, though it persisted as a commercial dye plant until Victorian times.[7]
When Caesar came to Britain, he found

[3] J. P. Hutchinson, R. A. Silow, and S. G.
Stephens, *The Evolution of Gossypium and the
Differentiation of the Cultivated Cottons* (Lon-
don: Oxford University Press, 1947).

[4] P. C. Mangelsdorf and R. G. Reeves, "The
Origin of Maize," *Proceedings of the National
Academy of Sciences*, XXIV (1938), 303–12.

[5] N. I. Vavilov, "Studies on the Origin of Cultivated Plants," *Bulletin of Applied Botany and
Plant Breeding*, XVI (Leningrad, 1926), 138–248.

[6] Edgar Anderson, *Plants, Man, and Life* (Boston: Little Brown, 1952), pp. 57–64.

[7] Jameison B. Hurry, *The Woad Plant and Its
Dye* (London: Oxford University Press, 1930).

468 · Edgar Anderson

our semisavage ancestors using it to paint their bodies. There are various other ornamentals (*Bixa, Amaranthus, Helianthus*) whose earlier associations were with dyes and body paints. Which is older, agriculture or body painting?

The cultivated grain amaranths (known to the Western world mainly through such bizarre late-summer annuals as love-lies-bleeding) demonstrate that we shall be in for some rude shocks when we make serious studies of these apparently trivial plants. J. D. Sauer[8] found that this whole group was domesticates, divisible into several different species, none of which could be equated to any wild amaranth; that the whole group was of American origin; and that the varieties cultivated since ancient times in Kashmir, China, and Tibet were not (as had previously been taken for granted) derived from Asiatic amaranths.

They are instead identical with those cultivated by the Aztecs and the Incas.

It is now becoming increasingly clear that the domestication of weeds and cultivated plants is usually a process rather than an event. None of them rose in one leap from the brain of Ceres, so to speak. The domestication of each crop or weed went on at various times and places, though by bursts rather than at a regular rate. For many it still continues. Our common weed sunflowers, for example, are at the moment being bred into superweeds. In California, by hybridization with a rare native sunflower, these weeds are increasing their ability to colonize the Great Valley.[9] In Texas,[10] by similar mongrelizations with two native species, they are adapting them-

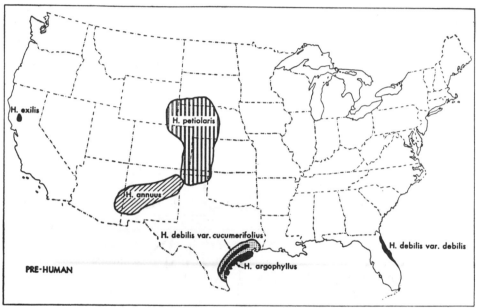

Fig. 1. Annual species of North American sunflowers as presumed to have existed in prehuman times: (1) *Helianthus exilis,* a highly localized endemic in the serpentine areas of California; (2) *H. petiolaris* on bare sandy areas in the western Great Plains; (3) *H. annuus* in playas and other raw-soil habitats of the southwestern deserts; (4) *H. argophyllus* on the sands of the Texas coastal plain; and (5) *H. debilis* in Florida and Texas.

[8] Jonathan D. Sauer, "The Grain Amaranths: A Survey of Their History and Classification," *Annals of the Missouri Botanical Garden,* XXXVII (1950), 561–632.

[9] Charles B. Heiser, Jr., "Study in the Evolution of the Sunflower Species *Helianthus annuus* and *H. bolanderi,*" *University of California Publications in Botany,* XXIII (1949), 157–208.

[10] Charles B. Heiser, Jr., "Hybridization in the Annual Sunflowers: *Helianthus annuus X H. debilis* var. *cucumerifolius,*" *Evolution,* V (1951), 42–51.

selves to life on the sandy lands of the Gulf Coast (see Figs. 1–3).

The story of the American sunflowers is significant because it demonstrates the kinds of processes which went on in the Stone Age and before, when our major crops were domesticated. It is because the domestication of weeds and cultivated plants (using the word "domestication" in its broadest sense) is a continuing process that it came to my professional attention.

his plant and animal companions into increased evolutionary activity? A growing body of observational and experimental data bears directly upon that question; rather than summarizing it, let me describe in considerable detail one particularly illuminating example. It concerns the hybridization of two California species of wild sage, *Salvia apiana* and *S. mellifera*. They have been meticulously studied by Epling —in the field,[11] the herbarium,[12] the

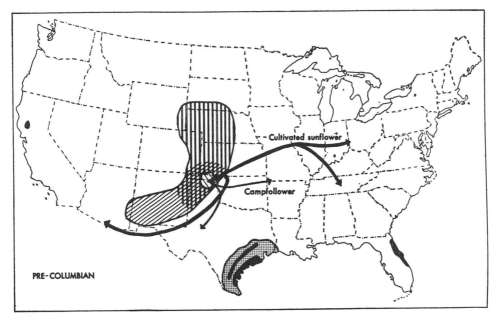

Fig. 2. Hypothetical origin of the North American sunflower as a weed and as a cultivated annual in pre-Columbian times. In the areas where *annuus* and *petiolaris* had begun to introgress, this process is being unconsciously accelerated by the activities of early man.

Thirty years ago I started out to study (and if possible to measure) such evolution as was still going on. As I analyzed example after example, the fact became increasingly clear that evolutionary activity is concentrated in (though by no means confined to) disturbed habitats—to times and places where man's interference with the prehuman order of things has been particularly severe. Post-Pleistocene evolution, it seems, has been very largely the elaboration of weedlike plants and animals.

Now why should this be? What is there about the presence of man that stimulates

laboratory, and the experimental plot.[13] Burton Anderson and I [14] have made an ex-

[11] Carl C. Epling, "Natural Hybridization of *Salvia apiana* and *Salvia mellifera*," *Evolution*, I (1947), 69–78.

[12] Carl C. Epling, "The California *Salvias*: A Review of *Salvia*, Section Audibertia," *Annals of the Missouri Botanical Garden*, XXV (1938), 95–188.

[13] Carl C. Epling and Harlan Lewis, "The Centers of Distribution of the Chaparral and Coastal Sage Associations," *American Midland Naturalist*, XXVII (1942), 445–62.

[14] Edgar Anderson and Burton R. Anderson, "Introgression of *Salvia apiana* and *Salvia mellifera*," *Annals of the Missouri Botanical Garden*, XLI (1954), 329–38.

haustively detailed analysis of the variation pattern of several populations, confirming and extending Epling's conclusions.

These two species of sage are so unlike that any ordinary amateur would immediately recognize them as radically different plants; only an occasional botanist would

fertility, hybrids were ordinarily not found in nature or occurred mainly at spots where the native vegetation had been greatly altered by man's activities. Yet on the rocky slopes where they were native, these two kinds of sage frequently grew intermingled. Burton Anderson and I worked with sam-

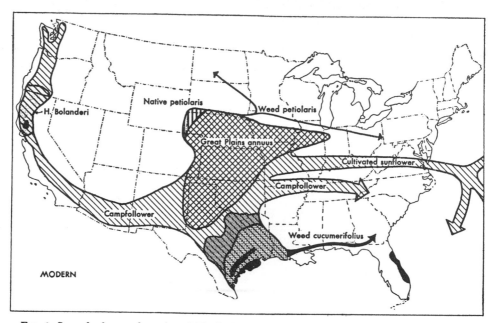

Fig. 3. Spread of annual species of North American sunflowers in modern times. In the Great Plains extensive introgression of *annuus* and *petiolaris* produced the Great Plains race of *Helianthus annuus*, which has spread eastward through the prairies as a somewhat weedy native. The camp-follower weed (sometimes mixed with Great Plains *annuus*) has spread as a weed throughout the East and to irrigated lands in the West. In California, by extensive and continuing introgression with *exilis*, it has created the semiweedy *H. bolanderi*, which is still actively spreading. Similarly, on the sands of the Texas coast and the Carrizo ridge, *H. argophyllus* is introgressing actively with *H. annuus* to produce weedier strains. Over an even wider area in Texas extensive introgression of *annuus*, *petiolaris*, and *cucumerifolius* is producing a coastal plain weed sunflower which is actively spreading along the coast. In spots it has already reached the North Carolina coastal plain. Eventually this will react actively with *H. debilis* var. *debilis*, breeding a superweed for the American Southeast but, fortunately, a not unattractive one. The Texas and California phenomena have already been documented by Heiser (1949, 1951), and research on other facets of the problem is going forward rapidly.

see that they are really quite closely related and that their differences, though conspicuous, are superficial. This was what first drew Epling's attention to them. He found that they hybridized readily when artificially cross-pollinated. The hybrids grew vigorously in an experimental plot and were fertile enough to produce abundant and variable offspring. In spite of this

ples of wild populations of both species so intensively that eventually we could distinguish between mongrels, seven of whose great-grandparents were from one species and one from the other, and plants with all eight grandparents from one species. With this yardstick we learned that, though the plants on the mountainside were prevailingly of one species or the other, yet along the pathway from which we collected them we could find a few mongrels. These were mostly plants closely resembling typical *Salvia mellifera* but showing slight indications of *S. apiana* in one character or another. Apparently the very rare hybrids which Epling had found were not completely without issue. Some of them had crossed back to *S. mellifera,* and, of these three-quarter bloods, a few of those similar to the recurrent parent had been able to fend for themselves.

At one point along the path we found conspicuous hybrids resembling those produced by Epling; careful investigation of this area gave us new understanding. With repeated visits we gradually realized that these bizarre mongrels were limited to a definitely circumscribed plot having a greatly altered habitat. It was at a point where the trail swung down along the slope. Originally a forest of live oaks had abutted on the rocky, sunny slopes where the salvias grow. The oaks had been cut and a small olive orchard planted and then abandoned—abandoned so long ago that native plants had flowed in and the whole site looked quite natural. A collection of salvias made exclusively from among the olives was almost entirely hybrids and hybrid descendants. Though the bulk of the plants looked somewhat like *Salvia apiana*, there was not a single plant which in all its characters agreed exactly with the *apianas* outside this plot. Furthermore, they resembled artificial backcrosses in that their differences from *apiana* were all in the direction of *S. mellifera*. These "sub-*apianas*" graded into plants closely resembling the first-generation hybrids raised by Epling. There were a few "sub-*melliferas*" similar to those we had detected along the pathway on the mountainside and a few plants which on our index scored as typical *melliferas*. However, in the field *none* of them looked quite average. Dr. Anderson and I had to work in St. Louis on pressed and pickled material previously collected in California. Had we been able to go back and add characters such as flower color and flower

pattern to our battery of measurable differences between *S. mellifera* and *S. apiana,* I believe we could have demonstrated that the entire plot was colonized with hybrids and mongrels, most of them first or second or third backcrosses from the original hybrids to one or the other species.

These results indicate that hybrids are being constantly produced on this mountainside, but one does not ordinarily find them, because there is no niche into which they can fit. The native vegetation had a long evolutionary history of mutual adaptation. Plants and animals have gradually been selected which are adapted to life with each other like pieces of a multidimensional jigsaw puzzle. It is only when man, or some other disruptive agent, upsets the whole puzzle that there is any place where something new and different can fit in. If a radical variant arises, it is shouldered out of the way before it reaches maturity. In a radically new environment, however, there may be a chance for something new to succeed. Furthermore, the hybrids and their mongrel descendants were not only something new; they varied greatly among themselves. If one of them would not fit into the strange new habitat, another might. Though virtually all of them had been at a selective disadvantage on the mountainside, a few of them (aided and abetted no doubt by the vigor which is characteristic of these and many other hybrids) were now at a selective advantage. They consequently flowed in and occupied the old olive orchard to the virtual exclusion of the two original species.

Furthermore, to take up an important fact about which biology as yet knows very little, the habitat among the olives was not only something new; it was *open*. It was not full of organisms which had been selected to fit together. Remember that for the mountainside, on those rare occasions where a first-generation hybrid plant had been able to find a foothold, virtually none of its highly variable descendants was able to persist. Such species crosses can father hundreds if not thousands of distinguishably different types of mongrel descendants. Only along the pathway had *any* of these been able to find a place for themselves and then only those which differed but slightly from *Salvia mellifera*. Hybridization does not advance in closed habitats.

The plants in the olive orchard had no such history of long association. The olives were new to California. The societies of micro-organisms in the soil were originally those which go with live oaks, not those accompanying the salvias on the sunny slopes. These must have been greatly changed during the time the olives were cultivated. Furthermore, the olives, being planted at considerable distances from each other, did not re-create either the fairly continuous shade of the oaks or the open sunshine of the upper slopes. The orchard became the site for evolutionary catch-as-catch-can, and under these circumstances, as we have seen, the new and variable had a decisive advantage.

Now that we know this much about these salvias, it would be interesting to work experimentally with them and the species with which they are associated to determine just what factors allow two different but closely related species to fit together with their associates so perfectly that all hybrid intermediates are excluded. From experience with other similar problems I should predict that among the most important factors would be fairly specific reactions between some of the other associated plants and these two sages. In our experimental work with sunflowers we have discovered that one of the strongest factors in determining where weed sunflowers may or may not grow is their reaction to grass. Many grasses apparently give off a substance highly toxic to weed sunflowers. The various species of weed sunflowers differ in their sensitivity to this poison. When two such sunflowers hybridize, one of the factors affecting the outcome is the grassiness of the site. Such relationships seem to be very general among plants. On the whole, many species grow where they do, not because they really prefer the physical conditions of such a site, but because they can tolerate it and many other organisms cannot.

Generally speaking, the plants which follow man around the world might be said to do so, not because they relish what man has done to the environment, but because they can stand it and most other plants cannot.

Are these salvias weeds? I would put forward the working hypothesis that those in the abandoned olive orchard are on the way to becoming weeds. The small exceptional communities of hybridizing colonies similar to this one, which can be found here and there over southern California, are worth considerably more attention than they have hitherto received. They demonstrate the way in which man, the great weedbreeder, the great upsetter, catalyzes the formation of new biological entities by producing new and open habitats.

The *Salvia* case is not unique. We now have over a score of similar well-documented studies of the connection between hybridization and weedy, disturbed habitats. The relationship had long been known to observant naturalists, though not until the last few decades was its significance stressed or experimental work undertaken. One other example demonstrates the role of man's operations on the habitat. Riley[15] studied the hybridization of two species of *Iris* on the lower delta of the Mississippi in a neighborhood where the land-use pattern had produced something as demonstrable and convincing as a laboratory experiment[16] (see Fig. 4). Property lines ran straight back from the river; the farms were small, only a few hundred yards wide, and very narrow. Under these conditions it was easy to see that the hybrids between these two irises were virtually limited to one farm. They grew in a swale which crossed several of the farms, yet were

[15] H. P. Riley, "A Character Analysis of Colonies of *Iris fulva, I. hexagona* var. *giganticaerulea* and Natural Hybrids," *American Journal of Botany*, XXV (1938), 727–38.

[16] Edgar Anderson, *Introgressive Hybridization* (New York: Wiley and Sons, 1949).

nearly all on one man's property. On his farm they went right up to the fences and stopped, and this could be demonstrated at either side of his property. Unlike his any of the neighboring farms. They had at length produced an open environment in which the pasture grasses were at a disadvantage and the resulting hybrid swarm of

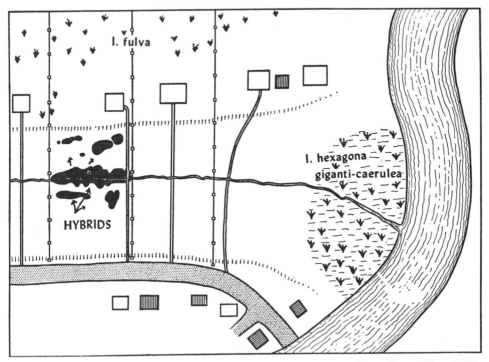

F̲ı̲g̲. 4. A demonstration of man's unconscious role in creating new plants (from Riley, 1938). At the far right one of the minor bayous of the lower Mississippi Delta. At right angles to it and running nearly across the figure is the abandoned channel of a former stream, now drained by a ditch. The natural levees of the stream are slightly higher than the surrounding country. Their sharp inner edges are indicated on the map by hachures. The road has been run along the lower levee, and houses have been built along the opposite one. The property lines (as in many old French settlements) produce a series of long narrow farms, which for our purposes serve as so many experimental plots. Each farm has its house on a low ridge with a long entrance drive connecting it across a swale to the public road on the opposite ridge. The farms (including a score of others which are out of sight to the left of the figure) were originally essentially similar. At the point where the ditch joins the bayou is a large population of *Iris hexagona giganti-caerulea.* Behind the levee on which the houses were built, *I. fulva* grows on the lower ground as well as farther upstream along the ditch. The key fact to be noted is that the hybrids are on only one farm, that they are abundant there, and that they go up to the very borders of the property on either side. Nature is evidently capable of spawning such hybrids throughout this area, but not until one farmer unconsciously created the new and more or less open habitat in which they could survive did any appear in this part of the delta. (See Anderson, 1949, for a more complete discussion.)

neighbors, he had kept the swale heavily pastured. His cattle had held in check the grasses which are serious competitors of swamp irises. They had also, tramping about in wet weather, turned the swale into more of a quagmire than existed on irises at a very real advantage. Hybrids in various patterns of terra cotta, wine, purple, and blue flooded out into this swale until it had almost the appearance of an intentionally created iris garden.

Though Riley never published the sequel,

it might be inserted here, parenthetically, since it points up some kind of a moral. The farmer himself did not remove the irises, even though they interfered seriously with the carrying capacity of his pasture. The irises were conspicuously beautiful, and garden-club members from New Orleans dug them up for their gardens, at so much per basket, until they were eventually exterminated. The hybridization which nature began in this and other pastures around New Orleans has been continued by iris fans. These Louisiana irises are now established as cultivated plants both in Europe and in America. Until the arrival of the garden-club ladies, they were nascent weeds (Fig. 5).

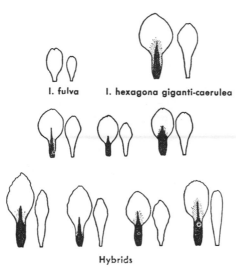

Hybrids

FIG. 5. Sepals and petals of some hybrids of *Iris hexagona giganti-caerulea* and *I. fulva* somewhat diagrammatic but accurately to scale. In each case the sepal (the so-called "fall" or iris fanciers) is shown to the left; the petal, "standard," to the right. *I. fulva* has small lax terra cotta sepals and petals. *I. hexagona giganti-caerulea* has large crisp petals and sepals of bright blue. The sepal has a brilliant yellow signal patch (shown in black) surrounded by a white area (shown by stipples) shading off into the blue. Note that in the various hybrids the small-sized flowers (characteristic of *I. fulva*) tend to be associated with the lack of a white area (another *fulva* characteristic). Note the variability of the hybrids. In color they varied from deep wine to very pale, light blue.

A little reflective observation will show that the ways in which man creates new and open habitats, though various, can mostly be grouped under a few headings: (1) dumps and other high nitrogen areas; (2) pathways; (3) open soil; (4) burns. The last is probably the oldest of his violent upsettings of the natural order of things. It must have stimulated evolutionary activity very early—whole floras or certainly whole associations must have come to a new adjustment with it here and there; fire should be, of all man's effects upon evolution, the most difficult to analyze. Until valid experimental and exact historical methods deal with this problem, it inevitably must spawn more polemic activity than scientific analysis.

In contrast to fire, the creation of open-soil habitats as a really major human activity belongs much more to the age of agriculture and industry than to prehistory. It may be that is why it seems to be the simplest to analyze. In Europe and eastern North America, in the humid tropics and subtropics, open soil—bare exposed earth —is scarcely part of the normal nature of things. Most of the flora truly native to these areas cannot germinate in open soil or, having germinated, cannot thrive to maturity. Make a series of seed collections from wild flowers and forest trees and plant them in your garden just like radishes or lettuce. You will be amazed to learn how small a percentage of them ever comes up at all. Make similar collections from the weeds in a vacant lot or from the plants (wanted and unwanted) of your garden. Nearly all of them will come up promptly and grow readily. Where did these open-soil organisms come from in the first place, these weeds of gardens and fields, these fellow-travelers which rush in after the bulldozer, which flourish in the rubble of bombed cities? Well, they must have come mostly from pre-human open-soil sites. River valleys did not supply all of them, but rivers are certainly, next to man, the greatest of weed-breeders. Our large rivers plow their banks at floodtimes, producing raw-soil areas. Every river system is provided with plants to fill this peculiar niche; all those known to me act as weeds in the uplands. One of the simplest and clearest examples is our common pokeweed, *Phytolacca americana,* native to eastern North America. It will be found growing up abundantly in the immediate valleys of our major rivers[17] (see Fig. 6). On the uplands it is strictly limited to raw soil, though, once established in such a habitat, it can persist vegetatively for a long time while other kinds of vegetation grow up around it. Being attractive to birds, its seeds are widely scattered. I remember, from my Michigan boyhood, how pokeweed came in when a woodland near our home was lumbered over. We had never noticed this weed in that community, but the birds had been planting it wherever they roosted. When the felling of the big oaks tore lesser trees up by the roots, pokeweed plants appeared as if by magic for the next few years in the new craters of raw soil. Man and the great rivers are in partnership. Both of them are upsetters. Both of them breed weeds and suchlike organisms. The prehuman beginnings of many of our pests and fellow-travelers are to be sought in river valleys. River valleys also must have been the ultimate source of some of the plants by which we live: gourds, squashes, beans, hemp, rice, and maize.

The examples of the salvias and irises show how quickly evolution through hybridization can breed out something new and different under man's catalytic influence. What we should most like to know is the extent to which weeds and suchlike organisms, created or at least extensively modified through man's influence, are built up into whole associations. It is clear that such things can happen; the *maqui* vegetation of the Mediterranean, the *shiblyak* and *karst* vegetation of the Balkans, the *carbón* scrub of Central America, are obviously very directly the results of man's inter-

ference. One would like to analyze the dynamics of these associations. We must do so if man is to understand his own past or to be the master of his own future. For such purposes we need ways of studying vegetation which are analytical as well as merely descriptive—methods not based upon preconceived dogmas. I should like to suggest that the methods used in analyzing the *Iris* hybrids and the *Salvia* hybrids, if combined with other experimental techniques, would allow us to get a long way into these problems. Let me illustrate what I mean by describing some recent studies of *Adenostoma,* a fire-resistant shrub, which is a common component of the California chaparral.[18]

Between the Great Valley and the Pacific Coast, *Adenostoma fasciculatum* is one of the commonest shrubs in the California landscape. Noting that it varied conspicuously from one plant to the next, I made collections of it near Palo Alto and applied to them the methods of pictorialized scatter diagrams and extrapolated correlates. The details of these techniques need not concern us here, since they have been adequately published elsewhere, both in technical journals and in books for the intelligent public. They allow us (through a meticulous examination of variability in such mongrel complexes as the salvias of the abandoned olive orchard) to determine precisely the good species (or subspecies or varieties) from which these complexes must ultimately have arisen. Furthermore, though it takes considerable hard work, these methods can be used successfully by one with no previous knowledge of the organisms or of the faunas and floras from which they may have come.

Using these methods, I have shown that the common *Adenostoma fasciculatum* of coastal California arose from the hybridization of two very different adenostomas. One of these was *A. fasciculatum* var. *obtusifolium,* a low-growing shrub of the head-

---

[17] Jonathan D. Sauer, "A Geography of Pokeweed," *Annals of the Missouri Botanical Garden,* XXXIX (1952), 113–25.

[18] Edgar Anderson, "Introgression in *Adenostoma,*" *Annals of the Missouri Botanical Garden,* XLI (1954), 339–50.

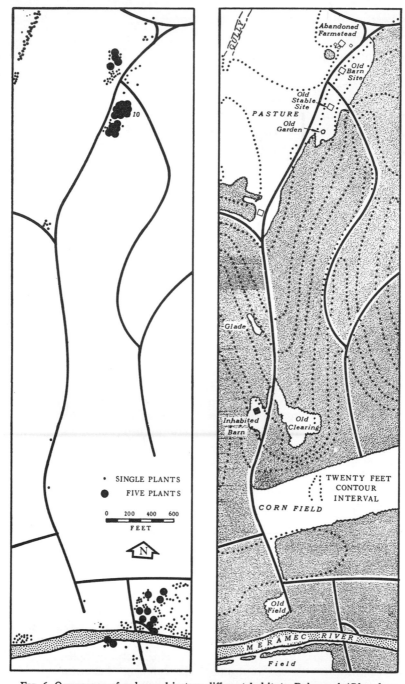

FIG. 6. Occurrence of pokeweed in two different habitats. Pokeweed (*Phytolacca americana*) is an example of a species which is apparently native in the open soil along American rivers but a weed in the open soil of disturbed habitats. (Map from J. Sauer, 1952.) Small dots represent single plants. Large dots represent five plants. It will be seen that the pokeweed is occurring in two quite different kinds of habitats: in a raw soil of repeatedly flooded woodlands on the immediate banks of the river and as a weed around farm buildings, gardens, and the like. (See J. Sauer, 1952, for further details and discussion.)

lands and islands along the California coast. The other is now found in its purest form in the Mother Lode country of the Sierra foothills, a tall, branching shrub which, when in flower, somewhat resembles a small-leaved white lilac. Each of these had its own contributions to make to life in coastal California. The coastal shrub brought in a tolerance of brilliant sunlight and the ability to grow in thin, rocky soil. However, it was accustomed to fog and drizzle even during the dry season. The inland form could go months without a drop of water, but it is used to deeper soil and to less extreme radiation. When these two centers of variation had been identified, it was easy to demonstrate that the common *Adenostoma* is a great, plastic, hybrid swarm, including approaches to these two extremes and many intermediates between them. On dry, rocky ridges in sites which are frequently foggy, one finds plants very close to the island extreme. On deeper soils and in the shade of small oaks are bushes scarcely different from those of the Mother Lode country. Around old ranch buildings and in other peculiar habitats one finds strange and bizarre recombinations of various sorts.

Just as these studies came to a close and it was time for me to leave California, I realized that many of the other plants in the chaparral association were similarly variable. There were swarms of hybrid oaks and hybrid ceanothus and hybrid manzanitas. The entire association seemed to be in a state of flux. Unlike the coastal sages which I had studied in southern California, there was room for hybrid recombinations within the association itself. The entire chaparral seemed to be ecologically in the same general class of disturbed habitat as the abandoned olive orchard.

I do not wish to jump to conclusions from one small experiment. I would merely suggest that these methods are appropriate for the analysis of such problems, particularly if combined with experimental work (for instance, the removal of a single specie or species complex from a small area using modern herbicides followed by measurement of the effect of this removal on the other complexes in the association). Here is a field in which we could very rapidly get down to some of the basic principles concerning closed versus open habitats. In my opinion, the degree to which such associations as the California chaparral are man-made is a better subject for study than for debate. They have certainly been greatly affected by man. To learn to what degree, I should prefer to look for more facts rather than to listen to more opinions.

Even among biologists there has been a strong tendency to avoid such problems —to study the plants and plant associations of mountaintops and jungles rather than those of dooryards and gardens, to think of plant and animal communities as they must have been in some blissfully innocent era before the advent of man. It seems to me far healthier and far more logical to accept man as a part of nature, to concentrate one's attention as a naturalist on man's activities, since he is the one species in the world we most nearly understand. It is because we know from inside ourselves the problems in which man is deeply involved that we appreciate their bewildering complexity; experiments with laboratory insects would not seem so beautifully simple if we knew as much about them as we do about man. The population genetics of garbage-pail flies[19] would appear more complex if we understood from within what it is like to be a *Drosophila*. The apparently standardized environment of flour in a bottle[20] would not seem undifferentiated to any investigator who had once been a flour beetle and who knew at firsthand

[19] Th. Dobzhansky, "Observations and Experiments on Natural Selection in *Drosophila*," in Gert Bonnier and Robert Larsson (eds.), *Proceeding of the Eighth International Congress of Genetics, Stockholm, 1948* (Lund, 1949), pp. 210–24.

[20] Thomas Park, "Studies in Population Physiology. VIII. The Effect of Larval Population Density on the Post-embryonic Development of the Flour Beetle, *Tribolium confusum* Duval," *Journal of Experimental Zoology*, LXXIX (1938), 51–70.

the complexities of flour-beetle existence. Imagine a non-human investigator of human populations recently arrived from Mars. What could he understand of the relationship of Catholics and Protestants? How long would it take him to discover that, though most of the shortest girls in New York City get married, the very tallest seldom do? Having discovered this phenomenon, how much longer would it take him to understand it? When we attempt to work with laboratory insects, our ignorance of their social complexities makes them seem far simpler material than they really are.

I must confess that when, from being a student of variation in natural populations, I was of necessity led to being a student of man's upsetting effects on his environment, my own thinking was too much colored by this attitude. Only gradually did I come to realize that, though man is now the world's great upsetter, he is not the first. There were others before him, and they played a similar role in evolution. Stebbins and I have recently suggested[21] that the great bursts of evolutionary activity in the past, the times of adaptive

[21] Edgar Anderson and G. L. Stebbins, Jr., "Hybridization as an Evolutionary Stimulus," *Evolution*, VIII (1954), 378–88.

radiation, were caused by such upsets. The formation *de novo* of a great fresh-water lake such as Lake Baikal produced a new and open habitat in which the organisms from various river systems could meet and mongrelize and, under the hand of selection, evolve as rapidly into new paths as did the salvias in the abandoned olive orchard. What must have happened when the first land vertebrates at last arrived on continents whose vegetation had no experience of such beasts? What occurred when the giant reptiles of the Mesozoic churned like gigantic bulldozers through the ferny swamps of that period? Must not the plants of those periods have gone through the same general experiences as are now facing the adenostomas of the California chaparral?

Man has been a major force in the evolution of the plants and animals which accompany him around the world, and in the midst of which he largely spends his days. The detailed study of this process (1) should illuminate for us the course of evolution in prehuman times; (2) should be as well one of our truest guides to the history of prehistoric man; (3) most importantly, should enable us at last to understand and eventually to control the living world around us.

ALDO SESTINI

REGRESSIVE PHASES IN THE DEVELOPMENT OF THE CULTURAL LANDSCAPE

Geography is no longer mere description of the earth, or a utilitarian compendium of data about this or that country. It does indeed remain description of the surface of our planet, but its aim is to explain phenomena, to inquire into their causes, and to study their relations and mutual effects.

With geography moving in this direction —the only scientific one, to be sure—it has not been difficult to recognize the variations to which the geographic content of telluric space may become subject in the course of time. In the latter half of the eighteenth century, the mutability of physical features began to appear in a clear light; it seems that that of the man-made features would have been obvious, but the study of its manifestations and modalities began, perhaps appropriately, a good deal later. Fluctuations in population, migratory movements, intensified exploitation of natural resources, and above all the modifications accomplished by man in the natural landscape, have been studied with scientific rigor from the geographic standpoint for no more than a century. Nevertheless, the variability of aspect within single regions of the earth, be its rhythm slow or rapid, today is one of the fundamental principles in the whole edifice of geography. In general, the present state of a physical or human feature is conceived as a particu-

lar phase of a development, as a link in a long series with roots in the past and ramifications into the future.

One may go even further: practical reasons impel us to give preference in geographic description to the present moment. From a purely scientific standpoint, however, a description of Tuscany in the year 1947 and a description of it as it looked at the end of the Middle Ages have equal value. In my judgment, historical chorology and modern chorology are on the same plane in the scientific system of geography. If the first is less cultivated than the second, and leads as a rule to more general or incomplete results, this is due not only to the mentioned practical utility of descriptions of modern conditions, but also to the difficulty of reconstructing geographic features of the past that no longer allow of direct observation—the method that has become basic to modern geographic research.

We should insist, in any case, that scientific study, no matter of what territory, cannot disregard conditions in the past. Often it is only by examining the development of a feature over time that its meaning can be grasped and its causes revealed. Many peculiar physical and cultural features of the regions of the earth cannot be interpreted or explained on the basis of the natural, social, economic, or political environments of our time. These features are relics of other epochs, adapted to physical and human conditions different from those of today. Hence the need for digging

Translated, with permission of the author, from "Le fasi regressive nello sviluppo del paesaggio antropogeografico," *Revista Geografia Italiana*, LIV (1947), 153–71. The author is professor of geography at the University of Florence, Italy.

479

into the past in order to illuminate the present, even in geography.

Having recalled these well-known ideas, let us return to the matter of the evolution of local and regional "cultural features"— meaning by this expression all the facts of relevance to human geography that are encountered in a place or region, and that characterize it.[1] These features emerge from a "human content," varied as to wealth and form, that can be summarized and schematized in three elements that always coexist and are closely linked among themselves: population, in its qualitative and quantitative aspects; economic activity and circulation; and finally, the cultural landscape. The last element is most interesting for us, both because it sums up somehow the other two, and because it preserves the traces of the past the longest and with the most evidence.

What is generally meant by anthropogeographic or human landscape, the *Kulturlandschaft* of the German authors, is well known. The natural features of the earth's surface undergo more or less profound modifications through man's work, especially that of the civilized and technically more advanced peoples. These modifications are mostly quite deliberate on man's part, and are made for the purpose of organizing the surface of the earth in such a way that they will better satisfy the needs of the human race. The improvement of river channels, the digging of canals, the drainage of swamps, the formation of artificial lakes, the substitution of fields and plantations for natural forests and prairies, the opening of mines and quarries, the construction of roads, railroads, dwellings,

[1] The expression "cultural geographic conditions" [*quadri antropogeografici*] will appear unfamiliar, but I have not found a better term to designate briefly the complex of anthropogeographic aspects of a given spatial unit. I do not believe that the denomination of "landscape" (anthropogeographic) sufficiently embraces such a complex; hence the title of this article sounds too restricted, but I preferred it for easier understanding.

ports, and so on—all these constitute a complex of the innumerable material works of man which are bequeathed to the land, and become a topographic testimonial to man's presence and activity. Thus the natural landscape of the earth's surface becomes changed into an anthropic landscape. It is obvious that a denser population must be translated, *ceteris paribus,* into a more profound transformation of the natural surroundings. Thus any form of economic activity, demanding a particular way of treating the soil, will impress a stamp of its own upon the human landscape. This is why it can be said that the human landscape subsumes the other two cultural geographic elements in a space on the earth.

A territory may be more or less rich in human content: that is, the imprint of human activity on the landscape may be more or less profound, depending on how numerous the population is and how intensive and advanced the exploitation of resources may be. Whoever looks at the evolution of the cultural geographic features of the world in recent centuries and especially at the expanding European civilization receives the impression of an ever more rapid, certain, and vigorous conquest of the earth by man, and of an enrichment of the human content of terrestrial space. In the middle of the seventeenth century, the total number of human beings was still less than 500 millions, and at the beginning of the nineteenth century it was nowhere near a billion, but today the world's population exceeds two billion, two hundred million. Immense expanses of forest, prairie, and savanna, under the most diverse climates, have given way to cultivation, enormous masses of minerals have been extracted from the subsoil, and men and goods have begun to circulate rapidly. And what shall we say of those typical features introduced into the geographic landscape by the presence of human settlements and especially cities? Cities are the highest expression of the human landscape, and the great urban centers, a few dozen at the beginning of the past century, today number almost seven hundred.

This rapid enrichment of the earth's surface in human content has certainly affected different territories in quite different degrees; it can be noted both in countries of old progressive civilization, like Europe, and in regions that, though possessing old cultures, were found by the Europeans in a state of stagnation (e.g., India, the Far East, and the Moslem countries). Finally, it occurs in the so-called "new countries" in America, Oceania, and elsewhere, with sparse population, light exploitation of natural resources, and scarce or scattered imprints of man upon the landscape.

Facts of this kind have captured men's imagination and have often given rise to the idea of an almost unlimited power of man within the bounds of the earth's surface. The notion has evoked emotional expression from writers of all periods, even well before the world-wide expansion of the Europeans, when a relatively limited horizon bounded rapid progress in cultural geographic forms. One can cite a well known passage in Tertullian:

All countries are henceforth accessible, all regions are known. . . . Cultivated fields have overcome the forests. . . . The sands are being planted, the rocks hewn, the swamps drained; there are more cities today than cabins some time back.

These words were re-echoed in Buffon, in the middle of the seventeenth century, when the expansion of the Europeans was still a long way from assuming the predominant role it has today in opening the way for human geographic landscapes in almost every corner of the world.[2]

What I most want to bring out here is

the extreme facility with which a conviction can become established: that the cultural geographic development of the various spaces of the earth always proceeds in the same direction—that is, the conviction that any territory tends to become enriched in human content, and that the imprint of culture in it constantly intensifies. This belief is mistaken, for exceptions to this type of development are numerous, widespread, and frequent. The cultural geographic features of a territory or a given place can be subjected relatively long and deeply to phases of regression.

To date, the modality of these phases of decadence has been little studied from the geographic standpoint, in contrast to the progressive phases that are continually being mentioned in any kind of chorographic work. Precisely for this reason, I am determined to outline briefly the extent of degenerative manifestations in cultural geography.

II

We shall begin by distinguishing between purely local manifestation and regional ones. The first are more numerous and commoner than the second, and generally mean something different. The clearest examples of local decadence are offered by cities: periods of growth, perhaps vertiginous, have usually alternated with periods of decline, and the regression may even go as far as the disappearance of an inhabited center. In a series of lectures on our city some years ago, a brilliant speaker, carried away by oratorical emphasis and love of argument, exclaimed: "Only creatures die; cities cannot die." But he forgot the poet's warning:[3]

If thou observe Luni and Urbisaglia,
　How they have gone, and how now after them
　Are going both Chiusi and Sinigaglia,
To hear how families degenerate

[2] Tertullian *De anima*, 30, 3; for Buffon, see J. Rouch, *Les traits essentiels de la géographie humaine* (Paris: Nathan, 1927), p. 10 [see also Clarence J. Glacken, "Count Buffon on Cultural Changes of the Physical Environment," *Annals of the Association of American Geographers*, L (1960), 1–21].

[3] Dante, "Paradise," *Divine Comedy*, XVI, 73–78. [The translation given here is that of J. B. Fletcher (New York: Columbia University Press, 1931).]

will seem to thee no novel thing nor hard,
Seeing that even cities have their date.

Examples are easy to find in the sphere
of the ancient civilizations of the East, as
in the Greco-Roman Mediterranean world.
Because this is so, I prefer not to give examples; another theme seems more important, although I can only give a hint of it.
The decline of ancient civilizations and
their corresponding cultural landscapes conveys the impression of something unitary
—although extremely complex—which cannot be repeated. We must show that in fact
such phenomena are not limited to a single
phase or form of civilization, nor only to
the Mediterranean environment and the
adjacent arid countries.

I refer in particular to the decadence of
urban centers, and I return therefore first
of all to the modern era, because this is on
the whole a period of growing urbanism.
So we shall begin with the so-called "new
countries," the countries colonized by Europeans in the last four centuries, where
cities have multiplied and grown at almost
prodigious rates. It is hardly necessary to
recall that I refer to the decadence of cities
in a geographic and not a political sense,
since history deals with the latter. These
are related matters, but the two phenomena
do not always proceed at the same rate or
in the same direction. Demographic, economic, constructional, and finally topographic decline are geographic manifestations of urban regression.[4]

Numerous old colonial cities have acquired and then lost splendor and riches in
the course of a few centuries, and are today
reduced to obscure villages or collapsing
little towns. What a difference there is between the description of the old Goa, left
by the Florentine Francesco Carletti, who
saw it at the beginning of the seventeenth

century, and what we read in a book of
Guido Gozzano! The first observer sees
nothing but the vivacity and opulence of
that emporium of Portuguese commerce in
India; the other, burdened with intimate
melancholy which finds response in the
atmosphere of the place, wanders about
deserted streets and among abandoned
churches, only the number and massiveness
of which evoke the former affluence of the
faithful.[5] Gorea, founded by the French
on a small island opposite modern Dakar,
has lost all the animation of the times when
it was a frequent port of call and a well-
stocked slave market; it has lost to Dakar
its functions as a port of call, its streets are
almost deserted, and more than half of the
houses are in ruins.[6] Something analogous
is repeated in Sofala, on the Mozambique
Channel, which was first an Arab trading
station and afterwards a Portuguese port.
The traffic that was generated by the demographic and topographic development has
turned away from these cities toward other
ports and other markets.

More rapid, and sometimes even downright violent, is the decadence of mining
centers, just as their rise is rapid and tu-
multuous, especially when its motive is exploitation of new deposits of gold, that
deceitful mirage of every age. During the
last century, the discovery of gold fields
in the Klondike, in California, and in western Australia provoked adventurous treas-
ure-hunts—"rushes." In California, gold
was discovered in 1848; as if by magic,
towns and cities grew like fungus. Only
traces of most of these remain: remnants
of houses, hostelries, inns, shops, even pub-

[4] In regard to natural actions which tend to destroy the material works of man, and so to cause
the anthropogeographic landscape to retrogress,
whenever the preventive efforts of man himself
cease, see Aldo Sestini: "Il paesaggio antropogeografico come forma d'equilibrio," *Bolletino della
Società Geografica Italiana,* serie 7, XII (1947),
1–8.

[5] Nevertheless, Goa, when Carletti sojourned
there, was already in decline. The book of Gozzano that is mentioned is *Verso la cuna del mondo*
(Milan: Treves, 1917). I admit that I have deliberately limited the citations to works containing specific notices upon the arguments given in
the text; I have not thought it necessary to give
citations for data that can easily be recovered
from common chorographic or general works, or
facts that are generally known.
[6] Derwent Whittlesey, "Dakar and Other Cape
Verde Settlements," *Geographical Review,* XXXI
(1941), 608–38.

lic buildings, abandoned suddenly, and so containing still the remains of their furniture or even merchandise. At Coloma, deserted dwellings and stores form two phantom files along the sides of a road without passers-by, and within the houses, invaded by grass and brush, one can still see some old iron trunks, ripped apart and rusted. It is said that a cluster of shacks, inhabited by 100 persons and responding to the pretentious name of Columbia, rocketed to a population of 60,000 in the most fervid moment of the fever; it has dropped again to a few dozen souls, who wander about among the signs of former prosperity; there is still a stage stop, a gold brokerage office, and a museum stuffed with relics, but all is silent.[7]

Outside the circle of European civilization, the remains of cities with imposing architecture, but half-buried in the rankness of the tropical forests of India, Indochina, Yucatan, and Central America, speak clearly. In Cambodia, for example, the French have partly liberated the ruins of Angkor, the great capital of the Khmer empire, from the tangled verdure. They extend over ten square kilometers, and include walls, fortresses, temples, sanctuaries, palaces, and pools, each of admirable architecture and with the richest decoration. The decadence of these cities goes back in general to the Middle Ages, but examples of later abandonment are not lacking. Thus in India there was Golconda, whose name evokes the sparkling diamonds of its old Moslem dynasty; today the city is only a ruin surrounded by a mighty wall of granite blocks, and the old bronze cannons on its pavements are kept for the curiosity of the visitor. The buildings of Bijapur occupy a very small part of the space surrounded by its walls; the remainder is a tangle of Indian figs rooted in the masonry of the old city, which is said to have contained a million people in the sixteenth and seventeenth centuries.

In Europe itself, there is no lack of

cities that have become totally extinct in the modern age. Of Byzantine Mistra only the suggestive remnants of churches, monasteries, palaces and fortifications remain; yet at the beginning of the eighteenth century it had about 40,000 inhabitants, and was then the marvel of the Peloponnese: *Mistra mostra tis Morias,* said a proverb. It was abandoned after being burned during the revolt of the Albanians in 1779. A similar story is told of Voscopoie, the metropolis of the Aromuni in southeastern Albania.

The local manifestations of human geographic regression in the countryside are less apparent. Very circumscribed physical events can lead to abandonment or destruction of particular settled places, and of limited tracts of cultivated land, roads, and other human works: e.g., violent floods, landslides, cyclones, and volcanic eruptions, to mention the most common cases. More general causes affecting entire regions can also bring about unwelcome but purely local effects, like those of economic or social crises, and new orientations of economic life. As long as these causes do not operate too profoundly, their effects appear only in places that offer the least favorable conditions for human activity: for example, lands of low fertility, inaccessible places, and places more exposed to natural or human damage. Many traces of abandoned dwellings and fields have been pointed out in the upper valley of the Indus. This, however, does not signify a general decadence of the region, since there are new settlements and cultivation to contrast with these traces.[8] Again, scattered indications of old terrace cultivation are found on several Mediterranean islands.

Let us go on to cases of regional decadence, remembering that the distinction between local and regional phenomena is far from precise. The regression of a city is a *local* phenomenon when it is unconnected with the general trend of human geographic

[7] G. Belloli, "L'oro californiano," *Le vie d'Italia e del Mondo,* III (1935), 379–92.

[8] G. Dainelli, "Le condizioni delle genti," in *Risultati scientifici della spedizione italiana De Filippi al Caracorum* . . . , serie 2, VIII (Bologna, n.d.), pp. 161–65.

development in the region to which it belongs. This applies particularly to cities that have been centers and nodes of traffic, or have received their life and drive from a single definite thing, like the exploitation of an isolated mine, a special industry, or function such as a state capital. Commercial currents dwindle away, minerals become exhausted, industrial transformation takes effect, or a state disappears; the vital lymph is wanting and the city retrogresses. But at other times the decline of a city is a direct consequence of a degenerative process throughout its territory, or city and region are both struck by the same cause of regression. When sources of information are scarce or fragmentary, the behavior of urban centers—discounting the special characteristics already mentioned—can give an index to regional development. Along a coastline of more than a hundred kilometers on the Gulf of Taranto, not one but four or five cities were distributed in antiquity, among which Sibari, Siri, and Metaponto were the most illustrious. It is hard to imagine this urban flourishing in the squalid and unhealthy landscape of our time; the countryside also must have been more populous and productive, for Metaponto imprinted a turgid spike of wheat on its coins, and the fertility of the territory of Siri is mentioned in the verses of a Greek poet.

The history of the Circum-Mediterranean and Near Eastern countries easily suggests the most important and extensive manifestations of regression in the cultural landscape. In good part the study of this problem from the geographical point of view has yet to be undertaken—at least such study has not gone beyond generic description and hence has not established the connection with transformations of the landscape. As usual, therefore, we turn back immediately to recent times and to countries outside the circle of the great ancient civilizations.

The death of mining cities has already been mentioned; let us add that depopulation can strike a whole region, as more ac-

cessible deposits are exhausted. For example, the Canadian Klondike territories, raised by gold fever to 99,000 inhabitants in 1891, declined in a decade to only 20,000, and then to less than 10,000.

It must be conceded that mining activity appears as something of an exception, whereas agricultural economy stands as a sign of the clear conquest of man on the earth, a conquest that spreads continually. Nevertheless, in various places in the interior of Latin America one still finds agricultural landscapes that are in decline. Until a few decades ago, vast areas of Misiones Province in Argentina and of Paraguay were dotted with the ruins of villages, churches, and Jesuit colleges, overgrown by the forest, which inspired a sense of loneliness and sadness. The departure of the Jesuits from the country in 1767 marked the beginning of a grave decline. The Jesuits had, as we know, established a kind of private state, organizing the Indians socially and economically, fixing them in stable villages, and developing agriculture. In eastern Venezuela, amid the forests of the upper Orinoco, numerous villages founded by the Spaniards appear too large for their present inhabitants, and many buildings are deserted and falling down. Some villages have completely disappeared and have been swallowed up, together with their fields, by the forest. Analogous cases recur in the neighboring Amazonian territories, in the zone of Portuguese as well as Spanish colonization. An occasional village was revived several decades ago by the search for rubber from forest plants, but has begun to decay again with the substitution of plantation rubber for wild rubber on the world market. We find similar developments in the Andean zone, and in this case I do not mean the traces and remains of cities, villages, forts, and agricultural terraces belonging to the ancient Peruvian civilization, for these were abandoned in part previous to the opening of the colonial period. I refer rather to the half-depopulated or altogether deserted villages recently discovered in some less frequented valleys of Peru. Some of these villages are Spanish establishments which go back to the reign of Felipe II.[9]

Abandonment of farmsteads and farmland has also taken place in the United States, and this relatively recent process is still going on. In New England the cultivated surface was reduced by one half in the four decades 1880–1920. Indeed, there are abandoned farmsteads in forested regions not far from the feverish life of New York.[10] There are also manifestations of agricultural regression in various central and western areas which were originally covered with prairie. Man's enemy here is a natural phenomenon that is assuming even greater proportions: the erosion of agricultural soils by water and in certain places also by sandstorms. The Americans are alarmed about erosion, and its study has gone further among them than in any other country.

Not even Europe — which seems so crowded and so much in need of land—is without examples of regression in agricultural territory. In some areas of southwestern France, and in several mountain ranges of Western and central Europe including the Alps, a considerable depopulation has been in progress for several decades; its immediate cause is permanent emigration, mostly toward the lower zones and cities. An extensive study, conducted on the spot, has delineated the picture of such depopulation in the Italian Alps. Where the phenomenon is worst it is accompanied by decadence of cultivation and the abandonment of higher settlements. This regression from the Alpine mountains is not exactly of regional character, since the lower parts of the valleys are seldom affected, but

neither can it be considered merely local, given its general distribution above a certain altitude. This distribution has a zonal character.

We find singular cases of decline in the cultural landscape of the plains themselves. Lands conquered for agriculture and settlement by hydraulic improvements are extraordinarily sensitive to variations in the natural and human environment. It is not enough to create improvements, they have to be maintained by a vigilant expenditure of energy. For example, in the second half of the sixteenth century, a wonderful work of improvement was completed by the Este family in the Ferrara plain. The principal sponsor of the project was the duke Alfonso II; when he died, the care necessary to maintain the works, the efficiency of which was then being undermined by subsidence, began to fail. Thus even in the course of the seventeenth century 40,000 hectares of land, reclaimed with much cost and effort, fell prey to waterlogging and desolation, to be restored for human use only in the last seventy years.[11]

Travelers and ethnologists have found numerous traces of regional decadence among less civilized peoples. However, the documents that might tell us the time and cause of such phenomena are almost always lacking, and the present natives are unable to explain them. This is true of one of the most famous examples, the fortifications and mines of Southern Rhodesia. Their traces and ruins are spread by the hundreds between the Limpopo and the Zambezi in an area as large as Italy. The main ones are those of Zimbabwe, from which the whole complex received its name. The ruins consist of dry walls that form more or less spacious enclosures. Within some of them traces of huts and many objects attesting to long and quite active life have been recovered. It seems that the time of the erection and peopling of these enclosures coincides with intensive mining of gold, copper,

[9] A. Lucchesi, *Nel Sudamerica* (Florence: Bemporad, 1936), *passim;* L. M. Nesbitt, *Orenoco* (Milan: Istituto per Studi di Politica Internazionale, 1938), *passim;* Earl Hanson, "Social Regression in the Orinoco and Amazon Basins," *Geographical Review,* XXIII (1933), 578–98; Robert Shipee, "Lost Valleys of Peru," *Geographical Review,* XXII (1932), 562–81.

[10] Pierre Deffontaines, *L'Homme et la forêt* (Paris: Gallimard, 1933), p. 31.

[11] C. Errera, "La bonifica estense nel basso Ferrarese," *Rivista Geografica Italiana,* XLI (1934), 49–53.

tin, and iron. Terrace works on the flanks of the hills, perhaps for agricultural purposes, and trenches that are interpreted as irrigation canals are also present. Altogether a set of cultural landscape features superior to what existed at the moment of European penetration has been reconstructed. To explain it, some ethnologists have had recourse to the hypothesis of distant origins, while others think that the present South African population cannot be denied the capacity for a development like that attested by the ruins of Zimbabwe. In any case, we see that the regression is independent of European influence.[12]

On the other hand, European influence is a factor in the decadence of many inferior cultures of Oceania and the Americas, but mostly this has to do only with matters of ethnographic regression, since the immigration and initiative of European peoples, and in part also of peoples from the Far East, have been able to impose a new progressive impulse on the cultural landscape of these territories. It must be added that in many cases the Europeans came on the scene when decadence was already evident, as in those strange villages of the farming folk, the so-called Pueblos of New Mexico and Arizona. Today very few of the pueblos are inhabited, although the Spaniards counted about sixty of them at their entry into the region in 1542. But numerous other ruins are without doubt pre-European, and among them are still found traces of larger villages. The arrival of the Europeans only accelerated a process already active, which certain people connect with a climatic change adverse to agriculture, to which the pressure of warlike nomad tribes of hunters and gatherers surely must be added.[13]

The causes cited for the Pueblo regression are in addition to those already mentioned. It is now appropriate to attempt a

general synthetic picture of all causes, by way of summary. With the search for causes one enters into the most delicate, and also the most purely scientific part of the investigation; the actual search is far from easy, not so much because of the variety of these causes in concrete cases, but chiefly because of the frequent interference of diverse factors that are themselves variable in time.

Physical influences are extremely varied, and do not spare any land. Physical mutations can of course produce cultural changes. Some kinds of physical mutations are of episodic character, even if frequently repeated: landslides, avalanches, very violent cyclones, sandstorms, and so on. But these have only local effects, causing destruction and impoverishment over very limited and scattered areas. Similarly, although floods may cover tremendous areas and directly or indirectly produce many victims, they do not leave too much of a mark in the cultural landscape, since the damage is usually repaired relatively quickly. China, for example, has been for millenniums a country of gigantic floods that have repeatedly spread carnage over territories several times as large as Italy. Nevertheless, China has remained a densely populated and intensely cultivated country, with a landscape rich in the imprints and works of man.

We can think of phenomena that are more frankly catastrophic: the unchained violence of endogenic forces, i.e., earthquakes and volcanic eruptions. Certainly the destruction sometimes produced by these forces is enormous, and we need no reminder here of the numbers of their victims. Nevertheless, even more terrifying manifestations should not be overestimated. Man soon returns to repopulate, repair, and reconstruct; this is especially true for volcanic regions, with their exceptionally fertile soil. Despite repeated disasters, have not the slopes of Etna and Vesuvius been densely settled and productive in every age? Regression in these cases is usually rather transitory, but the desertion of some

[12] Lidio Cipriani, *In Africa dal Capo al Cairo* (Florence: Bemporad, 1932), chap. 5.
[13] For the pueblos, see Renato Biasutti, *Le razze e i popoli della terra* (Turin: Unione Tipografico-Editrice Torinese, 1941), III, pp. 350–57 [3d ed., 1959, V, 445–60].

sites can be a lasting consequence. Although no city has formed again on the very ruins of Pompeii—luckily for the archeologists—numerous other centers have emerged to cluster on the rim of Vesuvius. After the destruction caused by the Calabrian earthquakes of 1783, many villages and small towns in the plain of Palmi were rebuilt on other sites;[14] similar cases are found in southeastern Sicily.

We can consider as more important the consequences of other kinds of physical variations: the slowly-acting variations that do not bring sudden death and destruction, but regularly and extensively modify the condition that nature offers to the human community. Such are the mutations of coastlines, river channels, and climates.

Passing over marine erosion, which has swallowed up various villages and ports of the British coast, let us think of the silting of low coasts, small bays, estuaries, river mouths and channels. In consequence of this process, many ports on these sites, considered the most suitable all through the Middle Ages, have become inaccessible in the course of centuries.

We could count dozens of ancient and medieval cities that have declined together with their sanded-up ports. More than one case of this sort is found on the French Mediterranean coast, where the most famous example is Aigues-Mortes. This little walled town on the level amphibious landscape of the Rhone Delta is only a memory of the maritime city that saw Saint Louis depart on his crusades. The outward spread of the fluvial deltas has withdrawn the sea from the old cities where the sea itself was one of the main domains of their economic and political life. Examples come to everyone's mind: Ephesus, Miletus, Adria, Ravenna, Pisa, etc.

The reality of climatic variations is a definitely established fact. A climatic mutation cannot be limited to a restricted area;

if it occurs it must affect vast regions. But at present the effects of such changes on the development of the cultural landscape can perhaps be appreciated only in a theoretical manner.

The thesis of a progressive desiccation has been maintained for northern and Saharan Africa, as well as for western and central Asia. Traces of more extensive human settlements in antiquity are found at every turn in this great arid and semiarid zone. Not only are there traces of urban sites and caravan cities, but the countryside also enjoyed a greater prosperity. It is known, for example, that the interior of Tunisia is full of the remains of ancient olive-oil presses.

We are talking about countries where water is scarce and has to be used with extreme care, and we understand how a slight fluctuation in the rainfall curve, or a small increase in evaporation can be enough to produce a deterioration of the conditions required for agriculture. Some people have gone so far as to suppose that a general process of climatic desiccation lay at the root of the decadence and death of the ancient Oriental civilizations, and especially those of Mesopotamia. Clear traces of an increase of aridity are demonstrated for the Saharan region, but they probably go back for the most part to prehistoric times. For historical times almost all recent studies, both on the North African countries and those of the Orient, affirm that the ancient prosperity could be imagined even with a natural environment identical to that of today. It may well be that the reaction to the first facile claims has gone too far; different evidence in other countries speaks of slow climatic changes even in historic times. In any case, the incidental climatic changes of the historical period cannot, it seems to me, be made responsible by themselves for human phenomena so profound as these.[15]

[14] L. Lacquaniti, "Spostamenti di sito di alcuni centri abitati della Piana di Palmi in relazione ai terremoti del 1783," *Bolletino della Società Geografica Italiana,* serie 7, VII (1942), 41–42.

[15] Certainly the ancient civilizations of anterior Asia were closely connected with the development of agriculture, from which the dependence on climate is equally obvious. Biasutti also appeals to

Climatic variations affect the volume and regime of watercourses, which in arid countries are the precious bringers of fertility to the ground. But in other ways, too, rivers and streams are subject to impoverishment of water volume, if we add the possibility, or in some cases the likelihood, of changes of course. Where irrigation is necessary, a change in the course of a river brings death to the area that was formerly fertilized by its waters. It is said that Albuquerque, the founder of Portuguese power in India, dreamed of diverting the Nile to destroy Egypt.

Notable traces of abandoned human settlements have been discovered in the desert basin of the Tarim, in Central Asia, where Sven Hedin and Aurel Stein have made precious finds of ancient Chinese and Buddhist civilizations. The city of Loulan, along an ancient silk road, is buried by the desert sands, but the place was once irrigated from the Konche-darya—a river that issues from the mountains, but now follows a different course. Even more revealing are the ruins of Niya, situated in the desert toward the southern margin of the basin about a hundred and fifty kilometers from the foot of the Kuen-lun mountains. The dryness of the air has permitted the preservation of the structure of houses and of the agricultural landscape. The trunks of fruit trees that have been dead for at least sixteen centuries are still standing. Water is far away today. A stream descends from the mountains in the direction of the ruins, but it becomes dry a little beyond the foot of the mountain, where the present oases are found. Until at least the third century of our era, this stream must have reached far enough to fertilize the fields of Niya. Anal-

ogous cases can be observed elsewhere in the desert.[16]

Certain diseases are connected with the natural environment, and first among them all is malaria. It is often regarded as particularly important in reducing entire regions to misery, and in the abandonment of cities and countrysides in the ancient Greco-Roman world, medieval Italy, etc. It is certain that malaria has plagued the inhabitants of many places until very recent times. But the problem in general is extraordinarily complex. To what extent has malaria caused decline in population and activity, and to what extent is it rather a consequence of such a decline? Apparently effect and cause are often changed about.[17]

I shall pass over the consequences of serious epidemics of episodic character, about which what has been said of catastrophic natural events might be repeated. Likewise, I shall say only a few words about another, and the saddest, scourge of humanity: war. War acts through direct destruction, and still more through its repercussions. It seems unnecessary to recall the many cities devastated by war and never rebuilt. Let us point out, rather, that entire territories can fall prey to manifestations of human geographic regression. During the Hundred Years' War, the forest grew up again on many fields in France, and in the Saintonge the people long repeated the proverb: "The forests came to France with the English." [18] In the western Caucasus, after the exodus of the Circassians in the face of Russian penetration, vigorous forests covered even the vestiges of native villages. A large part of Yun-nan, in southern China, was prostrated by the bloody Taiping Rebellion, and is now dotted, several decades later, with abandoned fields and villages.

---

climatic variations, but not to these alone: "Some climatic oscillations, the deforestation and the extension of nomadic pastoralism through the influence of invaders coming from Central Asia, can easily explain the periods of decadence in the economy, with the abandonment of villages and cities, the diminution of the population, and the impoverishment of their industries and their culture" (*op. cit.*, II, 509).

[16] Aurel Stein, "Innermost Asia: Its Geography as a Factor in History," *Geographical Journal*, XLV (1925), 378–403, 473–98.

[17] Maurice Le Lannou, "Le rôle géographique de la malaria," *Annales de Géographie*, XLV (1936), 113–35.

[18] Deffontaines, *op. cit.*, p. 31.

All the phenomena mentioned here as causes of human geographic regression carry with them direct destruction, or a deterioration of the physical environment. But decadence in some places and regions may also arise simply from the desertion of centers of human activity and means of communication, as mentioned in regard to old colonial emporia. In such cases, decadence in one place is balanced by progress in another. Certain technical advances, and the modern evolution of the general economy (especially in industry), have had this effect. Thus, an increase in the tonnage of ships has concentrated major maritime and mercantile activity in a limited number of well equipped ports, and this concentration has naturally caused decadence in various minor ports. In England, the clustering of large industries in the Carboniferous Basin at the time of the Industrial Revolution resulted in the ruin of numerous manufacturing towns of the south.

The evolution of the world economy— and the accompanying social evolution— has certainly been one of the most vast and profound causes acting on the cultural landscape of a region; it has touched all countries that do not live in an absolutely closed economic system. The recent depopulation in the European mountains has as one substantial motive the rupture of an old socioeconomic equilibrium. The demographic regression of these mountain zones does not depend upon an excess of deaths over births, but on permanent emigration toward the plains and cities that continue to exert a strong attraction on the mountaineer. Between 1870 and 1920 the isles of Greece saw their populations diminish because of the attraction exercised by distant countries. Even in the oases of the Sahara, which seem so remote and isolated, a human-geographic decadence has begun, caused primarily by a growing shortage of labor in the coastal cities.[19]

We are not talking about developments limited to our times. The great economic and social revolution of the late Middle Ages in parts of Europe, when the cities rapidly regained domination in economic and political life, was not without influence on the human geographic features of the countryside. To be sure, in some regions this influence was negative: for example, in Germany the influx of people from the country districts toward the cities seems to have brought about the abandonment of numerous rural sites and the partial depopulation of others.[20]

At this point we are getting into problems of landscape development that the geographer can only partly resolve. However, two observations seem to me to be pertinent.

In the first place, we must remember that major regressive manifestations rarely depend on a single, simple, or distinct cause. For example, we may ask ourselves why most cities destroyed by war or earthquakes have arisen again, despite the greatest injuries at the hands of man and nature. We must admit that the few cities which have declined may have suffered from conditions unfavorable to them, and that the additional destructive processes might simply have precipitated the catastrophe. Similarly, when slow or gradual deterioration of the physical environment saps away the equilibrium of the relations between man and the soil, additional destructive forces definitively break the equilibrium that has been undercut, and rapid decay begins.

In the second place, the effect of a given process will vary according to the natural environment, which may be more or less favorable to the life and progress of the human collectivity. Some environments are marginal for any kind of life except an extremely miserable one, and for any but an extremely sparse population: e.g., the marginal Arctic zone of the oikoumene, high mountains, arid regions, marshy areas.

[19] Marcel Larnaude, "La géographie du Sahara et l'Institut de Recherches Sahariennes," *Annales de Géographie*, LV (1946), 298.

[20] Kurt Scharlau, "Beiträge zur geographischen Betrachtung der Wüstungen," *Badische Geographische Abhandlungen*, Vol. XII (1933).

In these environments, even a process of little account in itself may be sufficient to bring about the partial or total abandonment of settlements, while in environments more favored by nature man will find the means and energy to react against light or temporary adversities, whether of a physical, economic, or political nature.[21] From such reactions a new equilibrium will be born, and there will be no decadence. In other words, we can say that the same causes will lead to the same effects only if they operate in an identical environment. Prior knowledge of this environment—i.e., the geographic facts—is therefore indispensable.

A final and more suggestive problem needs to be mentioned. History and ethnology tell us of the deep decadence and even of the death of some civilizations; the degeneration of the cultural landscape goes along with this trend. This is really a case of recalling the civilizations of antiquity, in that even less well developed cultures, in almost any part of the world, show us the same thing.

We cannot exclude the possibility that natural phenomena have contributed to the crises in these civilizations, particularly through the impoverishment of the human geographic content of a country: diminished population, decreased intensity of ex-

ploitation of the land, insufficiency of the means of defense against natural adversity, of irrigation works, etc. But in general it seems to me that the problem requires a different solution, that these regressive manifestations of landscapes are not the cause, but rather the effect of the decadence of a civilization; regression is the result of a weakening of the moral and material energies of a human collectivity. Let us leave aside the cases—not infrequent, to be sure—in which the ruin of a civilization is produced violently by the invasions of more backward peoples accustomed to a very different way of life. Let us restrict ourselves to the cases of civilizations that seem to decline or succumb to an internal crisis.

Here too the function of the geographer will not be that of a simple spectator, who takes note of the impoverishment of the human geographic content of a region, and to explain it invokes the decline of a civilization. We should not forget that this process has deep connections with all the human work designed to dominate the forces and the riches of nature, a subject within the compass of geography. Serious civil progress cannot be imagined apart from the understanding and the ever more vast exploitation of the possibilities that our planet offers us.

We must therefore consider ourselves to be at the point of juncture of three different branches of knowledge: ethnology, history, and geography. Only by means of their co-operation will it be possible to arrive at more than superficial conclusions on the course and causes of the most profound regressive phases of civilizations, peoples, and the corresponding cultural landscapes.

---

[21] Quite dissimilar difficulties confront the renewal of human action upon nature after a temporary period of decadence, according to environmental conditions, especially climatic ones. On the rocky Mediterranean mountains, where culture is necessary to conserve the thin mantle of humus, a renewal is far more laborious than in the slightly rolling and humid lands of Central and Western Europe. These, after man has abandoned them, grow up again in forest, but their soil does not lose its depth and fertility.

H. J. FLEURE

SOCIAL ORGANIZATION
AND ENVIRONMENT

As all modern men live in groups larger than that of man, wife and children, and as all evidence of former times points in the same direction, we can be fairly confident that a group-habitat is a general scheme, an expression of the fact that *Homo socialis* would be a useful designation for our species. The size and organization of the group-habitat depends upon the potentialities of the group and of its environment. When it is, or has been, a fairly small settlement in which the main occupation has been food production, we have no hesitation in calling the settlement a village; where it is large, with many expressions of corporate life in architecture and with diverse groups of craftsmen, we readily speak of a city or town. But between the two are many variants difficult to put into either group. Broadly, we know that the town or city represents an increment; it is evidence of differentiation of activities and of exchange on a larger scale than was the case in the, often, almost self-contained village.

May we now look at some questions and features of village and town in various re-

Reprinted, with permission of the author and editor, from *Some Problems of Society and Environment*, Publication XII, Institute of British Geographers (London: George Philip & Son, 1947). Only the second of the three lectures included in this publication is reproduced here. The lectures were given at University College, London in 1946. The author has been professor of geography and anthropology at the University College of Wales, Aberystwyth (1917–30), and professor of geography at Manchester University (1930–44). He now resides in London.

gions with this idea of possibilities of increment in mind, always remembering that any such possibilities tend to bring struggle for ownership, which in its turn gives scope to the power-quest so deeply rooted in human nature. Increment may therefore be, and often is, seized by some section of the community or some conquering immigrants, and the mass of the people may get very little.

Considering some special aspects of settlement-characteristics in Africa south of the Sahara and Abyssinia, we note first of all that this region has hitherto been subject to considerable disadvantages. It apparently received its early population mainly from farther north (probably including the Western Sahara before that area became desert), and early immigrants had, in the course of time, to face temperatures above the optimum, as we have already seen.[1] But it is particularly the difficulties attending the spread of items of equipment that must be emphasized. Millets acclimatized themselves, but wheat and barley did not, and cereal food remained on a low level, to be somewhat improved after introduction of American maize and manioc. Bananas, an ancient introduction, have been to some extent a compensation; but neither bananas nor millets brought the social organization that nearly always accompanies wheat.

The pastures all have tough grasses, poor

[1] [See the lecture on "Population and Environment" in the volume from which this essay is extracted.]

491

in Vitamin C; and animals are specially liable to attack by tsetse, tick and other parasites within as well as without. Cattle, sheep and pigs are all of poor quality under native conditions in inter-tropical and South Africa. Copper and tin both occur in Africa, but very far from one another, and the region under consideration seems to have missed a Bronze Age almost completely. This is of some importance, as bronze taught men elsewhere a good deal about trade and craft; especially through the need for bringing together from diverse sources the two main constituents (copper and tin). The African region mostly went from wood and stone to iron, crudely worked. We should here remember that the early and cruder stages of iron-working elsewhere acted as disintegrants socially; though, where trade had previously existed, it revived with the utilization of iron, and there were great advances, as in the Mediterranean of classical times. The poor quality of the farm animals in the region was a factor hindering the introduction of the plow, which hardly penetrated here before the intrusion of Europeans. The hoe and the digging-stick maintained their dominance, and hence the continued allocation of much routine of cultivation to women, who have, traditionally, and very naturally, looked upon such tasks as accessory and subordinate to motherhood. African cultivation has very widely meant using a patch until it was exhausted and then taking another and letting the first go back to the wild. Manuring, if practiced, is of rudimentary character, and care of the soil is unknown in most parts; the land belongs to the group, not to the household, so the incentive for family-increment through care of the soil is so much the weaker. Succession from generation to generation is not highly organized, and institutions are correspondingly limited—no written records and only rudiments of what might be called a priesthood. With all this naturally goes a paucity of specialized buildings expressive of the group life of units larger than a village, save that a special chieftain or king may have a special settlement for himself, his numerous wives and his servants. This settlement may be built for him, and is then a primary stage of a feature found in former times elsewhere, namely the idea of "new king, new capital." The general unit of settlement is the village, and, with the exception of a few towns in Nigeria and spreading slightly southward, and of the Arab commercial settlements once existing on the east coast, there were no cities or towns in Africa south of the Sahara and Abyssinia until modern Europeans brought the idea with them. Africa south of the Sahara has been a region of limitation, within which are regions of debilitation, areas in which herding has to be given up because of flies and ticks, and in which man finds it very difficult to maintain directive co-operative effort beyond a quite short-term plan. The almost self-contained village, the shifting use of land, the absence of records, the paucity of trackways, the slight development of trade, all were features of African life before Europeans affected it. They are all changing rapidly, but unevenly, and African peoples are accordingly being asked to step forward in a generation or two through stages which have occupied millenniums elsewhere. For so rapid change they need tutelage, which, unfortunately, does not always appreciate that what is most important is adjustment of the mental make-up, a process which, thus far, man has not been able to speed up very effectively.

A most dramatic contrast to Africa south of the Sahara is provided by the Nile-Syria-Euphrates region, the "Fertile Crescent" of Breasted. Here was a region in which, as desert conditions spread in a late phase of the Pleistocene, people gathered near the rivers, where the flood plains were no doubt obstructed with wet thicket. Here hunting came to be supplemented by the women's work in collecting seeds of grasses which were valuable food; tending the plants likely to give food was a natural development, and Eve became the pioneer of cultivation and civilization. The spring floods of Euphrates and Tigris, the summer (monsoonal rain) floods coming down the Nile from Abyssinia brought silt to the flood plain to renew its fertility year by year; and men learned to dig ditches and to use that flood plain to cultivate wheat (emmer), barley and other plants. In Mesopotamia and Syria, especially, it was possible to have domestic animals on the pastures, such as they were, near some rivers and on the hills (one recalls the psalmist's reference to the dews of Hermon); and the plow was developed as a consequence. The "Fertile Crescent" thus gave a flood-plain which could be cultivated year after year if the flood was controlled. This gave rise to durable village settlements with dwellings that, in the dry sunny climate, could be made of sun-dried brick and were typically made on the river bank for the sake of water supply, control of the ditches leading off from the river, possibilities of fishing and boat communication, and other allied reasons. It was an advantage that the sun-dried brick crumbled after a while and was replaced, as in this way the village came to be on a mound safer from the floods. But the village as such was durable, save that along the Euphrates changes in the braiding river introduced a factor of change in settlements.

The durability of the social equipment found expression toward the end of the fourth millennium B.C. in stone buildings connected with religion, and there is no need to give an elaborate account of the rise of cities—the oldest cities in the world—an increment of remarkable magnitude. The adjacent sites of Memphis and Cairo illustrate the inevitable and immense importance of the northern exit from the Nile Slot; the rise and fall of Ur, Nippur, Kish, Babylon and others bring out the vagaries of the Euphrates, changing the relative importance of its braided channels, silting up here and carving out there. Changing seats of power and of sanctity in Mesopotamia contrast with a greater constancy in Egypt, so long as it was self-contained. But when the isthmus of Suez became important as

an entry for warriors or an exit for armies, or, as in modern times, a commercial route, Egypt was gripped by change.

It was often characteristic of ancient Egypt, as it has been of modern Egypt, that her external commerce was in the hands of non-Egyptians. On the other hand, the changeability of conditions of cities in many parts of the Asiatic portion of the "Fertile Crescent" has carried with it recurrent struggles for power, dynasties founded by conquest (often by herders of the arid border) following which came organization, luxury, decadence and a new conquest, as ibn-Khaldun so insistently argued six centuries ago. The increment here has been seized by one group after another, and a general mobility had the characteristic effect of spreading features of Mesopotamian thought and equipment in antiquity in all directions. More and more as investigation develops is it seen how important Mesopotamia has been as a center of radiation to India and China, to the Mediterranean and via the Pontic Steppe to the loess lands of Europe. It is interesting that this radiation took effect in the third millennium B.C., and again and again afterwards until the tragic setback of the Turkish conquest. These later conquerors understood too little about management of an irrigation system; and an old region of increment, reduced to poverty for centuries, needs long and laborious effort to restore itself: today capital equipment from more technically advanced lands is needed, as the old standards of sufficiency and increment have been so revolutionarily changed by power machinery. It is interesting to note the comparative poverty of the remains of many monuments of early periods of increment in Mesopotamia. Hard stone was more difficult to get than in Egypt, and, even in Persepolis, a great deal of sun-dried brick was used and has long since crumbled, leaving stone lintels, doorposts, steps, window frames, and so on standing.

If we consider India in analogous fashion we see that, while there have been cities as elements of Indian life from the third millennium B.C. onwards, the village here is the typical social unit and hardly more than 10 per cent of India's huge population live in what may be called towns or cities. The cities have been in most cases expressions of the power and economic increment at the disposal of rulers. It is characteristic, for example, that quite a number of royal or imperial cities were built by one Mogul emperor after another in the neighborhood of Delhi, and a cynic has hailed New Delhi as a characteristic British addition to the future series of ruins. The deep divisions among the people of India from time immemorial are illustrated in the cliff-top sites and approaches to some of the cities—the nucleus of Gwalior, Golconda, and so on, but more important still are the facts of division illustrated in many villages. In the south, especially, the village of the caste-folk and the appendix where the pariah live can be distinguished, and sometimes the places within the village occupied by occupational caste groups are observably distinct.

The modern rise of Calcutta, Bombay, and Madras has been described at times as turning India inside out. Once largely self-contained, with external trade as a quite minor factor in its life, India has been drawn into external relations that have made Calcutta and Bombay its two largest cities, while Madras is of the same order of magnitude as the largest of the internal cities, Delhi and Hyderabad. It is the misfortune of India that the poor quarters of Bombay, especially, are a disgrace to all concerned, though parts of Bombay repeat features such as the craft groupings in various streets which suggest a better social order, but one which has been undermined by mass production and the jostling of peoples in a modern port, in a region in which the birth rate is still phenomenally high.

Looking at China, similarly, we see, here again, the vast number of villages, though there are more large native cities; but here again we have evidence of the "turning in-

side out." Shanghai, Canton, and Tientsin are all large, Shanghai the largest city on the mainland of Asia. Nevertheless, in China, these cities of external commerce are less "foreign-bodies" than are the corresponding ones in India, and Hankow-Wuchang-Hanyang, Peking, Nanking, Chungking, and so on, stand out strongly. The urban tradition is stronger in China than in India. China has less deeply contrasted fractions in its population, India was a *terminus ad quem* for many drifts of early groups and her jungles have allowed them to maintain their way of life. North China's loess has impressed a measure of uniformity of mode of life based on irrigated cultivation, generally more skilled than that of the great majority of Indian cultivation.

India and China both have had large increments which, in agricultural village-dwelling communities, have generally tended to become concentrated in relatively few hands, usually of rulers and religious organizations. The village dwellers have traditionally responded to increments by the birth rate. We should appreciate that the increment in these lands had also led to contributions to civilization. While much remains undetermined, it seems evident that the teaching of which Gautama Buddha gave the greatest expression has deeply affected subsequent religious thought beyond as well as within the Monsoon Lands. How far the teachings associated with Lao-Tzu and Confucius may have had effects outside China and Japan cannot be said. In the sphere of material culture, however, the contributions of China are notable, and include tea, the citrus fruits, porcelain, paper, perhaps printing. It is claimed also that the idea of paper money came from China. It is well to reserve judgment about origins of things and devices that may well have been invented independently more than once. The magnificence of Chinese art in painting and modeling is too well-known to need comment; it takes its place beside the greatest art of other lands.

It is an important fact concerning China

and India that both Peking and Delhi have imperial enclosures constructed under rulers who had come in with the aristocratic horseman tradition. The analogy in plan with the Kremlin at Moscow and elsewhere in European U.S.S.R. is very clear, though the Kremlin in European U.S.S.R is a monument built not by conquering horsemen of the steppe, but rather by rulers attempting to assert themselves against these horsemen.

The short references to Africa, the "Fertile Crescent," India, and China in preceding paragraphs are merely introductory to a consideration of some facts concerning Europe, but, before going into this, it may be well to notice a few relevant points concerning the lands of nomadism. The major arid belt of the Northern Hemisphere stretches, with small interruptions at rivers, from the Atlantic coast of the Sahara to Manchuria. The majority of its inhabitants are settled folk living near rivers or in oases, and cultivating, often intensively and with irrigation schemes. But around the settled folk are often pastoral groups who may be dependent to a considerable extent on exchanges with the cultivators. They should be looked upon as a specialized offshoot from the cultivators. The purely nomadic peoples, also often dependent upon exchange with cultivators, represent in all probability a further specialization. This is an important point in various ways, as it corrects an old error which constructed a general hypothetical sequence: hunter-collectors, nomad herdsmen, settled cultivators. It is not impossible that there may be a case for the hunter-collector groups having become nomad herdsmen, but all indications point to the sequence hunter-collector, hoe and digging-stick cultivator, mixed farmer with the plow.

Turning now to Europe, we note the very contrasted responses of Mediterranean lands on the one hand and Europe farther north on the other. The Mediterranean had cities in the third millennium B.C.; whereas, in some parts of Europe which have had great cities in recent times, there were none before A.D. 1000, or even a later date. A contrast of 4,000 years in this respect is dramatic, and we should realize some of the factors involved.

The climates of most of the Mediterranean coast lands give fairly reliable rain, and reliable sunshine almost to excess. "The rains are over and gone and the time of the singing of birds is come" is a famous phrase from the "Song of Songs."

The wheat of the Fertile Crescent could spread fairly directly to Mediterranean lands, and, on the way, the vine and the olive and the fig tree became important items of equipment.

Animal farming had its difficulties, for both the "Fertile Crescent" and the Mediterranean coast lands are summer-brown. "The grass withereth and the flower fadeth" when the Etesian winds blow in summer and the sun's rays beat down. For the Mediterranean lands, it was possible in many places to take the animals up to the heights for their summer pasture. The "rains are over and gone" by Easter (whence that festival), but the moisture they have left brings out flowers on the heaths and the humming and the honey of the bees has long been a Mediterranean feature. The islands of the Aegean offered bays for boat refuges, limestone and other bluffs for defensive sites near the ports, often with a spring gushing out from a joint in the rock. The joint may be hidden by solution of the lime and its deposition as it spread on the rock surface while the water evaporated, but Moses in the famous story knew where to strike this deposited crust so as to get joint-water.

The island habitat offered a measure of security and opportunities for fishing as well as for commercial odysseys. The city set on a hill, sometimes above an anchorage, is a Mediterranean feature. In some parts even a place of village size may be as closely compacted as a town, with narrow streets between tall houses, and with streets sometimes arched to help to support the houses as well as to increase shade.

One must add the oft-repeated fact that

the calcareous rocks of the region are often of the nature of free-stone, that is, stone which can be cut accurately in any direction. It is not difficult to picture the influence of this upon architecture among people who had a tradition of wooden pillars and had migrated to a less wooded region, but had found this new resource. More subtle is the bearing of all this on geometrical thought and the art of mensuration, especially as the clear skies and strong sun give sharp shadow effects. As the free-stone is often iron-stained, the effect of a pillared front on a hill-top facing the setting sun is impressive.

It is most natural that Mediterranean idealism emphasized the city—"The New Jerusalem" of the Apocalypse, the "City of God" of St. Augustine.

In addition to all this there is an almost more fundamental fact—namely, that the small, surface-scratching plow of the "Fertile Crescent" is also suitable on the yellowish and reddish Mediterranean soils, the color of which shows that evaporation draws up moisture through the soil, and iron salts are deposited at the surface. The plow should not go deep as the plant foodsalts are near the surface, but it must be used repeatedly and in criss-cross fashion to keep the surface from caking hard with lime and iron. The surface soil is usable in many places only in alternate years, and there are spots in Spain so dry that the field can be cultivated only one year in three. Alternation of crops is, often, no help.

The city grew as an expression of increment and a center of power, attaining great developments in periods which for one reason or another favored commerce. Knossos, Hissarlik and others in the third millennium B.C.; Hissarlik and Knossos again, Mycenae, Tiryns, Akrokorinth in the second; Athens and her rivals, and Rome and Italian cities in the last; Rome, Venice, Genoa, Naples, Ragusa, Florence, Bologna, Padua, Pavia, Milan, Barcelona in the Middle Ages; Barcelona, Marseilles, Rome, Milan, Genoa, Athens and Alexandria,

among others, in modern times, especially since the opening of the Suez Canal. And one might say much more of Constantinople as successor to Byzantium and predecessor to Istanbul, as well as of the various phases of Alexandria. We have here repeated, almost periodic, blossoming of cities (of increment) with commerce as a main factor, maritime commerce that found an appropriate nursery in the Aegean. Here little boats might navigate from island to island without losing sight of land; here, too, they might rely considerably on the Etesian winds in summer. Nowadays these conditions are of small account, but the Mediterranean is a maritime highway of the nations. Of old the obsidian of Melos, the emery of Naxos, the tin of Crissa on the gulf of Corinth were major factors; now it is the fruits of the Mediterranean lands that are a main basis of the region's trade. But modern through-routes from the Atlantic to the Indian Ocean, from the Black Sea to the opener waters, from northwestern Europe via Mediterranean ports to Monsoonal Asia, Australia and East Africa, from central and Eastern Europe via Trieste, Fiume, Salonika and the Dardanelles, all now surpass in importance the routes of Mediterranean traffic per se.

Yet, as Sir John Myres has so well shown,[2] the cities with their occasional, almost periodic, rise to affluence and power are set over a background of the rural poverty of those who have not the resources to plant groves of fruit trees and wait years for a return. And the sharp descent of streams from fold mountains brings mud to be laid on the plains below, so that, especially since forests have been reduced, the drainage of the lowland is poor and gives opportunities for malaria and other troubles that limit initiative and make an over-all organization hard to build up. The city, whether the city state of Greece or the trading city of the Middle Ages, has long tried to manage for itself; regional organization has been hindered and

[2] Sir John L. Myres, *Mediterranean Culture* (Cambridge: Cambridge University Press, 1943).

has had to face an ununderstanding mass of rural poverty. Still more, in the background are the mountains with their goatherds and shepherds, their transhumance, their wild kinship groups that in Greece and Macedonia today are a very discomfiting element in the political problem.

We thus have in the Mediterranean, with a background of rural poverty, a tradition of city life and power. We find a deep division between the representatives of larger power because of the split between eastern and western empires, perpetuated in the hostility between their heirs and successors, the Orthodox and the Roman Church. There is also an inevitable concern of peoples outside the Mediterranean in the routes through it. If we add to this the fact that the Mediterranean is poorly equipped for a phase of world-life in which power for machinery counts as it now does, we realize why the Mediterranean no longer leads, but we at the same time appreciate that some ports on it have grown wonderfully in the last seventy-five years.

It is to be remembered also that the long-ingrained habit of mind gathering around the city as a center of culture and of power held back development of linguistic nationalism, so that in Mediterranean lands a common measure of thought and aspiration within a language group can hardly be said to exist, and attempts at conscious national organization are recent and not very effective.

Were this lecture concerned with more aspects of Mediterranean life it would be necessary to refer to the intrusion and then the regression of Islamic power, which on the one hand helped to hand on a heritage from Greek thought, and, on the other, under the later Islamic invaders, put the clock back in so many respects.

Europe north of Mediterranean lands offers a dramatic contrast to the Mediterranean lands in the matter of village and city. Before men had iron axes they could make only a minor impression on the great forests of oak and elm, but patches of bush and small trees on the loess were cleared in the third millennium B.C., and the loess zones have been important belts of movement and of density of population for a long time, though an increment sufficient for development of cities came late.

The climate here, with its rain in summer (some from thunderstorms) and, east of the Rhine, its weeks or months of hard frost, does not promote evaporation on the scale felt in Mediterranean lands. Dissolved salts are not drawn up to the surface to the same extent. They remain distributed through the depth of the soil in the "brown earth"; and the humus decomposes more slowly—very slowly in the chernozem area, with its long frost and very dry summer. Towards the wetter and colder areas of the northeast and northwest the trend of dissolved salts is more markedly downwards, and bare soil after rain may even look grey; such soil has been called by Russian workers podsol. The farming of such soils as brown earth and podsol may easily exhaust the plant food near the surface, and it is most important to overturn the soil so as to get the accumulated food from below. The little plow used for the surface scratching in the Mediterranean was of little value save on loess here; and, so long as men were dependent on it, populations were small and cities did not grow in Europe north of the Alps, though one might try to turn over the garden soil with a spade. A larger plow for overturning soil became effective only when the plowshare could be shod with iron. Probably the iron plowshare began somewhere in western Europe some generations before the Roman conquest of Gaul, and the Belgae used it in Britain. But it was especially the conquering groups of post-Roman times who spread its use, at a time when the iron axe was making great attacks on the oak forests for building timber, ships and other purposes.

A heavy iron plowshare pulled by two, four or six oxen (references to eight oxen are almost certainly wrong) made a deep furrow and brought up the deeper, richer soil to be laid down by the ears of the plow or its mouldboard. A thorough plowing at the proper season was the important task, not the frequent surface scratching so important in Mediterranean lands. So agricultural routine was different. Instead of the small field of Mediterranean lands there was often the large field laid out in strips (the furrow-long or furlong measured as forty rods or poles or perches is a memory of this), and the peasant used or owned a strip or a part of a strip. Cultivation had, therefore, to be on one scheme for all the holders in the field. Where this scheme established itself the peasants were typically established in compact villages of a fair size with open fields around them.

There was little in this scheme to prompt early development of towns; and one rather finds in several areas traces of ancient earthworks that appear to have been refuges in times of trouble; the old nuclei of Poznań and Kraków illustrate this. As towns until relatively modern times were dependent on local food unless they were accessible by ship, the limited food supplies before the days of the iron plowshare hindered the larger agglomeration of population. It is of special interest in this connection to note that towns in the Aegean began about 3000 B.C., that only after 1000 B.C. did the idea of the city spread to the western Mediterranean, that only towards the change from B.C. to A.D. have we towns in France and Britain, mainly as a product of Roman influence, and that the idea of the city spread eastward from the Rhine, mainly as an imported idea, not long before A.D. 1000. The fact that the city still in the twentieth century has often been linked with immigrant populations, such as Germans and Jews, in Poland and Transylvania, has been one of the sources of lasting political and social difficulty, postponing the rise of native urbanism fit to take its important share in regional administration, as well as hindering growth of regional unity. The nation as we understand it has not truly developed in east-central Europe. Whether the huge transfers of population

of these years will change this old problem our successors may see.

Our wheat variety is a bread-wheat that was developed, perhaps, in lands north of Mesopotamia and that ultimately acclimatized itself in Europe north of the Mediterranean lands. It makes great demands on the soil, but, by pasturing cattle on the weeds of the stubble fields after harvest, the land was manured. With experience it became practicable in many places to have a rotation of wheat, barley and fallow, and, in due course, barley might be varied with oats or beans; and, where there was not sufficient strong sunshine for wheat, rye was planted. Rye and oats very probably began as weeds in wheat fields. The scheme of rotation and the fact that the fields were communally cultivated meant that leadership found special opportunities and lords of the manor arose to power, controlled cultivation, held the mill and sometimes owned the plow. But before going further we must glance at France.

In Mediterranean France conditions are interestingly different from those of most other lands around that sea. Standards of equipment are, on the whole, higher, and the factors of these differences would be an interesting topic for research. Malaria and summer lassitude are reduced to some extent by the presence of hills, and absentee ownership has been less common, at any rate since 1789; and government, whatever its failings, has been better and regional common measure more marked. There are also some economic factors. For example, all France is near enough to vineyards to like wine with its meals. The Bordeaux area supplies "Grand Vin" for luxury and for export; Languedoc, in its turn, supplies "Vin ordinaire," apart from a few very choice vintages. So there is scope both within France and in its export trade to supply a non–vine-growing population with wine on a fairly large scale. And, with skilled cultivation and rapid transport assured by the P.L.M., there is the possibility of *primeurs* (early vegetables, flowers and fruit) and of scented flowers for perfumes to be sold far and wide as they make their name and fame among the luxurious visitors to the Riviera.

Albigenses of the thirteenth century, Waldenses, Huguenots of the sixteenth century and onwards, the Marseillaise of the Revolution, and many more instances all tell us of an independence of mind and a power of thought that play their parts in Mediterranean France. There is, nevertheless, a great deal of rural poverty and dejection, with people streaming away from poor lands and sometimes with French peasants being replaced by Italian immigrants. Ariège, Aveyron, Cantal, Corrèze, Gers, Landes, Lozère, Puy-de-Dôme have tended to lose population lately.

In the Paris basin, the three-field system and feudal lordship of lay or ecclesiastical leaders has been a historic feature; but to understand the peasantry we must also remember that both towns, under the influence of the general revival after the Dark Ages in a region of urban Roman heritage, and villages, largely under Cistercian and other philanthropic effort, were growing together especially in the twelfth century. It is partly owing to this contemporaneity of growth that the French peasantry has developed its remarkable close-range exchange between village and town, the latter with a variety of small local industries, the former with few craftsmen save a smith and a carpenter.

Contemporaneity of factors of change is often a matter we must take into consideration along with environmental influences if we are to gain understanding. The case of the French peasantry during and after the Revolution of 1789 is further illustrative in this respect. The feudal lords had often become absentees, gathered at Paris by the king lest they should foment disorder in their home lands. Luxury and degeneration led to their impoverishment and to bad consciences, and greatly promoted the breakdown of the old autocracy, as it did in twentieth century Russia, and in both cases ecclesiastical decadence and persecu-

tion were other factors of breakdown. The good soil of France was a heritage to which the peasantry was attached, and, as the autocracy was breaking down, there was spreading the idea of root crops in the fields, parsnips, turnips, carrots, mangolds, and also of potatoes—more food for men and animals, provided control of the soil could be liberated from the old rotation. Add to this the fact that the root crops gave winter food to farm animals, and thus allowed improvements of their quality; and we see something of the character of the French Revolution, whereby, whatever else happened, the peasants got hold of the land. Eventually many of them have paid back their purchase mortgages in a depreciated currency, while selling their products at much appreciated prices, especially in war time.

Less difficult soil conditions, less malaria, less summer lassitude, better farm animals and food, more organic manure from animals folded on the stubble or fallow fields —these are some factors of advantages of the French peasantries over against those of southern Italy or parts of Spain and Greece.

Eastwards across the Rhine we find different conditions and different factors of change. In the first place winter is more severe and one soon gets to a region with one month's, and, farther east, to a region with two months' continuous frost, and consequent stoppage of outdoor work. Indoor work, especially in wood, with minor metal adjuncts, has become an important matter for the winter season. When this develops into craftsmanship, it has been found a useful introduction to the refined machine-making connected with the modern electrical industry in southern Germany.

The intricate and varied topography of Germany from Cologne to Leipzig and from Frankfurt to Hanover delayed political unity, and promoted the long maintenance of small principalities with the princes, dukes and so on, mostly in residence, maintaining the more or less feudal scheme and the three-field rotation down to the days of railways. Passivity of the peasantry as a consequence contrasts with their stubborn opposition to the lords in France. The French Revolution could not really infect Germany, and yet the German peasant, especially in the southwest, has craft skills beyond those of the great majority of French villagers, and, after immigration to towns, has contributed to industrial development.

When we look east beyond the Elbe we find still other evidences of rural character. On the morainic lands of the Prussian plain early forest clearing just east of the Elbe gave opportunity for founding villages around a green and often a church. The type is so well recognized that it has a name in common use, namely *Rundling*. As clearing went on eastwards, lines developed in and through the forest and the *Rundling* gave place to the line or street village, or to what one may call the mere-side village developed from an old fisher-farmer hamlet near inland water. In the forested areas, large hunting estates developed, and some have come down to modern times, but received an important increment of capital value when potatoes and root crops spread generally in the nineteenth century. Here, however, there was not the large peasant element with local town connections and centuries of experience that France possessed. Rather was it a population of poor hamlet-folk which found scope for increase, but had little experience that would have helped it to seize power, and little craftsmanship through which to express itself. The domination of the land-owning Junkers of Pomerania was hardly challenged until quite recently.

Somewhat farther south on the loess belts from Alsace and Saxony to the larger villages of the Ukraine, cultivation of grain and so on are well-established. The loess, as Dr. Alice Garnett has been arguing, was probably rich in trees and bushes at one time, but was perhaps not to any great extent covered with great oaks and the like.

Probably clearance of its trees and bushes makes regrowth difficult in parts like the Puszta. It seems to have been easier to clear; its friable soil was certainly easier to work than most of the boulder clay farther north. Here, then, might have occurred a richer development, but we are here in a zone that received the idea of the town through German and Jewish immigrants among a Slavonic-speaking peasantry. The division of language and often of religion, as between German Protestants, Magyar Romanists and Slavonic Greek Catholics (Uniates) or Orthodox is still and has long been an obstacle to regional unification, as the transfers of population after June, 1945, so tragically show. Associated with this, and with the remoteness of many villages from any town, we find the remarkable vitality of peasant crafts sometimes in individual homes (weaving and furniture), sometimes in villages (timber generally), sometimes in villages and very small towns (pottery).

It is important to see this, not only as an economic factor, but as a supplementary job, especially for the winter. It is also a mode of expression, and we have in this area an almost unself-conscious art, with styles that involve traditional loyalties rather than deliberate decisions, though individual fancy finds play somewhere at every turn. The shepherd may carve a wonderful distaff for his sweetheart, and she may embroider for him a border on a shirt that he will wear outside his trousers; while he, with his tougher fingers, embroiders sheepskin coats for them both. Weaving of rugs, skirts, sheets, blankets, house-building, especially with wood from the local forests, curing of skins for shoes as well as for coats—a multitude of home and village crafts have survived into the twentieth century. One has watched aniline dyes ousting garden products, factory yarn competing with the housewife's spinning, the transformation of the beautiful old distaffs more and more into museum pieces. The old art is threatened from many sides, and, with its decay, more of the social life will change than is sometimes imagined—the gifts at social events and festivals, the winter occupations, the old exchanges of goods and services, many an old custom and superstition. But, unless care is taken, there is likely to be a loss of productivity of the land as the often alien aristocrats fade out. Moneylenders step in. Winter supplements to the penurious livelihood are likely to diminish. More than all this, the self-contained village life has given very little experience of the outside world to its people, and they are easily the victims of political bosses and organized groups of various shades of opinion, a prey for party autocracy.

If, instead of working eastwards from the Rhine, we go northwards, the human scene changes. Denmark and southern Sweden might grow grain under some kind of old rotation system, with lords of the manor in more or less usual style, though hardly so rich and powerful in these more northerly lands. But, in this cooler region, oats were at least an alternative crop as food for man and beast, and some have claimed that rye, appropriate in the north, is less exhausting for the soil than wheat. Moreover, in the north, the downward trend of plant food in the soil is more marked, so there is more reserve to be plowed up. As oats are in the soil for only five months or so, there may be more time for stubble pasture while the snow is not too deep or the temperature too low. The soil used for oats has longer to rest, the rotation scheme is less essential, the baronial control less important and less powerful. And villagers may have a line of escape to the sea or to fishing in the many lakes and streams; they are less passive than so many south of the Baltic have been. These few remarks may give a background to the study of the transformation that has been enacted in modern times. How far that transformation should be credited to environmental and how far to personal and historical factors one cannot say; they interact all the time.

First let us note that, being far beyond the old Imperial Roman frontier, they naturally seceded easily, and without much bitterness, from the Empire's descendant, the Roman Church. They as naturally accepted the Lutheran ideas from across the Baltic and were thus led to emphasize the use of the Bible in the vernacular, with all that this meant in educational and nationalist directions. Denmark had compulsory general education in 1815, England in 1870. The growing of grain became less profitable after about 1870–75, but, ere that happened, the Danes had followed Grundtvig's advice in organizing folk high schools. And the villagers themselves, with their new education, quickly organized the co-operative system for buying and selling objects and products the farmers produced or needed. No doubt a purely economic geographical factor helped, namely, the Esbjerg bottleneck, through which passed a large proportion of the farm products exported to Britain. But here is a peasantry renovated, and the result is one in which they have themselves co-operated. It is a renovation that has greatly increased their regional and national consciousness on a scale far surpassing that of the village. The co-operatives are not matters of party or sect as they so often are elsewhere: they are national. And, if it is fairly true that traditional peasant crafts and arts are not very highly developed in Denmark (they are more so in Sweden), it is also true that the new education has spread social activities among the peasantry, especially for the winter time; and Denmark is fortunate in that proximity to the sea does limit the cold period, so that outdoor work can go on for a good part of the year.

What is most characteristic of rural Denmark is that the contrasts one so often finds in central Europe between peasant and townsman are much less marked. The folk high school education, of women as well as men, the co-operative system which has grown from the folk high school education, and the scientific interests developed through improved farming have deeply altered the old-time mentality. A contributory factor has been the effort of the

Danish Lutheran Church to become catholic in the sense of being comprehensive rather than authoritarian; nearly all rural Danes are at least nominally Lutherans. And, as it is the people themselves who created the co-operatives, the people have come to feel that the new social order is their own creation rather than something given to or imposed on them.

On the fringes of Europe, towards the ocean, north of France, wheat is a risky crop in many areas because of the possibility of heavy rain in summer. Spring corn (barley and oats) becomes more important, save in parts of England, and it occupies the land for only the spring and early summer months, allowing time for pasturing cattle on the fields and so for getting them manured. In Ireland, Wales, Scotland, and Norway there is much rough grazing, and therefore less need for a fallow field. The rain makes land-drainage, by ridges and furrows, more necessary than in many other areas. Patches of arable land, where possible in shelter from gales and with a southward aspect, make the nuclei of farms, which, in Scotland and Ireland, might be held conjointly by a small number of farmers, usually kinsfolk. A few such groups might have their habitations linked together in a hamlet, and a few hamlets adjacent to one another might form a clan under a leader for war. The arable field divided often into plowridges, that might be allocated year by year or might be more definite property, could be cultivated by co-operative plowing. Of the other land belonging to a hamlet some might be taken care of to a certain extent and cultivated in patches changed every year or every few years; and the patch to be cultivated next might be used beforehand for folding cattle. Other land was typically left as rough pasture.

In Wales the co-aration of a farm by a small group of co-heirs, which often obtained in Scotland, was abolished in Tudor times, and, in the late seventeenth century, sheep-keeping and wool became very important, but there are traces of former ridges, perhaps even of the three-field system in Flint and Denbigh, Cardiganshire, Pembrokeshire and Glamorganshire here and there.

In Norway the relation of the small patches of arable near fjord-shores to the custom of primogeniture-inheritance, to fishing, and to the summer pasturing of cattle on the heights has often been described.

Main features in oceanic European rural tradition are therefore the importance of animal husbandry and rough pasture, the subsidiary character of wheat where it is grown at all, frequently the sea as a means of employment and escape, the weak development and regional absences of the three-field system. The stock farmer typically lives very close to his animals with less taste and need for equipment than the wheat grower. His groups are smaller, his market towns simpler and farther apart. The contrast between the so-called Celtic fringe of Britain and the English Midlands is a striking fact of British life.

The contrast between the large open fields of Midland tradition and the old enclosed fields of the southeast is another matter that can be partly interpreted through clues given by historical geography and archeology. The Belgae appear to have had fairly large plows; they came, in all probability, as military lords over an earlier population, and that population, no doubt, had its enclosed fields after the old style. The new lords may not have had the open field and strip system in their experience; we hardly know how early that developed. In any case they came into a British system. If Fox is right in treating the great finds from Llyn Cerrig Bach as indicating gifts from many parts of Britain, including the southeast, to a sacred center, we may suppose that the old system went on after the Belgic conquests. Caesar's text suggests the same view. This possible sequence may help to interpret the rarity of the open field and strip system in the southeast compared with its one-time widespread occurrence in central England where the Roman invaders found a much less developed British population; also their withdrawal presumably left that region in utter weakness. By the time the Anglo-Saxons came the open field and strip system was developing, and, in a relatively empty region, there was an opportunity to impose it, and, in many places, the compact village with it.

Modes of agriculture, types of plow, forms of rural settlement, schemes of land tenure, crops, soils, climates, are all linked in intricate fashion and need to be studied regionally as well as generally.

A few points concerning cities in Europe north of Mediterranean lands are relevant to the purpose of this study. Roman cities were founded in Gaul and Britain, and, generally, as far as Rhine and Danube. The Celtic-speaking Belgae had probably something of the nature of towns in Gaul and Britain a few generations before the Romans came, but after ideas and material from the Mediterranean of classical times had infiltrated into the west. The fact that many of the Roman cities had Christian bishops in them before the empire fell helped those cities to survive and determined some directives of their revival after the barbarian lapse. The Gallo-Roman cities remained linked with Rome and had a bishop interested in their revival. The cathedral or town church is on the central square or market place, the craft streets, the walls and gates, the smithfield outside the town in one direction, the tanneries near a stream in another, and the fairground sometimes in still another, often with an abbey (Benedictine in many cases) near the fairground, and a church dedicated to St. Giles for the wandering merchants. (St. Giles at Edinburgh is in what was the strangers' location beyond the little old town clustering under the castle.) The growth of towns at the same time as the multiplication of villages in forest clearings in France in the twelfth century A.D. helped to make the French town a focus of a little region or *pays* which it supplied with craft goods. That system of town and country close-linked has persisted with minor

alterations to our own day in France. It is accompanied by the idea of local production of many types of consumers' goods, and the idea of export trade as a surplus matter, sending out specialities such as wines, perfumes, silks, jewellery and the like.

The French provincial town and its related *pays* are in a way the strength of France, and in another way its desperate problem in an age in which mass production and machinery count so heavily. This is the more difficult in that French iron ore in Lorraine has gone to Ruhr coke—it is less bulky than coke and less deteriorated by travel. So this large-scale industry aggravates the international problem.

The towns of Flanders and those near the Rhine typically have the town hall as their center, whereas only a few French towns, away from the northeast border, have old town halls. The central town hall usually means that the leading citizens in the Middle Ages were able to stand for themselves against the ecclesiastical nobility. Brussels, with its hotel de ville, its guild halls and its *maison du roi* on a central square is a classic example here.

Beyond the Rhine eastwards towns developed from the tenth century onwards, sometimes under ecclesiastical and sometimes under military leadership, sometimes with a permit gained by traders from a local prince or the emperor. Planted down usually by leaders from the Rhineland or influenced by the Rhineland, often boasting special courts and laws, they have not been so closely integrated with their immediate surroundings as the French ones have been. The physical geography of the tangled valleys east of the Rhine and north of the Main has preserved many small local sovereignties, at least nominally, until the twentieth century, so court cities with their attempts at aesthetic activity helped to set the fashion, and the contrast between peasant and townsman is the more marked as a result. The power of the medieval trade guilds, inevitably at that time with ecclesiastical linkage, made for the ostracism of people such as Jews whose religion kept them apart. The ghetto and the grim story of persecution is too well known to need comment. It illustrates the difficulty of social combination, and helps to make clear the desire of the Jews to escape eastwards as new towns grew in that direction.

It has been highly characteristic of Germany that, with coal near the northern fall line from hills to plain, the old cities of that fall line have become industrial centers, sometimes with common lands still public property and the city treasury reaping much increment. The contrast with British industrial cities, often previously quite small and not even incorporated, strikes every observer.

The spread of cities east of the Oder and of the Böhmer Wald brought further problems, especially that of a difference of language, sometimes of religion, between peasantries and townsfolk who may have been conquerors, and have been in any case apt to suffer from a superiority complex. The city may have an original nucleus, once a fortified enclosure, as at Poznan, Kraków, Prague, etc. A great rectangular lay-out by traders under German influence is characteristic, and its market square will have the town church and town hall (or cloth hall). German, Slavonic and Jewish quarters indicate the weakness of the common measure among the citizens. In Transylvania, the migrants of the early Middle Ages from lower Saxony (one thinks of the story of the Pied Piper of Hamelin) planned and built on a smaller scale and with a nostalgic reminiscence of the old home, as one cannot but observe at Sibiu and Brasov. They have held to their German tradition with great tenacity and remained in 1939 as "foreign bodies" in the Transylvanian complex. It is interesting to compare with them the bastides founded under Edward I in Wales—towns such as Conway, Carnarvon, and Aberystwyth. They were laid out on a rectangular scheme under the protection of a castle and they were for English and not for Welsh people. But the old prohibitions faded out under the Tudors, and intermarriage helped to make

these old towns as Welsh as any others. In an island environment, so long free from threat of military invasion, it was more possible for hostile confrontation to metamorphose into a working, if rarely a logical, compromise than in a country into which one or other great power might pour armies at any time.

The immense modern development of urbanism began in some parts in the seventeenth century and in many in the eighteenth century with landowners coming to spend winters in town and get their daughters married. We know in Britain many fine Georgian houses and can trace the process in Wales, for example, on into the early part of the nineteenth century. It is a process very different from the industrial massing of factories and dwellings. In some parts of Europe little of all this went on until the railway appeared, but, whenever it started in any region, it has gone on with an acceleration that made deliberate planning most difficult.

In Germany the multiplicity of little and big court cities no doubt hindered the growth of a large unity. On the other hand it fostered an element of taste and of show in German cities. Moreover, the industrial towns were fairly often old cities with proud traditions, owning their common lands and getting some of the increment of land values for the city's treasury. The municipality might be strong enough to direct the railway as to how it should approach or enter the city. Old lines of walls might become tree-lined promenades, and a feeling for cleanliness was a natural accompaniment.

In France the mental background of modern urban development has been different. The long struggle between royal and more localized powers in France in the Middle Ages emphasized the central authority and, with it, the city of Paris. The other cities, except Lyons to a certain extent, have rarely had the artistic activities of the corresponding (and usually larger) towns in Germany. On the other hand, they often have a more intimate link with the adjacent countryside, though this may be reflected in a lower degree of cleanliness. But the French are great road-makers, and we find, again, the tree-lined promenades of the old ramparts.

In Britain we have the towns which grew with residential quarters in the eighteenth century and those that have grown with nineteenth century industry, often from nuclei that had no corporations to control them, as was the case with Manchester, Liverpool, and Birmingham. The growth of towns on privately owned land with increment going into private hands, the ugliness and dirt, disease and degradation are too sadly known to need discussion. The fact that the towns just named did not have a mayor and corporation before the Victorian era had, however, had the effect of making it more possible for religious dissenters to have a measure of freedom in them, and, in this way, the industrial towns had acquired nuclei of sober, industrious men of initiative who played a considerable part in industrial development.

The growth and character of villages and towns and of their mutual relations is full of interest for those who will think of them in terms, not only of site and statistics, but also of the play of variously conditioned human minds.

ALBERT DEMANGEON

THE ORIGINS AND CAUSES
OF SETTLEMENT TYPES

In order to explain types of rural settlement, one can rely, according to time and place, upon quite different factors. It is permissible to say that the entire history of civilization is reflected in present forms of human establishments. Certain forms today are not the ancestral ones. We perceive here and there facts of evolution, and there have even been total revolutions. The description and classification of settlement forms can be achieved only through study of the influences that determine them. These influences fall into three main groups: (1) the influence of natural conditions, (2) the influence of social conditions, and (3) the influence of the agricultural economy.

INFLUENCE OF NATURAL CONDITIONS

Among the natural conditions that seem to have contributed to the establishment of settlement forms, we can recognize surface configuration, constitution of the soil, and water resources.

Surface configuration.—It cannot be denied that surface configuration effects settlement forms. For example, it has often

been observed that smooth relief seems to favor concentrated settlement, whereas rugged or broken relief tends to favor dispersed settlement. "The agglomerated village," wrote Vidal de la Blache, "is indigenous in districts where the arable area is continuous, all in one piece, thus permitting a uniform exploitation. Under the influence of communal needs, collective associations have been formed. The sinking and maintenance of wells, pools and ponds, and the necessity of building walls contribute to the crowding and concentration of settlement." [1] If plains are more favorable for villages, then mountains and broken land seem to encourage isolated houses or hamlets. This results from the small size and unequal distribution of arable land, which restrict the efforts of colonists and prevent them from living together in a single place. Debilitating factors include the necessary extensive movement of plows and wagons, difficulties of transportation that discourage distribution of fertilizers beyond a slight distance, and the encouragement of pastoral economy by expanses of open land. [2]

Translated, with permission of the publisher and the author's heir, from "La géographie de l'habitat rural," *Annales de Géographie,* XXXVI (1927), 1–23, 97–114; reprinted in Albert Demangeon, *Problèmes de géographie humaine* (Paris: A. Colin, 1942). Only the second of the three parts of this essay is translated here. A student of Vidal de la Blache, Albert Demangeon (1872–1940) was generally recognized as the leader of the second generation of French human geographers. From 1911 until his death, he was professor of geography at the Sorbonne.

[1] Paul Vidal de la Blache, *Principes de géographie humaine, publiés d'après les manuscrits de l'Auteur par Emmanuel de Martonne* (Paris: A. Colin, 1922), p. 195. [Translated by Millicent Todd Bingham as *Principles of Human Geography* (New York: Henry Holt, 1926).]

[2] Many authors are in agreement on this influence. See August Meitzen, *Siedlung und Agrarwesen der Westgermanen und Ostgermanen, der Kelten, Römer, Finner und Slaven* (3 vols. and atlas; Berlin: W. Hertz, 1895), II, 390; R. Lennard, "Englisches Siedlungswesen," in Johannes

These influences are clarified by numerous observations. In Great Britain prior to the enclosure movement, which upset settlement in the plains, many writers placed the settlement conditions of the plains in opposition to those of the mountains. In Harrison's "Description of England," drafted in the time of Queen Elizabeth, one finds this suggestive passage: "The mansion houses of our countrie townes and villages in the champaine ground [lowlands] stand altogether by streets and joining one to another, but in woodland soiles [uplands] [they are] dispersed here and there each upon the severall grounds of their owners." [3] At the time of the *Domesday Book* isolated farms often appear in the woods, i.e., in areas of broken terrain. Thus with respect to Eardisley (Hereford) one finds a text that is equally clear: *"In medio cujusdam silvae est posita et ibi est domus una defensabilis."* [4] At the same time, a mountain valley, Langdendale in Derbyshire, presents a very clear example of dispersal, with a series of small hamlets, formed by a couple of farms, succeeding one another at intervals of one or two miles.[5]

In France, such examples of a contrast between lowland and upland are repeated from one end of the country to the other. In the Vosges, dispersion increases toward the mountains: i.e., villages predominate to the west of the Coney on the plateaux of coquina limestone, while farms, with their orchards and fields, are scattered to the east of the stream.[6] In the Languedoc (regions of Lodève and Bédarieux), dispersion increases as one rises, and hamlets are

strung out like beads in the torturous folds of the land.[7] In Germany, the same opposition is frequently renewed: agglomerated settlement on the plains of the Württemberg *Unterland* and the plateau of the Rauhe Alb, versus dispersed settlement on the morainic hills extending north of Lake Constance and Allgäu.[8] Villages also appear in the great valleys that traverse the alpine region of Switzerland, Bavaria, and the Tyrol, whereas hamlets and isolated farmsteads are prevalent in the mountains.[9]

In the riparian lands of the Baltic countries, Scandinavia, and Finland, dispersion prevails wherever cultivation has been extended to the versants of the mountains or the rocky hillocks of the glaciated terrain. The mountaineers of Norway live in isolated dwellings (*gaards*); as soon as one reaches gentle and continuous surfaces, village settlement reappears (thus the Danish *by*). In Walachia, the hamlet or *catun* is the settlement type of the hills and mountains, whereas the village is the type of the plains.[10] Similarly, villages appear in the plains of Podolia and Galicia (Poland), and hamlets are found in the Carpathian hills.[11] In the Ukraine, the settlement type of the rugged regions of Poltava and Khorol is the isolated tenant farm, whereas the type of the plains of Zolotonocha and Kozelets is the large village.[12] The district of Kangra in the Punjab shows two types

Hoops (ed.), *Reallexikon der germanischen Altertumskunde* (Strasbourg: K. J. Trübner, 1911–19), I, 593–613; Hans Bernhard, "Die ländlichen Siedlungsformen," *Geographische Zeitschrift*, XXV (1919), 20–32.

[3] Cited by George L. Gomme, *The Village Community* (London: W. Scott, 1890), p. 64.

[4] Cited by Paul Vinogradoff, *English Society in the Eleventh Century* (Oxford: Clarendon Press, 1908), p. 267.

[5] Vinogradoff, *loc. cit.*

[6] A. Cholley, "La Vôge," *Annales de Géographie,* XXIII (1914), 219–35, ref. to 233–35.

[7] Max. Sorre, "La répartition des populations dans le Bas-Languedoc," *Bulletin de la Société Languedocienne de Géographie,* XXIX (1906), 106–36, 235–78, 365–87.

[8] Robert Gradmann, "Das ländliche Siedlungswesen des Königreichs Württembergs," *Forschungen zu der Landes- und Volkskunde,* XXI (1913), and *idem,* "Die ländlichen Siedlungsformen Württembergs," *Petermanns Geographische Mitteilungen,* LVI (1910), 183–86, 246–50, ref. to 184–86.

[9] A. Schoch, *Beiträge zur Siedlungs und Wirtschaftsgeographie des Zürichseegebietes* (Zurich: Lohnauer, 1917), pp. 74–80.

[10] Emmanuel de Martonne, *La Valachie* (Paris: A. Colin, 1902), chap. 17.

[11] P. Vidal de la Blache, *Principes de géographie humaine,* pp. 188–89.

[12] A. Woeikof, "Le groupement de la population rurale en Russie," *Annales de Géographie,* XVIII (1909), 13–23.

of juxtaposed settlements: in the plains, villages encircled by confused parcels of arable land; in the mountains, hamlets with scattered houses, each surrounded by its fields. The same facts are observed in China and Japan. Mountains and plains, so different by their forms of relief, are also opposed by different forms of settlement.

Yet this opposition, which seems so general and abrupt, does not explain everything, for dispersion is the predominant form of settlement in certain plains (e.g., the plains of Lucerne, Flanders, and Anglica), and villages are predominant in certain mountainous regions (e.g., central Italy, Kabylie, and the northern Riesengebirge). Gradmann observes that there is no coincidence in Upper Swabia between rugged relief and dispersed settlement, and, on the other hand, that large and continuous terraces with fertile soil do not have villages.[13]

Condition of the Soil.—To the extent that the soil presents a dry and solid or boggy and soft surface, radically different settlement conditions can be imposed. Whether the danger comes from rivers or the sea, the necessity to defend their homes against water has often induced men to agglomerate. In Italy, in the plain between Mincio and the Adige, the unhealthy conditions of the valleys has pushed human occupation to higher and more healthful sites where village settlement reigns. Likewise, in the delta of the Po, around Ferrara and Rovigo, settlement is concentrated in long lines on dikes. The same danger has imposed agglomeration in the parts of the Netherlands that are menaced by the sea. Before the construction of dikes, the inhabitants were grouped on elevated sites, usually artificial, and their bumpy silhouettes still attract attention: i.e., the *terpen* of Friesland, the *wierden* of Groningen, the *vluchtheuvels* of Betuwe, the *killen* and the *vliedbergen* of Zeeland. One often notices concentrated villages either in the north of the Netherlands or in the Marschen of the

region of Emden. Elsewhere in the land of polders, houses are concentrated along the roads, i.e., along the artificial causeways of the dikes. These dike-villages are counted by the score in Holland. They are also found on the edges of canals in the peat bog colonies of Overijssel, Drenthe, and Groningen.

We have the impression of a mandatory rule that low land susceptible to inundations obliges the inhabitants to concentrate on high points. Yet how can we explain the fact that in these same polder regions— e.g., in the maritime plain of Flanders and on the bottom of the former Haarlem Sea —we are in the domain of dispersion?

Water Resources. — Many people describe the influence of water resources on settlement in very simple terms and reason thus: In regions of permeable rocks, like limestone, the water escapes into the depths of the soil and can be reached only through deep wells and rare springs; hence the necessity for a concentration of settlement. And, inversely, in lands of impermeable rocks, where the water oozes from everywhere, the ubiquity of water promotes ubiquity of settlement.

Certainly the tyranny of water is imposed on rural settlement in arid lands, and, for example, in the Mediterranean region. In Friulia and Apulia, the Haut Tell of Tunisia, and Greece almost all of the population lives in villages, and each village is fixed close to a spring.[14] In his book on the Peloponnesos, Philippson demonstrates the close bond that unites inhabited places and sources of water.[15] He describes these strong and fresh springs, the pride and joy of the inhabitants, shaded by a large plane tree, and pouring their clear water into a stone basin. They are the heart of the village. In lands of irrigation, the law of water is rigorously imposed. There "every-

[13] Gradmann, "Das ländliche Siedlungsewesen des Königreichs Württembergs," p. 41.

[14] Th. Fischer, "Ansiedlung und Anbau in Apulien," *Mittelmeerbilder,* 1906, pp. 204–15, ref. to pp. 204–9; Ch. Monchicourt, *La région du Haut Tell en Tunisie* (Paris: A. Colin, 1913), pp. 391–99.

[15] Alfred Philippson, *Der Peloponnes* (Berlin: R. Friedländer & Son, 1892), p. 385.

thing is so subordinated to the life-giving element that there can be no manner of grouping other than that providing for the common enjoyment of water, whether of ponds or streams." [16] In the Punjab, as in the Dekkan, peasants are grouped together close to the essential organ on which their cultivation depends: the reservoir, well, or canal. Cohesion is necessary to retain control of the water. The village reservoir (tank) is the prerequisite of communal existence; with its fortress-like banks shaded by beautiful trees, it contains the source of life.

In the humid lands of frequent rain in Western Europe, it is impossible to affirm a similar close relation between hydrologic conditions and the distribution of settlement. Even in the case of scarcity, rain water can be collected and stored. Hence, the so-called law of water no longer applies. Regions of similar hydrologic conditions correspond to different types of settlement. On chalk subsoil and nearly analogous surface material, Picardy in France has concentrated villages, whereas the Chiltern plateau in England has isolated farmsteads. In a relatively homogeneous limestone region in France, the Caux, one notices dispersed settlement in the west and concentrated settlement in the east. On the plateau of the Ardennes, where there is a superabundance of springs, the inhabitants are grouped in villages. On the Hungarian *puszta* water is usually found at a shallow depth in a sheet that can be reached by the most elementary wells; nevertheless, the rural inhabitants are assembled in enormous villages. The question of water, above all in the past, seems secondary, and we would be wrong, with our present ideas, to imagine that it is decisive.[17]

[16] P. Vidal de la Blache, *Principes de géographie humaine*, p. 173.

[17] This opinion on the question of water is also given by Gradmann, "Das ländliche Siedlungswesen des Königreichs Württembergs," p. 38; and O. Marinelli, Notes to a discussion of "Agricultural Systems and Schemes of Distribution in Western Europe," *Geographical Teacher* [later *Geography*], XIII (1925), 202–4, ref. to 202.

INFLUENCE OF SOCIAL CONDITIONS

Forms of settlement may have been determined by the human milieu itself. It is conceivable that such forms, like other products of civilization, are manifestations of original tendencies or traditions proper to certain peoples. It is also conceivable that such tendencies or traditions were able at birth to respond to needs of defense, or that their evolution was conditioned by organization of property.

Original Tendencies.—We are hardly informed on the primordial conditions of human societies. The documents that we possess on primitive periods allow no more than hypotheses. But we cannot refrain from trying to imagine the beginnings of the civilization of rural settlement. Is agglomeration or dispersion the primary form? Or must we suppose that both are original forms recommended by different local conditions? We do not know. It seems probable that well before territories founded on permanent occupation of a geographically well-defined point became the material base of social organization, kinship relations were the bonds of social groups. From that time we probably should imagine that the habit of communal living developed among members of a family, i.e., descendants of a common ancestor. Isn't it reasonable to suppose that such people must have tried, by a quite natural instinct, to gather together for defense and pursuit of their common livelihood? Thus grouping would be the first effort of man, and this ancient familial organization would be the framework of the first village communities. Concentration rather than dispersion would be the primary stage of settlement. In Celtic Britain, the inhabitants lived in familial groups, formed of some hundreds of individuals and their flocks, which thus constituted villages. But we do not know if such has everywhere been the primordial type of settlement, nor if the familial community has always been accompanied by village settlement. In the west of Serbia, the persistence of familial communities (*zadrugas*) does not prevent dispersal of settlement in small hamlets, but we cannot say whether this dispersal is a primitive condition or the result of evolution. The transformation of grouped settlements into dispersed settlements, for which we have ancient examples, coincides with agricultural progress, since it permits a cultivator to establish himself close to his fields. But this evolution does not summarize all agricultural progress, since agricultural development has sometimes necessitated settlement in villages. According to H. J. Fleure, it was the use of the plow that induced communal cultivation and also, without doubt, a clustering of homes.

Ethnic Traditions.—The distinction between concentrated and dispersed settlement is explained, according to certain scholars, by the opposition of traditions common to different ethnic groups. August Meitzen was the first to describe the contrast between the domains of concentrated villages (*Dörfer*) and isolated farmsteads (*Einzelhöfe*), which is so marked in Western and central Europe. He attributes it to an original difference of population, the villages corresponding to Germanic peoples and the isolated farms to Celts. He describes the villages as being particularly numerous between the Weser, the Elbe, and the Danube (and wherever the "victorious conquests of the Germans" would have established them),[18] and the isolated farms as being very widespread in Ireland, Scotland, Wales, and the west of France.

This theory does not stand up to criticism. In spite of the prodigious accumulation of interesting facts that is found in Meitzen's work, it collides with unsolvable contradictions. For instance, it has not been demonstrated that concentrated settlement is the exclusive prerogative of the Germanic peoples. We see it among the Slavs who, as Meitzen recognizes, live in villages of quite

particular form, but definitely in villages; in the possession of Celtic settlers in Great Britain; in the possession of the Romans, some of whose "villas" or large domains formed, together with their personnel of agricultural laborers, the core of true villages; and in the possession of the Gauls, who lived in villages (*vici*) as well as on isolated farms. Among the Helvetii, Caesar counted no less than 400 *vici*, which he clearly distinguished from isolated houses (*aedificia*).[19] Neither is it demonstrated that isolated settlement is peculiar to the Celts, since in the heart of the Germanic country, to the west of the Weser, all of the rural population lives in dispersed houses. The same dispersal is observed in other Germanic lands, such as Flanders, the Swiss and Bavarian Alps, and the north of Scandinavia.[20] Moreover, even if facts supported the theory of ethnic influences, the solution of the problem would only be deferred, because we would still have to explain why a particular people adopted a particular settlement form.

Subsequent attempts to extend Meitzen's theory show that it is no more applicable to other countries. In India, some scholars would like to make an Aryan institution of the village. Actually, it is very widespread, even among the Dravidians.[21] In the alpine region of the Alto Adige, Schlüter contrasts villages of the Italian districts to the dispersed settlement of the Germanic country.[22] (In this case the Germans adopted dispersion rather than agglomeration.) But,

[18] Meitzen, *op. cit.*, I, 520. This theory has been reiterated and clarified by other authors. Cf. Otto Schlüter, "Die Formen der ländlichen Siedlungen," *Geographische Zeitschrift*, VI (1900), 248–62, and "Deutsches Siedlungswesen," in Hoops, *Reallexikon*, pp. 402–39.

[19] J. Flach, *L'Origine historique de l'habitation* (Paris: Larose, n.d.), pp. 10, 36–37; Karl Schumacher, *Siedlungs- und kulturgeschichte der Rheinlande von der Urzeit bis in das Mittelalter* (2 vols.; Mainz: L. Wilckens, 1921–23), II, 193–203; Frederic Seebohm, *The English Village Community* (2nd ed.; London: Oxford University Press, 1883), pp. 279–80.

[20] For criticism of the theory of Meitzen, see Gradmann, "Das ländliche Siedlungswesen des Königreichs Württembergs," p. 95; and Schoch, *op. cit.*, pp. 110–12.

[21] Gomme, *op. cit.*, pp. 23–32.

[22] Schlüter: "Deutsches Siedlungswesen," p. 437. See also Emmanuel de Martonne, *Les Alpes* (Paris: A. Colin, 1926), pp. 143–47.

as Marinelli observes,[23] the simplicity of this relationship is misleading: it is not ethnic traditions that impose their law, but rather economic necessities. One must look for an explanation in the different epochs of colonization and the nature of the respective agricultural economies.

Conditions of Security.—Necessities of common defense in times of insecurity impelled peasants to cluster together in villages. Correspondingly, with a return to security, they deserted villages and established themselves freely on the land of their choice. History provides numerous proofs of this relationship. The Mediterranean lands still show villages perched on high escarpments in a most paradoxical position vis-à-vis their distant fields. In the plain of the Po between Oglio and Adda, a region long exposed to the ravages of war, one still sees many fortified villages with dense clusters of houses.[24] According to Vidal de la Blache, "at the contact of steppe and districts characterized by other modes of life all structures take on the look of a fortress. Even the village, on the edge of the Sahara, Arabia, Turkistan, and Mongolia, becomes a prison and a refuge." [25] In the Aurès and Kabylie, villages are perched on very high points or crests which dominate the lowlands—"hundreds of elevated points separated by empty valleys in which eagles plunge with their spreading wings." [26] "The inhabitants of these houses seek safety in the concentration and defensive disposition of their constructions." [27] Certain Tunisian villages are perched on escarpments like acropolises and are further protected by thick plantations of cactus. On the southern slopes of the Atlas many villages are veritable citadels (*ksour*) in which the sedentary peasants store their grain, safe from the prowling nomads.

In France, several troubled periods have left traces characteristic of settlement. Brutails relates that fear of African corsairs in the twelfth and thirteenth centuries induced peasants in a large part of Roussillon to desert the plains and found new villages in the mountains.[28] Those who remained below entrenched and fortified themselves. For example, "at Corsavi a church consecrated in 1158 is now some distance from the village that abandoned it in order to reform around a fortified rock." In the southern Alps along the course of the Durance, one notices a tendency for houses to cluster more and more as one advances toward the exterior of the massif, i.e., toward the more accessible and threatened places. In order to escape from attacks of Saracen pirates, the villages were perched like fortresses.[29] In the Barronnies, as Mouralis has shown, Roman settlement was restricted to the plain and was not markedly concentrated. After the beginning of feudal troubles, the peasants moved into the highlands. "Certain villages, like Aubes, Condorcet, and Cornillon, were relocated on almost inaccessible cliffs, sometimes hundreds of meters above the river." [30]

Nevertheless, preoccupation with defense has not always or everywhere fostered agglomeration. Many isolated farms in Friulia and the Roman Campagna have been fortified, which makes it clear that insecurity does not always lead to agglomeration. It would be a mistake to regard all concentration as a defensive precaution, as has been alleged, without proof, for the Russian villages located south of Moscow and the Oka, and for the Hungarian villages of the Alfold. In France, nothing permits us to

[23] Marinelli, *op. cit.*, p. 202.

[24] *Loc. cit.* See also E. Bénévent, "La plaine du Po," *Revue de Géographie Alpine,* IV (1916), 189–236, ref. to 204–5.

[25] Vidal de la Blache; *Principes de géographie humaine,* pp. 195–96.

[26] Aug. Bernard, *Enquête sur l'habitation rurale des indigènes de l'Algérie* (Algiers: Fontana, 1921), pp. 82 ff.

[27] *Ibid,* pp. 75–76.

[28] Jean-Auguste Brutails, *Etude sur la condition des populations rurales du Roussillon au moyen âge* (Paris: Imprimerie Nationale, 1891), pp. 38–39, 43.

[29] Raoul Blanchard, *Les Alpes françaises* (Paris: A. Colin, 1925), p. 75.

[30] D. Mouralis, "Les phénomènes d'habitat dans le massif des Baronnies (Préalpes du Sud)," *Revue de Géographie Alpine,* XII (1924), 547–645.

affirm that the inhabitants of Picardy, Champagne, and Lorraine grouped themselves in villages for self-defense. Even the position of these villages, in open country, overrules any abiding concern with defense. On the contrary, the founders of these villages seem to have preferred sites in the middle of fertile land. As Vidal de la Blache remarks, "The aspect of the Meusiean village does not betray concern for security, quite the contrary . . . It is the preoccupation of agricultural life that appears in the choice of locations. Approaches are easy, without hedgerows or chicanery, in open land. The village itself opens to the fields on all sides, and from far away it is identified by its bell tower." [31]

The Agrarian Regime.—Social organization can also impose certain laws. In areas of large holdings and extensive exploitation, proprietors have often given their own rules for the placement of rural houses. The large villages of southern Italy are derived for the most part from the fact that landlords wanted to concentrate their tenants in order to keep them in hand.[32] According to Marinelli, these landlords have opposed the installation of their *contadini* in the country, not only to protect them from the dangers of malaria and to avoid the cost of constructing too many rural houses, but also in order that possession of an isolated farmstead would not become a reason for each family of laborers to claim ownership of its assigned parcel of land.[33] In Russia, the managers of large holdings preferred villages where the assembled peasants could be more closely supervised.[34] In the Balkan peninsula (e.g., the region south of Niš, the basins of the Maritsa, Kosovo, and the Metohija, Thessaly, central and southern Albania, and the platform of the lower Danube), the regime of

the *ciflik* (large estate), organized by the Turks, fostered the formation of villages by the grouping of the houses of the peasants (*rayas*) near the residence of the lord.[35] In Mexico, the large holding (*hacienda*) assembles its *peones* or agricultural laborers in a nearby village. In the same manner, some Gallo-Roman villages (*vici*) are derived from the grouping of colonists near a villa; later certain medieval villages developed from the agglomeration of serfs on a particular point of the seignorial domain. Nowadays in the Roman Campagna, farmers from Lombardy and Piedmont are founding large enterprises, and installing close to them families of permanent laborers, and thus nuclei for new villages have arisen. In Vercelli, Novara, Cremona, and the delta of the Po, large scale exploitation and the resulting concentration of laboring families also produce agglomerated settlements.

Elsewhere, when their interests have called for division of their domains among a crowd of small tenants, large landholders have adopted the system of the dispersed farmstead. The majority of the settlements in the Baltic countries (Latvia, Lithuania, Estonia) are small isolated farms; this is because the landed nobility in these countries was long accustomed to believe that exploitation is more successful when it is not tied to a village community.[36] According to Marinelli,[37] this preference also explains the dispersed colonization that was widespread in Tuscany at the end of the Middle Ages. Under this system, the unit of exploitation, the *podere,* had an extension sufficient to occupy and support a family, and the house of each tenant was built on the exploited land. A group of several of these tenant farms formed a domain, which the landowner entrusted to the direction of a manager.

[31] P. Vidal de la Blache, *Etude sur la vallée lorraine de la Meuse* (Paris: A. Colin, 1908), pp. 147–48.

[32] Bernhard, *op. cit.,* pp. 29–30.

[33] Marinelli, *op. cit.,* p. 203.

[34] Woeikof, *op. cit.,* pp. 20, 23.

[35] Jovan Cvijić, *La péninsule Balkanique* (Paris: A. Colin, 1918), pp. 223–24.

[36] Woeikof, *op. cit.,* p. 16.

[37] Marinelli, *op. cit.,* p. 203.

INFLUENCE OF THE
AGRICULTURAL ECONOMY

The conditions of the agricultural economy itself may recommend concentration or dispersion. According to whether it is sparse or dense and whether it possesses weak or powerful tools, an agricultural population exercises different holds on the soil, and the nature of land occupation can change even in the midst of the same area if economic conditions themselves have changed. Let us now consider how modes of livelihood can affect forms of settlement.

The Stage of Nomadic Cultivation.—One of the first stages of agriculture seems to have been nomadic or shifting cultivation, i.e., the perpetual displacement of cultivated fields across unlimited territory. This instability can be explained both by poverty of technology and sparseness of population. Under this system it is sufficient to burn the cover of shrubs and herbs, and bury the ashes by shallow plowing. After one or two crops, the field is abandoned to return to its wild state, and a new field selected from the reserve of uncultivated land is cleared. This nomadic form of cultivation was practiced by the Germans in the time of Tacitus, among the Irish in the sixteenth century, and among the Welsh of the Middle Ages. It is still practiced in the steppes of southern Russia and in the forested regions of northern Russia. In certain places, the colonist burns the forest, sows three or four crops in the ashes, and then abandons the field to revert again to forest. This practice persists in several districts of the provinces of Olonets, Arkhangelsk, and Perm.

With this unstable mode of cultivation, settlement is displaced like the fields. The movement of houses is facilitated by the lightness and simplicity of their construction. Under these conditions nothing, except perhaps the tendency of families to draw together, encourages agglomeration. From an economic point of view, many arguments encourage looser ties and dispersion: e.g., the necessity to dispose of poorly defined pastures, the frequent movement to new fields, and the obligation to preserve free land for hunting. Historical documents almost always show this primitive economy associated with isolated or dispersed settlement. Since the remote time when the extended family began to loosen its ties, we see dispersed settlement spread over Ireland and Wales. In the twelfth century, Giraldus Cambrensis described Welsh houses built of wood which were like the light and precarious dwellings of a semipastoral people living on the edge of the woods. The colonization of the Russian forest has been the work of isolated pioneers or small groups of merchants. On a fifteenth-century cadastral map of the Republic of Novgorod, cited by Woeikof, one finds mention of numerous free holdings and tenant farms. The clearings of the Middle Ages in Württemberg were accomplished by settlers who lived in hamlets. The penetration of the Swedes into the forests of Norrland and the advance of the Finns in their immense forests were also accomplished from isolated establishments.[38]

The Stage of Periodic Redistribution.— A new stage begins when population growth and scarcity of arable land oblige a society to limit individual rights of free appropriation: i.e., arable perimeters are delimited to regularize their distribution among various families. This periodic redistribution is designed to minimize inequalities of soil and provide new land for the younger generations. Close community ties are thus established among those who share land.

[38] For the stage of nomadic cultivation, see P. Lacombe, *L'Appropriation du sol* (Paris: A. Colin, 1912), pp. 10–11, 19–22; Seebohm, *op. cit.,* pp. 186, 342, 370, 368; Jan St. Lewiński, *The Origin of Property and the Formation of the Village Community* (London: Constable & Co., 1913), pp. 5–9, 15–18; Moritz J. Bonn, *Die englische Kolonisation in Irland,* (2 vols., Stuttgart and Berlin: J. G. Cotta, 1906), I, 255–59, II, 140–41; Bernhard, *op. cit.,* pp. 20–32; Woeikof, *op. cit.,* pp. 13–23; L. Beauchet, *Histoire de la propriété foncière en Suède* (Paris: Larose, 1904), pp. 10–15.

Redistribution applies only to the best land, i.e., land that yields the best harvests. Apart from these regularly tilled fields, there is an entire zone of vague land, pasture and woods, that is not partitioned and remains under common possession. These practices have long been conspicuous in numerous regions of Europe, e.g., in Russia, Sweden, and Germany. Redistribution was still practiced in Ireland under the eyes of Sir John Davies in the seventeenth century, and Hanssen calls attention to it at about 1835 in Eifel and Hunsrück.[39]

Does this stage of agricultural evolution coincide with an evolution of settlement? It does not appear to have the same consequences in all countries. In one area it leaves dispersed settlement intact; in another it encourages agglomeration. For medieval Ireland we have records of land cultivated in common, in *runnig,* where each person received an equal lot at periodical redistributions. According to Seebohm, complaints were made even in the seventh century that population pressure had reduced individual shares from thirty to twenty-seven bands or "ridges."[40] It is conceivable that this practice led the Irish to move their houses from these arable territories and regroup them in villages. Yet Ireland has remained a country of dispersed settlement. Actually, in this land of pastoral economy, parcels of good land represented only a minute portion of the exploited territory. To be sure, peasants met at more or less well established dates for plowing, seeding, and harvesting, but they placed their houses close to their pastures, each isolated from the others.

In Sweden, the custom of periodic redistribution existed prior to the twelfth century. This custom (*hamarskipt*) assigned to each inhabitant possession of a certain number of parcels for several years,

but with the provision that they should be surrendered to the community, in anticipation of a new distribution, at a time determined by law. Since Sweden is an agricultural country, one might believe that the necessity for periodical abandonment of fields would have encouraged cultivators to choose permanent sites, free from the obligations of sharing, where all their houses could be grouped. Actually, it appears that the ground on which the family house was erected (*topt*) was not privately owned and that it was even shared. Each dispossessed inhabitant had to clear away his dwelling and rebuild it on a new *topt*. However, the law granted a certain delay, in order to avoid the serious agitation that simultaneous demolition of all houses would have entailed. It is reasonable to suggest that the obligation to rebuild elsewhere did not involve a very difficult operation, for rural houses in Sweden were made of joists and assembled planks that could easily be dismounted and transported. Thanks to the *hamarskipt,* the habit of living in dispersed houses persisted in Sweden.[41]

In Russia, on the contrary, it seems that periodic redistribution favored village life. It was at a more recent date (sixteenth and seventeenth centuries) and under the influence of land scarcity and population pressure that a desire was felt for periodic redistribution of fields among the inhabitants of a single agricultural community. Thus was developed the *mir,* a Russian institution long mistaken for an ancient Slavic institution. On the territory of the *mir* each family head received parcels of land selected from each category of land value, which he kept until the next distribution, occurring, according to regions, every six, ten, fifteen, and even twenty years. This evolution, more recent than in Sweden, did not necessitate displacement of houses. The peasant had to establish his dwelling on a spot selected by the community to prevent emigration during the redistribution and to facilitate communal labor. In this case, it seems that the obligations of

[39] Lewiński, *op. cit.,* pp. 52–53, 60–61; Meitzen, *op. cit.,* I, 24.

[40] Seebohm, *op. cit.,* pp. 126–214, 230. Gilbert Slater, "The Inclosure of Common Fields," *Geographical Journal,* XXIX (1907), 35–55, ref. to 45–46.

[41] Beauchet, *op. cit.,* pp. 32–33, 43–54, 187.

the agricultural community moved peasants away from the system of isolated farms and made them adopt a system of agglomeration.[42]

The Stage of Permanent Possession in the Interior of an Agricultural Community.
—A new stage begins when further population growth necessitates a more favorable distribution of land. Peasants developed a desire to cultivate the same plot continuously rather than shifting from plot to plot. They could thus collect full profit from the care they had devoted to their fields. This agricultural formula does not date everywhere from the same epoch; but it reveals a systematic organization with fixed rules honored by all members of a community. In a large part of Europe, it was conceived in such a manner that it could be adapted during the year to production of cereals and livestock. It allowed a triennial rotation, i.e., a winter cereal the first year, a spring cereal the second year, and fallow the third year. This rotation was carried out according to rules that excluded dispersal of settlement. All the arable territory was divided into three portions (*soles, saisons, fields, Gewänne*), devoted to wheat, oats, and fallow respectively. On each of them the freedom of the farmer was limited by a discipline of communal labor and obligations of solidarity. It was necessary to carry out agricultural work and at the same time leave stubble and fallow for the common flock. Since each farmer had fields dispersed in each of the three *soles,* he could not place his house in the center of his fragmented domain. Houses were grouped around a central core formed of wells, a bridge, and, later, a church or castle. By living in such a village, the peasant found himself truly in the center of his domain. "It is understandable that necessity of agreement in the conduct of cultivation . . . created a need to centralize agricultural activity in some one place. A cooperative agreement as to dates in the agricultural calendar, and the time for certain

tasks is adopted for the advantage of all concerned. . . . The concentration of settlement . . . makes the village the common meeting ground, whither all paths lead" [43]

This organization, quite ancient in some countries, was born elsewhere in more recent periods and can be verified by historical records.

In Sweden, periodic redistribution of lands according to the *hamarskipt* system plus general agricultural progress led to a new system, the *solskipt,* which substituted collective for individual ownership of land. This revolution was nearly complete at the time of the drafting of provincial laws, i.e., in the course of the thirteenth and the beginning of the fourteenth centuries. However, it was optional and was realized only gradually as interests demanded. The result of this definitive redistribution of land was the choice of a village site where peasant houses were grouped. This site was divided among the cultivators according to the extent of their land, and each had to enclose the portion (*topt*) alloted to him. He was allowed to erect all the buildings he desired, but with the provision that he maintain a certain space between his houses and those of his neighbors to facilitate drainage and prevent the spread of fires.[44]

In the Javanese provinces of Cheribon and Tegal at the beginning of the nineteenth century one could see communal villages being substituted for isolated houses.[45] In the lands of rice cultivation, irrigation usually imposed concentration of settlement. Examples are numerous in India. In Puduvayal (Carnatic), thirty miles northwest of Madras, the village territory is divided into well defined sections according to the value of the soil, e.g., one section corresponds to land adjacent to the reservoir (the land least exposed to dryness), another to the lands farther away from the reservoir, and a third to lands

[42] Lewiński, *op. cit., passim.* Meitzen, *op. cit.,* I, 25, II, 213.

[43] Vidal de la Blache, *Principes de la géographie humaine,* pp. 185–86.

[44] Beauchet, *op. cit.,* pp. 32–33, 41–43.

[45] Lewiński, *op. cit.,* p. 30.

that receive sufficient water only one year in two or three.[46] Here again, the mandatory site of the settlement is found on a common point, the focus of all activity.

The Stage of Specialized Cultivation.— Further agricultural development and new dietary needs revealed to certain advanced peoples at a very early date the inefficiencies of nucleated settlement. The entanglement of plots held cultivators in narrow mutual dependence and obliged them to undertake a multitude of tasks, e.g., cultivation of the same crop on the same land, communal harvests, rights of common access to land, loss of time while commuting to distant fields, inability to undertake works of improvement without mutual understanding and collaboration, and inability to make a rational selection of crops. From a strict agricultural point of view, the isolated dwelling, placed in the middle of its fields, represents a superior arrangement. It allows the cultivator greater freedom, brings him closer to his land, and protects him from the inconveniences of community life. The isolated farm is a stronger economic unit and it is free of communal restraints.

Accordingly, certain countries penetrated by the commercial spirit and concerned to orient production as much toward urban markets as toward domestic consumption, deliberately consolidated the dispersed fields of the communal villages in compact blocks in order to form isolated farms. In England, this revolution, usually described under the heading of "enclosures," was accomplished in two periods, first in the fifteenth and sixteenth centuries and then in the eighteenth and nineteenth centuries. With the formation of independent farms,

[46] Gomme, *op. cit.*, pp. 23–34.

the farmer was permitted full initiative. He was able to orient his work and production according to his own choice, give clover and turnips a place in the rotation, feed more cattle, and fence his fields to provide better protection for his livestock. The consequence of this agricultural revolution was a settlement revolution, a shift from agglomeration to dispersion. It was the latter pattern that European colonists in the New World adopted as the most modern and economical form of rural settlement. Dispersal also favors the increased crop specialization that is now almost universal: e.g., market gardens and orchards in the Mediterranean region, pasturage and intensive livestock production in the plain of the Po.

Conclusion

In order to explain how certain men acquired the habit of settling in villages, while others preferred to live on isolated farms or in small hamlets, it is thus necessary to refer to all the natural, social, and economic conditions of their way of life. The study of settlement is a chapter in the study of rural civilizations. It must go back to their remote origins and follow their evolution until the present time. If we wish to classify types of settlement, we must treat them as manifestations of human enterprise that are not necessarily determined by physical geography. In a single country in the course of its history factors of settlement have not acted uniformly, and agricultural colonization has been able successively to adopt different forms of settlement. In a single country a well established type of settlement has been able to evolve into another one, if conditions of the human milieu have rendered such evolution necessary.

GLENN T. TREWARTHA

TYPES OF RURAL SETTLEMENT
IN COLONIAL AMERICA

This study of types of rural settlement in colonial America is an offshoot of an investigation of settlements, both early and modern, in the Driftless Hill Land along the upper Mississippi.[1] It grew out of a desire to know what colonial precedents, if any, existed for the various settlement types which developed in that section of the Middle West.

In the Atlantic-seaboard colonies of England were represented in relatively pure form the two extremes in rural settlement —the compact agricultural village and the isolated farmstead. Seventeenth-century New England, exemplifying the former type, was described by Edmund Burke as "a mosaic of little village republics." Virginia and the other planter colonies of the South exemplified almost equally well the dispersed variety. In the Middle Colonies the types were intermingled, though isolated farmsteads predominated.

THE NEW ENGLAND COLONIES

For the first hundred years and more of its history New England comprised a few score townships or towns (an area of land, not a small urban community), each con-

sisting of at least one principal farm-village nucleus and, commonly, several satellite clusters surrounded by cultivated fields, pastures, and woodlands.[2] There were few isolated farmsteads. For practically all of seventeenth-century New England there was a single general model for rural settlement, though in details there was great variety. So necessary to the New Englander's social, educational, and religious well-being was community living that he propagated the village type of settlement in outlying regions to which he migrated.[3]

MORPHOLOGY OF NEW ENGLAND TOWNS
AND THEIR FARM VILLAGES

Seventeenth-century New England towns, or townships, were grants of land ranging in area from four to ten miles square.[4] Fre-

Reprinted, with permission of the author and editor, from the *Geographical Review*, XXXVI (1946), 568–96 (copyright, 1946, by the American Geographical Society of New York). The author is professor of geography at the University of Wisconsin, Madison.

[1] See Glenn T. Trewartha, "The Unincorporated Hamlet: One Element of the American Settlement Fabric," *Annals of the Association of American Geographers*, XXXIII (1943), 32–81, and references 1 through 4 cited on p. 33.

[2] Good general descriptions of the New England type of settlement are found in the following publications: A. B. MacLear, "Early New England Towns," *Columbia University Studies in History, Economics, and Public Law*, vol. XXIX (1908); R. H. Akagi, *The Town Proprietors of the New England Colonies* (Philadelphia: University of Pennsylvania Press, 1924); P. W. Bidwell and J. I. Falconer, "History of Agriculture in the Northern United States, 1620–1860," *Carnegie Institution Publication No. 358* (1925), chap. 5; Edna Scofield, "The Origin of Settlement Patterns in Rural New England," *Geographical Review*, XXVIII (1938), 652–63.

[3] Herbert L. Osgood, *The American Colonies in the Seventeenth Century*, (3 vols.; New York and London: Macmillan, 1904–07), II, 47–48; Lois K. Mathews, *The Expansion of New England* (Boston and New York: Houghton Mifflin, 1909), p. 180.

[4] Melville Egleston, "The Land System of the New England Colonies," *Johns Hopkins Univer-*

quently the grants were not contiguous, and numerous "gores" were the result. In shape the towns were far from being regular, though they were more so than in the Middle and Southern Colonies. They were rarely square, though it was not unusual for them to be bounded by four straight lines. The term "miles square," commonly used to define a grant, referred primarily to the total area and not to the shape.

Somewhere near the geographical center of the town was the principal settlement, or the farm village, the nucleus of which was the town common. As a fairly standard village pattern, the church, the school, the burying ground and the home lots of some of the original settlers fronted on the town common. A home lot contained not only the farmhouse but, in addition, barns and other outbuildings, a garden, sometimes a small field of corn, and usually enclosures for feeding livestock. The degree of compactness of the village depended largely on the size of the home lots. In Salem they were two acres until 1635 and one acre thereafter. In Roxbury they averaged between two and five acres; in Cambridge one acre, though some were as small as a quarter of an acre; in Dorchester and Watertown four acres; in Charleston half an acre, in Marblehead two acres, and in Hingham five.[5] Many of the early villages were surrounded by palisades as a means of protection against the Indians.[6]

Often the earliest houses were dugouts in the hillsides. There were later supplanted by cottages of wattle, frequently daubed with clay, resembling those of an English

sity *Studies in History and Political Science,* Series 4, No. 11–12 (1886), p. 33; A. C. Ford, "Colonial Precedents of Our National Land System as It Existed in 1800," *Bulletin, University of Wisconsin No. 352* (History Series, II [1910]), pp. 15, 19, footnote 7.

[5] Osgood, *op. cit.,* I, 429; MacLear, *op. cit.,* p. 82.

[6] Ralph H. Gabriel, *Toilers of Land and Sea* (New Haven: Yale University Press, 1926), p. 43; H. B. Adams, "The Germanic Origin of New England Towns," *Johns Hopkins University Studies in History and Political Science,* Series 1, No. 2 (1883), pp. 5–38.

rural village. Still later, cabins constructed of vertical logs became common, and finally in the established communities larger houses of hand-hewn clapboards and shingles took the place of the wattle and log structures. New England frame houses, built by farmer carpenters, were simple of line and with a beauty begotten of this simplicity.

The farm of each villager was composed of several parcels of land lying in different directions and at different distances from the village residence. This fragmented type of farm, characteristic of areas with the village plan of rural settlement, resulted from the desire of each family to possess various types of land, and of the town proprietors to equalize the division of lands by compensating handicaps in quality or location with quantity, and vice versa. This was especially desirable in the diverse terrain, soil, and drainage environment of New England, where good cropland was limited in extent as well as scattered. The great diversity in natural features complicated the problem of land subdivision and led to considerable variety in the original village patterns and in their subsequent growth, in the location of fields and meadows, and in the routes of highways.

The town's arable lands and mowing lands were divided into large fields of several hundred acres, and these were partitioned into strips and distributed to the settlers by lot. A striking feature of many early New England towns was the regular arrangement of the planting lots (Figs. 1 and 2). The large fields were laid off in long tiers or rows, often parallel to one another, and the tiers in turn were divided into regular strips forming a series of small parallelograms, many of them equal in size. Such orderly and regular arrangement was not so characteristic of land subdivision in England and seems to have been a product of the American environment.

In addition to the home lots and the planting lots, which were held in fee simple, there were also the common lands, possessed and used by all the original settlers. Pasture

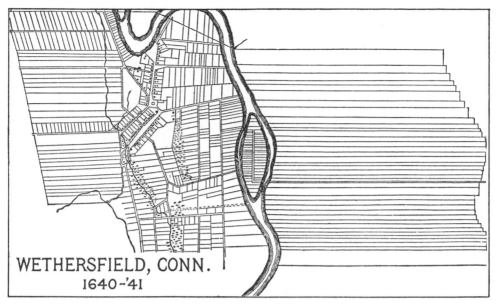

WETHERSFIELD, CONN.
1640-'41

Fig. 1. Wethersfield, Conn. Land subdivisions as of 1640–41. The town common with the meeting-house at its center stood in the middle of the village. Occupied home lots are indicated. Orderly arrangement of fields, which were usually long, narrow strips, is conspicuous. The home lots were generally about three acres in extent; the fields east of the river were three miles long. (Redrawn from map opposite p. 5 in C. M. Andrews, "The River Towns of Connecticut," *John Hopkins University Studies in History and Political Science,* Series 7, Nos. 7–9 [1889].)

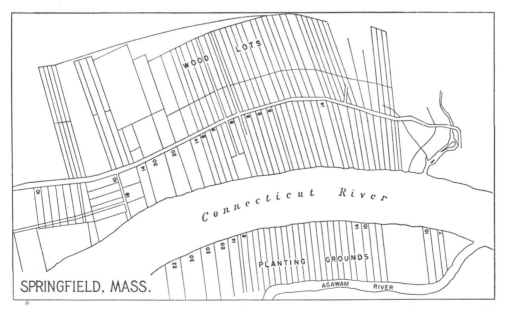

SPRINGFIELD, MASS.

Fig. 2. Land subdivided into long tiers, and the tiers in turn divided into regular, narrow strip fields of approximately equal size and shape, is very well developed in the part of the town of Springfield shown here. Most of the lots were eight rods wide. The top of the map is east. (Redrawn and simplified from frontispiece map in H. M. Burt, *The First Century of the History of Springfield* [Springfield, Mass., 1898].)

and woodland, and much of the meadow, were at first held absolutely in common, and even though the small planting lots were owned in severalty, they were subject to certain common regulations regarding choice of crops and the construction and maintenance of a fence around the large planting field—the individual lots were not enclosed—and were entirely common from harvest until sowing time.

Seventeenth-century New England farms were modest or even small in size, considering the abundance of virgin land. The system of allotments tended to prevent great inequalities in the sizes of original holdings and retarded as well the subsequent engrossment of land. In assigning home lots and fields, however, rigid numerical equality was rarely practiced. The largest grants were usually made to the minister and to the leaders of the town-founding enterprise. Wealth, size of family, original investment in the town's establishment, or the ability of a man to advance the interests of the community was taken into consideration. In Hartford, Conn., the first distribution of land resulted in average holdings of 27 acres. The largest farm was 160 acres, 10 were more than 20 acres, 70 from 10 to 20 acres, 41 from 1 acre to 10. In New Haven, Conn., the first land division gave the 123 grantees average allotments of 44 acres. A second division added 66 acres. The whole was contained in four separate parcels exclusive of the home lot. Nine farms were more than 300 acres, 34 between 100 and 300 acres, and 80 less than 100 acres. As successive subdivisions of the town's common lands were made and distributed among the villagers, a man's farm increased in size and in degree of fragmentation.

It is impossible to make up averages showing the degree to which New England farms were fragmented and the sizes of the separate plots. An example or two must suffice. In Groton, Mass., each settler held on the average 59 acres of upland or planting land in two or three parcels and 19½ acres of meadow divided into five

parcels. The farm of John White of Newton, Mass., on May 1, 1635, consisted of two small tracts of about three-quarters of an acre each, one of them his home lot; three tracts in "old field," one of 2½ acres and two of 1¼ acres; a one-acre lot on "long marsh hill"; a 3¼-acre lot in "long marsh"; 13½ acres in "the neck of land"; 11 acres in the "great marsh"; and one acre in "ox marsh." Altogether there were 36 acres in 10 separate parcels.[7] Another example is seen in Figure 3.

ORIGIN OF THE NEW ENGLAND FARM-VILLAGE TYPE OF SETTLEMENT

The neighborly, compact communities of New England were not so exclusively the result of defense needs against the Indians as some writers indicate.[8] Their origin is by no means so simple. Rather, the farm village resulted from a variety of intermingled forces, some of them indigenous to the New England social and physical environment, others inherent in the migrating groups.

The New England town, with its farm village and a land system involving intermingled holdings, with fields held both in common and in severalty, bears some resemblance to the English parish of the seventeenth century, caught in the midst of an agricultural revolution.[9] The American colonists, though well acquainted with the communal form of agricultural organization, were not ignorant of the compact enclosed farm with its single isolated farm-

[7] Osgood, *op. cit.,* I, 450.

[8] See, for example, Scofield, *op. cit.,* pp. 653–54.

[9] Some of the best descriptions of English agriculture at the time of the American colonization are to be found in the following references: Henry M. and Morton Dexter, *The England and Holland of the Pilgrims* (Boston and New York: Houghton Mifflin, 1905); Rowland E. Prothero (Lord Ernle), *English Farming Past and Present* (London and New York: Longmans, Green, 1912); *idem,* "Agriculture and Gardening," in *Shakespeare's England* (2 vols.; London, 1916), I, chap. 12; Mabel E. Seebohm, *Evolution of the English Farm* (London: Allen & Unwin, 1927); G. E. Fussell, "Social and Agrarian Background of the Pilgrim Fathers," *Agricultural History,* VII (1933), 183–202.

stead or of the economic advantages, and social disadvantages, that this type of farming offered.

The New England town, however, was no slavish copying of this ancestral type.[10] Such essential elements of the English system as the lord of the manor or the landlord, the general lack of ownership of land in fee simple, and the completely communal system of village agriculture were largely absent. The organization of the New England town evolved as a natural business process in possessing and developing a tract of land. It was designed to meet the needs of religious and social-minded Englishmen struggling to take root in a strange and relatively hostile physical and social environment. It was an indigenous product. Sanderson points out that wherever common lands, intermingled holdings, and free pasture are characteristic of an agricultural system, there the farm-village type of settlement results.[11] In other words, the settlement type grows out of the land system. The slow process of land clearing made the fragmented farm a likely development; for new parcels could be added to a farm as the timber was removed and new allotments made. Many times the home lot was all that was cleared and cultivated in the first year or two of settlement. During most of the seventeenth century the colonists were not aware that they could raise Indian corn among the girdled or burned trees without first plowing the land, and plowing required the removal of stumps, which was slow and difficult work.[12]

Of prime significance in understanding the origin of the farm village in seventeenth-century New England is the fact that settlement was by organized groups and not by individuals. These colonists came because they desired to worship as their consciences dictated. Commercial motives were not always absent, to be sure, for no doubt most of the emigrants hoped to improve their economic well-being, but this ambition was modestly restrained. Early New England was not colonized by promoters, in the form either of proprietors or of commercial companies, who looked on the new settlements only as a potential source of income. Often the migrating groups had been church congregations or neighborhoods in England. It seems reasonable that they should establish compact units of settlement knit together by religious and economic bonds. So important to the well-being and prosperity of the New England town was homogeneity in its residents that laws were passed in many towns forbidding the sale of land to outsiders without the consent of the town meeting. Much of the civil administration of an English parish was undertaken by church officials, so that vicar, vestry, and parishioners had just the kind of experience needed to fit them for the planting of a New World settlement.[13] It is not surprising, therefore, that most Puritan towns of New England were little ecclesiastical republics, in which the church existed as a covenanting body before the establishment of a civil government.

Closely associated with the practice of community migration was the policy of the New England colonizing organizations of making grants to groups rather than to individuals. Land was not sold but was awarded only after careful consideration to responsible groups in whom was reposed the destiny of the new town. In seventeenth-century New England land was neither a source of income for the colonies nor an object of speculation by individuals. It was held in trust for bona fide settlers who

[10] Osgood, *op. cit.*, I, 426; C. F. Adams, "The Genesis of the Massachusetts Town, and the Development of Town-Meeting Government," *Proceedings of the Massachusetts Historical Society,* 1891–92, Series 2, VII (1892), 172–263 (211–63, discussion).

[11] Ezra Dwight Sanderson, *The Rural Community* (Boston, New York, etc.: Ginn & Company, 1932), p. 178.

[12] R. R. Wolcott, "Husbandry in Colonial New England," *New England Quarterly,* IX (1936), 218–52, ref. to 226.

[13] C. M. Andrews, "The Rise and Fall of the New Haven Colony," *Tercentenary Commission of the State of Connecticut, Publication No. 48* (New Haven, 1936), pp. 3–4.

planned to use it as a livelihood and was granted to them in such amounts as their immediate and prospective needs indicated. In the granting of land to groups rather than to individuals the colonizing companies had in mind the stimulating of compact settlement. Indeed, regulations were passed restraining settlers from living apart from the village. This seems to have been necessary; for the more ambitious and adventurous very early tended to develop isolated farmsteads apart from the village. Bradford wrote concerning Plymouth:

And to every person was given only one acrre of land, to them and theirs, as nere the towne as might be, and they had no more till the 7 years were expired. The reason was, that they might be kept close together both for more saftie and defence, and the better improvement of the generall imployments.[14]

The General Court of the Massachusetts Bay Company decreed at its meeting of September 3, 1635, that "noe dwelling howse shalbe builte above halfe a myle from the meeteing howse, on any newe plantacon, . . . without leave from the Court."[15] A year later this order was extended to other towns in the colony, but in 1641 it was repealed. Concerning the Dorchester Company the record reads:

For purposes of mutual defence and the establishment of social order, the court held in London, May 21, 1629 contemplated that the settlements must be very compact and that a certain plot or pale should be marked out within which every one should build his house, and a half acre is named as the size of a house lot within the pale.[16]

When once the village community had been established, the centripetal forces generated by Puritan ideals of religion and education, and the New Englander's appreciation of the amenities of civilization, tended to hold the settlement together and retard disintegration into isolated farmsteads.[17]

The influence of his policy [settlement in compact units] can only be fully appreciated when standing by the side of the solitary settler's hut in the West, where even an Eastern man has degenerated to a boor in manners, where his children have grown up uneducated, and where the Sabbath has become an unknown day, and religion and its obligations have ceased to exercise control upon the heart and life.[18]

When a village outgrew its immediate land resource, or when increased size made attendance at the original meetinghouse a hardship, fission took place, and a part of the old community migrated to a new site where hearthsides were established about a new church-and-school nucleus.

Forces in the New England environment also made for community settlement. Chief of these was the hostility of the Indians on whose lands the colonists encroached and the need for organized defense against this menace. The need for defense was one of the reasons why all the colonizing companies at one time or another obliged the colonists to settle near together.[19] The regulations were tightened when the Indian menace was greatest and relaxed or repealed when relative security had been established. But there were parts of colonial America where hostile natives made life and property insecure in which settlement

[14] William Bradford, *Bradford's History of Plymouth Plantation, 1606–1646,* ed. William T. Davis (New York: Scribner's Sons, 1908), p. 175.
[15] N. B. Shurtleff (ed.), *Records of the Governor and Company of the Massachusetts Bay in New England,* Vol. I, 1628–41 (Boston, 1853), p. 157.
[16] *History of the Town of Dorchester, Massachusetts, by a Committee of the Dorchester Antiquarian and Historical Society* (Boston, 1859), p. 21.

[17] P. W. Bidwell, "Rural Economy in New England at the Beginning of the Nineteenth Century," *Transactions of the Connecticut Academy of Arts and Sciences,* XX (1915–16), 241–399; Frederick Jackson Turner, *The Frontier in American History* (New York: Henry Holt, 1920), pp. 73–74.
[18] Josiah G. Holland, *History of Western Massachusetts* (2 vols.; Springfield, Mass.: S. Bowles, 1855), I, 62.
[19] See statements by Bradford and rulings of the Dorchester Company quoted above.

was in large part by individuals on separate farms. This was the case in New Netherland, New Sweden, the Mohawk country, South Carolina, and Georgia. By itself the Indian menace does not seem to have been powerful enough to prevent dispersed settlement, though for more than a century it did retard the disintegration of the farm village. It was something more than defense that seventeenth-century New Englanders had in mind as they dotted the wilderness with compact communities.

The physical character of New England, as compared, for example, with that of tidewater Virginia or the Carolinas, seems to be less favorable for scattered, isolated farms. No great staple commercial crop was at home in the harsh New England environment, as tobacco, rice, and indigo were in the Southern Colonies. The general lack of commercial agriculture and the scarcity of servile labor militated against a plantation system with unified isolated farms.

EIGHTEENTH-CENTURY CHANGES IN NEW ENGLAND SETTLEMENT TYPES

No doubt the semicommunal system of husbandry was admirably suited to the period when the colonies were taking root. It was not, however, suited to a later stage of their development. In the beginning the proprietary town promoted democratic principles and harmony among the early settlers; on a rapidly expanding frontier it bred jealousy and inequality.

Even at an early date certain handicaps of village residence and scattered farm plots became obvious. Indian thievery was relatively easy in fields at some distance from the owner's house. Precious time was lost in going to and from the village farmstead and the outlying fields. Much land was wasted in the numerous roads leading to the individual plots within the larger planting fields. The long and narrow strips made cross-plowing and cultivation difficult. Restrictions regarding kinds of crops were annoying. When animals were herded in common, it was hard to control breeding and

foster improvement in livestock. The system in general tended to create a community dead level above which it was difficult for the more ambitious and industrious to rise.[20] As early as 1632 Governor Bradford bewailed the tendency of some Plymouth men, as their prosperity increased, to draw away from the meetinghouse and from the close communion of the village settlement to outlying settlements and isolated farms. In this change he professed to foresee the ruination of New England. He wrote:

For now as their stocks increased, and the increase vendible, ther was no longer any holding them togeather, but now they must of necessitie goe to their great lots; they could not other wise keep their catle; and having oxen growne, they must have land for plowing and tillage. And no man now thought he could live, except he had catle and a great deale of ground to keep them; all striving to increase their stocks. By which means they were scatered all over the bay, quickly, and the towne, in which they lived compactly till now [1632], was left very thine, and in a short time allmost desolate. . . . . And this, I fear, will be the ruine of New-England, at least of the churches of God ther.[21]

Apparently two opposite movements were proceeding simultaneously, one tending toward compact village settlement, common fields, and scattered farm plots, the other toward residence on a unified farm. As a town grew in years and in number of residents, more and more of its common lands were subdivided and allotments made to the original proprietors and to acceptable newcomers. By this means a farmer's scattered holdings grew more numerous and the distance from his village residence to the outlying fields increased. Contemporaneously, however, through buying and selling, exchanging, surrendering, and inheriting,

[20] Noah Porter, Jr., *A Historical Discourse Delivered by Request before the Citizens of Farmington . . . in Commemoration of the Original Statement . . .* , (Hartford, 1841), Note S, p. 83, quoting from manuscript of Governor Treadwell (1802 or 1803).

[21] Bradford, *op. cit.*, pp. 293–94.

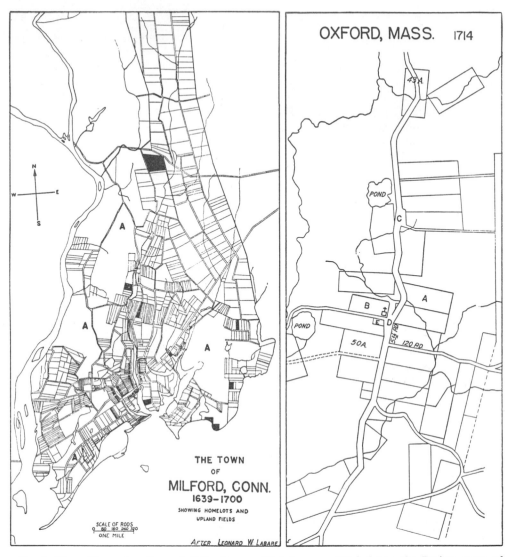

FIG 3. The settlement pattern of Milford exemplified to an unusual degree the Puritan town of seventeenth-century New England. Home lots, in the form of narrow rectangles, ranged in size from 2¾ to 7 acres. The farm of proprietor Deacon Richard Platt, which was fairly representative, was composed of fourteen parcels; the northernmost and southernmost fields were seven miles apart. The home lot and nine upland fields are shown on the map; four unfenced strips of meadow are not shown. (Modified from photograph of an original drawing prepared and copyrighted by Leonard W. Labaree and lent by him.)

FIG. 4. Oxford is typical of eighteenth-century towns with home lots so large that compact form had almost disappeared. The roughly 40-acre lots were relatively contiguous and fronted on a highway, with the longer dimension at right angles to it so that houses would be as close together as possible. The presence and central location of the meetinghouse (B), burying ground (E), common (C), and minister's lot (A) give evidence of a persisting Puritan type of community organization. (Redrawn and modified from map on p. 32 in G. F. Daniels, *History of the Town of Oxford, Massachusetts* [Oxford, Mass., 1892].)

farms were gradually being consolidated. As this took place, the village became less and less of a farm center and the farmer less and less of a villager.

Several specific forces were at work in the latter half of the seventeenth century, and more especially in the eighteenth, accelerating the disintegration of the New England farm village. According to the principles of town founding in early New England the land grant was made to the original nucleus of settlers (the proprietors), who usually had complete control over the dividing and disposal of the land. In the beginning, therefore, all the residents in a town were landowners, had rights in the use of common and undivided land, and were parts of the governing body in whose hands lay the management of the town's lands. It was pure democracy. But as population increased, both from natural births and from immigration, the governing body was often slow in extending the rights of land to the newcomers. This resulted in an increasing number of citizens who were without land or whose holdings and rights were definitely restricted. These landless citizens, eventually a majority, having no sentimental bonds with the town's historic past, formed a discontented group to whom the idea of founding a new home beyond the established settlements had great appeal. Many times it was a group migration that took place, but it was not unusual for a single family to strike out alone. An anonymous writer of 1775 remarks: "But the new comers do not fix near their neighbours and go on regularly, but take spots that please them best, though twenty or thirty miles beyond any others." [22]

Not only on the frontier, but in the general vicinity of the older established villages as well, where life and property were relatively secure against Indian attacks, there came to be an increasing number of isolated farm dwellings. Some of these were established by "squatters" or "cottagers,"

[22] *American Husbandry . . . , by an American* (2 vols.; London, 1775), I, 48.

the landhungry class previously described, who, with or without permission from the proprietors, occupied small tracts of the undivided land. Indentured servants who had completed their period of service were sometimes granted the privilege of building a home on the undivided land and of cultivating a small plot there. Proprietors whose distant fields made their husbandry difficult were inclined to establish residences closer to their principal farming areas. Or sons of the proprietors married and set up

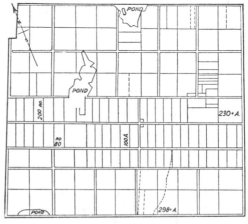

FIG. 5. The original plat of Pittsfield in 1738 called for 64 home lots, each to contain 100 acres. They were intended to be uniformly 80 rods wide and 200 rods deep, arranged in orderly fashion along parallel streets or roads; errors in surveying, however, caused slight variations in size. The later subdivisions provided for larger parcels, lying both north and south of the original fields. (Redrawn from map on p. 125 in J. E. A. Smith, *pflanzen und Hausthiere in ihrem Übergang nach*

homes of their own on a part of the parental estate. Not uncommonly the pioneer isolated farmstead attracted other settlers, so that a new community developed. These outlying centers that developed by accretion were rarely as compact as the original villages settled by groups. On the other hand, they were somewhat different from complete dispersion.

Foremost among the forces favoring dispersed settlement, particularly in newly created towns on the frontier, was the growth of the commercial incentive in land disposal. Alongside the discontented property-less class in the towns there came to exist a wealthy class possessed of surplus capital and land but having little desire to leave their comfortable and secure village surroundings. Out of this combination came a new method of settling the frontier. While continuing the historic practice of granting land to groups of bona fide settlers, the colonies at the same time introduced the new practice of selling and granting land in large blocks to wealthy or prominent citizens or to cities. These in turn sold it for a profit to individuals eager to pioneer. Massachusetts finding itself in financial difficulties, the General Court of the colony in 1760 ordered ten of its western townships offered for sale to the highest bidders. The use of public land as a source of income by the New England colonies was an innovation that had important repercussions in their later social and economic history. No particular attention was paid to the religious qualifications of the seeker for land, with the result that the frontier was frowned on by the Church because of its unreligious character. Towns settled by groups bound together by religious and social bonds became less common. Many besides Puritans were attracted by the freedom of the frontier, and in the records one finds numerous references to Dutch and Scotch-Irish settlers. The lull in Indian troubles after the first quarter of the eighteenth century quickened the tempo of colonial expansion and thereby hastened the decline of community settlement. The process was speeded up more especially after 1760 as a result of the defeat of the French and their Indian allies. The whole spirit of the expanding frontier, with its antisocial and unreligious tendencies and its emphasis on individualism, was the antithesis of all the conservative New England village stood for.

By the beginning of the nineteenth century the small farm village no longer contained a large proportion of the rural population. A Frenchman traveling in New England in the late eighteenth century wrote concerning its rural settlements:

For what is called in America, a *town* or *township,* is only a certain number of houses, dispersed over a great space, but which belong to the same incorporation. . . . The centre or head quarters of these towns, is the meeting-house or church. This church stands sometimes single, and is sometimes surrounded by four or five houses only.[23]

Two centuries had been required to complete a major transformation in settlement type.

SETTLEMENT TYPES IN THE MIDDLE ATLANTIC COLONIES

The spirit of the colonizing enterprise in the Middle Colonies was from the beginning very different from that prevailing for the first century in New England. Great proprietors, such as William Penn, Lord Baltimore, and Sir George Carteret, received from the British government vast tracts of land covering thousands of square miles that were their private estates and could be disposed of as they saw fit. Naturally they looked on these grants as potential sources of income, so that land was sold to individuals, including promoters and speculators, in tracts of various sizes. A universal form of revenue in the Middle Colonies was the quitrent, a fee required by the proprietor from the settlers in lieu of all services. The commercial motive was paramount, and speculation in land was rife; colonists were attracted through glowing advertisements. The tracts of land granted and sold were commonly of such size that development by the purchaser himself was impossible, which led him to subdivide and sell. Both the migration of colonists and the process of settlement were for the most part distinctly individualistic.

In the Middle Atlantic region homogeneity in the colonists was lacking. These

[23] Marquis de Chastellux, *Travels in North America, in the Years, 1780, 1781, and 1782, translated from the French by an English gentleman* (2 vols.; London, 1787), I, 20.

immigrants, originating in different parts of northwestern Europe, with different social, political, and religious backgrounds, were less amenable to a standardized pattern of living. Dutch, Swedes, Scotch-Irish, Germans, Quaker English, and others flocked to this region where substantial freeholds could be obtained at nominal prices, rubbed elbows with one another, and in the process lost some of that uncompromising attitude which was so prominent in Puritan New England. A mixture of religious faiths and creeds was represented with no one dominant, so that a spirit of compromise and tolerance was necessary. As a result the centripetal force of a cohesive ecclesiastical organization, which was so important in the community settlement of Massachusetts and Connecticut, was weak. Usually, however, the proprietors were aware of the advantages of community settlement and endeavored, at least mildly, to encourage it.[24]

THE JERSEYS

The characteristic Puritan settlement pattern of compact farm villages each with a meetinghouse nucleus was most strikingly developed in East Jersey, where settlement was strongly influenced by a wave of immigration from New England by way of Long Island.[25] The importance of this Puritan group and its influence on settlement are indicated by the fact that in 1682 two-thirds of the 5000 settlers in East Jersey were living in compact settlements.[26] Along

with the New Englander Puritans were Dutch, Quakers, Baptists, and Scotch Presbyterians. That the village form of settlement was not carried farther to the west may be attributed to the retarding influence of relief, which slowed up the New England invasion until Germans and Scotch-Irish had moved north to occupy the territory. Throughout East Jersey, at least after 1682, land grants to individual settlers were relatively large, estates of 500 to 1000 acres being common. In the areas settled by New Englanders the usual farm size was between 100 and 200 acres.[27]

West Jersey, largely in the hands of Quakers, was peopled by substantial farmers, tradesmen, and artisans direct from England. They did not settle in villages but on compact farms in dispersed farmsteads. In general the farms were relatively large.

NEW NETHERLAND

New Netherland, along the Hudson, was the development of the chartered United New Netherland Company, whose prime interest was not so much colonization as trade, more especially the Indian fur trade; hence the earliest Dutch settlements were chiefly fortified trading posts. But since the government of the Netherlands was also interested in colonies, a plan for settlement and land subdivision was eventually formulated. Two kinds of grants were made: enormous estates to patroons who would agree to plant a colony of some fifty souls on their land; and smaller grants of as much land as they could improve to individual bona fide farmers.[28] The patroon's estate represented a modified form of feudal tenure. Early settlement on the manors was relatively compact, but as the Indian menace abated, the tenants scattered out to develop the best land. The many restrictions associated with the patroon system of

[24] *Documents Relative to the Colonial History of the State of New-York,* Vol. II (Albany, 1858); Samuel Hazard, *Annals of Pennsylvania . . . , 1609–82* (Philadelphia, 1850), pp. 516–17; Samuel Smith, *The History of the Colony of Nova-Caesaria, or New-Jersey* (Burlington, 1765), p. 545.

[25] E. P. Tanner, "The Province of New Jersey, 1664–1738," *Columbia University Studies in History, Economics, and Public Law,* XXX (1908), 25–26; Thomas J. Wertenbaker, *The Founding of American Civilization: The Middle Colonies* (New York and London: Scribner's Sons, 1938), pp. 135–61.

[26] Tanner, *op. cit.,* p. 28.

[27] Bidwell and Falconer, *op. cit.,* p. 61.

[28] Irving Elting, "Dutch Village Communities on the Hudson River," *Johns Hopkins University Studies in History and Political Science,* Series 4, No. 1 (1886), p. 12.

settlement made it relatively unpopular, so that most of the estates were meagerly occupied. Some of the extensive manors had fewer than half a dozen tenants.

Because of the generous grants of land to individual colonists, early settlement outside the manors was dispersed. But as a result of the repressive acts of the administration, the Indian menace, and troubles with the Swedes and English, colonists were slow in coming. The "Report and Advice on the Condition of New Netherland" by the General Board of Accounts, dated December 15, 1644, admitted that the colony had not prospered as had been expected and attributed the condition in part to the fact that

the Colonists, each with a view to advance his own interest, separated themselves from one another, and settled far in the interior of the Country, the better to trade with the Indians . . .

In order to prevent war in future, the Colonists ought to settle nearer each other, on suitable places, with a view of being thus formed into villages and towns, to be the better able to protect each other in time of need.[29]

The next year instructions from the West India Company in Holland to the Director General and Council of New Netherland advised:

They shall endeavor as much as possible, that the colonists settle themselves with a certain number of families on some of the most suitable places, in the manner of villages, towns and hamlets, as the English are in the habit of doing, who thereby live more securely.[30]

In the year after the massacre of 1655 a proclamation went forth from the authorities in New Netherland ordering "all who resided in isolated places to collect together and form villages, 'after the fashion of our New England neighbors.' "[31]

But this order was difficult to enforce; for the Dutch colonists lacked local political powers, held no land in common, and probably lacked a genuine desire for an intimate church fellowship—three of the cohesive forces present in the New England towns.[32] The proclamation served mainly to guide the future policy of the authorities in the establishment of settlements, though it was put into effect to some degree in the older settlements. When in 1658 the

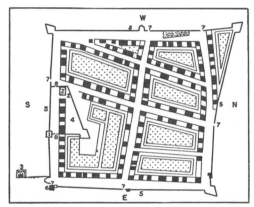

Fig. 6. A Dutch village, Wilttvick (now Kingston, N. Y.), 1695: 1, the blockhouse; 2, the church and burying place; 3, the minister's house; 4, the part separated and fortified; 5, the stockade; 6, the house where the governor was entertained; 7, the town gates; 8, the gates of the separate fortified part. (Redrawn from sketch in John Miller, *A Description of the Province and City of New York . . . in the Year 1695* [London, 1843; New York, 1862].)

settlers of the Pavonia area petitioned for exemption from the quitrent tithe, the governor agreed to a six-year exemption provided they would concentrate their farmsteads to form a village.[33] With the rapid increase in immigration after 1650 new rural settlements of the village type appeared in rapid succession. Population in-

[29] *Documents Relative to the Colonial History of the State of New-York,* I (Albany, 1856), 150–51.
[30] *Ibid.,* p. 161.
[31] Edmund B. O'Callaghan, *History of New Netherland* (2nd ed.; 2 vols.; New York: Appleton, 1855), II, 356.

[32] A. E. McKinley: "The English and Dutch Towns of New Netherland," *American Historical Review,* VI (1900–1), 1–18, ref. to p. 5.
[33] C. W. Rife, "Land Tenure in New Netherland," in *Essays in Colonial History Presented to Charles McLean Andrews by His Students* (New Haven: Yale University Press, 1931), pp. 41–73, ref. to p. 63.

creased from an estimated 2000 to 10,000 in 1664.[34] At least twelve villages were in existence by 1663.[35] The farm villages of the Dutch were patterned after those of New England, as were many of the features of land subdivision (Fig. 6). Home lots, tillage land, and meadow were held in severalty; pasture and woodland were used in common. But although in general morphology the later Dutch settlements bore a strong resemblance to those of New England, it should be emphasized that their origin was quite in contrast.

Under the English governors New York became essentially a colony of dispersed settlement with independent freeholders cultivating their own separate farms. Land was cheap, and quitrents were not oppressive. Grants of land were made largely to individuals, and for the first two decades of English sovereignty they were generally less than 1000 acres.[36] The New England form of settlement was not lacking, but it never assumed a prominent position except in Westchester County, where it was introduced by Puritan immigrants, chiefly from Connecticut.

NEW SWEDEN

Settlements along the Delaware, under the authority of the New Sweden Company, closely resembled those of early New Netherland. Here, too, the interest of the trading company was primarily in furs, and the first settlements were stockaded and garrisoned military posts designed to protect Swedish rights against the encroachments of the Dutch and English. What land was cultivated lay immediately outside the stockade. Many of the earliest immigrants were deserting soldiers and petty criminals who had come under duress and in consequence made unwilling farmers. As agricultural settlers became more numerous after 1642, they located on separate clearings in the general vicinity of the forts,

but not in compact villages.[37] This fact of dispersion is indicated by Stuyvesant's order to the Swedish settlers, after capture of their colony by the Dutch, to collect into small villages.[38]

PENNSYLVANIA

The proprietary colony of William Penn, cosmopolitan in the nationalities and religious faiths of its dominant immigrant groups, did not possess a favorable social environment for the development of community settlement. Pennsylvania Germans from the Rhine country had been reared in the economic and social environment of the rural village, though they were not unacquainted with dispersed settlement. But the cheapness of land and the ease with which it could be obtained were not conducive to duplication of the familiar German farm-village system. The colonist's desire was to possess land, and when he found that in Pennsylvania he could purchase 100 or 300 acres for the price of a dozen acres in the homeland, he bought to the limit of his means.[39] A farm of several hundred contiguous acres made village residence virtually impossible. As a result, the independent farmstead or *Einzelhöfe* became the basis of agricultural settlement among the Pennsylvania Germans. The same forces—individual grants, cheap land, and large farms—produced a similar pattern of settlement among the Scotch-Irish.

However, for those who desired "to sit together in a lot or township" Penn made provision that they should have their township "cast together." [40] He was well aware of the advantages of community living and endeavored in his settlement plans to bring the farmsteads of the colonists as close together as possible, considering the size of

[34] O'Callaghan, *op. cit.*, II, 540.
[35] Elting, *op. cit.*, p. 33.
[36] *Documents Relative to the Colonial History of the State of New-York*, IV (Albany, 1854), 392.

[37] Amandus Johnson, *The Swedish Settlements on the Delaware . . . , 1638–1664* (Americana Germanica [No. 13] (2 vols.; Philadelphia, 1911), I, 192–94, 202, 203, 303, 306.
[38] Benjamin Ferris, *A History of the Original Settlements on the Delaware* (Wilmington, 1846), p. 108.
[39] Wertenbaker, *op. cit.*, pp. 270–71.
[40] Hazard, *op. cit.*, p. 517.

the holdings. In his account of the province in 1685 he wrote:[41]

We do settle in the way of Townships or Villages, each of which contains 5,000 acres, in square, and at least Ten Families; the regulation of the Country being a family to each five hundred Acres. . . .

Our Townships lie square; generally the Village in the Center; the Houses either opposit, or else opposit to the middle, betwixt two houses over the way, for near neighborhood. We have another Method, that tho the Village be in the Center, yet after a different manner: Five hundred Acres are allotted for the Village, which, among ten families, comes to fifty Acres each: This lies square, and on the outside of the square stand the Houses, with their fifty Acres running back, where ends meeting make the Center of the 500 Acres as they are to the whole. Before the Doors of the Houses lies the high way, and cross it, every man's 450 Acres of Land that makes up his Complement of 500, so that the Conveniency of Neighbourhood is made agreeable with that of the Land.

Many settlers objected to Penn's planned townships:

Many that had right to more Land were at first covetous to have their whole quantity without regard to this way of settlement, tho' by such Wilderness vacancies they had ruin'd the Country, and then our interest of course. I had in my view Society, Assistance, Busy Commerce, Instruction of Youth, Government of Peoples manners, Conveniency of Religious Assembling, Encouragement of Mechanicks, distinct and beaten Roads, and it has answered in all those respects, I think, to an Universall Content.

Although Penn's arrangement of the 50-acre home lots and their farmsteads permitted some degree of neighborliness among the rural settlers, the final product was far from being a compact village. In some ways it resembled the shoestring settlements of New England during the transitional period

[41] Albert C. Myers (ed.), *Narratives of Early Pennsylvania, West New Jersey and Delaware, 1630–1707* (Original Narratives of Early American History) (New York: Scribner's Sons, 1912), p. 263.

of the eighteenth century. In all probability settlers in the planned towns did not constitute a very large part of the total population of Pennsylvania.

SETTLEMENT TYPES IN THE SOUTHERN PLANTER COLONIES

In the planter colonies of the South, which were the chief strongholds of dispersed settlement, early experimentation with the rural-village type of organization was common. For nearly two decades after the founding of Jamestown the Virginia population was held together in communities of various degrees of compactness. These villages were not neighborhood groups or church congregations but fortuitous collections of individuals, most of them serving as indentured laborers. The Virginia Company, which for seventeen years was responsible for the colonization procedure, was bent on obtaining a return on its investment rather than on settling a wilderness. The population at Jamestown, largely male, was housed within a stockaded village, and its energies went into the production of clapboards, pitch, tar, and soap ashes, for export to England, and into searching for precious metals. Agriculture was so neglected that hundreds died of starvation. There was no such thing as private ownership. Settlement was confined to the tiny peninsula on which Jamestown was located.

With the arrival in 1611 of new colonists and a more vigorous director active expansion began. Within five years Virginia, according to Rolfe, consisted of at least six distinct fortified settlement centers under military management scattered along the James from its mouth to a point about fifteen miles from the Fall Line. The total population of 351 was still predominantly male: there were only forty-five women and children. Tidewater Virginia is made up of numerous narrow necks of land between estuaries, a condition that made it possible for the settlements to protect themselves and their farmlands by building palings or palisades across the narrow interfluves.

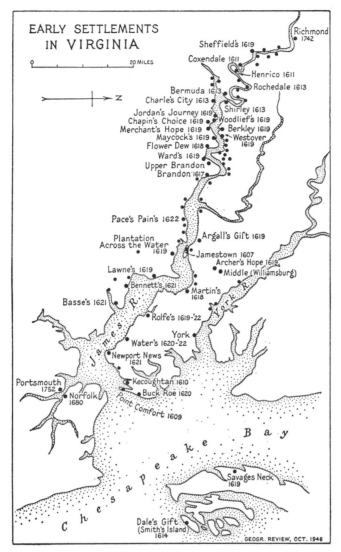

EARLY SETTLEMENTS
IN VIRGINIA

0 _____ 20 MILES

→—|—→ N

Richmond 1742

Sheffield's 1619
Coxendale 1611
Henrico 1611
Rochedale 1613
Bermuda 1613
Charles City 1613
Shirley 1613
Jordan's Journey 1619
Woodlief's 1619
Chapin's Choice 1619
Berkley 1619
Merchant's Hope 1619
Westover 1619
Maycock's 1619
Flower Dew 1618
Ward's 1619
Upper Brandon
Brandon 1617

Pace's Pain's 1622

Argall's Gift 1619
Plantation
Across the Water
1619
Jamestown 1607
Archer's Hope 1619
Middle (Williamsburg)

Lawne's 1619
Bennett's 1621
Martin's 1618
Basse's 1621

James R.
York R.

Rolfe's 1619-'22
York
Water's 1620-'22
Newport News
1621
Portsmouth
1752
Kecoughtan 1610
Buck Roe 1620
Norfolk
1680
Point Comfort 1609

Chesapeake Bay

Savages Neck
1619

Dale's Gift
(Smith's Island)
1614

GEOGR. REVIEW, OCT. 1946

Fig. 7. With three exceptions (Richmond, Portsmouth, and
Norfolk) the named and dated settlements were in existence by
1622. (Compiled from data contained on map opposite p. 201 in
Lyon G. Tyler, *The Cradle of the Republic*, 2nd ed. [Richmond,
1906]; and from maps prepared by Lyon G. Tyler in M. P. Robinson, "Virginia Counties," *Bulletin of the Virginia State Library*, IX,
Nos. 1–3 [1915], following p. 124. In the latter publication there
is a series of eight maps showing the progress of settlement in
Virginia from 1607 to 1671.)

Within the impaled area was the compact fortified village, which contained lodging quarters for the company's indentured laborers, and also storehouses and a church. In addition to the laborers there were "farmers," many of whom had families and who, besides working for the company, raised hogs, cattle, and food crops for the settlement and tobacco for export. The farmers did not always dwell within the compact village but often lived in scattered residences located along the protecting pales. In 1616 landholding in fee simple was still unknown in Virginia, even though the strict communism of early Jamestown had been relaxed. Most of the settlers had a small patch of cleared land which they could work for themselves. To each farmer with a family twelve acres of cleared land was allotted and a house of four rooms, tools, seeds, and animals were furnished.[42]

But the early semicompact settlement was short-lived in Virginia. The tendency to scatter out from the villages became particularly noticeable in the third decade of the seventeenth century. There is evidence that private enclosures were being established as early as 1620,[43] and it has been estimated that just before the massacre of 1622 there were nearly 80 farms along the James River, many of them owned by persons who had been granted a dividend of 100 acres by the company at the expiration of their term of service.[44] Dispersion seems to have been rather general by the middle of the third decade. Town life stagnated, and nowhere, except, perhaps, at Jamestown and Henrico, was

there a genuinely compact fortified settlement.[45]

A combination of events caused this transition period from compact to dispersed settlement in Virginia to be brief. The massacre of 1622 was quickly followed by vigorous warfare against the hostile Indians, so that they were cleared out of the tidewater country. Ownership of land in fee simple possibly began as early as 1619, until which time the colonists had been in the service of the company that brought them. After Virginia became a crown colony in 1624, private ownership of land was the universal policy. This was a potent force leading to the disintegration of the fortified community groups under military management. Tobacco, first planted by John Rolfe in 1612, became a staple crop within a few years. Ten years later, 60,000 pounds were exported to England, and it became necessary to pass a law compelling each head of a family to plant sufficient food crops to supply his dependents. The profits to be obtained from tobacco export urged men on to take up their own lands as quickly as possible. For two centuries tobacco shaped the destiny of Virginia.

Not alone in Virginia among the planter colonies was there early experimentation with the rural-village type of settlement. In almost all the Southern Colonies initial attempts were made to induce settlers to live in compact communities. In providing for the Ashley River Settlement the Carolina proprietors set aside twenty-five acres for a village, each family being assigned a home lot in the village and five acres outside as a planting lot.[46] The proprietors likewise in their instructions for the establishment of certain port towns stipulated that each of these should be surrounded by six tracts of 1200 acres each, to be known as colonies. Each colony was to contain a village type of settlement, and every free

[42] For descriptions of early Virginia settlements see *Virginia Historical Register*, Vol. 1, No. 3, Report of Rolfe of Virginia in 1616; Ralph Hamor, *A Trve Discovrse of the Present Estate of Virginia* (London, 1615), pp. 29–31; John Smith . . . : *Works, 1608–31*, ed. Edward Arber (Birmingham: The English Scholar's Library, No. 16, 1884), p. 510.

[43] Philip A. Bruce, *Economic History of Virginia in the Seventeenth Century* (2 vols.; New York and London: Macmillan, 1896), I, 316.

[44] L. C. Gray, "History of Agriculture in the Southern United States to 1860" (2 vols.; *Carnegie Institution Publication 430* [1933]), I, 320.

[45] John Fiske, *Old Virginia and Her Neighbours* (2 vols.; Boston and New York: Houghton Mifflin, 1897), I, 229.

[46] *Proceedings of the South Carolina Historical Association*, V (1897), 311, 315.

settler was to be allotted a building lot 300 feet square in the village, 80 acres in the same colony, and 400 acres in some other colony. In 1729 the king ordered eleven townships each of 20,000 acres to be laid out, in which settlers were to be assigned home lots in the villages and planting fields outside.[47] In accordance with this plan for compact settlements, groups of Germans founded New Berne, Orangeburg, Saxe-Gotha, and New Windsor; Swiss founded Purysburg; Moravians settled Salem, Bethany, and Bethabara; Scotch located at Kingston and Williamsburg; and a group of Welsh at Queensborough.[48] Most of these were cohesive national groups held together by religious ties.[49] Their pastors frequently came with them, and as in New England the church became the focal center of the new settlement. Where religious bonds were strong, a fairly compact community life was maintained for some time; where they were weak or lacking, disintegration was more rapid. In the Moravian settlements of North Carolina cohesiveness was present to an unusual degree.

Among the Southern Colonies, Georgia stood out as the one in which the earliest settlement was almost universally of the village type. This resulted from the unique purpose of the colony. It was to be a haven for the persecuted and the honestly unfortunate, most of whom had to be sent to the New World at public expense. At the same time the Carolinas were urging the establishment of a colony on their southern border to serve as a shield against the hostile Spanish and Indians. The charitable and military functions of the new colony combined to produce a special plan of set-

tlement. Trust deeds were made for tracts of several thousand acres of land, and these tracts were subdivided among settlers sent over by the trustees of the charity colony in England. In all, eight such large tracts, ranging in size from 2,500 to 10,000 acres, were laid out, so that most of the earliest inhabitants in Georgia were located in the rural villages that developed from the trust deeds.[50] They were, to a degree, garrisons in which the home lot was held as a military fief.

The earliest settlement, Savannah, served as a model for subsequent villages. Rectangular pattern was conspicuous. The town was divided into wards of 40 building lots each, and the wards in turn divided into tithings of 10 lots each. Wide streets and numerous squares were characteristic. Home lots measured 60 by 90 feet and had frontage on two streets. Each settler had a home lot in the village, a garden plot of nearly five acres not far from his residence, and a parcel of planting land amounting to 45 acres farther from the village.[51]

Settlements similar in origin and in plan were established at Ebenezer, Frederica, Sunbury, Abercorn, St. Joseph's Town, Highgate, and Hampstead.[52] Several of these were eventually abandoned because of unhealthful locations.

But although the settlement of charity

[47] Gray, *op. cit.*, I, 378.

[48] *Ibid.*, pp. 378–79; G. D. Bernheim, *German Settlements and the Lutheran Church in the Carolinas* (Philadelphia, 1872), pp. 67–161; *Colonial Records of North Carolina*, V, 1159–62; Alexander S. Salley, *The History of Orangeburg County, South Carolina* (Orangeburg, S.C.: R. L. Berry, 1898), p. 60.

[49] [See the sketch of Bethlehem, a Moravian settlement in Pennsylvania, reproduced on p. 588 of the original version of this article.]

[50] James R. McCain, *Georgia as a Proprietary Province* (Boston: R. G. Badger, 1917), p. 272.

[51] Peter Force (compiler), *Tracts and Other Papers Relating Principally to the Origin, Settlement, and Progress of the Colonies in North America* (4 vols.; Washington, 1836–46), I, No. 3, p. 21; Charles C. Jones, Jr., *The History of Georgia* (2 vols.; Boston and New York: Houghton Mifflin, 1883), I, 150–51.

[52] An old map of Georgia in the fourth decade of the eighteenth century, showing locations of some of these settlements along the lower course of the Savannah River, is to be found in Jones, *op. cit.*, I, opposite p. 148. Plans of several of the Georgia settlements, including Ebenezer and Frederica, are contained in Charles C. Jones, Jr., *The Dead Towns of Georgia* (Savannah, 1878). For a plat of early Savannah see the map opposite p. 36 in J. G. W. de Brahm, *History of the Province of Georgia* (Wormsloe, 1849).

colonists in compact villages was the usual method of early colonization in Georgia, it was not the only one. A colonist who could support himself and was able to bring ten servants at his own expense was granted

Savannah. Trust grants of large tracts of land to groups of charity settlers ceased in 1738, so that individual plantations soon came to be the common form of colonization.

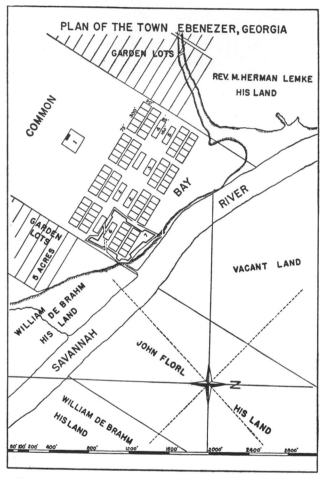

FIG. 8. Ebenezer is representative of early agglomerated settlements in the colony of Georgia. The estate of each man consisted of a home lot 60 feet by 90 feet, a garden plot of nearly 5 acres adjacent to the village, and 45 acres farther away. 1, burying ground; 2, parson's land; 3, church lot; 4, store; 5, opera house; 6, filature; 7, the fortified part. (Redrawn and modified from map opposite p. 24 in De Brahm, *History of the Province of Georgia* [cited in footnote 52].)

500 acres of land in fee simple. A quitrent of 20 shillings for each 100 acres was imposed. Thus even at the very beginning of the colony there were a number of small plantations along the lower course of the

FARM AND PLANTATION SETTLEMENTS

After a period of early and relatively unsuccessful experimentation with the village type of rural settlements the Southern Colonies shifted to the dispersed type characterized by the isolated residence on a compact individual farm or plantation. As in the Middle Colonies, land was looked on as a source of income for proprietors and colonies; the system of quitrents was almost universal; land was cheap and easy to obtain, chiefly through the headright system; grants were made to individuals in both large and small tracts; settlers were attracted through advertising and as a rule did not form a cohesive group. The settling process was largely a commercial undertaking. In Virgina, where, in order to stimulate immigration, the headright system of acquiring land was introduced in 1619, 50 acres were granted for each individual transported to the colony. Under this system large grants were made to individual promoters and land companies who undertook to import settlers. Later the colony inaugurated a new policy, namely the selling of land to prospective planters. The development of the plantation system was further strengthened by the rule of primogeniture, the emphasis on one staple crop, and, later, by the importation of African slaves in large numbers.

Virginia after the third decade of the seventeenth century was essentially a land of compact farms with isolated residences, strung out for miles along the estuaries and creeks of the Coastal Plain, their owners all engaged in raising tobacco. The riverine pattern of settlement was unusually striking, for practically all communication was by water. Almost every farm had its own wharf, and at many of them ocean-going boats could load and discharge cargo. Such an arrangement made the services of commercial towns unnecessary, and several attempts on the part of the government to stimulate the growth of towns came to naught. Virginia was strongly rural, even more so than the other Southern Colonies, where water transport was not so widely available. Town life held little appeal.

Thus neither the Interest nor Inclinations of the *Virginians* induce them to cohabit in Towns; so that they are not forward in contributing their Assistance towards the making of particular Places, every Plantation affording the Owner the Provision of a little Market: wherefore they most commonly build upon some convenient Spot or Neck of Land in their own Plantation.[53]

The popular concept of tidewater Virginia as a region of large estates owned by wealthy gentlemen-planters and tilled by Negro slaves is scarcely correct for the seventeenth century. Largely because of a labor shortage, the engrossment of land had not progressed far; Virginia was a colony of small to middle-sized farms, many of whose owners depended entirely on their own exertions for a living.[54] The seventeenth century was one of rapid immigration to Virginia, some 100,000 colonists arriving between 1607 and the end of the century. Many were indentured laborers, who were free at the close of their five years of service to take up land and marry, a circumstance that tended to keep Virginia at this stage fundamentally democratic. Ninety per cent of the population were independent small farmers. In 1704 the average number of workers, freeholders, and slaves on a farm was only 1.5. Negro slaves were not numerous until the eighteenth century.

The farmsteads of the seventeenth-century tobacco planters were, of necessity, modest.[55] The earliest residences were probably of crotch construction, in which curved tree trunks or limbs joined together at the top supported a roof of thatch weighted down with earth; the walls were of wattle plastered with clay. Houses of horizontal logs were unknown in the American colonies until 1635–36, when they were introduced by the Swedes along the Dela-

[53] Hugh Jones, *The Present State of Virginia* (London, 1724, reprinted [Sabin's Reports No. 5], New York, 1865), p. 35.

[54] Thomas J. Wertenbaker, *The Planters of Colonial Virginia* (Princeton: Princeton University Press, 1922), pp. 43–45.

[55] According to Dr. Wilmer L. Hall, state librarian of Virginia, original detailed maps or sketches of farmsteads and their houses in Virginia in the seventeenth century are non-existent. See also Harold R. Shurtleff, *The Log Cabin Myth*, ed. S. E. Morison (Cambridge, Mass.: Harvard University Press, 1939), p. 132.

ware.[56] The representative seventeenth-century houses were of local materials, chiefly frame cottages of one story besides the loft, with a chimney at each end. There was no pretense at beauty or design; even the homes of the most prominent planters were simple and plain. The plantation mansion belonged to a later period.

side by the ideals and blood of English country gentlemen.[57] Virginia owes much of the genteel flavor of its society to the cavaliers; for they exercised an influence in the colony far out of proportion to their numbers. As the influx of Negroes increased, the flow of white immigrants from England gradually dwindled and eventu-

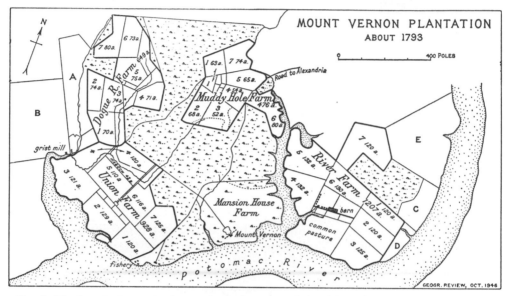

FIG. 9. The layout of an extensive southern plantation of the eighteenth century: George Washington's map of Mount Vernon, drawn in 1793, simplified from a copy of the original published by the University of Chicago Press, 1932. The cultivated part of Mt. Vernon was chiefly contained in four farms, the Mansion House Farm apparently having been more of a residential and service unit. The entire Potomac estate occupied about 10,000 acres. As was characteristic of Virginia plantations, a large part of Mount Vernon was woodland.

In the eighteenth century the tidewater country underwent a significant change in settlement form and landholding. The moderate-sized farms and small one-family farmsteads of the yeoman farmers gradually gave way to the extensive baronial estates of wealthy gentlemen-planters who lived in comparative luxury surrounded by scores of Negro slaves. Tidewater became aristocratic. This form of society, with its attendant settlement features, was supported on its economic side by an abundance of cheap black labor and on its social

ally ceased. Slave labor reacted disastrously on the small landowners, who were eventually ruined and forced to emigrate.

The settlement type represented by the eighteenth-century tidewater plantation does not fit readily into the simple classification consisting of only two subdivisions, agglomerated and dispersed. The plantation evolved out of the latter type and bore earmarks of it, in that it often supported only one free and independent rural family and its centralizing power was small. In the number of human beings at work or

[56] Henry C. Forman, *Jamestown and St. Mary's* (Baltimore: Johns Hopkins University Press, 1939), pp. 30–41.

[57] William Byrd, *The Writings of Colonel William Byrd, 1674–1744*, ed. J. S. Bassett (New York: Doubleday, Page, 1901), p. xi.

the number of buildings assembled, it represented an agglomeration, yet the plan of a village was lacking (Fig. 9). In addition to the pretentious mansion, which commonly fronted on a navigable stream, there were in the general vicinity the laundry, the

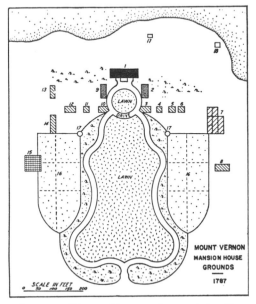

FIG. 10. Mount Vernon, about 1787. Slave quarters and many agricultural buildings are lacking, being on the individual farms of the plantation. 1, mansion house; 2, kitchen and servants' hall; 3, storehouse; 4, smokehouse; 5, washhouse; 6, coach house; 7, coach house and stables; 8, barn and carpenter's shop; 9, lodgings for white servants; 10, tailor and shoemaker's shop; 11, unknown; 12, spinning house; 13, blacksmith shop; 14, house for families; 15, hothouse; 16, kitchen gardens; 17, toilets; 18, springhouse. (Simplified from map by Samuel Vaughan in 1787, reproduced in *The George Washington Atlas* [Washington: George Washington Bicentennial Commission, 1937], Plate 7. Another plan of the central farmstead of a representative southern plantation is available in Gabriel, *Toilers of Land and Sea* [cited in footnote 6], Fig. 121, on p. 62.)

weaving and spinning quarters, kitchen, dairy, bakehouse, smokehouse, salthouse, servants' quarters, blacksmith shop, cobbler shop, distillery, carpenter shop, cooperage, stable, coach house, and perhaps others (Fig. 10). A grist and flour mill and a sawmill were normal plantation processing centers. Not too distant from the mansion were the slave quarters, the home of the overseer, and the barns and tobacco sheds. If the plantation was very extensive, there were likely to be outlying clusters of buildings containing slave cabins, overseer's home, and tobacco sheds. To an unusual degree these estates were self-sustaining settlement units.[58]

South of Virginia, where estuaries reaching deep into the Coastal Plain are lacking and the coast is fringed with shifting bars and shallow inlets leading into swamp-bordered sounds, plantation settlement developed much more slowly. At the close of the seventeenth century the Carolinas, still largely a frontier society, were occupied by many independent, thrifty small farmers, dwelling in isolation and carrying on a diversified type of agriculture. In the eighteenth century, with the expansion of tobacco culture in North Carolina and of rice and indigo in South Carolina and Georgia, a plantation system developed somewhat comparable with that of Virginia. South Carolina stands in contrast with the other planter colonies because of the early growth of a city, Charleston, on which the trade of the rural areas was focused. The unhealthfulness of the swamp country in which the rice plantations were located led the wealthier planters to leave more responsibility to their overseers while they themselves spent at least a part of the year in Charleston, where the opportunities for social life and education were concentrated.

Early in the eighteenth century land in tidewater Virginia had been largely laid out in private plantations and the frontier had reached the Fall Line. Aristocratic Church of England gentlemen engrossed in tobacco culture gave the Coastal Plain its social and economic stamp. But before this group

[58] An unusually good description and analysis of the life on one of these extensive eighteenth-century tidewater plantations is contained in Clifford Dowdey's novel, *Gamble's Hundred* (Boston: Little, Brown, 1939). See the pictorial map of Gamble's Hundred on the front and rear end papers.

could move on westward to dominate the
Piedmont and then the Ridge and Valley
Country beyond the Blue Ridge, a southward thrust of Scotch-Irish and Germans
from Pennsylvania, along with the un-
fortunates from tidewater country, had
taken possession. The Virginia Council
made plans for settling the frontier with
compact communities whose area should be
200 acres, shaped like a parallelogram with
a fort at the center of the village, but the
plan was unsuccessful.[59] The colonists migrated singly and in groups; and although
former neighbors commonly settled in the
same general locality, their farmsteads were
for the most part isolated. Farms were
smaller than in tidewater Virginia, riverine
settlement pattern was largely absent, subsistence grain-and-livestock farming took
the place of commercial tobacco culture,
and Negro slaves were lacking. There were
thus two Virginias, unlike in antecedents,
habits of thought, religion, and economic
interests; and although the integrated farm
and isolated farmstead were characteristic
of both, the farmstead units were markedly
in contrast.

The settlement forms and land systems
of the Southern and Middle Colonies differed in their institutional and legal backgrounds from those of New England. In
the former they were based on the proprietary grant, which induced strong commercial incentives in land dealings; in the
latter they had their inception in the town

[59] Frederick B. Kegley, *Virginia Frontier* (Roa-
noke, Va.: Southwest Virginia Historical Society,
1938), p. 136. See also the numerous plats showing boundaries of the individual landholdings.

grant, where community rather than individual interests were predominant. Outside
New England, almost from the beginning
of settlement, speculation in land and its
granting and sale to individuals were an
integral part of the scheme of colonization.
The system of quitrents was almost universal in the Southern and Middle Colonies,
and the early rise of such great staple crops
as tobacco, rice, and indigo tended to intensify the commercial spirit of the enterprise. Religious uniformity, which provided
a strong bond of community interest in
New England, was largely lacking farther
south. Out of these differences came two
contrasting forms of settlement, each suited
to its own social and economic environment. Seeds of community settlement were
freely sown throughout the seaboard from
New Netherland to Florida, but robust
plants capable of reproducing their kind
did not develop. In New England the socioeconomic climate of Puritanism was more
favorable, and for a century and more rural
villages prospered and multiplied. The system disintegrated in the face of a waxing
commercial spirit in matters pertaining to
land and of a weakening of the religious
bonds, especially on the frontier. The Indian menace as an influence favoring compact settlement in New England should
not be underestimated. Illustrations are not
wanting even outside New England of defense needs inducing proprietors and settlers alike to consider the advantages of
living together in villages. But where individualism was strong and land was cheap,
economic motives frequently outweighed
the appreciation of the greater security to
be obtained through village settlement.

CARL O. SAUER

THE AGENCY OF MAN
ON THE EARTH

As a short title for the present conference we have spoken at times and with hope of a "Marsh Festival," after the statesman-scholar, George Perkins Marsh, who a century ago considered the ways in which the Earth has been modified by human action.[1] The theme is the capacity of man to alter his natural environment, the manner of his so doing, and the virtue of his actions. It is concerned with historically cumulative effects, with the physical and biologic processes that man sets in motion, inhibits, or deflects, and with the differences in cultural conduct that distinguish one human group from another.

Every human population, at all times, has needed to evaluate the economic potential of its inhabited area, to organize its life about its natural environment in terms of the skills available to it and the values which it accepted. In the cultural *mise en valeur* of the environment, a deformation of the pristine, or prehuman, landscape has been initiated that has increased with

Reprinted, with permission of the author and publisher, from *Man's Role in Changing the Face of the Earth*, ed. William L. Thomas, Jr. (Chicago: University of Chicago Press, 1956), 49–60 (copyright, 1956, by the University of Chicago). The author is professor emeritus of geography at the University of California, Berkeley.
[1] George P. Marsh, *Man and Nature* (New York: Scribner, 1864), and *The Earth as Modified by Human Action* (2nd ed.; New York: Scribner's Sons, 1885). [See also David Lowenthal, *George Perkins Marsh: Versatile Vermonter* (New York: Columbia University Press, 1958).]

length of occupation, growth in population, and addition of skills. Wherever men live, they have operated to alter the aspect of the earth, both animate and inanimate, be it to their boon or bane.

The general theme may be described, therefore, in its first outline, as an attempt to set forth the geographic effects, that is, the appropriation of habitat by habit, resulting from the spread of differing cultures to all the *oikoumene* throughout all we know of human time. We need to understand better how man has disturbed and displaced more and more of the organic world, has become in more and more regions the ecologic dominant, and has affected the course of organic evolution. Also how he has worked surficial changes as to terrain, soil, and the waters on the land and how he has drawn upon its minerals. Latterly, at least, his urban activities and concentrations have effected local alterations of the atmosphere. We are trying to examine the processes of terrestrial change he has entrained or originated, and we are attempting to ask, from our several interests and experiences, relevant questions as to cultural behaviors and effects. Thus we come properly also to consider the qualities of his actions as they seem to affect his future well-being. In this proper study of mankind, living out the destiny ascribed in Genesis—"to have dominion over all the earth"—the concern is valid as to whether his organized energies (social behavior) have or should have a quality of concern with regard to his posterity.

On the Nature of Man

The primordial condition of man setting our kind apart from other primates involved more than hands, brain, and walking upright. Man owes his success in part to his digestive apparatus, which is equaled by none of his near-kin or by few other similarly omnivorous animals as to the range of potential food which can sustain him on a mixed, vegetarian, or flesh diet. The long, helpless infancy and the dependence through the years of childhood have forged, it would seem, *ab origine* a maternal bond that expresses itself in persistence of family and in formal recognition of kinship, system of kinship being perhaps the first basis of social organization. When humans lost the oestrous cycle is unknown; its weakening and loss is probably a feature of domestication, and it may have occurred early in the history of man, eldest of the domesticated creatures.

Built into the biologic nature of man therefore appear to be qualities tending to maximize geographic expansiveness, vigorous reproduction, and a bent toward social development. His extreme food range favored numerical increase; I question, for instance, any assumptions of sporadic or very sparse populations of Paleolithic man in any lands he had occupied. The dominant and continuous role of woman in caring for the family suggests further inferences. Maternal duties prescribed as sedentary a life as possible. Her collecting of food and other primary materials was on the short tether of her dependent offspring. Hers also was the care of what had been collected in excess of immediate need, the problem of storage, hers the direction toward homemaking and furnishing. To the "nature" of woman we may perhaps ascribe an original social grouping, a cluster of kindred households, in which some stayed home to watch over bairns and baggage

while others ranged afield. Baby-sitting may be one of the most ancient of human institutions.

Implicit in this interpretation of the nature of man and primordial society, as based on his trend to sedentary life and clustering, are territoriality, the provision of stores against season of lack, and probably a tendency to monogamy. These traits are familiar enough among numerous animals, and there is no reason for denying them to primitive man. Shifts of population imposed by seasons do not mean wandering, homeless habits; nomadism is an advanced and specialized mode of life. Folk who stuffed or starved, who took no heed of the morrow, could not have possessed the earth or laid the foundations of human culture. To the ancestral folk we may rather ascribe practical-minded economy of effort. Their success in survival and in dispersal into greatly differing habitats tells of ability to derive and communicate sensible judgments from changing circumstances.

The culture of man is considered in the main a continuum from the beginning; such is its treatment by archeology. The record of artifacts is much greater, more continuous, and begins earlier than do his recovered skeletal remains. Thereby hangs the still-argued question of human evolution, about which divergent views are unreconciled. If culture was transmitted and advanced in time and space as the archeologic record indicates, there would appear to be a linked history of a mankind that includes all the specific and generic hominid classifications of physical anthropology. Man, *sensu latiore,* therefore may conceivably be one large species complex, from archaic to modern forms, always capable of interbreeding and intercommunication. Variation occurred by long geographic isolation, blending usually when different stocks met. The former is accepted; the latter seems assured to some and is rejected by others, the Mount Carmel series of skulls being thus notoriously in dispute.

Neanderthal man, poor fellow, has had

a rough time of it. He invented the Mousterian culture, a major advance which appears to have been derived from two anterior culture lines. The Abbé Breuil has credited him with ceremonial cults that show a developed religious belief and spiritual ceremonial.[2] Boyd, in his serologic classification of mankind,[3] the only system available on a genetic basis, has surmised that Neanderthal is ancestral to a Paleo-European race. There is no basis for holding Neanderthal man as mentally inferior or as unable to cope with the late Pleistocene changes of European climate. Yet there remains aversion to admitting him to our ancestry. The sad confusion of physical anthropology is partly the result of its meager knowledge of hereditary factors, but also to *Homo's* readiness to crossbreed, a trait of his domestication and a break with the conservatism of the instinctive.

We are groping in the obscurity of a dim past; it may be better to consider cultural growth throughout human time as proceeding by invention, borrowing, and blending of learning, rather than by evolution of the human brain, until we know more of biological evolution in man. The little that we have of skeletal remains is subject to unreconciled evaluations; the record of his work is less equivocal. The question is not, could Peking man have left the artifacts attributed to him, as has been the subject of debate, but did he, that is, do the bones belong with the tools?

When primordial man began to spread over the earth, he knew little, but what he had learned was by tested and transmitted experience; he cannot have been fear-ridden but rather, at least in his successful kinds, was venturesome, ready to try out his abilities in new surroundings. More and more he imposed himself on his animal competitors and impressed his mark

[2] Henri Breuil and Raymon Lantier, *Les hommes de la pierre ancienne* (Paris: Payot, 1951), chap. 18.

[3] W. C. Boyd, *Genetics and the Races of Man* (Boston: Little, Brown, 1950).

on the lands he inhabited. Wherever he settled, he came to stay unless the climate changed too adversely or the spreading sea drove him back.

CLIMATIC CHANGES AND THEIR EFFECTS ON MAN

The age of man is also the Ice Age. Man may have witnessed its beginning; we perhaps are still living in an interglacial phase. His growth of learning and his expansion over the earth have taken place during a geologic period of extreme instability of climates and also of extreme simultaneous climatic contrast. His span has been cast within a period of high environmental tensions. Spreading icecaps caused the ocean to shrink back from the shallow continental margins, their waning to spread the seas over coastal plains. With lowered sea levels, rivers trenched their valley floors below coastal lowlands; as sea level rose, streams flooded and aggraded their valleys. Glacial and recent time have been governed by some sort of climatic pendulum, varying in amplitude of swing, but affecting land and sea in all latitudes, and life in most areas. The effects have been most felt in the Northern Hemisphere, with its large continental masses, wide plains, high mountain ranges, and broad plateaus. Millions of square miles of land were alternately buried under ice and exposed; here, also, the shallow seas upon the continental shelf spread and shrank most broadly.

This time of recurrent changes of atmosphere, land, and sea gave advantage to plastic, mobile, and prolific organisms, to plants and animals that could colonize newly available bodies of land, that had progeny some of which withstood the stresses of climatic change. The time was favorable for biologic evolution, for mutants suited to a changed environment, for hybrids formed by mingling, as on ecologic frontiers. To this period has been assigned the origin of many annual plant species dependent on heavy seed production for success.[4] Adaptive variations in human stocks, aided by sufficiently isolating episodes of Earth history, have also been inferred.[5]

The duration of the Ice Age and of its stages has not been determined. The old guess of a million years over all is still convenient. The four glacial and three interglacial stages may have general validity; there are doubts that they were strictly in phase in all continents. In North America the relations of the several continental icecaps to the phases of Rocky Mountain glaciation, and of the latter to the Pacific mountains, are only inferred, as is the tie-in of pluvial stages in our Southwest. That great lakes and permanent streams existed in many of the present dry lands of the world is certain, that these pluvial phases of intermediate latitudes correspond to glacial ones in high latitudes and altitudes is in considerable part certain, but only in a few cases has a pluvial state been securely tied to a contemporaneous glacial stage. The promising long-range correlation of Pleistocene events by eustatic marine terraces and their dependent alluvial terraces is as yet only well started. Except for northwestern Europe, the calendar of the later geologic past is still very uncertain. The student of further human time, anxious for an absolute chronology, is at the moment relying widely on the ingenious astronomical calendar of Milankovitch and Zeuner as an acceptable span for the Ice Age as a whole and for its divisions. It is not acceptable, however, to meteorology and climatology.[6] Slowly and bit by bit only

are we likely to see the pieces fall into their proper order; nothing is gained by assurance as to what is insecure.

The newer meteorology is interesting itself in the dynamics of climatic change.[7] Changes in the general circulation pattern have been inferred as conveying, in times of glacial advance, more and more frequent masses of moist, relatively warm air into high latitudes and thereby also increasing the amount of cloud cover. The importance now attached to condensation nuclei has directed attention again to the possible significance of volcanic dust. Synoptic climatological data are being examined for partial models in contemporary conditions as conducive to glaciation and deglaciation.[8] To the student of the human past, reserve is again indicated in making large climatic reconstructions. Such cautions I should suggest, with reserve also as to my competence to offer them, with regard to the following:

It is misleading to generalize glacial stages as cold and interglacial ones as warm. The developing phases of glaciation probably required relatively warm moist air, and decline may have been by the dominance of cold dry air over the ice margins. The times of climatic change may thus not coincide with the change from glacial advance to deglaciation. We may hazard the inference that developing glaciation is associated with low contrast of regional climates; regression of ice and beginning of an interglacial phase probably are connected (although not in each case) with accentuated contrast or "continentality" of climates. One interglacial did not repeat necessarily the features of another; nor must one glacial phase duplicate another. We need only note the difference in centers of continental glaciation, of direction of growth of ice lobes, of terminal moraine-building, of structure of till and of fluvio-

[4] Oakes Ames, *Economic Annuals and Human Cultures* (Cambridge, Mass.: Botanical Museum of Harvard University, 1939).

[5] As most recently by Carleton S. Coon, "Climate and Race," in Harlow Shapley (ed.), *Climatic Change* (Cambridge, Mass.: Harvard University Press, 1953), 13–34.

[6] See Shapley, *op. cit.;* H. C. Willett, "The General Circulation at the Last (Würm) Glacial Maximum," *Geografiska Annaler,* XXXII (1950), 179–87; G. C. Simpson, "World Climate during the Quaternary Period," *Quarterly Journal of the Royal Meteorological Society,* LX (1934), 425–78; *idem,* "Possible Causes of Change in Climate and Their Limitations," *Proceedings of the Linnean Society of London,* CLII (1940), 190–219.

[7] Shapley (*op. cit.*), and Carl Mason Mannerfelt, *et al.,* "Glaciers and Climate," *Geografiska Annaler,* Vol. XXXI (1949).

[8] John Leighly, "On Continentality and Glaciation," in Mannerfelt *et al., op. cit.,* pp. 133–46, ref. to pp. 133–34.

glacial components to see the individuality of climates of glacial stages. In North America, in contrast to Europe, there is very little indication of a periglacial cold zone of tundra and of permafrost in front of the continental icecaps. Questionable also is the loess thesis of dust as whipped up from bare ground and deposited in beds by wind, these surfaces somehow becoming vegetated by a cold steppe plant cover.

The events of the last deglaciation and of the "postglacial" are intelligible as yet only in part. A priori it is reasonable to consider that the contemporary pattern of climates had become more or less established before the last ice retreat began. Later, lesser local climatic oscillations were found but have been improperly extended and exaggerated, however, in archeological literature. In the pollen studies of bogs of northwestern Europe, the term "climatic optimum" was introduced innocently to note a poleward and mountainward extension of moderate proportions for certain plants not occurring at the same time over the entire area. Possibly this expansion of range means that there were sunnier summers and fall seasons, permitting the setting and maturing of seed for such plants somewhat beyond their prior and present range, that is, under more "continental" and less "maritime" weather conditions. This modest and expectable variation of a local climate in the high latitudes and at the changing sea borders of North Atlantic Europe has been construed by some students of prehistory into a sort of climatic golden age, existent at more or less the same time in distant parts of the world, without regard to dynamics or patterns of climates. We might well be spared such naïvely nominal climatic constructions as have been running riot through interpretations of prehistory and even of historic time.

The appearance or disappearance, increase or decrease, of particular plants and animals may not spell out obligatory climatic change, as has been so freely inferred. Plants differ greatly in rate of dis-

persal, in pioneering ability, in having routes available for their spread, and in other ways that may enter into an unstable ecologic association, as on the oft-shifted stage of Pleistocene and recent physiography. The intervention of man and animals has also occurred to disturb the balance. The appearance and fading of pines in an area, characteristic in many bog pollen columns, may tell nothing of climatic change: pines are notorious early colonizers, establishing themselves freely in mineral soils and open situations and yielding to other trees as shading and organic cover of ground increase. Deer thrive on browse; they increase wherever palatable twigs become abundant, in brush lands and with young tree growth; ecologic factors of disturbance other than climate may determine the food available to them and the numbers found in archeologic remains.

The penetration of man to the New World is involved in the question of past and present climates. The origin and growth of the dominant doctrine of a first peopling of the Western Hemisphere in postglacial time is beyond our present objective, but it was not based on valid knowledge of climatic history. The postglacial and present climatic pattern is one of extremes rarely reached or exceeded in the past of the earth. Passage by land within this time across Siberia, Alaska, and Canada demanded specialized advanced skills in survival under great and long cold comparable to those known to Eskimo and Athabascan, an excessive postulate for many of the primitive peoples of the New World. Relatively mild climates did prevail in high latitudes at times during the Pleistocene. At such times in both directions between Old and New World, massive migrations took place of animals incapable of living on tundras, animals that are attractive game for man. If man was then living in eastern Asia, nothing hindered him from migrating along with such non-boreal mammals. The question is of fundamental interest, because it asks whether man in the New World, within a very few thousand years, achieved independently a culture growth comparable and curiously parallel to that of the Old, which required a much greater span. There is thus also the inference that our more primitive aborigines passed the high latitudes during more genial climes rather than that they lost subsequently numerous useful skills.

FIRE

Speech, tools, and fire are the tripod of culture and have been so, we think, from the beginning. About the hearth, the home and workshop are centered. Space heating under shelter, as a rock overhang, made living possible in inclement climates; cooking made palatable many plant products; industrial innovators experimented with heat treatment of wood, bone, and minerals. About the fireplace, social life took form, and the exchange of ideas was fostered. The availability of fuel has been one of the main factors determining the location of clustered habitation.

Even to Paleolithic man, occupant of the earth for all but the last 1 or 2 per cent of human time, must be conceded gradual deformation of vegetation by fire. His fuel needs were supplied by dead wood, drifted or fallen, and also by the stripping of bark and bast that caused trees to die and become available as fuel supply. The setting or escape of fire about camp sites cleared away small and young growth, stimulated annual plants, aided in collecting, and became elaborated in time into the fire drive, a formally organized procedure among the cultures of the Upper Paleolithic *grande chasse* and of their New World counterpart.

Inferentially, modern primitive peoples illustrate the ancient practices in all parts of the world. Burning, as a practice facilitating collecting and hunting, by insensible stages became a device to improve the yield of desired animals and plants. Deliberate management of their range by burning to increase food supply is apparent among hunting and collecting peoples, in widely separated areas, but has had little study. Mature woody growth provides less food

for man and ground animals than do fire-disturbed sites, with protein-rich young growth and stimulated seed production, accessible at ground levels. Game yields are usually greatest where the vegetation is kept in an immediate state of ecologic succession. With agricultural and pastoral peoples, burning in preparation for planting and for the increase of pasture has been nearly universal until lately.

The gradually cumulative modifications of vegetation may become large as to selection of kind and as to aspect of the plant cover. Pyrophytes include woody monocotyledons, such as palms, which do not depend on a vulnerable cambium tissue, trees insulated by thick corky bark, trees and shrubs able to reproduce by sprouting, and plants with thick, hard-shelled seeds aided in germination by heat. Loss of organic matter on and in the soil may shift advantage to forms that germinate well in mineral soils, as the numerous conifers. Precocity is advantageous. The assemblages consequent upon fires are usually characterized by a reduced number of species, even by the dominance of few and single species. Recurrent burning has offered minor elements in a natural flora, originally mainly confined to accidentally disturbed and exposed situations, such as windfalls and eroding slopes, the chance to spread and multiply. In most cases the shift is from mesophytic to less exacting, more xeric, forms, to those that do not require ample soil moisture and can tolerate at all times full exposure to sun. In the long run the scales are tipped against the great, slowly maturing plants—the trees (a park land of mature trees may be the last stand of what was a complete woodland). Our eastern woodlands, at the time of white settlement, seem largely to have been in process of change to park lands. Early accounts stress the open stands of trees, as indicated by the comment that one could drive a coach from seaboard to the Mississippi River over almost any favoring terrain. The "forest primeval" is exceptional. In the end the success in a land occupied by man of whatever cultural level goes to the annuals and short-lived perennials, able to seed heavily or to reproduce by rhizome and tuber. This grossly drawn sketch may introduce the matter of processes resulting in what is called ecologically a secondary fire association, or subclimax, if it has historical persistence.

The climatic origin of grasslands rests on a poorly founded hypothesis. In the first place, the individual great grasslands extend over long climatic gradients from wet to dry and grade on their driest margins into brush and scrub. Woody growth occurs in them where there are breaks in the general surface, as in the Cross Timbers of our Southwest. Woody plants establish themselves freely in grasslands if fire protection is given: the prairies and steppes are suited to the growth of the trees and shrubs native to adjacent lands but may lack them. An individual grassland may extend across varied parent-materials. Their most common quality is that they are upland plains, having periods of dry weather long enough to dry out the surface of the ground, which accumulate a sufficient amount of burnable matter to feed and spread a fire. Their position and limits are determined by relief; nor do they extend into arid lands or those having a continuously wet ground surface. Fires may sweep indefinitely across a surface of low relief but are checked shortly at barriers of broken terrain, the checking being more abrupt if the barrier is sunk below the general surface. The inference is that origin and preservation of grasslands are due, in the main, to burning and that they are in fact great and, in some cases, ancient cultural features.

In other instances simplified woodlands, such as the pine woods of our Southeast, *palmares* in tropical savannas, are pyrophytic deformations; there are numerous vegetational alternatives other than the formation of grassland by recurrent burning. Wherever primitive man has had the opportunity to turn fire loose on a land, he seems to have done so, from time immemorial; it is only civilized societies that have undertaken to stop fires.

In areas controlled by customary burning, a near-ecologic equilibrium may have been attained, a biotic recombination maintained by similarly repeated human intervention. This is not destructive exploitation. The surface of the ground remains protected by growing cover, the absorption of rain and snow is undiminished, and loss of moisture from ground to atmosphere possibly is reduced. Microclimatic differences between woodland and grassland are established as effect if not as cause, and some are implicit in the Shelter Belt Project.

Our modern civilization demands fire control for the protection of its property. American forestry was begun as a remedy for the devastation by careless lumbering at a time when dreadful holocausts almost automatically followed logging, as in the Great Lakes states. Foresters have made a first principle of fire suppression. Complete protection, however, accumulates tinder year by year; the longer the accumulation, the greater is the fire hazard and the more severe the fire when it results. Stockmen are vociferous about the loss of grazing areas to brush under such protection of the public lands. Here and there, carefully controlled light burning is beginning to find acceptance in range and forest management. It is being applied to long-leaf pine reproduction in southeastern states and to some extent for grazing in western range management. In effect, the question is now being raised whether well-regulated fires may not have an ecologic role beneficent to modern man, as they did in older days.

Peasant and Pastoral Ways

The next revolutionary intervention of man in the natural order came as he selected certain plants and animals to be taken under his care, to be reproduced, and to be bred into domesticated forms increasingly dependent on him for survival. Their adaptation to serve human wants runs counter, as a rule, to the processes of natural selection. New lines and processes of organic evolution were entrained, widening the gap between wild and domestic forms. The natural land became deformed, as to biota, surface, and soil, into unstable cultural landscapes.

Conventionally, agricultural origins are placed at the beginning of Neolithic time, but it is obvious that the earliest archeologic record of the Neolithic presents a picture of an accomplished domestication of plants and animals, of peasant and pastoral life resembling basic conditions that may still be met in some parts of the Near East.

Three premises as to the origin of agriculture seem to me to be necessary: (1) That this new mode of life was sedentary and that it arose out of an earlier sedentary society. Under most conditions, and especially among primitive agriculturists, the planted land must be watched over continuously against plant predators. (2) That planting and domestication did not start from hunger but from surplus and leisure. Famine-haunted folk lack the opportunity and incentive for the slow and continuing selection of domesticated forms. Village communities in comfortable circumstances are indicated for such progressive steps. (3) Primitive agriculture is located in woodlands. Even the pioneer American farmer hardly invaded the grasslands until the second quarter of the past century. His fields were clearings won by deadening, usually by girdling, the trees. The larger the trees, the easier the task; brush required grubbing and cutting; sod stopped his advance until he had plows capable of ripping through the matted grass roots. The forest litter he cleaned up by occasional burning; the dead trunks hardly interfered with his planting. The American pioneer learned and followed Indian practices. It is curious that scholars, because they carried into their thinking the tidy fields of the European plowman and the felling of trees by ax, have so often thought that forests repelled agriculture and that open lands invited it.

The oldest form of tillage is by digging, often but usually improperly called "hoe culture." This was the only mode known in the New World, in Negro Africa, and in the Pacific islands. It gave rise, at an advanced level, to the gardens and horticulture of Monsoon Asia and perhaps of the Mediterranean. Its modern tools are spade, fork, and hoe, all derived from ancient forms. In tropical America this form of tillage is known as the *conuco,* in Mexico as the milpa, in the latter case a planting of seeds of maize, squash, beans, and perhaps other annuals. The *conuco* is stocked mainly by root and stem cuttings, a perennial garden plot. Recently, the revival of the Old Norse term *swithe,* or *swidden,* has been proposed.[9]

Such a plot begins by deadening tree growth, followed toward the end of a dry period by burning, the ashes serving as quick fertilizer. The cleared space then is well stocked with a diverse assemblage of useful plants, grown as tiers of vegetation if moisture and fertility are adequate. In the maize-beans-squash complex the squash vines spread over the ground, the cornstalks grow tall, and the beans climb up the cornstalks. Thus the ground is well protected by plant cover, with good interception of the falling rain. In each *conuco* a high diversity of plants may be cared for, ranging from low herbs to shrubs, such as cotton and manioc, to trees entangled with cultivated climbers. The seeming disorder is actually a very full use of light and moisture, an admirable ecologic substitution by man, perhaps equivalent to the natural cover also in the protection given to the surface of the ground. In the tropical *conuco* an irregular patch is dug into at convenient spots and at almost any time to set out or collect different plants, the planted surface at no time being wholly dug over. Digging roots and replanting may be going on at the same time. Our notions

[9] Karl Gustav Izikowitz, "Lamet: Hill Peasants in French Indochina," *Etnologiska Studier,* XVII (1951), 7; Harold C. Conklin, "An Ethnoecological Approach to Shifting Cultivation," *Transactions of the New York Academy of Sciences,* Series 2, XVII (1952), 133–42 [reprinted in this volume; see pp. 457–464].

of a harvest season when the whole crop is taken off the field are inapplicable. In the *conucos* something may be gathered on almost any day through the year. The same plant may yield pot and salad greens, pollen-rich flowers, immature fruit, and ripened fruit; garden and field are one, and numerous domestic uses may be served by each plant. Such multiple population of the tilled space makes possible the highest yields per unit of surface, to which may be added the comments that this system has developed plants of highest productivity, such as bananas, yams, and manioc, and that food production is by no means the only utility of many such plants.

The planting systems really do not deserve the invidious terms given them, such as "slash and burn" or "shifting agriculture." The abandonment of the planting after a time to the resprouting and reseeding wild woody growth is a form of rotation by which the soil is replenished by nutriments carried up from deep-rooted trees and shrubs, to be spread over the ground as litter. Such use of the land is freed from the limitations imposed on the plowed field by terrain. That it may give good yields on steep and broken slopes is not an argument against the method, which gives much better protection against soil erosion than does any plowing. It is also in these cultures that we find that systems of terracing of slopes have been established.

Some of the faults charged against the system derive from the late impact from our own culture, such as providing axes and machetes by which sprouts and brush may be kept whacked out instead of letting the land rest under regrowth, the replacement of subsistence crops by money crops, the world-wide spurt in population, and the demand for manufactured goods which is designated as rising standard of living. Nor do I claim that under this primitive planting man could go on forever growing his necessities without depleting the soil; but rather that, in its basic procedure and crop assemblages, this system has been most conservative of fertility at high levels of yield; that, being protective and intensive, we might consider it as being fully suited to the physical and cultural conditions of the areas where it exists. Our Western know-how is directed to land use over a short run of years and is not the wisdom of the primitive peasant rooted to his ancestral lands.

Our attitudes toward farming stem from the other ancient trunk whence spring the sowers, reapers, and mowers; the plowmen, dairymen, shepherds, and herdsmen. This is the complex already well represented in the earliest Neolithic sites of the Near East. The interest of this culture is directed especially toward seed production of annuals, cereal grasses in particular. The seedbed is carefully prepared beforehand to minimize weed growth and provide a light cover of well-worked soil in which the small seeds germinate. An evenly worked and smooth surface contrasts with the hit-or-miss piling of earth mounds, "hills" in the American farm vernacular, characteristic of *conuco* and milpa. Instead of a diversity of plants, the prepared ground receives the seed of one kind. (Western India is a significant exception.) The crop is not further cultivated and stands to maturity, when it is reaped at one time. After the harvest the field may lie fallow until the next season. The tillage implement is the plow, in second place, the harrow, both used to get the field ready for sowing. Seeding traditionally is by broadcasting, harvesting by cutting blades.

Herd animals, meat cattle, sheep, goats, horses, asses, camels, are either original or very early in this system. The keeping of grazing and browsing animals is basic. All of them are milked or have been so in the past. In my estimation milking is an original practice and quality of their domestication and continued to be in many cases their first economic utility; meat and hides, the product of surplus animals only.

The over-all picture is in great contrast to that of the planting cultures: regular, elongated fields minimize turning the animals that pull the plow; fields are cultivated in the off season, in part to keep them free of volunteer growth; fields are fallowed but not abandoned, the harvest season is crowded into the end of the annual growth period; thereafter, stock is pastured on stubble and fallow; land unsuited or not needed for the plow is used as range on which the stock grazes and browses under watch of herdboys or herdsmen.

This complex spread from its Near Eastern cradle mainly in three directions, changing its character under changed environments and by increase of population.

1. Spreading into the steppes of Eurasia, the culture lost its tillage and became completely pastoral, with true nomadism. This is controversial, but the evidence seems to me to show that all domestication of the herd animals (except for reindeer) was effected by sedentary agriculturists living between India and the Mediterranean and also that the great, single, continuous area in which milking was practiced includes all the nomadic peoples, mainly as a fringe about the milking seed-farmers. It has also been pointed out that nomadic cultures depend on agricultural peoples for some of their needs and, thus lacking a self-contained economy, can hardly have originated independently.

2. The drift of the Celtic, Germanic, and Slavic peoples westward (out of southwestern and western Asia?) through the northern European plain appears to have brought them to their historic seats predominantly as cattle- and horse-raisers. Their movement was into lands of cooler and shorter summers and of higher humidity, in which wheat and barley did poorly. An acceptable thesis is that, in southwestern Asia, rye and probably oats were weed grasses growing in fields of barley and wheat. They were harvested together and not separated by winnowing. In the westward movement of seed farmers across Europe, the weed grains did better and the noble grain less well. The cooler and wetter the summers, the less wheat and barley did the sower reap and the more of rye and oat seeds, which grad-

ually became domesticated by succeeding where the originally planted kinds failed.

Northwestern and Central Europe appear to be the home of our principal hay and pasture grasses and clovers. As the stock-raising colonists deadened and burned over tracts of woodland, native grasses and clovers spontaneously took possession of the openings. These were held and enlarged by repetition of burning and cutting. Meadow and pasture, from the agricultural beginnings, were more important here than plowland. Even the latter, by pasturing the rye fields and the feeding of oat straw and grain, were part of animal husbandry. Here, as nowhere else, did the common farmer concern himself with producing feed for his stock. He was first a husbandman; he cut hay to store for winter feed and cured it at considerable trouble; he stabled his animals over the inclement season, or stall-fed them through the year; the dung-hill provided dressing for field and meadow. House, barn, and stable were fused into one structure. The prosperity of farmstead and village was measured by its livestock rather than by arable land.

The resultant pattern of land use, which carries through from the earliest times, as recovered by archeology in Denmark and northern Germany, was highly conservative of soil fertility. The animal husbandry maintained so effective a ground cover that northern Europe has known very little soil erosion. Animal manure and compost provided adequate return of fertility to the soil. Man pretty well established a closed ecologic cycle. It was probably here that man first undertook to till the heavy soils. Clayey soils, rich in plant food but deficient in drainage, are widespread in the lowlands, partly because of climatic conditions, partly a legacy of the Ice Age. The modern plow with share, moldboard, and colter had either its origin or a major development here for turning real furrows to secure better aeration and drainage. Beneficial in northwestern and Central Europe, it was later to become an instrument of serious loss elsewhere.

3. The spread of sowing and herding cultures westward along both sides of the Mediterranean required no major climatic readjustment. Wheat and barley continued to be the staple grains; sheep and goats were of greater economic importance than cattle and horses. Qualities of the environment that characterized the Near East were accentuated to the west: valleys lie imbedded in mountainous terrain, the uplands are underlain by and developed out of limestone, and, to the south of the Mediterranean, aridity becomes prevalent. The hazard of drought lay ever upon the Near Eastern homeland and on the colonial regions to the west and south. No break between farmer and herdsman is discernible at any time; as the village Arab of today is related to the Bedouin, the environmental specialization may have been present from the beginning: flocks on the mountains and dry lands, fields where moisture sufficed and soil was adequate.

That the lands about the Mediterranean have become worn and frayed by the usage to which they have been subjected has long been recognized, though not much is known as to when and how. The eastern and southern Mediterranean uplands especially are largely of limestone, fertile but, by their nature, without deep original mantle of soil or showing the usual gradation of subsoil into bedrock and thus are very vulnerable to erosion. The less suited the land was or became to plow cultivation, the greater the shift to pastoral economy. Thus a downslope migration of tillage characterized, in time, the retreating limits of the fields, and more and more land became range for goats, sheep, and asses. Repeatedly prolonged droughts must have speeded the downslope shift, hillside fields suffering most, and with failing vegetation cover becoming more subject to washing when rains came.

Thus we come again to the question of climatic change as against attrition of surface and increased xerophytism of vegetation by human disturbance and, in particular, to what is called the "desertification"

of North Africa and the expansion of the Sahara. A case for directional change in the pattern of atmospheric circulation has been inferred from archeology and faunal changes. I am doubtful that it is a good case within the time of agricultural and pastoral occupation. Another view is that the progressive reduction of plant cover by man has affected soil and ground-surface climate unfavorably. Largely, and possibly wholly, the deterioration of the borders of the dry lands may have been caused by adverse, cumulative effects of man's activities. From archeologic work we need much more information as to whether human occupation has been failing in such areas over a long time, or whether it has happened at defined intervals, and also whether, if such intervals are noted, they may have a cultural rather than an environmental (climatic) basis.

No protective herbaceous flora became established around the shores of the Mediterranean on pastures and meadows as was the case in the north. Flocks and herds grazed during the short season of soft, new grass but most of the year browsed on woody growth. The more palatable feed was eaten first and increasingly eliminated; goats and asses got along on range that had dropped below the support levels required by more exacting livestock. As is presently true in the western United States, each prolonged drought must have left the range depleted, its carrying capacity reduced, and recovery of cover less likely. Natural balance between plants and animals is rarely reestablished under such exploitation, since man will try to save his herd rather than their range. A large and long deterioration of the range may therefore fully account for the poor and xerophytic flora and fauna without postulating progressive climatic desiccation, for the kinds of life that survive under overuse of the land are the most undemanding inhabitants.

Comparative studies of North Africa and of the American Southwest and northern Mexico are needed to throw light on the supposed "desiccation" of the Old World.

We know the dates of introduction of cattle and sheep to the American ranges and can determine rate and kind of change of vegetation and surface. The present desolate shifting-sand area that lies between the Hopi villages and the Colorado River was such good pasture land late in the eighteenth century that Father Escalante, returning from his canyon exploration, rested his travel-worn animals there to regain flesh. The effects of Navaho sheep-herding in little more than a century and mainly in the last sixty years are well documented. Lower California and Sonora are climatic homologues of the western Sahara. Against the desolation of the latter, the lands about the Gulf of California are a riot of bloom in spring and green through summer. Their diversity, in kind and form, of plant and of animal life is high, and the numbers are large. When Leo Waibel came from his African studies to Sonora and Arizona, he remarked: "But your deserts are not plant deserts." Nor do we have hammadas or *ergs,* though geologic and meteorologic conditions may be similar. The principal difference may be that we have had no millennial, or even centuries-long, overstocking of our arid, semiarid, and subhumid lands. The scant life and even the rock and sand surfaces of the Old World deserts may record long attrition by man in climatic tension zones.

IMPACT OF CIVILIZATION IN ANTIQUITY AND THE MIDDLE AGES

Have the elder civilizations fallen because their lands deteriorated? Ellsworth Huntington read adverse climatic change into each such failure; at the other extreme, political loss of competence has been asserted as sufficient. Intimate knowledge of historical sources, archeologic sites, biogeography and ecology, and the processes of geomorphology must be fused in patient field studies, so that we may read the changes in habitability through human time for the lands in which civilization first took form.

The rise of civilizations has been accomplished and sustained by the development of powerful and elaborately organized states with a drive to territorial expansion, by commerce in bulk and to distant parts, by monetary economy, and by the growth of cities. Capital cities, port cities by sea and river, and garrison towns drew to themselves population and products from near and far. The ways of the country became subordinated to the demands of the cities, the *citizen* distinct from the *miserabilis plebs.* The containment of community by locally available resources gave way to the introduction of goods, especially foodstuffs, regulated by purchasing, distributing, or taxing power.

Thereby removal of resource from place of origin to place of demand tended to set up growing disturbance of whatever ecologic equilibrium had been maintained by the older rural communities sustained directly within their metes. The economic history of antiquity shows repeated shifts in the areas of supply of raw materials that are not explained by political events but raise unanswered questions as to decline of fertility, destruction of plant cover, and incidence of soil erosion. What, for instance, happened to Arabia Felix, Numidia, Mauretania, to the interior Lusitania that has become the frayed Spanish Extremadura of today? When and at whose hands did the forests disappear that furnished ship and house timbers, wood for burning lime, the charcoal for smelting ores, and urban fuel needs? Are political disasters sufficient to account for the failure of the civilizations that depended on irrigation and drainage engineering? How much of the wide deterioration of Mediterranean and Near Eastern lands came during or after the time of strong political and commercial organization? For ancient and medieval history our knowledge as to what happened to the land remains too largely blank, except for the central and northern European periphery. The written documents, the testimony of the archeologic sites, have not often been interpreted by observation of the physical condition of the locality as it is and comparison with what it was.

The aspect of the Mediterranean landscapes was greatly changed by classical civilization through the introduction of plants out of the East. Victor Hehn first described Italy as wearing a dress of an alien vegetation, and, though he carried the theme of plant introduction out of the East too far, his study[10] of the Mediterranean lands through antiquity is not only memorable but retains much validity. The westward dispersal of vine, olive, fig, the stone fruits, bread wheat, rice, and many ornamentals and some shade trees was due in part or in whole to the spread of Greco-Roman civilization, to which the Arabs added sugar cane, date palm, cotton, some of the citrus fruits, and other items.

EUROPEAN OVERSEAS COLONIZATION

When European nations ventured forth across the Atlantic, it was to trade or raid, the distinction often determined by the opportunity. In Africa and Asia the European posts and factories pretty well continued in this tradition through the eighteenth century. In the New World the same initial activities soon turned into permanent settlement of Old World forms and stocks. Columbus, searching only for a trade route, started the first overseas empire. Spain stumbled into colonization, and the other nations acquired stakes they hoped might equal the Spanish territorial claim. The Casa de Contratación, or House of Trade, at Seville, the main Atlantic port, became the Spanish colonial office. The conquistadores came not to settle but to make their fortunes and return home, and much the same was true for the earlier adventurers from other nations. Soldiers and adventurers rather than peasants and artisans made up the first arrivals, and few brought

[10] Victor Hehn, *The Wanderings of Plants and Animals from their First Home* (London: Swan Sonnenschein, 1888) [first published as *Kulturpflanzen und Hausthiere in ihrem Übergang nach Griechenland und Italien sowie in das übrige Europa* (7th ed.; Berlin: Gebrüder Bornträger, 1902)].

their women. Only in New England did settlement begin with a representative assortment of people, and only here were the new communities transplanted from the homeland without great alteration.

The first colony, Santo Domingo, set in large measure the pattern of colonization. It began with trade, including ornaments of gold. The quest for gold brought forced labor and the dying-off of the natives, and this, in turn, slave-hunting and importation of black slaves. Decline of natives brought food shortages and wide abandonment of conucos. Cattle and hogs were pastured on the lately tilled surfaces; and Spaniards, lacking labor to do gold-placering, became stock ranchers. Some turned to cutting dyewoods. Of the numerous European plants introduced to supply accustomed wants, a few, sugar cane, cassia, and ginger, proved moderately profitable for export, and some of the hesitant beginnings became the first tropical plantations. One hope of fortune failing, another was tried; the stumbling into empire was under way by men who had scarcely any vision of founding a new homeland.

What then happened to the lands of the New World in the three colonial centuries? In the first place, the aboriginal populations in contact with Europeans nearly everywhere declined greatly or were extinguished. Especially in the tropical lowlands, with the most notable exception of Yucatán, the natives faded away, and in many cases the land was quickly repossessed by forest growth. The once heavily populous lands of eastern Panama and northwestern Colombia, much of the lowland country of Mexico, both on the Pacific and Gulf sides, became emptied in a very few years, was retaken by jungle and forest, and in considerable part remains such to the present. The highlands of Mexico, of Central America, and of the Andean lands declined in population greatly through the sixteenth and perhaps well through the seventeenth century, with slow, gradual recovery in the eighteenth. The total population, white and other, of the areas under

European control was, I think, less at the
end of the eighteenth century than at the
time of discovery. Only in British and
French West Indian islands were dense
rural populations built up.

It is hardly an exaggeration to say that
the early Europeans supported themselves
on Indian fields. An attractive place to live
for a European would ordinarily have been
such for an Indian. In the Spanish colonies,
unlike the English and French, the earlier
grants were not of land titles but of Indian
communities to serve colonist and crown.
In crops and their tillage the colonists of
all nations largely used the Indian ways,
with the diversion of part of the field crop
to animal feed. Only in the Northeast, most
of all in our Middle Colonies, were native
and European crops fused into a conservative plow-and-animal husbandry, with field
rotation, manuring, and marl dressing. The
Middle Colonies of the eighteenth century
appear to have compared favorably with
the best farming practices of Western Europe.

Sugar cane, first and foremost of the
tropical plantations, as a closely planted
giant grass, gave satisfactory protection to
the surface of the land. The removal of
cane from the land did reduce fertility unless the waste was properly returned to the
canefields. The most conservative practices
known are from the British islands, where
cane waste was fed to cattle kept in pens,
and manuring was customary and heavy.
Bagasse was of little value as fuel in this
period because of the light crushing rollers
used for extracting cane juice; thus the
colonial sugar mills were heavy wood users,
especially for boiling sugar. The exhaustion
of wood supply became a serious problem
in the island of Haiti within the sixteenth
century.

Other plantation crops—tobacco, indigo,
cotton, and coffee—held more serious erosion hazards, partly because they were
planted in rows and given clean cultivation,
partly because they made use of steeper
slopes and thinner soils. The worst offender
was tobacco, grown on land that was kept

bared to the rains and nourished by the
wood ashes of burned clearings. Its cultivation met with greatest success in our upper
South, resulted in rapidly shifting clearings
because of soil depletion, and caused the
first serious soil erosion in our country.
Virginia, Maryland, and North Carolina
show to the present the damages of tobacco
culture of colonial and early post-colonial
times. Southern Ohio and eastern Missouri
repeated the story before the middle of the
nineteenth century.

As had happened in Haiti, sharp decline
of native populations brought elsewhere
abandonment of cleared and tilled land and
thereby opportunity to the stockman. The
plants that pioneer in former fields which
are left untilled for reasons other than because of decline of fertility include forms,
especially annuals, of high palatability,
grasses, amaranths, chenopods, and legumes. Such is the main explanation for the
quick appearance of stock ranches, of
ganado mayor and *menor,* in the former
Indian agricultural lands all over Spanish
America. Cattle, horses, and hogs thrived
in tropical lowland as well as in highland
areas. Sheep-raising flourished most in early
years in the highlands of New Spain and
Peru, where Indian population had shrunk.
Spanish stock, trespassing upon Indian
plantings, both in lowland and in highland, afflicted the natives and depressed
their chances of recovery.[11] In the wide
savannas stockmen took over the native
habits of burning.

The Spaniards passed in a few years from
the trading and looting of metals to successful prospecting, at which they became
so adept that it is still said that the good
mines of today are the *antiguas* of colonial
working. When mines were abandoned, it
was less often due to the working-out of the
ore bodies than to inability to cope with
water in shafts and to the exhaustion of the
necessary fuel and timber. A good illustration has been worked out for Parral in

[11] Lesley B. Simpson, *Exploitation of Land in
Central Mexico in the Sixteenth Century* ("Ibero-
Americana," No. XXXVI [1952]).

Mexico.[12] Zacatecas, today in the midst of a high sparse grassland, was in colonial times a woodland of oak and pine and, at lower levels, of mesquite. About Andean mines the scant wood was soon exhausted, necessitating recourse to cutting mats of *tola* heath and even the clumps of coarse *ichu* (stipa) grass. Quite commonly the old mining *reales* of North and South America are surrounded by a broad zone of reduced and impoverished vegetation. The effects were increased by the concentration of pack and work animals in the mines, with resultant overpasturing. Similar attrition took place about towns and cities, through timber-cutting, charcoal- and lime-burning, and overpasturing. The first viceroy of New Spain warned his successor in 1546 of the depletion of wood about the city of Mexico.

I have used mainly examples from Spanish America for the colonial times, partly because I am most familiar with this record. However, attrition was more sensible here because of mines and urban concentrations and because, for cultural and climatic reasons, the vegetation cover was less.

Last Frontiers of Settlement

The surges of migration of the nineteenth century are family history for many of us. Never before did, and never again may, the white man expand his settlements as in that brief span that began in the later eighteenth century and ended with the first World War. The prelude was in the eighteenth century, not only as a result of the industrial revolution as begun in England, but also in a less heralded agricultural revolution over Western and Central Europe. The spread of potato-growing, the development of beets and turnips as field crops, rotation of fields with clover, innovations in tillage, improved livestock breeds—all joined to raise agricultural production to new levels in western Europe. The new agriculture was brought to our Middle Colonies by a mas-

sive immigration of capable European farmers and here further transformed by adding maize to the small grains–clover rotation. Thus was built on both sides of the North Atlantic a balanced animal husbandry of increased yield of human and animal foods. Urban and rural growth alike went into vigorous upswing around the turn of the eighteenth century. The youth of the countryside poured into the rising industrial cities but also emigrated, especially from Central Europe into Pennsylvania, into Hungarian and Moldavian lands repossessed from the Turks and into South Russia gained from the Tartars. The last *Völkerwanderung* was under way and soon edging onto the grasslands.

The year 1800 brought a new cotton to the world market, previously an obscure annual variant known to us as Mexican Upland cotton, still uncertainly understood as to how it got into our South. Cleaned by the new gin, its profitable production rocketed. The rapidly advancing frontier of cotton-planting was moved westward from Georgia to Texas within the first half of the century. This movement was a more southerly and even greater parallel to the earlier westward drive of the tobacco frontier. Both swept away the woodlands and the Indians, including the farming tribes. The new cotton, like tobacco, a clean cultivated row crop and a cash crop, bared the fields to surface wash, especially in winter. The southern upland soils gradually lost their organic horizons, color, and protection; gullies began to be noted even before the Civil War. Guano and Chilean nitrate and soon southern rock phosphate were applied increasingly to the wasting soils. Eugene Hilgard told the history of cotton in our South tersely and well in the United States Census of 1880. As I write, across from my window stands the building bearing his name and the inscription: TO RESCUE FOR HUMAN SOCIETY THE NATIVE VALUES OF RURAL LIFE. It was in wasting cotton fields that Hilgard learned soil science and thought about a rural society that had become hitched wholly to world commerce.

[12] Robert C. West, *The Mining Community in Northern New Spain: The Parral Mining District* ("Ibero-Americana," No. XXX [1949]).

Meantime the mill towns of England, the Continent, and New England grew lustily; with them, machine industries, transport facilities, and the overseas shipment of food.

The next great American frontier may be conveniently and reasonably dated by the opening of the Erie Canal in 1825, providing the cities with grain and meat on both sides of the North Atlantic, first by canal and river, soon followed by the railroad. The earlier frontiers had been pushed from the Atlantic Seaboard to and beyond the Mississippi by the cultivation of tropical plants in extratropical lands, were dominantly monocultural, preferred woodlands, and relied mainly on hand labor. For them the term "plantation culture" was not inapt. The last thrust, from the Mohawk Valley to the Mississippi, was West European as to agricultural system, rural values, settlers, and largely as to crops.

By the time of the Civil War, the first great phase of the northern westward movement had crossed the Missouri River into Kansas and Nebraska. New England spilled over by way of the Great Lakes, especially along the northern fringe of prairies against the North Woods. New York and Baltimore were gateways for the masses of continental emigrants hurrying to seek new homes beyond the Alleghenies. The migrant streams mingled as they overspread the Mississippi Valley, land of promise unequaled in the history of our kind. These settlers were fit to the task: they were good husbandmen and artisans. They came to put down their roots, and the gracious country towns, farmsteads, and rural churches still bear witness to the homemaking way of life they brought and kept. At last they had land of their own, and it was good. They took care of their land, and it did well by them; surplus rather than substance of the soil provided the foodstuffs that moved to eastern markets. Steel plows that cut through the sod, east-west railroads, and cheap lumber from the white-pine forests of the Great Lakes unlocked the fertility of the prairies;

the first great plowing-up of the grasslands was under way.

Many prairie counties reached their maximum population in less than a generation, many of them before the beginning of the Civil War. The surplus, another youthful generation, moved on farther west or sought fortune in the growing cities. Thus, toward the end of the century the Trans-Missouri grassy plains had been plowed up to and into the lands of drought hazard. Here the Corn Belt husbandry broke down, especially because of the great drought of the early nineties, and the Wheat Belt took form, a monocultural and unbalanced derivative. I well remember parties of landlookers going out from my native Missouri county, first to central Kansas and Nebraska, then to the Red River Valley, and finally even to the Panhandle of Texas and the prairies of Manitoba. The local newspapers "back home" still carry news today from these daughter-colonies, and still those who long ago moved west are returned "home" at the last to lie in native soil.

The development of the Middle West did exact its price of natural resources. The white-pine stands of the Great Lakes were destroyed to build the farms and towns of the Corn Belt; the logged-over lands suffered dreadful burning. As husbandry gave way westward to wheat-growing, the land was looked on less as homestead and more as speculation, to be cropped heavily and continuously for grain, without benefit of rotation and manuring, and to be sold at an advantageous price, perhaps to reinvest in new and undepleted land.

The history of the extratropical grasslands elsewhere in the world is much like our own and differs little in period and pace. Southern Russia, the Pampas, Australia, and South Africa repeat largely the history of the American West. The industrial revolution was made possible by the plowing-up of the great non-tropical grasslands of the world. So also was the intensification of agriculture in western Europe, benefiting from the importation of cheap overseas feedstuffs, grains, their by-products of milling (note the term "shipstuff"), oil-seed meals. Food and feed were cheap in and about the centers of industry, partly because the fertility of the new lands of the world was exported to them without reckoning the maintenance of resource.

At the turn of the century serious concern developed about the adequacy of resources for industrial civilization. The conservation movement was born. It originated in the United States, where the depletion of lately virgin lands gave warning that we were drawing recklessly on a diminishing natural capital. It is to be remembered that this awareness came, not to men living in the midst of the industrial and commercial centers of the older country-sides, but to foresters who witnessed devastation about the Great Lakes, to geologists who had worked in the iron and copper ranges of the Great Lakes and prospected the West in pioneer days, to naturalists who lived through the winning of the West.

THE EVER DYNAMIC ECONOMY

As a native of the nineteenth century, I have been an amazed and bewildered witness of the change of tempo that started with the first World War, was given an additional whirl on the second, and still continues to accelerate. The worry of the earlier part of the century was that we might not use our natural resources thriftily; it has given way to easy confidence in the capacities of technologic advance without limit. The natural scientists were and still may be conservation-minded; the physical scientists and engineers today are often of the lineage of Daedalus, inventing ever more daring reorganizations of matter and, in consequence, whether they desire it or not, of social institutions. Social science eyes the attainments of physical science enviously and hopes for similar competence and authority in reordering the world. Progress is the common watchword of our age, its motor-innovating techniques,

its objective the ever expanding "dynamic economy," with ever increasing input of energy. Capacity to produce and capacity to consume are the twin spirals of the new age which is to have no end, if war can be eliminated. The measure of progress is "standard of living," a term that the English language has contributed to the vernaculars of the world. An American industrialist says, roundly, that our principal problem now is to accelerate obsolescence, which remark was anticipated at the end of the past century by Eduard Hahn[13] when he thought that industrialization depended on the production of junk.

Need we ask ourselves whether there still is the problem of limited resources, of an ecologic balance that we disturb or disregard at the peril of the future? Was Wordsworth of the early industrial age farsighted when he said that "getting and spending we lay waste our powers"? Are our newly found powers to transform the world, so successful in the short run of the last years, proper and wise beyond the tenure of those now living? To what end are we committing the world to increasing momentum of change?

The steeply increasing production of late years is due only in part to better recovery, more efficient use of energy, and substitution of abundant for scarce materials. Mainly we have been learning how to deplete more rapidly the resources known to be accessible to us. Must we not admit that very much of what we call production is extraction?

Even the so-called "renewable resources" are not being renewed. Despite better utilization and substitution, timber growth is falling farther behind use and loss, inferior stands and kinds are being exploited, and woodland deterioration is spreading. Much of the world is in a state of wood famine, without known means of remedy or substitution.

[13] Eduard Hahn, *Wirtschaft der Welt am Ausgang des neunzehnten Jahrhunderts* (Heidelberg: Winter, 1900).

Commercial agriculture requires ample working capital and depends in high degree on mechanization and fertilization. A late estimate assigns a fourth of the net income of our farms to the purchase of durable farm equipment. The more farming becomes industry and business, the less remains of the older husbandry in which man lived in balance with his land. We speak with satisfaction of releasing rural population from farm to urban living and count the savings of man-hours in units of farm product and of acres. In some areas the farmer is becoming a town dweller, moving his equipment to the land for brief periods of planting, cultivating, and harvest. Farm garden, orchard, stable, barn, barnyards, and woodlots are disappearing in many parts, the farm families as dependent as their city cousins on grocer, butcher, baker, milkman, and fuel services. Where the farm is in fact capital in land and improvements, requiring bookkeeping on current assets and liabilities, the agriculturist becomes an operator of an outdoor factory of specialized products and is concerned with maximizing the profits of the current year and the next. Increasing need of working capital requires increased monetary returns; this is perhaps all we mean by "intensive" or "scientific" farming, which is in greater and greater degree extractive.

The current agricultural surpluses are not proof that food production has ceased to be a problem or will cease to be the major problem of the world. Our output has been secured at unconsidered costs and risks by the objective of immediate profit, which has replaced the older attitudes of living with the land. The change got under way especially as motors replaced draft animals. Land formerly used for oats and other feed crops became available to grow more corn, soybeans, cotton, and other crops largely sold and shipped. The traditional corn-oats-clover rotation, protective of the surface and maintaining nitrogen balance, began to break down. Soybeans, moderately planted in the twenties and then largely for hay, developed into a major

seed crop, aided by heavy governmental benefit payments as soil-building, which they are not. Soil-depleting and soil-exposing crops were given strong impetus in the shift to mechanized farming; less of the better land is used for pasture and hay; less animal and green manure is returned to fields. The fixation of nitrogen by clover has come to be considered too slow; it "pays better" to put the land into corn, beans, and cotton and to apply nitrogen from bag or tank. Dressing the soil with commercial nitrogen makes it possible to plant more closely, thus doubling the number of corn and other plants to the acre at nearly the same tillage cost. Stimulation of plant growth by nitrogen brings increased need of additional phosphorus and potash. In the last ten years the Corn Belt has more or less caught up with the Cotton Belt in the purchase of commercial fertilizer. The more valuable the land, the greater the investment in farm machinery, the more profitable the application of more and more commercial fertilizers.

The so-called row crops, which are the principal cash crops, demand cultivation during much of their period of growth. They give therefore indifferent protection to the surface while growing and almost none after they are harvested. They are ill suited to being followed by a winter cover crop. The organic color is fading from much of our best-grade farm lands. Rains and melting snow float away more and more of the top soil. There is little concern as long as we can plow more deeply and buy more fertilizer. Governmental restriction of acreage for individual crops has been an inducement to apply more fertilizer to the permitted acreage and to plant the rest in uncontrolled but usually also cash crops. Our commercial agriculture, except what remains in animal husbandry such as dairying, is kept expanding by increasing overdraft on the fertility of our soils. Its limits are set by the economically available sources of purchased nitrogen, phosphorus, potassium, and sulfur.

Since Columbus, the spread of European

culture has been continuous and cumulative, borne by immediate self-interest, as in mercantilist economy, but sustained also by a sense of civilizing mission redefined from time to time. In the spirit of the present, this mission is to "develop the underdeveloped" parts of the world, material good and spiritual good now having become one. It is our current faith that the ways of the West are the ways that are best for the rest of the world. Our own ever growing needs for raw materials have driven the search for metals and petroleum to the ends of the earth in order to move them into the stream of world commerce. Some beneficial measure of industry and transport facility thereby accrues to distant places of origin. We also wish to be benefactors by increasing food supply where food is inadequate and by diverting people from rural to industrial life, because such is our way, to which we should like to bring others.

The road we are laying out for the world is paved with good intentions, but do we know where it leads? On the material side we are hastening the depletion of resources. Our programs of agricultural aid pay little attention to native ways and products. Instead of going out to learn what their experiences and preferences are, we go forth to introduce our ways and consider backward what is not according to our pattern. Spade and hoe and mixed plantings are an affront to our faith in progress. We promote mechanization. At the least, we hold, others should be taught to use steel plows that turn neat furrows, though we have no idea how long the soil will stay on well-plowed slopes planted to annuals. We want more fields of maize, rice, beans of kinds familiar to us, products amenable to statistical determination and available for commercial distribution. To increase production, we prescribe dressing with commercial fertilizers. In unnoticed contrast to our own experience these are to be applied in large measure to lands of low productivity and perhaps of low effectiveness of fertilizers. Industrialization is recommended to take care of the surplus populations. We present and recommend to the world a blueprint of what works well with us at the moment, heedless that we may be destroying wise and durable native systems of living with the land. The modern industrial mood (I hesitate to add intellectual mood) is insensitive to other ways and values.

For the present, living beyond one's means has become civic virtue, increase of "output" the goal of society. The prophets of a new world by material progress may be stopped by economic limits of physical matter. They may fail because people grow tired of getting and spending as measure and mode of living. They may be checked because men come to fear the requisite growing power of government over the individual and the community. The high moments of history have come not when man was most concerned with the comforts and displays of the flesh but when his spirit was moved to grow in grace. What we need more perhaps is an ethic and aesthetic under which man, practicing the qualities of prudence and moderation, may indeed pass on to posterity a good earth.

INDEXES

INDEX TO AUTHORS

INDEX TO SUBJECTS